THE EMERGENCE OF LANGUAGE

Carnegie Mellon Symposia on Cognition

David Klahr, Series Editor

Anderson: Cognitive Skills and Their Acquisition

Carroll/Payne: Cognition and Social Behavior

Clark/Fiske: Affect and Cognition

Cohen/Schooler: Scientific Approaches to Consciousness

Cole: Perception and Production of Fluent Speech

Farah/Ratcliff: The Neuropsychology of High-Level Vision: Collected Tutorial Essays

Granrud: Visual Perception and Cognition in Infancy

Gregg: Knowledge and Cognition

Just/Carpenter: Cognitive Processes in Comprehension

Klahr: Cognition and Instruction

Lau/Sears: Political Cognition

MacWhinney: The Emergence of Language

MacWhinney: Mechanisms of Language Acquisition

Reder: Implicit Memory and Metacognition

Siegler: Children's Thinking: What Develops?

Sophian: Origins of Cognitive Skills

Steier/Mitchell: Mind Matters: A Tribute to Allen Newell

VanLehn: Architectures for Intelligence

THE EMERGENCE OF LANGUAGE

Edited by

Brian MacWhinney
Carnegie Mellon University

LEA

1999

LAWRENCE ERLBAUM ASSOCIATES, PUBLISHERS
Mahwah, New Jersey London

Lawrence Erlbaum Associates, Inc., Publishers
10 Industrial Avenue
Mahwah, New Jersey 07430

Cover design by Kathryn Houghtaling Lacey

Library of Congress Cataloging-in-Publication Data

The Emergence of language / edited by Brian MacWhinney.
p. cm.
Includes bibliographical references and index.
ISBN 0-8058-3010-3 (alk. paper). -- ISBN 0-8058-3011-1 (pbk. : alk. paper)
1. Language acquisition. I. MacWhinney, Brian.
P118.E43 1999
401'.93--dc21 98-47001
CIP

Books published by Lawrence Erlbaum Associates are printed on acid-free paper, and their bindings are chosen for strength and durability.

Printed in the United States of America
10 9 8 7 6 5 4 3 2 1

Contributors

Joseph Allen, Neuroscience Program HNB 18, University of Southern California, Los Angeles, CA 90089

Richard N. Aslin, Department of Psychology, Meliora Hall, University of Rochester, Rochester, NY 14627

Elizabeth Bates, Center for Research on Language, University of California, 9500 Gilman Drive, La Jolla, CA 92093

Barbara H. Bernhardt, Department of Linguistics, University of British Columbia, Vancouver BC, Canada

Gary S. Dell, Beckman Institute, University of Illinois, 405 North Matthews, Urbana, IL 61801

Jeffrey L. Elman, Center for Research on Language, University of California, 9500 Gilman Drive, La Jolla, CA 92093

T. Givón, Department of Linguistics, University of Oregon, Eugene, OR 97403

Adele E. Goldberg, Department of Linguistics, University of Illinois, Champaign, IL 61801

Roberta M. Golinkoff, College of Education, University of Delaware, Newark, DE 19711

Judith C. Goodman, Communication Science and Disorders, University of Missouri, 303 Lewis Hall, Columbia, MO 65211

Prahlad Gupta, Beckman Institute, University of Illinois, 405 North Matthews, Urbana, IL 61801

Kathy Hirsh-Pasek, Department of Psychology, Temple University, Philadelphia, PA 19122

George Hollich, Department of Psychology, Temple University, Philadelphia, PA 19122

Christopher T. Kello, Department of Psychology, Carnegie Mellon University, Pittsburgh, PA 15213

Maryellen C. MacDonald, Neuroscience Program HNB 18, University of Southern California, Los Angeles, CA 90089

Brian MacWhinney, Department of Psychology, Carnegie Mellon University, Pittsburgh, PA 15213

Marshall R. Mayberry, III, Department of Computer Sciences, The University of Texas at Austin, Austin, TX 78712

William E. Merriman, Department of Psychology, Kent State University, Kent, OH 44242

Risto Miikkulainen, Department of Computer Sciences, The University of Texas at Austin, Austin, TX 78712

Elissa L. Newport, Department of Psychology, Meliora Hall, University of Rochester, Rochester, NY 14627

David C. Plaut, Department of Psychology, Carnegie Mellon University, Pittsburgh, PA 15213

Jenny R. Saffran, Department of Psychology, University of Wisconsin–Madison, Madison, WI 53706

Mark S. Seidenberg, Neuroscience Program HNB 18, University of Southern California, Los Angeles, CA 90089

Linda B. Smith, Department of Psychology and Program in Cognitive Science, Indiana University, Bloomington, IN 47405

Catherine E. Snow, Graduate School of Education, Harvard University, Roy E. Larsen Hall, Cambridge, MA 02138

Joseph P. Stemberger, 51 East River Road, University of Minnesota, Minneapolis, MN 55455

Contents

Preface

If you spend time watching the checkout lines at a supermarket, you will find that the number of people queued up in each line stays roughly the same. There are rarely six people in one line and two in the next. There is no socially articulated rule governing this pattern. Instead, the uniformity of this simple social "structure" emerges from other basic facts about the goals and behavior of shoppers and supermarket managers.

Honeybees are certainly no smarter than shoppers. However, working together, bees are able to construct an even more complex structure. When a bee returns to the hive after collecting pollen, she deposits a drop of wax-coated honey. Each of these honey balls is round and approximately the same size. As these balls get packed together, they take on the familiar hexagonal shape that we see in the honeycomb. There is no gene in the bee that codes for hexagonality in the honeycomb, nor is there any overt communication regarding the shaping of the cells of the honeycomb. Rather, this form is an emergent consequence of the application of packing rules to a collection of honey balls of roughly uniform size.

Nature abounds with examples of emergence. The outlines of beaches emerge from interactions between geology and ocean currents. The shapes of crystals emerge from the ways in which atoms can pack into sheets. Weather patterns like the Jet Stream or El Niño emerge from interactions between the rotation of the earth, solar radiation, and the shapes of the ocean bodies. Biological patterns emerge in very similar ways. For example, the shapes of the stripes on a tiger are controlled by the timing of the expression of a pair of competing genes expressing color as they operate across the developing tiger embryo. No single gene directly controls these patterns. Rather, the stripes emerge from the interactions of the genes on the physical surface of the embryo. The shape of the brain is very much the same. For example, Miller, Keller, and Stryker have shown that the ocular dominance columns described by Hubel and Wiesel in their Nobel-prize-winning work may emerge as a solution to a competition between projections from the different optic areas during synaptogenesis in striate cortex.

Emergentist accounts of brain development provide useful ways of understanding the forces that lead to neuronal plasticity, as well as neuronal commitment. The chapters in the current volume derive from this basic theme and elaborate a vision of emergentism that extends to a wide variety of topics in language processing, structure, and acquisition. Sticking close to this biological grounding, Elman's chapter in this volume summarizes work showing how the wiring pattern of the brain emerges from the interaction of a variety of developmental pressures. For example, Ramachandran has shown that many aspects of reorganization depend on the elimination of redundant connectivity patterns. Moreover, Quartz and Sejnowski have shown that plasticity may also involve the growth of new patterns of connectivity. On the macro level, recent fMRI work by MacWhinney, Booth, Feldman, and Thulborn has shown how children with early brain lesions use a variety of alternative developmental pathways to preserve language functioning.

Students are often taught that the opposition between nativism and empiricism is the fundamental issue in developmental psychology. What they really end up learning, however, is that everything in human development depends on the interaction between nature and nurture. Unfortunately, students are given few conceptual tools to understand how this interaction occurs. As a result, they become confused about the underpinnings of the science of human development. Emergentism replaces the traditional opposition between nativism and empiricism with a new conceptual framework, explicitly designed to account in mechanistic terms for interactions between biological and environmental processes. The goal of emergentism is the construction of models that avoid stipulation regarding specific hard-wired neural circuitry. In the place of stipulation, emergentism provides accounts in which structures emerge from the interaction of known processes.

This strong formulation of the emergentist program must be tempered with practical reality. The primitive state of our understanding of basic neurological and developmental processes means that models often still have to rely on stipulation regarding structures that we do not yet fully understand. For example, a model of the effects of auditory processing deficits may need to include a hard-wired representation of information passed on to language processing from the auditory cortex. This type of stipulation regarding structures that are not at the core of a given model reflects the primitive nature of our current modeling techniques. It is not intended as a statement about how models should be constructed.

Emergentism should not be interpreted as a radical rejection of either nativism or empiricism. On the contrary, emergentism views nativist and empiricist formulations as partial components of a more complete account. The traditional contrast between nativism and empiricism revolves around the fact that they describe developmental processes that operate across different time frames. We can distinguish five separate time frames.

Evolutionary Emergence. The slowest moving emergent structures are those that are encoded in the genes. These structures, which are subject to more variability and competition than is frequently acknowledged, are the result of glacial changes resulting from the pressures of evolutionary biology. We can refer to this type of emergence as "evolutionary emergence."

Embryological Emergence. Translation of the DNA in the embryo triggers a further set of processes from which the initial shape of the organism emerges. Some structures are tightly specified by particular genetic loci. For example, the recessive gene for phenylketonuria or PKU begins its expression prenatally by blocking the production of the enzymes that metabolize the amino acid phenylalanine. Although the effects of PKU occur postnatally, the determination of this metabolic defect emerges prenatally. Other prenatal emergent structures involve a role for physical forces in the developing embryo. The formation of the stripes of the tiger is an example of this type.

Developmental Emergence. The emergentist accounts presented in the current volume focus primarily on the ways in which linguistic and cognitive structures emerge during learning and development. Jean Piaget's genetic psychology was the first fully articulated view of this type. Current emergentist accounts rely on perspectives such as connectionism, embodiment, and dynamic systems theory. Chapters in this book by Bates and Goodman, Elman, Goldberg, Smith, Stemberger and Bernhardt, and Merriman explore these aspects of language emergence.

Online Emergence. The briefest time frame for the study of emergent processes is that of online language processing. Chapters by Aslin, Saffran, and Newport, Gupta and Dell, Miikkulainen and Mayberry, MacWhinney, Allen and Seidenberg, and MacDonald investigate the ways in which language structure emerges from the activities of speaking and listening.

Diachronic Emergence. The changes that languages undergo across centuries can also be viewed in emergentist terms. The chapters by Givón and MacWhinney explore some aspects of this type of emergence.

In order to qualify as emergentist, an account of language functioning must tell us where a language behavior "comes from." In most cases, this involves accounting for a behavior in a target domain as emerging from some related external domain. For example, an account that shows how phonological structures emerge from physiological constraints on the vocal tract involves external determination, because the shape of one level of description is determined by patterns on a different level.

No full account of language emergence has yet been developed. However, emergentist accounts have been formulated for a wide variety of linguistic phenomena, including segmental inventories, stress patterns, phonotactic constraints, morphophonological alternations, lexical structures, pidginization, second language learning, historical change, online phrase attachment, and rhetorical structures. Formalisms that have been used to analyze the emergent nature of these forms include connectionist networks, dynamic systems theory, neuronal competition models, classifier systems, production-system architectures, Bayesian models, optimality theory, principles-and-parameters theory, corpora studies, and hermeneutic analysis. It is remarkable that approaches as apparently divergent as functionalist linguistics and principles-and-parameters theory share some common ground in terms of a mutual interest in emergentist accounts of both learning and processing.

The 16 chapters presented here were delivered between May 29 and 31, 1997, at the 28th Carnegie Mellon Symposium on Cognition with the theme "Emergentist Approaches to Language Acquisition" and sponsored by the National Science Foundation. Apart from the invited speakers, nearly a hundred additional researchers attended the symposium.

Many of the 16 papers presented at this symposium and published here adopt an explicitly emergentist approach. Elman examines issues in emergentist theory through the consideration of gene-gene interactions, neuronal plasticity, and the ways in which temporal interactions in neural structures can lead to emergent computational abilities. The background for the themes that Elman develops here is discussed in greater detail in the book entitled *Rethinking Innateness: A Connectionist Perspective on Development* that was recently published by MIT Press. In many ways the themes developed in the current symposium volume can be viewed as follow-ups to the issues raised in that book.

Two other chapters explore the ways in which grammar emerges from the lexicon. Using the Construction Grammar framework, Goldberg traces the emergence of the semantics of argument structure during language acquisition. Bates and Goodman apply a similar perspective to the understanding of individual differences in early language development. In both chapters, the authors view syntactic form as emerging from lexical learning. Goldberg grounds her account in linguistic analysis and recent experimental findings. Bates and Goodman rely more on the examination of correlations between lexicon and grammar across the first 2 years of language acquisition. Looking at a wide variety of special populations, including Down syndrome children, late talkers, precocious talkers, children with brain lesions, and Williams syndrome children, Bates and Goodman find little support for the nativist notion of a separate module for grammar.

The next two chapters look at adult sentence processing using the tools of connectionist modeling. Allen and Seidenberg study the ways in which judgments regarding degrees of grammaticality can emerge from competitive processing in connectionist networks. Their findings call into question the status of Chomsky's competence-performance distinction by showing how *competence* emerges from *performance.* Miikkulainen and Mayberry study ambiguity effects in sentence processing effects that have often been used to argue for a modular basis for sentence processing. They present an explicit connectionist model in which the process of settling on a particular interpretation for an ambiguous sequence emerges online from the interaction of a set of "soft" semantic, lexical, and syntactic constraints.

Three other chapters examine the emergence of the shape of grammar from language usage. Looking at data on competitive syntactic attachments, MacDonald argues that the incremental shape of sentence processing emerges from distributional forces in the language. However, she also notes that a full understanding of the role of these distributional pressures requires an understanding of the relations among comprehension, production, and acquisition. Like MacDonald, MacWhinney sees the form of comprehension, production, and acquisition as emerging from underlying cognitive pressures. MacWhinney presents a view of syntactic form as emergent from a process of perspective-taking in which both listener and speaker develop an embodied representation of the meaning of a sentence. He attempts to link linguistic form to the activity of perspective-taking across four cognitive levels, including affordances, spatial frames, causal action frames, and social frames.

Givón takes a slightly different approach to the way in which grammar formalizes cognitive operations. He argues that functional pressures have their greatest impact on incompletely consolidated forms of human language such as child language, pidgins, second language forms, and aphasic language. On the other hand, according to Givón, the full adult grammar of a language achieves a level of automaticity that escapes this direct type of direct functional pressure. Givón's analysis, like MacDonald's, suggests that we must reject simplistic attempts to account for all aspects of language form as emerging from any single source such as conversational pressure, distributional patterns, perspective-taking, or working memory load. Rather, we may need to view grammar as a rarefied response to the complete configuration of this entire set of dynamics.

Seven other chapters deal explicitly with language acquisition. In the lone chapter that explores specifically social influences, Snow challenges the relevance of accounts that attempt to view syntactic and semantic bootstrapping as the motors driving language learning. She suggests that we should take a close look at what children are good at, rather than those abilities they do not yet master. In particular, Snow believes that children have a precocious understanding of social relations and that their most advanced uses of language are grounded in this understanding. Like Bates and Goodman or Goldberg, Snow believes that grammatical advances are very much linked to lexical advances, and she adds to this perspective an emphasis on the role of parental input in fostering language development.

Three chapters examine emergentist mechanisms for early word learning. Smith argues for the idea that "general learning processes make specialized learning mechanisms." In a series of experiments, she shows how the child learns to learn new words. At first the child's guesses about the meanings of new words are relatively unfocused. However, as children learn more about language, these biases sharpen. Smith documents the emergence of these abilities in terms of both the shape bias for word learning and the ways in which the child uses linguistic frames to guess at the part of speech of a new word. Merriman articulates a point of view that is highly compatible with Smith's. He believes that children's word learning is governed primarily by the two basic forces of competition and attention. Attentional processes help the child focus in on possible candidate meanings for new words. Once these initial candidates emerge, they engage in a process of competition to control overgeneralizations. According to Merriman, the basic shapes of early words are determined not by innate constraints, such as Mutual Exclusivity, but by emergent processes. Golinkoff, Hirsh-Pasek, and Hollich present a slightly different approach to similar phenomena. They emphasize the extent to which an adequate account of early word learning must be based not only on cognitive principles, but also on social forces. Presumably, they have in mind the same types of social pressures emphasized by Snow, as well as the attentional focusing processes discussed by Merriman and Smith. Together, these articles paint a picture of early word learning in which the emergence of particular meanings is governed by a rich interaction between cognitive and social forces.

In the first year of life, before they approach the learning of the first words, children are exposed to a massive amount of auditory linguistic input. Until recently, our understanding of the child's processing of this input has focused on the acquisition of phonemic contrasts. Aslin, Saffran, and Newport present data on a new line of research with infants that goes well beyond this earlier literature. These new studies have shown us that 8-month-old children can group sequential auditory patterns solely on the basis of their distributional properties. They can use this ability to acquire the auditory forms of potential new words, as well as the intonational patterns of the language. Aslin et al. are careful to assume an agnostic approach to the interpretation of these findings as supporting an emergentist view, pointing out that the ability itself may be a part of an innate language acquisition device. However, they seem to recognize the fact that the child can use this ability as a powerful tool for language acquisition. Although this ability itself may not be treated as emergent, the action of the ability on input leads to emergent structures.

Plaut and Kello adopt a more specifically emergentist approach to phonological learning in a model that attempts to link up the child's learning of input, auditory forms to early articulatory productions. Using an innovative connectionist architecture, they show how many of the properties of early child articulations emerge from the way in which data is processed by these networks. This emergentist view of output phonology is very much in accord with Stemberger and Bernhardt's application of optimality theory to the study of child language. The theory of optimality provides a powerful constraint satisfaction formalism for describing certain types of emergent patterns, particularly in the area of phonology. Stemberger and Bernhardt view children's early articulations as strongly influenced by reduction of adult target forms. In order to move their pronunciations closer to the adult target, children must improve the ways in which they maintain "faithfulness" to the target. This application of optimality theory is important not only for its theoretical clarity, but also for its exploration of the roots of the constraints envisioned by optimality theory. In particular, Stemberger and Bernhardt see these constraints as emerging from both phonetic and cognitive processes.

Phonetic processes involving the movements of articulators such as the tongue and larynx are surely the sources of many phonological constraints. However, higher level lexical processes must also have a major impact. Gupta and Dell explore two possible ways in which phonological form emerges from lexical structure. First, they note that the serial organization of words into chains gives rise to a basic asymmetry between the beginnings of words and their ends. For example, a phrase like "smell bad" may have onsets exchanged, as in "bell smad" or rimes exchanged, as in "smad bell," but final consonants are seldom exchanged, as in "smed bal." Using a connectionist model, Gupta and Dell show that a good vocabulary is one in which words tend to be more differentiated at the beginning than at the end. Looking still more deeply into processing influences on the lexicon, Dell and Gupta show how many aspects of word learning can be viewed as emergent from basic facts about procedural learning and its neuronal implementation.

These chapters constitute a unique outpouring of creative energy. At the same time they personify an important new direction in thinking about language structure and language learning. By eschewing simplistic application of nativism and empiricism, these researchers have opened up rich new areas for theory and research. It would be a mistake to think that all of these works subscribe to some uniform emergentist "party line." For example, Aslin et al. explicitly declare their interest in pursuing nativist accounts for sequential learning. Aspects of the optimality theory formalism adopted by Stemberger and Bernhardt involve the provisional acceptance of a nonemergent level of formal representation. MacWhinney's views on perspective-taking make frequent reference to inborn processes and affordances. Finally, Givón emphasizes the extent to which grammar is nonfunctional, automatic, and nonemergent, at least in terms of what I have called online emergence, although Givón is willing to accept an important role for diachronic emergence.

This volume fails to include work from several related points of view. First, work on the emergence of grammar from conversation of the type presented by Hopper, Chafe, or Thompson is not represented. Second, recent work by Feldman, Lakoff, Narayanan, and associates on the linkage of language to fully embodied representations is missing, as is work on emergent properties in robotic and artificial life systems. Third, there is a lamentable absence of contributions from researchers in the tradition of generative grammar. Recent developments within the theory of generative grammar, as well as psycholinguistic extensions of the generative framework, have suggested that linguistic theory may eventually be compatible with an emergentist framework. However, these connections remain to be explored. Fourth, this volume includes no representative of the fascinating new work that is currently appearing on the emergence of language during the evolution of man from the primates. Finally, this volume has explicitly excluded studies grounded on cognitive neuroscience, as this would have taken us well beyond the scope of the conference. There is an enormous amount of work in cognitive neuroscience that strongly motivates an emergentist approach. Whether it be work on adult neuronal plasticity, organization of neural nets, or the development of the brain in the fetus and infant, each year sees new breakthroughs in our understanding of the biological bases of emergent processes. Fortunately, this omission is being addressed as this book goes to press. Just as the 28th Carnegie Symposium on Cognition focused on the emergence of language, the 29th symposium, that was held in October 1998, focused on the biological underpinnings of emergence.

Emergentism provides a conceptually solid way of linking our growing understanding of the brain with new theories of cognition, as well as new tools for simulation. By distinguishing levels of emergence across the five time scales mentioned earlier, we can incorporate the old opposition between nativism and empiricism into a detailed new research program. By linking these tools together in a single framework, we open up the promise that the next millennium will begin with a productive outpouring of new ways of thinking about the emergence of language.

Brian MacWhinney

Chapter 1

The Emergence of Language: A Conspiracy Theory

Jeffrey L. Elman
University of California, San Diego

Language is puzzling. On the one hand, there are compelling reasons to believe that the possession of language by humans has deep biological roots. We are the only species that has a communication system with the complexity and richness of language. There are cases of nonhuman primates who can be taught (sometimes only with heroic effort) some aspects of human language, but their performance comes nowhere close to that of a 6-year-old child. Second, although languages differ, there are also striking similarities across widely divergent cultures. Finally, there are significant similarities in the patterns of language acquisition across very different linguistic communities. These (and other considerations as well) all suggest that species-specific biological factors play a critical role in the ability of humans to acquire and process language.

So what is puzzling? First, it is not at all clear what the biological foundations are. What precisely do we mean when we say that the human propensity for language is innate—or as Pinker (1994) put it, is an "instinct"? Do we only mean, when we say that "language is innate," that one must possess a human genome in order to speak (hear, read, sign)? This is not terribly informative; after all, getting a driver's license also requires a human genome (although driving the freeways of Southern California, one sometimes wonders). But we do not view this as an especially useful explanation of the origin and nature of the skills and competencies that are required to drive a car. Second, when we actually look at the genome, we see little that suggests any obvious connection with language. The recurring lesson from recent genetic research is that behaviors typically rest on the interaction of large numbers of genes, each of which may participate in many other processes (e.g., Greenspan, 1995). Claims to the contrary notwithstanding (Gopnik & Crago, 1991; but see also Vargha-Khadem, Watkins, Alcock, Fletcher, & Passingham, 1995), there are no good examples of selective impairment of language that can be traced to defects in isolated genes.

Yet the fact remains that humans have language and chimpanzees do not. This is true no matter how human-like a chimp's environment and upbringing are made. Thus, we remain with a puzzling set of questions:

- Why does our species have language, and no other? What are the species differences that make language possible?
- Why does language take the forms it does, and not others?
- How does language emerge in the language-learning child?
- How do we account for both global patterns of similarity in language behavior as well as individual variations on those patterns?

In this chapter, I outline a connectionist perspective on language development with the goal of ultimately (if not now) providing answers to these questions. The particular perspective I put forward is one that has been developed together with my colleagues Elizabeth Bates, Mark Johnson, Annette Karmiloff-Smith, Domenico Parisi, and Kim Plunkett (see Elman et al., 1996, for a fuller account). In our view, biology plays a crucial role in determining the outcome of development, and in the case of humans, enabling language. However, rather than viewing the developmental process as one in which biology contributes some portion of the answer, and experience another (much like a jigsaw puzzle, in which biology assembles most of the pieces and experience fills in the rest), we see these two forces as engaged in a complex synergy. The challenge, of course, is to be able to clarify the way in which these interactions occur.

I begin by presenting a taxonomy for thinking about alternative ways in which behaviors might be constrained by biology. As it turns out, there are reasons to believe that some of these alternatives are more plausible than others and that what may be the most widely held view of innateness is highly unlikely in the case of language. After discussing other ways in which biological constraints might limit outcomes, I describe two simulations that illustrate how what appears to be a much weaker alternative constraint in fact has considerable power. Among other things, these simulations also suggest that domain-specific behaviors can be achieved through mechanisms that are themselves not domain specific. Finally, I discuss how these results fit in with more general findings regarding development into what I call a "conspiracy" theory of language origins.

WAYS TO BE INNATE

At least some of the controversy surrounding the nature–nurture debate arises from lack of clear notions regarding what is meant when it is claimed that a behavior is innate. In the framework outlined by Elman et al. (1996), we found it useful to think about development as a process that can occur at multiple levels (using *level* here in a heterarchical rather than hierarchical sense) and in which processes at different levels may interact. At all levels, the constraints may crucially depend on interactions with the environment. When we say that an outcome is innate, then, we mean that it is significantly constrained at one or more of these levels, given the expected inputs from the environment. The taxonomy that we developed makes reference to constraints at the levels of *representations, architectures,* and *timing.* These levels can be defined in terms of brain development, but we also find it useful to talk about their network analogs.

Representational Innateness

If cognitive behaviors are the immediate product of our mental states, and these are equivalent to brain states, then the most specific way of constraining a cognitive behavior is to constrain the brain states that underlie it. Brain states are patterns of activations across neurons, and their proximal cause lies in the pattern of synaptic connections that generate that activity. Thus, the most direct and specific way of constraining a behavior would be to specify in advance the precise pattern of neuronal connectivity that would lead to that behavior. In brains, then, a claim for representational innateness is equivalent to saying that the genome somehow predetermines the synapses between neurons. In neural networks, representational innateness is achieved by hand-wiring the network and setting the weights prior to learning.

At least some of the discussion regarding the origins of language appears to assume that representational innateness is what is assumed. Thus, for example, Pinker (1994) claimed the following:

> It is a certain wiring of the microcircuitry that is essential. . . . If language, the quintessential higher cognitive process, is an instinct, maybe the rest of cognition is a bunch of instincts too—complex circuits designed by natural selection, each dedicated to solving a particular family of computational problems posed by the ways of life we adopted millions of years ago. (pp. 93, 97)

Although this scenario is logically possible, and there are some animals for whom the genome appears to constrain the topology and connectivity of specific cells, we see next that representational innateness is highly dubious as a mechanism for ensuring language in humans.

Architectural Innateness

Outcomes can also be constrained by limiting the architectures that are available. As used here, *architecture* refers to organization that is at a higher level of granularity than the prespecified connections between neurons (or nodes) that guarantee representational innateness. Architectural constraints in fact can vary along a large number of dimensions, but in general fall into three broad classes: unit based, local, and global. *Unit-based architectural constraints* deal with the specific properties of neurons, including firing threshold, refractory period, and so forth; type of transmitter produced (and whether it is excitatory or inhibitory); nature of pre- and postsynaptic changes (i.e., learning), and so forth. In network terms, unit-level constraints might be realized through node activation functions, learning rules, temperature, or momentum. It is clear that unit-level constraints operate in brain development. There are a relatively small number of neuron types, for instance, and they are neither randomly nor homogeneously distributed throughout the brain. The unit-level constraints are fundamental to brain organization, because they concern the lowest level of computation in the brain. *Local architectural constraints* operate at the next higher level of granularity. In brains, these describe differences in the number of layers (e.g., the six-layered organization of the cortex), packing density of cells, types of neurons, degree of interconnectivity ("fan in" and "fan out"), and nature of interconnectivity (inhibitory vs. excitatory). In network terms, local architectural differences would include feedforward versus recurrent networks, or the layering of networks. Interestingly, the cortex itself appears to display relatively little in the way of local architectural differences at early stages of development. The much greater differentiation that is found in the adult cortex appears to result from development, and an interesting question is how these differences arise. This, in fact, is one of the goals of the second simulation that is described later. Finally, *global architectural constraints* specify the way in which the various pieces of a system—be it brain or network—are connected together. Local architecture deals with the ways in which the low-level circuitry is laid out; global architecture deals with the connections at the macrolevel between areas and regions and especially with the inputs and outputs to subsystems. If one thinks of the brain as a network of networks, global architectural constraints concern the manner in which these networks are interconnected. In brain terms, such constraints could be expressed in terms of (e.g., thalamo-cortical) pathways that control where sensory afferents project to and where efferents originate. Very few network models employ architectures for which this sort of constraint is relevant (because it presupposes a level of architectural complexity that goes beyond most current modeling). One might imagine, however, networks that are loosely connected, such that they function somewhat modularly but communicate via input–output channels. If the pattern of internetwork connections were prespecified, this would constitute an example of a global architectural constraint.

Chronotopic Innateness

A third way in which outcomes can be constrained is through the timing of events in the developmental process. Indeed, as Gould (and many other evolutionary biologists) argued eloquently, changes in the developmental schedule play a critical role in evolutionary change (Gould, 1977; see also McKinney & McNamara, 1991). In networks, timing can be manipulated through exogenous means, such as control of when certain inputs are presented. Or timing can arise endogenously, as seen in Marchman's simulations of the critical period (Marchman, 1993); in these networks, the gradual loss of plasticity in a network comes about as a result of learning itself. In brains, timing is sometimes under direct genetic control, but the control of timing may also be highly indirect and the result of multiple interactions. Hence, the onset and sequencing of events in development represents a schedule that is the joint product of genetic and environmental effects. Both of the simulations reported in this chapter deal with the effects of timing.

The differences between the three ways to be innate are shown in Table 1.1.

THE PROBLEM WITH REPRESENTATIONAL INNATENESS

Obviously, the most direct method for guaranteeing an outcome would be for the genome to specify a precise wiring plan for human cortex. Something like this appears to happen with the nematode, *C. elegans.* This animal has exactly 959 somatic cells, and genetically identical nematodes have virtually identical patterns of cell connectivity. This is quite unlike humans. No two humans, not even monozygotic twins, have identical neuronal connections. There is abundant reason to believe that representational nativism is simply not an option available for guaranteeing language in humans and that the cortex of higher vertebrates (and especially humans) has evolved as an "organ of plasticity" that is capable of encoding a vast array of representations.

TABLE 1.1
Ways To Be Innate

(Least specific/Indirect ← Most specific/direct)	*Source of Constraint*		*Examples in Brains*	*Examples in Networks*
	Representations		Synapses; specific microcircuitry	Weights on connections
		unit	Cytoarchitecture (neuron types); firing thresholds; transmitter types; heterosynaptic depression; learning rules (e.g., long-term potential	Activation function; learning algorithm, temperature; momentum; learning rate
	Architectures	*local*	Number of layers; packing density; recurrence; basic (recurring) cortical circuitry	Network type (e.g., recurrent, feed-forward); number of layers; number of units in layers
		global	Connections between brain regions; location of sensory and motor afferents/efferents	Expert networks; separate input/output channels
	Timing		Number of cell divisions during neurogenesis; spatiotemporal waves of synaptic growth and pruning/decay; temporal development of sensory systems	Incremental presentation of data; cell division in growing networks; intrinsic changes resulting from node saturation; adaptive learning rates

In a number of recent studies with vertebrates, for example, investigators have changed the nature of the input received by a specific area of the cortex, either by transplanting plugs of fetal cortex from one area to another (e.g., somatosensory to visual, or vice versa; O'Leary, 1993; O'Leary & Stanfield, 1989), by radically altering the nature of the input by deforming the sensory surface (Friedlander, Martin, & Wassenhove-McCarthy, 1991; Killackey, Chiaia, Bennett-Clarke, Eck, & Rhodes, 1994), or by redirecting inputs from their intended target to an unexpected area (e.g., redirecting visual inputs to auditory cortex; Frost, 1982, 1990; Pallas & Sur, 1993; Roe, Pallas, Hahm, & Sur, 1990; Sur, Garraghty, & Roe, 1988; Sur, Pallas, & Roe, 1990; see also Molnar & Blakemore, 1991). Surprisingly, under these aberrant conditions, the fetal cortex takes on neuroanatomical and physiological properties that are appropriate for the information it receives and quite different from the properties that would have emerged if the default inputs for that region had occurred. This suggests that cortex has far more representational plasticity than previously believed. Indeed, recent studies have shown that cortex retains representational plasticity into adulthood (e.g., radical remapping of somatosensory cortex after amputation, in humans, and in infrahuman primates; Merzenich, Recanzone, Jenkins, Allard, & Nudo, 1988; Pons et al., 1991; Ramachandran, 1993; see also Greenough, Black, & Wallace, 1993).

In fact, such a situation would seem to be inevitable, given the impossible burden that a direct gene-synapse specification would impose on the genome. Calow (1976) estimated that the adult human body contains approximately 5×10^{28} bits of information (taking into account that cell type, spatial position, and connectivity need to be specified for each of the 100 trillion cells in the body), but the genome contains only about 1×10^{9} bits (if it is construed as a bit-map). A better view of what genes do is provided by Bonner (1988), who suggested that much of development occurs through simple inertia of biochemical reactions that drive themselves. Genes play the role of catalysts and regulators that modulate these reactions, so their effects are typically highly indirect and opaque with regard to final outcomes. Furthermore, a very large number of genes may be involved in complex behaviors (e.g., courtship in the fruitfly; Greenspan, 1995), most of which are "reused" and participate in many other interactions.

Thus, although representational nativism is a logical possibility, it is not likely that it plays any role in the emergence of language.

THE IMPORTANCE OF TIME

If we reject representational nativism, this leads us to seek ways in which architectural and chronotopic (timing) constraints might be responsible for language. Architectural constraints are in fact very powerful, but in this chapter, I wish to focus on the role played by time.

Evolutionists have long known that dramatic changes in the timing of developmental events can produce remarkable differences in outcome (e.g., Gould, 1977; see also McKinney & McNamara, 1991). The dramatic distortions of body shape that Thompson (1961) described, involving simple allometric changes in Cartesian coordinates, easily arise from altered temporal growth gradients. In other cases, timing may alter the nature of tissue–tissue interaction and tissue induction. In adults, the length of long bones is partially determined by the number of mitotically active founder cells initially available. If the process of bone formation is delayed, these founder cells may in the interim be recruited to form other tissue types and so fewer cells will be available, leading to shortened bone length. Or timing may be so altered as to lead to a loss of interactions. The formation of teeth involves a complex interaction between several embryonic tissues.

In the case of birds, this interaction has been short-circuited but it can be artificially brought about by bringing together dental ectoderm from the chick and mesenchyme from a mouse (Kollar & Fisher, 1980). The genetic information necessary for tooth formation thus still seems to be present in birds (the last toothed bird dates to the Upper Cretaceous), but has been lost through a change in the timing of developmental events.

These are examples of closed systems, in which timing affects an interaction that is internal to the organism. I now describe two examples in which timing plays a crucial role in enabling an outcome that otherwise would not have occurred, but in which external input from the environment is also necessary.

THE IMPORTANCE OF STARTING SMALL

One of the most important things human children must learn to do is communicate. Language learning occupies a great deal of a child's time and it takes place over many years. The apparent inexorability of this process has led many people to conclude that there are powerful internal drives at work.

A fascinating feature of this behavior is that its form seems to be quite decoupled from its content. Manipulating words is not like manipulating a bicycle or using chopsticks or learning to walk. In these latter cases, the form of the activity is directly related to its function. Language is different in this respect. It is a highly symbolic activity. The relation between the symbols and the structures they form, on the one hand, and the things they refer to, on the other, is largely arbitrary. This too, has motivated many to seek biological explanations for the behavior, on the assumption that if the structures of language were functional, they could be learned.

Among the many peculiar features of language is the fact that whereas the sequence of words we speak occurs in a simple linear order (one word following another), the relations between these words are complex and often involve hierarchical organization. Thus, in the sentence *The cat who the dogs chase runs toward me,* the main thrust of the sentence is that the cat is running toward me, and the fragment *who the dogs chase* is subsidiary. One way to capture the relations between the different parts of the sentence is through a tree diagram of the sort shown in Fig. 1.1. This sort of tree encodes our intuitions about the relative relation of the words in the sentence by explicitly representing their constituent structure (e.g., *the cat* and *who the dogs chase* are constituents—parts—of the top level NP, which, along with the VP, is a constituent of the top level S).

In traditional linguistic theory, such representations are supposed to do several things for us. First, a theory of meaning (semantics) should be able

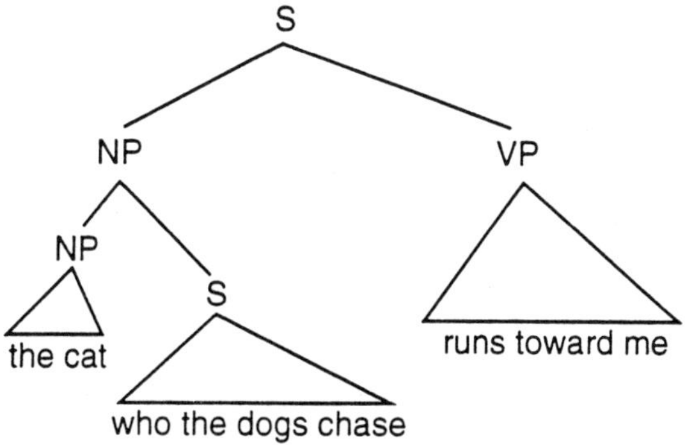

FIG. 1.1. A simplified phrase structure tree corresponding to the sentence *The cat who the dogs chase runs toward me.* Triangles simplify additional structure; S, NP, and VP stand for sentence, noun phrase, and verb phrase.

to use these representations to determine how the meaning of the sentences is built up from its constituents, given their structural relations. Second, these representations should provide a vocabulary for expressing important formal generalizations about what sorts of structures are grammatical. A very simple but important grammatical generalization in English and many other languages is that the exact form of the verb depends on whether its subject noun is singular or plural. Thus, we rule out *The cat who the dogs chases run toward me* as ungrammatical; *cat* requires that its verb (*runs*) be in the singular, and *dogs* requires that its verb (*chase*) be in the plural. The generalization that guarantees this agreement between noun and verb can be readily captured by the tree diagram in Fig. 1.1, because it allows us to appeal to notions of *level* or *clause*; *cat* and its verb are in the same clause, even though embedded material intervenes in the linear string.

Embedding is a basic property of human language. Whatever theory of language one adopts must provide some way to represent the complex hierarchical relations that occur in many sentences. The ability to maintain such representations would appear to be an ideal candidate for something that must be innate in language users and absent in nonhuman species.

Indeed, in a well-known mathematical proof, Gold (1967) was able to show that formal languages of the class that allow embeddings of the sort seen earlier cannot be learned inductively on the basis of positive input only. A crucial part of Gold's proof relied on the fact that direct negative evidence (e.g., of the explicit form in which the parent tells the child, "The following sentence, 'Bunnies is cuddly', is not grammatical") seems virtually nonexistent in child-directed speech (but see MacWhinney, 1993). Because children eventually do master language, Gold (1967) suggested that this may be because they already know critical things about the possible form of natural language. That is, learning merely takes the form of fine-tuning.

Although there are many reasons to believe that Gold's proof is actually not relevant to the case of natural language acquisition, it would be a mistake to take the extreme opposite position and claim that language learning is entirely unconstrained. Children do not seem able to learn any arbitrary language, and nonhuman young are not able to learn human languages. To return to the example at hand, what sort of constraint might permit a language user to represent abstract hierarchical relations of the sort found in sentences? To study this question, I created an artificial language that possessed a number of characteristics that are presumably problematic (in the aforementioned sense) and attempted to teach a simple recurrent network to process them (see Elman, 1993, for full account). The artificial language had the following characteristics:

1. Grammatical categories: Words belonged to different categories (e.g., noun, verb).
2. Basic sentence structure: Simple sentences consisted of a noun followed by a verb; if the verb was transitive then a second noun followed.
3. Number agreement between subject noun and verb: Singular nouns required the singular form of the verb; plural nouns required plural verbs.
4. Verb argument structure: Some verbs were transitive; others were intransitive; and others were optionally transitive.
5. Relative clauses: Nouns could be modified by a relative clause (e.g., *who the dogs chase*); both subject relatives (*girl who sees the boy*) and object relatives (*girl who the boys see*) were possible.

The words in the language were represented by vectors in which all elements were 0 except for a single bit that was set to 1. Because these vectors are all orthogonal to each other, there was no similarity of form that the network could use to determine that a given vector was a noun or verb, or even that two vectors might be related (as in *boy* and *boys*).

The task of the network was to take one word at a time and predict what the next word would be. Because the grammar that generated the sentences was nondeterministic, any given word might be followed by a number of different possibilities. Short of memorizing the entire training corpus (which was not feasible, given the size of the corpus and the resources available to the network), the optimal strategy would be for the network to predict all the possible words that might occur in a given context. Thus, after having heard the sequence *the girl who the dogs see . . .* , the network should predict all the words that might occur in that position, namely, singular transitive verbs. But in order to do this, the network had to have identified which words were verbs, which were singulars, and which were transitive. Furthermore, and most relevant to the issue at hand, the network must have somehow learned to associate the first verb it encounters in the sequence (*see*) with the second noun it has heard (*dogs*), and that the word that follows *see* must be the verb that goes with the very first noun (*girl*), and therefore a singular. This is exactly the sort of information tree diagrams are intended to convey. How would a network—or *could* a network—represent this information?

Because the task involved processing a sequence of information presented over time, a simple recurrent network with the architecture shown in Fig. 1.2 was used. The recurrent connections provide the network with the memory it needs to process the serially ordered inputs.

The results of the first trials were quite disappointing. The network failed to master the task, even for the training data. Performance was not uniformly bad. Indeed, in some sentences, the network would correctly coordinate the number of the main clause subject, mentioned early in a sentence, with the number of the main clause verb, mentioned after many embedded relative clauses. But it would then fail to get the agreement correct on some of the relative clause subjects and verbs, even when these were close together. (For example, it might predict *The boys who the girl*

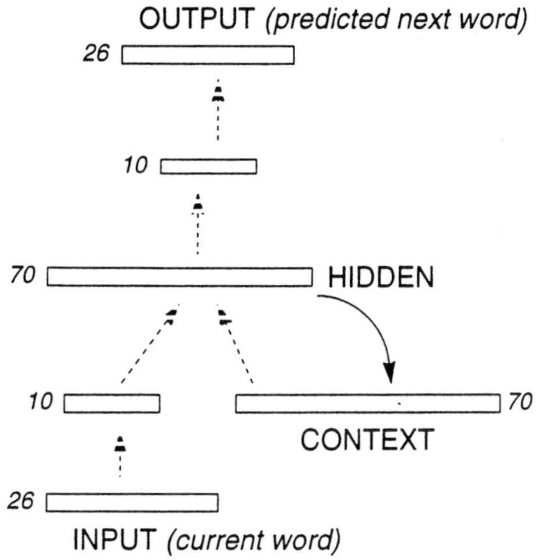

FIG. 1.2. The simple recurrent network used in the prediction task. Rectangles represent groups of nodes; the numbers are shown adjacent to each layer. Lines with arrows indicate connections between layers and the flow of information. Broken lines represent connections whose weights can be changed by learning; the solid line represents connections that are fixed at the value of 1.0.

**chase see the dog*, getting the number agreement of *boys* and *see* right, but failing on the more proximal—and presumably, easier—*girl chases*.) This failure, of course, is exactly what might have been predicted by Gold.

In an attempt to understand where the breakdown was occurring, and just how complex a language the network might be able to learn, I devised a regimen in which the training input was organized into corpora of increasing complexity, and the network was trained first with the simplest input. There were five phases in all. In Phase 1, 10,000 sentences consisting solely of simple sentences were presented. The network was trained on five exposures (*epochs*) to this database. At the conclusion of this phase, the training data were discarded and the network was exposed to a new set of sentences. In Phase 2, 7,500 of the sentences were simple and 2,500 complex sentences were also included. As before, the network was trained for five epochs, after which performance was also quite high, even on the complex sentences. In Phase 3, the mixture was 5,000 simple and 5,000 complex sentences, for five epochs. In Phase 4, the mixture was 2,500 simple and 7,500 complex; and in Phase 5, the network was trained on 10,000 complex sentences. At the conclusion of training, the network's performance was quite good, for complex as well as simple sentence. Furthermore, the network generalized its performance to novel sentences.

This result contrasts strikingly with the earlier failure of the network to learn when the full corpus was presented at the outset. Put simply, the network was unable to learn the complex grammar when trained from the outset with the full "adult" language. However, when the training data were selected such that simple sentences were presented first, the network succeeded not only mastering in these, but then going on to master the complex sentences as well.

In one sense, this is a pleasing result, because the behavior of the network partially resembles that of children. Children do not begin by mastering the adult language in all its complexity. Rather, they begin with the simplest of structures and build incrementally until they achieve the adult language.

There is an important disanalogy, however, between the way in which the network was trained and the way children learn language. In this simulation, the network was placed in an environment that was carefully constructed so that it only encountered the simple sentences at the beginning. As learning and performance progressed, the environment was gradually enriched by the inclusion of more and more complex sentences. But this is not a good model for the situation in which children learn language. Although there is evidence that adults modify their language to some extent when interacting with children, it is not clear that these modifications affect the grammatical structure of the adult speech. Unlike the network, children hear exemplars of all aspects of adult language from the beginning.

If it is not true that the child's environment changes radically (as in this first simulation), what is true is that the *child* changes during the period he or she is learning language. A more realistic network model would have a constant learning environment, but some aspect of the network itself would undergo change during learning. One candidate for a developmental change that might interact with learning is working memory; working memory and attention span in the young child are initially limited and increase over time. Could such changes facilitate learning?

To study a possible interaction between learning and changes in working memory, another new network was trained on the "adult" (i.e., fully complex) data that had initially been problematic. This time, at the outset of learning, the context units (which formed the memory for the network) were reset to random values after every two or three words. This meant that the temporal window within which the network could process valid information was restricted to short sequences. The network would of course see longer sequences, but in those cases the information necessary to make correct predictions would fall outside the limited temporal window; such sequences would effectively seem like noise. The only sequences that would contain usable information would in fact be short, simple sentences. After training the network in this manner for a period of time, the "working memory" of the network was extended by injecting noise into the context units at increasingly long intervals and eventually eliminating the noise altogether.

Under these conditions, the performance at the conclusion of training was just as good as when the training environment had been manipulated. Why did this work? Why should a task that could not be solved when starting with "adult" resources be solvable by a system that began the task with restricted resources and then developed final capacities over time?

It helps to understand the answer by considering just what was involved when learning was successful. At the conclusion of learning, the network had learned several things: distinctions between grammatical categories, conditions under which number agreement obtained, differences between verb argument structure, and how to represent embedded information. As was the case in the simulation involving simple sentences, the network uses its internal state space to represent these distinctions. It learns to partition the state space such that certain spatial dimensions signal differences between nouns and verbs, other dimensions encode singular versus plural, and other dimensions encode depth of embedding.

In fact, we can actually look at the way the network structures its internal representation space. Let us imagine that we do the equivalent of attaching electrodes to the network that successfully learned the complex grammar, by virtue of beginning with a reduced working memory. If we record activations from this network while it processes a large number of sentences, we can plot the activations in a three-dimensional space whose coordinates are the principal components of hidden unit activation space (we use the second, third, and eleventh principal components). The plot shown in Fig. 1.3b shows the regions of this space that are used by the network.

As can be seen, the space is structured into distinct regions, and the patterning is used by the network to encode grammatical category and number. Once the network has developed such a representational scheme, it is possible for it to learn the actual grammatical rules of this language. The representations are necessary prerequisites to learning the grammar, just because these internal representations are also play a role in encoding memory (remember that the hidden unit activation patterns are fed back via the context units). Without a way to meaningfully represent the (arbitrarily encoded) inputs, the network does not have the notational vocabulary to capture the grammatical relations. Subjectively, it is the same problem we would have if we tried to remember and repeat back words in an unfamiliar language—it all sounds like gibberish. Note that this creates a bit of a problem, however. If the network needs the right internal representations to work with, where are these to come from? The truth is that these representations are learned in the course of learning the regularities in the environment. It learns to represent the noun–verb distinction because it is grammatically relevant. But we just said it could not learn the

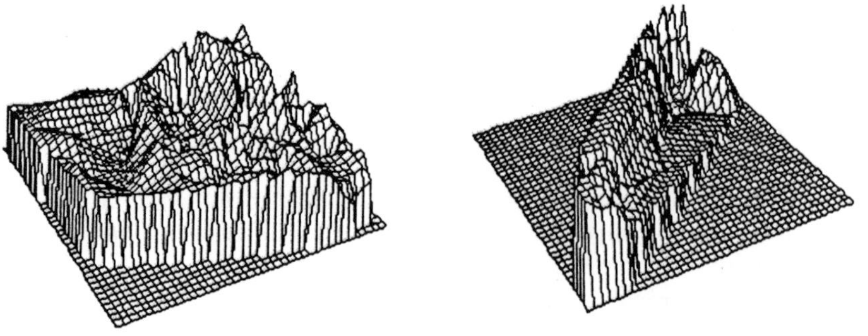

(a) (b)

FIG. 1.3. View of hidden unit space (in 3 of 70 dimensions) of a network that fails to learn the grammar (a), and that succeeds (b). The surfaces are plotted by passing a large number of test sentences through each network and recording the hidden unit activation vector following each word. In the case of successful learning, the hidden unit state space is structured and can be interpreted in terms of various dimensions of relevance for the task (e.g., noun vs. verb, singular vs. plural). In the case of the unsuccessfully trained network, the state space is poorly organized and no clearly interpretable dimensions are found.

grammar without having the representations. Indeed, this chicken-and-egg problem is exactly the downfall of the network that starts off fully developed (but lacking the right representations). If we look at the internal space of this network after (unsuccessful) training, shown in Fig. 1.3a, we see that the space is poorly organized and not partitioned into well-defined areas. The network that starts off with limited resources, on the other hand, actually is at an advantage. Although much of what it sees is now "noise," what remains—the short, simple sentences—is easier to process. More to the point, they provide a tractable (because they are short and impose fewer demands on a well-developed representation–memorial system) entry point into the problem of discovering the grammatical patterns and categories latent in the environment. Once these categories have been induced, they provide the bootstrap by which the network can go on, as its working memory improves, to deal with increasingly complex inputs and refine its knowledge.

Seen in this light, maturational limitations take on a very positive character. If a domain to be mastered is complex, it helps to have some clues about where to start. Certainly the solution space for inducing a grammar from the data is extremely large, and finding the right grammar might be an intractable problem. It makes sense therefore that children (or networks) might need cues to help guarantee they discover the right grammar. The question is, what do these cues look like?

One possibility is that children (or networks) might be prewired in such a way that they know about concepts such as "noun" and "verb" at birth. We might endow them as well with special knowledge about permissible classes of structures, or grammatical operations on those structures. The role of experience would be to help the learner figure out which particular structures or operations are true of the language being learned. This is the hypothesis of Parameter Theory (Chomsky, 1981).

The simulation here suggests another solution to the problem of finding the needle in the grammatical haystack. Timing the development of memory has the effect of limiting the search space in exactly the right sort of way as to allow the network to solve a problem that could not be solved in the absence of limitations.

Is there any evidence that this positive interaction between maturational limitations and language learning plays a role in children, as it seems to in networks? Newport (1988, 1990) suggested that indeed, early resource limitations might explain the apparent critical period during which languages can be learned with native-like proficiency. Newport calls this the "less is more" hypothesis.

It is well known that late learners of a language (either first or second) exhibit poorer performance than early or native learners. What is particularly revealing is to compare the performance of early (or native) learners when it is at a comparable level to that of the late learners (i.e., early on, while they are still learning). Although gross error scores may be similar, the nature of the errors made by the two groups differs. Late learners tend to have incomplete control of morphology and rely more heavily on fixed forms in which internal morphological elements are frozen in place and therefore often used inappropriately. Young native learners, in contrast, commit errors of omission more frequently. Newport suggested that these differences are based in a differential ability to analyze the compositional structure of utterances, with younger language learners at an advantage. This occurs for two reasons. Newport pointed out that the combinatorics of learning the form–meaning mappings that underlie morphology are considerable and grow exponentially with the number of forms and meanings. If one supposes that the younger learner is handicapped with a reduced short-term memory, then this reduces the search space (because the child will be able to perceive and store a limited number of forms). The adult's greater storage and computational skills work to the adult's disadvantage. Secondly, Newport hypothesized that there is a close correspondence between perceptually salient units and morphologically relevant segmentation. With limited processing ability, one might expect children to more attentive to this relation than adults, who might be less attentive to perceptual cues and more inclined to rely on computational analysis. Newport's conclusions are thus very similar to what is suggested by the network performance: There are situations in which maturational constraints play a positive role in learning. Counterintuitively, some problems can only be solved if you start small. Precocity is not always to be desired.

The starting-small and less-is-more hypotheses suggest a new interpretation to the "critical period" phenomenon. Many people have interpreted the fact that language learning occurs with greatest success (e.g., learners achieve native fluency) during childhood as evidence for a Language Acquisition Device that operates only during childhood. Once its job is done, it ceases to function. But the simulation here, and Newport's hypothesis, suggest rather that the ability children have for learning language derives not from a special mechanism that they possess and adults do not but just the reverse. It is children's *lack* of resources that enables them to learn languages fluently.

Finally, how do these hypotheses bear on the issue of innateness? If in fact developmental limitations of the sort discussed here can impose constraints that are crucial for achieving a target behavior, and these developmental limitations arise from biological factors, then we may say that the network described here is "innately constrained" to discovering the proper grammar. But note that this is a very different sort of innateness than that envisioned by the prewired-linguistic-knowledge hypothesis.

HOW DOES THE CORTEX GET ITS ARCHITECTURE?

One of the arguments I advanced earlier against the hypothesis of representational innateness (i.e., direct specification of cortical microcircuitry) rested on experimental data that suggest that the regional mapping of functions in the human cortex is not prespecified. Initially, the cortex appears to possess a high degree of pluripotentiality. Over time, however, a complex pattern of spatially localized regions develops, and the pattern of localization is relatively consistent across individuals. The mystery is how the specific functional organization of the cerebral cortex arises. Shrager and Johnson (1996) and Rebotier and Elman (1996), building on earlier work by Kerszberg, Dehaene, and Changeux (1992), offered a preliminary account of at least one factor that might provide an answer to this question. Let me describe these simulations.

Shrager and Johnson (1996) began with the assumption that the cortex is organized through a combination of endogenous and exogenous influences, including subcortical structuring, maturational timing, and the information structure of an organism's early environment. Their goal was to explore ways in which these various factors might interact in order to lead to differential cortical function and to the differential distribution of function over the cortex. They began with several simple observations.

First, Shrager and Johnson pointed out that although there are signals that pass through the cortex in many directions, subcortical signals (e.g., from the thalamus) largely feed into primary sensory areas, which then largely feed forward to various secondary sensory areas, leading eventually into the parietal and frontal association areas. Each succeeding large-scale region of the cortex can be thought of as processing increasing higher orders of invariants from the stimulus stream. The image is that of a cascade of filters, processing and separating stimulus information in series up toward the integration areas.

Second, Shrager and Johnson noted that a very striking aspect of development of the cerebral cortex is the initial overproduction and subsequent loss of neural connections, resulting in the relatively sparsely interconnected final functional architecture. This process of overproduction of synapses and subsequent (or simultaneous) thinning out of the arbor is thought to be key in cortical ontogeny. As Thatcher (1992) suggested, when initially heavily connected, the cortex is like a lump of stone that, in the hands of the sculptor, is shaped by removal of bits and pieces into its final form. But curiously, this sculpting does not occur everywhere simultaneously. Instead, there appears to be a general developmental dynamic in which, grossly speaking, the locus of maximum neural plasticity begins in the primary sensory and motor areas and moves toward the secondary and parietal association areas, and finally to the frontal regions

(Chugani, Phelps, & Mazziotta, 1987; Harwerth, Smith, Duncan, Crawford, & von Noorden, 1986; Pandya & Yeterian, 1990; Thatcher, 1992). Thus, there is a parallelism between the final architecture of the cortex, in which information proceeds from sensory to secondary to association areas, and the dynamics of cortical development, which also proceeds from sensory to secondary to association areas.

Given these observations, Shrager and Johnson (1996) posed the question, How might such a developmental wave of plasticity—in which different regions of the cortex are more plastic at different points in time—affect the outcome of learning? To study this question, Shrager and Johnson developed a connectionist network that was designed to test the hypothesis that under certain regimes of wave propagation, we might expect a tendency toward the development of higher order functions in later parts of the cortical matrix. In this way, the model might account for spatial distribution of function in the cortex without having to encode the localization directly.

The Shrager and Johnson model is shown in Fig. 1.4. The model consists of an abstract "cortical matrix" composed of a 30 × 30 matrix of artificial neurons. Each neuronal unit has afferent and efferent connections to nearby units and also receives afferent inputs from external signals designated A and B. For our purposes, we consider the case in which afferent and efferent connection weights are initially set at random, and in which the external signals A and B provide simultaneous inputs of 0 and 1, also at random.

The matrix weights are changed according to a Hebbian learning rule, so that connection strength grows between units whose activations are more highly correlated. Under the default conditions just described, the outcome after learning is that some units become active only when their A input is on, others become sensitive only to the presence of the B input, and still others become sensitive to A and B simultaneously (logical AND) or to either A or B (logical OR). A very large number of units are always off. No units develop that are sensitive to exclusive OR (XOR), which is not surprising because Hebbian learning does not typically lead to such higher order functions.

Shrager and Johnson (1996) then considered what might happen if the Hebbian learning is modulated by a trophic factor (TF) that passed through the matrix in a wave, from left to right. The effect of the wave was that the columns of units underneath it, at any given point in time, were more plastic and therefore able to learn. During the first training cycle, for example, a modulation vector was produced for the 30-column matrix that might be [1.0, 0.86, 0.77, 0.66, 0.53, . . . , 0.0, 0.0]. That is, TF transmission at Location 1 in the matrix took place normally, whereas TF transmission at Location 2 was reduced to 86% of what would have been moved, and

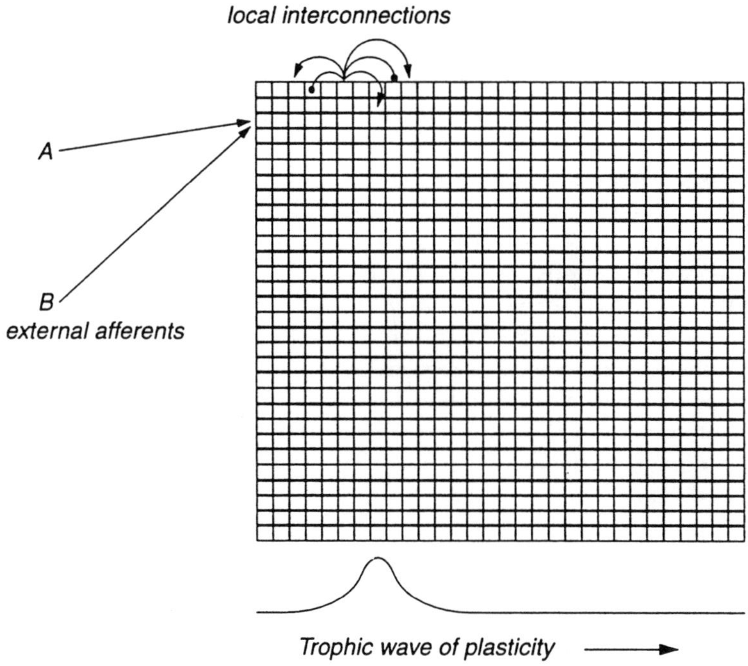

FIG. 1.4. Shrager and Johnson (1996) model. Each unit has short local connections (excitatory and inhibitory) to close neighbors and also receives afferents from the external afferents, A and B (shown here as excitatory, but initially set as excitatory or inhibitory at random). In some simulations, a tropic wave of plasticity spreads from left to right across the matrix and has the effect of modulating learning in the columns under this wave.

so forth. On the next cycle, the wave moved to the right a small amount: [0.86, 1.0, 0.86, 0.77, 0.66, . . . , 0.0, 0.0]. The progress of the wave thus modulated the transmission of TF, leading to a dynamic plasticity in the cortical matrix. Leftward columns were plastic early and also lost their plasticity early on; whereas rightward columns did not become plastic until later on, but were plastic toward the end of the simulation when most of the neurons were reaching asymptote on the stabilization and death curves.

Under certain regimes of wave propagation, Shrager and Johnson (1996) expected to observe a tendency toward the development of higher order functions in the cortical matrix. (Higher order functions are those that depend on both A and B inputs; lower order functions are those that depend solely on A or B.) The reason for this may be envisioned by considering two steps in the propagation of the wave from some leftward set of columns to the next set of columns to the right. We shall call these columns COL1 and COL2 (which is immediately to the right of COL1). COL1, initially more plastic than COL2, determines its function during receipt of input from A and B afferents, as has been the case all along. However, COL1 becomes fixated in its function relatively early, as the wave moves on to COL2. Now, however, COL2 is receiving input that, in addition to the input coming from A and B afferents, includes the combined functions fixated by the earlier plasticity in COL1. Thus, COL2 has, in effect, three afferents: A, B, and COL1.

In fact, Shrager and Johnson (1996) found that the number of first-order functions (A, ~A, B, and ~B) differed significantly from the number of second-order functions (B-AND--A, A-AND--B, A-XOR-B, ~[A-AND-B], A-AND-B, A=B, A>=B, A<=B, and A-OR-B), when the wave was present, but not without the wave. Furthermore, as predicted, the density of higher order functions increased in regions of the matrix that were plastic later on, as determined by the propagation of the TF wave. Finally, when the propagation rate of the wave was tripled from the initial rate, a different picture emerged. Again, the first- and second-order functional densities were significantly different, but this time the mean values were inverted. In the slow-wave case, the second-order functions were emphasized, whereas in the fast-wave case, the first-order functions were emphasized.

There is another result that is of great significance and was the focus of a replication and extension by Rebotier and Elman (1996). This result has to do with the problem of how to reconcile the desire for a learning rule that is both biologically plausible and sufficiently powerful. On the one hand, Hebbian learning has a greater biological plausibility than back propagation learning. Also, Hebbian learning is a form of self-organizing behavior, which is attractive because it means an explicit teacher is not required (as in back propagation). On the other hand, Hebbian learning cannot be used to learn certain important problems. These include XOR and other functions in which classification cannot be done on the basis of correlations. This is unfortunate, because it means that the learning mechanism that is most natural on biological grounds seems to lack necessary computational properties.

Rebotier and Elman (1996) constructed a network of the form Shrager and Johnson (1996) devised and allowed Hebbian learning to take place through all parts of the network ("instant cortex"). Not surprisingly, Rebotier and Elman (1996) found no units that responded to the XOR of the inputs A and B. Rebotier and Elman then repeated the experiment, but this time they allowed learning to be modulated by a spatial wave of TF, which passed over the network from left to right. This time, a small percentage of units were found that computed XOR. These units tended to be on the right side of the network (i.e., the late maturing regions). The reason they could compute XOR is that they did not learn until later, after early units had developed which learned simpler functions such as AND and OR. These early learning units then became additional inputs to the later learning units. Because XOR can be decomposed into the AND and OR functions, this made it possible to learn a function that could not otherwise have been learned.

There are thus two important lessons to be learned from the Shrager and Johnson (1996) and Rebotier and Elman (1996) studies. First, the models demonstrate how the differential functional architecture of the cortex might arise in early development as an emergent result of the combination of organized stimulus input and a neurotrophic dynamic (whether produced by a natural wave of TF or by some other endogenous or exogenous phenomenon). Second, development provides the key to another puzzle. The studies show how some complex functions that are not normally learned in a static mature system can be learned when learning is carried out over both time and space rather than occurring everywhere simultaneously.

A CONSPIRACY THEORY OF LANGUAGE

I began at the outset with a set of questions and I would like to return to them now, if not to provide answers, at least to say how the aforementioned simulations suggest we might think about what kinds of answers are likely.

The questions—about species uniqueness, the form of language, language learning, universals, and variation—might be answered by simply stipulating that language is an innate property of our species and takes the form it does "just because it does." This is not only not a very illuminating answer, but to the extent that it relies on representational innateness, is also highly implausible. Yet language does emerge only in our species; it does assume a constrained set of forms; and patterns of acquisition and usage are remarkably similar across languages. How might we account for this?

The two simulations described earlier (and considerable other evidence discussed in detail in Elman et al., 1996) suggest what might be called the "language as conspiracy" view. This view is in fact consistent with two very robust findings in the embryological and developmental genetics literature: (a) the nonlinear effects of small developmental changes on outcome, and (b) the conservative nature of the genome and the importance of interactions in development.

At the turn of the century, the naturalist D'Arcy Thompson published a now-classic treatise called *On Form and Growth* (1961). Thompson pointed out that relatively simple transformations of the Cartesian coordinates underlying body plans could produce dramatic differences in body morphology. Thus, the skulls of the human, chimpanzee, baboon, and dog bear a striking resemblance once the transformation is made apparent (see Fig.

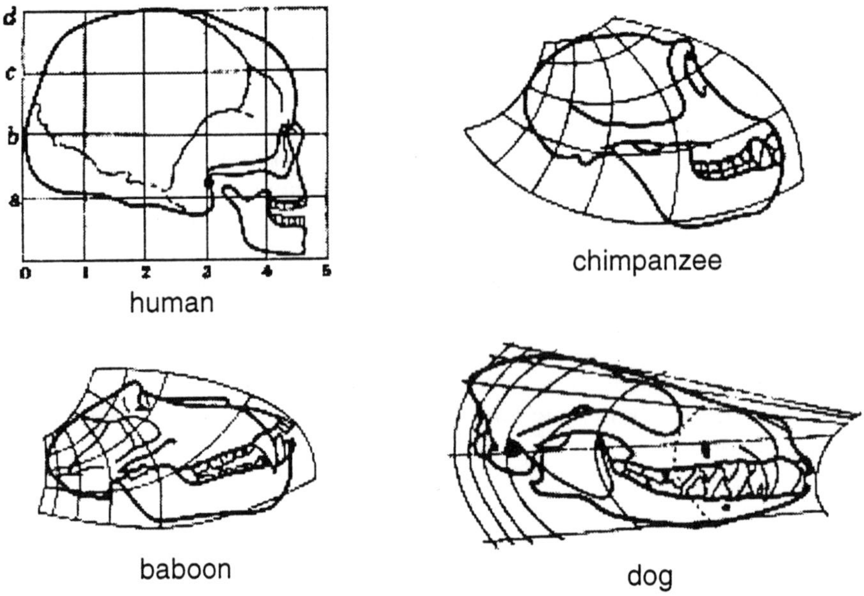

FIG. 1.5. Skulls of human, chimpanzee, baboon, and dog, drawn with respect to a single Cartesian coordinate system. Differences in skull size and shape can be produced by transformations on the coordinates. From Thompson (1961, pp. 318–319, 322).

1.5). Thompson suggested that what appear to be large morphological differences in species might be misleading in that they involve far simpler changes in growth.

We know now that in fact there are a variety of developmental mechanisms that can accomplish transformations of the sort described by Thompson (see McKinney & McNamara, 1991, for an extensive review). It is clear that small changes in a developmental trajectory can indeed lead to very great differences in outcome. Earlier, in discussing the role of timing, I gave the examples of long-bone growth. Similar accounts have been offered for a variety of other changes associated with speciation. Flightlessness, for example, is common among birds that live on islands without large mammalian predators; maintenance of the bone and muscle mass necessary for flight are energetically expensive and will be selected against unless there is some adaptive advantage to flight. Some groups of birds, such as rails, have evolved to delay sternum formation until relatively late in development. Delaying this important developmental process until after hatching pre-adapts the group so that further changes leading to flightlessness (in environments where this is advantageous) are easy to achieve.

An even more dramatic example concerns the process of tooth formation (or lack thereof) in the modern bird. The formation of teeth involves a complex interaction between several embryonic tissues. One layer of tissue (epithelium) must be brought into contact with another layer of tissue (mesenchyme). The mesenchyme induces the epithelium to differentiate into an enamel-producing organ; the organ-producing epithelium then induces the mesenchyme to differentiate into tissue that secretes dentin. In the absence of this second interaction, the mesenchyme would become spongy bone. Birds are known to descend from ancestral species that possessed teeth, but such toothed birds have not been seen since the Upper Cretaceous. Does this mean that the genetic information necessary to form teeth has been lost in birds and replaced by "beak-forming genes"? Apparently not. Rather, it seems that in birds, this interaction has merely been short-circuited. The interaction can be artificially brought about by bringing dental epithelium from the chick into contact with mesenchyme from a mouse (Kollar & Fisher, 1980). Under these conditions, the chick epithelium will form enamel organs, and further interactions may lead to formation of complete teeth.

This last example also illustrates the second major lesson concerning development: In mammals, most important developmental phenonena rest on a complex set of interactions. These include virtually every possible interaction imaginable, for example, gene–gene, gene–environment, tissue–tissue, tissue–environment, organ–organ, organ–environment, and so forth. The early view, for example, that complex behaviors might be directed by single genes, has given way over the past several decades to the realization that even apparently simple traits such as eye color reflect the coordinated interaction of multiple genes. For more complex traits, the number of genes involved may figure in the thousands. Furthermore, genes typically play multiple roles, participating in the formation of very different traits.

As an example of this last point, consider courtship in the fruit fly, *Drosophila melanogaster*. Courtship involves at least six distinct phases, each with a different set of behaviors. A great deal has been discovered about the mechanisms that are required for the sequence of behaviors that lead to successful mating. The total repertoire depends on nine or more different regions of the central nervous system. The genetic basis for the behaviors is also beginning to be worked out, with the discovery that the genes that are involved in courtship also play a role in other behaviors. Thus, the *period* gene, which is involved in controlling the rhythm of the courtship song, also plays a role in regulating the fly's circadian rhythms. Other aspects of the courtship require that the male respond adaptively to the female's behavior; the *CaMKII* and *eag* genes, which are known to play a role in learning and memory in the fruit fly, are then called into play (Greenspan, 1995; see Hall, 1994, for a full review of the genetic basis of courtship behavior).

The complex interactions and the importance of genes as regulators may occasionally give rise to what looks like a one gene–one trait relation. For instance, two (of the many) species of fruit fly found only in Hawaii differ minimally (and are in fact interfertile), primarily in head shape. One species, *D. silvestris*, has the normal round-shaped head. The other, *D. heteroneura*, has a bizarrely shaped head that looks like a hammerhead shark. This difference is mostly associated with a single gene—but this gene is involved with complex epistatic interactions with three or four other genes, and it is a quantitative change in the interaction that gives rise to a qualitative change in trait (Val, 1976).

Or consider the recent discovery of a family in Costa Rica that has a family history, going back more than 200 years, of acquired deafness (Lynch et al., 1997). The onset of deafness is around puberty and leads to hearing loss, initially in the low-frequency range but eventually becoming total. Because of the very high family incidence and the long family history (and the total lack of incidence in the family's village), a genetic basis for the disorder was sought and eventually found. It turned out that the deafness could be attributed to a mutation in a single gene. The mutation's effect was that the last 52 of the 1,265 amino acids coded for by the gene were incorrectly specified.

A gene for deafness? Not at all. A nearly similar gene called *Diaphonous* is also found in the fruit fly. The *diaphanous* gene produces a protein that controls the assembly of actin. Actin is one of the most prevalent proteins found in the body; it organizes the tiny fibers found in cell plasma that determine a cell's structural properties (rigidity, ability to move, to deform, etc.). It seems likely that the mutation was selectively producing deafness only because the hair cells in the ear are particularly sensitive to loss of stiffness. Because the mutation was slight, the degenerate form of the protein was sufficient for most of its uses in the rest of the body. It was only in the hair cells that the deficiency could not be tolerated.

The recurring lesson, whenever one looks at complex phenotypic traits in mammals, is that the traits are produced by a sometimes large number of interactions. The underlying genetic substrate is enormously conservative, evolutionarily. What makes innovation possible is that the interactions are sufficiently complex and that small alterations in developmental pathways can lead to very large differences in outcome.

Seen in this light, we should doubt that the novelty of language lies in having evolutionary and developmental origins that differ radically from those underlying communicative behaviors in similar species. Rather, it makes sense to view language as a behavior that results from allometric transformations (à la D'Arcy Thompson) over a set of behaviors that are present as well in other closely related species. Language is simply the result of a number of tweaks and twiddles, each of which may in fact be quite minor, but which in the aggregate and through interaction yield what appears to be a radically new behavior. It is in this sense that language is a conspiracy.

Of course, in very significant ways, language *is* a radically new behavior. At a phenomenological level, it is quite unlike anything else that we (or any other species) do. It has features that are remarkable and unique. The crucial difference between this view and the view of language as a separable domain-specific module (in the sense of Tooby & Cosmides, 1992) is that the uniqueness emerges out of an interaction involving small differences in domain-nonspecific behaviors.

If this view of language as conspiracy is correct, then it should be possible to list in detail the behaviors that participate in the conspiracy. We should be able to identify the ways in which the human version of those behaviors differs from that in other species. We should ultimately be able to formulate a theory of interaction that provides an account not only for human language but for other nonhuman primate communication systems. They too are unique, in their own ways. Although we are probably far from having such a full account, I believe that the simulations offered here illustrate such an account's viability.

REFERENCES

Bonner, J. T. (1988). *The evolution of complexity.* Princeton, NJ: Princeton University Press.

Calow, P. (1976). *Biological machines: A cybernetic approach to life.* London: Arnold.

Chomsky, N. (1981). *Lectures on government and binding.* New York: Foris.

Chugani, H. T., Phelps, M. E., & Mazziotta, J. C. (1987). Positron emission tomography study of human brain functional development. *Annals of Neurology, 22,* 487–497.

Elman, J. L. (1993). Learning and development in neural networks: The importance of starting small. *Cognition, 48,* 71–99.

Elman, J. L., Bates, E. A., Johnson, M. H., Karmiloff-Smith, A., Parisi, D., Plunkett, K. (1996). *Rethinking innateness: A connectionist perspective on development.* Cambridge, MA: MIT Press.

Friedlander, M. J., Martin, K. A. C., & Wassenhove-McCarthy, D. (1991). Effects of monocular visual deprivation on geniculocortical innervation of area 18 in cat. *The Journal of Neuroscience, 11,* 3268–3288.

Frost, D. O. (1982). Anomalous visual connections to somatosensory and auditory systems following brain lesions in early life. *Brain Research, 255,* 627–635.

Frost, D. O. (1990). Sensory processing by novel, experimentally induced cross-modal circuits. *Annals of the New York Academy of Sciences, 608,* 92–109, 109–112.

Gold, E. M. (1967). Language identification in the limit. *Information and Control, 16,* 447–474.

Gopnik, M., & Crago, M. B. (1991). Familial aggregation of a developmental language disorder. *Cognition, 39,* 1–50.

Gould, S. J. (1977). *Ontogeny and phylogeny.* Cambridge, MA: Harvard University Press.

Greenough, W. T., Black, J. E., & Wallace, C. S. (1993). Experience and brain development. In M. Johnson (Ed.), *Brain development and cognition: A reader* (pp. 290–322). Oxford, UK: Blackwell.

Greenspan, R. J. (1995, April). Understanding the genetic construction of behavior. *Scientific American, 272,* 72–78.

Hall, J. C. (1994). The mating of a fly. *Science, 264,* 1702–1714.

Harwerth, R. S., Smith, E. L. I., Duncan, G. C., Crawford, M. L. J., & von Noorden, G. K. (1986). Multiple sensitive periods in the development of the primate visual system. *Science, 232,* 235–238.

Kerszberg, M., Dehaene, S., & Changeux, J. P. (1992). Stabilization of complex input output functions in neural clusters formed by synapse selection. *Neural Networks, 5,* 403–413.

Killackey, H. P., Chiaia, N. L., Bennett-Clarke, C. A., Eck, M., & Rhoades, R. (1994). Peripheral influences on the size and organization of somatotopic representations in the fetal rat cortex. *Journal of Neuroscience, 14,* 1496–1506.

Kollar, E. J., & Fisher, C. (1980). Tooth induction in chick epithelium: Expression of quiescent genes for enamel synthesis. *Science, 207,* 993–995.

Lynch, E. D., Lee, M. K., Morrow, J. E., Welsch, P. L., León, P. E., & King, M. (1997). Nonsyndromic deafness DFNA1 associated with mutation of a human homolog of the *Drosophila* gene *diaphanous. Science, 278,* 1315–1318.

MacWhinney, B. (1993). Connections and symbols: Closing the gap. *Cognition, 49,* 291–296.

Marchman, V. (1993). Constraints on plasticity in a connectionist model of the English past tense. *Journal of Cognitive Neuroscience, 5,* 215–234.

McKinney, M. L., & McNamara, K. J. (1991). *Heterochrony: The evolution of ontogeny.* New York: Plenum.

Merzenich, M. M., Recanzone, G., Jenkins, W. M., Allard, T. T., & Nudo, R. J. (1988). Cortical representational plasticity. In P. Rakic & W. Singer (Eds.), *Neurobiology of neocortex* (pp. 41–67). New York: Wiley.

Molnar, Z., & Blakemore, C. (1991). Lack of regional specificity for connections formed between thalamus and cortex in coculture. *Nature, 351 (6326),* 475–477.

Newport, E. L. (1988). Constraints on learning and their role in language acquisition: Studies of the acquisition of American Sign Language. *Language Sciences, 10,* 147–172.

Newport, E. L. (1990). Maturational constraints on language learning. *Cognitive Science, 14,* 11–28.

O'Leary, D. D. (1993). Do cortical areas emerge from a protocortex? In M. Johnson (Ed.), *Brain development and cognition: A reader* (pp. 323–337). Oxford, UK: Blackwell.

O'Leary, D. D., & Stanfield, B. B. (1989). Selective elimination of axons extended by developing cortical neurons is dependent on regional locale: Experiments utilizing fetal cortical transplants. *Journal of Neuroscience, 9(7),* 2230–2246.

Pallas, S. L., & Sur, M. (1993). Visual projections induced into the auditory pathway of ferrets: II. Corticocortical connections of primary auditory cortex. *Journal of Comparative Neurology, 337(2),* 317–333.

Pandya, D. N., & Yeterian, E. H. (1985). Architecture and connections of cortical association areas. In A. Peters & E. G. Jones (Eds.), *Cerebral cortex: Vol. 4: Association and auditory cortices* (pp. 3–61). New York: Plenum.

Pinker, S. (1994). *The language instinct: How the mind creates language.* New York: Morrow.

Pons, T. P., Garraghty, P. E., Ommaya, A. K., Kaas, J. H. Taub, E., & Mishkin M. (1991). Massive cortical reorganization after sensory deafferentation in adult macaques. *Science, 252(5014),* 1857–1860.

Ramachandran, V. S. (1993). Behavioral and magnetoencephalographic correlates of plasticity in the adult human brain. *Proceedings of the National Academy of Sciences, 90,* 10413–10420.

Rebotier, T. P., & Elman, J. L. (1996). Explorations with the dynamic wave model. In D. Touretzky, M. Mozer, & M. Haselmo (Eds.), *Advances in neural information processing systems 8* (pp. 549–556). Cambridge, MA: MIT Press.

Roe, A. W., Pallas, S. L., Hahm, J. O., & Sur, M. (1990). A map of visual space induced in primary auditory cortex. *Science, 250 (4982),* 818–820.

Shrager, J., & Johnson, M. H. (1996). Dynamic plasticity influences the emergence of function in a simple cortical array. *Neural Networks, 8,* 1–11.

Sur, M., Garraghty, P. E., & Roe, A. W. (1988). Experimentally induced visual projections into auditory thalamus and cortex. *Science, 242,* 1437–1441.

Sur, M., Pallas, S. L., & Roe, A. W. (1990). Cross-modal plasticity in cortical development: Differentiation and specification of sensory neocortex. *Trends in Neuroscience, 13,* 227–233.

Thatcher, R. W. (1992). Cyclic cortical reorganization during early childhood. *Brain and Cognition, 20,* 24–50.

Thompson, D. W. (1961). *On growth and form.* Cambridge, UK: Cambridge University Press.

Tooby, J., & Cosmides, L. (1992). The psychological foundations of culture. In J. Barkow, L. Cosmides, & J. Tooby (Eds.), *The adapted mind: Evolutionary psychology and the generation of culture* (pp. 19–136). New York: Oxford University Press.

Val, F. C. (1976). Genetic analysis of the morphological differences between two interfertile species of Hawaiian Drosophila. *Evolution, 31,* 611–620.

Vargha-Khadem, F., Watkins, K., Alcock, K., Fletcher, P., & Passingham, R. (1995). Praxic and nonverbal cognitive deficits in a large family with a genetically transmitted speech and language disorder. *Proceedings of the National Academy of Sciences USA, 92,* 930–933.

Chapter 2

On the Emergence of Grammar From the Lexicon

Elizabeth Bates
University of California, San Diego

Judith C. Goodman
University of Missouri, Columbia

Where does grammar come from? How does it develop in children? Developmental psycholinguists who set out to answer these questions quickly find themselves impaled on the horns of a dilemma, caught up in a modern variant of the ancient war between empiricists and nativists. Indeed, some of the fiercest battles in this war have been waged in the field of child language. Many reasonable individuals in this field have argued for a middle ground, but such a compromise has proven elusive thus far, in part because the middle ground is difficult to define.

So let us begin with some definitions. The core of this debate is about epistemology, a branch of philosophy that we can define as the study of knowledge, its form, and source, and the process by which it comes to be. Within this framework, empiricism can be defined as the belief that knowledge originates in the environment and comes into the mind or brain through the senses, an epistemology that can be traced back to Aristotle, with variations over the centuries by Hume, Locke, and the American Behaviorist School. Nativism can be defined as the belief that fundamental aspects of knowledge are inborn, and that experience operates by filling in preformed categories, selecting, activating, or "triggering" these latent mental states. This epistemology can be traced back to Plato, with historical variations that have included Kant and Descartes.

Many researchers follow the lead of Chomsky, subscribing explicitly to the nativist doctrine as we just defined it. Chomsky himself has consistently and clearly articulated a nativist approach to the nature and origins of grammar, treating grammar as an organ of the brain not unlike an organ of the body, unfolding on a strict maturational schedule, governed by a specific genetic program. Some sample quotes from Chomsky (1988) illustrate these claims, including an unambiguous endorsement of Plato:

> The evidence seems compelling, indeed overwhelming, that fundamental aspects of our mental and social life, including language, are determined as part of our biological endowment, not acquired by learning, still less by training, in the course of our experience. Many find this conclusion offensive. They would prefer to believe that humans are shaped by the environment, not that they develop in a manner that is predetermined in essential respects. (p. 161)

> Now this illustrates a very general fact about biology of organs. There has to be sufficiently rich environmental stimulation for the genetically determined process to develop in the manner in which it is programmed to develop. The term for this is "triggering"; that is, the experience does not determine how the mind will work but it triggers it, it makes it work in its own largely predetermined way. (p. 172)

> How can we interpret [Plato's] proposal in modern terms? A modern variant would be that certain aspects of our knowledge and understanding are innate, part of our biological endowment, genetically determined, on a par with the elements of our common nature that cause us to grow arms and legs rather than wings. This version of the classical doctrine is, I think, essentially correct. (p. 4)

Of course Chomsky acknowledges that French children learn French words, Chinese children learn Chinese words, and so on. But he believes that the abstract underlying principles that govern language in general and grammar in particular are not learned at all, arguing elsewhere ". . . that a general learning theory does exist, seems to me dubious, unargued, and without any empirical support or plausibility at the moment" (Chomsky, 1980, p. 110).

Because this theory has been so influential in modern linguistics and child language, it is important to understand exactly what Chomsky means by "innate." Everyone would agree that there is something unique about the human brain that makes language possible. But in the absence of evidence to the contrary, that "something" could be nothing other than the fact that our brains are very large, a giant all-purpose computer with trillions of processing elements. Chomsky's version of the theory of innateness is much stronger than the "big brain" view and involves two logically and empirically separate claims: that our capacity for grammar is innate, and that this capacity comprises a dedicated, special-purpose learning device that has evolved for grammar alone. The latter claim is the one that is really controversial, a doctrine that goes under various names including *domain specificity, autonomy,* and *modularity.* Putting the separable but correlated claims of innateness and domain specificity together, Kandel, Schwartz, and Jessell (1995) provided a concise textbook summary of Chomsky's theory that provides a fair representation of this view as it has been received and interpreted outside of linguistics, in the outer reaches of cognitive science and neuroscience:

> Chomsky postulated that the brain must have an organ of language, unique to humans, that can combine a finite set of words into an infinite number of sentences. This capability, he argued, must be innate and not learned, since children speak and understand novel combinations of words they have not previously heard. *Children must therefore have built into their brain a universal grammar, a plan shared by the grammars of all natural languages.* (p. 639, italics added)

Strong and explicit illustrations of this view can also be found within child language as well, with emphasis on the genetic and the neural bases of a mental organ for grammar:

> A distinguishing feature of recent linguistic theory, at least in the tradition of generative/transformational grammar, is that it postulates universal (hence, putatively innate) principles of grammar formation, rather than characterizing the acquisition of language as the product of general cognitive growth. . . . This theoretical framework is often referred to as the theory of Universal Grammar, a theory of the internal organization of the mind/brain of the language learner. (Crain, 1991)

> It is a certain wiring of the microcircuitry that is essential . . . if language, the quintessential higher cognitive process, is an instinct, maybe the rest of cognition is a bunch of instincts too—complex circuits, each dedicated to solving a particular family of computational problems posed by the ways of life we adopted millions of years ago. (Pinker, 1994, pp. 93, 97)

> It is not unreasonable to entertain an interim hypothesis that a single dominant gene controls for those mechanisms that result in a child's ability to construct the paradigms that constitute [grammatical] morphology. (Gopnik & Crago, 1991, p. 47)

In contrast with the relatively large group of linguists and psycholinguists who are willing to embrace a nativist view, few modern investigators proclaim themselves to be empiricists as we define it here. Instead, those who disagree with Chomsky tend to argue in favor of an interactionist account, where learning plays a central role but does so within biological constraints. In its weaker form, interactionism constitutes little more than an eclectic mix of nativist and empiricist claims. A stronger form of interactionism, alternatively called *constructivism* or *emergentism,* constitutes a genuine third alternative. However, emergentism is also a much more difficult idea than either nativism or empiricism, and its historical roots are less clear. In the 20th century, the constructivist approach has been most closely associated with the Swiss psychologist Piaget (e.g., 1970). More recently, it has appeared in a new approach to learning and development in brains and brain-like computers alternatively called *connectionism, parallel distributed processing*, and *neural networks* (Elman et al., 1996; Rumelhart & McClelland, 1986), and in a related theory of development inspired by the nonlinear dynamical systems of modern physics (Thelen & Smith, 1994). To understand this difficult but important idea, we need to distinguish between simple interactions (black and white make gray) and real cases of emergence (black and white get together and something altogether new and different happens).

In an emergentist theory, outcomes can arise for reasons that are not obvious or predictable from any of the individual inputs to the problem. One might expect, for example, that the spherical shape of soap bubbles derives from some specific property of soap; instead, it turns out that soap bubbles are round because a sphere is the only possible solution to achieving maximum volume with minimum surface (i.e., their spherical form is not explained by the soap, the water, or the little boy who blows the bubble). The honeycomb in a beehive takes a hexagonal form because that is the stable solution to the problem of packing circles together (i.e., the hexagon is not predictable from the wax, the honey it contains, or from the packing behavior of an individual bee—see Fig. 2.1). Piaget

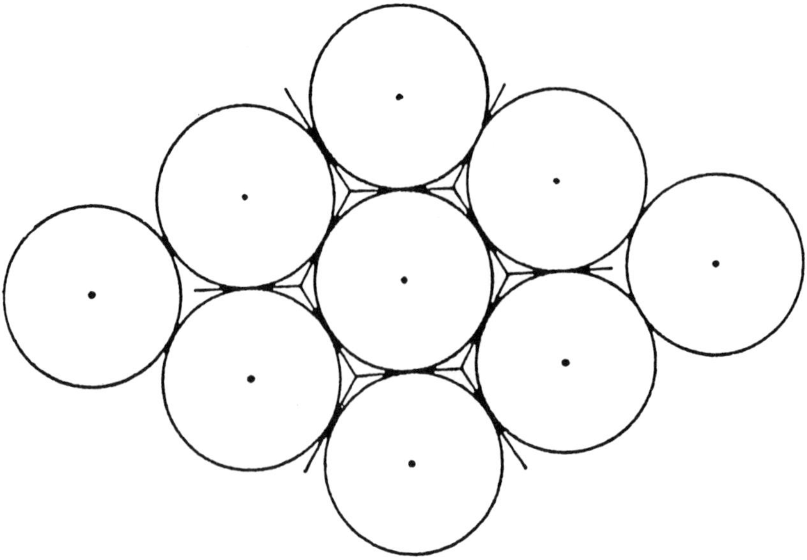

FIG. 2.1. Diagram of hexagonal cells. After Bonanni.

argued that logic and knowledge emerge in just such a fashion, from successive interactions between sensorimotor activity and a structured world. A similar argument has been made to explain the emergence of grammars, which represent the class of possible solutions to the problem of mapping a rich set of meanings onto a limited speech channel, heavily constrained by the limits of memory, perception, and motor planning (Bates & MacWhinney, 1989). Logic and grammar are not given in the world, but neither are they given in the genes. Human beings discovered the principles that comprise logic and grammar, because these principles are the best possible solution to specific problems that other species just simply do not care about and could not solve even if they did. Proponents of the emergentist view acknowledge that something is innate in the human brain that makes language possible, but that "something" may not be a special-purpose, domain-specific device of the sort proposed by Chomsky and his followers, that is, an autonomous device that evolved for language and language alone. Instead, language may be something that we do with a large and complex brain that evolved to serve the many complex goals of human society and culture (Tomasello & Call, 1997).

So the debate today in the field of language development is not about nature versus nurture, but about the "nature of nature," that is, whether language is something that we do with an inborn language device, or whether it is the product of (innate) abilities that are not specific to language. The horned beast in Fig. 2.2 provides another metaphor of the process by which nature finds idiosyncratic outcomes through simple quantitative change in a much more general structure. The elegant headgear displayed in Fig. 2.2 is striking; confronted with such an odd display, we are tempted to speculate about its specific purpose for that species (e.g., to appeal to females, to frighten competing males). However, Thompson (1917/1968) pointed out long ago that the curvature of a more general "standard horn" will twist into just such a shape if the animal continues

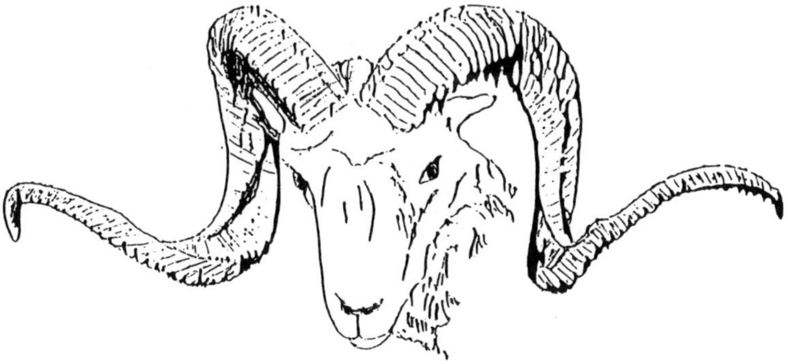

FIG. 2.2. Marco Polo's sheep: *Ovis poli.* From Cook.

to grow past the age at which horn growth normally comes to an end. Hence, a relatively simple quantitative change in patterns of growth can yield an exotic and (apparently) peculiar outcome (of course, the female sheep may have grown quite fond of the resulting display in the intervening years, but that is another story).

Yet another metaphor for the evolution of grammar comes from the giraffe (Fig. 2.3). Consider in particular the giraffe's neck, a striking adaptation if ever there was one. Because of this adaptation, giraffes can feast on leaves high up in the trees, with no competition from birds, monkeys, and other creatures that reach the same heights by other means. Should we conclude that the giraffe's neck is a "high-leaf-eating organ"? Not necessarily. First of all, the giraffe's neck is still a neck, that is, it still does all the jobs that necks perform in less specialized species. Second, the giraffe's neck is built out of a basic blueprint that is used in all vertebrates, for example, it has the same number of bones that necks contain up and down the mammalian line, elongated to provide extra potential for reaching up high in the trees. As a result of this particular adaptation (resulting from quantitative changes in the Basic Neck Plan), other adaptations have

FIG. 2.3. The giraffe as a metaphor for the evolution of specialized organs.

been necessary as well, including cardiovascular changes (to pump blood all the way up to the giraffe's brain), shortening of the hind legs relative to the forelegs (to ensure that the giraffe does not topple over), and so on. If we insist that the neck is a leaf-reaching organ, then we have to include the rest of the giraffe in that category too, including cardiovascular changes and adjustments in leg length.

We suggest that the human "grammar organ" has evolved in a similar fashion: Because of quantitative adjustments in neural mechanisms that exist in other mammals, human beings have walked into a problem space that other animals cannot perceive, much less solve. However, once it finally appeared on the planet, it is quite likely that language itself began to apply adaptive pressure to the organization of the human brain, just as the leaf-reaching adaptation of the giraffe's neck applied adaptive pressure to other parts of the giraffe. All of the neural mechanisms that participate in grammar still do other kinds of work (i.e., they have kept their "day jobs"), but they have also grown to meet the language task. Candidates for this category of "language-facilitating mechanisms" might include our social organization, our extraordinary ability to imitate the things that other people do, our excellence in the segmentation of rapid auditory stimuli, our fascination with joint attention (looking at the same events together, sharing new objects just for the fun of it), and perhaps above all our ability to create and manipulate symbols, letting one object, sound, or action stand for an object, event, or idea that is not currently present or perceivable in the immediate environment (Bates, Benigni, Bretherton, Camaioni, & Volterra, 1979; Bates, Thal, & Marchman, 1991). These abilities are present in human infants within the 1st or 2nd year, and they are clearly involved in the process by which language is acquired. Thus, even though none of these basic cognitive and communicative abilities are specific to language, they permit the emergence of language in general, and grammar in particular.

In this chapter, we explore a particular variant of the emergentist approach to grammar, emphasizing the union between grammar and the lexicon. We define grammar as the class of possible solutions to the problem of mapping back and forth between a high-dimensional meaning space with universal properties and a low-dimensional channel that unfolds in time, heavily constrained by limits on information processing (see also MacWhinney & Bates, 1989). This is a constraint satisfaction problem, and it is also a dimension reduction problem. In problems of this kind, complex solutions are likely to emerge that are not directly predictable from any individual component (Elman et al., 1996; Rumelhart & McClelland, 1986). Grammars do not "look like" anything else that we do—not even the quintessentially linguistic act of naming. However, such idiosyncratic products can be explained without postulating a grammar-specific learning device or a grammar-specific neural mechanism in the brain. Two related lines of evidence are marshaled in favor of this approach. First, we provide evidence for a strong form of lexicalism, showing that grammar and the lexicon are acquired and mediated by the same mental–neural mechanisms. Evidence for this claim includes the strong relation between grammar and lexical development during the early stages of language learning, the striking overlap between lexical and grammatical symptoms observed in neurological patients, and the absence of evidence for a systematic difference in the cortical areas that mediate grammatical and lexical information. Second, we include evidence suggesting that the mental–neural mechanisms responsible for both lexical and grammatical processing are not unique to language. Like the giraffe's neck (which is highly specialized but also handles many tasks), the neural mechanisms that "do" language also do a lot of other things.

The link between emergentism and the lexicalist approach to grammar is also discussed by Goldberg (chap. 7, this volume), but is important enough for our arguments here that it merits some attention before we proceed. The autonomy of grammar from other aspects of language has been a key element in Chomsky's arguments for innateness. A critical aspect of this argument revolves around the Poverty of the Stimulus: Grammars (as Chomsky defines them) are not learnable in finite time in the absence of negative evidence (i.e., in the absence of clear feedback concerning forms that are not possible within the language—see especially Gold, 1967); because children do not receive systematic negative evidence, they must possess enough innate knowledge about their grammar to permit learning to go through. In other words, grammar cannot be learned bottom up, through the application of inductive learning procedures, because such learning requires exploration of an infinite search space. Even if this were true, one still might argue that grammar could be learned top down, through the application of deductive procedures that map linguistic forms onto a finite set of meanings, including meanings that are not specific to language (e.g., negation, agency, causality, location, and change of location). This meaning-driven approach to the acquisition of grammar might narrow the search space enough to permit successful learning in finite time. It also requires no assumptions about the modularity–autonomy of grammar, because the same top-down mechanisms that are used to acquire words (e.g., mapping the sounds CAT and DOG onto their respective categories) can be used to acquire grammatical structures (e.g., mapping nominative case and preverbal position onto an emerging category of agency). To counter such claims, Chomsky and his colleagues underscored the peculiarity and functional opacity of grammar, emphasizing the difference between grammatical development and word learning. Although word learning may involve innate constraints of some kind (for a discussion and rebuttal, see Smith, chap. 10, this volume), most nativists concede that the lexicon is finite, varies markedly over languages, and must be learned (at least in part) through brute-force inductive procedures that are also used for other forms of learning, linguistic and nonlinguistic (Bates & Elman, 1996; Saffran, Aslin, & Newport, 1996). Because core grammar is universal, functionally opaque, and infinitely generative, the domain-general procedures that are used to acquire words cannot (it is argued) work for the acquisition and processing of grammar (cf. letters in *Science*, 1997, by Pesetsky, Wexler, & Fromkin; Pinker; Jenkins & Maxam; Clark, Gleitman, & Kroch; Saffran, Aslin, & Newport). Additional arguments in favor of this dual-mechanism approach include (a) differences in the onset and pattern of development observed for words versus grammar in normal children, (b) patterns of dissociation between grammar and the lexicon in children and adults with language disorders, and (c) different patterns of brain localization for lexical versus grammatical processing in lesion studies and in studies of normal adults using neural imaging techniques (e.g., Jaeger et al., 1996; Pinker, 1991, 1994; Ullman et al., 1997).

In this chapter, we argue against the autonomy of grammar, in favor of a unified lexicalist approach to the processes by which grammar is acquired, used, and represented in the brain. This is only one part of a more general emergentist theory of grammar, but it counters many of the arguments that have been used to date against the emergentist account. Although we are building a theory of linguistic performance, our lexicalist account is compatible with a number of independently motivated proposals within modern linguistics. A general trend has characterized recent proposals in otherwise very diverse theoretical frameworks within linguistics: More and more of the explanatory work that was previously handled by the grammar has been moved into the lexicon. In some frameworks (e.g., recent versions of Chomsky's generative grammar—Chomsky, 1981, 1995), the grammatical component that remains is an austere, stripped-down system characterized by a single rule for movement and a set of constraints on the application of that rule. In this theory, the richness and diversity of linguistic forms within any particular language are now captured almost entirely by the lexicon, which includes complex propositional structures and productive rules that govern the way those elements are combined. The trend toward lexicalism is even more apparent in alternative frameworks like Lexical Functional Grammar (Bresnan, 1982, 1996) and Head-Driven Phrase Structure Grammar (Pollard & Sag, 1994). It reaches its logical conclusion in a framework called Construction Grammar (Fillmore, Kay, & O'Connor, 1988; Goldberg, 1995 and chap. 7, this volume), in which the distinction between grammar and the lexicon has disappeared altogether (see also Langacker, 1987). In Goldberg's Construction Grammar, all elements of linguistic form are represented within a heterogeneous lexicon that contains bound morphemes, free-standing content and function words, and complex phrase structures without terminal elements (e.g., the passive). This lexicon can be likened to a large municipal zoo, with many different kinds of animals. To be sure, the animals vary greatly in size, shape, food preference, lifestyle, and the kind of handling they require. But they live together in one compound, under common management.

The remainder of this chapter is divided into three parts:

1. First, we look at recent evidence on the relation between lexical development and the emergence of grammar in normally developing children between 8 and 30 months of age. This includes longitudinal data from a group of normal infants followed across a crucial phase of language development. The evidence shows that the emergence and elaboration of grammar are highly dependent on vocabulary size throughout this period, as children make the passage from first words to sentences and go on to gain productive control over the basic morphosyntactic structures of their native language.

2. Second, we compare these results for normal children with studies of early language development in several atypical populations, including late and early talkers, and children with focal brain injury, Williams Syndrome, Down Syndrome, and Specific Language Impairment (SLI). Results show that (a) grammar and vocabulary do not dissociate during the early stages of development in late talkers, early talkers, or in children with focal brain injury; (b) grammatical development does not outstrip lexical growth at any point in development, even in the Williams population (a form of retardation in which linguistic abilities are surprisingly spared in the adult steady state); and (c) grammatical development can fall behind vocabulary in some subgroups (e.g., Down Syndrome and SLI), but this apparent dissociation can be explained by limits on auditory processing, without postulating isolated deficits in a separate grammar module.

3. Having reviewed the developmental findings in some detail, we provide a brief critical review of evidence for and against the idea that grammar and the lexicon are mediated by separate neural systems in the adult brain. We raise questions about the interpretation of differences in neural activity for grammatical and lexical stimuli in neural imaging studies of normal adults, and we will show that there is no solid evidence for a double dissociation between these putative modules in adult aphasia. This does not mean that all linguistic deficits are alike. Different kinds of lexical impairments have been observed (e.g., in fluent vs. nonfluent aphasic patients), and these lexical contrasts are typically accompanied by different kinds of grammatical breakdown. In other words, our municipal zoo can be damaged in a number of different ways. We argue, however, that these diverse patterns can be explained within a unified lexicalist account.

We should note before proceeding that our arguments for the unity of grammar and the lexicon might be acceptable to Fodor (1983), who (unlike Chomsky) argues for a large and relatively undifferentiated language module, separate from the rest of cognition. However, the evidence we present also suggests that the acquisition and neural representation of grammar and the lexicon are accomplished by domain-general mechanisms that transcend the boundaries of language proper, a conclusion that is incompatible with both the Fodorian and the Chomskian accounts.

GRAMMAR AND THE LEXICON IN NORMALLY DEVELOPING CHILDREN

One of the nine criteria that define a *mental module* (Fodor, 1983) is the observance of a "characteristic maturational course." At first glance, it looks like the basic modules of 1960s generative linguistics emerge on a fixed and orderly schedule. Phonology make its first appearance in reduplicative babbling, between 6 and 8 months of age. Meaningful speech emerges sometime between 10 and 12 months, on average, although word comprehension may begin a few weeks earlier. Vocabulary growth is typically very slow for the first 50 to 100 words, and many children spend between 4 and 8 months in what has come to be called the *one-word stage*. Between 16 and 20 months, most children display a "burst" or acceleration in the rate of vocabulary growth, and first word combinations usually appear between 18 and 20 months. At first, these combinations tend to be rather spare and telegraphic (at least in English). Somewhere between 24 and 30 months, most children show a kind of "second burst," a flowering of morphosyntax characterized as the ivy coming in between the bricks. By 3 to 3.5 years of age, most normal children have mastered the basic morphological and syntactic structures of their language (defined by various criteria for productivity, including rule-like extension of grammatical structures to novel words). Hence, one might characterize early language development as the successive maturation of separate modules for phonology, the lexicon, and grammar.

Of course, this textbook story is not exactly the same in every language (Bates & Marchman, 1988; MacWhinney & Bates, 1989; Slobin, 1985, 1992, 1997), and perfectly healthy children can vary markedly in rate and style of development through these milestones (Bates, Dale, & Thal, 1995; Fenson et al., 1994; Shore, 1995). At a global level, however, the passage from sounds to words to grammar appears to be a universal of child language development. A quick look at the relative timing and shape of growth in word comprehension, word production, and grammar can be seen in Fig. 2.4, taken from our own longitudinal study of language development from

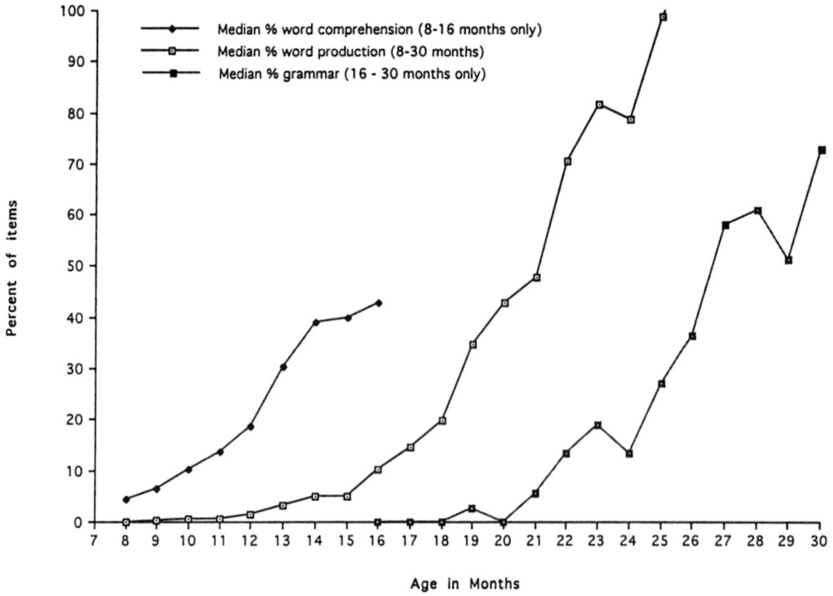

FIG. 2.4. Median growth scores for word comprehension, production, and grammar expressed as a percentage of available items.

8 to 30 months (Goodman, 1995). The word comprehension and production estimates are based on the same word checklist, and the grammar estimate is based on a 37-item scale for sentence complexity (note that these comprehension data were only collected from 8 to 16 months, and measurement of grammar did not begin until 16 months—see following text for additional methodological details). Assuming for a moment that we have a right to compare the proportional growth of apples and oranges, this figure shows that all three domains follow a dramatic, nonlinear pattern of growth across this age range. However, the respective "zones of acceleration" for each domain are separated by many weeks or months.

Bickerton (1984) took this succession quite seriously. Following Chomsky,[1] he argued that the period of babbling and single-word production prior to 2 years of age is essentially "prelinguistic." True language only begins when sentences begin, around 2 years of age. Locke (1983, 1997) argued for a similar discontinuity, albeit in a more subtle form. He sug-

[1]"Observation of early stages of language acquisition may be quite misleading in this regard. It is possible that at an early stage there is use of languagelike expressions, but outside the framework imposed, at a later stage of intellectual maturation, by the faculty of language—much as a dog can be trained to respond to certain commands, though we would not conclude, from this, that it is using language" (Chomsky, *Reflections on language*, p. 53. New York, Pantheon Books, 1975).

gested that the phase of single-word production (including some formulaic phrases like *I wan' dat* or *Love you*) is governed by an "utterance collecting" mechanism that may be mediated primarily by the right hemisphere. The emergence of productive, lawful grammar between 2 and 3 years of age reflects the discontinuous emergence of a separate linguistic mechanism, possibly one that is mediated by the left hemisphere. Unlike Bickerton, Locke believed that there is a causal relation between these two phases. Specifically, if the rule mechanism "turns on" before a critical mass of utterances has been stored, it will not operate properly. However, the two phases are mediated by distinct neural mechanisms, and each matures (turns on) according to its own genetic timetable (i.e., vocabulary size does not "cause" the grammatical device to mature).

Is this passage from first words to grammar discontinuous, as Bickerton and Locke proposed? We have known for some time that, within individual children, the content, style, and patterning of first word combinations is strongly influenced by the content, style, and patterning of single-word speech (Bates, Bretherton, & Snyder, 1988; Bloom, Lightbown, & Hood, 1975; Braine, 1976; Horgan, 1978, 1979, 1981). But of course, no one has ever proposed that grammar can begin in the absence of words. As Locke noted, any rule-based device is going to have to have a certain amount of lexical material to work on. The real question is: Just how tight are the correlations between lexical and grammatical development in the 2nd and 3rd year of life? Are these components dissociable, and if so, to what extent? How much lexical material is needed to build a grammatical system? Can grammar get off the ground and go its separate way once a minimum number of words is reached (e.g., 50–100 words, the modal vocabulary size when first word combinations appear—Bates et al., 1988; Nelson, 1973; Shore, 1995; Shore, O'Connell, & Bates, 1984)? Or will we observe a constant and lawful interchange between lexical and grammatical development, of the sort that one would expect if the lexicalist approach to grammar is correct, and grammar does not dissociate from the lexicon at any point in life?

Our reading of the evidence suggests that the latter view is correct. As we shall see, the function that governs the relation between lexical and grammatical growth in this age range is so lawful that it approaches Fechner's law in elegance and power. The successive bursts that characterize vocabulary growth and the emergence of morphosyntax can be viewed as different phases of an immense nonlinear wave that starts in the single-word stage and crashes on the shores of grammar a year or so later.

Our first insights into this tight correlation came in a longitudinal study of 27 children who were observed at 10, 13, 20, and 28 months of age, using a combination of structured observations (at home and in the laboratory) and parental report (Bates et al., 1988; see also Bretherton, McNew,

TABLE 2.1
Relations Between Vocabulary Size and Mean Length of Utterance in Morphemes From 20 to 28 Months

	20-Month Vocabulary	*20-Month MLU*[a]	*28-Month vocabulary*	*28-Month MLU*[a]
20-month Vocabulary	—			
20-month MLU[a]	+ .54**	—		
28-month Vocabulary	+ .64**	+ .47*	—	
28-month MLU[a]	+ .83**	+ .48*	+ .73**	—

[a]Mean length of utterance in morphemes.
*p <.05. **p < .01.

Snyder, & Bates, 1983; Snyder, Bates, & Bretherton, 1981). Among other things, we examined the concurrent and predictive relation between vocabulary size and grammatical status at 20 and 28 months of age. Vocabulary size was assessed with a combination of video observations and parental report (for a discussion of why parental report provides a faithful estimate of lexical size and content, see Bates et al., 1995; Fenson et al., 1994; Marchman & Bates, 1994). In this study, grammatical development was assessed in a rather standard fashion, calculating mean length of utterance (MLU) in morphemes from speech transcriptions, following the rules outlined by Brown (1973).[2] Table 2.1 summarizes the cross-lag correlations we found between lexical and grammatical development within and across these two age levels. Results were very clear: The single best estimate of grammatical status at 28 months (right in the heart of the "grammar burst") is total vocabulary size at 20 months (measured right in the middle of the "vocabulary burst"). In fact, the correlation coefficient in this and related analyses with other grammatical variables hovered consistently between +.70 and +.84. Because we know that no measure can correlate with another variable higher than it correlates with itself (i.e., Spearman's Law of Reliability), it is interesting to note that separate samples of MLU at 28 months of age also tend to intercorrelate in the +.75 to +.80 range. What this means, in essence, is that 20-month vocabulary and 28-month MLU scores are statistically identical; one could be used as a stand-in for the other in predicting a child's rank within his or her group. Of course this kind of correlational finding does not force us to conclude that grammar and

[2]We also looked at many other metrics of grammatical development, including propositional complexity and morphological productivity. After all that work we were surprised to find that, at least in this period of development, MLU is so highly correlated with other, more sophisticated measures, that there was no point in using any other estimate of grammar in correlational analyses with other variables; for a discussion of this point, see Bates et al., 1988.

vocabulary growth are mediated by the same developmental mechanism. Correlation is not cause. At the very least, however, this powerful correlation suggests that the two have something important in common.

In a more recent series of studies, we developed a new parental report instrument called the MacArthur Communicative Development Inventory (CDI) to study the relation between lexical and grammatical development in a much larger sample of 1,800 normally developing children, primarily middle class, all growing up in English-speaking households (see Bates et al., 1995; Bates et al., 1994; Dale, 1991; Dale, Bates, Reznick, & Morisset, 1989; Fenson et al., 1993, 1994). The CDI relies primarily on a checklist format to assess word comprehension (8–16 months), word production (8–30 months) and the emergence of grammar (16–30 months). Numerous studies in many different laboratories have shown that these parental report indices provide a reliable and valid assessment of lexical development from 8 to 30 months (including both comprehension and production) and grammatical developments in the period from 16 to 30 months (see Fenson et al., 1994, for a review). Because these scales are published, and widely used in clinical and research settings, we refer the reader to other sources for methodological details.

The complete word production checklist in the CDI contains 680 words that are typically acquired by children exposed to American English before 30 months of age. It was much less obvious how to assess grammar through parent report, because the class of possible sentences is infinite. One solution was a checklist of 37 sentence pairs, each reflecting a single linguistic contrast that is known to come in across the 16- to 30-month period (e.g., "KITTY SLEEPING" paired with "KITTY IS SLEEPING"). Parents were asked to indicate which sentence in each pair "sounds more like the way that your child is talking right now," yielding scores that varied from 0 (no multiword speech at all) to 37 (the more complex form checked in every pair). Studies show that this measure correlates very highly with traditional laboratory measures of grammatical complexity (Dale, 1991; Dale et al., 1989), including correlations with MLU up to the statistical ceiling (i.e., as high as MLU correlates with itself in reliability studies). It is thus fair to conclude that these measures provide valid and reliable estimates of individual differences in grammatical development across the period from 16 to 30 months of age.

As reported by Fenson et al. (1994), the relation between grammatical complexity and vocabulary size in their large cross-sectional sample replicates and extends the powerful grammar–vocabulary relation that had emerged in Bates et al. (1988). Figure 2.5 illustrates the relation between performance on the 37-item sentence complexity scale with productive vocabulary size (collapsed over age, with children divided into groups reflecting fewer than 50 words, 50 to 100 words, 101 to 200 words, 201 to

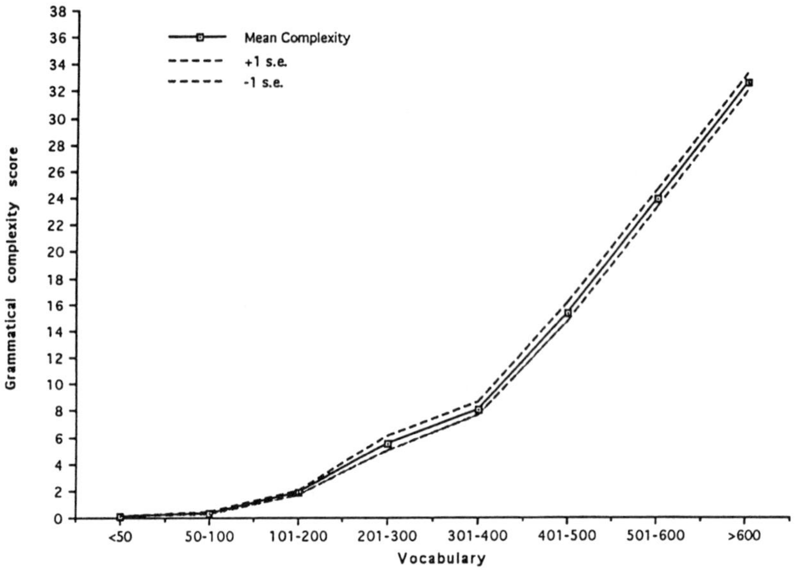

FIG. 2.5. Mean and standard errors for grammatical complexity in children at different vocabulary levels. From Bates and Goodman (1977).

300 words, 301 to 400 words, 401 to 500 words, 501 to 600 words, and more than 600 words). The linear correlation between these two measures is +.84 ($p < .0001$), but it is clear from Fig. 2.5 that the function governing this relation is nonlinear in nature.

Of course there is some individual variation around this function. This is illustrated by the standard error of the mean in Fig. 2.5, and by the separate lines in Fig. 2.6a, which indicate scores for children at the 10th, 25th, 50th, 75th, and 90th percentiles for grammar within each vocabulary group. These variance statistics make two points: (a) individual differences around the grammar-on-vocabulary function are relatively small and (b) the variance is consistent in magnitude at every point along the horizontal axis beyond 50 to 100 words. Both these points are clarified further if we compare the tight correlation between grammar and vocabulary with the clear dissociation between word comprehension and word production observed at an earlier point in language development. Figure 2.6b displays the relation between expressive vocabulary (on the vertical axis) and receptive vocabulary (on the horizontal axis), collapsed over age in children between 8 and 16 months (redrawn from the MacArthur norming study, Fenson et al., 1994). Analogous to Fig. 2.6a, Fig. 2.6b illustrates the relation between domains by plotting scores at the 10th, 25th, 50th, 75th, and 90th percentile for word production within each comprehension group. What we see in Fig. 2.6b is a classic fan-shaped pattern of variation, including

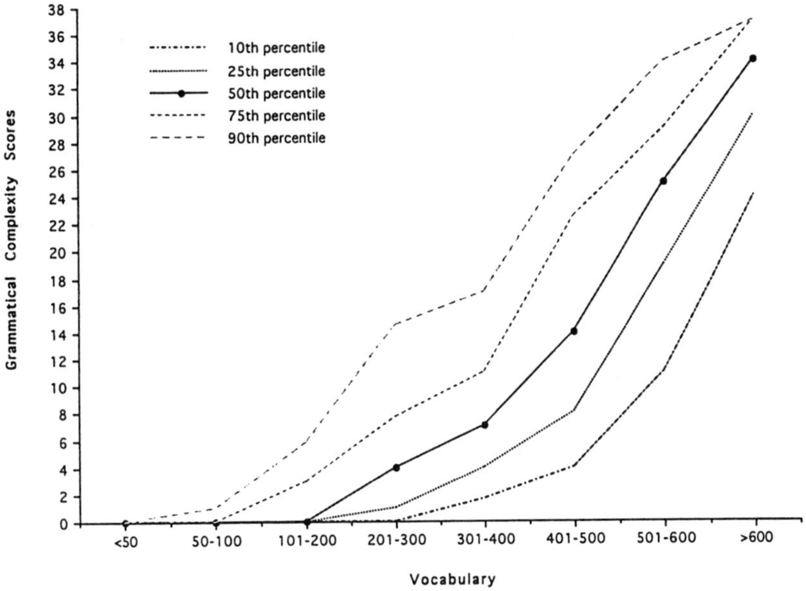

FIG. 2.6a. Relation between grammar and vocabulary size: variation within each vocabulary level.

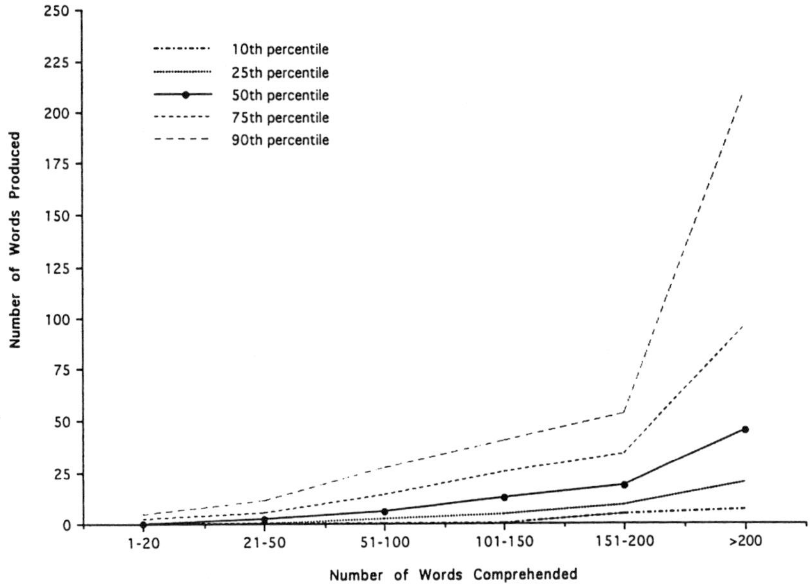

FIG. 2.6b. Variability in word production as a function of comprehension vocabulary size. From Fenson et al. (1994).

children who are still producing virtually no meaningful speech at all despite receptive vocabularies of more than 200 words. Hence, this figure captures a well-known phenomenon in the child language literature: Comprehension and production can dissociate to a remarkable degree. A certain level of word comprehension is prerequisite for expressive language to get off the ground, but comprehension (although necessary) is apparently not sufficient. If the same thing were true for the relation between vocabulary and grammar, we would expect the same kind of fan-shaped variance in Fig. 2.6a. That is, we might expect vocabulary size to place a ceiling on grammatical development up to somewhere between 50 and 200 words (when most children make the passage into multiword speech). After that point, the variance should spread outward as the two domains decouple and grammar takes off on its own course. Instead, we find that grammar and vocabulary are tightly coupled across the 16- to 30-month age range.

To understand the relevance of this finding, it is important to keep in mind that normally developing children are able to produce most of the basic morphosyntactic structures of their language by 3 to 3.5 years of age, including passives, relative clauses, and other complex forms (Bates & Devescovi, 1989; Crain, 1991; Demuth, 1989; Marchman, Bates, Burkhardt, & Good, 1991; Slobin, 1985, 1992, 1997). Hence, the function in Fig. 2.5 follows children right into the very heart of grammatical development, when productive control over crucial morphological and syntactic structures is well underway (Brown, 1973). We also note that this powerful function is not an artifact of age, because it remains very strong when age is partialed out of the correlation (Fenson et al., 1994). Indeed, age is a surprisingly poor predictor of both vocabulary and grammar within this 16- to 30-month window for this large sample of healthy English-speaking children. Taken together, age and vocabulary size account for 71.4% of the variance in grammatical complexity. When age is entered into the equation after vocabulary size is controlled, it adds a statistically reliable but exceedingly small 0.8% to the total variance accounted for. However, when vocabulary size is entered into the equation after age is controlled, it adds a reliable and robust 32.3% to the variance in grammar scores.

Given the power of this relation, we might suspect that another kind of artifact is lurking beneath the surface. After all, the vocabulary checklist includes grammatical function words like prepositions, articles, auxiliary verbs, pronouns, and conjunctions. Perhaps all that we really have in Fig. 2.5 is a tautological relation of grammar with itself! To control for this possibility, we recalculated total vocabulary size for the full MacArthur sample, subtracting out grammatical function words for each individual child. Figure 2.7 illustrates the relation between grammar and vocabulary that is observed when vocabulary counts are based entirely on the remain-

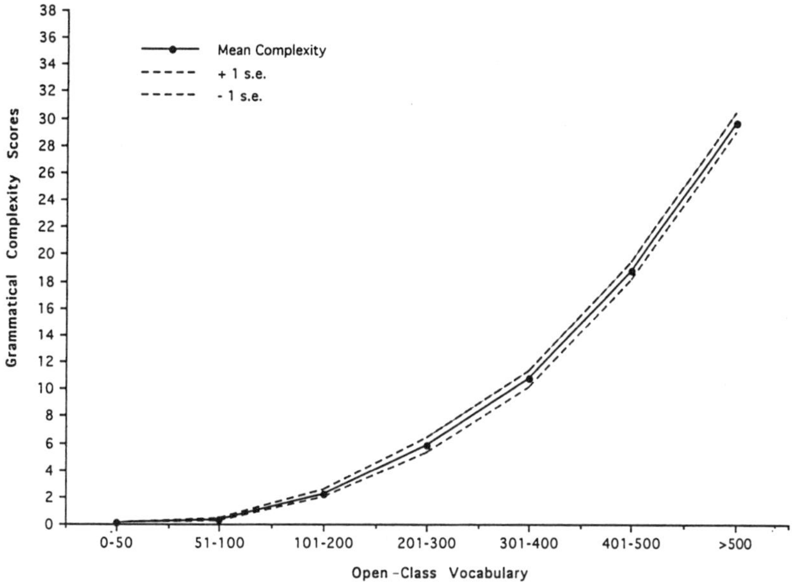

FIG. 2.7. Grammatical complexity as a function of open class vocabulary only.

ing content words. The nonlinear function that remains is, if anything, even more powerful than the original function where all words are included in the vocabulary total.

The data we have reported so far are all based on English. More recently, Caselli and Casadio (1995) developed and normed a version of the MacArthur CDI for Italian. Although the word checklist for Italian is equivalent to the English list in length, it is not a mere translation; instead, the words listed within each category were selected specifically for Italian, based on prior studies of lexical and grammatical development in this language. Similarly, because the grammar of Italian is quite dissimilar from that of English, Caselli and Casadio constructed a 37-item sentence complexity scale designed to tap those structures that are known to develop in Italian between 16 and 30 months of age (Bates, 1976; Caselli, 1995; Cresti & Moneglia, 1995; Devescovi & Pizzuto, 1995; Pizzuto & Caselli, 1992; Volterra, 1976). Detailed cross-linguistic comparisons are provided elsewhere (Caselli, Casadio, & Bates, 1998; Caselli et al., 1995; Pizzuto & Caselli, 1994). For our purposes here, we note that the function linking grammar and vocabulary size is quite similar in English and Italian—this despite striking differences between the two languages in the content of vocabulary and grammar.

Another possible objection to these findings revolves around the cross-sectional nature of the normative sample. Because the functions in Figs. 2.4

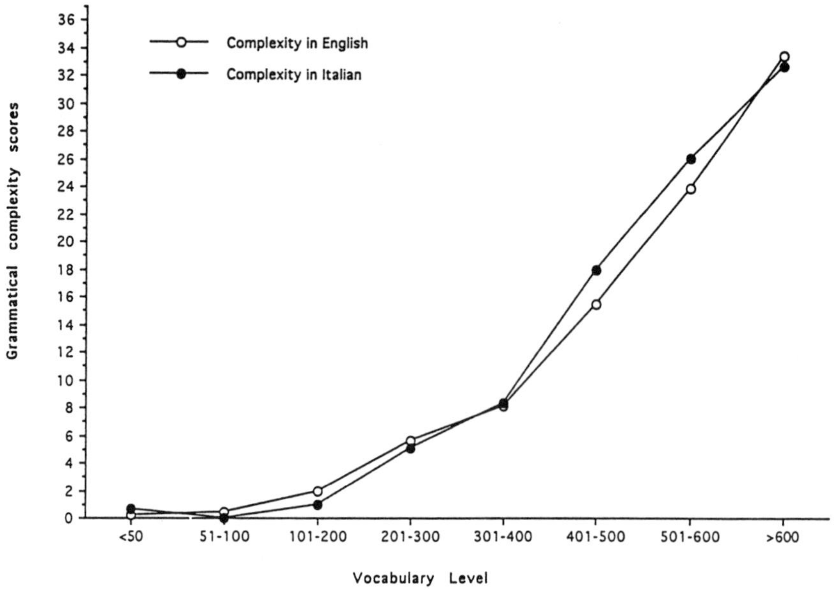

FIG. 2.8. Grammatical complexity as a function of vocabulary size. From Caselli, Casadio, and Bates (1998).

to 2.8 are collapsed across different children at different age levels, we cannot assume that they represent patterns of growth for any individual child. In a more recent study (Goodman, 1995; Jahn-Samilo, 1995; Thal, Bates, Goodman, & Jahn-Samilo, 1997), we used the MacArthur CDI to follow individual children longitudinally, with parents filling out the forms on a monthly basis from 8 to 30 months of age. From 12 to 30 months, we also saw the children monthly in the laboratory, videotaping free speech and free play and administering structured measures of word comprehension, word production, and comprehension of grammar. Thirty-four children enrolled in the study in the first few months, and 28 stayed with us through the 30-month end date. The sample was predominantly middle class, screened to exclude cases with serious medical complications (including mental retardation and prematurity). All children were growing up in homes in which English was the primary language spoken by both parents. Additional details about this sample and the cross-correlations between CDI and laboratory measures are available in Bates and Goodman (1997) and Jahn-Samilo, Goodman, Bates, and Appelbaum (1997). For present purposes, we note that the correlations between laboratory and parent report are very high in this sample, further evidence for the reliability and validity of the CDI as a measure of early grammar and vocabulary.

The finding that is most important for our purposes here concerns the relation between grammar and vocabulary in individual children followed across the 17- to 30-month period (i.e., from the point at which we began to collect measures of grammatical abilities until the end of the study). Figure 2.9 compares the nonlinear function linking sentence complexity and vocabulary size in the respective cross-sectional and longitudinal samples. The two functions are remarkably similar, separated only by a very small lag (i.e., slightly lower complexity rates per vocabulary group in the longitudinal sample), well within the range of variation that we observe for the cross-sectional sample in Figs. 2.5 and 2.6a.

Although this comparison does suggest that a common growth function is observed in both designs, we are still looking at group data in both cases (i.e., results collapsed over many different children at each data point). We might therefore ask whether the growth curves in the longitudinal study look similar for individual children, or whether the commonalities in Fig. 2.9 represent group trends that mask sharp dissociations in at least some individual cases. To address this issue, we graphed the individual grammar-on-vocabulary functions for all 28 children. Results suggest a remarkable degree of similarity between these individual growth curves and the range of curves (from the 10th to the 90th percentile) summarized at the group level in Fig. 2.6a (for details, see Bates & Goodman, 1997).

We are convinced by these data that there is a powerful link between grammar and lexical growth in this age range, a nonlinear growth function that holds for both cross-sectional and longitudinal designs, at both indi-

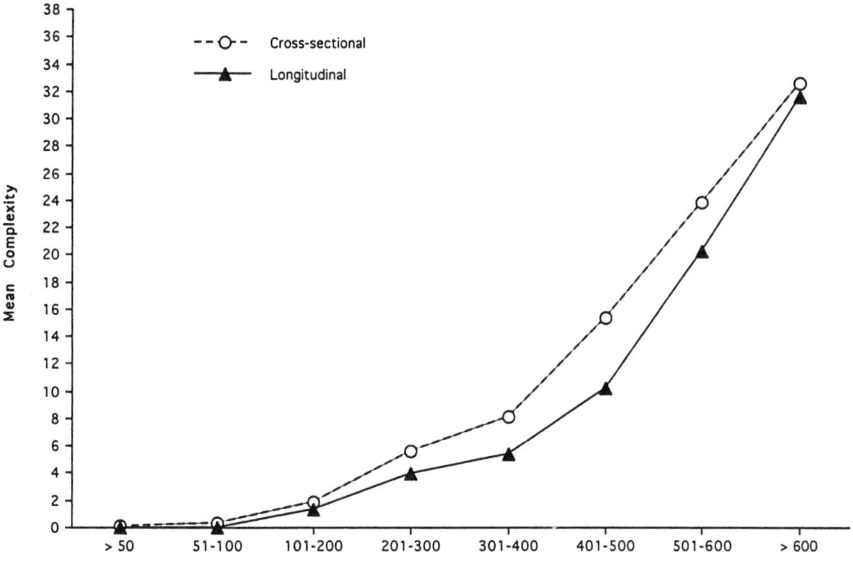

FIG. 2.9. Grammatical complexity as a function of vocabulary level for the cross-sectional versus longitudinal samples.

vidual and group levels, and perhaps across languages as well (although two languages is a very small sample of the possibilities that the world has to offer). These results (even for individual children) are collapsed across a range of different grammatical structures. What does the relation look like when we look at specific aspects of the grammar? Presumably, because we know that different grammatical structures come in at different points within this developmental window, we ought to expect individual forms to display different degrees and (perhaps) different types of lexical dependence. For example, individual grammatical structures might require a different critical mass across the whole vocabulary, or they might require a critical number of lexical items within a specific class. Marchman & Bates (1994) addressed this issue, using the MacArthur norming data to investigate the relation between the number of verbs that children use and their progress on the verb morphology subscales on the CDI (i.e., the checklists of irregular, regular, and overregularized forms noted earlier). They reported a powerful nonlinear relation between the number of verbs in the child's vocabulary (based on the subset of verbs that are used in the vocabulary checklist and in the past tense scale) and three forms of past tense marking: zero stem (the child is reported to use the verb in the citation form only), correct irregulars, and incorrect overgeneralizations (see Fig. 2.10). Results were similar to those observed in connectionist

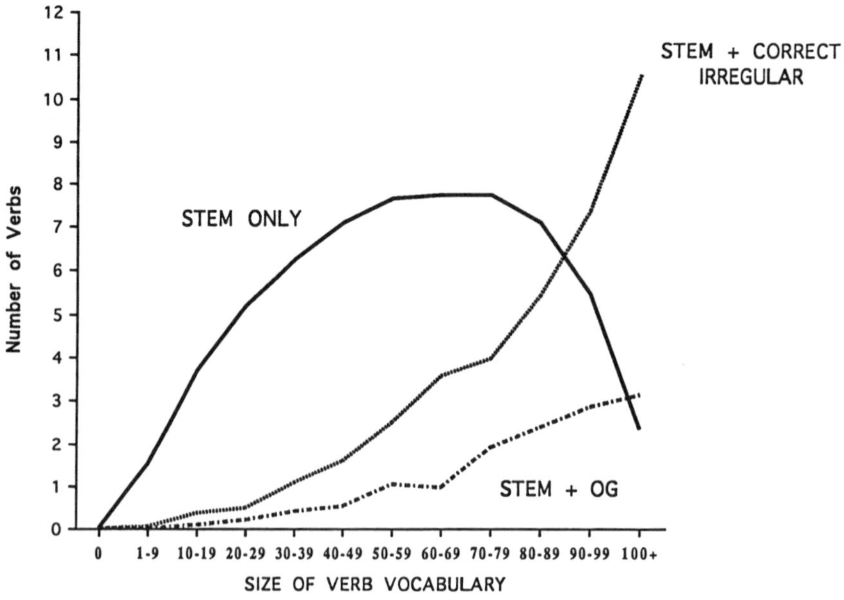

FIG. 2.10. Reported production of 16 irregular verbs as a function of verb vocabulary size.

simulations of past tense learning (Plunkett & Marchman, 1991, 1993; Rumelhart & McClelland, 1986), providing further evidence in favor of the idea that regular and irregular morphemes are acquired by the same learning mechanism and tightly tied to the size and distribution of the child's verb vocabulary at any given point in development.

This demonstration of a link between verb vocabulary and past tense morphology is the only example we have right now of a link between specific grammatical structures and their requisite critical mass of lexical items. A great deal more work could be done in this area to determine the lexical prerequisites (if any) for specific grammatical forms. Results of such investigations are likely to vary markedly within and across languages, despite the solid trends that we find by collapsing over lexical and grammatical types.

Explaining the Link

Why is the relation between grammar and the lexicon so strong in this period of development? In children who are developing on a normal schedule, the same basic nonlinear relation appears in longitudinal and cross-sectional data, in at least two dramatically different languages, in different domains of grammar. The dependence of early grammar on vocabulary size is so strong and the nonlinear shape of this function is so regular that it approaches the status of a psychological law, akin to the reliable psychophysical functions that have been observed in perception (e.g., Weber's Law, Fechner's Law). But explanation by legislation is not very satisfactory, and it is particularly unsatisfactory if better explanations are available. We can offer five reasons why grammar and the lexicon are so closely related in this phase of development. None of these explanations are mutually exclusive.

1. Perceptual Bootstrapping. Nusbaum and Goodman (1994) and Nusbaum and Henly (1992) proposed that efficient word perception requires a certain amount of top-down processing, permitting the listener to weed out inappropriate candidates from a large pool of items that overlap (at least partially) with the blurred word tokens that so often occur in fluent speech (see also Hurlburt & Goodman, 1992; Marslen-Wilson, 1987; McQueen, Cutler, Briscoe, & Norris, 1995). To the extent that this is true, it is probably even more true for the perception of grammatical function words and bound inflections. For a variety of reasons, these units are particularly hard to perceive (Cutler, 1993; Goodglass & Menn, 1985; Grosjean & Gee, 1987; Kean, 1977; Leonard, 1998; Shillcock & Bard, 1993). They tend to be short and low in stress, even in speech that is produced slowly and deliberately. In informal and rapid speech, speakers have a tendency to exploit the frequency and predictability of function words and bound morphemes by giving them short shrift, deforming their phonetic structure and blurring the boundaries between these morphemes and the words that surround them. In fact, when grammatical function words are clipped out of connected speech and presented in isolation, adult native speakers can recognize them no more than 40% to 50% of the time (Herron & Bates, 1997). This is true of speech directed to children as well as speech directed to adults (Goodman, Nusbaum, Lee, & Broihier, 1990). Under these circumstances, we should not be surprised that young children are unable to acquire grammatical forms until they have a critical mass of content words, providing enough top-down structure to permit perception and learning of those closed-class items that occur to the right or left of "real words."

2. Logical Bootstrapping. Studies in several different languages have shown that verbs and adjectives are acquired later than nouns (Au, Dapretto, & Song, 1994; Caselli et al., 1995; Gentner, 1982; Pae, 1993; for a dissenting view, see Gopnik & Choi, 1990, 1995). Except for a few terms like *up* and *no* that can stand alone, function words tend to appear later still, well after the first verbs and adjectives appear (Bates et al., 1994). Furthermore, many relatively early prepositions (e.g., *up*) may not be used in the same way by children as by adults. Adults use them to specify a relation between objects or a location. Children, on the other hand, use them to refer to events (Smiley & Huttenlocher, 1995; Tomasello & Merriman, 1995) instead of using them as "grammatical glue." It has been suggested that this progression from names to predication to grammar is logically necessary, based on a simple assumption: Children cannot understand relational terms until they understand the things that these words relate. One can argue about the extent to which this assumption holds for individual structures, but it may provide a partial explanation for the dependence of grammar on lexical growth.

3. Syntactic Bootstrapping. The perceptual and logical bootstrapping accounts both presuppose that the causal link runs from lexical growth to grammar. However, studies from several different laboratories have shown that children between 1 and 3 years of age are able to exploit sentential information to learn about the meaning of a novel word (Goodman & McDonough, 1996; Goodman, McDonough, & Brown, 1996; Naigles, 1988, 1990; Naigles, Gleitman, & Gleitman, 1993; Sethuraman, Goldberg, & Goodman, 1996; Tomasello, 1992). Naigles et al. (1993) referred to this process as *syntactic bootstrapping,* although it has been shown that children can use many different aspects of a sentence frame for this purpose, including sentence-level semantics, morphological cues, word order, and prosody. It is therefore possible that the accelerating function in Figs. 2.2 to 2.10 is due in part to the effect of the child's emerging grammar on lexical growth.

4. Nonlinear Dynamics of Learning in a Neural Network. The previous three accounts all support a link between lexical and grammatical development, but it is not obvious from these accounts why the function ought to take the nonlinear form that appears so reliably across populations and age levels. We noted earlier that the nonlinear functions governing the relation between verb vocabulary and the emergence of regular and irregular past tense marking appear in a similar form in English-speaking children and in neural network simulations of past tense learning (MacWhinney, Leinbach, Taraban, & McDonald, 1989; Marchman & Bates, 1994; Plunkett & Marchman, 1991, 1993). This is only one example of a more general point: Multilayered neural networks produce an array of nonlinear growth functions, reflecting the nonlinear dynamics of learning and change in these systems (Elman et al., 1996, chap. 4). The kinds of critical-mass effects that we have proposed to underlie the relation between lexical and grammatical growth may be a special case of this more general approach to the nonlinear dynamics of learning (see also Port & van Gelder, 1995; Smith & Thelen, 1993; Thelen & Smith, 1994; van Geert, 1994).

5. Lexically Based Grammar. Finally, as we noted at the outset of this chapter, the historical trend in modern linguistics has been to place in the lexicon more and more of the work that was previously carried out in a separate grammatical component. The powerful relation between grammatical and lexical development that we observed here is precisely what we would expect if grammar is an inherent part of the lexicon.

Points 1 to 4 all pertain to learning. Point 5 is a stronger claim, extending to the relation between grammar and the lexicon in the adult steady state. The data that we reviewed so far may be relevant only to the early stages of language development, the period in which the fundamental properties of language-specific morphosyntax are laid down. It is entirely possible that a modular distinction between grammar and the lexicon may emerge at a later point in development, in accordance with the processes of *modularization* described by Karmiloff-Smith (1992); see also Bates et al., 1988; Friederici, 1990). This question is best addressed by looking at the literature on language disorders in children and adults, where strong claims about the modularity of grammar and the lexicon have been made.

GRAMMATICAL DEVELOPMENT AND THE LEXICON IN ATYPICAL POPULATIONS

As we shall see later, the literature on older children with SLI and adults with language disorders gives us reason to expect selective impairments in early grammar. What happens in the early stages of development in children who are acquiring language on an atypical schedule? Are there any individual children or any specific pediatric population in which we can find a dissociation between early grammar and the lexicon, that is, a deviation from the functions displayed in Figs. 2.5 to 2.9?

Late and Early Talkers

If grammar and vocabulary really are separate modules, each maturing on a separate schedule, then it should be possible to locate at least a few individual children who are developing grammar at a normal rate, despite vocabulary scores that are abnormally high or low for their age. Thal and her colleagues examined this issue within a larger program of research on late and early talkers. Later talkers are defined as children between 18 and 24 months who are in the bottom 10th percentile for expressive vocabulary, in the absence of retardation, frank neurological impairment, autism, deafness, or any other obvious biomedical cause for their delay (Bates et al., 1995; Thal, 1991; Thal et al., 1997; Thal & Katich, 1996). Early talkers are defined, conversely, as children between 12 and 24 months who are in the top 10th percentile for expressive vocabulary (Robinson, Dale, & Landesman, 1990; Thal et al., 1997; Thal, Bates, Zappia, & Oroz, 1996). To date, no evidence for such a dissociation between grammar and vocabulary has appeared in any of these samples. Instead, grammatical development appears to be tied to lexical level even in children at the far ends of the continuum.

To illustrate this point, we present the grammar-on-vocabulary functions for two individual children in Fig. 2.11, for each session between 16 and 30 months. These children were selected to represent extremes in rate of vocabulary growth, including one very late talker and one very early talker. The contrast between these two cases is particularly interesting for our purposes here, because there is absolutely no overlap in their vocabulary size across this longitudinal study from 17 to 30 months of age. Our late talker had a vocabulary of only 272 words on the CDI in the last session at 30 months. By contrast, our early talker already had a vocabulary of 315 words on the CDI at 17 months, when we began to administer the grammar scales. It is clear from Fig. 2.11 that both children are making progress in grammar that is directly commensurate to their lexical abilities, even though they reach their respective grammar-on-vocabulary levels at widely different ages within this period of development.

Some further insights into this issue come from two case studies of children with extremely precocious language development (Thal & Bates, 1988; Thal et al., 1996). In one of these children, grammar does appear to lag behind vocabulary level, suggesting some degree of dissociation. However, a detailed comparison of the free speech data and parent report data

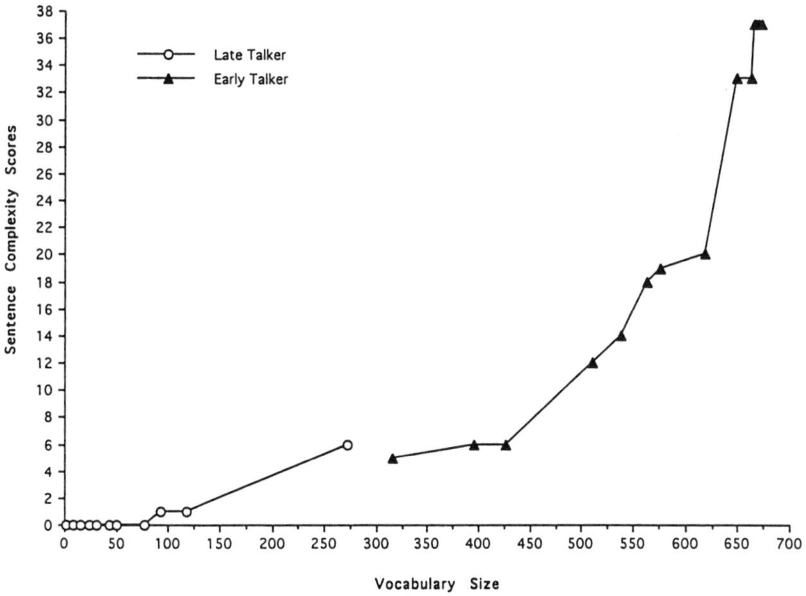

FIG. 2.11. Relation between grammatical complexity and vocabulary size for one late talker and one early talker. From Bates and Goodman (1997).

reveals an unexpectedly strong association between vocabulary development and inflectional morphology for both these children, even though one of them has barely moved out of the single-word stage. Table 2.2 (from Thal et al., 1996) provides examples of the utterances produced by M.W. (17 months old with an expressive vocabulary of 596 words in the CDI) and S.W. (21 months old with an expressive vocabulary of 627 words on the CDI). With an MLU of 2.13, M.W. is right where we would expect her to be in grammar, given her vocabulary size (equivalent to performance by an average 28- to 30-month-old child in both domains). By contrast, S.W. has just begun to combine words (MLU = 1.12) despite her huge vocabulary. In fact, her grammatical abilities are quite average for a 21-month-old child. However, the examples in Table 2.2 reveal a very curious phenomenon: production of words with contrasting inflections (e.g., *falling . . . fell*) in single-word utterances. Applying the criteria for morphological productivity developed by Brown (1973), Thal et al. (1996) discovered that both children have about as much control over English morphology as we would expect to find in a 2.5-year-old child. In fact, S.W. was actually more advanced than M.W. in grammatical morphology (i.e., productive control over more morphemes according to Brown's rules), and both children were well within the range of morphological development that we would expect for children with more than 500 words (Marchman & Bates, 1994). In other words, there is no

TABLE 2.2
Examples of Language Production by Two Very Early Talkers

MW:		*SW:*	
Age:	17 months	Age:	21 months
Vocabulary	596 words	Vocabulary:	627 words
Vocabulary age:	30 months	Vocabulalry age:	> 30 months
MLU:	2.13	MLU	1119
MLU age:	28 months	MLU age:	20 months

Where cup went?	Pretty.
Where chair went?	Cute.
Teddy bear went?	Big.
Baby doing?	Round.
	Dry.
Wanna walk e baby.	Hungry.
Wanna put it on.	Wet.
Wanna go ride it.	Different.
Want mom get off.	Enough.
	Else.
Daddy take her. (referring to self)	More.
Help with the apple.	Minute.
Can't get the teddy bear.	Brushing.
Teddy bear the bath.	Hiding.
	Baby crying.
Too much carrots on the disk.	
	Hold.
Move it around,	Hold it.
Clean e bottom.	Dropped it.
	Bring it.
Put ne sofa.	
Put in eye.	Falling.
	Fell.
Mommy wear hat.	
Mommy smell it.	Talk.
Mommy read the book.	Talking.
Mommy sit down.	
	Wash'em.
Find Becky.	Shirt on.
See Becky in the morning.	Teddy up.
Becky is nice.	Mommy shoe.
Saw Becky and goats.	

Note. From Thal, Bates, Zappia, and Oroz (1996).

dissociation between vocabulary size and grammatical morphology, although there is substantial variation in average utterance length. Thal et al. (1996) suggested that these two children differ primarily in the size of the unit that they are able to store in auditory memory, the size of the unit that they are able to retrieve and reformulate in speech production, or both (see also Peters, 1977). As we shall see shortly, this kind of processing account will prove useful in explaining the apparent dissociations observed in other clinical populations.

Early Focal Lesions

If there are separate neural mechanisms in the brain for grammar versus the lexicon, then we might expect to find dissociations between these two aspects of language learning in children with congenital injuries to one side of the brain. Specifically, based on claims in the literature on adult aphasia (discussed later), we might expect to find greater delays in grammar among children with left frontal damage (including Broca's area) and greater lexical delays in children with left posterior damage (including Wernicke's area). Although these are reasonable predictions, there is virtually no evidence in their favor. When cases with intractable seizures or other medical complications are excluded, most studies of older children with a history of congenital brain injury report language abilities within the normal range, regardless of lesion side, size, or site (for reviews, see Bates, Vicari, & Trauner, in press; Eisele & Aram, 1995; Vargha-Khadem, Isaacs, & Muter, 1994). As a group, these children do tend to perform below neurologically intact controls on many measures of language and cognition (including an average IQ difference of 3–10 points). However, they rarely qualify for a diagnosis of aphasia. Even more important, language outcomes are not reliably different for children with left- versus right-hemisphere damage.

Some interesting exceptions to this general conclusion come from a handful of prospective studies that have looked at the first stages of language learning, before the plastic reorganization for which this population is famous has taken place. If we look early enough, we do find evidence for specific effects of lesion site—but these findings still do not map in any obvious way onto the adult aphasia literature, and they provide no evidence whatsoever for a dissociation between grammar and the lexicon. Some particularly relevant findings for our purposes here come from a series of studies by Bates, Vicari, et al. (in press) and Reilly, Bates, and Marchman (1998), covering a period of development from 10 months to 12 years of age:

Absence of Left–Right Differences. There are few global differences between children with left- versus right-hemisphere injuries on expressive language measures across this range of development, in sharp contrast with more than 100 years of research on brain injury in adults. There are also few differences in receptive language, except for a small but reliable disadvantage in word comprehension between 10 and 17 months in children with right-hemisphere damage—the opposite of what we would predict based on the adult aphasia literature.

Surprising Findings for Wernicke's Area. Differences in hemispheric specialization do emerge when one considers only those children who have injuries involving the left temporal cortex, compared to children who have damage to any other sites in the right or left hemispheres. In particular, children with left temporal damage are selectively delayed in expressive language across the period from 10 to 60 months, on a succession of age-appropriate lexical *and* grammatical measures. This finding is surprising from the point of view of classical aphasiology, where lesions to the left temporal cortex (the presumed site of Wernicke's area) are usually associated with fluent aphasia with mild to severe deficits in comprehension.

Surprising Findings for Broca's Area. Bates et al. (in press) and Reilly et al. (1998) found no selective effects of damage to the left frontal cortex (the presumed site of Broca's area) at any point from 10 months to 12 years of age. Frontal damage does make a difference in the period between 19 and 31 months, a period that includes dramatic changes in both lexical and grammatical development (i.e., the vocabulary burst and the emergence of grammatical morphology). However, this frontal effect is bilaterally symmetrical. That is, children whose lesions included *either* the left frontal *or* right frontal cortex are more delayed in vocabulary size and grammatical complexity. Putting these lines of evidence together, Bates et al. (in press) concluded that the temporal regions of the left hemisphere appear to be specialized in some way from the beginning of language learning, but the frontal regions of the left hemisphere do not have a special status until some point much later in normal development.

Disappearance of the Left Temporal Effect. After 5 to 7 years of age, children with a history of early focal brain injury tend (as a group) to perform below their age-matched normal controls on a range of lexical, grammatical, and discourse measures (Reilly et al., 1998). However, there are no effects due to side or site of lesion. In particular, the left temporal disadvantage observed in younger children is no longer detectable, suggesting that a great deal of reorganization must have occurred in the period between 1 and 6 years of age.

In addition to these group data, Bates et al. (in press) and Reilly et al. (1998) also found no evidence for a selective dissociation between grammar and lexical development in individual children. To illustrate this last point, Fig. 2.12 shows the relation between grammar and vocabulary for 19 individual children in the Bates et al. (in press) study, compared with the means for normal controls at different vocabulary levels between 19 and 31 months of age from the MacArthur CDI norming study (Fenson et al., 1994). We plotted grammatical complexity against vocabulary size in this figure in a form that facilitates comparison between the focal lesion data and the other populations considered so far.[3] Separate symbols are pro-

[3]Bates et al. described the relation between vocabulary and grammar using the CDI subscale on which parents record the three longest utterances their children have produced in the last two weeks. Scores on the 37-item complexity scale were only available for children from 2 of the 3 research sites participating in that study. For our purposes here, we have

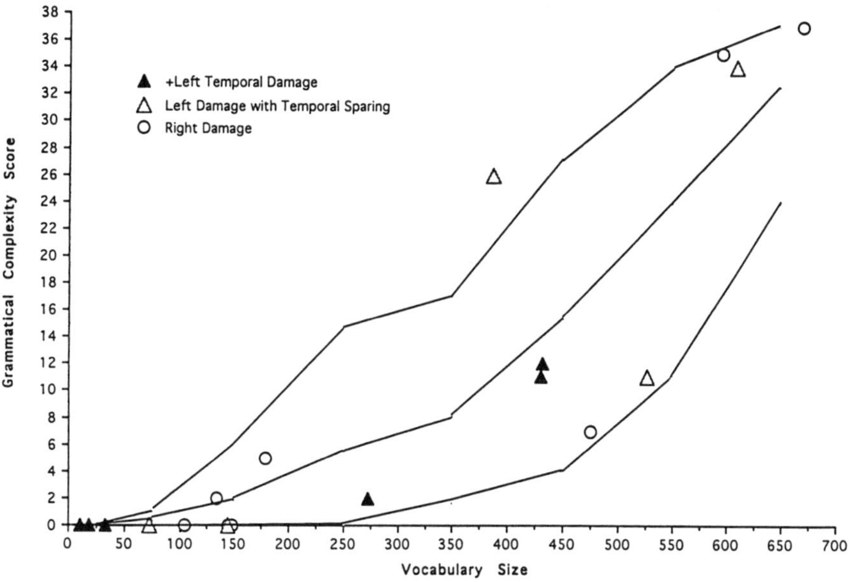

FIG. 2.12. Grammar as a function of vocabulary size in children with focal brain injury (lines = 10th, 50th, and 90th percentile for normals).

vided to distinguish cases with left-hemisphere injuries involving the temporal lobe, left-hemisphere injuries that spare the temporal lobe, and right-hemisphere damage. The three lines in Fig. 2.12 represent the 10th, 50th, and 90th percentiles for grammar as a function of vocabulary size in the Fenson et al. (1994) normative sample. It should be clear from this figure that children with focal brain injury display the normal nonlinear relation between grammar and vocabulary, even though some of them are markedly delayed on both (clustered in overlapping symbols in the bottom left quadrant). Of course there is some variance around this function, but the variance is no greater than we observe with normal children. Out of 19 focal lesion cases, 18 fall within the 10 to 90 window for normal children, and 1 falls outside; we would expect between 1 and 4 cases to fall outside that window if we were drawing children randomly from the normal population. In short, there is no evidence for a dissociation between vocabulary and grammar in this phase of development, even in children who have

---

used the 37-item complexity scale data, available only for the San Diego and New York populations. In addition, we excluded data for one child who was dropped from the focal lesion sample one year after the Bates et al. study, due to extraneous medical complications. Despite these differences, the results in Figure 12 for 19 children on the complexity scale are comparable to the results reported by Bates et al. for 30 children on the longest-utterance scale.

suffered pre- or perinatal injuries to the classical language zones within the left hemisphere.

Williams Syndrome and Down Syndrome

Williams Syndrome (WMS) and Down Syndrome (DNS) are genetically based forms of mental retardation. In both groups, mean IQs generally hover between 40 and 60, although a broader range of IQ scores can be observed at every stage from infancy through adulthood. Despite similarities in global IQ and in life experience, recent studies have revealed sharp contrasts between the two groups. For our purposes here, we are particularly interested in the claim that WMS and DNS represent a double dissociation between lexical and grammatical aspects of language processing.

Children with DNS are markedly delayed in the acquisition of language. More important, their language abilities at virtually every stage (including the adult steady state) fall below the levels that we would expect based on their mental age (Chapman, 1995; Miller, 1987, 1992a, 1992b). Furthermore, children and adults with DNS appear to be especially impaired in the production of bound and free grammatical morphemes, constituting a form of congenital agrammatism that is even more severe than the selective delays in grammatical morphology reported for children with SLI (discussed subsequently). The function word omissions and structural simplifications produced by older children with DNS are especially salient in a richly inflected language like Italian (Contardi & Vicari, 1994).

By contrast, older children and adults with WMS display levels of linguistic knowledge and language use that are surprisingly good when they are compared with the low levels of performance that the same individuals show on most measures of visual-spatial cognition, problem solving, and reasoning (Bellugi, Bihrle, Neville, Jernigan, & Doherty, 1992; Karmiloff-Smith, Klima, Bellugi, Grant, & Baron-Cohen, 1995; Mervis & Bertrand, 1993). This does not mean that individuals with WMS are "language savants." Those studies that have used normal controls have shown that the linguistic performance of WMS individuals falls invariably below their chronological age—which is, of course, not surprising for participants with an IQ score of around 50. When WMS individuals are compared with younger normals matched for mental age, the picture is mixed. Some studies report performance above mental-age controls on a handful of measures (including phonological memory and acquisition of novel words), but most studies report performance close to mental age on tests of vocabulary comprehension, sentence comprehension, sentence repetition, and spontaneous sentence production (Capirci, Sabbadini, & Volterra, 1996; Giannotti & Vicari, 1994; Vicari, Brizzolara, Carlesimo, Pezzini, & Volterra, 1996;

Volterra, Pezzini, Sabbadini, Capirci, & Vicari, 1996). For present purposes, the point is that older individuals with WMS and DNS differ markedly in their control over language, particularly grammatical morphology. In view of these differences, a number of studies have begun to explore the early stages of language development in WMS and DNS. When do these two groups separate? Is the emergence of syntax dissociated from vocabulary development for either the WMS or the DNS group at any point in development?

In fact, studies suggest that both groups are severely and equally delayed on early language milestones (Mervis & Bertrand, 1993; Thal, Bates, & Bellugi, 1989). In other words, despite their ultimate proficiency with language, children with WMS are late talkers. This conclusion is underscored in a recent study by Singer Harris, Bellugi, Bates, Rossen, and Jones (1997), who used the MacArthur CDI to obtain early language data from a large sample of children between the ages of 1 and 6 with WMS or DNS. In the period of development covered by the infant scale (equivalent to normal children between 8 and 16 months), WMS and DNS participants were equally and severely delayed in both word comprehension and word production. The predicted separation between WMS and DNS did not emerge until the period of development covered by the toddler scale (equivalent to normal children between 16 and 30 months). Both groups were still delayed by approximately 2 years at this point, with no significant difference in overall vocabulary size. However, Singer et al. found striking differences in the emergence of grammar. Interestingly, this difference reflects a DNS disadvantage rather than a WMS advantage. To facilitate comparison across groups, we plotted the data for individual WMS and DNS participants from Singer et al. in Fig. 2.13, in the same format adapted throughout this chapter. Within the WMS sample, grammatical development appears to be paced by vocabulary size, in the normal fashion. In fact, when these children are compared with lexically matched normal controls from the CDI sample, the relation between grammar and vocabulary size is identical, following the same nonlinear accelerating function described earlier for normals and for children with focal brain injury. In short, there is no evidence for a dissociation between grammatical and lexical development in the WMS sample—at least not in this early phase of grammatical development. By contrast, the DNS sample provides our best evidence to date for a significant dissociation between grammar and the lexicon. In particular, DNS children scored significantly below the grammatical levels displayed by normal children and by WMS children matched for vocabulary size (Fig. 2.13).

Note that this finding for DNS constitutes our first evidence so far for a dissociation between grammar and lexical development. Singer Harris

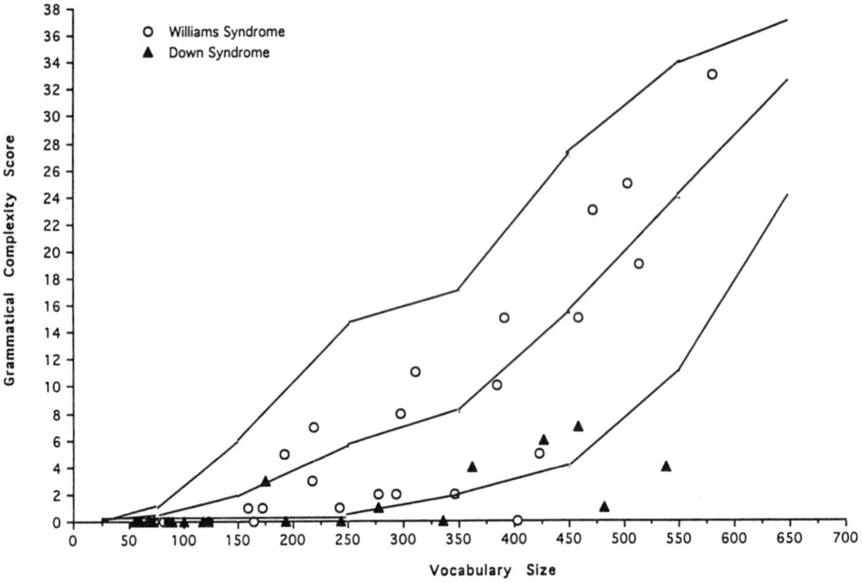

FIG. 2.13. Grammar as a function of vocabulary size in children with Williams vs. Down syndrome (lines = 10th, 50th, and 90th percentiles for normals).

et al. (1997) concluded that lexical size is a necessary but not sufficient condition for the acquisition of grammatical function words, the onset of word combinations, and growth in sentence complexity. This finding is compatible with reports on the selective impairment of grammar displayed by older DNS individuals, although the basis of the impairment is still unknown. Of course it could be due to impairment of some domain-specific grammatical processor (e.g., Pinker, 1991). Alternatively, it may derive from aspects of information processing that are only indirectly related to grammar. Wang and Bellugi (1994) reported a double dissociation in these two groups between auditory short-term memory (significantly better in WMS individuals) and visual short-term memory (significantly better in DNS individuals). It appears that DNS individuals suffer from a selective impairment in one or more aspects of auditory processing, a deficit that is superimposed on their more general cognitive delay. Under these circumstances, it is perhaps not surprising the DNS individuals are selectively impaired in the ability to detect, store, or retrieve those aspects of their linguistic input that are lowest in phonological salience (as Leonard, Bortolini, Caselli, McGregor, & Sabbadini, 1992, reported for children with SLI) and lowest in visual imagery (as Goodglass & Menn, 1985, reported for adults with Broca's aphasia). This brings us to a consideration of grammatical deficits in older children.

Specific Language Impairment

SLI is defined as a delay in expressive language abilities that is at least 1 standard deviation below the mean for the child's chronological age, in the absence of mental retardation, frank neurological impairment, social-emotional disorders (e.g., autism), or any other serious biomedical risk factors that could account for the delay. A diagnosis of SLI is usually given only after 3 to 4 years of age, beyond the period in development that we have considered so far. To some extent, research on this population does support the notion that grammar can dissociate from lexical (and cognitive) abilities. However, as we already saw in the case of DNS, it may be possible to explain this dissociation on perceptual grounds.

There is general agreement about the nature of the language impairment in SLI. However, there is considerable disagreement about its cause and even more controversy regarding its specificity (i.e., whether the deficit really is restricted to language). After 30 years of research looking for deviant patterns of language development, most investigators in this field have concluded that SLI represents a pattern of delay rather than deviance (for recent reviews, see Bishop, 1997; Leonard, 1998). That is, within every linguistic domain that has been studied to date, the expressive and receptive abilities of children with SLI are qualitatively similar to those of younger normal children. However, a specific kind of deviance can be detected if one looks across rather than within linguistic domains (Johnston & Schery, 1976). In particular, grammatical morphology appears to be more delayed than any other area of language development. Thus, much of the debate in this field concerning the nature and causes of SLI revolves around the disproportionate problems that children with SLI experience in this aspect of grammar, with some investigators arguing that the deficit is due to a problem that is strictly linguistic in nature (Clahsen, 1991; Gopnik & Crago, 1991; Rice, 1996; van der Lely, 1994), whereas others argue that the morphological problems observed in SLI are secondary to processing deficits that may transcend the boundaries of language (Bishop, 1997; Leonard, 1998; Tallal et al., 1996).

By definition, the term *specific language impairment* implies a deficit that is restricted entirely to language. However, some investigators report that children with SLI score significantly below age-matched controls on at least some nonlinguistic measures, including mental imagery and mental rotation (Johnston, 1994), symbolic play (Thal & Katich, 1996), and shifting attention (Townsend, Wulfeck, Nichols, & Koch, 1995). Tallal and her associates proposed that the specific vulnerability of morphology is a by-product of a subtle deficit in the ability to perceive rapid temporal sequences of auditory stimuli (Tallal et al., 1996; Tallal, Stark, & Mellits, 1985). Leonard (1998) and Bishop (1997) agreed with this proposal in spirit, although they argued for a perceptual deficit that involves degree of internal detail (e.g., spectral features) as well as temporal resolution. There has been strong resistance to Tallal's proposal among investigators like Mody, Studdert-Kennedy, and Brady (1997), who proposed that the basis of congenital language impairment (particularly the impairments resulting in dyslexia) is phonological rather than acoustic in nature. In fact, the phonological and acoustic proposals are not mutually exclusive: If one takes a developmental perspective, it is clear that an acoustic deficit could result in incomplete and faulty phonological learning, with consequences for the ability to segment and acquire phonologically weak elements of grammatical morphology. Furthermore, it has been shown that degradations at the phonetic level lead to a reduction in semantic activation even in normal adults (Utman, 1997). Hence, an initial deficit at the perceptual level could create a cascade of deficits at higher levels of language processing, even though children do make progress and learning does occur. The fact that children with DNS and children with SLI both experience a selective deficit in the use of grammatical morphology is compatible with this account. This brings us at last to a consideration of the case for and against a modular dissociation between grammar and the lexicon in adults.

GRAMMAR AND THE LEXICON IN THE ADULT BRAIN

The evidence reviewed so far on the interdependence of lexical and grammatical development is compatible with a unified lexicalist approach to grammar. However, it is at least possible that a modular dissociation between grammar and the lexicon emerges over time, a "modularization" process (Karmiloff-Smith, 1992) that is the outcome rather than the cause of development. We end this chapter with a necessarily brief consideration of the claim that grammar and the lexicon are mediated by distinct neural systems in the adult brain, a hypothesis that is compatible with our developmental findings but would not be compatible with a unified lexicalist account of grammar in the adult steady state.

Two kinds of evidence are relevant to this claim: neural imaging studies of grammatical and lexical processing in normal adults, and dissociations between grammar and the lexicon in patients with focal brain injury. To evaluate this evidence, we need to keep the following points in mind:

1. **All knowledge is in the brain**. Where else would it be? Even if we could show that a given class of stimuli is correlated with specific patterns of neural activity in normals, and with specific lesion sites in aphasics, we cannot conclude anything about the source of that knowledge, namely, whether it is innate, acquired, or an emergent property of interactions at

many levels. If we could demonstrate that a specific pattern of neural mediation is present at birth, prior to any experience with the stimuli in question, we might be justified in concluding that this pattern is innate. This does not appear to be the case for grammar and the lexicon in children with focal brain injury (discussed earlier).

2. **Any difference in experience or behavior must be accompanied by differences in neural activity.** This is a logical consequence of (1): If an individual responds differently to two classes of stimuli, then these two classes must be associated with different patterns of activity in the brain (whether or not we are able to detect those differences with current technology is a separate question). There are, for example, recent demonstrations of differences in brain activity for content versus function words (Nobre & Plunkett, 1997), regular versus irregular morphemes (Jaeger et al., 1996), and grammatical violations versus lexical violations (Osterhout & Holcomb, 1993). There are also demonstrations of differences in brain activity for high- versus low-frequency words (Indefrey et al., 1997), nouns versus verbs (Nobre & Plunkett, 1997), and tool words versus animal words (Martin, Wiggs, Ungerleider, & Haxby, 1996). None of these demonstrations are sufficient to establish the existence of separate brain systems. If every difference in neural activity is interpreted as a difference in kind, then we would have to postulate separate brain systems for chess, for English spelling, for high- versus low-frequency words—in short, for just about every systematic distinction between classes of stimuli.

3. **Localization and domain specificity are not the same thing.** Even if we could show that a given brain region is correlated with a specific kind of processing from the beginning of life, we could not conclude (without further evidence) that the pattern is domain specific, that is, that the neural region in question is dedicated to that class of stimuli and no other. It has been shown, for example, that every single component of the complex called Broca's area shows significant activation during one or more nonverbal motor planning tasks (Erhard, Kato, Strick, & Ugurbil, 1996). Is Broca's area involved in speech? Yes. Is Broca's area unique to speech? No. The same argument applies to demonstrations of a neural difference between grammatical and lexical violations, content words versus function words, nouns versus verbs, and tool words versus animal words. Such differences could reflect differences in the kind of processing required (e.g., high demands on memory for stimuli that are long or low in imageability; high demands on perception and attention for stimuli that are short and low in acoustic salience), rather than a modular parcellation of the brain for specific kinds of content.

In our view, the burgeoning literature on lexical and grammatical processing using event-related brain potentials, positron emission tomography, or functional magnetic resonance imaging reflects confounds along all these dimensions. There are indeed some demonstrations that grammatical and lexical stimuli lead to different patterns of brain activity. However, findings are quite variable from one study to another (reflecting variations in task, stimuli, and instructions), providing little evidence for separate, domain-specific neural systems for grammar versus the lexicon.

A more interesting challenge comes from the adult aphasia literature, where some strong claims about the dissociability of grammar and semantics have been made (Grodzinsky, 1993; Kean, 1985). Briefly, it has been argued that nonfluent Broca's aphasia constitutes a form of "central agrammatism," a specific difficulty with grammatical processing that shows up in all modalities, including agrammatic speech (syntactically simplified, with few inflections or function words) and receptive agrammatism (difficulty processing sentences like *The boy who chased the girl is tall*, in which the patient cannot rely on semantic or pragmatic information). Because Broca's aphasia is correlated with damage to the inferior frontal region of the left hemisphere (especially Broca's area), some have concluded that Broca's area stands at the center of a specific neural system for grammar. This position is illustrated in the following quote from Zurif and Caramazza (1976):

> The particular effects of anterior brain damage are not limited to speech; nor are these effects due to an economy of effort. Rather, *at no level* does the agrammatic patient appear fully capable of processing the small words of language, epecially those words that function as syntactic markers for implicit grammatical structure. (p. 270, italics added)

Although this was a promising hypothesis through the 1970s and 1980s, most aphasiologists have now abandoned the doctrine of central agrammatism in favor of a position in which the same deficits are explained with reference to more general processing deficits that transcend the boundaries of grammar. This change in position is illustrated in the following quote from Zurif, Swinney, Prather, Solomon, and Bushell (1993):

> The brain region implicated in Broca's aphasia is *not* the locus of syntactic representations *per se*. Rather, we suggest that this region provides processing resources that sustain one or more of the fixed operating characteristics of the lexical processing system—characteristics that are, in turn, necessary for building syntactic representations in real time. (p. 462)

The reasons for this sea change are complex, and have been reviewed in some detail elsewhere (Bates & Goodman, 1997; Bates & Wulfeck, 1989; Bates, Wulfeck, & MacWhinney, 1991; Blackwell & Bates, 1995; Devescovi et al., 1997; see also Menn & Obler, 1990). We restrict ourselves here to a brief summary of arguments against a lexical–grammatical dissociation and the separate neural system for grammar that such a dissociation seemed to require.

All Aphasic Patients Have Lexical Deficits

Anomia refers to a deficit in word retrieval. Although many different forms of anomia have been described, one fact is very clear: Anomia is reported in every form of aphasia, including the nonfluent agrammatic syndrome associated with lesions to Broca's area. This point is illustrated in Table 2.3, which provides a classical taxonomy of the seven major aphasia subtypes. Despite ample variation in comprehension, fluency, and repetition, anomia is observed in all seven subgroups. Simply put, this means that there is no evidence of a full double dissociation between grammar and the lexicon. Grammatical deficits are always accompanied by at least some form of anomia.

Agrammatic Patients Still "Know" Their Grammar

Starting in the 1980s, a series of studies have shown that so-called agrammatic patients can perform above chance on grammaticality judgment tasks, including some very subtle morphosyntactic judgments (Linebarger, Schwartz, & Saffran, 1983; Shankweiler, Crain, Gorrell, & Tuller, 1989; Wulfeck, 1988; Wulfeck, Bates, & Capasso, 1991). These studies are complemented by a growing cross-linguistic literature showing that agrammatic patients retain language-specific profiles in their performance on both expressive and receptive tasks (Bates, Wulfeck, et al., 1991; Menn & Obler, 1990), suggesting that their performance is still governed (in considerable detail) by language-specific grammatical knowledge.

TABLE 2.3
Traditional Aphasia Classifications

Aphasia Type	*Production: Naming*	*Production: Fluency*	*Comprehensio n ("bedside")*	*Repetition*
Broka	-	-	+	-
Wernicke	-	+	-	-
Transcortical motor	-	-	+	+
Transcortical sensory	-	+	-	+
Conduction	-	+	+	-
Anomia	-	+	+	+
Global	-	-	-	-

Expressive Agrammatism Is Not Specific to Any Syndrome

The idea that grammar is impaired in Broca's aphasia but preserved in fluent patients with Wernicke's aphasia was proposed in the 1970s, based almost exclusively on data for English-speaking patients. In fact, it has been known for almost 100 years that Wernicke's aphasics also display grammatical deficits (Pick, 1913/1973). However, these deficits are only apparent in richly inflected languages. As Pick noted (based on his own research with German and Czech patients), nonfluent patients tend to err by omitting inflections and function words (*agrammatism*), whereas fluent patients err by producing the wrong inflection or function word (*paragrammatism*). Because English has so little inflectional morphology (and because function word substitution errors are multiply interpretable), there are few opportunities to observe frank paragrammatic symptoms. Hence, the belief that expressive agrammatism is restricted to Broca's aphasia is a by-product of research conducted in English! Table 2.4 (see also Bates & Goodman, 1997, p. 549) presents a summary of populations who are known to display some form of expressive agrammatism, including some of the congenital populations already described (DNS, WMS, SLI). At least three different forms of expressive agrammatism have been reported: the nonfluent variety, characterized by omission (a predominant symptom in Broca's aphasia, DNS, and SLI); the fluent or hyperfluent variety, characterized by substitution and occasional inappropriate additions (a predominant symptom in Wernicke's aphasia, Italian children with WMS, and the spoken and written language of some congenitally deaf adults); and a third variety that we call *syntactic simplification*, characterized by a reduction in the use of complex syntactic forms in the absence of frank errors of omission or substitution (a symptom that has been reported in Alzheimer's disease and in normal aging). For present purposes, the key point is that expressive agrammatism is not restricted to any specific clinical group, and it is not associated uniquely with damage to any particular region of the brain.

Patients Display Similar Grammatical and Lexical Symptoms

Table 2.4 also summarizes the lexical symptoms that are characteristic of each patient group. Although this is an idealization (most patients display more than one symptom type), a characterization of patients by their predominant lexical and grammatical symptom reveals some striking similarities. For example, patients who display an omission pattern in grammar tend to produce lexical omissions as well (i.e., complete word-finding failures). This is particularly true of Broca's aphasics, but a similar pattern can be detected in the underproduction of content words reported for

TABLE 2.4
Varieties of Expressive Agrammatism and Their Relation to Lexical Symptoms

Group	*Predominant Grammatical Symptom*	*Predominant Lexical Symptom*
Broca's aphasia	Omission of function words and inflections	Word-finding failure
Specific Language Impairment	Omission of function words and inflections	Word-finding failure
Down syndrome	Omission of function words and inflections	Word-finding failure
Wernicke's aphasia	Substitution of function words and inflections	Word substitutions (paraphasia)
Williams syndrome	Substitution of function words and inflections	Word substitutions (paraphasia)
Neurologically intact deaf speakers of an oral language	Substitutions, additions of function words	??
Anomic aphasia	Reduction in syntactic complexity without frank errors of omission of substitution	Empty speech (heavy use of pronouns and "light forms")
Alzheimer's dementia	Reduction in syntactic complexity without frank errors of omission or substitution	Empty speech (heavy use of pronouns and "light forms")
Normal aging	Reduction in syntactic complexity without frank errors of omission or substitution	Empty speech (heavy use of pronouns and "light forms")

Note. Adapted from Bates and Goodman (1997).

DNS and SLI. Patients who display a substitution pattern in grammar tend to produce lexical substitutions as well (referred to as *semantic paraphasias*). This is particularly true for Wernicke's aphasics, but similar phenomena have been reported in WMS. The one dissociation here involves the congenitally deaf, who reportedly do make grammatical substitutions and additions in the absence of frank lexical paraphasias. Finally, those individuals who produce a reduced and restricted range of syntactic forms in the absence of frank grammatical errors also have a tendency to overproduce pronouns, light verbs (e.g., *make* and *do*), and other underspecified lexical forms, in the absence of frank lexical errors. This joint lexical–grammatical pattern has been reported in Alzheimer's disease and in studies of language production in normal aging. Taken together, these results suggest that grammatical and lexical deficits have a common cause, compatible with the heterogeneous but unified lexicalist approach to grammar described in the introduction.

Receptive Agrammatism Is Not Specific to Any Syndrome, and Can Be Observed in Normals Under Stress

Finally, it is now quite clear that the profiles of receptive agrammatism reported for Broca's aphasics are not unique to patients with left anterior lesions and can be observed in a host of different populations including normals processing language under stress. Receptive agrammatism is characterized by a marked difficulty in processing inflections and closed-class words, together with the reduction or loss of the ability to process noncanonical word order types (e.g., passives like *Tom is kissed by Mary* are harder than actives like *Tom kisses Mary*; object relatives like *It's the boy that the girl kisses* are harder than subject relatives like *It's the boy that kisses the girl*. Table 2.5 (see also Bates & Goodman, 1997, p. 549) summarizes the

TABLE 2.5
Varieties of Receptive Agrammatism Across Populations

Group	*Difficulty Processing Closed-Class Morphemes*	*Difficulty Processing Rare or Complex Syntactic Frames*
Broca's aphasia	XX	XX
Wernicke's aphasia	XX	XX
Anomic aphasia	X	X
Alzheimer's dementia	≈	X
Neurologically intact deaf speakers of an oral language	X	≈
Specific Language Impairment	X	X
Down syndrome	X	X
Williams syndrome	X	X
Elderly controls and nonaphasic patients	≈	≈
College students under perceptual degradation (noise or compression)	≈	≈
College students under cognitive overload (dual-task conditions)	≈	no deficit

Note. Adapted from Bates and Goodman (1997).
XX = severe deficit. X = moderate deficit (worse than age- or IQ-matched normal controls). ≈ mild deficit (worse than normal young adults).

populations in which these two receptive symptoms have been observed. Simply put, the same elements that are difficult for Broca's aphasics are difficult for everybody! The same specific profiles of morphological vulnerability observed in Broca's aphasia (e.g., difficulty detecting agreement errors despite preserved ability to detect word order errors) are observed in a wide range of patient groups, and in normal college students who are asked to process the same stimuli under perceptual degradation (e.g., a partial noise mask), temporal degradation (compressed speech), or cognitive overload (e.g., digit load). A similar story holds for complex noncanonical sentence structures, with one interesting exception. For Broca's aphasics, Wernicke's aphasics, even anomic aphasics with no history of expressive agrammatism, it is invariably the case that active sentences and subject relatives elicit more accurate performance than passive sentences or object relatives. This same order of difficulty is observed in normals as well, albeit at a much higher accuracy level, and it is exaggerated in the aphasic direction when college students are forced to process the same sentence stimuli under a noise mask or with compressed speech. However, in contrast with results for grammatical morphemes, the two "hard" sentence structures appear to be resistant to the effects of a cognitive overload: Participants in a dual-task condition perform no worse than participants with processing under ideal conditions. This is our first evidence to date that the effect of generic stressors on normal processing is different depending on the kind of morphosyntactic structure that participants are required to process. This is an interesting result, but the general message is the same: Receptive agrammatism is not unique to any form of aphasia and may reflect "weak links in the processing chain" that show up in neurologically intact individuals under adverse processing conditions.

Putting these lines of evidence together, we conclude that there is no compelling evidence for a "hard" dissociation between grammar and the lexicon, and hence no evidence for the claim that grammar and the lexicon are mediated by separate, dedicated, domain-specific neural systems. This does not mean that grammar does not exist (it does), or that grammatical and lexical structures are identical (they are not). As we already noted, we should expect different classes of stimuli to elicit different patterns of brain activity, depending on the task, the specific nature of the stimuli, and the kind of processing that each requires. Big and small, short and long, loud and soft, frequent and rare—any systematic difference in stimulus characteristics may require a different configuration of processors. The brain, like the hand, is a flexible and dynamic system that responds with exquisite precision to the demand characteristics of the task and the object to be manipulated. The human brain is the only system on earth that is capable of acquiring a fully grammaticized language. It is also the only system capable of musical composition, ice hockey, and international finance. The mix of systems that has evolved to make these accomplishments possible is still unknown, but one thing is certain: There is (at this writing) no evidence that requires postulation of a mental organ for grammar. The emergentist account of grammar is viable, and is, in our view, the most coherent and parsimonious account currently available.

ACKNOWLEDGMENTS

Support for the research reported here has been provided by a grant to Judith Goodman by the John D. and Catherine T. MacArthur Foundation Research Network on Early Childhood Transitions, and by NIDCD 401-DC00216, NINDS P50 NS22343, NIDCD P50 DC01289-0351 and NIH 1-R01-AG13474 to Elizabeth Bates. Portions of this chapter are adapted from E. Bates and J. Goodman, "On the inseparability of grammar and the lexicon," *Language and Cognitive Processes*, 1997.

REFERENCES

Au, T. K. F., Dapretto, M., & Song, Y. K. (1994). Input vs constraints: Early word acquisition in Korean and English. *Journal of Memory and Language, 33,* 567–582.

Bates, E. (1976). *Language and context: Studies in the acquisition of pragmatics.* New York: Academic Press.

Bates, E., Benigni, L., Bretherton, I., Camaioni, L., & Volterra, V. (1979). *The emergence of symbols.* New York: Academic Press.

Bates, E., Bretherton, I., & Snyder, L. (1988). *From first words to grammar: Individual differences and dissociable mechanisms.* New York: Cambridge University Press.

Bates, E., Dale, P., & Thal, D. (1995). Individual differences and their implications for theories of language development. In P. Fletcher & B. MacWhinney (Eds.), *Handbook of child language* (pp. 96–151). Oxford, UK: Basil Blackwell.

Bates, E., & Devescovi, A. (1989). A cross-linguistic approach to sentence production. In B. MacWhinney & E. Bates (Eds.), *The crosslinguistic study of sentence processing* (pp. 225–256). New York: Cambridge University Press.

Bates, E., & Elman, J. (1996). Learning rediscovered: A perspective on Saffran, Aslin & Newport. *Science, 274,* 1849–1850.

Bates, E., & Goodman, J. C. (1997). On the inseparability of grammar and the lexicon: Evidence from acquisition, aphasia and real-time processing. In G. Altmann (Ed.) (Special issue on the lexicon), *Language and Cognitive Processes, 12,* 507–586.

Bates, E., & Marchman, V. (1988). What is and is not universal in language acquisition. In F. Plum (Ed.), *Language, communication and the brain* (pp. 19–38). New York: Raven.

Bates, E., Marchman, V., Thal, D., Fenson, L., Dale, P., Reznick, S., Reilly, J., & Hartung, J. (1994). Developmental and stylistic variation in the composition of early vocabulary. *Journal of Child Language, 21,* 85–124.

Bates, E., Thal, D., & Marchman, V. (1991). Symbols and syntax: A Darwinian approach to language development. In N. Krasnegor, D. Rumbaugh, R. Schiefelbusch, & M. Studdert-Kennedy (Eds.), *Biological and behavioral determinants of language development* (pp. 29–65). Hillsdale, NJ: Lawrence Erlbaum Associates.

Bates, E., Vicari, S., & Trauner, D. (in press). Neural mediation of language development: Perspectives from lesion studies of infants and children. In H. Tager-Flusberg (Ed.), *Neurodevelopmental disorders: Contributions to a new framework from the cognitive neurosciences.* Cambridge, MA: MIT Press.

Bates, E., & Wulfeck, B. (1989). Comparative aphasiology: A cross-linguistic approach to language breakdown. *Aphasiology, 3,* 111–142, 161–168.

Bates, E., Wulfeck, B., & MacWhinney, B. (1991). Crosslinguistic research in aphasia: An overview. *Brain and Language, 41,* 123–148.

Bellugi, U., Bihrle, A., Neville, H., Jernigan, T., & Doherty, S. (1992). Language, cognition, and brain organization in a neurodevelopmental disorder. In M. Gunnar & C. Nelson (Eds.), *Developmental behavioral neuroscience* (pp. 201–232). Hillsdale, NJ: Lawrence Erlbaum Associates.

Bishop, D. V. M. (1997). *Uncommon understanding: Development and disorders of comprehension in children.* Hove, UK: Psychology Press/Erlbaum.

Blackwell, A., & Bates, E. (1995). Inducing agrammatic profiles in normals: Evidence for the selective vulnerability of morphology under cognitive resource limitation. *Journal of Cognitive Neuroscience, 7,* 228–257.

Bloom, L., Lightbown, L., & Hood, L. (1975). Structure and variation in child language. *Monographs for the Society for Research in Child Development, 40*(Serial No. 160). Issue 2

Braine, M. D. S. (1976). Children's first word combinations. With commentary by Melissa Bowerman. *Monographs of the Society for Research in Child Development, 41*(Serial No. 164). Issue 1

Bresnan, J. (Ed.). (1982). *The mental representation of grammatical relations.* Cambridge, MA: MIT Press.

Bresnan, J. (1996). *Lexical functional syntax.* Manuscript submitted for publication.

Bretherton, I., McNew, S., Snyder, L., & Bates, E. (1983). Individual differences at 20 months. *Journal of Child Language, 10,* 293–320.

Brown, R. (1973). *A first language: The early stages.* Cambridge, MA: Harvard University Press.

Capirci, O., Sabbadini, L., & Volterra, V. (1996). Language development in Williams syndrome: A case study. *Cognitive Neuropsychology, 13,* 1017–1039.

Caselli, M. C. (1995). Il primo sviluppo lessicale [Early lexical development]. In G. Sabbadini (Ed.), *Manuale di neuropsicologia dell'età evolutiva* ([Handbook of developmental neuropsychology], pp. 242–258). Bologna, Italy: Zanichelli.

Caselli, M. C., & Casadio, P. (1995). *Il primo vocabolario del bambino: Guida all'uso del questionario MacArthur per la valutazione della comunicazione e del linguaggio nei primi anni di vita* ([The child's first words: Guide to the use of the MacArthur questionnaire for the assessment of communication and language in the first years of life], pp. 94–100). Milan: FrancoAngeli.

Caselli, M. C., Casadio, P., & Bates, E. (in press). A cross-linguistic study of the transition from first words to grammar. *Journal of Child Psychology.*

Chapman, R. S. (1995). Language development in children and adolescents with Down Syndrome. In P. Fletcher & B. MacWhinney (Eds.), *The handbook of child language* (pp. 664–689). Oxford, UK: Basil Blackwell.

Chomsky, N. (1980). The linguistic approach. In M. Piattelli-Palmarini (Ed.), *Language and learning* (pp. 109–130). Cambridge, MA: Harvard University Press.

Chomsky, N. (1981). *Lectures on government and binding.* New York: Foris.

Chomsky, N. (1988). *Language and problems of knowledge: The Managua Lectures.* Cambridge, MA: MIT Press.

Chomsky, N. (1995). *The minimalist program.* Cambridge, MA: MIT Press.

Clahsen, H. (1991). *Child language and developmental dysphasia: Linguistic studies of the acquisition of German.* Amsterdam: Benjamins.

Clark, R., Gleitman, L., & Kroch, A. (1997, May). Acquiring language [Letter to the editor]. *Science, 276(5316),* p. 1177.

Contardi, A., & Vicari, S. (Eds.). (1994). *Le persone Down: Aspetti neuropsicologici, educativi e sociali* [Persons with Down Syndrome: Neuropsychological, educational, and social aspects]. Milan: FrancoAngeli.

Crain, S. (1991). Language acquisition in the absence of experience. *Behavioral and Brain Sciences, 14,* 597–611.

Cresti, E., & Moneglia, M. (1995). *Ricerche sull'acquisizione dell'italiano* [Research on the acquisition of Italian]. Rome: Bulzoni.

Cutler, A. (1993). Phonological cues to open- and closed-class words in the processing of spoken sentences. *Journal of Psycholinguistic Research, 22,* 109–131.

Dale, P. S. (1991). The validity of a parent report measure of vocabulary and syntax at 24 months. *Journal of Speech and Hearing Sciences, 34,* 565–571.

Dale, P. S., Bates, E., Reznick, S., & Morisset, C. (1989). The validity of a parent report instrument of child language at 20 months. *Journal of Child Language, 16,* 239–249.

Demuth, K. (1989). Subject, topic and Sesotho passive. *Journal of Child Language, 17,* 67–84.

Devescovi, A., Bates, E., D'Amico, S., Hernandez, A., Marangolo, P., Pizzamiglio, L., & Razzano, C. (1997). An on-line study of grammaticality judgments in normal and aphasic speakers of Italian. In L. Menn (Ed.), (Special issue on cross-linguistic aphasia), *Aphasiology, 11,* 543–579.

Devescovi, A., & Pizzuto, E. (1995). Lo sviluppo grammaticale [Grammatical development]. In G. Sabbadini (Ed.), *Manuale di neuropsicologia dell'età evolutiva* ([Handbook of developmental neuropsychology], pp. 242–258). Bologna, Italy: Zanichelli.

Eisele, J., & Aram, D. (1995). Lexical and grammatical development in children with early hemisphere damage: A cross-sectional view from birth to adolescence. In P. Fletcher & B. MacWhinney (Eds.), *The handbook of child language* (pp. 664–689). Oxford, UK: Basil Blackwell.

Elman, J., Bates, E., Johnson, M., Karmiloff-Smith, A., Parisi, D., & Plunkett, K. (1996). *Rethinking innateness: A connectionist perspective on development.* Cambridge, MA: MIT Press.

Erhard, P., Kato, T., Strick, P. L., & Ugurbil, K. (1996). Functional MRI activation pattern of motor and language tasks in Broca's area [Abstract]. *Society for Neuroscience, 22,* 260.2.

Fenson, L., Dale, P., Reznick, J., Bates, E., Thal, D., & Pethick, S. (1994). Variability in early communicative development. *Monographs of the Society for Research in Child Development, 59*(5, Serial No. 242).

Fenson, L., Dale, P., Reznick, J. S., Thal, D., Bates, E., Hartung, J., Pethick, S., & Reilly, J. (1993). *The MacArthur Communicative Development Inventories: User's guide and technical manual.* San Diego, CA: Singular.

Fillmore, C. J., Kay, P., & O'Connor, C. (1988). Regularity and idiomaticity in grammatical constructions: The case of Let Alone. *Language, 64,* 501–538.

Fodor, J. A. (1983). *The modularity of mind: An essay on faculty psychology.* Cambridge, MA: MIT Press.

Friederici, A. D. (1990). On the properties of cognitive modules. *Psychological Research, 52,* 175–180.

Gentner, D. (1982). Why are nouns learned before verbs: Linguistic relativity versus natural partitioning. In S. A. Kuczaj II (Ed.), *Language development, Vol. 2: Language, thought and culture.* Hillsdale, NJ: Lawrence Erlbaum Associates.

Giannotti, A., & Vicari, S. (Eds.). (1994). *Il bambino con sindrome di Williams* [Children with Williams Syndrome]. Milan, Italy: FrancoAngeli.

Gold, E. (1967). Language identification in the limit. *Information and Control, 16,* 447–474.

Goldberg, A. E. (1995). *Constructions: A construction grammar approach to argument structure.* Chicago: University of Chicago Press.

Goodglass, H., & Menn, L. (1985). Is agrammatism a unitary phenomenon? In M.-L. Kean (Ed.), *Agrammatism* (pp. 1–26). Orlando, FL: Academic Press.

Goodman, J. C. (1995). The shape of change: Longitudinal evidence about language development. *Society for Research in Child Development Abstracts, 10,* 111.

Goodman, J. C., & McDonough, L. (1996). *The role of context in the acquisition of novel verbs.* Manuscript in preparation.

Goodman, J. C., McDonough, L., & Brown, N. (1996). *Lexical bootstrapping: Toddlers' acquisition of new words heard in sentence contexts.* Manuscript submitted for publication.

Goodman, J. C., Nusbaum, H. C., Lee, L., & Broihier, K. (1990). The effects of syntactic and discourse variables on the segmental intelligibility of speech. *The Proceedings of the 1990 International Conference on Spoken Language Processing* (pp. 393–396). Kobe, Japan: The Acoustical Society of Japan.

Gopnik, A., & Choi, S. (1990). Do linguistic differences lead to cognitive differences? A cross-linguistic study of semantic and cognitive development. *First Language, 10,* 199–215.

Gopnik, A., & Choi, S. (1995). Names, relational words, and cognitive development in English and Korean speakers: Nouns are not always learned before verbs. In M. Tomasello & W. Merriman (Eds.), *Beyond names for things: Young children's acquisition of verbs* (pp. 63–80). Hillsdale, NJ: Lawrence Erlbaum Associates.

Gopnik, M., & Crago, M. B. (1991). Familial aggregation of a developmental language disorder. *Cognition, 39,* 1–50.

Grodzinsky, Y. (Ed.). (1993). Special issue: Grammatical investigations of aphasia. *Brain and Language, 45*(3).

Grosjean, F., & Gee, J. P. (1987). Prosodic structure and spoken word recognition. In U. Frauenfelder & L. K. Tyler (Eds.), *Spoken word recognition* ([Special issue of *Cognition*], pp. 135–155). Cambridge, MA: MIT Press.

Herron, D., & Bates, E. (1997). Sentential and acoustic factors in the recognition of open- and closed-class words. *Journal of Memory and Language, 37,* 217–239.

Horgan, D. (1978). How to answer questions when you've got nothing to say. *Journal of Child Language, 5,* 159–165.

Horgan, D. (1979, May). *Nouns: Love 'em or leave 'em.* Address to the New York Academy of Sciences, New York.

Horgan, D. (1981). Rate of language acquisition and noun emphasis. *Journal of Psycholinguistic Research, 10,* 629–640.

Hurlburt, M. S., & Goodman, J. C. (1992). The development of lexical effects on children's phoneme identifications. In J. J. Ohala, T. M. Nearey, B. L. Derwing, M. M. Hodge, & G. E. Wiebe (Eds.), *ICSLP 92 Proceedings: 1992 International Conference on Spoken Language Processing* (pp. 337–340). Banff, Canada: University of Alberta.

Indefrey, P., Brown, C., Hagoort, P., Herzog, H., Sach, M., & Seitz, R. J. (1997). A PET study of cerebral activation pattern induced by verb inflection. *Neuroimage, 5(4),* Part 2, S548.

Jaeger, J. J., Lockwood, A. H., Kemmerer, D. L., van Valin, R. D., Murphy, B. W., & Khalak, H. G. (1996). Positron emission tomographic study of regular and irregular verb morphology in English. *Language, 72,* 451–497.

Jahn-Samilo, J. (1995). Language comprehension and production in children from 8 to 30 months of age: A comparison of parent report and laboratory measures from a longitudinal study. *Society for Research in Child Development Abstracts, 10,* 112.

Jahn-Samilo, J., Goodman, J. C., Bates, E., & Appelbaum, M. (1997). *Parent and laboratory measures of production from 12 to 30 months of age.* Manuscript submitted for publication.

Jenkins, L., & Maxam, A. (1997, May). Acquiring language [Letter to the editor]. *Science, 276*(5316), pp. 1178–1179.

Johnston, J. R. (1994). Cognitive abilities of language-impaired children. In R. Watkins & M. Rice (Eds.), *Specific language impairments in children: Current directions in research and intervention* (pp. 107–122). Baltimore: Paul Brookes.

Johnston, J. R., & Schery, T. K. (1976). The use of grammatical morphemes by children with communication disorders. In D. M. Morehead & A. E. Morehead (Eds.), *Normal and deficient child language* (pp. 239–258). Baltimore: University Park Press.

Kandel, E., Schwartz, J., & Jessell, T. (Eds.). (1995). *Essentials of neural science and behavior.* Norwalk, CT: Appleton & Lange.

Karmiloff-Smith, A. (1992). *Beyond modularity: A developmental perspective on cognitive science.* Cambridge, MA: MIT Press.

Karmiloff-Smith, A., Klima, E. S., Bellugi, U., Grant, J., & Baron-Cohen, S. (1995). Is there a social module? Language, face processing, and theory of mind in subjects with Williams Syndrome. *Journal of Cognitive Neuroscience, 7,* 196–208.

Kean, M.-L. (1977). Linguistic interpretation of aphasia syndromes. *Cognition, 5,* 9–46.

Kean, M.-L. (Ed.). (1985). *Agrammatism.* Orlando, FL: Academic Press.

Langacker, R. (1987). *Foundations of cognitive grammar.* Stanford, CA: Stanford University Press.

Leonard, L. B. (1998). *Children with specific language impairment.* Cambridge, MA: MIT Press.

Leonard, L. B., Bortolini, U., Caselli, M. C., McGregor, K., & Sabbadini, L. (1992). Morphological deficits in children with specific language impairment: The status of features in the underlying grammar. *Language Acquisition, 2,* 151–179.

Linebarger, M., Schwartz, M., & Saffran, E. (1983). Sensitivity to grammatical structure in so-called agrammatic aphasics. *Cognition, 13,* 361–392.

Locke, J. L. (1983). *Phonological acquisition and change.* New York: Academic Press.

Locke, J. L. (1997). A theory of neurolinguistic development. *Brain and Language, 58,* 265–326.

MacWhinney, B., & Bates, E. (Eds.). (1989). *The crosslinguistic study of sentence processing.* New York: Cambridge University Press.

MacWhinney, B., Leinbach, J., Taraban, R., & McDonald, J. (1989). Language learning: Cues or rules? *Journal of Memory and Language, 28,* 255–277.

Marchman, V., & Bates, E. (1994). Continuity in lexical and morphological development: A test of the critical mass hypothesis. *Journal of Child Language, 21,* 339–366.

Marchman, V., Bates, E., Burkhardt, A., & Good, A. (1991). Functional constraints on the acquisition of the passive: Toward a model of the competence to perform. *First Language, 11,* 65–92.

Marslen-Wilson, W. (1987). Functional parallelism in spoken word recognition. In U. Frauenfelder & L. K. Tyler (Eds.), *Spoken word recognition* ([Special issue of *Cognition*], pp. 71–102). Cambridge, MA: MIT Press.

Martin, A., Wiggs, C. L., Ungerleider, L. G., & Haxby, J. V. (1996). Neural correlates of category-specific knowledge. *Nature, 379,* 649–652.

McQueen, J. M., Cutler, A., Briscoe, T., & Norris D. (1995). Models of continuous speech recognition and the contents of the vocabulary. *Language and Cognitive Processes, 10,* 309–331.

Menn, L., & Obler, L. K. (Eds.). (1990). *Agrammatic aphasia: Cross-language narrative sourcebook.* Amsterdam: John Benjamins.

Mervis, C. B., & Bertrand, J. (1993, March). *Early language and cognitive development: Implications of research with children who have Williams Syndrome or Down Syndrome.* Paper presented at the 60th Anniversary Meeting of the Society for Research in Child Development, New Orleans, LA.

Miller, J. (1987). Language and communication characteristics of children with Down Syndrome. In S. Pueschel, C. Tingey, J. Rynders, A. Crocker, & D. Crutcher (Eds.), *New perspectives on Down Syndrome* (pp. 233–262). Baltimore: Brookes.

Miller, J. (1992a). The development of speech and language in children with Down Syndrome. In E. McCoy & I. Lott (Eds.), *Clinical care for persons with Down Syndrome.* Orlando, FL: Academic Press.

Miller, J. (1992b). Lexical acquisition in children with Down Syndrome. In R. S. Chapman (Ed.), *Child talk: Advances in language acquisition.* Year Book Medical Publishers, Inc.

Mody, M., Studdert-Kennedy, M, & Brady, S. (1997). Speech perception deficits in poor readers: Auditory processing or phonological coding? *Journal of Experimental Child Psychology, 64,* 199–231.

Naigles, L. (1988). Syntactic bootstrapping as a procedure for verb learning. *Dissertation Abstracts International, 49*(6), 2396B.

Naigles, L. (1990). Children use syntax to learn verb meanings. *Journal of Child Language, 17,* 357–374.

Naigles, L. G., Gleitman, H., & Gleitman, L. R. (1993). Children acquire word meaning components from syntactic evidence. In E. Dromi (Ed.), *Language and cognition: A developmental perspective* (pp. 104–140). Norwood, NJ: Ablex.

Nelson, K. (1973). Structure and strategy in learning to talk. *Monographs of the Society for Research in Child Development, 38*(1 & 2, Serial No. 149).

Nobre, A. C., & Plunkett, K. (1997). The neural system of language: Structure and development. *Current Opinion in Neurobiology, 7(2),* 262–268.

Nusbaum, H. C., & Goodman, J. C. (1994). Learning to hear speech as spoken language. In J. C. Goodman & H. C. Nusbaum (Eds.), *The development of speech perception: The transition from speech sounds to spoken words* (pp. 299–338). Cambridge, MA: The MIT Press.

Nusbaum, H. C., & Henly, A. S. (1992). Listening to speech through an adaptive window of analysis. In B. Schouten (Ed.), *The processing of speech: From the auditory periphery to word recognition.* Berlin, Germany: Mouton-De Gruyter.

Osterhout, L., & Holcomb, P. J. (1993). Event-related potentials and syntactic anomaly: Evidence of anomaly detection during the perception of continuous speech. *Language and Cognitive Processes, 8,* 413–437.

Pae, S. (1993). *Early vocabulary in Korean: Are nouns easier to learn than verbs?* Unpublished doctoral dissertation, University of Kansas.

Pesetsky, D., Wexler, K., & Fromkin, V. (1997, May). Acquiring language [Letter to the editor]. *Science, 276*(5316), p. 1177.

Peters, A. (1977). Language-learning strategies: Does the whole equal the sum of the parts? *Language, 53,* 560–573.

Piaget, J. (1970). *Genetic epistemology* (E. Duckworth, Trans.). New York: Columbia University Press.

Pick, A. (1973). *Aphasia* (J. Brown, Ed. & Trans.). Springfield, IL: Charles C. Thomas. (Original work published 1913)

Pinker, S. (1991). Rules of language. *Science,* 253, 530–535.

Pinker, S. (1994). On language. *Journal of Cognitive Neuroscience, 6(1),* 92–97.

Pinker, S. (1997, May). Acquiring language [Letter to the editor]. *Science, 276*(5316), p. 1178.

Pizzuto, E., & Caselli, M. C. (1992). The acquisition of Italian morphology: Implications for models of language development. *Child Language, 19,* 491–557.

Pizzuto, E., & Caselli, M. C. (1994). The acquisition of Italian verb morphology in a cross-linguistic perspective. In Y. Levi (Ed.), *Other children, other languages* (pp. 137–187). Hillsdale, NJ: Lawrence Erlbaum Associates.

Plunkett, K., & Marchman, V. (1991). U-shaped learning and frequency effects in a multi-layered perceptron: Implications for child language acquisition. *Cognition, 38,* 43–102.

Plunkett, K., & Marchman, V. (1993). From rote learning to system building: Acquiring verb morphology in children and connectionist nets. *Cognition, 48,* 21–69.

Pollard, C., & Sag, I., (1994). *Head-drive phrase structure grammar* (Center for the Study of Language and Information, Rep. No. CSLI-88-132). University of Chicago.

Port, R., & van Gelder, T. (1995). *Mind as motion: Dynamical perspectives on behavior and cognition.* Cambridge, MA: MIT Press.

Reilly, J., Bates, E., & Marchman, V. (1998). Narrative discourse in children with early focal brain injury. In M. Dennis (Ed.), Discourse in children with anomalous brain development or acquired brain injury. *Brain and Language* (Special issue), *61,* 335–375.

Rice, M. (Ed.). (1996). *Toward a genetics of language.* Mahwah, NJ: Lawrence Erlbaum Associates.

Robinson, N. M., Dale, P. S., & Landesman, S. (1990). Validity of Stanford-Binet IV with linguistically precocious toddlers. *Intelligence, 14,* 173–186.

Rumelhart, D., & McClelland, J. L. (Eds.). (1986). *Parallel distributed processing: Explorations in the microstructure of cognition.* Cambridge, MA: MIT Press.

Saffran, E., Aslin, R., & Newport, E. (1996). Statistical learning in 8-month-olds. *Science, 274,* 1926–1928.

Saffran, J. R., Aslin, R. N., & Newport, E. L. (1997, May). Acquiring language [Letter to the editor]. *Science, 276*(5316), 1180, 1276.

Science. (1997). Letters, *Vol. 276,* pp. 1176–1181, 1276.

Sethuraman, N., Goldberg, A. E., & Goodman, J. C. (1997). Using the semantics associated with syntactic frames for interpretation without the aid of context. *Proceedings of the 28th Annual Child Language Research Forum* (pp. 283–294). Stanford, CA: Center for the Study of Language and Information.

Shankweiler, D., Crain, S., Gorrell, P., & Tuller, B. (1989). Reception of language in Broca's aphasia. *Language and Cognitive Processes, 4,* 1–33.

Shillcock, R. C., & Bard, E. G. (1993). Modularity and the processing of closed class words. In G. T. M. Altmann & R. C. Shillcock (Eds.), *Cognitive models of speech processing: The Second Sperlonga Meeting* (pp. 163–183). Hove, UK: Lawrence Erlbaum Associates.

Shore, C. M. (1995). *Individual differences in language development.* Thousand Oaks, CA: Sage.

Shore, C. M., O'Connell, C., & Bates, E. (1984). First sentences in language and symbolic play. *Developmental Psychology, 20,* 872–880.

Singer Harris, N., Bellugi, U., Bates, E., Rossen, M., & Jones, W. (1997). Emerging language in two genetically based neurodevelopmental disorders. In D. Thal & J. Reilly (Eds.), Special issue on Origins of Communication Disorders. *Developmental Neuropsychology, 13,* 345–370.

Slobin, D. (Ed.). (1985). *The crosslinguistic study of language acquisition* (Vols. 1 & 2). Hillsdale, NJ: Lawrence Erlbaum Associates.

Slobin, D. (Ed.). (1992). *The crosslinguistic study of language acquisition* (Vol. 3). Hillsdale, NJ: Lawrence Erlbaum Associates.

Slobin, D. (Ed.). (1997). *The crosslinguistic study of language acquisition* (Vols. 4 & 5). Mahwah, NJ: Lawrence Erlbaum Associates.

Smiley, P., & Huttenlocher, J. (1995). Conceptual development and the child's early words for events, objects, and persons. In M. Tomasello & W. E. Merriman (Eds.), *Beyond names for things.* Hillsdale, NJ: Lawrence Erlbaum Associates.

Smith, L. B., & Thelen, E. (Eds.). (1993). *A dynamic systems approach to development: Applications.* Cambridge, MA: MIT Press.

Snyder, L., Bates, E., & Bretherton, I. (1981). Content and context in early lexical development. *Journal of Child Language, 8,* 565–582.

Tallal, P., Miller, G., Bedi, G., Byma, G., Jenkins, W. M., Wang, X., Nagarajan, S. S., & Merzenich, M. M. (1996). Language comprehension in language-learning-impaired children improved with acoustically modified speech. *Science, 271*(5245), 81–84.

Tallal, P., Stark, R., & Mellits, D. (1985). Identification of language-impaired children on the basis of rapid perception and production skills. *Brain and Language, 25,* 314–322.

Thal, D. (1991). Language and cognition in late-talking toddlers. *Topics in Language Disorders, 11,* 33–42.

Thal, D., & Bates, E. (1988). Language and gesture in late talkers. *Journal of Speech and Hearing Research, 31,* 115–123.

Thal, D., Bates, E., & Bellugi, U. (1989). Language and cognition in two children with Williams Syndrome. *Journal of Speech and Hearing Research, 3,* 489–500.

Thal, D., Bates, E., Goodman, J., & Jahn-Samilo, J. (1997). Continuity of language abilities in late- and early-talking toddlers. In D. Thal & J. Reilly (Eds.), Special issue on Origins of Communication Disorders, *Developmental Neuropsychology, 13,* 239–273.

Thal, D., Bates, E., Zappia, M. J., & Oroz, M. (1996). Ties between lexical and grammatical development: Evidence from early talkers. *Journal of Child Language, 23,* 349–368.

Thal, D., & Katich, J. (1996). Does the early bird always catch the worm? Predicaments in early identification of specific language impairment. In K. Cole, P. Dale, & D. Thal (Eds.), *The measurement of communication and language: Vol. 6. Assessment* (pp. 1–28). Baltimore: Brookes.

Thelen, E., & Smith, L. B. (1994). *A dynamic systems approach to the development of cognition and action.* Cambridge, MA: MIT Press.

Thompson, D. W. (1968). *On growth and form* (2nd ed., reprinted). Cambridge, UK: Cambridge University Press. (Original work published 1917)

Tomasello, M. (1992). *First verbs: A case study of early grammatical development.* Cambridge, UK: Cambridge University Press.

Tomasello, M., & Call, J. (1997). *Primate cognition.* New York: Oxford University Press.

Tomasello, M., & Merriman, W. (Eds.). (1995). *Beyond names for things: Young children's acquisition of verbs.* Hillsdale, NJ: Lawrence Erlbaum Associates.

Townsend, J., Wulfeck, B., Nichols, S., & Koch, L. (1995). *Attentional deficits in children with developmental language disorder* (Tech. Rep. No. CND-9503). La Jolla: University of California, San Diego, Center for Research in Language, Project in Cognitive and Neural Development.

Ullman, M., Corkin, S., Coppola, M., Hickok, G., Growdon, J. H., Koroshetz, W. J., & Pinker, S. (1997). A neural dissociation within language: Evidence that the mental dictionary is part of declarative memory, and that grammatical rules are processed by the procedural system. *Journal of Cognitive Neuroscience, 9,* 266–276.

Utman, J. (1997). *Effects of subphonetic acoustic differences on lexical access in neurologically intact adults and patients with Broca's aphasia.* Unpublished doctoral dissertation, Brown University.

Van der Lely, H. K. J. (1994). Canonical linking rules: Forward versus reverse linking in normally developing and specifically language-impaired children. *Cognition, 51,* 29–72.

Van Geert, P. (1994). *Dynamic systems of development: Change between complexity and chaos.* New York: Harvester Wheatsheaf.

Vargha-Khadem, F., Isaacs, E., & Muter, V. (1994). A review of cognitive outcome after unilateral lesions sustained during childhood. *Journal of Child Neurology, 9*(Suppl.), 2S67–2S73.

Vicari, S., Brizzolara, D., Carlesimo, G. A., Pezzini, G., & Volterra, V. (1996). Memory abilities in children with Williams syndrome. *Cortex, 32,* 503–514.

Volterra, V. (1976). A few remarks on the use of the past participle in child language. *Italian Linguistics, 2,* 149–157.

Volterra, V., Pezzini, G., Sabbadini, L., Capirci, O., & Vicari, S. (1996). Linguistic abilities in Italian children with Williams syndrome. *Cortex, 32,* 663–677.

Wang, P. P., & Bellugi, U. (1994). Evidence from two genetic syndromes for a dissociation between verbal and visual short-term memory. *Journal of Clinical and Experimental Neuropsychology, 16,* 317–322.

Wulfeck, B. (1988). Grammaticality judgments and sentence comprehension in agrammatic aphasia. *Journal of Speech and Hearing Research, 31,* 72–81.

Wulfeck, B., Bates, E., & Capasso, R. (1991). A crosslinguistic study of grammaticality judgments in Broca's aphasia. *Brain and Language, 41,* 311–336.

Zurif, E., & Caramazza, A. (1976). Psycholinguistic structures in aphasia: Studies in syntax and semantics. In H. Whitaker & H. A. Whitaker (Eds.), *Studies in neurolinguistics, Vol. I* (pp. 260–292). New York: Academic Press.

Zurif, E., Swinney, D., Prather, P., Solomon, J., & Bushell, C. (1993). An on-line analysis of syntactic processing in Broca's and Wernicke's aphasia. *Brain and Language, 45,* 448–464.

Chapter 3

Generativity and Variation: The Notion 'Rule of Grammar' Revisited

T. Givón
University of Oregon

1. CONTEXT

In a well-known early paper titled "On the notion 'rule of grammar' ", Chomsky (1961) outlined his logical-mathematical perspective on the structure of language, one that has haunted generative linguistics ever since:

> ". . . By "grammar of the language *L*" I will mean a device of some sort (that is, a set of rules) that provides, at least, a complete specification of an infinite set of grammatical sentences of *L* and their structural description. In addition to making precise the notion "structural description", the theory of grammar should meet requirements of the following kind. It should make available:
>
> (1) (a) a class of possible grammars *G1, G2* . . .
> (b) a class of possible sentences *S1, S2* . . .
> (c) a function *f* such that *f(i,j)* is a set of structural descriptions of the sentence *Si* that are provided by the grammar *Gj*,
> (d) a function *m(i)* which evaluates *Gi*,
> (e) a function *g* such that *g(i,n)* is the description of a finite automaton that takes sentences of (b) as input and gives structural descriptions assigned to these sentences by *Gi* . . ." (1961, p. 6)

As has been transparent since the dawn of generative grammar, Chomsky's vision of grammar as algorithmic—or 'logic machine'—likens rules of grammar to rules of logic or mathematics. Like those, rules of grammar were asserted to be exceptionless and governed by necessary and sufficient criteria.

A diametrically opposed approach to grammar has been offered in the recent writings of Paul Hopper (see Hopper 1987), most specifically in connection with his concept of 'emergent grammar':

> ". . . The notion of emergence is a pregnant one. It is not intended to be a standard sense of origins or genealogy, not a historical question of "how" the grammar came to be the way it "is", but instead it takes the adjective emergent seriously as a *continual movement toward structure*, a *postponement* or *"deferral" of structure*, a view of *structure as always provisional, always negotiable*, and in fact as *epiphenomenal* . . . Structure, then, in this view is not an overarching set of abstract principles, but more a question of *a spreading of systematicity* from individual words, phrases and smalls sets . . ." (1987, p. 142; emphases added)

To the extent that such richly metaphoric prose can be interpreted with precision, Hopper seems to assert that grammar is *totally* flexible, is *always* negotiated for the occasion, and is thus 100% dependent on its communicative context. Whatever systematicity, rigidity or generality can be detected in grammar are presumably nothing but a mirage of the linguist's arbitrary analytic habits.

In a later work, Hopper (1991) further elaborates his initial argument by suggesting that since the boundary between grammatical, semantic and phonological change are *not absolute*, it is therefore *non-existent*. This proposition is somehow supported by the early contention that grammar does not 'really' exist, in the traditional sense of relatively stable relationships between structure and its paired semantic or pragmatic values:

> ". . . The more extensive definition of grammaticalization implicit in this work raises the question of whether, when grammaticalization has done its work, there would in the end be any room left for the notion of grammar in a sense of static structural relationships . . . If grammar is not a discrete, modular set of relationships, it would seem to follow that no set of changes can be identified which distinctively characterise grammaticalization as opposed to, say, lexical change of phonological change in general . . ." (1991, pp. 18–19)

The logic of both extreme positions is founded on the very same fallacious reasoning. In Chomsky's case, the implicit inference is something like this:[1]

---

[1]To be fair to Hopper, I myself indulged in the same fallacious argument in Givón (1981), where I endeavored to conclude that because some or even many instances of graduality and continuum in grammatical categories can be shown, grammar is non-discrete. A similar—and logically just as fallacious—argument has been recently advanced by Dryer (1995, 1996) in his denial of the universality of grammatical relations.

(1) • rules of grammar are *not 100% flexible*
• therefore rules of grammar must be *100% rigid*

In Hopper's case, the implicit reasoning is:

(2) • rules of grammar are *not 100% rigid*
• therefore rules of grammar must be *100% flexible*

It is perhaps worth noting that a third position has existed in linguistics for a long time, a middle-ground position that has recognized that both Chomsky and Hopper must be right—but only partially. That position was espoused by both Edward Sapir and Otto Jespersen. Consider, for example, Sapir's (1921) celebrated quotation:

> ". . . Were a language ever completely "grammatical", it would be a perfect engine of conceptual expression. Unfortunately, or luckily, no language is tyrannically consistent. *All grammars leak* . . . " (1921, p. 38; emphases added)

If I am not misinterpreting Sapir, I believe he did not assert here that *all* rules of grammars leak *all the time,* but rather that no grammar is totally leak-free.

A similar perspective on the partial fallibility of grammar was expressed by Jespersen (1924), in his discussion of lexical classes:

> ". . . Most of the definitions given in even recent books are little better than sham definitions in which it is extremely easy to pick holes. . . . Not a single one of these definitions is either exhaustive or cogent . . ." (1924, pp. 58–59)

Again, it seems to me that Jespersen is not objecting here to the existence of *some* rigidity in grammatical generalizations ('rules'), but only to the tyrannical assumption—a la Chomsky—that *all* rules of grammar are exceptionless and squeaky clean.

One may wish to note, in passing, that the perspectives espoused by Chomsky and Hopper have, not surprisingly, much in common. Both subscribe to the Platonic (or 'Platonistic') position that for something to be a "rule"—i.e. a generalization—it must be exceptionless. From this common premise, Chomsky goes on to insist that only rules that conform to this rigid criterion can be "rules of grammar". While Hopper, in turn, concludes that since grammar never displays such complete rigidity, it therefore possesses no rigidity at all.

Since the facts of natural communication support neither extreme inference (1) nor (2), how could such positions be credibly upheld by rational scholars? In Chomsky's case, the logical sleight of hand is made possible by a well-known trick, the radical sanitization of the facts of natural language use. I refer here to Chomsky's (1965) fateful distinction between "competence" (knowledge) and "performance" (use), and his insistence that we study and build a model only of "competence". But the spirit of this distinction already hovers over the early work:

> ". . . A grammar, in the sense described above, is essentially a theory of the sentences of a language . . . It is not, however, a model of the speaker or hearer . . ." (1961, p. 7)

The rather undignified ruse of performance vs. competence has allowed generative linguists for almost forty years now to consider only language data produced for the analytic occasion out of the linguist's "native" competence, and to ignore performance-tainted data of natural communication.

Hopper (1987, 1991), likewise, gets away with *his* sleight of hand by selectively citing only instances of flexibility, indeterminacy or "emergence" in natural language use, ignoring all the textual instances where grammar displays rigidity.

Neither Chomsky nor Hopper, it seems, support their radical positions the only honorable way this should be done in an empirical science: by an exhaustive sampling of a large enough continuous chunk of natural communication (say, a narrative or conversational text); by quantifying the *distribution* of instances of grammatical flexibility vs. grammatical rigidity in the sampled population, and then letting the empirical chips fall as they may.

In this chapter I would like to explain why neither Chomsky's nor Hopper's extreme position could possibly represent the facts of grammar in natural language. Rather, the facts of grammar in natural language use tend to uphold a middle-ground position, one akin to that of Sapir and Jespersen.

I will begin by outlining a cognitively and biologically based approach to natural categories, one that should, in my view, serve as the foundation for any empirically-responsible discussion of the notion "rule of grammar".

2. CATEGORIES

The two extreme approaches to grammar, Chomsky's and Hopper's, are but the latest recapitulation of similar extreme postures in philosophy and psychology, both within the context of the theory of categories. I propose to first outline the antecedents of the two extreme approaches in both philosophy and psychology, and then to describe the alternative, middle-ground empirical approach initially developed within cognitive psychology. I will then point out the adaptive, bio-cognitive foundations of the middle-ground alternative.

2.1. Philosophical Antecedents

In philosophy, Chomsky's position can be traced back to Plato's **essentialist** doctrine of meaning, as depicted by Plato's *Cratylus* and other dialogues.[2] Categories of meaning within the Platonic tradition are clean and discrete, with no possible hedges, ambiguities or gradations. This idealization was passed on through an illustrious logic-oriented tradition, via Descartes and the Logical Positivists (see Russell, 1918).

The Platonic approach to categories can be illustrated with a Venn diagram, which allow individuals either membership or non-membership in a category—but never partial membership along a continuum of similarity.

(3)

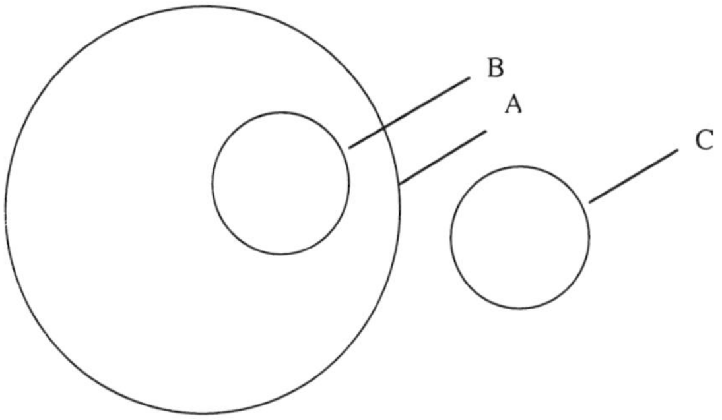

In terms of the distribution of the populations of token-members of two different category-types across a categorial continuum-space, it is implicit in the Platonic approach that all members cluster equally well around the categorial mean, so that no variability, or "degree of membership", is tolerated. That is:

---

[2]See Everson (1994), Bostock (1994), Williams (1994). It may well be the case that Plato did not advocate this Platonic position, but simply describe it as a possible position, one among others. But it certainly has been ascribed to him by later-era self-described Platonists (St. Augustine, Descartes). The idealization involved in Plato's "essences" (*eidon*) is essentially the same intellectual gambit as Chomsky's *competence* or Saussure's *langue*. The argument developed in *Cratylus* and *Parmenides* (as well as in *Phaedo, Phaedrus, Meno, Republic*) is that natural usage is disorderly, graded, ambiguous and context-dependent. For this reason, one cannot base a reliable theory of meaning on such data. One must therefore resort to the cleaner, discrete, idealized *essences* of linguistic concepts. The Platonist thus takes it for granted that a theory of meaning can only be based on discrete categories.

(4)

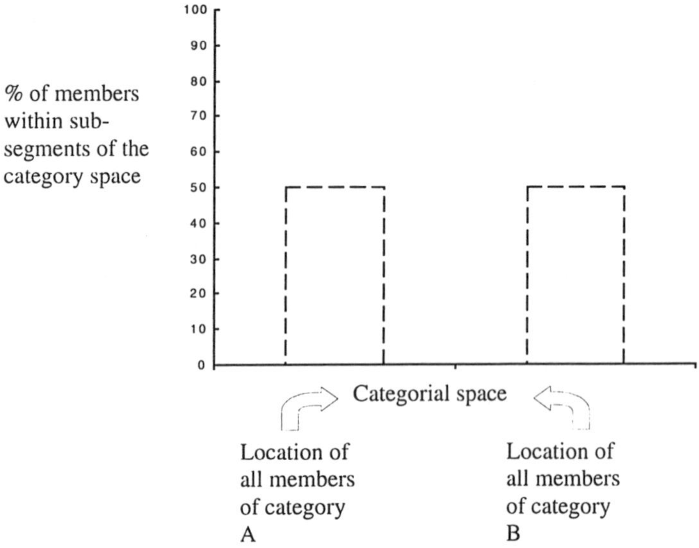

The philosophical antecedent of Hopper's position can be traced back to passages in both Aristotle and Plato,[3] but has been most forcefully expressed in this century by Ludwig Wittgenstein. Wittgenstein (1953) argued first that meaning is profoundly context-dependent and usage-driven:

> ". . . A move in chess doesn't consist simply in moving a piece in such-and-such way on the board—nor yet in one's thoughts and feelings as one makes the move; but in the *circumstances* that we call "playing a game of chess", "solving a chess problem", and so on . . ." (1953, 33; p. 17; emphases added)

> ". . . For a large class of cases—though not for all—in which we employ the word "meaning" it can be defined as thus: the meaning of a word is its *use* in language . . ." (1953, 43; p. 20; emphasis added)

Second, meaning is non-discrete, i.e. involves graded continua.[4] His celebrated metaphor of semantic relatedness as "family resemblance" runs as follows:

---

[3]See Givón (1989, chapter 1) for some discussion of the pragmatic antecedents in Plato and Aristotle.

[4]An essentially similar approach to 'graded' meaning has been espoused by Lakoff (1987), through his notion of "radial categories". In this approach, protracted historical meaning extensions do not ever split a semantic category, but merely include more and more member (senses) in it. This is of course implicit in the Lakoff and Johnson (1980) approach to metaphors, which in essence asserts that "once a metaphoric connection, forever a metaphoric connection".

". . . (we) can see how similarities crop up and disappear. And the result of this examination is this: we see a complicated network of similarities overlapping and criss-crossing, sometimes overall similarities, sometimes similarities of detail. I can think of no better expression to characterize these similarities than *"family resemblances"*; for the various resemblances between members of a family: build, features, colour of eyes, gait, temperament etc. etc. overlap and criss-cross in the same way.—And I shall say: 'games' form a family . . ." (1953, 66,67; p. 32.; emphases added)

Expressed as a Venn diagram, Wittgenstein's "family resemblance" approach to categories of meaning may be given as:

(5)

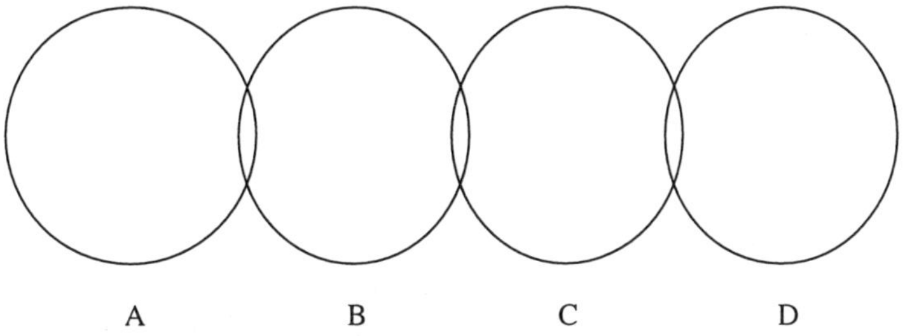

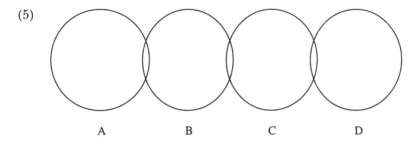

The frequency distribution of token-members of Wittgensteinean category-types along the categorial continuum-space may be given as:

(6)

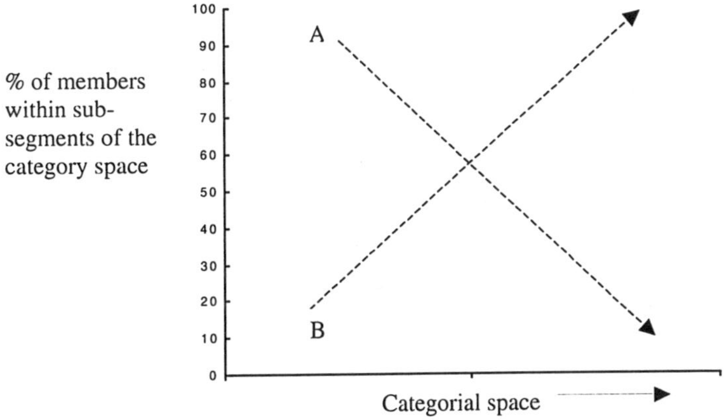

2.2. Antecedents in Psychology

The very same dichotomy between the extreme discreteness and extreme continuum approach to categories also crops up in psychology. A close analog of the discrete, Platonic approach to categories may be seen in the work of Smith *et al.* (1974), where lexical-semantic concepts are characterized in terms of lists of their **discrete, atomic features**. Semantic similarities between words are then expressed in terms of words containing one or more identical features.[5]

A close analogue to the Wittgensteinean account of meaning and meaning relatedness is can be seen in the **semantic networks** cum **spreading activation** model of Collins and Quillian (1972) or Collins and Loftus (1975). Concepts are likened in this model to nodes in a connected network. Adjacent nodes activate each other and such activation can, in principle, spread on and on. This spreading activation is reminiscent of both Wittgenstein's 'family resemblance' and Lakoff's (1987) "radial categories". Semantic similarity within such a system may be expressed in terms of distance, i.e. the number of intervening connections between two nodes. In principle, at least, this approach view meaning as graded and non-discrete.

2.3. Prototypes: The Cognitive Middle Ground

The elaboration of the pragmatic middle ground in both psychology and linguistics is due to the work of Eleanor Rosch (1973, 1975). Rosch's approach is intellectually an extension of the Collins and Quillian (1972) network model, but with some crucial differences. Its salient properties are as follows:

(a) **Multiple criterial features**:
Membership in a natural category, unlike that in a logical category, is not determined by a single either/or criterial feature, but rather by a large basket of features. Some of those features may be "more criterial", in the sense that more members will display them.

(b) **Prototypes and graded membership**:
The most prototypical member of a category is the one displaying the largest number of criterial features. But other members may display fewer features and still be members.

(c) **Strong feature association**:
The criterial features of a natural category tend to be strongly associated, so that in the majority of cases, having one features implies having many of the others.

(d) **Clustering around the categorial mean (prototype)**:
As a logical consequence of strong feature association (c), the vast majority of token-members of a natural category will tend to cluster around the categorial mean, i.e. the prototype. Outliers and am-

[5]This approach is essentially the same as the one advocated by Katz and Fodor (1963), and may have been adapted from there.

biguous members tend to be a relatively small minority within the total population.

Properties (a) and (b) of the prototype-based categories represent the Wittgensteinean (or Collins-Quillian) side of Rosch's approach, allowing for gradation of membership (prototypicality) along a continuum. On the other hand, properties (c) and (d) represent the Platonic of prototype-based categories, their substantial discreteness; i.e. the fact that the vast majority of the members of a category will be easily distinguishable from the vast majority of the members of a contrasting category.

A Venn-diagram representation of Roschean categories may be given as:

(7)

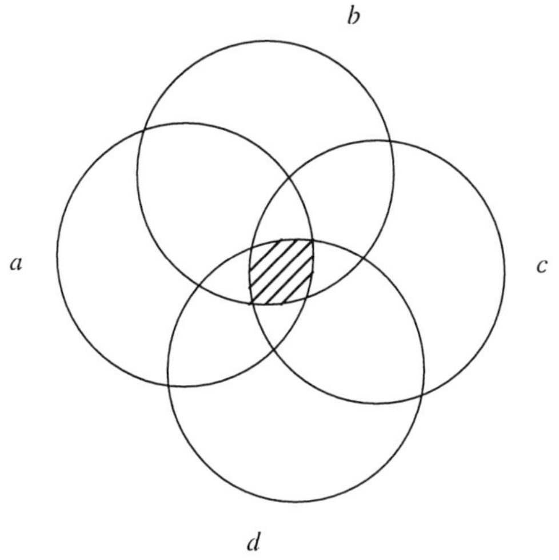

A frequency distribution of token-members of Roschean categories along the categorial space may be given in:

(8)

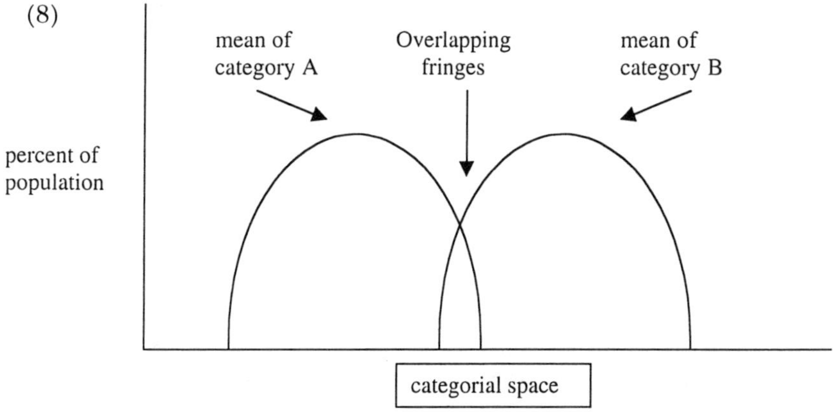

2.4. A Cognitive-Adaptive Perspective

The hybrid nature of prototype-based categories—partly Platonic, partly Wittgensteinean—is not a philosophical choice. Rather, it is due to an adaptive compromise designed to accommodate two conflicting demands on biologically based information processing.

The first demand is that of **rapid processing** of categories that are either very frequent, highly predictable, or carry great adaptive urgency. In biological organisms, the processing of such information tends to become highly automated. And **automated processing**, in turn, is heavily dependent of clear, discrete, hierarchic structures.[6]

The most salient adaptive pressure toward automated processing is the need to draw rapid conclusions about category membership from a relatively quick scan of a few salient, observable features. In a nutshell, **stereotyping**. This is precisely where features (c) and (d) of prototype-based categories become a crucial adaptive advantage.

The more prototypical members of a category tend to be processed automatically. Since they comprise the vast majority of the population, this is where the heavy investment in the development of automaticity yields the highest dividends.

As an illustration, consider the task of deciding, when walking in the bush, whether a tiger-size animal with the characteristic tiger-like stripes, viewed only briefly and scantily, is a dangerous predator or not. While encounters with tigers may be infrequent, there is a powerful, highly predictable association between the innocuous visual feature "stripes" and the lethal behavioral feature "dangerous predator". This informational predictability, coupled with a highly adaptive urgency of avoiding tigers, is what impels us to react rapidly, indeed automatically, to the mere perception of the telltale stripes, and thus extract "tiger" from "stripes" with little regard to the fine gradation of the specific context.

The second, conflicting demand on categorial decisions is that of **fine discrimination**. In contexts of low frequency, low predictability, high uncertainty but, paradoxically, again high adaptive urgency, categorization decisions tend to be slow and conscious. Finer features and subtle contextual gradations must be scanned and analyzed, carefully and thus slowly. The characteristic modus operandi here is that of **attended processing**.

Attended, context-dependent processing is the more Wittgensteinean facet of information processing, where the organism must perform context-sensitive tasks of subtle discriminations along the phenomenological continuum.

Marginal, non-prototypical members of a category, those that tend to occupy the ambiguity-plagued inter-categorial space, are precisely the ones

---

[6]For an extensive review of the relation between categorization and information processing, see Givón (1989, chapters 2 and 7).

that tend to be processed slowly, and in an attended, context-dependent fashion.

But why doesn't the organism just ignore the small ambiguous minority, or "write it off for a loss"? Well, it turns out that however small, the minority may on occasion be just as crucial adaptively as the more prototypical majority. In performing delicate brain surgery, for example, one operates slowly, deliberately and consciously, scanning multiple contextual features, weighing multiple options, remaining attentive to contingencies and alternative strategies.

But another, broader and highly adaptive context also depends on the more flexible, graded aspect of categorization. Change, learning, development and evolution thrive on subtle, gradual re-interpretations of categorial boundaries.

Cognitively, learning is heavily dependent on judgements of similarity, analogy and metaphoric extension. Such judgements are, in principle, impossible to accommodate within a rigid, discrete categorial system. It is only the residual flexibility of prototype-based categories that can accommodate growth and learning, historical change and, ultimately, phylogenetic evolution.

When one compares grammaticalized language processing to pre-grammatical communication (pidgin, early child language, aphasic communication), the parallel between grammar vs. pre-grammar and automated vs. attended processing, respectively, leaps out:[7]

(9) **Pre-grammatical vs. grammatical discourse processing**:
(after Givón 1979, 1989, 1995)

properties	grammatical mode	**pre-grammatical mode**
STRUCTURAL		
a. **Grammatical morphology:**	abundant	absent
b. **Syntactic constructions:**	complex/ embedded	simple/ conjoined
c. **Use of word-order:**	grammatical (subj/obj)	pragmatic (topic/comment)
d. **Pauses:**	fluent	halting
FUNCTIONAL		
e. **processing speed:**	fast	slow
f. **Mental effort:**	effortless	laborious

[7]See also general discussion in Polinsky (1995).

g. **Error rate:**	lower	higher
h. **Context dependence:**	lower	higher
COGNITIVE		
i. **Processing mode:**	automated	attended
j. **acquisition:**	late	early
k. **evolution:**	late	early

One may, finally, note that in an earlier era, Jespersen (1924) identified the conflicting demands on categorization rather succinctly. Indeed, he alludes to the need for a clustering approach, whereby each criterion is neither necessary nor sufficient:

> ". . . the trained grammarian knows whether a given word is an adjective or a verb not by referring to such *definitions*, but in practically the same way in which we all on seeing an animal know whether it is a cow or a cat, and children can learn it much as they learn to distinguish familiar animals, by practice, being shown a sufficient number of specimens and having their attention drawn successively *now to this* and *now to that* distinguishing feature . . ." (1924, p. 62; emphases added)

2.5. Variation: A Bio-Adaptive Perspective

Modern evolutionary biologists treat biological species and their populations in a manner essentially identical to the Roschean approach to natural categories. While species are reasonably distinct and cluster around their categorial means, they still display a considerable amount of genetic and phenotypical (behavioral) variation. The evolutionary biologist Douglas Futuyma (1986) has the following to say concerning trait variability within a species:

> ". . . Most characteristics vary to at least some extent; commonly, the phenotypic standard deviation (the square root of the phenotypic variance) is about 5-10 percent of the mean . . ." (1986, p. 90)

Futuyma notes the intimate connection between variation and evolutionary change, contrasting variationism with Platonic essentialism:

> ". . . Variation is the heart of the scientific study of the living world. As long as *essentialism*, the outlook that ignored variation in its focus on fixed essences, held sway, the possibility of evolutionary change could hardly be conceived, for variation is both the product and the foundation of evolution. Few other

sciences make variation as primary a focus of study as does evolutionary biology . . ." (1986, p. 82; emphases added)

Futuyma also recapitulates what, in Linguistics, has come to be known as **the Labov principle** concerning the intimate connection between (synchronic) variation and (diachronic) change:

". . . At many loci, allele frequencies differ from one population to another, so that the variation that arises within populations becomes transformed into variation among populations . . ." (1986, p. 102)

What makes variation such a crucial adaptive necessity in biological populations is its intimate connection to adaptive evolutionary change. As Bonner (1988) notes, both excessive variability and excessive homogeneity within a species can prove maladaptive. Excessive homogeneity (integration), approximating a Platonic category, decreases the species' potential to respond to novel contexts, thus the species' ability to adapt and change. Excessive variability (isolation), on the other hand, leads to speciation, whereby innovative populations do not plow their adaptive innovations back into the general population's gene-pool.

3. EMPIRICAL SUPPORT

In the following sections I will cite a range of facts about the grammar in human language, pertaining to both grammatical categories and grammar-governed behavior. In each case, the facts support neither an extreme generative (Chomsky) nor extreme emergentist (Hopper) approach. Rather, the facts support a hybrid, middle-ground approach in which both flexibility and rigidity are accommodated.

4. THE UNIVERSALITY OF GRAMMATICAL RELATIONS

4.1. Subjecthood Criteria

The various generative schools have taken structural-relational categories such as "subject" and "direct object" for granted, assuming—on the basis of an impoverished and skimpily analyzed sample of related Indo-European languages—that single necessary and sufficient criteria such as word-order, nominal case-marking or pronominal verb agreement can determine unambiguously what is or isn't the subject or direct object.

The traditional Platonic approach to grammatical relations blatantly disregards the massive empirical evidence, both cross-linguistic and within any single language, that points to the prototype-based nature of grammatical relations.

The development of a prototype-based approach to grammatical relations is due to Keenan (1975, 1976). Keenan lists first a large basket of functional (semantic, pragmatic) properties of grammatical subjects:

(10) **Functional properties of grammatical subjects**:
(Keenan 1976):
a. independent existence
b. indispensability
c. absolute, presupposed or persistent reference
d. definiteness
e. topicality
f. agentivity

With the exception of agentivity (10f), which is obviously misplaced,[8] Keenan's functional properties are all reference-related, and thus reducible to a single property—**topicality**. That is, they are all predictable reflections of the fact that the clause's grammatical subject tends to code the current discourse topic at the time when the clause is being processed.

Turning to formal—grammatical—properties, Keenan (1975, 1976) divides them into two clusters: overt coding properties and behavior-and-control properties. The first are:

(11) **Overt coding properties of grammatical subjects**:
(Keenan, 1975, 1976)
a. word-order
b. verb agreement
c. nominal case morphology

The second cluster, behavior-and-control properties, list the grammatical rules ("processes") that operate on particular grammatical relations:

(12) **Behavior-and-control properties of grammatical roles**:
(Keenan, 1976)
a. promotion to direct object
b. demotion from direct object (antipassive)
c. passivization
d. reflexivization

[8]For further discussion of the discourse-pragmatic control of extraposition, see Bolinger (1992).

e. causativization
f. equi-NP reference in complementation
g. raising
h. possessor promotion
h. anaphoric co-reference in chained clauses
i. co-reference in relativization, WH-question, cleft constructions and participial clauses

The applicability—or relevance—of formal properties in either (10) or (11) to a particular grammatical relation is determined by answering the question:

- Does one need to mention a particular grammatical relation in the definition of a particular grammatical property?

4.2. Cross-Linguistic Variation

In comparing the applicability of formal subject properties across languages, one sees a wide range of variation. Thus consider table (13) below, comparing six subject-related properties in nine nominative languages.

(13) **Distribution of formal subject properties in a sample of nominative languages properties** (Givón, 1995):

	overt coding prop.			behavior-and-control prop.		
	word order	**verb agreement**	**case marking**	**equi**	**reflexive**	**zero anaphora**
English	+	+/−	−	+	+	+
Mandarin	+	−	−	+	+	−
Japanese	+	−	+	+	+	−
Spanish	−	+	−	+	+	+
Bibl. Hebrew	−	+	−	+	+	+
Ute	−	+/−	+	+	+	−
Early Latin	+	+	+	+	+	+
Late Latin	−	+	+	+	+	+
Krio	+	−	−	+	+	+

The languages in our sample clearly display **degrees of grammaticalization** of their subjects, with Early Latin displaying the most properties (6) and Mandarin the least (3).

A similar gradation can be shown for direct objecthood. In table (14) below, seven languages are listed in order, according to the degree to which the category direct-object is completely de-semanticized—i.e. detached from the semantic case of "patient" and is thus a syntactic rather than semantic category.

(14) **Continuum of grammaticalization toward a de-semanticized DO** (Givón, 1995):

language	type of object-role	freedom of promotion to direct-object
	most semantic	
a. Japanese	patient	no promotion
b. Hebrew	definite patient	no promotion
c. Spanish	dative, human patient	no promotion
Provençal	dative, pronoun patient	no promotion
Newari	dative, topical patients	no promotion
d. Ute	patient, dative, benefactive	no promotion
e. Tzotzil	patient, dative, benefactive, possessor of object	oblig. promotion
f. English	direct object	some promotion
g. Nez Perce, KinyaRwanda	direct object	full promotion
	most grammatical	

The cross-linguistic variation of formal properties of grammatical relations is hardly capricious. Rather, the consistent gradation in terms of universality seems to be observed:

(15) **Ranking of all properties of grammatical roles according to universality** (Keenan, 1975, 1976; Givón, 1995):

most universal

a. Functional reference-and-topicality properties
b. Behavior-and-control properties
c. Word-order
d. Grammatical agreement
e. Nominal case-marking

least universal

This gradation may be explained as follows by the correlation between formal and functional properties. Thus, all the processes subsumed under behavior-and-control-properties (12) involve referential coherence, i.e. topicality. Word-order is strongly associated with topicality (Givón, 1988). Grammatical agreement springs originally from pronominalization (Givón, 1976), thus related back to reference and topicality. The two most morphological RG properties—agreement and case-marking—are the most grammaticalized and thus, eventually, the most detachable from functional constraints.

One may thus conclude that:

(16) **Correlation between universality and functional transparency of subject and object properties**:
"The more closely a formal property of subjects and objects is associated with their pragmatic function of topicality, the more universal it is likely to be in its cross-language distribution".

The cross-linguistic variation in the properties of GRs can, of course, be interpreted in a Wittgensteinean way, by disregarding all its profound underlying regularities. Thus, for example, Dryer (1995, 1996) argues that only the topic-related functional properties of GRs are universal, but all formal properties are strictly language specific. The categories "subject" and "object" are thus not universal, he suggests.

Dryer's argument, however Wittgensteinean its conclusions, is surprisingly Platonic. He first selects two morphological coding properties of subjects—the least universal ones, pronominal agreement and case-marking, as the sole criteria for subjecthood. Ignoring all the more universal criteria, in particular behavior-and-control properties, Dryer's argument boils down to, in essence:

(17) • no single property applies equally to GRs in all languages
• therefore, GRs cannot be universal

The Platonic foundations of such an argument have already been noted earlier.

4.3. Intra-Linguistic Variation

*4.3.1. **Preamble.*** The phenomenon I will describe here boils down to the following observation: The subjects of some constructions (clause-types) in the very same language display more subject properties than the subjects of other constructions.

Keenan (1975, 1976) has noted that the subjects of "non-basic" clauses tend to display fewer subject properties than those of "basic"—main, declarative, affirmative, active—clauses. The subject of de-transitive clauses, further, assumes the overt coding properties of the subject of the corresponding active clause in a hierarchically predictable order:

(18) **Implicational hierarchy of assumption of overt coding properties by subjects of passive clauses** (Keenan, 1975):
nominal case-marking > verb agreement > word-order

That is, if "non-basic" subjects assume any "basic" subject property at all, it will be its word-order, followed by control of subject agreement and, last, the characteristic nominal case-marking.

Keenan's observations can only be accommodated by a graded, Prototype approach to the category "subject". They are incompatible with a discrete, Platonic approach to categories. In the following sections I will illustrate the problem with three specific examples

*4.3.2. **Existential-Presentative Clauses.*** Clausal subjects tend to be, overwhelmingly, definite, anaphoric, topical. This is the human-universal prototype. But there exists a construction type, the existential-presentative clause, with a referring-indefinite subject. And this clause-type exhibits many structural peculiarities relative to the structure of clauses with a definite subject. Most saliently, the REF-indefinite subject of the existential clause displays only a sub-set of the subject preoperties observed in DEF-subject clauses. As illustration, contrast the DEF-subject (19a) with the INDEF-subject (19b) clause in Swahili (Bantu):

(19) a. **Definite SUBJ clause**:
watoto **wa**-li-kuwa nyumba-ni
children **they**-PAST-be house-LOC
'The children were in/at the house'
b. **Existential-presentative clause**:
nyumba-ni **ku**-li-kuwa (na) watoto
house-LOC **there**-PAST-be (with) children
'In/at the house there were children'

The DEF-subject of (19a) behaves prototypically; it controls pronominal agreement on the verb and is pre-verbal (SVO). The INDEF-subject of (19b) behaves aberrantly; it relinquishes control of pronominal agreement to the locative 'in the house', and follows the verb (OVS). Similar deviations from the DEF-subject prototype are widespread cross-linguistically (Hetzron 1971, 1975). But in some languages, the INDEF-subject of existential clauses may retain some subject properties. Thus, for example, the subject of existential clauses in English retains control over singular/plural verb agreement in English, but displays the non-prototypical post-verbal (OVS) order:

(20) a. There **is** a fly in my soup
b. There **are** flies in my soup

A Platonic, Generative approach to grammatical categories cannot accommodate such facts, which point to a graded membership in the category "subject". But neither can an extreme Wittgensteinean approach accommodate the behavior of the majority of clause, whose subjects are much more prototypical.

4.3.3. Non-Promotional Passives. In many, probably most, languages, the passive clause is typically agent-suppressing and non-promotional. That is, the agent cannot appear in the passive clause, and the non-agent topic of the clause—patient or other—retains its characteristic active-clause case-marking. As an illustration, consider the *se*-marked impersonal passive in Spanish:

(21) a. **Active**:
la policía le-encontró **a** Juan borracho en la calle
the police him-found **OBJ** John drunk in the street
'The police found John drunk in the street'
b. **se**-le-encontró **a** Juan borracho en la calle
REF-him-found **OBJ** John drunk in the street
'Someone found John drunk in the street'
'They found John drunk in the street'
'John was found drunk in the street'
c. ***se**-le-encontró **a** Juan borracho por la policía
REF-him-found **OBJ** John drunk by the police

The topic of the *se*-passive in Spanish thus retains its active-clause object case-marking and its object agreement, and does not control subject agreement. In terms of formal subject properties, it is thus much less prototypical than the subject of the corresponding active clause.

A more complex situation may be seen in Ute (Uto-Aztecan). The passive clause in Ute is, much like the *se*-passive in Spanish, non-promotional and agent-suppressing. Ute is a flexible-order language that tends to pre-pose topicalized NPs. As in the Spanish *se*-passive, the topicalized non-agent in the Ute passive retains its active-clause case-marking:

(22) a. **Active**:
ta'wach siveetuch-**i** tata-xa
man/SUBJ goat-**OBJ** kicked-PERF
'The man kicked the goat'
b. **Passive**:
siveetuch-**i** tata-**ta**-xa
goat-**OBJ** kick-**PASS**-PERF
'Someone kicked the goat'
'The goat was kicked (by someone)'

Grammatical agreement is more complex in Ute. Obligatory plural agreement is vested in the 'underlying' subject/agent of the active even in passivization. The topic of the passive never assumes control of this type of agreement. Thus compare:

(23) a. **Active**:
taata'wachi-u siveetuch-**i** tata-**qa**-xa
men/SUBJ-PL goat-**OBJ** kick-**PL**-PERF
'The men kicked the goat'
b. **Passive**:
siveetuch-**i** tata-**qa**-ta-xa
goat-**OBJ** kick-**PL**-PASS-PERF
'Someone (pl.) kicked the goat'
'The goat was kicked (by some agents)'

Pronominal agreement, on the other hand, is optional in Ute. In the active, such agreement can be controlled by either the agent or the patient, pending on which one is topicalized. Thus:

(24) a. **Agent topic**:
taata'wachi-u siveetuch-**i** tata-qa-xay-**am**
men/SUBJ-PL goat-**OBJ** kick-PL-PERF-**they**
'The men, they kicked the goat'
b. **Patient topic**:
siveetuch-**i** taata'wachi-u tata-qa-xay-**'u**
goat-**OBJ** men/SUBJ-PL kick-PL-PERF-**him**
'The goat, the men kicked it'

In the passive, however, only the non-agent topic-of-passive can control pronominal agreement:

(25) a. ***Agent topic**:
*taata'wachi-u siveetuch-**i** tata-qa-**ta**-xay-**am**
men/SUBJ-PL goat-**OBJ** kick-PL-**PASS**-PERF-**they**
b. **Patient topic**:
siveetuch-**i** tata-qa-**ta**-xay-**'u**
goat-**OBJ** kick-PL-**PASS**-PERF-**him**
'The goat, it was kicked (by some agents)'

Again, a Platonic-generative approach to grammatical categories cannot accommodate subject properties in Ute, where the non-agent topic of the passive displays some properties of the prototype active-clause subject, but not others. But equally, an extreme Wittgensteinean approach cannot account for the strong clustering of subject properties in the active prototype.

4.3.4. Object-Topic Clauses in Dzamba. Dzamba (Bantu) is a rigid SVO language with obligatory subject agreement. If the object is L-dislocated, SVorder is retained and both subject and object pronominal agreement is required.

In the object-topicalizing inverse clause (Y-movement), pre-posing the object automatically deprives the subject of two of its overt coding properties—clause-initial position (word-order) and pronominal agreement. Thus (Bokamba 1971, 1976):

(26) a. **Active clause**:
o-Poso **a**-kom-aki i-mukanda
DEF-Peter **he**-write-PAST DEF-letter
'Peter wrote a litter'

b. **L-dislocation**:
i-mukanda, o-Poso a-**mu**-kom-aki
DEF-letter DEF-Peter he-**it**-write-PAST
'The letter, Peter wrote it'

c. **Inverse clause (Y-movement)**:
i-mukanda **mu**-kom-aki o-Poso
DEF-letter **it**-write-PAST DEF-Peter
'The letter Peter wrote (rather than tear it)'

The very same changes seen in the object-topicalizing inverse (26c) are observed in object relativization (as well as object clefting and object WH-questions). The subject of such object-topicalizing clauses in Dzamba is post-posed and loses its typical pronominal agreement:

(27) o-Zaki a-tom-aki i-mukanda i-**mu**-kom-aki o-Poso
DEF-Jack he-send-PAST def-letter DEF-**it**-write-PAST DEF-Peter
'Jack sent the letter that Peter wrote'

In these object-topicalizing "non-basic" clauses in Dzamba, the agent cedes the subject-related properties of word-order and verb agreement to the patient—but not quite. The patient does not become a prototypical subject, since it now controls *object* agreement rather than subject agreement.

5. SYNCHRONIC VARIABILITY IN RULE APPLICATION

5.1. Gradation and Non-Discreteness Due to Ongoing Change

As has been noted in numerous studies on grammaticalization and diachronic change,[9] grammatical change—much like semantic and phonological change—is most commonly gradual, invading a domain at a relatively

[9]See Givón (1979), Hopper and Traugott (1993), Traugott and Heine (eds 1991), Heine et al. (1990), inter alia.

narrow "beachhead" and then gradually spreading and generalizing. In grammaticalization, this is just as true of the spread of functional extension as it is of structural adjustment. When a grammatical domain is in the midst of change, non-discrete, graduated, messy, partial rules are only to be expected. These are indeed the kind of examples cited by Hopper (1991). I see no need to further belabor the issue of principle here, although the issue of frequency remains.

5.2. Residual Semantic-Pragmatic Sensitivity of Synchronic Grammar

5.2.1. Exceptions to Phonological Rules. The semantic (or paradigmatic) motivation for exceptions to the application of otherwise quite rigid and general phonological rules has been noted by Vennemann (1971). The scope and generality of phonological changes is routinely circumscribed, and strategic lacunae are left behind, in order to save paradigmatic information.

Similarly, socio-linguistic motivations for exceptions to phonological rules and/or changes have been noted by Labov (1966). What these facts suggest is that when speakers expand the application of presumably rigid, automated, largely-unconscious phonological rules/changes, they remain sensitive to functional considerations, and make well-chosen exceptions to accommodate them.

5.2.2. Causativization and Predicate Raising in Spanish. The application of rules of grammar, whether fully synchronic or still in the midst of grammaticalization, displays the same residual flexibility. Most commonly, a rule of grammar is not governed by a single criterion of application, but rather by a **cluster of criteria**. Some of the criteria are more general. That is, the rule has become more entrenched, more "grammaticalized". To the generative linguist, these rules seem to be the whole story. But other rules are less general, retaining higher sensitivity to the semantic or pragmatic context. In other words, rules of grammar behave very much like prototype-based categories.

Consider, first, the fairly general application of the rule of *predicate raising* in Spanish causativization:

(28) a. **Simple intransitive clause**:
Juan cantaba
John sang/3s
'John sang'

b. **Causativized**:
le-hice cantar a Juan
him-made/1s sing OBJ John
'I made John sing'

c. **Simple transitive (inanimate object)**:
Juan comió la manzana
John ate/3s the apple
'John ate the apple'

d. **Causativized**:
le-hice comer la manzana a Juan
him-made/1s eat the apple OBJ John
'I made John eat the apple'

e. **Simple transitive, human object**:
Juan vio a María
John saw/3s OBJ Mary
'John saw Mary'

f. **?Raised causativization**:
?le-hice ver a Maria a Juan
?le-hice ver a Juan a Maria

g. **Non-raised causativization**:
hice que Juan viera a María
him-made/1s SUB John see/SUBJUN/3s OBJ Mary
'I made John see Mary'

h. **Pronominal causee**:
le-hize ver a María
him-made/1s see OBJ Mary
'I made him/her see Mary'

i. **Topicalized causee**:
a Juan, le-hice ver a María
OBJ John him-made see OBJ Mary
'As for John, I made him see Mary'
'*As for John, I made Mary see him'

The potential ambiguity of semantic-role assignment—underlying patient vs. underlying causee—suspends the application of predicate-raising in (28f) and forces us into either the un-raised alternative (28g) or, if the context permits, the anaphoric causee version in (28h). Likewise, topicalization of the causee renders predicate-raising acceptable, but the underrelying patient cannot be topicalized, thus again avoiding ambiguity in (28i).

Presumably, before the dative preposition had spread to human direct objects in Spanish, predicate raising in the causativization of (28e) would have been as unproblematic as in the case of the inanimate object in (28c,d).[10]

---

[10]See Givón (1979, 1989, 1995), Liberman (1984), Bloomstein and Milberg (1983), Schnitzer (1989), inter alia.

5.2.3. Extraposed Relative Clauses in English. Consider next the variation in the grammar of extraposed REL-clauses in English:

(29) a. A woman **who** had no shoes on came over and . . .
b. ?A woman had no shoes on came over and . . .
c. A guy **whom** I used to know came over and . . .
d. A guy I used to know came over and . . .

The insubordinate *subject* REL-clause (29b) is acceptable in non-standard spoken American English, where it is rescued by an appropriate intonation pattern, one that distinguishes between REL-clauses and main clauses. In contrast, the insubordinate *object* REL-clause in (29d) is acceptable in both non-standard and standard English.

In extraposition, the rules are modified to accommodate potential ambiguities. Consider first extraposed subject REL-clauses:

(30) a. ?A woman came to see John who had no shoes on
b. A woman came over who had no shoes on
c. *A woman came over had no shoes on

We have now pitted, in head-on competition, two cognitively transparent—indeed iconic—processing principles in grammar:

- place a modifier (operator) adjacent to the modified (operand)
- place a subject adjacent to its relevant predicate

Example (30a) is problematic because of potential ambiguity. In (30b) ambiguity is removed and the very same extraposition is unproblematic. Put another way, the decision whether to apply or reject extraposition is sensitive to semantic considerations. Example (30c) is acceptable in neither standard nor non-standard English. Piling up the non-standard removal of 'who' on top of the non-adjacency of head and modifier apparently yields excessive processing complexity.

Consider, finally, the extraposition of object REL-clauses:

(31) a. A woman I used to like in college came into the room
b. A woman came into the room I used to like in college
c. A woman came into the room who I used to like in college
d. *A woman came over I used to like in college
e. A woman came over who I used to like in college

Example (31b) can only be interpreted as 'the room' being the object of 'like', not 'the woman'. The insertion of the human-specific subordinator 'who' in (31c) tips the scale toward 'the woman' as object. No potential ambiguity exists in (31d), but still neither standard nor non-standard English would accept this insubordinate extraposed clause.[11] But the mere insertion of 'who' again rescues the extraposition.

Again, multiple considerations, some quite subtle, some semantic or pragmatic, seem to govern the application of grammatical rules. Such interaction supports neither rigid Platonic generativity nor Wittgensteinean free-for-all. Once again, grammar seems to display a complex mix of both.

6. TEXT-DISTRIBUTION OF "GENERATIVE" VS. "EMERGENT" GRAMMAR

If grammar is substantially—though never 100%—rigid, as I have tried to suggest all along, then natural communication, or at least unedited informal face-to-face communication, ought to reflect this distributionally. That is, I should be able, at least in principle, to back up my claims with the **percent distribution** of "emergent" (variable) vs. "generative" (rigid) usage in a contiguous sample of natural communication.

In this section I attempt to make one such assessment, using an English conversational text. The conversation was elicited under the following conditions (Dickinson and Givón, 1997): The two participants watched the same 6-minute video movie. They were then told that they saw similar but non-identical movies. They were urged to converse with the aim of clarifying the similarities and differences between the respective movies. Their conversation was tape-recorded, and the entire transcript is given in the appendix.

In detecting "emergent" features in this text, I have considered as baseline "non-emergent" usage the grammar of informal conversational English. As is well known, such usage is replete with features that are unique to informal face-to-face communication:

- pauses
- repetitions
- truncations
- run-on clauses
- hedges
- overlaps
- zero-anaphoric reference
- dislocations

It is also replete with oral discourse operators such as 'kinda', 'like' and 'you know'. All these feature should not, by themselves, be considered

[11]Many verbs are stative and thus cannot an agent as subject. The fact that they may be a minority of all verbs is not due to agent being a subject property, but rather to the fact that the majority of stereotyped events categorized by humans relate to volitional human actions.

"emergent grammar", since they are stable, predictable features of oral communication. Grammatical change—and to a lesser extent its Siamese twin, variation—is almost exclusively the province of spoken language.

Further, in trying to identify true features of "emergent grammar", I have elected to err on the side of caution by over-representing instances of "emergence", thus going against my own hypothesis.

In the four pages of transcript of the conversation, only *four* (4) instances were found of what can, by any stretch of the imagination, be identified as, at least potentially, "emergent grammar" of conversational English. They are underscored in the full transcript (see appendix), and are given in (32) below together with their equivalent standard English translation. In the standard version, I underscore the crucial difference.

(32)

"emergent version"	translated into standard
a. That the same?	*Is* that the same?
b. All th't I really remember 'bout the dress there was a dress . . .	All that I really remember about the dress *is that* there was a dress . . .
c. . . . kind of little mountain of brush she was hauling to around . . .	. . . kinda little mountain of brush she was hauling *it around to* . . .
d. maybe a half an inch	maybe *half an* inch maybe *a half*-inch

There were a total of 187 lines of text in the transcript. The majority of the lines include at least 3 clauses each. So, erring on the side of caution again, I have selected to express the perecent distribution of "emergent grammar" in conversation as a ratio of instances per lines as follows:

$$\mathbf{4/187 = 2.01\%.}$$

7. DISCUSSION

There are excellent reasons for grammar to be *largely* rigid: It is a partially automated, partially conventionalized system of rapid speech processing. Pre-grammatical communication—Pidgin—is slow, halting, error-prone and extremely dependent on the immediate communicative context. The process of grammaticalization—be it in first and second language acquisition, in history or in evolution—has an unimpeachable cognitive-cultural adaptive motivation, that of streamlined communication.

But there are also excellent reasons why grammar remains *residually* flexible. Change, adaptive innovation and learning cannot proceed without this residual flexibility. And in contexts of high informational uncertainty, ambiguity or adaptive urgency, communication can be de-coupled from automated grammar, so that richer and more specific features of context can be scanned, evaluated and acted upon.

The argument between extreme generativists and extreme emergentist folks is not a rational argument, but rather a tug of war between two—opposing but in some way rather similar—reductionist perspectives. The generativists, following the Platonic tradition, are so impressed with the substantial rigidity of grammar, that they would like to ignore its adaptively-crucial residual slop. They do so—following Plato, Saussure and Chomsky—by ruling the relevant data out of bounds ("performance").

The emergentists are so impressed with the persistent residue of flexibility in natural communication, or as communication is reflected in historical change, that—following Wittgenstein—they insist on ignoring the huge component of grammatical rigidity in natural communication.

Each of the two warring extremes, generativist and emergentist, cluster rather naturally as two well-known perspectives on cognition and cognitive science:

generative extreme	**emergentist extreme**
• modular	• distributive
• domain-specific	• domain-general
• innate/evolved	• emergent
• invariant	• variable
• generative/rigid	• emergent/flexible
• discrete	• scalar/graduated
• input-independent	• input-driven
• context-free	• context-sensitive

They are both reductionist perspectives on a complex domain that fairly cries for a non-reductionist approach, an approach that would recognize both extremes as facets of a complex, interactive whole. The mind-brain is *both* modular and interconnected. It depends on *both* domain-specific (sensory, motor) and domain-general (executive attention, episodic memory) capacities. Parts of it are mature at birth (thus 'innate'), others mature during—and in interaction with—lifetime experience (emeregent). It has highly automated (invariant, rigid, discrete, input-independent, context-free) modules. But they interact with more flexible (context-sensitive, input-dependent, scalar) mechanisms. To insist on one to the exclusion of the other is to short-change the enormous complexity of this quintessentially **hybrid** system, the mind-brain.

Reductionism is the intellectual scourge of immature science. I wonder how long we must persist in oscillating between reductive philosophical extremes. How long must we allow Chomsky's (1959) fatal insistence—either Skinner or Descartes, no room in the middle—to continue to haunt us with its crude intellectual Stalinism?

Perhaps it is time we heeded S.J. Gould's (1977) observation, in the context of another futile war between reductive extremes in a complex science:

> " . . . the solution to great arguments is usually close to the golden mean . . . (1977, p. 18)
>
> " . . . I doubt that such a controversy could have arisen unless both positions were valid (though incomplete) . . . " (1977, p. 59)

REFERENCES

Bloomstein, S. and W. Milberg (1983) "Automatic and controlled processing in speech/language deficit in aphasia", **Symposium on Automatic Speech**, Minneapolis: Academy of Aphasia

Bokamba, G.E. (1971) "Specificity and definiteness in Dzamba", **Studies in African Linguistics**, 2.3

Bokamba, G.E. (1976) **Question Formation in Some Bantu Languages**, PhD dissertation, Bloomington: Indiana University (ms)

Bolinger, D. (1992) "The role of accent in extraposition and focus", **Studies in Language**, 16.2

Bonner, J.T. (1988) **The Evolution of Complexity**, Princeton, NJ: Princeton University Press

Bostock, D. (1994) "Plato on understanding language", in S. Everson (ed. 1994)

Chomsky, N. (1959) "Review of B.F. Skinner's **Verbal Behavior**", **Language**, 35

Chomsky, N. (1961) "On the notion 'rule of grammar' ", in **The Structure of Language and its Mathematical Aspects**, Providence, RI: American Mathematical Society

Chomsky, N. (1965) **Aspects of the Theory of Syntax**, Cambridge, Mass.: MIT Press

Collins, A.M. and E.F. Loftus (1975) "A spreading activation theory of semantic processing", **Psychological Review**, 82

Collins, A.M. and M.R. Quillian (1972) "How to make a language user", in E. Tulving and W. Donaldson (eds) **Organization of Memory**, NY: Academic Press

Dickinson, C. and T. Givón (1997) "Memory and conversation", in T. Givón (ed.) **Conversation: Cognitive, Communicative and Social Perspectives**, TSL #34, Amsterdam: J. Benjamins

Dryer, M. (1995) "Grammatical relations in Ktunaxa (Kutenai)", **The Belcourt Lecture**, Winnipeg: University of Manitoba

Dryer, M, (1996) "Are grammatical relations universal?", SUNY at Buffalo (ms)

Everson, S. (1994) "Introduction", in S. Everson (ed., 1994)

Everson, S. (ed. 1994) **Companion to Ancient Thought, 3: Language**, Cambridge: Cambridge University Press

Futuyma, D. J. (1986) **Evolutionary Biology**, Sunderland, MA: Sinauer (2nd edition)

Givón, T. (1979) **On Understanding Grammar**, NY: Academic Press

Givón, T. (1981) "Logic vs. pragmatics, with human language as the referee", **J. of Pragmatics**,

Givón, T. (1988) "The pragmatics of word-order: Predictability, importance and attention", in E. Moravcsik (ed.) **Typology and Language Universals**, TSL #16, Amsterdam: J. Benjamins

Givón, T. (1989) **Mind, Code and Context: Essays in Pragmatics**, Hillsdale, NJ: Erlbaum

Givón, T. (1995) **Functionlism and Grammar**, Amsterdam: J. Benjamins

Gould, S.J. (1977) **Ontogeny and Phylogeny**, Cambridge: Harvard University Press

Heine, B. U. Claudi and F. Hünnemeyer (1991) **Grammaticalization: A Conceptual Framework**, Chicago: University of Chicago Press

Hopper, p. (1987) "Emergent grammar", **BLS #13**, Berkeley: Berkeley Linguistics Society

Hopper, P. (1991) "On some principles of grammaticalization", in E.C. Traugott and B. Heine (eds) **Approaches to Grammaticalization, TSL # 19**, vol. I, Amsterdam: J. Benjamins

Hopper, P. and E.C. Traugott (1993) **Grammaticalization**, Cambridge: Cambridge University Press

Jespersen, O. (1924/1965) **The Philosophy of Grammar**, NY: Norton

Katz, J.J. and J.A. Fodor (1993) "The structure of a semantic theory", **Language**, 39.1

Keenan, E. (1975) "Some universals of passive in relational grammar", **CLS #11**, University of Chicago: Chicago Linguistics Society

Keenan, E. (1976) "Toward a universal definition of 'subject' ", in C. Li (ed.) **Subject and Topic**, NY: Academic Press

Labov, W. (1966) **The Social Stratification od English in New York City**, Washington, DC: Center for Applied Linguistics

Lakoff, G. (1987) **Women, Fire and Dangerous Things**, Chicago: University of Chicago Press

Lakoff, G. and M. Johnson (1980) **Metaphors We Live By**, Chicago: University of Chicago Press

Liberman, P. (1984) **The Biology and Evolution of Language**, Cambridge: Harvard University Press

Plato, **The Dialogues**,

Polinsky, M. (1995) "Double object causatives: Toward a study of coding conflict", **Studies in Language**, 19.1

Rosch, E. (1973) "On the internal structure of perceptual and semantic categories", in T.E. Moore **Cognitive Development and the Acquisition of Language**, NY: Academic Press

Rosch, E. (1975) "Cognitive representation of semantic categories", **J. of Experimental Psychology: General**, 104

Russell, B. (1981) "The philosophy of logical atomism", in R.C. Marsh (ed.) **Bertrand Russell: Logic and Knowledge** (selected essays 1901-1950), London: Routledge

Sapir, E. (1921/1929) **Language**, NY: Harcourt, Brace & Co., Harvest Books

Schnitzer, M. (1989) **The Pragmatic Basis of Aphasia**, Hillsdale, NJ: Erlbaum

Smith, E.E., L.J. Rips and E.J. Shoben (1974) "Semantic memory and psychological semantics", in G. Bowers (ed.) **The Psychology of Learning and Motivation**, vl. 8, Hillsdale, NJ: Erlbaum

Traugott, E.C. and B. Heine (eds 1991) **Approaches to Grammaticalization**, **TSL # 19**, vol. I, Amsterdam: J. Benjamins

Vennemann, T. (1973) "The phonology of Gothic vowels", **Language**, 77.1

Williams, B. (1994) "Cratylus theory of names and its refutation", in S. Everson (ed. 1994)

Wittgenstein, L. (1953) **Philosophical Investigations**, NY: MacMillan

1. APPENDIX: CONVERSATION BETWEEN LORI AND VICKY

VICKY: [. . .] first what was the guy wearing?

LORI: He was wearing, uh, red shorts and a white T-shirt. No shoes . .

V: No shoes?

L: No shoes.

V: My guy was wearing [foot . . .] or something . . .

L: OK . . . Now, first [. . .] the guy came in carrying three long tools and a . . uh, hatchet . . . and, uh, he walked over to a tree, set them down, they fell down once and he brought . . . and then . . . he picked them up . .

V: OK, mine . . . I'd, you know I didn't really count . . . I think mine had two . . .

L: Yeah.

V: And, they dropped and he picked them back up.

L: OK. And then what did he do?

V: And he had, uh . . . a hatchet.

L: Yeah

V: And he went over to the wood pile, ove' to where the wood was . . . and he started chopping, it was rather ineffective, but he was chopping, and . . .

L: Pieces of wood? [OVERLAP]

V: Yeah they were about . . . boy, maybe, two inches in diameter . . .

L: Yeah . . . [OVERLAP]

V: three . . . pieces about . . . foot-and-a-half long . . .

L: OK

V: And . . . uh he would . . . chop them and throw them over the side . . . uh there're maybe seven or eight . . . of them . . .

L: There may have been more, I think [. . .] more [. . .]

[TG: **You got to speak louder.**]

V: [. . .] my guess is there were four or five . . . Umm . . . and then the woman came in, she's wearing uh a pink skirt and, a white . . . blouse, a light shirt with color . . . she was rearing . . . red shoes . . . <u>That the same?</u>

L: Umm, <u>all th't I really remember 'bout the dress there was a dress</u> . . . I think it was a skirt and a blouse . . .

V: OK.

L: And the blouse was white, or was a light color . . . it was half color . . .

V: OK . . . uh . . . what did she do?

L: Well, they talked, they conversed . . . and . . . ummm . . . it sounded to me like she was telling him . . . you know "Right [. . .] enough with the wood . . ." you know, "go . . . go hoe . . ." you know, the . . . the field or whatever . . .

V: "I'll take care of the fire . . . "

L: Yes . . . and so she collects the wood, and she goes over to like, one of those little umm . . . lean-to, or shed . . . and . . . she, collects some . . . uh . . . some kindling, or some little twigs . . . OK, what's up?

V: My lady she went over and kinda yelled at him for . . . sounded like she yelled at him for doing whatever . . . and then she took, his, pile of wood and went over to a big . . . uh . . . <u>kind of a little mountain of brush</u> . . . <u>she was hauling to around</u> . . . and she . . . took out about a dozen a . . . took them and broke them . . . and collected them all in a . . . bundle . . .

L: You're right, I'm wrong . . .

V: [laughter; long pause]

L: it was a mountain of brush . . .

V: OK . . .

L: and then she went to [. . . .] a whole pile . . .

V: yes [. . . . long pause]

L: she walked down the [. . .] and came over to some area, of, uh, under the shade . . . of the tree . . . and there was . . . uh, prob'ly two sitting benches . . . and . . . uh . . . uh . . . she . . . started to make . . .

V: No, she put the brush down and she walked back over near the lean-to and picked up . . . [a] box of matches I think . . . and then went back over and started a fire in a little box . . . fire thing . . . What was then? . . . . . .

L: . . . Well . . . she . . . went to over by the shed, she sat down . . . uh . . . if I remember correctly she was sitting in the sun . . . and . . . she . . . was . . . she got the matches . . . yes she went up and she went to the lean-to . . . looks to me if I remember correctly she went around to the back side of the lean-to and got some matches . . . I don't think she went into it . . .

V: Hmmm, OK.

L: And, uh . . . I can be wrong . . . but, and then she anyway, she got the matches and the pot . . .

V: She never sat down . . . in mine . . .

L: Mine too . . . she just never sat down . . .

V: OK . . .

L: Did she, put the wood over there by the fire before she?

V: No. And she didn't in mine she didn't do it she didn't go into the lean-to or around it to get there . . . not that I think it was, kind-of on the edge between the two of them [. . .] . . . OK . . .

L: She went around my lean-to . . . the very beginning

V: OK. Ummm and after that she made a fire . . . umm she picked up . . a little . . . bad-old tin pail, and she went over next to the lean-to the white bucket of water, and she poured the water into the pail and then took the pail back and put it on the fire . . . OK? . . . What's she doing next? . . .

L: She put the wood into the little fire-thing . . .

V: Uh-huh . . .

L: OK of course she . . . she walked over to where the fire-pit was . . .

V: Huh-huh . . .

L: She put the wood into the fire-pit . . . and then she uh . . . she started the uh . . . fire . . . and uh she put . . . [. . .] I thought she put a little bit of kindling in to get it going? . . .

V: Huh-huh . . .

L: And then once it was going good she went over and she got the pot of water . . .

V: huh . . .

L: and took the pot . . . took the pot out and put it back on the fire . . . and then . . . she went . . . around . . . behind the shed . . .

V: yes [OVERLAP]

L: just she went behind the shed . . . she got the chicken . . .

V: yeah . . .

L: She had this big-old butcher knife . . .

V: Yes!

L: And she was trr[laugh]yying . . .

V: [laughing] . . . [OVERLAP]

L; She was try . . . [laughter] . . .

V: [laughter] [OVERLAP]

L: Try . . . Trying to, y'know, slit the chicken's throat . . .

V: Yes, she was, the chicken was just a wild little guy . . .

L: Yeah I don't think she really had the heart to do it, yeah . . .

V: I think [OVERLAP] she woulda done it! She was trying.

L: Well uh, to me . . . uh, uh . . . a woman like that she probably kills these chickens all the time . . .

V: Yes . . .

L: I don't think . . I just don't think she tried hard enough . . . but, anyway . . .

V: No, she didn't try very hard because the chicken she . . .

L: Yeah . . . [OVERLAP]

V: . . . she kinda rearranged it a coupla times and he was squawking, and then the chicken got away, and she chased after him for about . . . ten feet . . . and then . . . gave up . . .

L: Right, and let him run [away] . . .

V: threw up her arms and said "yeah", and let him go . . .

L: Did they get dinner? . . .

V: Huh . . . [laughing] . . . umm . . . uh . . . OK, then after that she went back . . . she went and opened . . . to the side of the lean-to and opened the door and went inside an' got a bundle of . . . something [. . .] . . . something wrapped in a white, and then she went back over to the shade . . . put it down, on one of the benches . . . and unwrapped it . . . and there was a plastic bag, of something . . . chip . . . chip-like . . . a clear plastic bag, and, she, cut . . . she took the knife and she cut a couple of things with the knife . . and kind of . . . looked like she was kinda making a sandwich? . . . and then . . . she folded things back in a bundle, and . . . walked off . . . [. . . .]

L: OK, in mine . . . the chicken got away, she threw up her hands, she went back around, she went int . . . she opened up . . . the, shed and she, got the stuff up . . . maybe it was cheese or something like that . . .

V: that right . . .

L: and, it was, in a plastic bag, a bag of some sort . . . uh . . . and she unwrapped the bag, and then she, she, she cut the . . .

V: It was a bag, not a cloth . . . [?]

L: It was a cloth, but, had like, paper in th' bag, I'd say it was . . . it was cloth . . . she'd a cloth I think she had like inside a wrapping inside it that she . . .

V: OK . . .

L: and um . . . she made two cuts . . .

V: close to three . . . [. . . .]

L: she . . . she made a coupla slices and it looked like cheese, it was like, y'know . . .

V: yes . . .

L: maybe a half an inch . . .

V: yeah . . .

L: and then, like you said, she put it . . . she, she put it together like a little bit of a sandwich like, she . . . and then she put everything back, everything back up . . . and . . . then let's see then . . .

V: OK . . .

L: and in the next scene, she uh . . . went and . . . she went to where her husband was hoeing . . . out in the field, now it's also very ineffective [. . .] . . .

V: What was he doing? [OVERLAP]

L: I don't know . . .

V: He wasn't hoeing!

L: [. . .] . . . [OVERLAP]

V: He wasn't doing much of anything!

L: But anyway, that's what he was doing . . . and she's . . . basically she's bringing lunch, but I assume she's doing . . . or a snack or something . . .

V: Yeah . . .

L: . . . so he goes over to the tree to sit down . . . and she follows him . . . and . . . when he looks at what . . . he, she brought him . . . he gets up

V: He [. . .] [OVERLAP]

L: and he takes his hoe 'n he starts chasing her around . . .

V: Yes . . . And he chased around in a circle . . . twice . . . and she was yelling, and then he yelled after a while, and going on back and forth

L: Yeah . . .

V: And it stopped. . . .

L: Then it stopped . . .

V: Before he murdered his wife. Which was good. [laughter]

Chapter 4

The Emergence of Grammaticality in Connectionist Networks

Joseph Allen
Mark S. Seidenberg
University of Southern California

Linguistic theory in the generative tradition is based on a small number of simple but important observations about human languages and how they are acquired. First, the structure of language is extremely complex—so complex that it is often argued that it would be impossible to learn without prior knowledge as to its general character (Chomsky, 1965). Second, children learn languages rapidly and seemingly effortlessly. Although clearly limited with respect to other sorts of cognitive tasks, every normal child raised under normal circumstances learns the basic syntax of language within a few years of birth. Third, the world's languages exhibit structural commonalities—so-called linguistic universals. Together, these observations have led many researchers to the conclusion that language involves domain-specific forms of knowledge that are largely innate. In the generative approach, the faculty of mind dedicated to language is called *linguistic competence.* A generative grammar is a formal description of this faculty, in the form of a system that generates the set of possible sentences of a given language, and thereby bestows on its possessor the ability to distinguish between grammatical and ungrammatical utterances. Grammars developed within this tradition (which we will call the *standard approach*) typically consist of primitives, operations, and principles intended to describe the knowledge of an idealized speaker–hearer in a homogeneous speech community. In this approach, cognitive representations are hierarchically structured sets of symbols, and cognitive processes are operations on them.

Although the standard approach has been very successful in promoting the discovery of descriptive generalizations about linguistic structure and variation, it presents several problems when considered as the basis for a theory of how language is acquired and used. These problems arise from the competence–performance distinction that is one of the foundational assumptions of the approach. The distinction between what people know about language and what they do with that knowledge is easy to recognize. However, the relation between competence grammars and performance is more complex.

One issue concerns the systematic ambiguity in the field regarding the extent to which competence grammar should figure in accounts of performance. Chomsky has often suggested that competence grammars describe procedures for relating different levels of representation, but are not characterizations of the computations involved in using language. In Chomsky (1995), he reiterated this view: "The ordering of operations [in grammatical theory] is abstract, expressing postulated properties of the language faculty of the brain, with no temporal interpretation implied" (p. 380). However, many researchers have pursued a more literal-minded interpretation of grammar as the basis for accounts of how language is acquired, used, or impaired as a consequence of brain injury. In acquisition, a well-known example is the work of Borer and Wexler (1992), in which acquisition phenomena are characterized in terms of the maturation of principles ascribed to Universal Grammar, such as the bi-uniqueness relations and A-bar chains. Within this approach, acquisition is characterized as movement along a trajectory from not knowing to knowing rules of grammar (Gold, 1967). In the area of language processing, Frazier and Fodor (1978) developed a theory of parsing based on heuristics applying to grammatical representations developed within generative theory. In neurolinguistics, Grodzinsky (1995) argued for an account of agrammatic aphasia in which patients fail to represent traces, a particular aspect of grammatical theory. Uncertainty about the relation between competence grammar and performance has existed throughout the history of generative linguistics (see Berwick & Weinberg, 1984; Bresnan, 1978; Fodor, Bever, & Garrett, 1974).

A second problem created by the competence–performance distinction is that it motivates disregarding data that actually may be crucial to understanding basic characteristics of language. The competence approach excludes performance mishaps such as false starts, hesitations, and errors, but also more central aspects of linguistic performance. It is assumed, for example, that language should be characterized independently of the perceptual and motor systems employed in language use, memory capacities that limit the complexity of utterances that can be produced or understood, and reasoning capacities used in comprehending text or discourse. The competence theory also systematically excludes information about statistical and probabilistic aspects of language; the fact that *that* is used more often than *than,* for example, or that the word *the* is followed more often by a noun than a verb are not seen as relevant to this deeper characterization of linguistic knowledge. However, recent studies have emphasized the important roles these aspects of language and cognition play in acquisition and processing (Kelly, 1992; MacDonald, Pearlmutter, & Seidenberg, 1994; Saffran, Aslin, & Newport, 1996; Trueswell, Tanenhaus, & Kello, 1993).

In the standard view, the child is learning a system of rules (or constraints) that governs the relations among abstract linguistic entities. The child attends to the structure of utterances guided by innate capacities in order to set language-specific parameters. Poverty of the stimulus arguments are used to suggest that knowledge of language is underdetermined by evidence available to language learners and therefore must be attributable to innate Universal Grammar (Chomsky, 1981). Statistical and probabilistic properties of the input are presumed to play no role in this process, and their influence is excluded from generative accounts of acquisition, implying that children also ignore these aspects of input. Excluding the use of these factors from theories of acquisition is seen as positive, in that it avoids a possible combinatorial explosion of intercorrelations among linguistic properties that would make acquisition difficult. The fallacy in this argument is that the statistical and probabilistic aspects of language might actually facilitate acquisition. Allowing that children attend to all aspects of linguistic input—even speech errors—is not a problem because the low frequency of particular errors means that they will not seriously influence the statistical model of language developed in the course of learning.

The apparent complexity of language and its uniqueness vis-à-vis other aspects of cognition, which are taken as major discoveries of the standard approach, may derive in part from the fact that these "performance" factors are not available to enter into explanations of linguistic structure. If, in fact, the properties of the language faculty are to some extent determined by a combination of general neural information processing procedures applied to the unique types of tasks that language processing represents, then an approach to the characterization of the language faculty that excludes reference to these factors runs the risk of mischaracterizing the nature of linguistic cognition in a fundamental way.

A third issue concerns the role of performance data in deriving the competence theory itself. The mapping between competence grammar and performance is at best complex, as we have noted; it is also largely unknown. A problem arises because the primary data on which the standard approach relies—grammaticality judgments—are themselves performance data (Bever, 1972). The methodology of the standard approach holds that properties of the hypothesized language faculty can be identified on the basis of experts' intuitive judgments of the well-formedness of utterances. However, the relation between grammaticality judgment and the structure of the grammar is no more transparent than between other aspects of competence and performance.

In the standard view, a grammatical sentence is one that is generated by the competence grammar. This definition entails that every sentence is either grammatical (generated by the grammar) or not. The metaphor here is that of a Turing machine that recognizes some strings but not others as members of a language. A grammaticality judgment, in contrast, is a particular way of querying one's grammatical knowledge. Among nonexperts (i.e., nonlinguists), performance on this task is affected by the memory limitations, distractions, shifts of attention and interest, errors, false starts, and hesitations characteristic of other aspects of performance. For these informants, linguistic competence is only one factor in the judgment process.

For linguists, using grammaticality judgments to infer properties of the underlying computational system can only be justified if they are able to abstract away from these "grammatically irrelevant" distractions. The notion that linguists are partly in the business of looking beyond actual behavior (determined by a mix of performance and competence) to discover true underlying competence was suggested by Grimshaw and Rosen (1990), who argued against equating subjects' performance on a judgment task with grammatical knowledge: "To determine properties of the underlying system requires inferential reasoning, sometimes of a highly abstract sort" (p. 188). Linguists assume that they are capable of reasoning from intuitions about grammaticality to underlying competence. This type of reasoning obviously requires awareness of the types of factors that influence grammaticality judgments. The problem with this logic is that no general theory of how grammaticality judgments are made has ever been proposed. Considering the enormous number of performance factors that have been identified as able to influence the judgment process, and how poorly they are understood, it is not surprising that a careful review of the evidence led Schutze (1996) to conclude that "it is hard to dispute the general conclusion that metalinguistic behavior is not a direct reflection of linguistic competence" (p. 193).[1]

[1]The fact that sentences afford different degrees of ungrammaticality has long been recognized in the linguistics literature (e.g., Chomsky, 1961, 1965), but the issue of how to deal with this fact within grammatical theory has never been resolved. One way of reconciling the paradox entailed by a competence grammar that either generates a sentence or not with graded judgment data is to have the grammar assign degrees of badness to strings that violate grammatical principles. Another is to say that the judgment process itself results in graded judgments because it includes nonsyntactic information. A third possibility is that constructions are underlyingly grammatical to different degrees (Lakoff, 1973). The existence of all of these possibilities makes distinguishing the effects of grammatical knowledge versus processing on judgment data difficult (Clark & Haviland, 1974), and the assumption that it is possible to determine the properties of an underlying grammar from judgment data even more problematic.

Given the three issues noted thus far—the uncertainties about whether competence grammar should figure in accounts of performance, the exclusion of data concerning statistical and probabilistic aspects of language, and the difficulty involved in "reverse-engineering" grammar from performance data—it is quite possible that the formalisms of the standard approach really are only metaphorically related to the brain processes involved in producing and comprehending language. This alternative is sometimes recognized in the literature, but rarely taken seriously. For example, Schutze (1996) has noted,

> It is conceivable that competence in this sense of a statically represented knowledge does not exist. It could be that a given string is generated or its status computed when necessary, and that the demands of the particular situation determine how the computation is carried out, e.g., by some sort of comparison to prototypical sentence structure stored in memory. Since such a scenario would demand a major rethinking of the goals of the field of linguistics, I will not deal with it further. (p. 20)

The remainder of this chapter represents a step toward just such a rethinking of the linguistic endeavor.

AN ALTERNATIVE FRAMEWORK

In recent years, a framework has begun to develop that differs significantly from the standard approach with respect to what it means to know a language. The goal of this work is not to devise primitives and principles that describe the set of sentences an idealized speaker–hearer would accept but rather to make explicit the experiential and constitutional factors that account for the development of knowledge structures underlying linguistic performance. Whereas the standard approach is committed to the uniqueness of linguistic representations vis-à-vis other cognitive domains, and to the existence of representations whose fundamental character is shaped by the repertoire of innate ideas, the alternative view sees cognitive representations as one component of a system that includes both the organism and its environment. Cognitive processes are taken to be the manipulation of representations such that the organism is able to interact successfully with its environment (Van Gelder, in press). Linguistic representations emerge as a function of the interplay among several factors, including the physical components of the human brain that are active during language processing (and their characteristic manner of processing information), the tasks such components are engaged in, and characteristics of the language signals to which they are exposed, particularly their statistical aspects. This view has arisen contemporaneously with and partly as a consequence of connectionism, which has provided novel views of both the nature of mental representation and the ways in which such representations might be learned.

A consequence of this move away from a commitment to the uniqueness of linguistic representations is a renewed interest in the possibility of relating factors typically considered nonlinguistic to linguistic regularities. For example, regularities in the sound system could be seen as arising out of a complex set of conspiracies and compromises among factors affecting production, such as the shape of the articulators; constraints arising from the serial nature of language; and efficiency, that is, the need to minimize effort expended while simultaneously remaining as communicative as possible. This perspective is beginning to be applied most productively to phonology (Browman & Goldstein, 1989; Maddiesson, 1997) and has the potential for being applied productively to other aspects of language behavior. Similarly, because there is no a priori commitment to describing knowledge of language in terms of formal primitives, functional considerations are not excluded from entering into explanations of what knowledge of language consists of (Bates & MacWhinney, 1982).

The alternative framework also entails a different view of the nature of language acquisition (Allen, 1997; Seidenberg, 1997; Seidenberg, Allen, & Christiansen, 1997). On the standard approach, to know a language is to know the rules that define a computational system that generates the set of sentences in that language. It follows that to learn a language is to learn the rules of this computational system. The child's task is to identify the grammar (the rule set) that characterizes the target language. This identification paradigm has played a central role in linguistic theories of acquisition (Gold, 1967; Wexler & Cullicover, 1980; Wexler & Hamburger, 1973).

We view the task of learning a language differently. The task that children are engaged in is learning to use language. In the course of mastering this task, they develop various types of knowledge representations that allow communication to proceed. These knowledge representations are shaped by many factors, including nonlinguistic ones, which should, in our view, provide the primitives of a theory of linguistic knowledge. The primary function of this knowledge is producing and comprehending utterances, whether grammatical or otherwise. A by-product of this knowledge is the capacity to distinguish grammatical from ungrammatical sentences.

As an analogy, consider the problem of learning to read. The beginning reader's problem is to learn how to read words. There are various models of how the knowledge relevant to this task is acquired (e.g., Seidenberg & McClelland, 1989). Once acquired, this knowledge can be used to perform many other tasks, including the many tasks that psychologists have used in studying language and cognition. One such task is lexical decision: judging whether a stimulus is a word or not. Even young readers can reliably determine that *book* is a word but *nust* is not. Note, however, that the task confronting the beginning reader is not learning to make lexical decisions. By the same token, the task confronting the language learner is not learning to distinguish well- and ill-formed utterances. In both cases, knowledge that is acquired for other purposes can eventually be used to perform these secondary (metalinguistic) tasks. Such tasks may provide a useful way of assessing people's knowledge but should not be construed as the goal of acquisition.

This perspective shares with Chomsky the view that the competence grammar is only metaphorically related to acquisition and processing. However, in our view, it is also only indirectly related to the knowledge that underlies these and other aspects of language use. Knowledge of language is construed as one or more neural networks that are engaged in producing and comprehending utterances. Grammars represent high-level, idealized descriptions of the behavior of these networks that abstract away from the computational principles that actually govern their behavior. Grammatical theory has enormous utility as a framework for discovering and framing descriptive generalizations about languages and performing comparisons across languages, but it does not provide an accurate representation of the way knowledge of language is represented in the mind of the language user.

GRAMMATICALITY JUDGMENTS

The approach that we have briefly summarized is beginning to be applied to a range of questions about acquisition, processing, and breakdown following brain injury (e.g., MacDonald et al., 1994; Plaut, McClelland, Seidenberg, & Patterson, 1996; Chater & Christiansen, in press). Here, we want to return to the concept of grammaticality and to the task of making grammaticality judgments, both of which are central to the standard approach. We have suggested that knowledge of language is not a set of rules for generating sentences and that the child's task is not grammar acquisition. We therefore owe an account of how it is that people can nonetheless make grammaticality judgments.

The capacity to make these judgments emerges out of the ability to process language normally. The task requires informants to establish criteria for deciding whether to call a sentence grammatical or ungrammatical. One important property of the task is that different decision criteria may be used, depending on the properties of the sentences being judged. Thus, judging the utterance *The the the the the* as ungrammatical may not rely on the same information as judging *The boy tried Bill to go* or *The boy fell the chair.* The first sentence can be judged on the basis of whether it even potentially conforms to an interpretable object; superficial properties such as the absence of nouns and verbs provide a reliable basis for deciding that it does not. These criteria will be not sufficient for the second and third sentences, which require using other sorts of information. A second point is that for a broad range of sentence types, judgments may be reliably cued by local statistical information concerning subsequences of words. For example, recognizing that *The boy fell the chair* is an instance of the pattern *NP fell NP* may be sufficient to make a decision based on properties of the verb *fall.* People can apparently make use of information derived from a complete analysis of the utterance if it is required for further processing (e.g., as in formulating a correction), but this level of analysis is not required in many cases.

One reason to believe that judgments of well-formedness reflect statistical information is that in many cases, such judgments reflect ambiguity resolution procedures that also rely on this information. For example, so-called garden paths can arise when a word has two meanings, one of which is very frequent and one relatively rare. In a sentence such as *The horse raced past the barn fell, raced* is used much more frequently as a transitive verb than as a past participle in a reduced passive. In such cases, the frequent meaning quickly dominates the rarer meaning, often to the point that the reader is unaware of the alternate structural interpretation. Such sentences are often judged ungrammatical by speakers who fail to recompute the relations among the lexical items in the sentence after an initial parse. Statistical information of this type (the relative frequency with which a lexical item is used in one way rather than another) is thus required to account for the conditions under which judgments of well-formedness are made.

The usual argument against this approach to grammaticality is that there are sentences containing low-probability sequences of words that can nonetheless be judged as grammatical (e.g., *Colorless green ideas sleep furiously*). The treatment of such sentences turns on the levels over which sequential statistics are being computed. Although the ungrammaticality of many sentences can be determined by detecting local anomalies defined over sequences of lexemes, others may depend on statistics involving other types of information. Assume, for example, that comprehension involves computing high-level semantic types of words; for example, that a *dog* is a thing and that *pushing* is an action. This information would provide the basis for deciding that the sequence *Colorless green ideas sleep furiously* is acceptable because each of the local (high-level) semantic sequences *property property thing action manner* is quite normal English. The sequence *Ideas colorless sleep furiously green* would be rejected on this basis because the sequence *Thing property action manner property* does not occur.

Given this account of grammaticality judgments, the fact that the standard approach excludes most of this statistical information is important. If grammaticality judgments can be based on statistical information derived from experience with the target language, then it cannot be assumed that the task requires computing the kinds of representations assumed within the standard approach.

AGRAMMATISM

We can now use this account to explore some puzzling data concerning apparent dissociations between knowledge of grammar and the capacity to make grammaticality judgments. The speech of agrammatic aphasics (Broca-type patients with lesions in the anterior portion of the dominant hemisphere) is typically restricted to telegraphic utterances that rely heavily on open-class lexical items. This production impairment is frequently accompanied by impaired comprehension: Broca's aphasics tend to experience difficulty on comprehension tasks when syntax alone furnishes critical aspects of meaning (Caramazza & Zurif, 1976; Saffran, Schwartz, & Marin, 1980). Linguists have been interested in this form of aphasia because it was thought to provide another kind of evidence bearing on the nature of linguistic competence, specifically, the existence for a syntactic module that can be selectively impaired.

The work of Linebarger, Schwartz, and Saffran (1983) raised important questions about the interpretation of agrammatic behavior. They described four agrammatic patients who exhibited comprehension difficulties but retained the ability to judge the grammaticality of many sentences. These results are important because they represent a dissociation between grammaticality judgment and other aspects of performance. Attempts to relate agrammatic comprehension to syntactic theory assume that a failure to structurally represent a sentence causes a failure to comprehend that sentence. If grammaticality judgments represent evaluations over syntactic representations, then the failure to syntactically represent a sentence should also affect the ability to make appropriate grammaticality judgments. Linebarger et al.'s (1983) data provided evidence against the claim that agrammatism represents a selective loss of syntactic capacity, in that patients who performed at chance levels on comprehension tasks performed at high levels when judging the grammaticality of similar sentence types.

These findings generated considerable controversy. One response was the formulation of revised theories that attempted to maintain the idea that agrammatism has a grammatical basis (e.g., Grodzinsky, 1990; Hildebrandt, Caplan, & Evans, 1987; Zurif & Grodzinsky, 1983). However, these proposals have run into other problems (Druks & Marshall, 1991; Milekic, Boskovic, Crain, & Shankweiler, 1995; Tesak & Hummer, 1994). In the model presented in the next section, we develop an alternative account in which a "syntactic" processing deficit is created by damaging parts of a neural network that computes from form to meaning and from meaning to form.

A second issue concerns the assumption that the grammaticality judgment task provides direct evidence about a person's syntactic knowledge. We suggested that grammaticality judgments in many cases do not require evaluations of complete syntactic representations but instead can be based on how well an utterance conforms (sometimes quite locally) to statistical regularities, acquired in the course of learning, and generally excluded on the standard approach from descriptions of linguistic competence. Knowledge of such regularities might provide the basis for making well-formedness judgments even when normal comprehension processes are significantly impaired. In the next section, we present a simulation model that exhibits just this outcome.

SIMULATING GRAMMATICALITY JUDGMENTS

We now describe a connectionist model of language processing that provides a basis for differentiating between several classes of grammatical and ungrammatical utterances and, when damaged, exhibits partial retention of this capacity. The model learned to perform two mappings. Given a sequence of words as input, it computed their semantic representations. This form-to-meaning mapping is an analogue of comprehension. Conversely, given an input sequence of meanings, the model computed the appropriate words, the meaning-to-form mapping involved in production. Our hypothesis about grammaticality judgment is that it involves computing the meaning of a sentence and then passing that derived representation through the production system. The mismatch between the form presented as input and the form computed on the backward pass through production provides the basis for judging grammaticality. In the implemented model, this mismatch was quantified as the distance between relevant vectors. We assume that if these differences are large enough, subjects can set a decision criterion that allows them to distinguish the grammatical and ungrammatical utterances, as in the standard signal detection paradigm, although this decision process was not explicitly modeled.

Put simply, the judgment process is modeled by querying the network for its version of an input sentence. Given a particular input utterance, would the model have said it the same way? This is accomplished by processing the input sentence normally, computing as far as possible the corresponding meaning, generating a sentence that corresponds to that meaning, and then measuring how far apart the input and output forms are.

This way of implementing well-formedness judgments was inspired by a view of grammaticality in which a grammatical structure is seen as one that best satisfies the various constraints developed over the course of learning (MacDonald et al., 1994; Smolensky, 1986). Sentence structures reflect the interaction of innate constraints (whether linguistic or nonlinguistic) and the input to which the learner has been exposed. It follows that an ungrammatical structure is one that is suboptimal, meaning that there is some other structure that better satisfies the relevant set of constraints given a particular input. As an example, let us take the input to a sentence-generating system (production) to be a conceptual representation. In this view, the form produced on the basis of this conceptual representation will be that which best satisfies the multiple constraints that make up the speaker's knowledge of form–meaning relations.

It follows that the grammaticality of an utterance is defined with respect to a particular meaning. Unlike the Turing machine metaphor of string recognition, the grammaticality of an utterance cannot be defined with respect to the form of that sentence alone, but must make reference to the meaning that gave rise to it. It further follows that an (absolutely) ungrammatical utterance is one to which no meaning maps. Note that this is not equivalent to saying that an ungrammatical utterance is one that maps to no meaning, because presumably there is always some semantic representation that best satisfies the constraints given the ungrammatical utterance as input. If we now take the input to the metatask of grammaticality judgment to be a sentence, and we generate a hypothetical space of all possible meaning candidates (comprehension), there will always be some best (semantic) candidate, even for (absolutely) ungrammatical utterances. On the other hand, if we take the semantic output generated by that ungrammatical input and map it back to form (production), we will not get the sentence form that we started with, if it is the case that no meaning maps to that form.

The hypothesis, then, is that a mismatch between the form that is the input to the comprehension system and the form produced on the basis of what was comprehended could be used as the basis for detecting ungrammaticality. We further hypothesize that in some types of aphasia, the linguistic system is impaired enough to interfere with comprehension and production, but still support the ability to judge the grammaticality of many sentences.

Network Implementation

The network used in these simulations was trained on a set of utterances like those given by Linebarger et al. (1983) to their agrammatic subjects. As a consequence of training on the form-to-meaning and meaning-to-form mappings, the network developed a type of symmetric knowledge, that is, that form *a* entailed meaning *b* and that meaning *b* entailed form *a*. Because both mappings had a shared computational substrate, these two skills were not independent of one another. After training, the network was evaluated by supplying either novel forms or novel meanings and recording the network's behavior. In the course of training, the network developed sensitivity to the statistical properties of the sentences to which it was exposed and as a consequence, behaved differently when provided with grammatical and ungrammatical versions of these utterances.

When normal processing was disrupted by "damaging" the network, it exhibited behaviors seen in agrammatic patients such as a failure to produce high-frequency items that are low in semantic content (function words) and impaired comprehension (i.e., failure to activate the correct sequence of semantic representations for a given lexical input sequence). Although impaired in these ways, the damaged network retained the ability to distinguish between many grammatical and ungrammatical utterances.

Architecture

The architecture used in the simulations is shown in Fig. 4.1, and consisted of three main layers. The semantic layer consisted of 297 units that served to represent the semantics of an utterance (see the section on Representation). This layer was connected to itself via a set of 15 clean-up units.

The pathway from the semantic units to the clean-up units and back to semantics allows for the semantic units to interact with one another during processing. The purpose of the layer of clean-up units along this pathway is to allow for interactions to develop among semantic units during processing. By providing an intermediate layer of units (the clean-up units) along the pathway from semantics to semantics, it becomes possible to encode in the weights of these pathways a more complex set of relations among semantic units. For example, exclusive *or*- relations among sets of semantic units become learnable when a clean-up layer is used to connect the semantic layer to itself, whereas only linearly separable relations (e.g., *and* or *or*) would be learnable if the semantic layer were to be connected to itself directly without an intermediate layer. The pathways between the semantic units and the clean-up units thus allow for combinations of se-

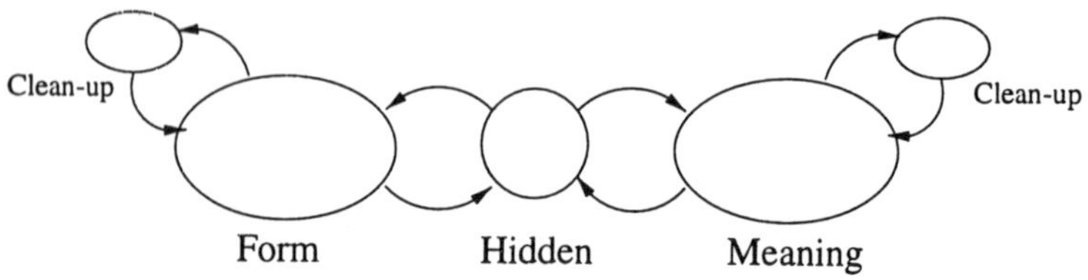

FIG. 4.1. Architecture of the grammaticality judgment model. Arrows represent full connectivity between layers.

mantic features to influence the patterns that develop over time on the semantic units (see Hinton & Shallice, 1991, for discussion).

Futhermore, in processing an exemplar through time, the semantic units and their associated clean-up units serve to form an attractor network, where an initial activity on the semantic layer may be coerced over time toward the nearest fixed-point attractor developed during training.[2] The semantic layer was also connected to a hidden layer consisting of 50 units. These hidden units were connected to each form unit, each semantic unit, and to each other. The 97 form units were also connected to each other via a set of 15 clean-up units, allowing fixed-point attractors to develop in the form representation as well. All connection sets were fully connected, and all weights were initially set to random values between −1 and 1.

Network Dynamics

The implemented network developed sensitivity to the characteristics of sequences of words in an utterance. Our strategy for accomplishing this was in some ways quite similar to that used in simple recurrent networks (Elman, 1990), in which sequential dependencies are developed by representing sequences through time. Our network differs from the standard simple recurrent network in several ways, however. First, we exploited the advantages provided by the continuous activation function described in Pearlmutter (1989), in which the state of a unit changes smoothly over time in response to input from other units. This approach significantly improves the ability of networks to "reach back in time," that is, to develop sensitivity to longer sequences than is possible in standard discrete time nets. This continuous approach is approximated by dividing the normal time steps of discrete back prop through time (Williams & Zipser, 1990) into ticks of some shorter duration. An infinite number of such ticks would represent truly continuous activation. The number of time steps per tick (called the *integration constant*) changes the grain at which activation is propagated and error injected into the network. Details of the implementation are given in the Appendix.

Second, unlike a simple recurrent network that freezes a set of weights (copy back connections) from the hidden units to the "context" units, all connection sets in this network were trainable. In this sense, the simple recurrent net represents a strict subset of the weight values that our network can take on. Like the simple recurrent network, however, this network does not suffer from the problem associated with providing a distinct set

[2]If a separate dimension is assigned to each unit's current activation value, then each fixed-point attractor corresponds to a particular point in a space whose dimensionality is defined by the number of units in the vector. The set of patterns that are attracted to any of the fixed points form the basin of attraction for that fixed point.

of units and connections for each distinct sequential element (letter, phoneme, word, etc.) in a representation, where the set of weights encoding knowledge about an element in one position is completely independent of the weights encoding knowledge about the same word in a different position. Rather, in this network, information derived from experience about an element occurring at time t is available to the network when that element occurs at time $t \pm n$.

For purposes of the simulation, we defined an exemplar as a sequence of states, each representing either a word or a word's semantics. Under the version of continuous back propagation utilized here, the network does a forward pass on the entire string (all of the words), integrating activity up, and remembering its state for the whole utterance at every tick. On the backward pass, error is injected for each tick based on the integration constant, the error associated with each unit for each tick, and on what flowed backward from the following tick.

The targets for each utterance thus form a *trajectory* that the network attempts to learn to follow. For semantic targets, this trajectory is the sequence of points defining the semantic values of each word in the utterance. For form targets, this trajectory is the sequence of points representing the individual words of the utterance.

Use of this system allows the network to develop sensitivity to the sequences of state transitions defined by the training utterances. At word n, information about word $n - 1$, $n - 2$, and so forth, is available to the network in the form of the state of the target, hidden, and clean-up units when the processing of word n begins. Recurrent connections allow the state of the hidden units at any time to be influenced by their own state at previous times. The network learns to rely on regularities in these sequences to the extent that they minimize error.

Each utterance in the training set was presented for 65 "seconds," with an integration constant of .2 (five ticks per second). Each word was presented for a window of 3 seconds, thus 15 ticks. Inputs were clamped only for the initial seven ticks of the word's window, and feedback was given only on the final eight ticks of each 3-second window. This offset between the time at which the input is clamped and the time at which the target is required forces the network to depend on its current state as well as its input. Thus, for example, activity on the semantic vector corresponding to the semantics of the word (e.g., *car*) was made to depend not only on the input from the formal representation of *car,* but also on the state of the network before and after the time that the form vector for the word *car* was clamped as input.

This technique forces the network to use information earlier in the sequence to begin to activate what it is predictable about the next item in order to minimize error. Given the attractor network implemented via clean-up units at the meaning layer, if the prediction can get the semantic vector into the right neighborhood, the actual word presented will sharpen the representation quickly. Of course, only parts of the next word can be predicted (e.g., the *entity* feature after a determiner is a good guess). But if a wrong prediction is made, it takes the network a long time to recover, because both the current state of the semantic attractor and the identity of the current word have an effect on the semantic output.

Representation

Meaning. It is notoriously difficult to represent the semantics of propositions. It is even more difficult, if not impossible, to represent the semantics of propositions without a system for binding arguments and roles. In order to simplify the simulations, the semantics of utterances were represented by sequences of word-level semantic representations. As a consequence, many relations like coreference, binding, predication, and a host of others relevant to the semantics of propositions (whether semantic or syntactically represented) are not captured by this approach.

This simplification means that our model does not represent phrasal- and propositional-level relations among words such as *subject of predicate* or *object of verb.* Although we assume that a good deal of knowledge concerning the formal expression of these higher level structures is also emergent from form–meaning pairings available in the learner's environment, the technical challenges involved in modeling such knowledge are considerable. This *role filler* (or *binding*) problem arises in many cognitive domains and has received considerable attention elsewhere, for example, in the area of vision, Hummel and Biederman (1992); von der Malsburg and Schneider (1986); for phrase structure, Omlin and Giles (1995); for grammatical category assignment, Elman (1990); for verb argument structure, Allen (1997). Although the techniques used in these approaches vary, much of this work suggests that temporal dynamics of processing will play a crucial role in understanding how such relations are represented. The approach adopted here is compatible with this general view in that both this work and that focused on binding assume that understanding cognitive representation will involve the analysis of dynamical systems that change through time. In short, our model does not deal with all aspects of language but its limitations are not relevant to the idea that is our main focus, that many grammatical and ungrammatical utterances can be distinguished using much simpler and more local types of knowledge representations than are required for complete syntactic analysis or semantic interpretation.

Features for the semantic representations of words were based on the semantic hierarchy associated with each word from the Wordnet database (Miller, 1990) and then augmented by hand. Although Wordnet includes entries for many open-class items, features for the closed-class words in the training set were developed by hand. An example of the set of features used for the word *house* appears in (1).

(1) *house:* house housing lodging structure construction artifact object physicalobject entityhouse

Because pronouns, prepositions, and determiners do not appear in the Wordnet database, these items were given semantic features that represented their relation both to each other and to other words in the training set. For example, the pronoun *he* was given the features *singular, male,* and *animate.* In addition, features such as *plural* were added to words such as *men, them,* and *ducks* to distinguish between plural and singular versions of the same word. We used these representations because they form a series of hierarchies, with some features (e.g., *entity*) applying to many different words, and others (e.g., *vehicle*) applying to many fewer. The semantic representations thus have an internal structure that the network can take advantage of during learning. Units higher on the hierarchy tend to be positively correlated with those lower on the hierarchy, and to develop positive weights between them. As a consequence, units higher on the hierarchy will tend to activate those below them, and those lower on the hierarchy will tend to activate those above them. In contrast, units at similar levels tend to inhibit each other.

The semantics of each word, then, was represented as the state of a space whose dimensionality was defined by the number of units (297) in the semantic representation, and the semantics of an utterance was represented by a series of such states.

Form. The forms of utterances were represented as a series of words presented over time. Words were represented locally, that is, each word was represented by a single unit. The vector representing each word was thus extremely simple, consisting of a single unit being on and all other form units being off for the appropriate time steps. The form of an utterance was presented to the network by activating the units representing each word of the utterance in sequence. There were 97 distinct words used in the example sets, so the form layer consisted of 97 units.

Training and Testing Materials

Agrammatic performance on 10 sentence types was reported by Linebarger et al. (1983). These types formed the basis of the training and testing sets used in the simulations. Grammatical and ungrammatical versions of these 10 types are listed in Table 4.1.

TABLE 4.1
Grammatical and Ungrammatical Examples of Sentence Types in Training and Test Corpora

	Type	*Example*
I.	Strict subcategoritization	
	Grammatical	He came to my house at noon.
	Ungrammatical	*He came my house at noon.
II.	Particle movement	
	Grammatical	She went up the stairs in a hurry.
	Ungrammatical	*She went the stairs up in a hurry.
III.	Sub–Aux inversion	
	Grammatical	Did the old man enjoy the view?
	Ungrammatical	*Did the old man enjoying the view?
IV.	Empty elements	
	Grammatical	Frank was expected to get the job.
	Ungrammatical	*The job was expected Frank to get.
V.	Tag questions, Pronoun agreement	
	Grammatical	The little boy fell down, didn't he?
	Ungrammatical	*The little boy fell down, didn't it?
VI.	Left-branch condition	
	Grammatical	Which old man did you invite to the party?
	Ungrammatical	*Which old did you invite man to the party?
VII.	Gapless relatives	
	Grammatical	Mary ate the bread that I baked.
	Ungrammatical	*Mary ate the bread that I baked a cake.
VIII.	Phrase structure	
	Grammatical	The paper was full of mistakes.
	Ungrammatical	*The paper was full mistakes.
IX.	Reflexive agreement	
	Grammatical	I helped myself to the birthday cake.
	Ungrammatical	*I helped themselves to the birthday cake.
X.	Tag questions, Aux copying	
	Grammatical	John is very tall, isn't he?
	Ungrammatical	*John is very tall, doesn't he?

A training and testing corpus was developed by providing *partial paradigms* for each of the sentence types listed above. Twenty sentences were created for each of the 10 sentence types for a total of 200 utterances. The partial paradigm for each type was created by replacing individual words with others that might be used grammatically in those positions. For example, one of the sentence types was a reflexive (*The little boy cut himself while playing*). The paradigm created for this sentence type included the following:

- The little boy cut himself while playing.
- The little girl cut herself at noon.
- The big boy cut himself while playing.
- A little boy fell while running.
- An old man cut himself while shaving.

Half of this training set was used to train the network, and half was used to assess learning after training. The training corpus consisted of 100 utterances and 665 words (97 types). The mean number of words per utterance in the training corpus was 6.65, and the mean number of content words per utterance was 3.1. The testing corpus consisted of 100 utterances and 652 words (97 types). The mean number of words per utterance in the testing corpus was 6.52, and the mean number of function words per utterance was 2.8. Two examples were developed per utterance, one for each mapping.

An ungrammatical corpus was developed by creating ungrammatical versions of each of the sentence types listed previously. Each of the ungrammatical utterances deviated from the grammatical version in the way picked out by the category name. For example, the ungrammatical phrase structure utterances were all examples of phrase structure violations (e.g., *He came to my town* → **He came my town*). The ungrammatical corpus consisted of 100 utterances and 653 words (97 types). The mean number of words per utterance in the ungrammatical corpus was 6.53, and the mean number of function words per utterance was 2.8.

Training the network consisted of presenting two types of trials. The model was trained on grammatical sentences only. On form-to-meaning trials, the unit representing each word in the utterance was activated in sequence. The task of the network was then to compute the correct semantic representation of each word in the sequence. On meaning-to-form trials, the requirements were reversed. Word meanings were presented one at a time to the network, and the task of the model was to compute the formal trajectory that constituted the representation of the utterance by activating the appropriate word units in the right sequence at the right times. The network was trained for 25,000 iterations, where an iteration consisted of a presentation and feedback on either a form-to-meaning example or a meaning-to-form example. After 25,000 iterations, the network produced the correct trajectories for all utterances on which it had been trained.

After training, the model's performance on three types of tasks was assessed under two different conditions. The three tasks were a comprehension task, a production task, and a grammaticality judgment task. The comprehension and production tasks are assessments of the model's ability to handle the primary task of form-to-meaning and meaning-to-form mappings under normal and impaired conditions. The grammaticality judgment task is a test of the model's ability to discriminate two types of stimuli. In the *normal* condition, performance of the undamaged model was assessed. In the *impaired* condition, 10% of connections between the semantic and hidden units were lesioned by setting their weights to 0. This represents an impairment to the network's ability to successfully perform the mappings on which it was trained.

RESULTS

Normal Comprehension

The model's ability to produce the correct semantic representations for novel utterances was tested by supplying the 100 novel utterance forms of the testing corpus to the network and recording activation of the semantic vector at the center of the target period (tick 11). The results are shown in the first columns of Tables 4.2 and 4.3. Table 4.2 shows the proportion of words correctly identified by the network. These figures were computed as follows. The semantic vector computed by the network 11 ticks after the form of a word was presented was compared with the vector representing the semantic target for that word. If the computed vector was both closer to the target vector than any other word's vector and each unit of the computed vector was within .2 of its target, the word was considered recognized. The Euclidean distance between the computed and target vectors for each sentence type is shown in Table 4.3. Together these figures give an overall view of the network's performance on the comprehension tasks. The first column of Table 4.2 shows that the normal network is easily able to accommodate novel utterances. The range of identification is between 88% and 100% for comprehension in the normal network. Thus, although the network had not been trained on the sentence *A little boy fell at noon*, it had no trouble producing the correct vector for each word at the correct time step.

TABLE 4.2
Proportion of Words Correctly Comprehended or Produced for Normal and Impaired Network

	Comprehension		*Production*	
Sentence Type	*Normal*	*Inpaired*	*Normal*	*Impaired*
Subcategorization	1.00	0.66	0.93	0.76
Particle movement	0.93	0.36	0.99	0.47
Inversion	1.00	0.37	0.93	0.41
Empty elements	0.91	0.45	0.94	0.59
Tag questions (PN)	0.94	0.41	0.86	0.46
Left-branch condition	0.99	0.45	0.88	0.56
Gapless relatives	0.98	0.49	0.93	0.51
Phrase structure	0.94	0.34	0.97	0.51
Reflexive agreement	0.90	0.54	0.97	0.54
Tag questions (Aux)	0.88	0.31	0.89	0.57
Mean	0.95	0.43	0.93	0.53

Note. PN = pronoun agreement; Aux = auxiliary copying.

TABLE 4.3
Distances Between Target and Computed Vectors for Normal and Impaired Production and Comprehension

	Comprehension		*Production*	
Sentence Type	*Normal*	*Inpaired*	*Normal*	*Impaired*
Subcategorization	0.97	1.77	0.64	0.87
Particle movement	0.87	1.86	0.68	0.92
Inversion	1.01	2.41	0.75	0.94
Empty elements	1.11	1.98	0.75	1.00
Tag questions (PN)	1.06	2.21	0.65	1.06
Left-branch condition	1.00	2.34	0.61	0.83
Gapless relatives	1.00	2.21	0.77	1.02
Phrase structure	1.10	2.10	0.97	0.95
Reflexive agreement	1.06	1.81	0.68	0.91
Tag questions (Aux)	1.00	2.04	0.60	0.94
Mean	1.01	2.07	0.69	0.94

Note. PN = pronoun agreement; Aux = auxiliary copying.

These results show that under normal conditions, computing the correct semantics for sequences that form novel grammatical utterances is a simple problem for the network. The ability to recognize the elements of novel grammatical sequences is facilitated by the fact that the same weights are being used for words regardless of a word's position in the utterance. Thus, regardless of whether the network had been exposed to *boy* in the third position of an utterance, the weights from the unit representing *boy* are still those used when *boy* appears in this position in a novel utterance.

In the impaired condition, comprehension performance is significantly worse. The second columns of Tables 4.2 and 4.3 show that when damaged, the network is less likely to produce the correct word's semantics, and that the average distance between the correct vector and that produced by the network is higher than in the undamaged network. (All differences between the first and second columns of Tables 4.2 and 4.3 are significant at $p < .05$ or lower.)

Production

The model's ability to produce the correct formal representation for novel utterances was then tested by supplying 100 novel meaning sequences representing the testing corpus. As in the comprehension task, 10 sentences of each type were presented. The results are shown in the third columns of Tables 4.2 and 4.3. As in the comprehension task, for each word, the form vector that was computed by the network 11 ticks after the semantics of a word was presented was compared with the vector representing the formal target for that word. If the computed form vector was closer to the target vector than to any other formal vector, and the activation of each unit was within .2 of its target, the correct word was considered produced. As in the comprehension task, this task is fairly straightforward for the normal network, and performance was quite high, ranging from 86% to 99% of words correctly produced.

Impairment to the network also significantly affects its ability to compute the correct sequence of words. The impaired model's ability to produce the correct formal representation for novel meanings sequences was tested as for the normal network. The results are shown in the final columns of Tables 4.2 and 4.3. Again, under damaged conditions, the proportion of words correctly produced is lower, and the mean distance between target and computed vectors is higher, than under normal conditions. All differences between the third and fourth columns of Tables 4.2 and 4.3 are significant at or below the .05 level.

An interesting aspect of the production tests on the impaired model was the differential impairment on grammatical morphemes as a consequence of their semantic "shallowness." As can be seen in Table 4.4, closed-class words are more likely to fail to be produced and to be further from their targets than open-class words. Why are function and content words differentially affected by damage to the connections between hidden and semantic representations? Activation of the correct semantic pattern for a word relies both on the word input to the model and on the semantic attractors that move the initial representation to its target. Because the hierarchy is typically deeper for content than for function words, content

TABLE 4.4
Impaired Network: Content Versus Function Word Production

Sentence Type	*Open Class*	*Closed Class*
Subcategorization	0.81	0.69
Particle movement	0.60	0.35
Inversion	0.57	0.25
Empty elements	0.63	0.56
Tag questions (PN)	0.55	0.38
Left-branch condition	0.74	0.46
Gapless relatives	0.52	0.50
Phrase structure	0.73	0.30
Reflexive agreement	0.65	0.47
Tag questions (Aux)	0.63	0.51
Mean	0.64	0.44

Note. PN = pronoun agreement; Aux = auxiliary copying.

words are more resilient to damage to the system. The influence of semantic representations on agrammatic production may be an additional factor to those already recognized concerning why closed-class items may be impaired when, for other reasons, they might be expected to be easy to produce (e.g., Stemberger, 1985).

Grammaticality Judgments

The network was trained by interleaving form-to-meaning and meaning-to-form exemplars. This interleaved training caused the network to develop knowledge of the probable contingencies among elements in sequences of both form and meaning. The dynamics of the grammaticality judgment task rely on the following property of the trained network: When a formal pattern is supplied to the network, the semantic pattern associated with it is activated because of the form-to-meaning connections. Activation then flows back to the form vector along the normal meaning-to-form path. This activation results in the re-creation of the original form vector several ticks after it is released. Thus, the form that was presented to the network is normally reproduced as activation flows back to the form layer. However, when the form of an utterance deviates from the type the network is familiar with, the computed semantics deviate from normal, and as a consequence, the form that is created deviates from the form presented. We simulate the metalinguistic notion of grammaticality as the accurate reproduction of a supplied form, measured in terms of distance. The results show that ungrammatical utterances of the type used in Linebarger et al.'s (1983) study produce more deviant re-creations of the input than do novel grammatical sentences.

Ten ungrammatical versions of each sentence type were presented to both the impaired and normal networks. Although impairment to the network significantly disrupts the ability of the model to compute the correct meanings of novel forms and the correct forms of novel meanings, the ability to distinguish grammatical from ungrammatical utterances is retained for 7 of the 10 utterance types.

Figures 4.2 and 4.3 show the mean distance between the form vector supplied and that produced 11 time ticks after the onset of each word for normal and impaired networks. For example, the first set of bars in Fig. 4.2 shows that the normal network (re-)produced vectors with a mean distance of .56 from those supplied on novel grammatical versions of the subcategorization sentences like *He left my house at noon*, but (re-)produced vectors with a mean distance of 1.27 from that supplied on novel ungrammatical sentences such as *He left to my house at noon.* For the normal network, 7 of the 10 sentence types produced significant differences between grammatical and ungrammatical distances at or below the .05 level. The sentence

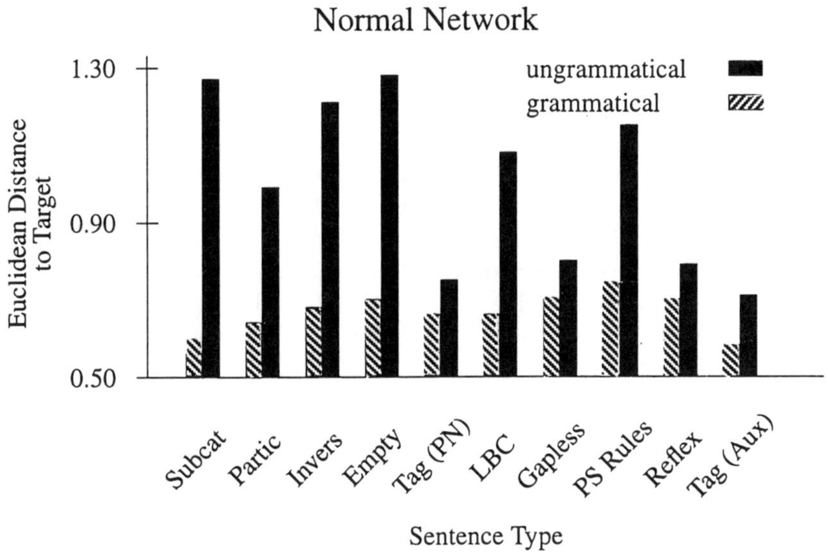

FIG. 4.2. Mean distance between form supplied to network and form computed by network for grammatical and ungrammatical novel utterances for normal network.

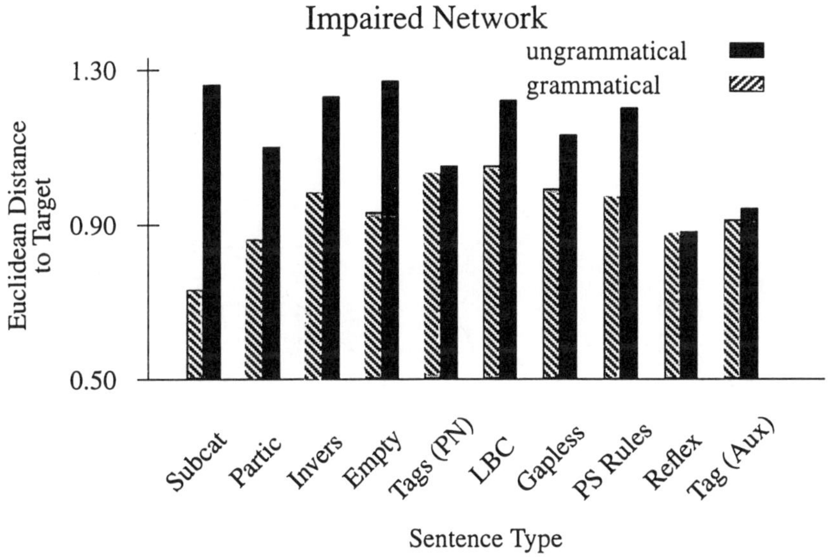

FIG. 4.3. Mean distance between form supplied to network and form computed by network for grammatical and ungrammatical novel utterances for impaired network.

types on which the network did not detect ungrammaticalities by this measure were the two types of tag questions and reflexive agreement. Figure 4.3 shows these distances for the grammatical and ungrammatical utterances produced by the impaired network. As seen in the first set of bars, the impaired network (re-)produced vectors with a mean distance of .73 from those supplied on novel grammatical versions of the subcategorization sentences, and vectors with a mean distance of 1.26 from that supplied on novel ungrammatical subcategorization sentences. Like the normal network, in the impaired network, 7 of the 10 sentence types produced significant differences between grammatical and ungrammatical utterances at or below the .05 level. The sentence types on which the network did not exhibit distinctions between grammatical and ungrammatical utterances by this measure were the same types as before.

Interestingly, Linebarger et al.'s (1983) patient data exhibit essentially the same pattern as the impaired simulation. Although the patients were able to judge the grammaticality of most types of sentences, they were impaired on the same three sentence types as the model. For the seven sentence types the patients were able to judge correctly, Linebarger (1989) reported performance with a range of 81.2% to 90.4% correct. For the other three sentence types, the patients performed at levels that were not reliably different from chance.

Figure 4.4 illustrates a comparison between the processing of the grammatical and the ungrammatical versions of an utterance of the subcategorization type in the normal network. The utterances differ with respect

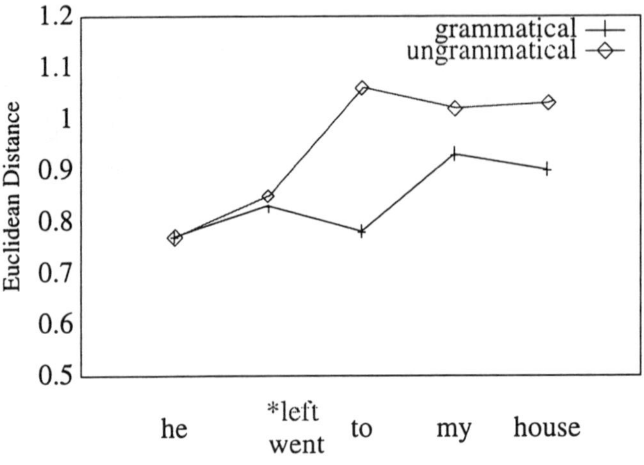

FIG. 4.4. Distance between form presented and form reproduced for a single sentence from the subcategorization set.

to the subcategorization frames of the verbs. The verb *left* does not subcategorize for the preposition *to*, but the verb *went* does. The distance between presented and calculated values of the form vector at tick 11 are plotted for each word of the utterance. At the point of ungrammaticality, the distance between what is presented and what is computed rises. Although the continuations of the sentences are identical, the network continues to produce formal vectors that deviate from their targets more than in the grammatical case. This effect shows the impact of sequential processing in the network.

The opposite case is illustrated in Fig. 4.5, where the verb *left* is used correctly, but the verb *went* (which is consistently used with *to* in the training set) is used in a violation of its *subcategorization frame*. Again, the network responds to this noncanonical sequence by producing vectors that continue to deviate from their targets for the next two words.

Why does this result obtain? Although the comprehension and production results reported earlier are consistent with the idea that the network was only responding on a word-by-word basis, its performance actually relies on more than merely a local mapping between the current form and meaning pair. Because the network was encouraged to develop a reliance on its current state as well as its current input, anomalous sequences such as *went the store* produce state trajectories in the semantic units that do not correspond to the regularities on which the network has come to rely. As a consequence, anomalous local sequences tend to produce anomalous semantics, and anomalous semantics produce formal vectors that deviate from the form supplied. This result is partly brought about by the use of continuous time training. Because targets are supplied prior

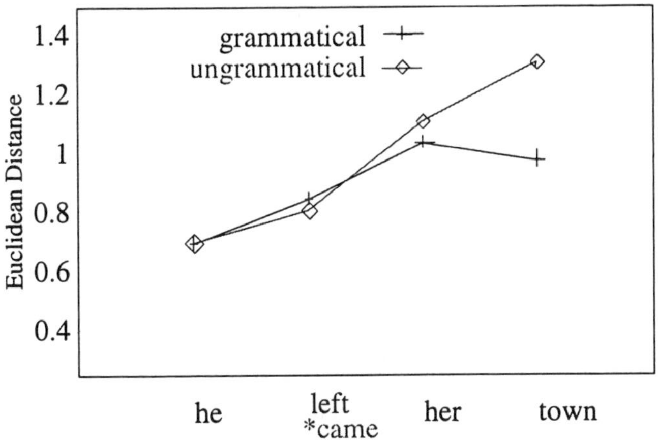

FIG. 4.5. Distance between form presented and form reproduced for a single sentence from the subcategorization set.

to the time at which clamping the current word form can activate the correct units on their own (because of the built-in rise time), the network learns to rely on information that is available, namely, material prior in the sequence. Because only some parts of the prior sequence are reliable, the network learns to take advantage of those regularities and ignore other aspects of its input.

A related issue concerns the fact that in our results, the absolute value for the distance between grammatical and ungrammatical utterances varies between sentence types. Is it reasonable to suppose that different cutoffs are required for different sentence types? Although no single line can distinguish between grammatical and ungrammatical versions across sentence types, it is not clear what the significance of such a line would be. Our basic theory is that an ungrammatical utterance results in a deviation from the normal course of processing, which we measure in terms of a comparison between grammatical and ungrammatical versions. Our method assumes a sensitivity to this distinction and not to an absolute level of difference.

Colorless Green Ideas

Earlier, we noted the existence of sentences such as *Colorless green ideas sleep furiously,* which contain low-probability sequences of words that nonetheless can be judged as grammatical, and suggested that the treatment of such sentences turns on the levels over which sequential statistics are being computed. We claimed that a sentence such as the *Colorless* one might be rated as more acceptable than a random permutation of words based on sequential regularities in the high-level semantic properties of these items.

The network we have presented was designed to be sensitive to statistical regularities in lexical and semantic sequences simultaneously. The network was sensitive to sequences of lexical items because the input form of both the training task and the grammaticality judgment task consisted of local representations of lexical items. At the same time, the network was sensitive to the sequences of semantic representations of words, in that processing involves computation of these semantic representations.

In order to demonstrate that the network is sensitive to both of these levels simultaneously, we tested the network under four conditions that manipulated two factors: the transitional probabilities between words and the transitional probabilities of the semantic types that the words represented.

In the first condition (HH), the network was presented with sentences in which the transitional probabilities between both lexical items and semantic types were high. These are normal sentences. The second condition (LH) consisted of sentences in which the transitional probabilities between words were low, but the transitional probabilities between semantic types were high. This type of sentence corresponds to *Colorless green ideas sleep furiously,* in which the semantic subsequences [property property entity act manner] are consistent with semantic sequences that appeared in the training set, but the bigram frequencies of the words (e.g. *colorless-green, green-ideas,* etc.) were low or zero in the training corpus. The third condition (HL) consisted of sentences in which the transitional probabilities between words were high, but the transitional probabilities between semantic types were low. This condition is possible because there are sequences with high word transitional probabilities such as *mother cares,* where the semantic type represented by the first word in the pair predicts a different semantic continuation more strongly than that of the second word. The fourth condition (LL) consisted of sentences in which both types of transitional probabilities were low. This condition corresponds to random sequences of words such as *sleep ideas green furiously colorless.* Ten sentences of each type matched in terms of the overall frequencies of the words they contained were presented to the network.

Table 4.5 provides the mean transitional probabilities between words (WTP), the mean transitional probabilities between semantic types (STP), and an example sentence for each condition. The semantic type for lexical items was determined by taking the most frequent semantic feature that appeared in the word. For example, the representation for the word *mother* included the following features:

> *mother:* femaleparent parent female relative human livingthing organism animate entity

The most frequent of these features in the training vocabulary is the *entity* bit. The semantic type of the word *mother* was thus taken to be *entity.*

The final column of Table 4.5 gives the mean grammaticality score of the network in these four conditions. As in the earlier grammaticality judgment task, these scores reflect the mean Euclidean distance between the vector representing the form supplied to the network and that com-

TABLE 4.5
Effects of Word and Semantic Transition Probabilities on Comprehension

Condition	*Example*	*WTP*	*STP*	*Score*
HH	Which girl did you invite	.33	.32	.68
LH	Which street invited a cake on time	.02	.26	.77
HL	My mother was expected to arrive	.30	.07	.80
LL	On invited cake street time the which	.00	.00	1.10

Note. WTP = word transition probability; STP = Semantic transition probability. Probabilities calculated with respect to the training corpus.

puted by the network for each sentence type. The LL condition, corresponding to a random sequence of words, is the sentence type that yielded the largest deviation, as would be expected if it is the least grammatical. The HH sentence types yielded the least deviation. The other two conditions resulted in scores that were intermediate in value. The differences between the random-word condition (LL) and the other three conditions were significant below the .01 level. The differences between the HH, LH, and LH conditions were not significant, although this may reflect the relatively small number of test sentences in each condition.

In summary, the model yielded graded performance on the four types of sentences and pseudosentences. The model can be seen as defining a metric in which sentences differ in degree of grammaticality. The largest differences were between the random-word condition (LL) and the other three conditions, providing a basis for treating the LL items as ungrammatical and the other stimuli—including the model's version of a *colorless green ideas* sentence—as grammatical. The model also suggests that it should be harder to judge sentences of the HL and LH types as grammatical than the HH items, an observation that appears to be consistent with human performance.

DISCUSSION

The simulations presented here represent a step in the development of the alternative framework described at the beginning of this chapter. The implemented model illustrates how knowledge of language can be represented in a network rather than a grammar. The network acquired this knowledge in the course of learning to comprehend and produce utterances. The implemented model is clearly limited in scope, addressing only a fragment of the grammar of one language, but these results invite further investigations along the same lines and we have by no means approached the limit of what can be represented in such systems (for related work, see Chater & Christiansen, in press).

We also took a step toward developing a theory of how grammaticality judgments are made. In the absence of such a theory, linguists have interpreted performance on the task in different ways. Sometimes it is assumed that the judgments of native speakers, children, or aphasic patients more or less directly reflect the state of their grammatical knowledge. Sometimes it is noted that factors outside the scope of grammatical theory can influence decisions, but what is involved in filtering out these performance factors and whether this can be achieved in a consistent manner is unclear.

Our account of grammaticality judgment has three main features. First, we note that the capacity to perform the task emerges in the course of acquiring a language but does not play a central role in the acquisition process itself. In this sense, it is like being able to make lexical decisions. Second, there are no absolute criteria for making such decisions; the criteria that people use vary depending on the nature of the sentences they are being asked to judge. Third, making the decision involves generating an error signal based on discrepancies between the sentence presented and what the linguistic system computes. In our model, we generated this error signal by passing the computed semantic representation back through production. This was undoubtedly a simplification insofar as other error signals could be derived from the model and these are probably relevant to performance under some circumstances. For example, Plaut (1997) described how anomalous patterns of semantic activation can provide a basis for making a lexical (word–nonword) decision, and it is easy to imagine the same kind of mechanism being used to judge grammaticality.[3] The results suggest that for a fairly broad range of sentence structures, local anomalies provide a sufficient basis for making correct responses. This means that it cannot be assumed that decisions necessarily require deriving a full syntactic representation of the utterance.

The method we used to implement well-formedness judgments was inspired by a view in which a grammatical structure is one that best satisfies the various probabilistic constraints encoded over the course of learning. In this view, a sentence is one that best satisfies the constraints that make up the speaker's knowledge of language-specific form-to-meaning and meaning-to-form relations given a particular semantic intention. The acceptability of an utterance in this view is defined with respect to a particular meaning. This account differs in kind, of course, from the view that a structure may be ill-formed solely on the basis of the syntactic features of its lexical items.

Implementing these ideas provided the basis for addressing questions concerning the bases of aphasia and the nature of grammaticality judgments raised by Linebarger et al.'s (1983) study of agrammatic patients. Damaging the network impaired its performance on the tasks on which it was trained, yet it was still able to distinguish between grammatical and ungrammatical representations of several sentence types. These results provide a basis for explaining how Linebarger et al.'s patients could perform above chance on such sentences even when their comprehension

[3]Plaut (1997) used a measure called *stress*, based on the entropy of sets of units. This measure reflects how far unit activation deviates from 0.5, in that the stress of a unit is 0 when its state is 0.5 and approaches 1 as its state approaches either 0 or 1. In a model simulating grapheme-to-semantic mappings, the target semantic patterns for words were binary, and thus they showed maximum stress. Because nonwords shared structure with sets of words that had conflicting semantic features, nonwords typically failed to drive semantic units as strongly as words did, producing semantic patterns with much lower average stress.

was significantly impaired. Given the simplicity of the input data that the model had to work with, the fit between the model and the Linebarger et al. data was quite good. Although there was some variation among the patients, overall they were impaired on the same types of sentences as the model. This outcome suggests that our explanation for the basis of grammaticality judgments is a viable one.

The sentences that both the network and patients could judge correctly are ones containing local sequential anomalies. The three sentence types on which both network and patients failed to distinguish between grammatical and ungrammatical versions were the ones for which these anomalies are not readily apparent. Examples of the ungrammatical versions of the 10 sentence types are reproduced in Table 4.6. Sentence Type I includes the local sequence *came my*. Type II contains the sequence *went the stairs*. Type III includes *man enjoying*. Type IV includes *Frank to get*. Type VI includes *which old did*, and Type VII includes *full mistakes*. None of these sequences are consistent with the types of lexical-semantic sequences that appear in either the training set or in the novel grammatical testing set.[4]

There were three sentence types on which the model was unable to detect differences between grammatical and ungrammatical versions. These were the same sentence types that Linebarger et al.'s (1983) patients had the most difficulty with. In both cases, the basis for impaired performance on these items is unclear. There are a number of reasons why the network might have been unable to detect these types of ungrammaticalities. One possibility is that although these sentences, like the others, contain sequential anomalies, they are not sufficiently local. That is, although all 10 sentence types involve violations of lexical or semantic sequences, or both, the distances over which the anomalies are defined are too long in these three cases for the current architecture to pick up. The sentence in Table 4.6 illustrating Type V, for example, requires holding information about *boy* for five lexical items prior to processing *it*. Similarly, the example shown for Type X requires holding information about the auxiliary for

[4]Obviously, these sequences are only anomalous relative to the training set: Simple two-word sequences, such as *full mistakes*, are less anomalous relative to the language as a whole (we can imagine sentences such as *Full mistakes are penalized less than partial mistakes*, for example) and therefore would not be expected to trigger a judgment of ungrammaticality by themselves.

Given the knowledge of the average human speaker, the specific sequence types that provide the basis for deciding that an utterance is ungrammatical will in many cases differ from those to which the model is sensitive, but the same principles will apply. For example, anomalies may be defined over longer stretches such as *was full mistakes*, where the use of *was* forces a particular interpretation of *full*, and with that interpretation in hand, the use of *mistakes* becomes an anomalous sequence.

TABLE 4.6
Ungrammatical Example Sentences

	Type	*Example*
I.	Strict subcategoritization	*He came my house at noon.
II.	Particle movement	*She went the stairs up in a hurry.
III.	Sub–Aux inversion	*Did the old man enjoying the view?
IV.	Empty elements	*The job was expected Frank to get.
V.	Tag questions (PN)	*The little boy fell down, didn't it?
VI.	Left-branch	*Which old did you invite man to the party?
VII.	Gapless relatives	*Mary ate the bread that I baked a cake.
VIII.	Phrase structure	*The paper was full mistakes.
IX.	Reflexive agreement	*I helped themselves to the birthday cake.
X.	Tag questions (Aux)	*John is very tall, doesn't he?

Note. PN = pronoun agreement; Aux = auxiliary copying.

four lexical items. This possibility can be addressed by conducting a larger scale simulation involving more sentences and adjusting the number of units in the network.

A second possibility is that the differences between the grammatical and ungrammatical forms involve kinds of dependencies that our simple network does not encode. The model obviously does not encode all aspects of language, including aspects that might provide the basis for judging the ungrammaticality of some types of sentences. Addressing this issue requires developing models that provide broader coverage of the language. A third possibility is that the poorer performance on these three sentence types derives from the fact that there happened to be less overlap between them and the other sentence types in the corpus. For example, the knowledge that the model brings to bear on sequences such as *came my* relies on exposure to all of the other sequences involving verbs in the training set. In contrast, knowledge concerning the relation between reflexives and antecedents in the network comes only from exposure to sentence Type IX. Poorer performance on Type IX might simply reflect exposure to fewer relevant examples. Again, this possibility can be addressed in larger scale simulations of the same type we explored.

Although additional research is required in order to determine which of these factors is relevant to the model's performance, it is clear that there are two general limiting factors. First, the network was only given access to a fraction of the information that enters into the formation of the dynamic representations that underlie language behavior. It is likely that in humans, performance on the sentence types we tested benefits from exposure to a broad range of other structures not included in the training set. Second, the model's architecture limits its capacity to represent important aspects of the semantics of utterances. For example, although we represent the semantics of propositions as a trajectory of semantic values, it is clearly the phrases of language that refer to conceptual units. Similarly, propositions have semantic characteristics that are compositional, that is, built up out of the semantics of the phrases and clauses that make up the form of a proposition. There are all sorts of semantic relations that occur across multiword windows, including coindexation, predication, dependencies, thematic role binding, and others. In many cases, grammaticality judgments are made on the basis of more information than is provided by the sequential regularities of semantic sequences that we were able to represent in our network.

Although it is clear that a meaningful treatment of these more complex relations within our approach must await technical advances in both representation and learning, a good deal of work within the general framework suggests that progress is being made. For example, implementing the types of conceptual representations people use will almost certainly require the ability to represent hierarchies where parts of a representation are identified with roles that those parts play with respect to larger structures. Implementing the binding of roles to arguments has been studied in references cited earlier. Other limitations on our ability to represent relevant structure arise as a consequence of general questions concerning the basic character of semantic representations (e.g., Fodor, 1985; Jackendoff, 1990; Langacker, 1986), issues that are not specific to connectionist implementations.

In closing, we suggest that this model illustrates an approach to thinking about language acquisition, processing, and breakdown that shows considerable promise. Given the simplicity of the model's architecture and the limited corpus on which it was trained, it seems quite surprising that it was able to develop a basis for performing the grammaticality judgment task at levels comparable to normal and aphasic subjects. The claim that subjects can base their grammaticality judgments on statistical cues such as sequential probabilities of words clearly differs from the view that grammaticality judgments reflect access to principles of grammar. These differences can be seen clearly by considering Linebarger's (1989) discussion of the various bases on which sentence Type IV (Empty elements) might be judged ungrammatical:

> We might reject "Frank thought was going to get a job" for any number of reasons. If the empty category is PRO, then it violates the requirement that PRO be ungoverned, so we might reject it as a violation of the binding theory. Or we might take the empty category to be an NP trace of Frank, assigning the D-Structure "__ thought Frank was going to get the job"; under this analysis [the utterance] represents, inter alia, a violation of the theta criterion since the moved NP is now assigned two theta roles. Recognition of any of these principles might trigger a rejection. On the other hand, perhaps the sentence is ultimately rejected because the grammar, —by dis-

allowing PRO and NP trace in this position, provides us with no NP for the verb phrase 'get the job' to be predicated of, and the sentence simply 'makes no sense' unless it expresses who it is that is expected to get the job. (p. 236)

We take our results to indicate that many grammaticality judgments are made on the basis of knowledge of sequential regularities of the type that humans apparently cannot help but absorb in the course of language learning (Saffran, Aslin & Newport, 1996). The degree to which this approach can be extended to other aspects of linguistic structure is an important question that remains to be answered.

ACKNOWLEDGMENTS

This research was supported by Grant MH PO1-47566 from the National Institute of Mental Health and a Research Scientist Development Award to Mark S. Seidenberg (NIMH KO2-01188), which we gratefully acknowledge. We thank Maryellen MacDonald, David Plaut, and Brian MacWhinney for comments on an earlier draft.

APPENDIX

The continuous approach to activation is approximated by dividing the normal time steps of discrete back prop through time (Williams & Zipser, 1990) into ticks of some shorter duration. An infinite number of such ticks would represent truly continuous activation. The number of time steps per tick (called the *integration constant*) changes the grain at which activation is propagated and error injected into the network.

Under this approach to approximating continuous time, the instantaneous change in the activation of each unit in a network is dependent both on its current state and on the input it is receiving from other units. Rather than the more commonly used discrete activation function then, change in the activity of units in the network was governed by the formula given in Equation 2:

$$\tau \frac{\partial y_i}{\partial t} = -y_i + \sigma(x_i) \tag{2}$$

$$\sigma(x) = (1 + e^{-x})^{-1} \tag{3}$$

where $\sigma(x)$ is the output of the normal sigmoidal activation function applied to inputs to unit y (seen in Equation 3), and y_i is the state of $unit_i$.

The final parameter τ is a time constant, also normally ranging between 0 and 1, which multiplicatively alters the rate at which units rise in activation. A value of τ close to 0 will mean that a unit rises in activation very slowly, and a value of 1 would mean that the unit would rise in activity at the rate of $1 - e^{-t}$, where t is the number of time steps at which input is provided at a constant rate. In all cases, there is some rise time associated with the activity of a unit.

The activation function described in Equation 2 defines a leaky integrator in which the closer a unit's activation is to its goal output (defined by the output of the standard sigmoidal transformation of Equation 3), the more slowly it approaches its target. Use of this system allows us to vary targets continuously over the course of an example and to train the network to be sensitive both to the current state of its units and to the inputs it is currently processing.

In order to apply back propagation through time to targets with continuous units, the backward propagation of error must also be made continuous. The network was thus trained using a variant of back propagation through time adapted for continuous units (Pearlmutter, 1989), shown in Equation 4. After a forward pass, weights are updated in the direction and to a magnitude made dependent on how much a small change in their values would affect error in the units to which they are connected. More concretely, the change in weight from unit i to unit j is made proportionate to the partial derivative of the overall error with respect to that weight.

$$\Delta w_{i,j} = -\varepsilon \frac{\partial E}{\partial w_{i,j}} \tag{4}$$

where ε is a small constant (the learning rate, set at .1 in our simulations), and

$$\frac{\partial E}{\partial w_{i,j}} = \frac{1}{\tau_j} \int_{t_1}^{t_0} y_i \, \sigma(x) z_j dt \tag{5}$$

where z is defined by the differential Equation 6:

$$\frac{dz}{dt} = \frac{1}{\tau_i} z_i - e_i - \sum j \frac{1}{\tau_j} w_{ij} \, \sigma_t \, (x_j) z_j \tag{6}$$

Importantly, in this version of back prop, the τ values of Equation 2 were also a trainable parameter of the network, and were also made sensitive to how minute changes in τ at time t would affect error rates, holding everything else constant, as in Equation 7:

$$\Delta\tau = -\mu \frac{\partial E}{\partial \tau_i} \tag{7}$$

where μ is another small constant (set at .005 in our simulations), and

$$\frac{\partial E}{\partial \tau} = -\tau \int_{t_0}^{t_i} z \frac{\partial y_i}{\partial t} dt \tag{8}$$

The τ values for all units in the network were initially set to 1, but (only) those of the hidden units and the clean-up units were trained and thus allowed to take on values that tended to minimize error in the network. In particular, some units could ramp up quickly while others ramp up more slowly. This aspect of the training regime is what allows the network to reach back somewhat further in time than the more standard discrete back propagation training regimes.

REFERENCES

Allen, J. (1997). Probabilistic constraints in acquisition. In A. Sorace, C. Heycock, & R. Shillcock (Eds.), *Proceedings of the GALA '97 Conference on Language Acquisition.* Edinburgh: University of Edinburgh Human Communications Research Centre.

Bates, E., & MacWhinney, B. (1982). A functionalist approach to language development. In E. Wanner & L. Gleitman (Eds.), *Language acquisition: The state of the art* (pp. 173–218). Cambridge, UK: Cambridge University Press.

Berwick, R., & Weinberg, A. (1984). *The grammatical basis of linguistic performance.* Cambridge, MA: MIT Press.

Bever, T. G. (1972). The limits of intuition. *Foundations of Language, 8,* 411–412.

Borer, H., & Wexler, K. (1992). Bi-unique relations and the maturation of grammatical principles. *Natural Language & Linguistic Theory, 10*(2), 147–189.

Bresnan, J. (1978). A realistic transformational grammar. In M. Halle, J. Bresnan, & G. Miller (Eds.), *Linguistic theory and psychological reality* (pp. 1–59). Cambridge, MA: MIT Press.

Browman, C., & Goldstein, L. (1989). Articulatory gestures as phonological units. *Phonology, 6,* 151–206.

Caramazza, A., & Zurif, E. (1976). Dissociation of algorithmic and heuristic processes in language comprehension. *Brain and Language, 3,* 572–582.

Chater, N., & Christiansen, M. H. (in press). Connectionism and natural language processing. In S. Garrod & M. Pickering (Eds.), *Language processing.* London: University College London Press.

Chomsky, N. (1961). Some methodological remarks on generative grammar. *Word, 17,* 219–239.

Chomsky, N. (1965). *Aspects of the theory of syntax.* Cambridge, MA: MIT Press.

Chomsky, N. (1981). *Lectures on government and binding.* Dordrecht, Netherlands: Foris.

Chomsky, N. (1995). *The minimalist program.* Cambridge, MA: MIT Press.

Clark, H. H., & Haviland, S. E. (1974). Psychological processes as linguistic explanation. In D. Cohen (Ed.), *Explaining linguistic phenomena* (pp. 91–124). Washington DC: Hemisphere.

Druks, J., & Marshall, J. C. (1991). Agrammatism: An analysis and critique, with new evidence from four Hebrew-speaking aphasic patients. *Cognitive Neuropsychology, 8*(6), 415–433.

Elman, J. L. (1990). Finding structure in time. *Cognitive Science, 14,* 179–211.

Fodor, J., Bever, T., & Garrett, M. (1974). *The psychology of language.* New York: McGraw-Hill.

Fodor, J. A. (1985). Precis of the modularity of mind. *Behavioral & Brain Sciences, 8*(1), 1–42.

Frazier, L., & Fodor, J. (1978). The sausage machine: A new two stage parsing model. *Cognition, 6,* 291–326.

Gold, E. M. (1967). Language identification in the limit. *Information and Control, 10*(16), 447–474.

Grimshaw, J., & Rosen, S. T. (1990). Knowledge and obedience: The developmental status of the binding theory. *Linguistic Inquiry, 21*(2), 187–222.

Grodzinsky, Y. (1990). *Theoretical perspectives on language deficits.* Cambridge, MA: MIT Press.

Grodzinsky, Y. (1995). Trace deletion, theta-roles, and cognitive strategies. *Brain and Language, 51*(3), 469–497.

Hildebrandt, N., Caplan, D., & Evans, K. (1987). The man_i left t_i without a trace: A case study of aphasic processing of empty categories. *Cognitive Neuropsychology, 4*(3), 257–302.

Hinton, G. E., & Shallice, T. (1991). Lesioning an attractor network: Investigations of acquired dyslexia. *Psychological Review, 98,* 74–95.

Hummel, J., & Biederman, I. (1992). Dynamic binding in a neural network for shape-recognition. *Psychological Review, 99*(3), 480–517.

Jackendoff, R. (1990). *Semantic structures.* Cambridge, MA: MIT Press.

Kelly, M. H. (1992). Using sound to solve syntactic problems: The role of phonology in grammatical category assignments. *Psychological Review, 99*(2), 349–364.

Lakoff, G. (1973). Fuzzy grammar and the performance competence terminology game. In C. Corum, C. T. Smith-Stark, & A. Weiser (Eds.), *Papers from the ninth regional meeting* (pp. 271–291). Chicago: Chicago Linguistic Society.

Langacker, R. W. (1986). An introduction to cognitive grammar. *Cognitive Science, 10*(10), 1–40.

Linebarger, M. C. (1989). Neuropsychological evidence for linguistic modularity. In G. N. Carlson & M. K. Tanenhaus (Eds.), *Linguistic structure in language processing* (pp. 197–238). Norwell, MA: Kluwer Academic.

Linebarger, M. C., Schwartz, M. F., & Saffran, E. M. (1983). Sensitivity to grammatical structure in so-called agrammatic aphasics. *Cognition, 13,* 361–392.

MacDonald, M. C., Pearlmutter, N. J., & Seidenberg, M. S. (1994). The lexical nature of syntactic ambiguity resolution. *Psychological Review, 101*(4), 676–703.

Maddiesson, I. (1997). Phonetic universals. In W. Hardcastle & J. Laver (Eds.), *The handbook of phonetic sciences.* Oxford, UK: Blackwell.

Milekic, S., Boskovic, Z., Crain, S., & Shankweiler, D. (1995). Comprehension of nonlexical categories in agrammatism. *Journal of Psycholinguistic Research, 24*(4), 299–311.

Miller, G. (1990). Wordnet: An on-line lexical database. *International Journal of Lexicography, 3*(4).

Omlin, C. W., & Giles, C. L. (1996). Extraction of rules from discrete-time recurrent neural networks. *Neural Networks, 9,* 41–52.

Pearlmutter, B. A. (1989). Learning state space trajectories in recurrent neural networks. *Neural Computation, 1,* 263–269.

Plaut, D. C. (1997). Structure and function in the lexical system: Insights from distributed models of word reading and lexical decision. *Language and Cognitive Processes, 12,* 765–805.

Plaut, D., McClelland, J., Seidenberg, M., & Patterson, K. (1996). Understanding normal and impaired word reading: Computational principles in quasi-regular domains. *Psychological Review, 103,* 56–115.

Saffran, J., Aslin, R., & Newport, E. (1996). Statistical learning by 8-month old infants. *Science, 274*(5294), 1926–1928.

Saffran, E., Schwartz, M., & Marin, O. S. M. (1980). The word order problem in agrammatism. *Brain and Language, 10,* 249–262.

Schutze, C. T. (1996). *The empirical base of linguistics.* Chicago: University of Chicago Press.

Seidenberg, M. (1997). Language acquisition and use—learning and applying probabilistic constraints. *Science, 275*(5306), 1599–1603.

Seidenberg, M. S., & McClelland, J. L. (1989). A distributed, developmental model of word recognition and naming. *Psychological Review, 96*(4), 523–568.

Smolensky, P. (1986). Information processing in dynamical systems: Foundations of harmony theory. In J. McClelland & D. Rumelhart (Eds.), *Parallel distributed processing: Explorations in the microstructure of cognition. Vol. 2: Psychological and biological models* (pp. 194–281). Cambridge, MA: MIT Press.

Stemberger, J. P. (1985). Bound morpheme loss errors in normal and agrammatic speech: One mechanism or two? *Brain and Language, 25*(2), 246–256.

Tesak, J., & Hummer, P. (1994). A note on prepositions in agrammatism. *Brain and Language, 46*(3), 463–468.

Trueswell, J., Tanenhaus, M. K., & Kello, C. (1993). Verb specific constraints in sentence processing: Separating effects of lexical preference from garden-paths. *Journal of Experimental Psychology: Learning, Memory and Cognition, 19*(3), 528–553.

van Gelder, T. (in press). The dynamical hypothesis in cognitive science. *Behavioral and Brain Sciences.*

von der Malsburg, C., & Schneider, W. (1986). A neural cocktail party processor. *Biological Cybernetics, 54,* 29–40.

Wexler, K., & Cullicover, P. (1980). *Formal principles of language acquisition.* Cambridge, MA: MIT Press.

Wexler, K., & Hamburger, H. (1973). On the sufficiency of surface data for the learning of transformational languages. In K. Hintikka, J. Moravcsik, & P. Suppes (Eds.), *Approaches to natural languages* (pp. 169–179). Boston: D. Reidel.

Williams, R., & Zipser, D. (1990). *Gradient based learning algorithms for recurrent connectionist networks* (Tech. Rep. No. NU-CCS-90-9). Boston, MA: College of Computer Science, Northeastern University.

Zurif, E., & Grodzinsky, Y. (1983). Sensitivity to grammatical structure in agrammatic aphasics: A reply to Linebarger, Schwartz and Saffran. *Cognition, 15,* 207–213.

Chapter **5**

Disambiguation and Grammar as Emergent Soft Constraints

Risto Miikkulainen
Marshall R. Mayberry, III
The University of Texas at Austin

How do people arrive at an interpretation of a sentence? The thesis put forth by this chapter is that sentence processing is not a crisp symbolic process, but instead emerges from bringing together a number of soft constraints, such as the syntactic structure of the sentence and semantic associations between its constituents. Consider the following sentence:

`The girl who the boy hit cried.`

This sentence has a relative clause attached to the main noun `boy`. Relative clauses have a simple structure, and it is easy to form deeper embeddings by repeating the structure recursively:

`The girl who the boy who the girl who lived next door blamed hit cried.`

This sentence contains no new grammatical constructs. The familiar embedded clause is used just three times, and the resulting sentence is almost incomprehensible. If humans were truly symbol processors, the number of levels would make no difference. It should be possible to handle each new embedding just like the previous one. Now consider a similar sentence:

`The car that the man who the dog that had rabies bit drives is in the garage.`

This sentence has the same grammatical structure as the previous one, and for a symbol processor it should be equally easy, or hard, to process. Yet somehow this sentence is understandable, whereas the previous one was not. The reason is that the previous sentence can only be understood based on syntactic analysis, whereas this one has strong semantic constraints between constituents. We know that dogs have rabies, people drive cars, and cars are in garages. These constraints make it possible for a human to understand the sentence even when they lose track of its syntactic structure.

These examples suggest that people are not pure symbol processors when they understand language. Instead, all constraints—grammatical, semantic, discourse, pragmatic—are simultaneously taken into account to form the most likely interpretation of the sentence. What could be the underlying mechanism for representing and combining such constraints?

A viable hypothesis is that the constraints arise from correlations with past experience. For example, if the sentence understander has often heard about dogs with rabies, rarely about people with rabies, and never about cars with rabies, he or she has a semantic constraint that favors attaching `rabies` to `dog` in the earlier sentence. It is not a hard rule, because it might also be that the man had rabies, but it is a soft constraint that makes those interpretations of the sentence where dog has rabies more prominent. When several such constraints are simultaneously taken into account, what results is the most likely interpretation of the sentence, given the past experience.

The theory of sentence processing as soft constraints can be made concrete in subsymbolic neural network models. Processing in neural networks is based on precisely the same principles. Trained to associate a set of input patterns to a set of output patterns, the network learns correlations in the data. For each new input pattern, the network then forms the most likely output given the training data (Hertz, Krogh, & Palmer, 1991). If the sentence interpretation task can be cast as a mapping from a sequence of input words to a representation of the meaning of the sentence, sentence processing can be modeled with neural networks. Such models can give us insight into the processes underlying sentence processing and suggest further hypotheses that can be tested experimentally.

Several subsymbolic models of sentence processing have been built around this idea (Elman, 1991; McClelland & Kawamoto, 1986; Miikkulainen & Dyer, 1991; St. John & McClelland, 1990). This chapter aims at two goals: (1) providing a clear, concrete example of soft constraints and how they are combined in sentence processing, and (2) showing how systems based on soft constraints can process language productively and systematically, while at the same time maintaining cognitive validity (as in the previous examples).

DISAMBIGUATION AS SOFT CONSTRAINTS

In understanding ambiguous sentences, humans seem to employ automatic and immediate lexical disambiguation mechanisms even when they are compelled to alternate between two or more senses of an ambiguous word. Consider the following sentence:

`The diplomat threw the ball in the ballpark for the princess.`

As a reader processes this sentence, he or she is inclined to interpret the word `ball` first as a dance event, then as baseball, and lastly again as dance. Yet this processing seems to occur at such a low level that the reader will hardly be aware that there was any conflict in his or her interpretation. There does not seem to be any conscious inferencing required, no moment's cogitation as might be observed if, say, the reader were instead asked to compute the product of two double-digit numbers.

Several models have been proposed to account for how ambiguities are resolved during reading. The three most prominent in recent years have been the context-dependent, the single-access, and the multiple-access models. The context-dependent model (Glucksberg, Kreutz, & Rho, 1986; Schvaneveldt, Meyer, & Becker, 1976) is based on the assumption that only one meaning of a word is activated at any given time, namely, the one most appropriate to the context in which the word occurs. The primary reason is that the context primes the meaning that is most applicable, while suppressing others. The single-access (or ordered-access) model (Forster & Bednall, 1976; Hogaboam & Perfetti, 1975; Simpson & Burgess, 1985) posits that only one active interpretation of an ambiguous sentence is maintained at any one time. If, in the course of processing the sentence, information is encountered that does not accord well with the active interpretation, then that interpretation is abandoned and a representation that accounts for the established information as well as for the current ambiguity is sought, most probably through backtracking to the point of ambiguity. The activation level of an interpretation is determined by the relative frequencies of the meanings of the word or words that are the source of the ambiguity. The search process for the appropriate meaning takes place serially, terminating when a fit is made, or retaining the most dominant meaning when no contextually relevant match can be found. In the strongest statement of the model (Hogaboam & Perfetti, 1975), only the most dominant meaning of an ambiguous word is retrieved first, regardless of whether the context supports a subordinate meaning.

The multiple-access model (Onifer & Swinney, 1981; Seidenberg, Tanenhaus, Leiman, & Bienkowski, 1982; Tanenhaus, Leiman, & Seidenberg, 1979), which is the most widely accepted, suggests that several interpretations may be actively maintained when ambiguous information is encountered. At a later time, when additional input allows resolving the ambiguity, only the appropriate interpretation is retained. However, not all of the interpretations may be maintained with equal activation levels. Rather, the strength of a particular activation would be proportional to the likelihood of that interpretation being the correct one. Unlike the single-access model, in which a single meaning is sought and selected, the multiple-access model claims that all meanings are activated simultaneously, regardless of context, but the context later influences selection of the most appropriate one. As is not unusual when aspects of behavior are supported by several more or less opposing models, refinements are proposed to include elements from several models. For example, Burgess and Simpson (1988) supported the multiple-access model, but suggested that meaning frequencies determine which interpretations reach the recognition threshold first. The role of context is to select which of the meanings remains activated.

This is where a subsymbolic neural network model can be used to gain insight into the process. It is possible to build a model of sentence understanding where ambiguity resolution occurs as an integral part of the task. Observing the behavior of the network, we see that multiple activation levels are maintained simultaneously during the processing of a sentence, and the various meanings of each word are activated to the degree that corresponds to the frequency with which that word has been associated to the previous words in the sentence in the past. This way, the model confirms Burgess and Simpson's (1988) theory computationally and suggests that semantic frequencies could play an even more fundamental role: Lexical ambiguity resolution emerges from combining the soft constraints posited by the semantic frequencies of the sentence constituents.

The Sentence Disambiguation Model

The sentence processing model is based on the Simple Recurrent Network (SRN) architecture (Elman, 1990), which has recently become a standard tool in subsymbolic natural language processing, including sentence and story understanding (Miikkulainen, 1993, 1996; St. John, 1992; St. John & McClelland, 1990) and learning grammatical structure (Elman, 1991; Servan-Schreiber, Cleeremans, & McClelland, 1991). In modeling disambiguation, the idea is to train the SRN to map a sequence of words to the case-role representation (Cook, 1989; Fillmore, 1968) of the sentence and observe the evolution of the sentence representation during parsing an ambiguous sentence. The parser was trained on sentences generated from two basic sentence templates:

1. `The` *agent* `threw the ball in the` *location* `for the` *recipient.*

2. The ball was thrown in the *location* for the *recipient* by the *agent.*

The fixed words in the template are indicated by courier typeface. The *location, recipient,* and *agent* stand for slots to be filled by actual content words. Depending on these words, the sentences could be interpreted as statements about baseball (e.g., The pitcher threw the ball in the ballpark for the fans), dance (The emcee threw the ball in the ballroom for the princess), or something rather ambiguous (The visitor threw the ball in the court for the victor). The output of the parser is one of two possible case-role representations:

1. *agent act:*tossed *patient:*baseball *location recipient*

2. *agent act:*hosted *patient:dance location recipient.*

Which of these two representations were used in the output depended on how strongly the words occupying the *location, recipient,* and *agent* slots were associated with baseball and dance.

Training Data. There were a total of 26 words in the lexicon: five for each of the three slots, two interpretations of throw and ball, and seven fixed words for the input sentences. Each were given hand-coded representation vectors according to the eight features shown in Table 5.1. The last component, sense, indicates how strongly the word is associated with tossed baseball (0) and hosted dance (1). For example, if a word rep-

TABLE 5.1
The Word Representation Vectors

Feature		*Set to 1 for words*
1.	Ball	ball, baseball, and dance
2.	Verb	thrown, tossed, and hosted
3.	Other	the and was
4.	Preposition	in, for, and by
5.	Location	the five *location* words and in
6.	Recipient	the five *recipient* words and for
7.	Agent	the five *agent* words and by
8.	Sense	Graduated according to word sense

Note. The words in the lexicon were encoded by these eight features. The first seven components were set to either 0 or 1; the right column lists those words that had the value 1. The *Sense* feature was used to indicate the degree of association to the two senses of throw and ball.

resentation has a sense of 0.25, it is more strongly associated with baseball than dance. Tables 5.2 and 5.3 summarize the sense values of each word.

This representation strategy was chosen because it makes the disambiguation process transparent. To see what the network is thinking, it is enough to look at the values of the sense units at its output. Distributed word representations (e.g., Miikkulainen, 1993) could be used as well, but sense would then have to be calculated based on distances between representation vectors.

The sense values were then used to put together a set of training sentences that made the sense associations explicit. For each possible sentence, the sense was computed by averaging the sense values of the individual words. Because these values were graduated in fourths, averaging over the three content words (per sentence) would result in twelfths. Thus, each input sentence was repeated 12 times in the training corpus, with the two possible case-role representations (i.e., senses) assigned in proportion of the sense value of the sentence. For example, if the passive sentence template is instantiated with the words `clubroom` (sense: 0.75), `fans` (0.00), and `emcee` (1.00), the following sentence is obtained:

```
The ball was thrown in the clubroom for the fans by the emcee.
```

Averaging the sense values gives $\frac{7}{12}$, or 0.5833. Accordingly, this sentence was repeated 12 times in the training corpus, with seven of the sentences assigned to `hosted dance` at the output and five to `tossed baseball`. Thus, in the experience of the parser, $58\frac{1}{3}\%$ of the contexts in which `ball`,

TABLE 5.2
Sense Values for the Content Words

Location	*Recipient*	*Agent*	*Sense*
ballpark	fans	pitcher	0.00
stadium	press	coach	0.25
count	victor	visitor	0.50
clubroom	vips	diplomat	0.75
ballroom	princess	emcee	1.00

TABLE 5.3
Sense Values for the Fixed Words

Fixed Words	*Sense*
tossed, baseball (output only)	0.00
ball, thrown, threw, the, was, in, for, by	0.50
hosted, dance (output only)	1.00

`clubroom`, `fans`, and `emcee` appeared were associated with `hosted dance`, and the remaining with `tossed baseball`. Hence, the dance sense would be slightly more dominant in this context and would be the preferred interpretation.

There are 125 possible combinations of the five words in the three categories. Each combination was used to instantiate the two sentence templates, giving a total of 250 sentences. Because each sentence is repeated 12 times, the training corpus is composed of 3,000 sentences. These sentences constitute the contextual history of the ambiguous words `throw` and `ball`. Active and passive constructions were used to contrast whatever priming effects the words might have on the general sense of the sentence; the fact that they represent different voices is not significant in this experiment.

Network Architecture. The SRN parser network (Fig. 5.1) has a single input assembly consisting of eight units, corresponding to the eight components in the word representation. The output layer is a concatenation of five word-representation assemblies, corresponding to the case-role assignment of the sentence.

At each step in the sequence, a word representation is loaded in the input assembly and the activity is propagated through the hidden layer to the output. The activity in the hidden layer (60 units wide) is saved in the previous hidden layer assembly, and used together with the word repre-

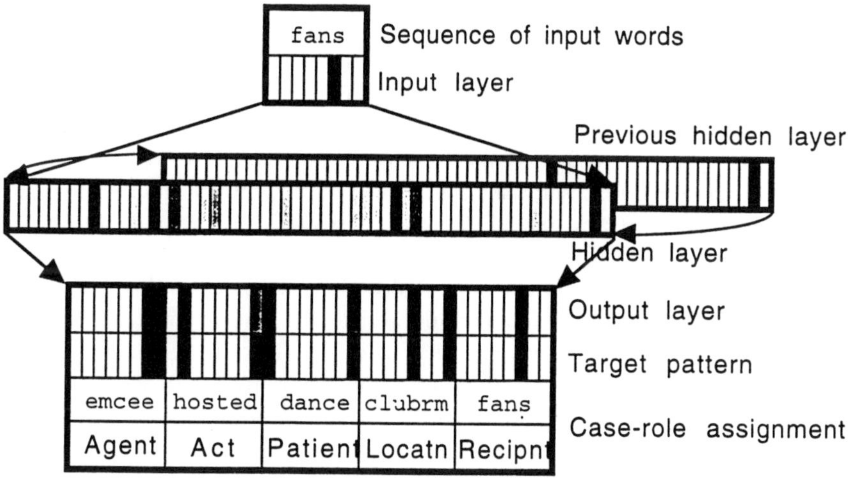

FIG. 5.1. The simple recurrent parser architecture. The model consists of a simple recurrent network trained through backpropagation to map a sequence of input word representations into a case-role representation of the sentence.

sentation as input to the hidden layer in the next step. Throughout the sequence, the complete case-role assignment is used as the training target, and the error is propagated and the weights are changed (through the backpropagation algorithm) at each step.

In effect, the network is trained to shoot for the complete sentence interpretation from the first word on. As a result, it learns to indicate the current sense of the sentence in the sense components of the *act* and the *patient* assemblies at its output. If the current interpretation is predominantly `hosted dance`, these components have high values, and if it is `tossed baseball`, they have low values. A completely ambiguous interpretation is indicated by activation 0.5.

In this experiment, the parser was trained with a 0.5 learning rate for 100 epochs, then 0.1 for 50 epochs, 0.05 for 5, and finally 0.01 until epoch 200. At this point, the average error per unit after reading a complete sentence was 0.024. The exact shape of the training schedule is not crucial: As long as the learning rate is gradually decreased, good results can be achieved reasonably quickly and reliably.

Disambiguation Results

The parser was tested with the same set of sentences used to train it to determine how well it captured the sense for each sentence. The theoretically optimal values for the sense outputs were obtained from the training data based on the distribution of the words in the sentences. The sense outputs of the network were then compared to the theoretical values. Generalization was not tested in this study because tight control over the theoretical frequencies was desired, and because good generalization is common for models of this type and offers no new perspective on the disambiguation problem.

The network captured the sense frequencies very accurately: The average error across the entire data set was found to be 0.0114 (0.0122 for the active constructions and 0.0107 for the passive). Moreover, all sentences where at least one of the content words was associated to a sense opposite of that of the other content words resulted in semantic flipping behavior. The processing of two sentences, one active and one passive, is analyzed in detail below. These examples are particularly interesting because they require revising the semantic interpretation twice during processing.

In reading the following active sentence,

```
The diplomat threw the ball in the ballpark for the princess
```

(see Fig. 5.2), the average of the two sense unit activations is initially very nearly 0.5, indicating no bias one way or the other (i.e., complete ambiguity) because the two senses of `ball` were equiprobable in the training set. After

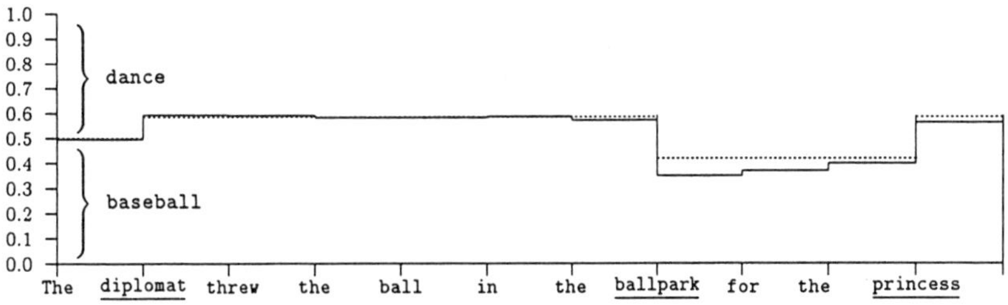

FIG. 5.2. Evolution of the interpretation of an active construction. The dotted line represents the theoretical sense level during processing the sentence, and the solid line indicates the average of the two sense output units. The content words have been underlined. The average error per unit on this sentence was 0.0180.

processing the word `diplomat`, the activation level rises to 0.5921 because a slight majority ($58\frac{1}{3}\%$) of the sentences in the training set in which `diplomat` occurs have the sense `dance`. In effect, `diplomat` has a priming effect on the interpretation of the rest of the words. The activation remains at roughly this level until the word `ballpark` is encountered. At this point, the semantic bias flips to 0.3481 in favor of `baseball`, because in the experience of the parser, a majority ($58\frac{1}{3}\%$) of the sentences in which both `diplomat` and `ballpark` appear have the sense of `baseball`. The activation stays below 0.5 until `princess` is read in as the last word, whereupon it flips back to 0.5610, indicating that the sentence is once again interpreted as `diplomat hosted dance`. The theoretical expectation of those sentences containing the words `diplomat`, `ballpark`, and `princess` is 0.5833, which is close to the activation level the parser finally settled on.

Similarly, in processing the following passive sentence,

```
The ball was thrown in the clubroom for the fans by the emcee
```

(see Fig. 5.3), after a long sequence of neutral fixed words, the network encounters `clubroom` and the interpretation becomes biased toward `dance`,

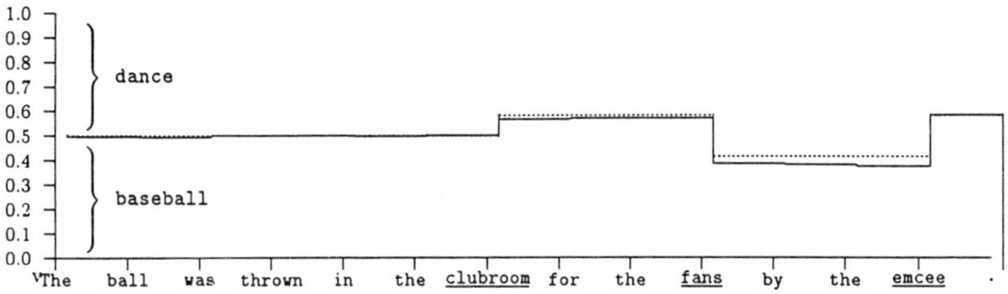

FIG. 5.3. Interpretation of a passive construction. The average error per unit on this sentence was 0.0123.

because $58\frac{1}{3}\%$ of the training sentences with `clubroom` have this sense. On reading `fans`, the interpretation flips toward `baseball`, because now the majority of sentences (again $58\frac{1}{3}\%$) with both `clubroom` and `fans` have the sense `baseball`. When the last word is read, the bias flips again back to `dance`, because a sentence with `clubroom`, `fans`, and `emcee` has an overall sense average 0.5833.

The biases and flips in the sense values are not particularly dramatic because the frequency differences are small in the training corpus. For a more stark contrast, these allocations could be adjusted; however, it is important that even such minor differences will result in reliable semantic revision behavior. In real-world data, there is a lot of noise in terms of accidental correlations, originating from many simultaneous tasks and goals. Even if the semantic regularities are only slightly stronger than the noise, the system will be able to utilize them to perform semantic interpretation reliably.

Conclusions From the Sentence Disambiguation Model

The most salient effect was that the semantic sense of an input sentence as a whole varied as a function of the semantic senses of its component words. It is this variation that accounts for the flipping behavior that we set out to model. Let us examine what insights the model can provide into human language comprehension.

A reader has experienced each word in a variety of contexts. Instead of regarding the word semantics as a collection of discrete and disjoint definitions in the lexicon, it is possible to view semantics simply as an encoding of all these past contexts. For most words, these contexts share much in common. For an ambiguous word, however, there are two or more distinctly different contexts, some of them more frequently observed than others. As a reader processes a sentence, there is an interaction between the semantics (i.e., past contexts) of each word and the evolving interpretation of the current sentence. Each word primes the interpretation according to the frequency with which the word has been associated with the current context in the past. After reading the whole sentence, all the past contexts of its constituent words are combined into the most likely interpretation. In other words, the interpretation emerges from the soft constraints among the sentence constituents.

Although sense disambiguation is just one small part of language processing, the same mechanisms could in principle be at work in language processing in general. Syntactic, semantic, discourse, and pragmatic structures manifest themselves as regularities in how language is used. These regularities can be captured and represented in the mind—and modified continuously with experience—to make language comprehension possible.

This approach is sufficient for capturing the statistical, automatic aspect of sentence comprehension, where the meaning of the sentence can be derived by combining prior contexts. However, it is not sufficient for explaining how dynamic inferencing comes about, where constraints that have previously been seen only in separate contexts must be combined. For example, in the following sentence (from Lange & Dyer, 1989),

`John put the pot in the dishwasher because the police were coming,`

if dishwasher and police have never been seen together before, there is no basis for statistically combining the contexts they represent. Washing dishes and waiting for the police to come does not combine into using a dishwasher to hide things. Such cases require a high-level process that has access to the statistical semantics but can use higher level constraints to combine constituents into novel representations. An approach and an example of such a process is described next.

PROCESSING GRAMMATICAL STRUCTURE

The problem of dynamic inferencing is particularly obvious in processing sentences with relative clauses. A subsymbolic neural network can be trained to form a case-role representation of each clause in a sentence like `The girl who liked the dog saw the boy`, and it will generalize to different versions of the same structure, such as `The dog who bit the girl chased the cat` (Miikkulainen, 1990). However, such a network cannot parse sentences with novel combinations of relative clauses, such as `The girl who liked the dog saw the boy who chased the cat`. This sentence has a relative clause in a new place in an otherwise familiar sentence structure and processing it would require combining contexts that the network has never seen together before. Such a lack of generality is a serious problem, given how effortlessly people can understand novel sentences.

This section demonstrates that dynamic inferencing is possible if the soft constraints are combined with high-level control. In the Subsymbolic Parser for Embedded Clauses (SPEC) model (Miikkulainen, 1996), the basic idea is to separate the tasks of segmenting the input word sequence into clauses, forming the case-role representations, and keeping track of the recursive embeddings into different modules. Each module is trained with only the most basic relative clause constructs, and the combined system is able to generalize to novel sentences with remarkably complex structure. Importantly, SPEC is not a neural network reimplementation of a symbol processor. It is a self-contained, purely subsymbolic neural network system, and exhibits the usual properties of such systems. For example, unlike symbolic parsers, the network exhibits plausible memory degradation as the depth of the center embeddings increases, its memory is primed by the earlier constituents in the sentence, and its performance is aided by semantic constraints between the constituents.

The SPEC Architecture

SPEC receives a sequence of word representations as its input, and for each clause in the sentence, forms an output representation indicating the assignment of words into case roles. The case-role representations are read off the system and placed in a short-term memory (currently outside SPEC) as soon as they are complete. SPEC consists of three main components: the *parser*, the *segmenter*, and the *stack* (Fig. 5.4).

The Parser. The parser is similar to the disambiguation network discussed earlier. It performs the actual transformation of the word sequence into the case-role representations. Words are represented distributively as vectors of gray-scale values between 0 and 1. The component values are initially assigned randomly and modified during learning by the FGREP method (Forming Global Representations by Extended backPropagation; Miikkulainen, 1993; Miikkulainen & Dyer, 1991) so that similar words will have similar representations. FGREP is a convenient way for forming these representations, but SPEC is not dependent on FGREP. The word representations could have been obtained through semantic feature encoding (McClelland & Kawamoto, 1986) as well, or even assigned randomly.

The case-role assignment is represented at the output of the parser as a case-role vector (CRV), that is, a concatenation of those three-word representation vectors that fill the roles of agent, act, and patient in the sentence (the representation was limited to three roles for simplicity). For example, the word sequence `the girl saw the boy` receives the case-role assignment agent = `girl`, act = `saw`, patient = `boy`, which is represented as the vector |`girl saw boy`| at the output of the parser network. When the sentence consists of multiple clauses, the relative pronouns are replaced by their referents: `The girl who liked the dog saw the boy` parses into two CRVs: |`girl liked dog`| and |`girl saw boy`|.

The parser receives a continuous sequence of input word representations as its input and its target pattern changes at each clause boundary. For example, in reading `The girl who liked the dog saw the boy`, the target pattern representing |`girl saw boy`| is maintained during the first two words, then switched to |`girl liked dog`| during reading the embedded clause, and then back to |`girl saw boy`| for the rest of the sentence. The CRV for the embedded clause is read off the network after `dog` has

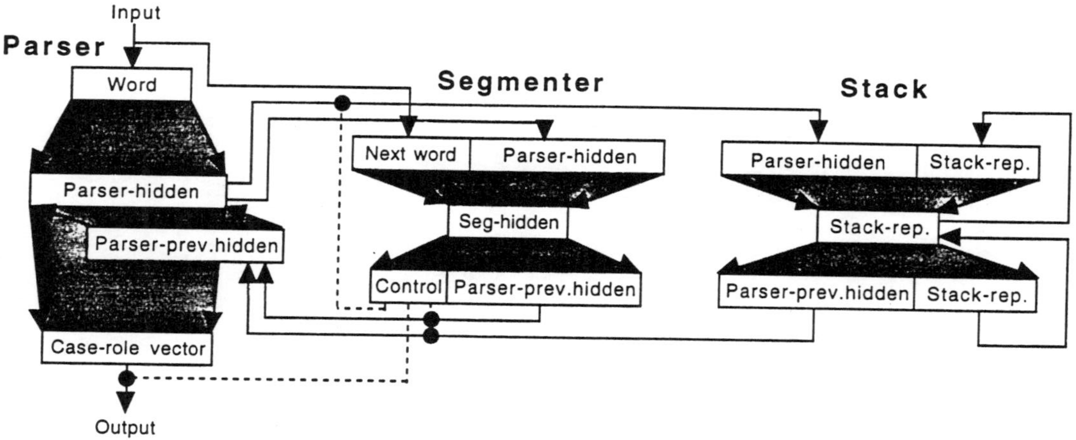

FIG. 5.4. The SPEC sentence-processing architecture. The system consists of the parser (a simple recurrent network), the stack (a RAAM network), and the segmenter (a feedforward network). The gray areas indicate propagation through weights, the solid lines stand for pattern transport, and the dashed lines represent control outputs (with gates).

been input and the CRV for the main clause after the entire sentence has been read.

When trained this way, the network is not limited to a fixed number of clauses by its output representation. Also, it does not have to maintain information about the entire past input sequence in its memory, making it possible in principle to generalize to new clause structures. Unfortunately, after a center embedding has been processed, it is difficult for the network to remember earlier constituents. This is why a stack network is needed in SPEC.

The Stack. The hidden layer of a simple recurrent network forms a compressed description of the sequence so far. The stack has the task of storing this representation at each center embedding and restoring it on return from the embedding. For example, in parsing `The girl who liked the dog saw the boy`, the hidden-layer representation is pushed onto the stack after `The girl`, and popped back to the parser's previous-hidden-layer assembly after `who liked the dog`. In effect, the SRN can then parse the top-level clause as if the center embedding had not been there at all.

The stack network is a model of one specific task of the human working memory. Although the working memory must be responsible for several different functions, in SPEC it is only required to perform the function of the symbolic stack; hence, it is called the stack network. It would of course be possible to just use a symbolic stack in SPEC, but as we will see in a later section, many of the cognitive effects in SPEC depend on subsymbolic representations of memory traces.

There are many ways to form such memory traces: for example, in the hidden layer of an SRN, or as attractors in a recurrent network (Hinton & Shallice, 1991; Plaut, 1991). From the point of view of SPEC, it is only important that the subsymbolic representation of the current state is a combined representation of the previous state and the new item. The most direct architecture for this task is the Recursive Auto-Associative Memory (RAAM; Pollack, 1990). RAAM is a three-layer backpropagation network trained to perform an identity mapping from input to output. As a side effect, its hidden layer learns to form compressed representations of the network's input–output patterns. These representations can be recursively used as constituents in other input patterns, and a potentially infinite hierarchical data structure, such as a stack, can be compressed this way into a fixed-size representation.

The input–output of the stack consists of the stack's top element and the compressed representation for the rest of the stack. Initially the stack is empty, which is represented by setting all units in the "stack-rep" assembly to 0.5 (Fig. 5.4). The first element, such as the hidden-layer pattern of the parser network after reading `The girl`, is loaded into the "parser-hidden" assembly, and the activity is propagated to the hidden layer. The hidden-layer pattern is then loaded into the stack-rep assembly at the input, and the stack network is ready for another push operation.

When the parser returns from the center embedding, the stored pattern needs to be popped from the stack. The current stack representation is loaded into the hidden layer, and the activity is propagated to the output layer. At the output, the "parser-prev. hidden" assembly contains the stored parser-hidden-layer pattern, which is then loaded into the previous-hidden-layer assembly of the parser network (Fig. 5.4). The stack-rep assembly contains the compressed representation for the rest of the stack, and it is loaded to the hidden layer of the stack network, which is then ready for another pop operation.

The Segmenter. The parser + stack architecture alone is not quite sufficient for generalization into novel relative clause structures. For example, when trained only with examples of center embeddings (such as in the previous section) and tail embeddings (like `The girl saw the boy who chased the cat`), the architecture generalizes well to new sentences such as `The girl who liked the dog saw the boy who chased the cat`. However, the system still fails to generalize to sentences like `The girl saw the boy who the dog who chased the cat bit`. Even though the stack takes care of restoring the earlier state of the parse, the parser has to learn all the different transitions into relative clauses. If it has encountered center embeddings only at the beginning of the sentence, it cannot generalize to a center embedding that occurs after an entire full clause has already been read.

The solution is to train an additional network, the segmenter, to divide the input sequence into clauses. The segmenter receives the current hidden-layer pattern as its input, together with the representation for the next input word, and it is trained to produce a modified hidden-layer pattern as its output (Fig. 5.4). The output is then loaded into the previous-hidden-layer assembly of the parser. In the middle of reading a clause, the segmenter passes the hidden-layer pattern through without modification. However, if the next word is a relative pronoun, the segmenter modifies the pattern so that only the relevant information remains. In the previous example, after `boy` has been read and `who` is next to come, the Segmenter generates a pattern similar to that of the parser's hidden layer after only `The boy` in the beginning of the sentence has been input.

In other words, the segmenter (1) detects transitions to relative clauses, and (2) changes the sequence memory so that the parser only has to deal with one type of clause boundary. This way, the parser's task becomes sufficiently simple so that the entire system can generalize to new structures.

The segmenter plays a central role in the architecture, and it is very natural to give it a complete control over the entire parsing process. Control is implemented through three additional units at the segmenter's output (Fig. 5.4). The units "push" and "pop" control the stack operations, and the unit "output" indicates when the parser output is complete and should be read off the system. This way the segmenter implements the high-level strategy of parsing sentences with relative clauses.

Although the segmenter was originally found necessary for computational reasons (i.e., for generalization to new sentence structures), it can also be motivated in a more general cognitive framework of perspective shifts in processing relative clauses (MacWhinney, 1977, 1988). When a relative pronoun is encountered, a perspective shift is initiated: The current clause is temporarily suspended, and a new clause is started with possibly new agent or patient, introducing a new perspective. The segmenter is a mechanism for carrying out this shift. It has a global view of the parsing process, allowing it to decide when a shift is necessary. It then utilizes the low-level mechanisms of working memory of the stack and the sequence memory of the parser to carry it out.

Experiments

The training and testing corpus was generated from a simple phrase structure grammar (Table 5.4). Each clause consisted of three constituents: the agent, the verb, and the patient. A relative `who`-clause could be attached to the agent or the patient of the parent clause, and `who` could fill the role of either the agent or the patient in the relative clause. In addition to `who` and `the`, the vocabulary consisted of the verbs `chased`, `liked`, `saw`, and `bit`, and the nouns `boy`, `girl`, `dog`, and `cat`. Certain semantic restrictions were imposed on the sentences. A verb could only have certain nouns as its agent and patient, as listed in Table 5.5. The grammar was used to generate all sentences with up to four clauses, and those that did not match the semantic restrictions were discarded. The final corpus consisted of 49 different sentence structures, with a total of 98,100 different sentences.

The SPEC architecture divides the sentence parsing task into three subtasks. Each component needs to learn only the basic constructs in its

TABLE 5.4
The Sentence Grammar

<table>
<tr><td>S</td><td>→</td><td>NP VP</td></tr>
<tr><td>NP</td><td>→</td><td>DET N | DET N RC</td></tr>
<tr><td>VP</td><td>→</td><td>V NP</td></tr>
<tr><td>RC</td><td>→</td><td>who VP | who NP V</td></tr>
<tr><td>N</td><td>→</td><td>boy | girl | | dog | cat</td></tr>
<tr><td>V</td><td>→</td><td>chased | liked | saw | bit</td></tr>
<tr><td>DET</td><td>→</td><td>the</td></tr>
</table>

TABLE 5.5
Semantic Restrictions

Verb	*Case-Role*	*Possible Fillers*
chased	Agent:	boy, girl, dog, cat
	Patient:	cat
liked	Agent:	boy, girl
	Patient:	boy, girl, dog
saw	Agent:	boy, girl, cat
	Patient	boy, girl
bit	Agent:	dog
	Patient:	boy, girl, dog, cat

task, and the combined architecture forces generalization into novel combinations of these constructs. Therefore, it is enough to train SPEC with only two sentence structures: (a) the two-level tail embedding (e.g., The girl saw the boy who chased the cat who the dog bit) and (b) the two-level center embedding (e.g., the girl who the dog who chased the cat bit saw the boy). The training set consisted of 100 randomly selected sentences of each type. In addition, the stack was trained to encode and decode up to three levels of pushes and pops.

The word representations consisted of 12 units. Parser's hidden layer was 75 units wide, segmenter's 50 units, and stack's 50 units. All networks were trained with online backpropagation with 0.1 learning rate and without momentum. Both the parser and the segmenter developed word representations at their input layers (with a learning rate of 0.001). The networks were trained separately (i.e., without propagation between modules) and simultaneously, sharing the same gradually developing word and parser-hidden-layer representations. The convergence was very strong. After 400 epochs, the average error per output unit was 0.018 for the parser, 0.008 for the segmenter (0.002 for the control outputs), and 0.003 for the stack.

SPEC's performance was then tested on the entire corpus of 98,100 sentences. The patterns in the parser's output assemblies were labeled according to the nearest representation in the lexicon. The control output was taken to be correct if those control units that should have been active at 1 had an activation level greater than 0.7, and those that should have been 0 had activation less than 0.3. Measured this way, the performance was excellent: SPEC did not make a single mistake in the entire corpus, neither in the output words nor in control. The average unit error was 0.034 for the parser, 0.009 for the segmenter (0.003 for control), and 0.005 for the stack. There was very little variation between sentences and words within each sentence, indicating that the system was operating within a safe margin.

The main result, therefore, is that the SPEC architecture successfully generalizes not only to new instances of the familiar sentence structures, but to new structures as well, thereby demonstrating dynamic inferencing. However, SPEC is not a mere reimplementation of a symbol processor. As SPEC's stack becomes increasingly loaded, its output becomes less and less accurate; symbolic systems do not have any such inherent memory degradation. An important question is whether SPEC's performance degrades in a cognitively plausible manner, that is, whether the system has similar difficulties in processing recursive structures as people do.

To elicit enough errors from SPEC to analyze its limitations, the stack's performance was degraded by adding 30% noise in its propagation. Such an experiment can be claimed to simulate overload, stress, cognitive impairment, or lack of concentration. The system turned out to be remarkably robust against noise. The average parser error rose to 0.058, but the system still got 94% of its output words right, with very few errors in control. As expected, most of the errors occurred as a direct result of popping back from center embeddings with an inaccurate previous-hidden-layer representation. For example, in parsing `The girl who the dog who the boy who chased the cat liked bit saw the boy`, SPEC had trouble remembering the agents of `liked`, `bit`, and `saw`, and patients of `liked` and `bit`. The performance depends on the level of the embedding in an interesting manner. It is harder for the network to remember the earlier constituents of shallower clauses than those of deeper clauses (Fig. 5.5). For example, SPEC could usually connect `boy` with `liked` (in 80% of the cases), but it was harder for it to remember that it was the `dog` who `bit` (58%) and even harder that the `girl` who `saw` (38%) in the previous example.

Such behavior seems plausible in terms of human performance. Sentences with deep center embeddings are harder for people to remember than shallow ones (Foss & Cairns, 1970; Miller & Isard, 1964). It is easier to remember a constituent that occurred just recently in the sentence than one that occurred several embeddings ago. Interestingly, even though SPEC was especially designed to overcome such memory effects in the parser's sequence memory, the same effect is generated by the stack architecture. The latest embedding has noise added to it only once, whereas the earlier elements in the stack have been degraded multiple times. Therefore, the accuracy is a function of the number of pop operations instead of a function of the absolute level of the embedding.

When the SPEC output is analyzed word by word, several other interesting effects are revealed. Virtually in every case where SPEC made an error in popping an earlier agent or patient from the stack, it confused it with another noun. In other words, SPEC performs plausible role bindings: Even if the exact agent or patient is obscured in the memory, it "knows"

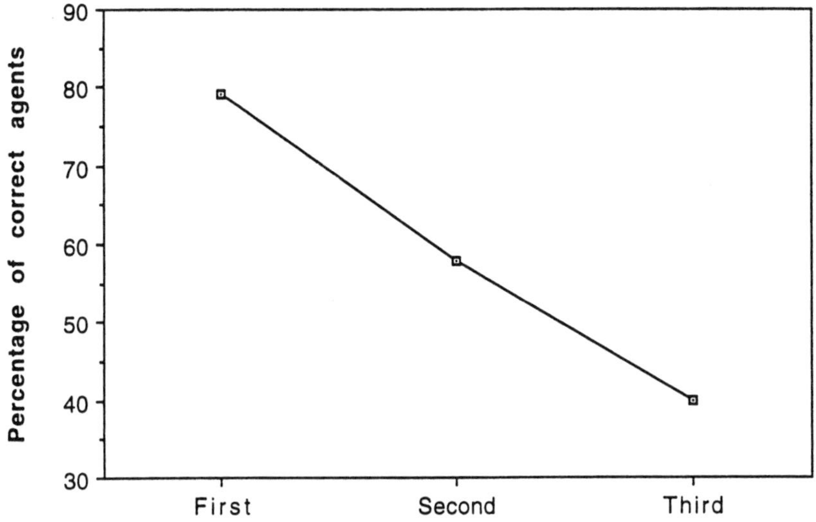

FIG. 5.5. Memory accuracy after return from center embeddings. The percentage of correctly remembered agents is plotted after the first, second, and third pop in sentences with three levels of center embeddings. Each successive pop is harder to do correctly. Similarly, SPEC remembers about 84% of the patients correctly after the first pop, and 67% after the second pop. The stack representations were degraded with 30% noise to elicit the errors.

that it has to be a noun. Moreover, SPEC does not generate the noun at random. Out of all nouns it output incorrectly, 75% had occurred earlier in the sentence. It seems that traces for the earlier nouns are discernible in the previous-hidden-layer pattern, and consequently, they are favored at the output. Such a priming effect is rather surprising, but it is very plausible in terms of human performance.

The semantic constraints (Table 5.5) also have a marked effect on the performance. If the agent or patient that needs to be popped from the stack is strongly correlated with the verb, it is easier for the network to remember it correctly (Fig. 5.6). The effect depends on the strength of the semantic coupling. For example, `girl` is easier to remember in `The girl who the dog bit liked the boy`, than in `The girl who the dog bit saw the boy`, which is in turn easier than `The girl who the dog bit chased the cat`. The reason is that there are only two possible agents for `liked`, whereas there are three for `saw` and four for `chased`. Whereas SPEC gets 95% of the unique agents right, it gets 76% of those with two alternatives, 69% of those with three, and only 67% of those with four.

A similar effect has been observed in human processing of relative clause structures. Half the participants in Stolz's (1967) study could not decode

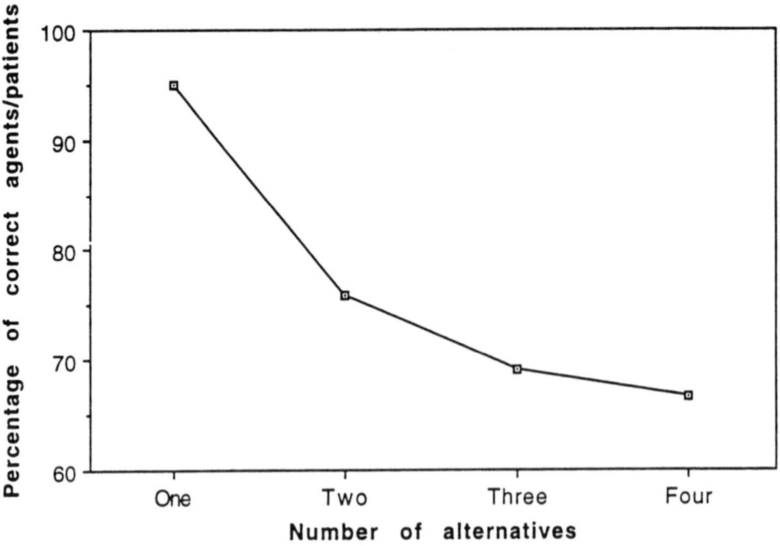

FIG. 5.6. Effect of the semantic restrictions on the memory accuracy. The percentage of correctly remembered agents and patients over the entire corpus is plotted against how strongly they were semantically associated with the verb. When there was only one alternative (e.g., `dog` as an agent for `bit` or `cat` as the patient of `chased`), SPEC remembered 95% of them correctly. There was a marked drop in accuracy with two, three, and four alternatives. The stack representations were degraded with 30% noise to elicit the errors.

complex center embeddings without semantic constraints. Huang (1983) showed that young children understand embedded clauses better when the constituents are semantically strongly coupled, and Caramazza and Zurif (1976) observed similar behavior in aphasics. This effect is often attributed to limited capability for processing syntax. The SPEC experiments indicate that it could be at least partly due to impaired memory as well. When the memory representation is impaired with noise, the parser has to clean it up. In propagation through the parser's weights, noise that does not coincide with the known alternatives cancels out. Apparently, when the verb is strongly correlated with some of the alternatives, more of the noise appears coincidental and is filtered out.

SPEC Conclusions

The main insight from SPEC is that whereas soft constraints alone may not be sufficient for dynamic inferencing, when combined with a high-level control mechanism, novel inputs can be processed productively and systematically. Trained on only the basic sentence constructs, SPEC generalized to a wide range of new sentence structures. At the same time, the model maintained cognitively valid behavior that arises from combining soft constraints. Deep embeddings are difficult, and semantic constraints aid in interpreting the sentence. The errors that the model produces are similar to human performance. This way SPEC goes a long way in answering the challenge posed in the beginning: how seemingly symbolic behavior such as sentence processing can emerge from interacting subsymbolic soft constraints.

The segmenter in SPEC is a first step toward high-level control in subsymbolic models. The segmenter was designed specifically for this task: It monitors the input sequence and the state of the parsing network, and issues input–output control signals for the stack memory and the parser itself at appropriate times. It has a high-level view of the parsing process, and uses it to assign simpler tasks to the other modules. In this sense, the segmenter implements a strategy for parsing sentences with relative clauses. It may be possible to build similar control networks for other linguistic tasks, or perhaps one sophisticated control network for language processing in general. Such control networks could play a major role in subsymbolic models of natural language processing and high-level reasoning in the future.

FUTURE OUTLOOK

If we adopt the view that language processing emerges from soft constraints, and that subsymbolic neural networks are a good model of this process, where will it take us? What are some of the future challenges and opportunities of this approach?

Although the subsymbolic models have been successful in demonstrating the utility of the approach, they are still mostly demonstrations of capabilities on toy problems. There are several technical challenges that need to be met before modeling language processing in a more realistic scale is possible. First, how can complex linguistic representations be encoded on subsymbolic neural networks? For example, how can an indefinite number of agents in a clause be represented, or clauses in a sentence, or sentences in a story, when there is a limited and fixed number of units in the network? Humans do not have a fixed upper bound, although there clearly are memory limits. It is possible that some kind of reduced descriptions, similar to those modeled by RAAM, are being formed. However, so far it has turned out to be very difficult to make the RAAM architecture generalize to new structures.

Second, how can we come up with training examples for realistic language processing? Although large corpora of unprocessed text are readily available, subsymbolic systems usually require more sophisticated information as targets, such as case-role representations for parsing. Building such corpora is very laborious, and it is unclear whether it is ever possible to have large enough training sets. It is also unclear what form the targets should take. In many cases, the targets represent some form of "language of thought," or internal representations of meaning, which are difficult to justify.

If these problems can be solved, however, it may be possible to build a subsymbolic model of sentence understanding that is capable of dynamic inferencing on general linguistic structure and that generates cognitively valid emergent behavior. The inferencing capabilities can be verified against the corpora. Cognitive validity can be tested at least in part by comparing the model with grammaticality judgments in humans (Gibson, 1997). What is difficult for humans should also be difficult for the model.

The model could then be used to generate predictions on areas where not much is known about human performance and processes. For example, predicting semantic complexity of sentences, or why is `pot + dishwasher + police` harder than `diplomat + ballpark + princess`? Predictions could be made on how ambiguities are resolved in general, showing how soft constraints on syntax, semantics, and frequency interact. The model can be lesioned, the resulting behavior observed and matched with human impairments, and predictions on possible sources of deficits made. More efficient ways of retraining the model could translate to suggestions on better ways of rehabilitating aphasics. Such a model could serve as a platform for motivating and testing theories about human language processing and its breakdown.

CONCLUSION

This chapter demonstrated, through subsymbolic neural network modeling, how sentence understanding could emerge from soft constraints. The constraints arise from regularities in the input and are applied through correlating the current input with past contexts, as illustrated in the sentence disambiguation task. The same processes may be active in complex grammar processing as well, as demonstrated by the SPEC model of relative clauses. Augmented by a high-level control process, soft constraints combine for productive and systematic processing of new sentence structures, with plausible cognitive effects. This way a seemingly symbolic linguistic behavior may in fact be an emergent property of soft constraints. The approach may eventually lead to testable, cognitively accurate natural language processing models with good predictive power.

ACKNOWLEDGMENT

This research was supported in part by the Texas Higher Education Coordinating Board under Grant ARP-444.

NOTE

Source code and online demos of the systems described in this chapter are available in the World Wide Web under URL http://www.cs.utexas.edu/users/nn.

REFERENCES

Burgess, C., & Simpson, G. B. (1988). Neuropsychology of lexical ambiguity resolution. In S. L. Small, G. W. Cottrell, & M. K. Tanenhaus (Eds.), *Lexical ambiguity resolution: Perspectives from psycholinguistics, neuropsychology and artificial intelligence* (pp. 411–430). San Mateo, CA: Morgan Kaufmann.

Caramazza, A., & Zurif, E. B. (1976). Dissociation of algorithmic and heuristic processes in language comprehension: Evidence from aphasia. *Brain and Language, 3*, 572–582.

Cook, W. A. (1989). *Case grammar theory*. Washington, DC: Georgetown University Press.

Elman, J. L. (1990). Finding structure in time. *Cognitive Science, 14*, 179–211.

Elman, J. L. (1991). Distributed representations, simple recurrent networks, and grammatical structure. *Machine Learning, 7*, 195–225.

Fillmore, C. J. (1968). The case for case. In E. Bach & R. T. Harms (Eds.), *Universals in linguistic theory* (pp. 0–88). New York: Holt, Rinehart & Winston.

Forster, K. I., & Bednall, E. S. (1976). Terminating and exhaustive search in lexical access. *Memory and Cognition, 4*, 53–61.

Foss, D. J., & Cairns, H. S. (1970). Some effects of memory limitation upon sentence comprehension and recall. *Journal of Verbal Learning and Verbal Behavior, 9*, 541–547.

Gibson, E. (in press). Syntactic complexity: Locality of syntactic dependencies. *Cognition*.

Glucksberg, S., Kreutz, R. J., & Rho, S. (1986). Context can constrain lexical access: Implications for interactive models of language comprehension. *Journal of Experimental Psychology: Learning, Memory, and Cognition, 12*, 323–335.

Hertz, J., Krogh, A., & Palmer, R. G. (1991). *Introduction to the theory of neural computation*. Reading, MA: Addison-Wesley.

Hinton, G. E., & Shallice, T. (1991). Lesioning an attractor network: Investigations of acquired dyslexia. *Psychological Review, 98*, 74–95.

Hogaboam, T. W., & Perfetti, C. A. (1975). Lexical ambiguity and sentence comprehension. *Journal of Verbal Learning and Verbal Behavior, 14*, 265–274.

Huang, M. S. (1983). A developmental study of children's comprehension of embedded sentences with and without semantic constraints. *Journal of Psychology, 114*, 51–56.

Lange, T. E., & Dyer, M. G. (1989). High-level inferencing in a connectionist network. *Connection Science, 1*, 181–217.

MacWhinney, B. (1977). Starting points. *Language, 53*, 152–168.

MacWhinney, B. (1988). The processing of restrictive relative clauses in Hungarian. *Cognition, 29*, 95–141.

McClelland, J. L., & Kawamoto, A. H. (1986). Mechanisms of sentence processing: Assigning roles to constituents. In J. L. McClelland & D. E. Rumelhart (Eds.), *Parallel distributed processing: Explorations in the microstructure of cognition, Volume 2: Psychological and biological models* (pp. 272–325). Cambridge, MA: MIT Press.

Miikkulainen, R. (1990). A PDP architecture for processing sentences with relative clauses. In H. Karlgren (Ed.), *Proceedings of the 13th International Conference on Computational Linguistics* (pp. 201–206). Helsinki, Finland: Yliopistopaino.

Miikkulainen, R. (1993). *Subsymbolic natural language processing: An integrated model of scripts, lexicon, and memory.* Cambridge, MA: MIT Press.

Miikkulainen, R. (1996). Subsymbolic case-role analysis of sentences with embedded clauses. *Cognitive Science, 20,* 47–73.

Miikkulainen, R., & Dyer, M. G. (1991). Natural language processing with modular neural networks and distributed lexicon. *Cognitive Science, 15,* 343–399.

Miller, G. A., & Isard, S. (1964). Free recall of self-embedded English sentences. *Information and Control, 7,* 292–303.

Onifer, W., & Swinney, D. A. (1981). Accessing lexical ambiguities during sentence comprehension: Effects of frequency of meaning and contextual bias. *Memory and Cognition, 9,* 225–226.

Plaut, D. C. (1991). *Connectionist neuropsychology: The breakdown and recovery of behavior in lesioned attractor networks.* Doctoral dissertation, Computer Science Department, Carnegie Mellon University, Pittsburgh, PA. Technical Report CMU-CS-91-185.

Pollack, J. B. (1990). Recursive distributed representations. *Artificial Intelligence, 46,* 77–105.

Schvaneveldt, R. W., Meyer, D. E., & Becker, C. A. (1976). Lexical ambiguity, semantic context, and visual word recognition. *Child Development, 48,* 612–616.

Seidenberg, M. S., Tanenhaus, M. K., Leiman, J. M., & Bienkowski, M. (1982). Automatic access of the meanings of ambiguous words in context: Some limitations of knowledge-based processing. *Cognitive Psychology, 14,* 489–537.

Servan-Schreiber, D., Cleeremans, A., & McClelland, J. L. (1991). Graded state machines: The representation of temporal contingencies in simple recurrent networks. *Machine Learning, 7,* 161–194.

Simpson, G. B., & Burgess, C. (1985). Activation and selection processes in the recognition of ambiguous words. *Journal of Experimental Psychology: Human Perception and Performance, 11,* 28–39.

St. John, M. F. (1992). The story gestalt: A model of knowledge-intensive processes in text comprehension. *Cognitive Science, 16,* 271–306.

St. John, M. F., & McClelland, J. L. (1990). Learning and applying contextual constraints in sentence comprehension. *Artificial Intelligence, 46,* 217–258.

Stolz, W. S. (1967). A study of the ability to decode grammatically novel sentences. *Journal of Verbal Learning and Verbal Behavior, 6,* 867–873.

Tanenhaus, M. K., Leiman, J. M., & Seidenberg, M. S. (1979). Evidence for multiple stages in the processing of ambiguous words in syntactic contexts. *Journal of Verbal Learning and Verbal Behavior, 18,* 427–440.

Chapter 6

Distributional Information in Language Comprehension, Production, and Acquisition: Three Puzzles and a Moral

Maryellen C. MacDonald
University of Southern California

One of the unwritten rules of psycholinguistics is that acquisition, comprehension, and production research each keeps to itself—the questions addressed in these three fields, and the researchers who ask them, overlap in only the most general ways. In acquisition, for example, researchers of necessity use comprehension and production measures in assessing children's progress, but the primary goal of much acquisition research is to understand how the child comes to acquire the grammar, or knowledge of the language, not how the child develops comprehension or production abilities. Production and comprehension research are similarly isolated; neither one digs deeply into the question of how the nature of these adult systems is constrained by the acquisition process, or whether production and comprehension processes exert significant constraints on each other. Research in each field has made a great deal of progress using this isolationist strategy, and there are clearly unique questions in each field for which the neighboring fields offer little insight. There do appear to be some important domains, however, where it appears that the isolationist approach is a distinct limitation. This is the theme of this chapter, which reviews three interrelated findings in comprehension, production, and acquisition research. In each case, the puzzling results in one field appear to have solutions in another. The intricate relationships between these puzzles hold important implications for the nature of the human language faculties and for the isolationist research strategies that currently dominate psycholinguistic research.

PUZZLE #1: A CURIOUS FINDING IN SYNTACTIC AMBIGUITY RESOLUTION

Syntactic processing, or *parsing*, is the subfield of language comprehension research that investigates how comprehenders uncover the syntax and meaning of sentences from the linear string of spoken or written input. Much of this research has used syntactic ambiguities, strings that temporarily have more than one syntactic interpretation, to study the parsing process. A great deal of recent parsing work shows the importance of lexical information in the ambiguity resolution process. This interest in lexical information is shared to some degree by every major approach to sentence processing but is represented most clearly within what is called the *constraint-based* approach, in which comprehension is achieved through the parallel satisfaction of multiple probabilistic constraints, including constraints from lexical representations. For example, MacDonald, Pearlmutter, and Seidenberg (1994) applied this approach to three major types of syntactic ambiguities in English and suggested that the initial interpretation of each of them is strongly guided by distributional information in the linguistic input concerning the relative frequencies of alternative lexical interpretations. An example of one of these ambiguities, the Main Verb/Reduced Relative ambiguity, is shown in (1):

1. a. *Temporary Main Verb/Reduced Relative Ambiguity:* The three men arrested . . .
   b. *Main Verb Interpretation:* The three men arrested the bombing suspects in a parking garage.
   c. *Reduced Relative Interpretation:* The three men arrested in the parking garage were wanted in connection with the bombing of the oil refinery.

In this case, interpretation of the ambiguity is constrained by the frequency with which the ambiguous verb (here, *arrested*) participates in transitive and passive structures, of which reduced relative clauses are a special type (MacDonald, 1994; MacDonald et al., 1994; Trueswell, 1996). Interpretation of this structure is also constrained by combinatorial lexical information, such as the plausibility of the initial noun phrase (NP) filling the agent or patient role of the verb (MacDonald, 1994; McRae, Spivey-Knowlton, & Tanenhaus, 1998; Pearlmutter & MacDonald, 1992; Tabossi, Spivey-Knowlton, McRae, & Tanenhaus, 1994; Trueswell, Tanenhaus, & Garnsey, 1994). Similar simple and combinatorial lexical effects for this and other ambiguities have made a strong case for the importance of distributional information, particularly lexical information, in the earliest stages of syntactic processing, a key claim of constraint-based models of language comprehension.

One syntactic ambiguity stands out as a prominent exception to this pattern of lexical sensitivity. This ambiguity is a particular kind of modification ambiguity, in which a phrase can modify (or in syntactic structure terms, *attach to*) one of several elements earlier in the sentence. The particular modification ambiguity of importance here is one in which a prepositional or adverbial phrase can modify one of two verbs, as in (2). Example (2a) shows a fully ambiguous structure; (2b) shows an example in which verb tense disambiguates the sentence in favor of the *local modification* interpretation, in which the adverb *yesterday* modifies the nearby verb *left* rather than the more distant phrase *will say*; and (2c) shows a sentence with distant modification, in which *tomorrow* is not modifying the local verb, *left*, but is instead modifying the distant verb, *will say*.

2. a. *Verb Modification Ambiguity:* John said that Bill left yesterday.
   b. *Local Modification:* John will say that Bill left yesterday.
   c. *Distant Modification:* John will say that Bill left tomorrow.

English speakers have an extremely strong preference for local modification for this structure, as in (2b), and sentences like (2c) are typically perceived to be very difficult and awkward. Many researchers have assumed that this preference emerges from a general operating principle of the syntactic parsing mechanism to prefer the most local modification; such principles have been variously called Right Association (Kimball, 1973), Late Closure (Frazier, 1987), and Recency (Gibson, Pearlmutter, Conseco-Gonzales, & Hickok, 1996). A striking feature of the verb modification ambiguity is that unlike so many other syntactic ambiguities in English, the choice of words in the sentence seems to have little effect on the local modification preference. Thus, we could change the verbs *say* and *left* in (2) to different verbs and change the modifying adverb to a different word or even a prepositional phrase like *in the morning*, and the local modification preference persists across all of these variations in the lexical content. This resistance to lexical influence is one of the primary reasons why these ambiguities have been thought to support a principle-based approach and to be the Achilles' heel of the constraint-based approach to syntactic processing, as lexical information is such a crucial kind of constraint within that framework.

On closer examination, the situation is both more complicated and more interesting than this short description would lead us to believe. If this ambiguity were truly immune to lexical effects, that fact would be a problem for every theory of sentence processing, as essentially every theory incorporates lexical information during at least some stage of the syntactic ambiguity resolution process. Thus, models in which lexical information does not affect initial interpretation but constrains later interpretation and reanalysis, such as the Garden Path Model (Frazier, 1987) and Tuning (Mitchell, Cuetos, Corley, & Brysbaert, 1995), would be faced with the question of why the lexical information in (2) seems so ineffective in promoting the distant modification case, whereas lexical information in other ambiguities appears to have a strong effect in eventual interpretation. Fortunately for all theories, it turns out that there are real, although extremely subtle, effects of lexical information on the interpretation of these ambiguities. For example, Fodor and Inoue (1994) noted that when the modifying expression contains a negative polarity item, such as *any more,* which must modify a negated verb, this ambiguity is readily interpreted with distant modification, as in (3), where *any more* modifies the distant negated verb *doesn't tell* rather than the local verb *thinking.*

3. John doesn't tell us what he's thinking about any more.

The question still remains, however, why lexical information typically carries so little weight in the interpretation of this ambiguity. From the perspective of constraint-based theories, which stress the sensitivity to distributional information in the language, a likely answer is that there is something about the distributional information in the input that causes other constraints to be weighed much more heavily than lexical ones in interpreting sentences with this ambiguity. Of course framing the question in this way is not itself a solution, but it offers a particular direction for the research, namely identifying the nature of the relevant distributional information and exploring how this information constrains the ambiguity resolution process. This is the approach that I pursue here. The account is both distributional and rather Gricean in character, in the sense outlined by Frazier and Clifton (1996), in that I suggest that the sequence *verb . . . verb modifier* has come to be interpreted with the modifier modifying the local verb because this is essentially the only syntactic structure that can convey this meaning, whereas there exist better alternative syntactic structures to convey the distant modification interpretation. These alternative structures are "better" not from the point of view of comprehension, but from production. In other words, the solution to the puzzle of comprehending verb modification ambiguities is revealed in part through an understanding of how production processes work.

Phrase Length and Production Constraints

When there is an option for ordering phrases in alternative ways in English, choice of phrase order is strongly governed by the length of the phrases, such that the short phrase tends to be uttered first (Hawkins, 1994; Ross, 1967; Wasow, 1997). Some common examples include verb + particle constructions, as in (4), and *heavy-NP shift* constructions in (5). In both of these constructions, there is a general preference to place the direct object NP immediately after the verb, as in the (a) examples; an alternative ordering, as in the (b) examples, is quite awkward or ungrammatical, indicated by the asterisk. When the NP becomes particularly long, however, preferences to produce a short-before-long phrase order promotes an alternative phrase ordering in which the NP is not adjacent to the verb (V), as in the (c) examples. Most speakers of English rate the (c) versions to be at least as acceptable as the (d) versions, in which the V–NP adjacency is maintained despite the long NP.

4. a. Mary threw it out.
   b. *Mary threw out it.
   c. Mary threw out the old chicken salad that had sat in the refrigerator for four days.
   d. ?Mary threw the old chicken salad that had sat in the refrigerator for four days out.

5. a. Mary ate chicken for lunch.
   b. *Mary ate for lunch chicken.
   c. Mary ate for lunch the old chicken salad that had sat in the refrigerator for four days.
   d. ?Mary ate the old chicken salad that had sat in the refrigerator for four days for lunch.

Within most accounts of speech production, this preference for the short–long phrase ordering is assumed to stem from the incremental nature of speech production processes (Bock, 1987; Kempen & Hoenkamp, 1987). In this view, the ordering of words and phrases in production is constrained in part by these elements' accessibility, where more accessible words and phrases are ones that are higher in frequency, have more recently been primed, or have some other property that makes retrieval of word forms relatively easy (Bock, 1987). Several researchers have hypothesized that on average, short phrases should require less processing and be more accessible than long ones, so that on many occasions, a shorter phrase is ready to be articulated before a longer phrase (DeSmedt, 1994; Stallings, MacDonald, & O'Seaghdha, 1997).

Given these production constraints, speakers and writers will tend to produce utterances in which short phrases precede long phrases, creating particular distributional patterns in the language. Moreover, exceptions to this phrase ordering should tend to appear for a reason, for example, if the long–short order is necessary to convey a particular meaning; some of the modification ambiguities discussed earlier are exceptions of just this sort. Consider the examples in (6), where the local site for modification, the second verb (*left*), is part of an embedded sentential complement of the distant verb (*said*). From the perspective of length and phrase ordering, such sentences are interesting in that a long (underlined) phrase, that John had left, precedes a short (italicized) phrase, *yesterday,* seeming to violate the length ordering constraints in English. This phrase order is necessary, however, to modify the second verb and convey the meaning that the leaving event, not the saying event, was yesterday. Alternative orders that follow the general short–long phrase ordering preference, as in (6b–c), do not convey the intended meaning; they instead unambiguously convey distant modification, such that the saying event was yesterday.

6. a. Bill said that John had left *yesterday*. (Long–short order)
   b. Bill said *yesterday* that John had left. (*Short*–long order)
   c. *Yesterday*, Bill said that John had left. (*Short*–long order)

This example shows that the technically ambiguous construction *verb . . . verb . . . modifier,* as in (6a), is actually the required ordering for expressing the meaning in which the modifier modifies the local site (the second verb, *left*). This construction can also be used to express the meaning in which the distant verb is modified by *yesterday*, but production constraints in English discourage this usage in favor of structures like (6b–c), in which the short phrase can precede the long one. Production constraints therefore create a distributional pattern in the language in which the long–short order is strongly associated with local modification rather than distant modification. Comprehenders have been shown to be exquisitely sensitive to distributional information of this sort, and they should therefore tend to interpret modification ambiguities in a way that is consistent with distributional information. If so, the local modification preference for structures such as (6a) emerges from comprehenders' sensitivity to distributional information, which in turn emerges from the incremental nature of speech production. There is therefore no need to postulate some local modification parsing principle such as Right Association (Kimball, 1973), Late Closure (Frazier, 1987), or Recency (Gibson et al., 1996) in order to account for interpretation preferences in this construction.

Not only does this account obviate the need for a parsing principle, it makes predictions for variations in the degree of local modification preference across individual sentences, whereas the parsing principles do not. The distributional information relevant to ambiguity resolution in this case specifically concerns those sentences in which a long phrase precedes a short phrase, because the distributional patterns emerge directly from length-sensitive production constraints. Pressure to utter the modifying adverbial expression before the embedded verb phrase (VP) should not exist if the embedded phrase is not longer than the modifier, as in (7). Here, the modifying adverbial phrase (*very much* or *very slowly*) is longer than the embedded phrase (*swimming*), in contrast to (6). For sentences with short embedded phrases, therefore, comprehenders should not show a strong tendency to interpret a sentence-final ambiguous modifier in favor of local modification, because the length-based production constraint that promotes this interpretation in (6) is not present for sentences with short embedded phrases such as (7).

7. a. Short embedded phrase, Distant modification Mary likes swimming very much.
   b. Short embedded phrase, Local modification Mary likes swimming very slowly.

Thornton and MacDonald (1998) tested these length-based predictions in a self-paced reading experiment. They manipulated the length of the phrase containing the local verb in ambiguous verb modification constructions. In one condition, shown in (8), the embedded phrase was quite long and substantially longer than the modifying phrase at the end of the sentence. In another condition, shown in (7), the embedded phrase was only one or two words long and was as short or shorter than the modifying phrase. Thornton and MacDonald also manipulated the material in the modifying phrase so that it clearly modified either the distant verb (7a, 8a) or the local verb (7b, 8b), thereby providing a disambiguation to the temporary modification ambiguity.

8. a. Long embedded phrase, Distant modification Mary likes it when the dolphins at Sea World are swimming very much.
   b. Long embedded phrase, Local modification Mary likes it when the dolphins at Sea World are swimming very slowly.

Whereas a local attachment parsing strategy would predict shorter reading times for local modification than distant modification independent of the length of phrases in the sentence, the distributional hypothesis advanced here predicts an interaction, such that modification of the local verb is preferred over the distant only when the local verb is embedded in a long phrase. This long phrase creates a sentence with a long–short phrase order, which is the obligatory order for local modification but is strongly dispreferred for distant modification, owing to violations of the short–long constraint. When the local verb is embedded in a short phrase, however, this phrase and the ambiguous modifier are about the same length, so no ordering constraints are violated. In this case, either modification should be acceptable, and no differences in reading times are predicted.

These predictions were confirmed with a reliable Phrase Length × Interpretation interaction in reading times at the disambiguation region. In the long condition, reading times at the disambiguation (*very much* vs. *very slowly*) were a reliable 20 msec per word longer for the distant modification than for the local modification. When the phrase containing the local verb site was short, however, reading times actually revealed a nonsignificant preference for distant modification. In other words, manipulations of phrase length dictated the presence or absence of a local modification preference in ambiguity resolution, supporting the importance of distributional information concerning phrase length in interpretation of this ambiguity.

Summary

By using an independently motivated account of production (Bock, 1987; Kempen & Hoenkamp, 1987) and an independent account of comprehenders' sensitivity to distributional regularities in the input (e.g., MacDonald et al., 1994; Tabossi et al., 1994), an approach to modification ambiguity emerges that does not require any local modification parsing principles in order to account for interpretation preferences. Moreover, this distributional account offers an explanation of why these preferences vary with the length of certain phrases in the sentence, in contrast to the parsing principles.

This account also sketches a direction for future research into the interpretation of other kinds of modification ambiguities. It offers an explanation for why there is a strong local modification preference for structures in which the local site is a verb phrase like (6) but much weaker interpretation preferences in two other constructions in which the local site is an NP, as in complex NP modification such as (9), in which both local and distant sites are NPs, and ambiguities in which a modifying prepositional phrase (PP) can attach to either a VP (the distant site) or an NP (the local site), as in (10). In each of these examples, the modifier and the head of the phrase being modified are underlined.

9. a. Distant modification: The cat on the rug with long whiskers
   b. Local modification: The cat on the rug with long tassels

10. a. Distant modification: Cynthia saw the woman from the balcony.
    b. Local modification: Cynthia saw the woman from Toledo.

The explanation for the stronger preferences in verb modification ambiguities than in the complex NP constructions (9) or VP–NP constructions (10) is that the verb modification ambiguity is created by embedding an entire sentence (containing the local verb site) within a VP (6). Embedded sentences tend to be long, so that a large number of words typically intervenes between the distant site and the modifier. By contrast, in the complex NP construction (9) and the VP–NP construction (10), there is no embedded sentence, and the local site is an NP that tends not to be longer than the modifying phrase at the end of the sentence. Phrase length therefore exerts little effect on the ordering of phrases in the constructions exemplified in (9–10), so that distributional information concerning phrase length does not strongly promote local attachment in these cases.[1] The preferences that are observed for these constructions are largely due to other constraints, primarily lexical and discourse factors (Altmann & Steedman, 1988; Spivey-Knowlton & Sedivy, 1995; Thornton, MacDonald, & Gil, 1998).

The answer to the first puzzle, then, comes from an understanding of production processes and how these processes might provide distributional information relevant to language comprehension. The next puzzle arises from a deeper scrutiny of the very same production processes that lead to the solution of Puzzle #1. A closer look at length effects in production reveals that these processes may actually pose a problem for the incremental models of production that proved so useful for solving Puzzle #1. Again, framing the solution in terms of distributional information offers a perspective that is not a dominant theme in syntactic production research.

PUZZLE #2: EXCEPTIONS TO INCREMENTAL SPEECH PRODUCTION?

English is relatively inflexible in its ordering of phrases, but as we have seen, variations in the length of phrases promote some nonstandard (typically called *shifted*) phrase orders in production. One such structure, illustrated in (5c), has been termed *heavy-NP shift* because it appears when the direct object NP is very long or "heavy" (see Hawkins, 1994; Wasow, 1997, for review). More recent research has suggested that the relative length of the NP and the other constituent (a prepositional or adverbial phrase) is a better determinant of shifting than simply the length of the NP alone (Hawkins, 1994). Sensitivity to the relative length of the phrases is exactly what would be expected from an incremental production account, so that the choice of ordering of phrases in the VP appears to be constrained by

[1]One prediction of this account is that manipulations of the length of the local NP site in (9–10) should affect attachment preferences in these constructions just as in the VP site attachment structure. However, it is very difficult to test this prediction, because manipulation of the length of the NP requires manipulating the amount of prenominal modification the NP receives, and this prenominal modification has been shown to affect attachment ambiguities in at least complex NP constructions (Thornton et al., 1998). Thus, any manipulation of length is confounded with another factor with demonstrated effects on ambiguity resolution.

how accessible each phrase is for the next phase of the production process (DeSmedt, 1994). Moreover, Firbas (1966) suggested that there is a discourse component to heavy-NP shift, in that previously described, or *given* information tends to precede new information in utterances. In this view, the length of the NP is not the basic motivation for shifting but rather a correlate of givenness; new information tends to be expressed using more words than previously given information. The incremental approach clearly has something to say here, in that the words and phrases conveying given information have typically been recently uttered in the discourse, and they will tend to be primed and thus more accessible than the words and phrases that convey the new information. The incremental approach is attractive in that it suggests that phrase length and givenness are not competing explanations for heavy-NP shifting, but rather that phrase accessibility, by virtue of length, givenness, or other factors, governs phrase ordering and thus heavy-NP shifting during production.

The puzzle concerning heavy-NP shifting and incremental production processes is that there seem to be some significant aspects of heavy-NP shifting that are not compatible with a strictly incremental approach to production processes. Stallings et al. (1998) investigated the role of verbs in shifting behavior in a series of experiments in which participants uttered sentences using a set of phrases that they saw on a computer screen. In critical trials, the phrases could be combined to make either a heavy-NP shifted sentence or a sentence with a "basic" V NP PP order in the VP. Stallings et al. measured the frequency with which speakers uttered shifted versus basic order sentences.

Stallings et al. (1998) manipulated the kind of verb that appeared in the sentence fragments on the screen. In one condition, the verb was a simple transitive verb that did not allow other argument structures (except possibly intransitive structures), such as *transferred* or *reviewed.* In a second condition, the verbs, in addition to allowing transitive structures, also permitted sentential complement constructions, in which one sentence, often introduced with *that,* is embedded in another sentence, as in *Mary revealed that the book was missing.* Such verbs are called NP/S verbs in the sentence comprehension literature, reflecting the fact that they can take both NP direct objects (the simple transitive structure) and sentential (S) complements. In all cases, the verbs appeared on screen with a subject, direct object, and PP (never an S-complement); thus, the verb type manipulation refers to the number and kinds of other structures afforded by verbs, and the critical stimulus items always formed simple transitive sentences.

Stallings et al. (1998) found that sentence fragments containing NP/S verbs were uttered in a shifted form about twice as often as those with the simple transitive verbs. This result, which was replicated across a series of experiments using three different production methods, indicates that lexical properties of the verb constrained the ordering of phrases later in the sentence. In other words, something about the distributional properties of verbs in transitive and S-complement structures affects whether transitive structures will be uttered in a shifted versus basic form.

Why would verb properties affect the ordering of postverbal phrases during sentence production? Stallings et al. (1998) hypothesized that each verb has a "shifting disposition" reflecting past experiences with various syntactic structures. A key feature of this argument is the observation that in heavy-NP shift, the verb and direct object NP are not adjacent to one another in the sentence. Stallings et al. suggested that the frequency with which a verb participates in various kinds of nonadjacent constructions affects a verb's disposition to allow shifting of the material in the VP. They identified two other nonadjacent constructions in addition to heavy-NP shift itself. One is the so-called verb-particle structures previously shown in (4), in which the verb and direct object are separated by a verb particle such as *up, out, on,* and so forth, as in *throw out the trash, clean up the room, reel in the fish.* The second kind of nonadjacent structure appears in S-complement constructions. When a verb that has a sentential complement is modified with a prepositional or adverbial phrase in English, the modification may appear between the verb and the complement, as in the examples in (11), where the underlined modifying phrases separate the verb from its S-complement.

11. a. The eccentric director reported <u>in a loud voice</u> that the cast party was canceled.
    b. The young woman discovered <u>almost immediately</u> that her new roommates were slobs.

Given that verb modification is a common occurrence in English, verbs that participate in S-complement constructions will often participate in the constructions shown in (11), which place the verb's complement nonadjacent to the verb. Stallings et al. (1998) hypothesized that a verb's participation in nonadjacent S-complement structures increases a verb's disposition to participate in other nonadjacent structures, including heavy-NP shift.[2] For example, the fact that the NP/S verbs *reported* and *discovered*

[2]Wasow (1997) suggested that the relevant generalization is not about nonadjacent structures but rather about the adjacency of verbs and prepositional phrases, that is, verbs that frequently occur adjacent to PPs are frequently found in shifted constructions. In support of this claim, he cited corpus data showing a large number of heavy-NP shifted sentences containing verbs that enter into verb-particle constructions. This account is simpler than the one proposed by Stallings et al. (1998), in that it refers to adjacency of two elements rather than the nonadjacency of two elements because of an intervening third element. The two accounts make different predictions concerning the rate of shifting in sentences with

participate in nonadjacent structures like those in (11) makes them more able to participate in the heavy-NP shift structures shown in (11), whereas simple transitive verbs such as *sang* and *uncovered,* which have not had the nonadjacent experience in S-complement structures like (12), are less compatible with shifting. This comparison between verb types is shown in (12-13); the NP/S verbs in (12) tend to be much better in shifted structures than the simple transitive verbs in (13) in both production measures and acceptability ratings (Stallings et al., 1998). Thus, the choice of syntactic structure in production, although clearly influenced by the accessibility of various planned constituents during the production process, is also strongly influenced by distributional information.

12. a. The eccentric director reported in a loud voice the songs that would be used during the opening act of the play.
    b. The young woman discovered almost immediately the richly embroidered sack of semi-precious stones.

13. a. The eccentric director sang in a loud voice the songs that would be used during the opening act of the play.
    b. The young woman uncovered almost immediately the richly embroidered sack of semi-precious stones.

Stallings et al. (1998) argued that shifting disposition was a property of the distributional information for each individual verb concerning its frequency of participation in nonadjacent structures. This sort of precise lexical knowledge, the frequency with which verbs participate in alternative syntactic structures, is exactly the sort of information that proponents of constraint-based accounts of language point to in accounting for a large number of syntactic processing phenomena (e.g., MacDonald, 1994; MacDonald et al., 1994; McRae et al., 1998; Pearlmutter & MacDonald, 1992; Tabossi et al., 1994; Trueswell et al., 1994). Thus, production, although it does appear to have an incremental component, also appears to have a

---

biased-intransitive verbs, which are verbs that can be used transitively but are more often used intransitively, such as *walk, move, work,* and so forth. These verbs do not enter into verb-particle constructions, but they often occur adjacent to a prepositional phrase (e.g., *walk in the park, move to the left*), and thus Wasow's (1997) formulation predicts that these verbs should frequently appear in heavy-NP shifted sentences. The Stallings et al. (1998) nonadjacency account makes the opposite prediction: These verbs do not typically occur with direct objects in nonadjacent position, by virtue of the fact that they rarely occur with any direct objects, and they are therefore poor candidates for shifted sentences. MacDonald, Stallings, and O'Seaghdha (1998) presented corpus data indicating that the biased-intransitive verbs are in fact quite rare in shifted sentences, supporting the nonadjacency characterization of verb shifting disposition.

sensitivity to distributional lexical information in a way that has not typically played a dominant role in production theories to date.

These results suggest important parallels between production and comprehension in the use of distributional information, and they raise questions about the extent to which the same distributional information is used by both comprehension and production systems. A number of different scenarios are possible. For example, the system might be entirely modular, such that a person's comprehension system uses distributional information accrued from the history of sentences comprehended but not from those uttered by the person, whereas the production system uses distributional information only from the person's prior utterances. A more likely scenario is that prior comprehension and production events constrain both comprehension and production. Certainly, prior productions should influence comprehension, because the utterances that a speaker produces are also perceived and comprehended by this speaker. From the point of view of production, it is clear that prior comprehension experiences do have some effects on syntactic production (Levelt, 1989; Potter & Lombardi, 1998), although it is possible to imagine scenarios in which distributional information from prior productions are weighed more heavily than information from prior comprehension events. These topics will be interesting ones for future research, but whatever their outcome, it is clear that they have introduced a new puzzle, namely, how and why the adult speaker and comprehender could come to possess all of this tremendously detailed lexical information. In other words, now that we have seen that comprehension and production research have a great deal to say to each other, it becomes clear that both of these fields must also pay attention to research in language acquisition.

PUZZLE #3: HOW IS DISTRIBUTIONAL INFORMATION ACQUIRED?

The sorts of distributional information that we have discussed in comprehension and production are really phenomenally detailed, and these examples represent only a small sample of the kinds of information that have been shown to be important in language processing. A brief survey of some current findings in Table 6.1 attests to both the varied nature of distributional information and the rapidity with which new kinds of distributional information are being uncovered. Such varied information would seem daunting to learn, and indeed some researchers have suggested that it is beyond the capability of humans to attend to, store, and use such information efficiently (Mitchell et al., 1995). Clearly, an account of production or comprehension that relies so heavily on distributional informa-

TABLE 6.1
A Sampling of Distributional Information Hypothesized to be Important in Comprehension and Production

Type of Information	*Source*
Frequency of past tense versus past participle uses of a verb	MacDonald, 1994; MacDonald, Pearlmutter & Seidenberg, 1994; Trueswell, 1966
Frequency of transitive versus intransitive uses of a verb	MacDonald, 1994; MacDonald et al., 1994; Trueswell, Tanenhaus, & Garnsey, 1994
Frequency of transitive versus sentential complement uses of a verb	Garnsey, Pearlmutter, Myers, & Lotocky, 1997, Trueswell, Tanenhaus, & Kello, 1993
Frequency with which a verb takes S-complements with and without overt *that*	Trueswell, Tanenhaus, & Kello, 1993
Frequency of long–short phrase order in verb modification ambiguities	Thornton & MacDonald, 1998
Frequency with which verb and complement are nonadjacent	Stallings, MacDonald, & O'Seaghdha, 1998
Frequency with which a verb co-occurs with a PP conveying an Instrument role	Taraban & McClelland, 1988; Spivey-Knowlton & Sedivy, 1995

tion cannot afford to ignore the question of how such information is acquired.[3]

An important related question is why such information is acquired—why would a speaker of a language spend a lifetime encoding a finely detailed history of many co-occurrences between words and structures? This question may actually not be that difficult to answer, or at least to frame the shape of a response, as the basis for an answer has long existed in the acquisition literature: Distributional information appears to be crucial for acquiring a large amount of (at least) language-particular information, so that an acquisition system that did not pay attention to distributional information would not in fact successfully acquire language. This view can be seen most explicitly in Bates and MacWhinney's (1989) Competition Model, but the central role for distributional information is not limited to this perspective. For example, a number of researchers have suggested that information in the speech signal can be used by children to aid in a number of acquisition tasks, including finding word boundaries in the speech stream and identifying lexical categories and syntactic structure (Gleitman & Wanner, 1982; Morgan, 1986; Morgan & Demuth, 1996; Saffran, Aslin, & Newport, 1996). These accounts are inherently distributional—the information in the speech signal is probabilistic, and the child must attend to the distributional properties of the input over some time

[3]This is not to say that one must have a full account of the origins of distributional information in order to pursue constraint-based accounts of processing. Indeed, MacDonald (1997) argued that the origin question and the question of how distributional information is used can be profitably investigated separately.

in order to obtain useful information. Similar claims can be made about semantic bootstrapping accounts (Pinker, 1984, 1987), in which the child combines innate syntax–semantics linking rules with information in the environment to learn the syntactic properties of words in the language. The mapping between the world and the linguistic context is of course complicated and probabilistic (Gleitman, 1990), so that a distributional analysis is an important component for the success of this sort of account. Finally, syntactic bootstrapping approaches, in which mappings between syntactic structure and the world aid the child in acquiring semantic information about words (e.g., Gleitman, 1990; Landau & Gleitman, 1985), are also reliant on distributional information, as the mappings between the events and the syntactic structure of utterances are variable. An important emphasis in this work is on the role of noun information in the acquisition of verbs, particularly the identification of noun arguments of a verb. This sensitivity to the relation between verbs and nouns should also underlie the acquisition of distributional information affecting what Stallings et al. (1998) called a verb's *shifting disposition*—information about the (non)adjacency of verbs and their complement thought to constrain heavy-NP shifting. In other words, the very same information that is crucial in the acquisition of verb semantics in childhood appears to constrain the production of heavy-NP shift in the adult state.

This sort of claim, that the same general kinds of distributional information that guide the acquisition process in childhood continue to have an important role in adult performance, emerges from an alternative account of the nature of the acquisition process. Posed in the traditional way, the process of language acquisition is acquiring a grammar and a lexicon, and in this view it is mysterious why a lifetime of distributional information must be recorded after the grammar and lexicon are in place. Another perspective (e.g., Seidenberg, 1997) suggests that the acquisition process is not so isolated from the immediate demands of comprehension and production, in that the goal of the child is not acquiring an adult grammar but rather understanding others and being understood as much as possible in each communicative event. In this view, there is not an "acquisition device" separate from comprehension and production processes.

An illustration of these ideas can be found in a connectionist model of verb acquisition developed by Allen (1998). This model acquired verb semantics from the pairing of child-directed speech taken from the CHILDES (Child Language Data Exchange System; MacWhinney, 1995) corpus, particularly verb argument structure information, and an interpretation—the set of events accompanying the speech. For example, for the transitive sentence *Peter broke the pencil*, the model received the argument structure information that there were two arguments, one before the verb and one after, and that the verb was *break*. This information was paired with the interpretation that there were two participants, one the agent and one the patient, and that the event consisted of a breaking event. The goal of the modeling effort was to use knowledge acquired from exposure to these pairings to activate both appropriate argument role interpretations and verb semantics for each utterance, including constructions on which the model had not been trained, such as *the bottle broke.* Allen's model performed well, exhibiting both the ability to supply role interpretations for novel constructions and to activate appropriate verb semantics for novel verbs given information about both the argument structure and the semantics of the arguments in the utterance.

More important for our purposes, Allen (1998) showed that the model took advantage of a great deal of distributional information in the input to acquire its verb representations. This information included, in approximately descending order of importance, the frequency with which a verb was used, the set of constructions the verb appeared in, the frequency with which a verb was used in particular constructions, the semantic relation between a verb and other verbs used in similar constructions, the combined frequencies of related verbs, and the size of the set of semantically related verbs. These factors combined to form neighborhoods of verbs with semantically mediated privileges of co-occurrence. As is obvious from comparisons between this list and the adult comprehension and production studies shown in Table 6.1, Allen's model acquired distributional information that looks very similar to the constraints that are used in adult performance. This similarity is not accidental, because the task of the model was not acquisition per se but rather a primitive version of what human adult comprehenders do, namely, assign a representation to each input sentence. In the course of assigning these representations, Allen's model passes activation across various levels of representation, and each utterance affects the weights between connections in the network. In this system, encoding of distributional information does not stem from some specialized acquisition mechanism but is rather an inevitable consequence of this kind of processing architecture when applied to the task of comprehension or production.

THE PATH THROUGH THE PUZZLES, AND A MORAL

In this chapter, I argued that a sensitivity to distributional information is an important link between comprehension, production, and acquisition. In the case of comprehension, I suggested that a set of seemingly puzzling modification ambiguities reveal comprehenders' sensitivity to distributional patterns concerning the relative length of phrases in the input. The distributional patterns are thought to emerge from pressures on the production system to produce phrases in a certain order. The production system itself was also shown to be extremely sensitive to distributional information, such that information about the typical location of verb complements, probably acquired from both comprehension and production, constrains the choice of syntactic structure during production. This wealth of distributional information in the adult state forces us to grapple with acquisition issues concerning how such information comes to be encoded. The answer suggested here was that in many constraint-satisfaction theories of acquisition, production, and comprehension, each comprehension or production event changes the nature of the linguistic representation. Such changes are substantial in early phases of learning and very minor in later phases, but they still serve to encode the distributional patterns of the language as a natural consequence of the comprehension and production processes.

This view suggests a moral: If this general account is on the right track, then the acquisition, comprehension, and production processes have links between them that cannot be safely ignored. First, work in comprehension is likely to have a lot to learn from constraints imposed on the production system, well beyond the ones discussed here. For example, consider the problem of how a comprehender determines whether a phrase such as *she* or *the cat* refers to some new entity in the discourse or whether it is coreferential with some earlier-mentioned entity (and if so, what entity). Speakers' choices for nominal expressions, for example, *she, the cat, Trinity,* and so forth, appear to be guided by a number of constraints such as whether the referred-to entity is the topic of the discourse, whether the entity has been previously referenced, the grammatical role of the entity in the sentence in its current or past mention, and many other factors (Ariel, 1990; Givón, 1976; Gordon, Grosz, & Gilliom, 1993). These constraints clearly create distributional patterns in the input that are likely to be extremely helpful to the comprehender, and they clearly are not the only examples of the intricate interplay between comprehension and production processes.

Similarly, the vast amount of distributional information available in the adult state has implications for acquisition research. For example, there is some debate in this literature whether one kind of bootstrapping mechanism—syntactic, semantic, or prosodic—is *the* mechanism underlying lexical acquisition. Many researchers adopt the position that multiple kinds of bootstrapping are likely to be at work (e.g., Jusczyk, 1997; Morgan, 1986; cf. Pinker, 1984). The variety of distributional information evidenced in the adult state points toward the multiple constraints approach. Of course, demonstrating sensitivity to distributional information in the adult state is not the same thing as showing that a child actually uses such information at a particular time to solve a particular problem, but the fact that such a huge variety of information is demonstrable in adults minimally requires that comprehenders have encoded the information, and it encourages us to place our bets in favor of a system in which a variety of constraints simultaneously shape the comprehension and production processes not only in the adult state but also in the child. Examples such as these suggest that the traditional distinctions between acquisition, production, and comprehension are not actually realized in language users, and that psycholinguistic researchers should find it increasingly profitable to break the traditional rule about keeping these subfields separate.

ACKNOWLEDGMENTS

This research was supported by National Science Foundation Grant SBR-9511270. I thank Joe Allen, Robert Thornton, and Lynne Stallings for helpful comments on an earlier draft of this chapter. Correspondence may be directed to Maryellen MacDonald, Hedco Neuroscience Building, University of Southern California, Los Angeles, CA 90089-2520.

REFERENCES

Allen, J. (1998). *Argument structures without lexical entries.* Unpublished doctoral dissertation, University of Southern California, Los Angeles.

Altmann, G. T. M., & Steedman, M. (1988). Interaction with context during human sentence processing. *Cognition, 30,* 191–238.

Ariel, M. (1990). *Accessing noun-phrase antecedents.* London: Routledge.

Bates, E., & MacWhinney, B. (1989). Functionalism and the competition model. In B. MacWhinney & E. Bates (Eds.), *The crosslinguistic study of sentence processing* (pp. 3–76). New York: Cambridge University Press.

Bock, J. K. (1987). An effect of the accessibility of word forms on sentence structure. *Journal of Memory and Language, 26,* 119–137.

DeSmedt, K. J. M. J. (1994). Parallelism in incremental sentence generation. In G. Adriaens & U. Hahn (Eds.), *Parallelism in natural language processing.* Norwood, NJ: Ablex.

Firbas, J. (1966). On defining the theme in functional sentence perspective. *Travaux Linguistiques de Prague, 2.*

Fodor, J. D., & Inoue, A. (1994). The diagnosis and cure of garden paths. *Journal of Psycholinguistic Research, 23,* 407–434.

Frazier, L. (1987). Sentence processing: A tutorial review. In M. Coltheart (Ed.), *Attention and Performance XII: The psychology of reading* (pp. 559–586). Hillsdale, NJ: Lawrence Erlbaum Associates.

Frazier, L., & Clifton, C. (1996). *Construal.* Cambridge, MA: MIT Press.

Garnsey, S. M., Pearlmutter, N. J., Myers, E., & Lotocky, M. A. (1997). The contributions of verb bias and plausibility to the comprehension of temporarily ambiguous sentences. *Journal of Memory and Language, 37,* 58–93.

Gibson, E., Pearlmutter, N. J., Conseco-Gonzales, E., & Hickok, G. (1996). Recency preference in the human sentence processing mechanism. *Cognition, 59,* 23–59.

Givón, T. (1976). Topic, pronoun, and grammatical agreement. In C. N. Li (Ed.), *Subject and topic.* New York: Academic Press.

Gleitman, L. R. (1990). The structural sources of verb meanings. *Language Acquisition, 1,* 1–55.

Gleitman, L. R., & Wanner, E. (1982). The state of the state of the art. In E. Wanner & L. Gleitman (Eds.), *Language acquisition: The state of the art* (pp. 3–48). Cambridge, England: Cambridge University Press.

Gordon, P. C., Grosz, B. J., & Gilliom, L. (1993). Pronouns, names and the centering of attention in discourse. *Cognitive Science, 17,* 311–348.

Hawkins, J. A. (1994). *A performance theory of order and constituency.* Cambridge, England: Cambridge University Press.

Jusczyk, P. W. (1997). *The discovery of spoken language.* Cambridge, MA: MIT Press.

Kempen, G., & Hoenkamp, E. (1987). An incremental procedural grammar for sentence formulation. *Cognitive Science, 11,* 201–258.

Kimball, J. (1973). Seven principles of surface structure parsing in natural language. *Cognition, 2,* 15–47.

Landau, B., & Gleitman, L. (1985). *Language and experience: Evidence from the blind child.* Cambridge, MA: Harvard University Press.

Levelt, W. J. M. (1989). *Speaking: From intention to articulation.* Cambridge, MA: MIT Press.

MacDonald, M. C. (1994). Probabilistic constraints and syntactic ambiguity resolution. *Language and Cognitive Processes, 9,* 157–201.

MacDonald, M. C. (1997). Lexical representations and sentence processing: An introduction. *Language and Cognitive Processes, 12,* 121–136.

MacDonald, M. C., Pearlmutter, N. J., & Seidenberg, M. S. (1994). The lexical nature of syntactic ambiguity resolution. *Psychological Review, 101,* 676–703.

MacDonald, M., Stallings, L., & O'Seaghdha, P. G. (1998). *Distributional information and heavy-NP shift.* Manuscript in preparation.

MacWhinney, B. (1995). *The CHILDES project: Tools for analyzing talk* (2nd ed.). Hillsdale, NJ: Lawrence Erlbaum Associates.

McRae, K., Spivey-Knowlton, M., & Tanenhaus, M. K. (1998). Modeling the influence of thematic fit (and other constraints) in on-line sentence comprehension. *Journal of Memory and Language, 38,* 283–312.

Mitchell, D. C., Cuetos, F., Corley, M. M. B., & Brysbaert, M. (1995). Exposure-based models of human parsing: Evidence for the use of coarse-grained (nonlexical) statistical records. *Journal of Psycholinguistic Research, 24,* 469–488.

Morgan, J. (1986). *From simple input to complex grammar.* Cambridge, MA: MIT Press

Morgan, J., & Demuth, K. (Eds.). (1996). *From signal to syntax.* Mahwah, NJ: Lawrence Erlbaum Associates.

Pearlmutter, N. J., & MacDonald, M. C. (1992). Plausibility and syntactic ambiguity resolution. In *Proceedings of the 14th Annual Conference of the Cognitive Society* (pp. 498–503). Hillsdale, NJ: Lawrence Erlbaum Associates.

Pinker, S. (1984). *Language learnability and language development.* Cambridge, MA: Harvard University Press.

Pinker, S. (1987). The bootstrapping problem in language acquisition. In B. MacWhinney (Ed.), *Mechanisms of language acquisition* (pp. 399–441). Hillsdale, NJ: Lawrence Erlbaum Associates.

Potter, M. C., & Lombardi, L. (1998). Syntactic priming in immediate recall of sentences. *Journal of Memory and Language, 38,* 265–282.

Ross, J. R. (1967). *Constraints on variables in syntax.* Unpublished doctoral dissertation, MIT, Cambridge, MA.

Saffran, J. R., Aslin, R. N., & Newport, E. L. (1996). Statistical learning by 8-month-old infants. *Science, 274,* 1926–1928.

Seidenberg, M. S. (1997). Language acquisition and use: Learning and applying probabilistic constraints. *Science, 275,* 1599–1603.

Spivey-Knowlton, M. J., &. Sedivy, J. (1995). Resolving attachment ambiguities with multiple constraints. *Cognition, 55,* 227–267.

Stallings, L. M., MacDonald, M. C., & O'Seaghdha, P. G. (1998). Phrasal ordering constraints in sentence production: Phrase length and verb disposition in heavy NP shift. *Journal of Memory and Language, 39,* 392-417.

Tabossi, P., Spivey-Knowlton, M. J., McRae, K., & Tanenhaus, M. K. (1994). Semantic effects on syntactic ambiguity resolution: Evidence for a constraint-based resolution process. In C. Umilta & M. Moscovitch (Eds.), *Attention and Performance XV* (pp. 589–616). Cambridge, MA: MIT Press.

Taraban, R., & McClelland, J. L. (1988). Constituent attachment and thematic role assignment in sentence processing: Influences of content-based expectations, *Journal of Memory and Language, 27,* 597–632.

Thornton, R., & MacDonald, M. C. (1997). *The role of phrase length in interpretation of modification ambiguities.* Manuscript in preparation.

Thornton, R., MacDonald, M. C., & Gil, M. (1998). *Pragmatic constraints on modifier attachment to complex NPs in English and Spanish.* Manuscript submitted for publication.

Trueswell, J. C. (1996). The role of lexical frequency in syntactic ambiguity resolution. *Journal of Memory and Language, 35,* 566–585.

Trueswell, J. C., Tanenhaus, M. K., & Garnsey, S. M. (1994). Semantic influences on parsing: Use of thematic role information in syntactic disambiguation. *Journal of Memory and Language, 33,* 285–318.

Trueswell, J. C., Tanenhaus, M. K., & Kello, C. (1993). Verb-specific constraints in sentence processing—separating effects of lexical preference from garden-paths. *Journal of Experimental Psychology: Learning, Memory and Cognition, 19,* 528–553.

Wasow, T. (1997). Remarks on grammatical weight. *Language Variation and Change, 9,* 81–105.

Chapter 7

The Emergence of the Semantics of Argument Structure Constructions

Adele E. Goldberg
University of Illinois, Urbana–Champaign

In the traditional view of argument structure, the main verb directly determines the overall form and meaning of the sentence. That is, the verb is assumed to *project* its argument structure. This view has been widely accepted on the basis of basic sentences such as the following:

(1) a. Pat went down the street.
b. Pat did her homework.
c. Pat gave Chris a cake.
d. Pat made Chris happy.
e. Pat put the book on the table.

In 1a, for example, the main verb *go* seems to be responsible for the fact that the sentence has a subject and a prepositional phrase complement, and *go* also seems to be responsible for the interpretation of motion. In 1b, *do* is arguably responsible for both the transitive form and transitive meaning. Similarly, *give* in 1c is a three-argument verb and lexically specifies the meaning of transfer apparent in the overall expression. *Make* in 1d is arguably responsible for the resultative form and interpretation, and *put* insures the particular three-complement configuration in 1e and the interpretation of caused motion.

However, if we look beyond these basic sentences, we find other cases in which it is not as natural to attribute the overall form and meaning to the main verb. For example, consider the following:

(2) a. The truck rumbled down the street.
b. Pat eyebrow'd her surprise.
c. We will overnight you that package.
d. He kissed mother unconscious.
e. They couldn't manage to pray the two little girls home again.

Rumble in 2a, for example, is a verb of sound emission, not motion, but the sentence nonetheless entails motion. *Eyebrow* and *overnight* are not even normally verbs and yet they appear in 2b and 2c as verbs with transitive and ditransitive argument structures, respectively. *Kiss* normally has a simple transitive form, but in 2d appears with a causative interpretation and the resultative complement. *Pray*, normally an intransitive verb, is used in 2e with a directional phrase in an expression that implies caused motion. In none of these cases is it plausible to attribute the overall form and meaning of the sentence to the main verb.

Another reason why it is not always useful to attribute the overall form and meaning directly to the main verb is that verbs generally appear in multiple argument structures. That is, verbs typically underdetermine the overall form and meaning of a clause. For example *type* appears in at least the following five argument structures:

(3) a. She typed for 3 hours.
(intransitive construction)
b. She typed a letter.
(transitive construction: creation)
c. She typed her fingers raw.
(resultative construction)
d. She typed 40 characters onto the page.
(caused-motion construction)
e. She typed her way to a promotion.
(*way* construction)

Similarly, *sneeze*, a parade example of an intransitive verb, can appear in at least the following five different argument structures:

(4) a. Pat sneezed.
(intransitive construction)
b. Pat sneezed the foam off the cappuccino.
(caused-motion construction)
c. She sneezed a terrible sneeze.
(cognate object construction)
d. She sneezed her nose red.
(the resultative construction)
e. She sneezed her way to the emergency room.
(the *way* construction)

TABLE 7.1
English Argument Structure Constructions

Construction/Example	*Meaning*	*Form*
1. **Intransitive motion** The fly buzzed into the room.	X moves to Y	Subj V Obl
2. **Transitive** Pat cubed the meat.	X acts on Y	Subj V Obj
3. **Resultative** She kissed him unconscious.	X causes Y to become Z	Subj V Obj XCOMP
4. **Double object** Pat faxed Bill the letter.	X causes Y to receive Z	Subj V Obj Obj2
5. **Caused-motion** Pat sneezed the foam off the cappuccino.	X causes Y to move Z	Subj V Obj Obl

At the same time that the verb is not reliably responsible for the form and meaning of the clause, there are clearly regularities between the form and meaning themselves. For example, Subj V $\text{Obl}_{location}$ is associated with the interpretation of motion; Subj V Obj Obl is associated with the meaning of caused motion; Subj V Obj1 Obj2 is associated with the meaning of transfer, and so on (see Goldberg, 1995, for discussion). One way of capturing the contribution of form and meaning that is not attributable to the main verb is to posit abstract *constructions* that pair form with meaning, independently of the verbs that appear in them.[1]

The following is a definition of *construction*: C is a CONSTRUCTION iff_{defn} C is a pairing of form and function such that some aspect of the form or some aspect of the function is not strictly predictable from C's component parts. Knowledge of language in general is understood as the knowledge of interrelated constructions (see Fillmore & Kay, in preparation; Goldberg, 1995; Langacker, 1987, 1991; Pollard & Sag, 1987).

A partial list of the constructions that correspond to basic argument structures in English is given in Table 7.1.

The argument structures listed in Table 7.1 are constructions because their form and associated meaning are not necessarily predictable from the words that appear in them (cf. examples 2a–e, and discussion in Goldberg, 1995). The rest of this chapter offers an account of how the meaning associated with argument structure constructions is acquired: The meaning can be understood to emerge from generalizing over lexical instances. That is, constructions associated with basic argument structure patterns can be seen to be learned through a process of categorization and generalization over the input. No innate linking rules need to be posited.

[1]See also Hovav and Levin (1998) for a related way of capturing these generalizations by allowing a distinction between a verb's core meaning and the meaning associated with argument structure frames.

It should be mentioned that the emergentist framework adopted here differs from that advocated by Hopper (1987). Whereas Hopper viewed grammar as constantly emerging during ongoing discourse, this present account takes the position that grammar emerges primarily during initial acquisition, from a combination of linguistic input, the functional demands of communication, and general cognitive abilities and constraints. Once grammar is acquired, it is assumed that it has a highly conventionalized status, and that although minute changes in the system constantly occur, the system as a whole is fairly stable.

THE EMERGENCE OF ARGUMENT STRUCTURE MEANING

Initial acquisition of argument structure patterns has been widely argued to be on a verb-by-verb basis (Akhtar, 1998; Akhtar & Tomasello, 1997; Bates & MacWhinney, 1987; Bowerman, 1982; MacWhinney, 1982; Schlesinger, 1977; Tomasello, 1992; Tomasello & Brooks, 1998; see also Gropen, Epstein, & Schumacher, 1997, for discussion of the somewhat more productive use of nouns). Children initially tend to conservatively produce the patterns they have heard.

At the same time, it is clear that children cannot continue to learn argument structure patterns on a verb-by-verb basis indefinitely or we might expect to find a language in which argument structures varied on a verb-by-verb basis in an unrestrained way. For example, we might expect to find a language in which the transitive form is expressed by SVO word order for the verb *see*, but by SOV word order for *kiss*, and by case-marking for *hate*:

(5) a. Pat saw Chris
    b. Pat Chris kissed
    c. Hate Pat-nom Chris-acc

However, languages do not vary in this way; they are much more regular, having a few argument structure constructions that are systematically related. Moreover, semantically similar verbs show a strong tendency to appear in the same argument structure constructions (Fisher, Gleitman, & Gleitman, 1991).[2]

[2]Possible exceptions are mental experience or *psych verbs*, which often do vary within a single language in the way the arguments are expressed. For example, in English we say *It pleases her*, with the experiencer as object, but *She likes it*, with the experiencer as subject. Yet even this class has been widely argued to vary in a fairly systematic way, with causative psych verbs encoding the stimulus as subject, and stative psych verbs encoding the experiencer as subject (see Grimshaw, 1990, and references therein).

Further evidence that children generalize over particular instances to form more abstract representations comes from their ability to use constructions productively. For example, by the age of 3 or 4, children produce spontaneous overgeneralizations such as *Don't laugh me* or *She falled me down* (Bowerman, 1982). They are also able to successfully manipulate and comprehend new or nonsense verbs in unmodeled constructions in experimental settings (e.g., Akhtar & Tomasello, 1997; Gropen et al., 1989; Naigles, 1990). Because children do not hear such sentences in the input, their occurrence is evidence that children recognize an abstract pattern in their language and know how to productively exploit it for new cases. Therefore, it seems that learners must be attempting to categorize the instances they hear into patterns (cf. also Allen, 1997; Morris, 1998; Tomasello & Brooks, 1998).

Akhtar (1998) provides experimental evidence that nicely demonstrates both the strategy of learning on an item-by-item basis and the growing trend toward generalization. Children aged 2, 3, and 4 were taught novel actions for two novel verbs modeled in SOV or VSO orders:

(6) a. Elmo the car gopping.
    b. Dacking Elmo the car.

Recording spontaneous productions of these verbs and elicited responses to queries of *what happened?*, Akhtar found that 2- and 3-year-olds matched SOV or VSO patterns roughly half the time and corrected order to SVO order roughly half the time. The fact that the 2- and 3-year-old children produced the modeled, non-English orders of the novel verbs so often demonstrates that they were willing to learn the argument structures of these verbs on an individual basis. This finding supports the idea that initial acquisition is highly sensitive to word-specific patterns. At the same time, the fact that these same children corrected the order for these same verbs half the time to make it standard English SVO order demonstrates that they were also aware of and making use of a generalization over the instances they had already learned. The language-particular SVO generalization played a much greater role for the 4-year-olds. These older children rarely matched the modeled order and were much more likely to correct to SVO order.

In a control condition, Akhtar performed the analogous experiment with familiar verbs, for example *push* and *hit*:

(7) a. Elmo the car pushing.
    b. Hitting Elmo the car.

This condition was designed to test whether children might have been simply accommodating the experimenter's strange word orders for pragmatic reasons that did not necessarily have to do with acquisition. If so, then we might expect the children to produce these known verbs with the novel word orders as well, because the same experimental context applied. On the other hand, if the children were truly learning how to use the novel verbs in the earlier experiment, the production of known verbs should be different. We would expect that the children would be more likely to change to SVO order, because this order of arguments was already mastered for these verbs. The latter scenario is exactly what Akhtar found. In the control condition involving known verbs, even the youngest children were far more likely to correct to SVO than to use the order that was modeled.

The Basis of Constructional Meaning

Returning to the argument structure constructions listed in Table 7.1, it is worth considering more specifically how their meaning emerges from learned instances. I would like to suggest that the generalization to constructional meaning is based largely on the meanings of highly frequent "light" verbs: verbs with very general meanings. Notice that the meanings of the light verbs *go, do, make, give,* and *put* correspond closely to the meanings associated with argument structure constructions (see Table 7.1) as given in Table 7.2.

Clark (1978) noted that these light verbs are among the first verbs to be learned cross-linguistically, citing Bowerman (1973) for Finnish, Grégoire (1937) for French, Sanches (1978) for Japanese, and Park (1977) for Korean. Children were observed to use these verbs with a general meaning close to that of adults.

The following are examples of early uses of these verbs, with data from the Howe (1981) and Bloom (1970) corpora on CHILDES (MacWhinney, 1995):

(8) a. put it there (Kevin, MLU 1.87)
b. make @ car under bridge (Kathryn, MLU 1.92)
c. go back # Mum (Ian, MLU 1.53)
d. give it brush (Kevin, MLU 1.87)
e. Daddy do that (Ian, MLU 1.53)

TABLE 7.2
Light Verbs and Corresponding Constructions

go	X moves Y	Intransitive construction
do	X acts on Y	Transitive construction
make	X causes Y to become Z	Resultative construction
give	X causes Y to receive Z	Ditransitive construction
put	X causes Y to move Z	Caused motion construction

TABLE 7.3
Frequencies From Carrol et al. (1971)

do	1,2695	take	4,089	eat	1,616
make	8,333	put	3,942	hold	1,192
find	6,916	give	3,366	fall	824
get	5,700	read	3,057	sit	549
go	5,388	play	2,113	fit	461
come	4,676	draw	1,623	fix	156

Clark (1978) also noted that these verbs are the most frequent verbs in children's early English. The high frequencies of these verbs reflect the children's input. That is, the relatively high frequency of the set of light verbs in children's speech is mirrored by the high frequency of the same set of verbs in the input. The following raw frequencies are from the frequency list of Carroll, Davies, and Richman (1971), based on a 5-million-word corpus of texts used for third through ninth graders: The light verbs *do, make, find, get, go, come, take, put,* and *give* are more frequent than other early verbs.[3]

Eaton (1940) provided word frequency counts for French, German, and Spanish as well as English. Translations of the previously mentioned light verbs all appear in the list of the 1,000 most frequent words in each of these languages.

Why is it that light verbs tend to be so frequent cross-linguistically? Bybee (1985; Bybee, Perkins, & Pagliuca, 1994) observed that there is a strong correlation between high frequency and general semantics, because lexical items with more general meanings are applicable in a larger number of situations. Comparing *go* with *amble, crawl, limp, run,* or *waltz,* for example, or comparing *put* with *shelve, box, hide, tuck in,* or *stuff,* we can see that *go* and *put* apply in a wider range of contexts. Importantly, light verbs also code meanings that are highly relevant to daily human experience: scenes of motion, action, causation, transfer, and so on. These basic scenes are arguably the building blocks for much of human cognition through processes of metaphorical extension and abstraction (Goldberg, 1995; Lakoff, 1987).

High frequency in the input begets high frequency in children's speech for several reasons. Slobin (1997) noted that high frequency is a necessary condition for automatization and facilitates accessibility, leading to ease of production and comprehension. High frequency also correlates strongly

[3]*Read* is the next highly frequent verb on the list, but this may be the result of a bias of the corpus, as the corpus consists of children's school texts. *Do* is especially frequent because it can be used as an auxiliary as well as a main verb; however, in a small corpus study I performed on the CHILDES database, *do* is used as frequently as other light verbs by children who are not yet using this or any auxiliaries.

with shorter forms (Zipf, 1935), leading highly frequent verbs to be shorter and therefore easier to learn and use. Slobin (1997) observed that these factors, in addition to (or instead of) input frequency per se, encourage language learners to rely heavily on light verbs in their own speech.

In fact, children's reliance on light verbs goes beyond the frequency in adult speech to some extent. Clark (1994, p. 29) observed that children seem to use light verbs in circumstances when adults would generally select a more specific verb. For example:

(9) a. You . . do . . doing that
(as adult builds blocks into a tower)
b. Uh oh, I did.
(as he turned off the tape-recorder by pushing a knob)
c. make name!
(telling adult to write the child's name)

This fact is most likely explainable by the same factors that lead to the light verbs' early acquisition. Because the light verbs are more frequent and thus easier to produce, it is natural that children sometimes use a light verb instead of a more specific verb that may be somewhat harder to retrieve.

The fact that children learn the light verbs so early and use them so frequently may play a direct role in the acquisition of argument structure constructions in the following way. Children are likely to record a correlation between a certain formal pattern and the meaning of the particular verb(s) used most early and frequently in that pattern. This meaning would come to be associated with the pattern even when the particular verbs themselves do not appear. Because light verbs are more frequent than other verbs and are also learned early, these verbs tend to be the ones around which constructional meaning centers.

For example, the syntactic frame, Subj V Obl_{loc}, is associated with the meaning of intransitive motion. This explains the interpretation of sentences like the following, which do not involve verbs that lexically designate motion:

(10) a. The truck rumbled down the alley.
b. The runner huffed and puffed up the hill.

The expressions in 10a–b entail motion when put in the constructional frame associated with motion, roughly the meaning of *go*.

It turns out that the verb *go* accounts for a full 53.8% of the tokens (105/195) of this syntactic pattern in the Bates, Bretherton, and Snyder

(1988) corpus of 27 children at 28 months of age.[4] Other verbs appear in the pattern, but with much less frequency, for example, *fall* (6.2%), *get* (5.6%), *look* (4.1%), and *live* (4.1%). Similarly, the syntactic frame Subj V Obj Obl_{loc} is associated with the meaning of caused motion, which accounts for the interpretation of the following expressions:

(11) a. She sneezed the foam off the cappuccino.
b. We will overnight you that package.

Put is the verb that encodes the meaning of caused motion most directly, and *put* accounts for a full 38.1% (16/42) of the tokens in the corpus. Again, other verbs appear in this pattern, but with much less frequency. The next most frequent verbs are: *get* (19%), *take* (9.5%), *do* (7.1%), *throw* (4.8%).

The ditransitive form, Subj V Obj1 Obj2, is associated with the meaning of transfer, roughly the meaning of the lexical verb, *give* (e.g., Goldberg, 1995). The present hypothesis predicts therefore that *give* should be the most frequently used verb in the ditransitive frame. Because the ditransitive construction does not appear to be frequently used at 28 months, relevant data reported in Gropen et al. (1989) were reanalyzed to test the current hypothesis.[5]

Gropen et al. (1989) collected ditransitive utterances in longitudinal corpora from the Brown (1973) corpus of Adam, Eve, and Sarah's speech, and MacWhinney's (1995) corpus of the speech of his two sons, Ross and Mark. Adam was recorded in 55 two-hour samples taken every 2 to 4 weeks between the ages of 2;3 and 5;2. Eve was recorded in 20 two-hour samples taken every 2 to 3 weeks between the ages of 1;6 and 2;3. Sarah's speech was recorded in 139 one-hour samples taken at 2- to 19-day intervals between the ages of 2;3 and 5;1. Ross and Mark were recorded in 62 samples of varying sizes at varying intervals, between the ages of 2;7 and 6;6 in the case of Ross, and 1;5 and 4;7 in the case of Mark.

A chart of the most frequent verbs recorded in the ditransitive construction, together with the percentage of tokens, are given in Table 7.4.[6]

As the current hypothesis predicts, *give* was the most frequent verb for four out of the five children. In fact, it appeared more than twice as frequently as the next most frequent verb for each of these children. In the case of one child, Mark, 10 instances of *give* were observed as compared

---

[4]I am indebted to Nitya Sethuraman for collecting this data by hand from the Bates et al. corpus (which is part of the CHILDES database).

[5]The ditransitive construction appeared a total of only six times in the Bates et al. corpus.

[6]Uses determined to be idiomatic would have increased the overall frequency of *give*; we nonetheless excluded them from the following analysis.

TABLE 7.4
Most Frequent Verb Used Distransitively for Each Child

Chile	*Verb Used*	*Percentage of Distransitives*
Adam	*give*	52.7% (59/112)
Eve	*give*	36.4% (4/11)
Sarah	*give*	43.3% (29/67)
Ross	*give*	43.1% (69/160)
Mark	*tell*	32.4% (11/34)
	(give)	29.4% (10/34)

Note. Based on data summarized in Gropen et al. (1989).

with 11 instances of *tell.* Thus, *give* was also among the first or second earliest recorded verbs in the ditransitive frame for each of the five children.

The claim is that because the light verbs are the most frequent verbs used in their respective syntactic patterns and are also among the earliest verbs to be used in those patterns, the interpretations of expressions with light verbs act as a center of gravity for other expressions having the same form. The end result of this categorization is the direct association of the meaning of the light verb with the formal pattern, giving rise to the constructional meaning. The strong effect of early acquisition and frequency has been documented in connectionist net simulations (Elman, 1993; Elman et al., 1996; see also Allen, 1997, for connectionist modeling of argument structure constructions).

It is likely that the categorization and generalization into more abstract patterns is driven by an increase in vocabulary size. That is, in order to learn an ever increasing vocabulary and the associated syntactic patterns, it may be necessary to categorize individual instances into classes. This idea is supported by Bates and Goodman (1997) (chap. 2, this volume), who argue that syntactic proficiency is strongly correlated with vocabulary size. In particular, they argue that the single best estimate of grammatical status at 28 months, which is when syntactic encoding becomes produced more regularly as measured by the MacArthur Communicative Development Inventory (CDI), is the total vocabulary size at 20 months, which is the heart of the vocabulary burst. In fact Bates and Goodman (1997) showed that grammar and vocabulary stay tightly coupled across the 16- to 30-month range. This correlation would be expected if the increasing vocabulary size is in fact directly forcing certain syntactic generalizations.

Further empirical support for the present view of the acquisition of argument structure comes from Ninio (1996). Ninio noted that children often begin using a single verb in a particular grammatical pattern long before other verbs begin to be used in the pattern. In particular, the first uses of SVO and VO patterns were studied in two Hebrew-speaking populations: 15 children in a longitudinal study and eighty-four 18-month-old children in a cross-sectional study.[7] Ninio noted the overwhelming tendency for the "pathbreaking" verbs to be drawn from the set of light verbs. In particular, in both the longitudinal and cross-sectional studies, the children tended to use the following verbs transitively before other verbs were used: *want, make/do, put, bring, take out,* and *give.*

In the longitudinal study, Ninio further observed that SVO and VO patterns were initially produced with only one or at most a few verbs for a prolonged period lasting between 2 and 15 weeks. More and more verbs came to be used in an exponentially increasing fashion; that is, there seemed to be more facilitation after 10 verbs than after 5, and so on. She suggested that this increase stems from the fact that children gradually abstract a more general syntactic pattern on the basis of the early verbs, and that the growing generalization allows them to use new verbs in this pattern more and more easily.

These facts accord well with the account proposed here. Patterns are learned on the basis of generalizing over particular instances. As vocabulary increases, so does the strength of the generalization, making it progressively more and more easy to assimilate new verbs into the patterns. With Ninio, it is proposed here that the instances that play an initial, crucial role are those involving light verbs.

Ninio's (1996) explanation for the early acquisition of the light verbs is somewhat different from the present account. She suggested that the tendency for light verbs to be used early in the VO and SVO patterns stems from a high degree of semantic transitivity in these light verbs.[8] She stated that "the 'pathbreaking verbs' that begin the acquisition of a novel syntactic rule tend to be generic verbs expressing the relevant combinatorial property in a relatively undiluted fashion; this is what makes them such good candidates for acquisition" (p. 25).

The account seems to assume that the semantics of the verbs match the semantics of an independently existing "combinatorial property" and

---

[7]Ninio (1996) includes data from one English-speaking child in the longitudinal study as well.

[8]That these light verbs are all highly semantically transitive is not entirely clear. As Ninio (1996) noted, they are not according the transitivity criteria laid out by Hopper and Thompson (1980). In the present account, meanings of constructions emerge from generalizations over particular verbs; because the transitive pattern appears with a range of highly frequent verbs, including verbs with low semantic transitivity, such as *get* and *want,* the association of semantic transitivity with simple syntactic SVO status is predicted not to be overwhelmingly strong. In fact, a good number of SVO sentences are not highly transitive (including statives and generics as well as expressions with main verbs such as *get* and *want*).

that it is this correspondence that results in the verbs' early use in the construction. The combinatorial property and its associated semantics is in effect a schematic construction: a pairing of form and meaning. The account seems to assume, therefore, that a construction exists prior to the first verbs being used in it; verbs whose meanings match the constructional meaning are used earliest. We might call this the Match Proposal.

If semantic transitivity is associated with the language's two-argument construction from the start, and if it is the match between the meaning and form that facilitates the early use of particular verbs, we might expect that all verbs that are semantically transitive should be acquired equally quickly and easily. That is, it is not clear exactly why or how the early use of light verbs should facilitate the use of the construction with other verbs, as it seems to do according to Ninio's (1996) empirical data. The Match Proposal also does not explain why the verbs that are learned earliest are the most frequent verbs in children's (and adults') speech.

The present account suggests that the semantics that comes to be associated with a syntactic pattern emerges from early uses of the pattern with particular verbs. Thus, it is an account of how the construction itself, that is, the pairing of form with meaning, comes to exist in the minds of speakers. The child categorizes learned instances into more abstract patterns, associating a semantic category with a particular formal pattern; the meaning of the most frequent and early verbs occurring in a particular pattern form the prototype of the category.[9] In the present account, then, the simple transitive pattern is associated with the semantics of certain light verbs as the result, and not the cause, of these verbs being used so early and frequently in this pattern.

The fact that light verbs are used so early and frequently in turn results from their high frequency in the input language, which stems from their generally applicable meanings. The early acquisition and high frequency of light verbs are correlated because high frequency facilitates acquisition.

This account generalizes to other light verbs that are not transitive, but are also very frequent, and can be seen to form the basis of argument structure meaning. For example, we have seen that the verb *go* is the most frequent verb used in the intransitive motion construction and corresponds to the meaning of that construction. The same is true of the ditransitive pattern, Subj V Obj1 Obj2, which comes to be associated with the meaning of *give*, the caused-motion pattern, Subj V Obj Obl, which comes to be associated with the meaning of *put*, and so on. More generally, the specific formal patterns associated with particularly frequent verbs come to be associated with the meanings of those verbs. The Match Proposal would

[9]See Goldberg (1995) for discussion of the family of related meanings typically associated with constructions.

need to assume that each of these constructions and its associated meaning were known to the child at the time of the child's first verbs. How the constructions themselves come to exist is not explained. Finally, the Match Proposal predicts cross-linguistic uniformity in the acquisition of verbs and argument structure patterns. The present proposal allows for some cross-linguistic variability given the central role of input frequencies.

Cross-Linguistic Variation

It was noted earlier that light verbs are very frequent and among the first to be learned cross-linguistically. It is therefore expected that light verbs should form the basis of the argument structure constructions in a number of languages (including, e.g., Hebrew and English). In other languages, a small set of light verbs is used in conjunction with nominal, adjectival, or participial hosts to form the basis of all verbal meaning (cf., e.g., Mohanan, 1994, for Hindi; Mohammad & Karimi, 1992, and Karimi, 1997, for Persian).

At the same time, the idea that constructional meaning emerges from generalizing over lexical instances allows for some variation cross-linguistically as well. Whereas we expect general verbs to be highly frequent, and we further expect highly frequent verbs to form the basis of argument structure constructions, which frequent verbs actually form the basis of constructional generalization may be somewhat idiosyncratic and language specific (see Bowerman, 1990, for discussion of cross-linguistic variability in the linking between form and meaning).

Conclusion

This chapter proposed an account of how constructional meaning emerges from the categorization and generalization of the input. Although verbs and associated argument structures are initially learned on an item-by-item basis, increased vocabulary leads to categorization and generalization. Light verbs, because they are typically acquired early and are highly frequent, act as a center of gravity, forming the prototype of the semantic category associated with the formal pattern.

The relation between the main verb and the constructional pattern in the basic sentences given at the outset (examples 1a–e) was argued to play an important role in the acquisition of the constructions associated with these basic argument structures. Although such a direct relation is not representative of all verb–construction combinations (cf. examples 2a–e), the frequency of examples such as those in (1) allows speakers to record a correlation of form and meaning that ultimately gives rise to the abstract construction that can then be used in novel ways with new verbs.

ACKNOWLEDGMENTS

I would like to thank Brian MacWhinney, Bill Morris, and Nitya Sethuraman for comments on earlier versions of this chapter.

REFERENCES

Akhtar, N. (1998). Learning basic word order. In E. Clark (Ed.), *Proceedings of the 29th Annual Child Language Research Forum* (pp. 161–169). Stanford, CA: CSLI Publications.

Akhtar, N., & Tomasello, M. (1997). Young children's productivity with word order and verb morphology. *Developmental Psychology, 33*(6), 952–965.

Allen, J. (1997). *Argument structures without lexical entries.* Unpublished doctoral dissertation, University of Southern California.

Bates, E., & Goodman, J. (1997). On the inseparability of grammar and the lexicon: Evidence from acquisition, aphasia and real time processing. In G. Altmann (Ed.), Special Issue on the Lexicon, *Language and Cognitive Processes, 12*(5–6), 507–584.

Bates, E., Bretherton, I., & Snyder, L. (1988). *From first words to grammar: Individual differences and dissociable mechanisms.* Cambridge, MA: Cambridge University Press.

Bates, E., & MacWhinney, B. (1987). Competition, variation and language learning. In B. MacWhinney (Ed.), *Mechanisms of language acquisition* (pp. 157–193). Hillsdale, NJ: Lawrence Erlbaum Associates.

Bloom, L. (1970). *Language development: Form & function in emerging grammars.* Cambridge, MA: MIT Press.

Bowerman, M. (1973). *Early syntactic development: A cross-linguistic study with special reference to Finnish.* Cambridge, England: Cambridge University Press.

Bowerman, M. (1982). Reorganizational processes in lexical and syntactic development. In E. Wanner & L. R. Gleitman (Eds.), *Language acquisition: The state of the art* (pp. 319–346). New York: Cambridge University Press.

Bowerman, M. (1990). Mapping thematic roles onto syntactic functions: Are children helped by innate linking rules? *Linguistics, 28,* 6.

Brown, R. (1973). *A first language: The early stages.* Cambridge, MA: Harvard University Press.

Bybee, J. (1985). *Morphology: A study of the relation between meaning and form.* Amsterdam: Benjamins.

Bybee, J., Perkins, R., & Pagliuca, W. (1994). *The evolution of grammar: Tense, aspect and modality in the languages of the world.* Chicago: University of Chicago Press.

Carroll, J., Davies, P., & Richman, B. (1971). *Word frequency book.* New York: Houghton Mifflin.

Clark, E. V. (1978). Discovering what words can do. In *Papers from the parasession on the lexicon, Chicago Linguistic Society* (pp. 34–57).

Clark, E. V. (1994). *The lexicon in acquisition.* Cambridge, England: Cambridge University Press.

Eaton, H. S. (1940). *An English-French-German-Spanish word frequency dictionary: A correlation of the first 6000 words in four single-language frequency lists.* New York: Dover.

Elman, J. (1993). Learning and development in neural networks: The importance of starting small. *Cognition, 48,* 71–99.

Elman, J., Bates, E., Johnson, M. H., Karimiloff-Smith, A., Parisi, D., & Plunkett, K. (1996). *Rethinking innateness.* Cambridge, MA: MIT Press.

Fillmore, C., & Kay, P. (in preparation). *Construction grammar.* Berkeley: University of California.

Fisher, C., Gleitman, H., & Gleitman, L. (1991). On the semantic content of subcategorization frames. *Cognitive Psychology, 23*, 331–392.

Goldberg, A. E. (1995). *Constructions: A construction grammar approach to argument structure.* Chicago: University of Chicago Press.

Grégoire, A. (1937). *L'apprentissage du langage*, vol. 1 [Language learning, Volume 1]. Paris: Droz.

Grimshaw, J. (1990). *Argument structure.* Cambridge, MA: MIT Press.

Gropen, J., Epstein, T., & Schumacher, L. (1997). Context sensitive verb learning: Children's ability to associate conceptual and semantic information with the argument of the verb. *Cognitive Linguistics, 8*(2), 137–182.

Gropen, J., Pinker, S., Hollander, M., Goldberg, R., & Wilson, R. (1989). The learnability and acquisition of the dative alternation in English. *Language, 65*(2), 203–257.

Hopper, P. (1987). Emergent grammar. In J. Aske, N. Beery, L. Michaelis, & H. Filp (Eds.), *Proceedings of the Thirteenth Annual Meeting of the Berkeley Linguistics Society* (pp. 139–157). Berkeley, CA: Berkeley Linguistics Society.

Hopper, P. J., & Thompson, S. A. (1980). Transitivity in grammar and discourse. *Language, 56*, 251–299.

Hovav, M. R., & Levin, B. (1998). Building verb meanings. In M. Butt & W. Geode (Eds.), *The projection of arguments: Lexical and compositional factors* (pp. 97–134). Stanford: Center for the Study of Language & Information.

Howe, C. (1981). *Howe corpus of 16 Scottish mother-child pairs at ages 1;6-1;8 and again at age 1;11-2;1.* Glasgow, Scotland: Department of Psychology, Strathclyde University.

Karimi, D. (1997). *Complex predicates in Persian.* Unpublished doctoral dissertation, University of Essex, England.

Lakoff, G. (1987). *Women, fire & dangerous things.* Chicago: University of Chicago Press.

Langacker, R. (1987). *Foundations of cognitive grammar 1.* Stanford, CA: Stanford University Press.

Langacker, R. (1991). *Foundations of cognitive grammar 2.* Stanford, CA: Stanford University Press.

MacWhinney, B. (1978). The acquisition of morphophonology. *Monographs of the Society for Research in Child Development, 43*, 1–2.

MacWhinney, B. (1982). Basic syntactic processes. In S. A. Kuczaj II (Ed.), *Language development, syntax and semantics Vol. 1.* Hillsdale, NJ: Lawrence Erlbaum Associates.

MacWhinney, B. (1995). *The CHILDES project: Tools for analyzing talk* (2nd ed.). Hillsdale, NJ: Lawrence Erlbaum Associates.

Mohammad, J., & Karimi, S. (1992). Light verbs are taking over: Complex verbs in Persian. In J. Nevis & V. Samiian (Eds.), *Western conference on linguistics* (pp. 195–213). Department of Linguistics, Fresno, CA: Cal State University Fresno.

Mohanan, T. (1994). *Argument structure in Hindi.* Stanford, CA: CSLI Publications.

Morris, W. (1998). *Emergent grammatical relations.* Unpublished doctoral dissertation, University of California, San Diego.

Naigles, L. (1990). Children use syntax to learn verb meanings. *Journal of Child Language, 17*, 357–374.

Ninio, A. (1996, July). *Pathbreaking verbs in syntactic development.* Paper presented at the 7th International Congress for the Study of Child Language, Istanbul, Turkey.

Park, T.-Z. (1977). *Emerging language in Korean children.* Unpublished manuscript, Institute of Psychology, Bern, Switzerland.

Pollard, C., & Sag, I. (1987). *Information-based syntax and semantics 1: Fundamentals* (CSLI Lecture Notes Series No. 13). Stanford, CA: Center for the Study of Language and Information.

Sanches, M. (1978). *On the emergence of multi-element-utterances in the child's Japanese.* Unpublished manuscript, University of Texas at Austin, Department of Anthropology.

Schlesinger, I. M. (1977). *Production and comprehension of utterances.* Hillsdale, NJ: Lawrence Erlbaum Associates.
Slobin, D. I. (1997). The origins of grammaticizable notions: Beyond the individual mind. In D. I. Slobin (Ed.), *The crosslinguistic study of language acquisition: Vol. 5: Expanding the contexts.* Mahwah, NJ: Lawrence Erlbaum Associates.
Tomasello, M. (1992). *First verbs: A case study of early grammatical development.* Cambridge, England: Cambridge University Press.
Tomasello, M., & Brooks, P. J. (1998). Early syntactic development: A construction grammar approach. In M. Barrett (Ed.), *The development of language.* London: UCL Press.
Zipf, G. K. (1935). *The psycho-biology of language.* Boston: Houghton Mifflin.

Chapter **8**

The Emergence of Language From Embodiment

Brian MacWhinney
Carnegie Mellon University

> *"Man is the measure of all things."*
>
> –Protagoras

The basic function of language is communication. When the listener succeeds in decoding the message intended by the speaker, the communication has been a success. But exactly how does the speaker package information to make sure that the listener will succeed? What does the listener have to do to build up a mental representation that echoes the original representation in the speaker's mind?

The traditional approach to this problem is one that has focused on the construction of propositional representations (Clark & Clark, 1977; Kintsch, 1974; Levelt, 1989; Schank & Abelson, 1977; Sowa, 1984). In this standard model, a message is represented by a directed graph in which words are joined together by labeled arcs. Although these graphs allow for multiple attachments to a single node, they otherwise resemble the phrase structure tree used in linguistics. This standard, graph-based approach provides a good way of depicting patterns of connectedness between words, but it fails in terms of providing a deeper account of meaning. There is a big gap between the schematic representation provided in a propositional graph and our actual understanding of the activity underlying a sentence. When we look at a picture of a boy letting a frog out of a glass jar, we can form a dynamic representation of the boy turning the lid of the glass jar and the frog hopping out of the jar. Although we could notate structural aspects of this action sequence through a propositional graph, we cannot use this graph to capture the actual flow of action or the unitized nature of the whole scene. The graph tells us little about the ways in which we move our elbow and wrist to unscrew the lid or the ways in which the frog leaps and jumps.

To deepen the linkage of propositional representations to cognition, cognitive linguists have often sought to unpack lexical forms into component propositional structures. For example, generative semantics provided an account of the meaning of a verb like *kill* that unpacked its lexical form into the predicate structure (cause(become(not(alive)))). Pursuing this form of decompositional semantic analysis, Miller and Johnson-Laird (1976) showed how the meaning of a simple noun like *table* can be unpacked into a series of propositions that explain how the top of the table fits onto its legs, how we place things on tables, and how we work at tables. Langacker (1989) and Talmy (1988) showed how we can enrich propositional representations by linking them to pictorial representations based on the theory of space grammar. These decompositional approaches succeed at enriching propositional representations by unpacking the meaning components of individual lexical items. However, they still leave us with a large gap between the notational system being used and our actual understandings of the meanings of sentences.

By treating communication as the construction of links between abstract symbols, or even pictorial configurations, the standard approach has implicitly accepted a fully Platonic characterization of sentence meaning. In this Platonic view, the meaning of a sentence has its truest existence outside of the minds of individual speakers and listeners. The "true" meaning of an utterance is not dependent on the cognitions of individual speakers or listeners; rather, it is a general cultural possession, or perhaps even a reflection of abstract semantic theory. Although this view makes good sense to those who wish to construct a logical theory of linguistic meaning, it cannot provide a psychologically satisfying account of the processing of meaning. The core problem with the propositional account is that it encourages us to think of representations in terms of disembodied graphs and schematic diagrams.

There is an interesting alternative to the standard propositional account. This alternative account treats language processing as a process of "perspective taking." According to this view, language comprehension and production are embodied processes whose goal is the creation and extraction of embodied meanings. Speakers and listeners use language as a way of working through various perspectives and shifts in perspective grounded on the objects and actions described by language. We can refer to these processes of active embodiment as the *perspective-taking system.* In order to understand sentences, we must become actively involved with a starting point or initial perspective. We use this perspective as the foundation for building an embodied understanding of the sentence. For example, when we listen to a sentence such as *The skateboarder vaulted over the railing,* we take the perspective of *the skateboarder* and imagine the process of crouching down onto the skateboard, snapping up the tail, and jumping into the air, as both rider and skateboard fly through the air over a railing and land together on the other side. Identifying with the skateboarder as the agent, we can evaluate the specific bodily actions involved in crouching, balancing, and jumping. The more we know about skateboarding, the more deeply we understand this utterance. If we know only a little about skateboarding, the perspective we assume will be monochromatic and superficial. We will simply imagine the skateboard and rider somehow jumping over a railing. This superficial interpretation will not include a real understanding of body movements and physical dynamics. In general, the extent to which we elaborate our understanding of any particular sentence depends on our ability to assume a perspective from which we can enact the entire sentence. The more time that we have available, the more deeply we can understand the sentence.

FOUR PERSPECTIVAL SYSTEMS

The human mind constructs perspectives on four levels: (1) affordances, (2) spatio-temporal reference frames, (3) causal action chains, and (4) social roles. The hypothesis being developed here is that these four perspectival systems are grounded on specific brain structures that have evolved to solve major adaptive challenges. Each of the four perspectival systems relies on cognitive simulation—also known as *representation* (Karmiloff-Smith, 1982) and *redintegration* (Horowitz & Prytulak, 1969)—to construct meaning by reenacting the sensory and motoric experiences. Let us take a brief glance at how perspective taking works in each of these four perspectival systems.

In the first perspectival system, language and cognition relate to individual objects and actions through affordances. When we think of an object like a banana, we think of it in terms of its colors, textures, and odors. All of these properties provide us with intimate affordances regarding this object. The perspective we assume when we evaluate the affordances provided by the banana is invariably the perspective of our own body as it acts on the banana.

The second perspectival system is the set of competing spatio-temporal reference frames. The three alternative spatial frames are an object-centered frame, a speaker-centered frame, and an environment-centered frame. Temporal relations are also perceived through three analogous frames. Shifting between these frames involves competition and cooperation between perspectives.

The third perspectival system is the one that is most centrally involved in the emergence of grammar. This is the system of causal action frames that allows us to understand the action of a verb from the perspective of the subject in nominative-accusative language or the focus in ergative-absolutive languages.

The fourth perspectival system is the one that allows us to adopt the social and cognitive perspectives of other human beings. In terms of its linguistic reflexes, this system supports the use of discourse devices such as anaphora, deixis, aspect, conjunction, and backgrounding. Perspective switching on this highest level places heavy demands on working memory, planning, strategy selection, and social referencing.

Three Examples

To get a sense of the ways in which perspectives can be instantiated and modified in discourse, consider Sentence (1):

1. As far as the eye could see, stalks of corn were bending in waves under the battering force of a surging curtain of rain.

If we listen to this sentence in a fairly passive way, we may extract a vague picture of strong rain coming down on a large field of corn. However, if we take a more embodied stance, it allows us to "get into" the meaning of the sentence. To do this, we first assume the perspective of an *eye* that scans the full distance from the foreground out to the end of vision at the horizon. This scanning sets up a spatial frame for grounding *as far as the eye can see.* We then shift perspective to the *stalks of corn.* After constructing *stalks* as an initial perspective, we hear the word *corn.* At this point, we see *stalks* as a distributive figure located against the general ground of *corn.* From this distributive perspective, we trace the bending across repeated *waves* or rows of corn. As we begin to do this, we use the word *under* to spawn a secondary causal perspective for the *battering force* that is seen to emerge from a *surging curtain of rain.* All of these shifts in perspective are driven by specific linguistic devices such as *under, of,* and *as far as.* An embodied understanding of this sentence involves a movement across at least four perspectives: eyes, stalks of corn, battering force, and curtain of rain. Because we used the *corn* as our starting point for the main clause, we end up with an understanding that emphasizes the corn as the actor responding to external pressures, rather than an understanding that starts with the rain as the first mover. In this sense, the exact syntactic form we select when speaking constrains the dynamics of the listener's understanding of the flow of perspective in a sentence.

Let us look at a second example of a slightly different type. Sentence (2) allows us to examine ways in which two alternative perspectives are yoked together in terms of a reciprocal interaction.

2. The harder you try to clamp the pipe, the more the water spurts out into the room.

To understand this sentence fully, we imagine clamping a pipe by using some tool that we either squeeze or turn. Because the tool is not specified, the exact shape of the action cannot be precisely embodied, but we feel ourselves exerting some type of pressure against the pipe. At the same time, we assume the secondary perspective of a stream of water that shoots out into the room. In order to understand the yoked relation between these two perspectives, we must notch up our hold on the pipe by degrees and imagine corresponding increases in the stream of water. In fact, one such imagining of a notching up of pressure on the pipe and subsequent increase in the water spurt is enough to give us the embodied sense of an ongoing linkage between the two yoked processes. We then simply assume that repeated increases of pressure on the pipe will lead to repeated increases of spurting by the water.

As a third example of the process of embodied representation, let us take a look at how we understand Sentence (3) with a more metaphoric content.

3. Casting furtive glances at the seamstress, he wormed his way into her heart.

To understand this sentence, we begin by embodying its literal meaning. We first take the viewpoint of the implied subject and imagine casting glances at a seamstress. Next we assume the guise of a worm and imagine trying to enter into the seamstress. Of course, we would avoid interpreting this too graphically. The repulsiveness of assuming the guise of a worm triggers selection of a more metaphorical interpretation for *worming his way into her heart.* In this metaphorical interpretation, the suitor merely acts like a guileful person who is trying to get emotionally closer all the time and the seamstress accepts these advances, allowing the suitor to enter into her affections. However, the juxtaposition of the figurative and literal interpretation gives this metaphor its unique flavor.

The shape of human language is strongly influenced by the way in which perspective promotes the extraction of embodied meanings. To put this more succinctly, we can say that language emerges from embodiment. The grammatical systems that mark functions such as tense, transitivity, deixis, aspect, and agency have as their sole purpose the elaboration of embodied representations through perspective taking. Although languages vary widely in the ways they mark these basic functions, the need to mark these relations is universal. When children learn language, they use perspectival relations (MacWhinney & Bates, 1989) as a key to acquiring lexical and grammatical forms. They do this by focusing on activities that correspond to their own embodied perspectives (Huttenlocher, Smiley, & Charney, 1983).

Having sketched out the basics of the impact of perspective taking on the emergence of language, we next turn to a more detailed look at the four levels of perspective taking: affordances, spatial reference systems, causal action, and social referencing. We begin with an examination of the role of perspective taking in organizing affordances.

AFFORDANCES

Affordances (Gibson, 1966) are sensations that we experience when we interact with individual objects. When we grab a banana, our hands experience the texture of the banana peel, the ridges along the peel, the smooth extensions between the ridges, and the rougher edges where the banana connects with other bananas into a bunch. These haptic affordances are coordinated with visual affordances such as a perception of the yellow and brown colors of the banana and its curving shape. When we hold or throw a banana, we appreciate its weight and balance. An overripe banana can assault us with its pungent smell. When we peel a banana, we encounter still further affordances involving the action of peeling, as well as the peel itself. With the peel removed, we can access new affordances from the meat of the banana. When we eat a banana, our whole body becomes involved in chewing, swallowing, and digestion. All of these affordances in vision, smell, taste, touch, skeletal postures, haptic actions, and even locomotion are provided by a single object that we categorize as a "banana." It is this rich and diverse set of affordances that constitutes the fullest grounding for our understanding of the word *banana*. Of course, we know other things about bananas. We know that they are rich in potassium and Vitamin E, that they are grown in Central America by United Fruit cooperatives, and so on, but these are secondary, declarative facts. Our first line understanding of the word *banana* is grounded not on these declarative facts, but on affordances. When we hear the word *banana*, each of these affordances becomes potentially activated. The visual affordances or images may be the quickest to receive activation. If the sentence requires nothing more, this may be all that we experience. However, just activating the raw visual image is enough to enable embodied processing of the word *banana*.

Affordances are thoroughly grounded in both the motor and the sensory systems. The perspective that we adopt to understand these individual words is one that reactivates our normal, personal encounters with these objects. These encounters involve both motoric actions and sensory perceptions. When we hear the word *banana*, we activate neural pathways that are involved in our nonfictive interactions with real bananas. In this sense, understanding of the meaning of an object involves running a "cognitive simulation" of our interactions with that object in terms of its most salient affordances.

Sometimes languages reflect affordances directly in their names for things. For example, in Navajo, a chair is *bikáá'dah'asdáhí* or "on-it-one-sits." In this example, the object is being characterized primarily in terms of the actions it affords. Or to take a more familiar example, many languages refer to a corkscrew as a "cork puller." Here, again, the object is being characterized in terms of the action that it affords. In their work on procedural semantics, Miller and Johnson-Laird (1976) showed that definitions of nouns in terms of criterial attributes were often not as effective as definitions in terms of affordances. For example, they found that attempts to define a "table" in terms of the number or the placement of its legs or the shape of the top often failed to capture the possible variation in the shape of what counts as a table. It works better to define a table instead as an object that provides a space on which we can place work. In this way, Miller and Johnson-Laird eventually came to the same conclusion that the Navajo reached when they called a table *bikáá'dání* or "at-it-one-works."

Verbs and adjectives also provide affordances. When we hear the word *walk*, we immediately activate the basic elements of the physical components of walking. These include alternating motions of the legs, counterbalanced swinging of the arms, pressure on the knees and other joints, and the sense of our weight coming down on the earth. Although all of these affordances are eventually available, only the tip of this iceberg of is activated unless the sentence calls for the activation of the full set. Adjectives and adverbs also activate affordances, but only in consort with accompanying nouns and verbs. Consider the combination of the adjective *red* with different nouns. A red tomato is redder than is red lettuce. Squeezing a towel affords different sensations from squeezing a sugar cube. Pointing a football toward something involves different orientations and affordances from pointing a tennis ball toward something. The various affordances provided by these words interact through a system of competitive interactions and polysemic processes, as discussed in MacWhinney (1989).

Children tend to learn new words by matching up their concepts to the affordances provided by these words. Lise Menn (personal communication, 1997) observed her son looking at a bird and declaring "have no hands." It appears that the child was relating to the bird by assuming its perspective and this led immediately to the observation that the bird had no hands. Similarly, Marilyn Shatz (personal communication, 1997) reported the case of a child who, after looking at a tiger's tail, turned around to see if she had a tail too. Such anecdotes reflect the ways in which children attempt to understand new animate objects by mapping them onto their own human perspective. This mode of apperception can also extend to nonanimate agents, as we take an embodied approach to understanding the shapes, postures, and positions of trees, cars, house, and even waterfalls (Werner & Kaplan, 1963).

Languages often directly reflect the embodied nature of object name affordances. In English, we speak of the hands of a clock, the teeth of a zipper, and the foot of the mountain. In Apache, this penchant for body-part metaphors carries over to describing the parts of an automobile. The tires are the feet of the car, the battery is its heart, and the headlights are its eyes. Such perspectival encodings combine with the basic affordances we discussed earlier in the case of *banana* to flesh out the meanings of words, even before they are placed into syntactic combination.

Psychologists have often noted that the compatibility between ideas tends to facilitate recall and recognition. Sometimes this compatibility also provides evidence for the construction of embodied representations. For example, Klatzky, Pellegrino, McCloskey, and Doherty (1989) asked participants to judge whether phrases such as *aim a dart* or *close a nail* made sense or not. When the phrases were preceded by hand-shape names that matched the action, such as *pinch* for *aim a dart*, these judgments were facilitated. It appears that generating the appropriate hand shape facilitated construction of the representation. This occurs because the affordances provided by a word like *dart* match up well with the hand-shape cues given by Klatzky et al. Affordances can also involve emotional and affectual attitudes. Ertel and Bloemer (1975) asked participants to verify sentences that sometimes contained negative elements. They found that judgments for negative sentences were facilitated when participants were separating blocks, rather than putting them together. Similar findings for a relation between physical states such as smiling or frowning and affective judgments about people mentioned in sentences were reported by Berkowitz and Trocolli (1990).

This view of perception as requiring active motoric involvement is supported by a wide variety of neurological and physiological findings. Psychophysiologists have often noted a general match between emotions, thoughts, and efferent responses (Cuthbert, Vrana, & Bradley, 1991). For example, when we imagine performing bicep curls, there are discharges to the biceps. Similarly, when we imagine eating, there is an increase in salivation. However, the precise match between such efferent discharge and particular linguistic structures has not been delineated using these techniques. For example, studies of galvanic skin response (GSR) and salivation rate have not been able to tell us how people understand words like *stab* or *lettuce.*

SPACE, TIME, AND MOTION

The second major perspective-taking system is the one that deals with position in and through space and time. Researchers have shown that there are three major spatial frames that speakers can use to specify the positions and movements of objects. These are (1) the ego-centered frame, (2) the object-centered frame, and (3) the environment-centered frame.

The most basic of these three frames is the ego-centered frame, because it encodes the perspective of the speaker. The spatial position of the speaker is given by the deictic term *here* and locations away from the speaker are given by the deictic term *there*. The function of deixis is absolutely fundamental to all perspective taking in space and time, because everything must eventually be referenced to the here and now. The speaker may modify the initial deictic perspective to include the listener as a part of ego. In that case, *here* can refer to the position of the speaker and the listener, and *there* can refer to a position away from the speaker and listener. Other terms that are grounded in the self's position and perspective include *forward, backward, up, down, left,* and *right*.

Within the object-centered frame, locations are defined in terms of their position relative to an external object. For example, *in front of the house* defines a position relative to a house. In order to determine exactly where the front of the house is located, we need to assume the perspective of the house. We can do this by placing ourselves into the front door of the house where we would face people coming to the front door to "interact" with the house. Once its facing is determined, the house functions like a secondary human perspective, and we can use spatial terms that are designed specifically to work with the object-centered frame, such as *under, behind,* or *next to*. If we use these terms to locate positions with respect to our own bodies as in *behind me* or *next to me,* we are treating our bodies as the centers of an object-centered frame. In both ego-centered and object-centered frames, positions are understood relative to a figural perspective that has an orientational field like that of the upright human body.

The use of the ego-centered frame as the basis for the object-centered frame leads to a variety of consequences for both sentence processing and memory. In their classic sentence-picture verification study, Chase and Clark (1972) examined reaction times to sentences like *the star is above the line* or *the star is under the line*. They found that participants were quicker to verify the sentence when it contained an unmarked preposition like *above* instead of a marked preposition like *under*. Clark (1973) noted that unmarked prepositions like *above* or *in front of* tend to reflect orientation to the favored human perspective, whereas marked prepositions like *under* or *behind* deviate from this preferred human perspective. Additional support for the notion of a basic human spatial perspective comes from a study by Bryant, Tversky, and Franklin (1992) in which participants were asked to memorize spatial layouts from particular perspectives. For example, in the hotel scene, they were told "To your left, you see a shimmering indoor fountain." Each object was located at some point in reference to the observer in the imagined scene. After the scene was stored in memory, the time taken to retrieve a particular object was measured. Participants responded most quickly to objects located on the head–feet axis, followed by the front–back axis, followed by the left–right axis. This ordering of perspective reflects the fact that the head–feet axis is the most fundamental human dimension, followed by front–back and then left–right.

Shifts in spatial perspective can lead to strange alternations of the perspectival field. For example, if we are lying down on our backs in a hospital bed, we might refer to the area beyond our feet as "in front of me," even though the area beyond the feet is usually referred to as "under me." To do this, we may even imagine raising our head a bit to correct the reference field, so that at least our head is still upright. We may also override the normal shape of the object-centered field by our own ego perspective. For example, when having a party in the back of a house, we may refer to the area on the other side of the house as "in back of the house," thereby overriding the usual reference to this area as "the front of the house." In this case, we are maintaining our current ego position and perspective as basic and locating the external object within that ego-centered perspective.

Just as the self may be treated as an object, external objects can be treated as the centers of a complete ego perspective. For example, when we say that the "supermarket is up from the police station" we mean that one can take the perspective of the police station and then use ego-centered deictic reference to describe the position of another object. In this sense, object-centered reference is best viewed as an extension of ego-centered reference grounded on a shift of perspective from ego to an external object. Both ego-centered and object-centered perspectives are governed by the basic human perspective. All that is involved in moving between ego-centered and object-centered reference frames is explicit tracking of perspective shift in a way that allows the two frames to be active in parallel.

The third spatial reference system, the environment-centered frame, enforces a perspective based on fixed external landmarks, such as the position of a mountain range, the North Star, or a river. These landmarks must dominate a large part of the relevant spatial world, because they are taken as the basis for a full-blown Cartesian coordinate system. The Guugu Yimithirr language in northeast Queensland (Haviland, 1993) makes extensive use of this form of spatial reference. In Guugu Yimithirr, rather than asking someone to "move back from the table," one might say "move a bit to the west." Of course, we can use this type of geocentric or environment-centered reference in English too, but our uncertainty about whether our listener shares our judgments about which way is "west" makes use of this system far less common. On the other hand, we often make use of specific local landmarks in English. For example, we can describe a position as being *50 yards behind the school.* In this case, we are adopting an initial perspective that is determined either by our own ego-centered location (e.g., facing the school) or by the object-centered perspective of the school for which the entry door is the front. If we are facing the school, these two reference frames pick out the same location. When we describe the position as being located *50 yards toward the mountain from the school,* we are taking the perspective of the mountain, rather than that of the speaker or the school. We then construct a temporary Cartesian grid and use a measurement like *50 yards* to locate a given object.

In all three reference systems, there is a perspective (ego, object, or reference landmark), a reference object (the school), and a location being specified (the position 50 yards away from the school). As long as we are working in the real world, the shifting of perspective within and between these three frames is not that difficult. However, there is always a certain preference for the ego-centered and object-centered frames over the more difficult environment-centered frame. Children who are learning languages, like Tzotzil, that make extensive use of all three frames tend to begin with ego-centered and object-centered frames and only later acquire environment-centered frames (de Leon, 1994). It makes sense that children learn to make spatial reference by first starting out from their own point of view (Piaget, 1952).

The major tasks involved in spatial processing are choice of a reference frame, assignment of position within a frame, shifting between reference frames, and managing competing reference frames. Language use places particularly high demands on frame shifting and integration. Consider a sentence like *I found a ring over there under the bench east of the swimming pool.* The phrase *over there* invokes an ego-centered reference frame that points the listener's attention to a position distant from either the speaker or the listener. The phrase *under the bench* invokes an object-centered reference frame that locates the position under a bench. However, the position of the bench in the overall field is not yet well determined. The phrase *east of the swimming pool* completes the identification of the location by invoking the environment-centered frame of compass positions. As long as we are clear about the locations of the perspectives involved, these shifts between perspectives are easy to manage.

Asking participants to construct coherent maps of new spatial arrays from sketchy verbal descriptions is a more difficult task. Studies have shown that participants shift between multiple competing frames in accord with task demands (Carlson-Radvansky & Logan, 1997; De Vega, 1994; Franklin, Tversky, & Coon, 1992; Klatzky, Loomis, Beall, Chance, & Golledge, 1998; Maki & Marek, 1997), and that learning to manipulate these competing frames is a skill that develops gradually through the school-age years (Rieser, Garing, & Young, 1994).

Mental Models and Spatial Perspectives

The effects of perspective are not confined to linguistic expression; rather, they also extend to the mental models that we extract from linguistic descriptions. The impact of perspective on mental models can be seen both in the process of constructing internalized models and in the use of these models, once they are constructed. Studies of comprehension often emphasize the online incremental nature of the comprehension process (Hess, Foss, & Carroll, 1995; Marslen-Wilson, 1975; Marslen-Wilson & Tyler, 1980; Tanenhaus, Spivey-Knowlton, Eberhard, & Sedivy, 1995). It also appears that incrementality is facilitated when interpretations can be organized about the perspective of the main character or protagonist. The following example passages adapted from Sanford and Moxey (1995) illustrate these effects:

4. While measuring the wall, Fred laid the sheet of wallpaper on the table. Then he put his mug of coffee on the wallpaper.

5. After measuring the wall, Fred pasted the wallpaper on the wall. Then he put his mug of coffee on the wallpaper.

A propositional analysis does not reveal anything odd about (5), but an embodied perspectival analysis reveals that, when Fred comes to put his mug onto the wallpaper, it is glued to the wall. For Fred to carry out the action of putting his mug on the wallpaper would require placing it onto a vertical surface using glue or magnets, which seems like a strange thing to do. Sanford and Moxey (1995) used passages of this type to argue that textual coherence depends on the construction of full representations of passages.

If we look at other studies in the discourse comprehension literature, we find further evidence that readers use perspective to construct mental models. For example, Murray, Klin, and Meyers (1993) and Keefe and

McDaniel (1993) provide evidence that readers tend to follow along closely with the perspective of the protagonist in the passage. In their experiments, subjects may read a sentence like "After standing through the three-hour debate, the tired speaker walked over to his chair." Alternatively, they may read the sentence "The tired speaker moved the chair that was in his way and walked to the podium to continue his three-hour debate." After reading one of these two sentences, subjects were asked to pronounce the visually presented probe word "sat." They were faster at pronouncing the probe when it followed the first sentence, and slower when it followed the second. In the first sentence, the speaker is about to sit down and it makes a lot of sense to pronounce the probe word "sat." In the second sentence, it makes no sense to suddenly have the speaker sitting down when he is actually ready to continue his debate. Glenburg, Meyer, and Linden (1987) report similar results using a probe recognition latency measure.

Morrow, Bower, and Greenspan (1989) asked subjects to read passages describing buildings and the rooms and objects in those buildings. They then read a passage that told about how a protagonist moved through the building. Their task was to decide if particular objects were in particular rooms. It turns out that they were quicker to make this judgment when the rooms and the objects were on the path that the protagonist had taken. The fact that they were quicker in assessing the position of objects directly along the path is consistent with the idea that the path is being encoded from the viewpoint of the imagined protagonist who is touring the imagined building.

O'Brien and Albrecht (1992) gave subjects sentences to read, such as "As Kim stood outside the health club, she felt a little sluggish." Having read this, subjects would then be given the sentence, "She decided to go outside. . . ." Because the continuation is not congruent with the previous spatial arrangement, subjects had trouble reading these continuation sentences.

These experiments in text comprehension have shown that mental models are constructed from the perspective of the protagonist. Relations between objects that lie outside of the main path followed by the protagonist are not as fully encoded as relations between on-path objects and the movements of the protagonist. Embodied representations include not only spatial relations, but also information about the body position of the protagonist (Keefe & McDaniel, 1993), orientations of objects (Sanford & Moxey, 1995), shapes of objects (Klatzky et al., 1989), and other affordances. In addition to information about spatial perspectives and affordances, embodied representations also include information organized around causal action perspectives and social reference perspectives, as we discuss in the next two sections.

Tense, Aspect, and Modality

The processing of temporal relations through adverbials, tense-aspect marking, and modality parallels the processing of spatial relations. Processing of the verb features of tense, aspect, and modality involves movement through the worlds of time, fictive action, and social obligation. Our movements through these worlds are all conducted from a specified perspective that matches up with the aspect or tense given in the sentence. As in the case of spatial processing, the initial basis for temporal deixis is the time of the speech act in which the ego is present. Often, we need to deal with shifts and splits in perspective across time. Vendler (1957) showed how tense can encode three different temporal perspectives: speaking time, action time, and reference time, which are parallel to ego-centered, object-centered, and environment-centered spatial frames, respectively.

Several recent experimental studies have shown that listeners use tense-aspect markings to add richness to the mental models they construct. Earlier, we saw how listeners use spatial relations to construct mental models that embody alternative perspectives. This same principle also extends to the processing of temporal relations through aspects and tense. For example, Carrieras, Carriedo, Alonso, and Fernández (1997) found that, when a protagonist's activities are discussed in the present tense, additional information about that protagonist is quicker to process than when the activities are discussed in the past tense. Zwaan (1996) produced a similar effect by introducing time shifts into narratives such as *a moment later*, as opposed to *an hour later*. The more that a temporal reference pushes an event into the background, away from the main focus of the perspective of the protagonist, the slower we are to reinstantiate that secondary perspective.

CAUSAL ACTION CHAINS

The two levels of perspectival organization we have discussed so far provide grounding for many of the basic units of language. Affordances ground individual open-class words such as *banana, warm,* and *run.* Spatial relations ground closed-class words such as *now, behind,* and *until.* Spatial relations also link up objects in terms of attachment of prepositional phrases to heads, as in *the bench in the park.* However, these affordances and orientations by themselves do not provide us with a rich enough relational system to understand the ways in which objects act on other objects. In particular, a major problem facing both language and cognition is the task of understanding who has acted on what in a causal action chain. Language provides a separate series of devices for solving this problem.

Intransitive Verbs

Predications using intransitive verbs constitute the lowest level building blocks from which causal action chains are constructed. Intransitives can describe actions (e.g., *run* or *jump*), changes of state (e.g., *fall* or *redden*), constant states (e.g., *rest* or *stand*), or processes (e.g., *rain* or *relax*). In each case, the verb being described is interpreted from the perspective of the object that is intimately involved in the action, process, state, or change of state. We can talk about corn growing, dominoes falling, geese flying, or a boy standing. In each case, we interpret the growing, falling, flying, or standing from the viewpoint of the nominal perspective. In fact, we can often go beyond simply seeing a distant object undergoing a change. We can actually embody this change through our own imagined physical activities. When we think about geese flying, we can imagine using our own limbs in this way, even though we cannot really fly. When we talk about a tree standing, we can imagine ourselves as the tree and interpret this ongoing state through the perspective we have when we stand still. In this way, we can treat intransitive verbs as a rich set of embodied affordances. Unlike the affordances provided by nouns, we are not evaluating our actions on an external object. Instead, with intransitive verbs, we are actually performing a cognitive simulation of the activity or process, as we ourselves would execute it. For intransitive verbs such as *twist* or *spread*, this requires us to imagine large whole-body movements that are often fairly complex. When verbs like *twist* or *spread* are used transitively, the basic embodied perspective is still that of the object that is twisting or spreading.

Transitivity Systems

Causal action chains arise from the linking of intransitive activities first into transitive descriptions that are then chained together to form longer narratives. Consider a simple transitive sentence like *The farmer grew the corn.* In this relation, the basic intransitive process of growing is evaluated from the perspective of the corn. However, in terms of causation, it is the farmer who acts on the corn and makes it grow. The farmer plays the role of the agent and the corn plays the role of the patient. When describing relations of this type, languages have to decide whether to focus on the external causal actor or the more directly embodied patient. Nominative-accusative languages, like English, place focus on the actor by treating it as the perspective for the clause. In these languages, the grammatical role of subject is tightly linked to the function of perspective taking. Even in a passive sentence, like *The corn was grown by the farmer,* the subject still marks the farmer as the initial causor. In this case, however, the sentence is understood from the perspective of the patient (the corn), rather than the agent (the farmer).

In ergative-absolutive languages, like Basque or Djirbal, the primary focus is on the participant undergoing change, rather than on the participant causing the change. In the sentence *The farmer grew the corn*, the farmer is placed into the ergative case and the corn is in the absolutive case. The absolutive is also the case that is used for the word *corn* in the intransitive sentence *The corn grew.* This means that ergative-absolutive languages place default focus on the patient, rather than the agent. They do this in order to focus not on the act of causation, but on the processes of change that occur in the patient. Ergative-absolutive languages place a narrow, close focus on process and leave causation as a secondary fact, which is then assigned to the ergative case role. Du Bois (1987) noted that this tendency may be supported by the fact that the actors in transitive sentences are often omitted or pronominalized in causal discourse. English has some minor constructions that can illustrate the effect of the ergative perspective. In a sentence like *This tent sets up in about ten minutes*, we assume the perspective of the tent and imagine it changing shape almost without the intervention of an outside actor, although we realize that this actor is involved on the sidelines.

Just as a nominative-accusative language like English can illustrate occasional ergativity effects, languages like Hindi or Samoan can illustrate incomplete or "split" ergativity (Delancey, 1981; Silverstein, 1976). In Hindi and Gujarati, ergative-absolutive marking is used in the perfective tense, but not the imperfective. This means that a sentence in the imperfective tense, like *The farmer was growing the corn*, is nominative-accusative, but a sentence in the perfective, like *The farmer grew the corn*, shifts into ergative-absolutive. In order to understand why this happens, consider the way in which perspective taking interacts with tense. When we describe an event in the present or the imperfective, we equate our perspective with the ongoing perspective of the actor and the action. However, for an event that occurred in the past and is fully completed, we assume the perspective of the present and describe the past as a separate reality. As a result, we are relatively less involved and less inclined to assume the perspective of the actor. This split allows us to focus on the patient and move the causor into the ergative role.

A second way in which ergative marking can be split is in accord with the person of the agent. When the actor is in third person, nearly all Australian languages and many languages in North America use ergative-absolutive marking. However, when the actor is in first or second person, these languages often use nominative-accusative marking. This split reflects the fact that we are more deeply involved with the first and second person perspectives, for which we can more directly infer causality. For third person actors, we are often on safer ground to defocus their causal activities and focus instead on the perspective of the patient. Other factors that can lead to splits in ergative marking include inferential markers and certain discourse structures.

Ergative marking can also be used to mark intentionality. Delancey (1981) described this for the Caucasian language Batsbi, which uses ergative case for the subject of a sentence like (6) when the falling is intentional and absolutive marking of the subject when the falling is unintentional.

6. Bill fell to the ground.

This use of alternative constructions to mark intentionality closely resembles a similar use of the passive in English.

Variations in transitivity can also be used as a way of shifting between various causal perspectives in discourse. In an example like (7), perspective is initially assigned to the first noun (*car*) as starting point.

7. The car was struck by a falling limb.

However, in order to fully construct the meaning of the utterance, a secondary perspective is established for the falling limb. Studies by Sachs (1967) and Lombardi and Potter (1992) indicate that passives are eventually reshaped into actives in discourse memory. However, when the discourse is structured in ways that properly support the passive structure, it is more likely to be maintained in its full form (Keenan, MacWhinney, & Mayhew, 1977). The English passive is used when the agent is not the focus. Other languages achieve this effect using topicalization devices (as in Hungarian), verbal conjugations (as in Tagalog), or additional types of ergative marking (as in Jacaltec).

Packaging and Conflation

Individual clauses are the basic links in causal action chains. However, in order to break up larger chains of cause and effect, we have to decide how to package and conflate actions into clauses. Consider the following alternative ways of viewing a situation:

8. The beam fell.
9. The beam fell when the crane operator released a lever.
10. The crane dropped the beam.

11. The crane operator released the beam.
12. The crane operator pulled a lever to release the beam.
13. The crane operator dropped the beam by pulling a lever.

The selection of one of these ways of depicting the action over another depends on the perspective we take. If we take the perspective of the falling beam, we will select either of the first two sentences. If we choose (8), we restrict our perspective entirely to *the beam.* If we select (9), we take *beam* as our first perspective, but then add *the crane operator* as a secondary perspective. In (10) through (13), we adopt the perspective of *the crane operator* and include or exclude the way in which the operator dropped the beam.

Perspectives can be conflated in a variety of ways. Consider the contrast between these four sentences describing the movements of small toys:

14. The lion pushed the giraffe, and the giraffe bumped into the table.
15. The lion hit the giraffe and it bumped into the table.
16. The lion bumped the giraffe into the cube.
17. The lion bumped the giraffe, sending it flying toward the table.

In (14), the two actions are packaged into separate full clauses. First, we assume the perspective of the lion hitting the giraffe. Then perspective shifts to the giraffe that bumps into the table. Sentence (15) has the same structure, but the pronoun *it* refers ambiguously to either the initial perspective of *lion* or the new perspective of *giraffe.* In (16) and (17), the two separate actions are conflated into one with *lion* as the dominant perspective and *giraffe* as the subordinate perspective. The conflation of multiple actions into a single verb is also exemplified in (18):

18. So far, the people of this small textile town in northwestern Carolina have been unable to pray Mrs. Smith's two little boys home again.

In this example, the verb *pray* conflates the action of praying and the action of bringing home the two little boys. As in example (16), the perspective of the subject controls two actions at once. When verbs conflate actions in this way, they are forced to accommodate to all the meanings being combined (MacWhinney, 1989). Consider these examples:

19. The light bulb flashed.
20. The light bulb flashed until morning.

In Example (19), the default reading is that the light bulb flashed no more than once or twice. However, in (20) we have to assume that the light bulb flashed iteratively until the morning. In other words, when we take the perspective of the light bulb and then evaluate the temporal frame *until morning*, we have to understand the action of flashing as occurring repeatedly across a period.

Fictive Action

Language provides various devices and forms to support the interpretation of causal action from the viewpoint of a dynamic perspective. Often, that perspective is an animate, human perspective. However, even when the perspective is nonanimate, it still carries the full force of a causal perspective. Sentence (21) illustrates this effect:

21. The library contains three major collections.

Here, the library is viewed as an agent that actively holds collections of books. As Talmy (1988) noted, this is only a fictive agency, because the library is not a real agent and the act of "holding collections" is not a real dynamic action. Nonetheless, the syntax of the sentence invokes a causal action frame with an agential perspective. To further illustrate this, consider the contrast between Sentences (22) and (23).

22. She walked down through the cornfields, out to the river.
23. The path winds down through the cornfields, out to the river.

In (22), the human agent moves over a real path. In (23), on the other hand, the path moves fictively over the same path. Similarly, in (25) the screws are selected as the perspective and this tends to elevate the static force they are exerting to the level of a full causal action.

24. The carpenter holds the four legs firmly against the center pedestal.
25. The screws hold the four legs firmly against the center pedestal.

These examples of fictive motion and fictive causation illustrate the extent to which perspective taking dominates our general view of causal relations in the physical universe. These same forces work for fictive social causation. For example, in (26) the activities of the initial perspective (Tim) trigger a series of activities in the secondary perspective (Mary).

26. Tim's failure to reply to her invitation led to Mary's breaking off their relation.

Here the notion is that one social action leads to another. In fact, both actions are really nonactions. Although this causation is on the social level, we apply a basic physical causal model to even these social effects.

C-Command and Starting Points

Perspective taking in causal action chains impacts certain key aspects of the grammar of pronominal coreference. This effect results from a basic fact about language use, which is that starting points must be fully referential (MacWhinney, 1977). Gernsbacher (1990) discussed this requirement in terms of her theory of "structure building," which holds that the incremental nature of sentence comprehension requires the starting point to be fully identified, because it is the basic building block on which the rest of the interpretation will be constructed. In dozens of psycholinguistic investigations, Gernsbacher has shown that the initial nominal phrase has the "advantage of first mention." This advantage makes it more memorable and more accessible for further meaningful processing. However, when the first noun is not sufficiently referential, the foundation is unclear and the process of comprehension through structure building is thwarted. If the starting point is a nominal, referentiality is not at issue. However, if the starting point is a pronoun, then there must be a procedure for making it referential. One way of doing this is to link the pronoun up to an entity mentioned in the previous discourse. In a sequence like (27), it is easy to link up *he* in the second sentence with *John* from the first sentence, because John has already been established as an available discourse referent. However, in (28) there is nothing to link *he* to and the second sentence seems awkward without this previous link.

27. John was listing the guests at last week's party. He says Bill came, along with Mary and Tom.
28. Only a few of the guests arrived on time. He says Bill came early.

The theory of perspective taking attributes these effects to the fact that starting points serve as the basis for the construction of the embodied mental model conveyed by the clause.

The generative theory of Government and Binding (Chomsky, 1982) treats this same phenomenon in terms of structural relations in a phrase-marker tree. According to this theory, the problem in the second sentence in (28) is that Bill does not "c-command" the pronoun *he* and cannot be coreferential. The phrase marker involved is given in (29):

29.

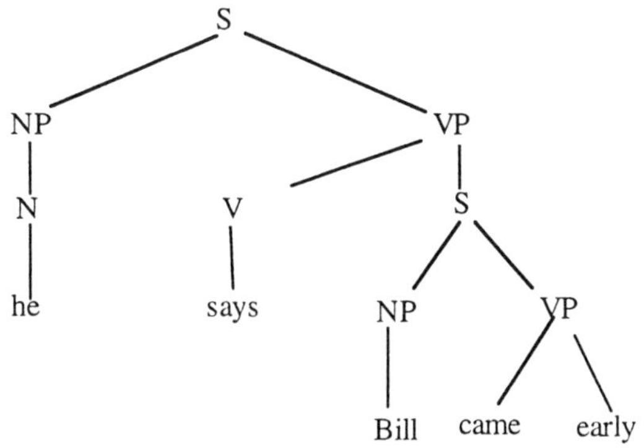

Here, the topmost S node dominates both *he* and *Bill.* However, the VP node and the lower S node only dominate *Bill* and not *he.* Therefore the noun *Bill* does not c-command the pronoun and cannot be coreferential with the pronoun. However, if we shift *Bill* and *he* in this tree, we get (30):

30.

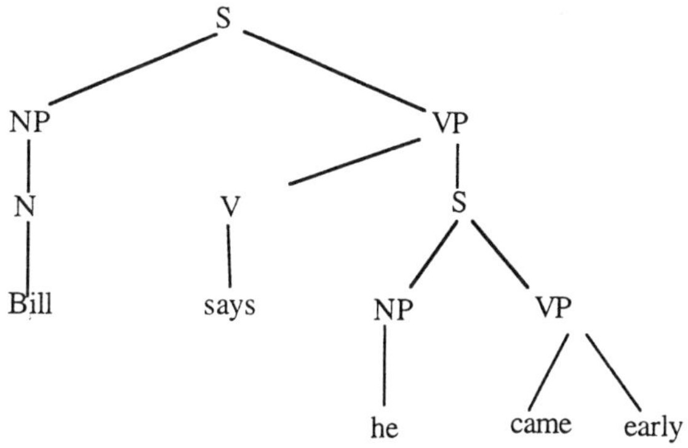

Here, *Bill* c-commands *he* because the only node dominating *Bill* also dominates *he.* Because *Bill* c-commands *he,* it can bind the pronoun and the noun and the pronoun can be coreferential. As a result, there is no problem with (31).

31. Only a few of the guests arrived on time. Bill says he came early.

This effect is not a simple matter of linear order, because coreference between a pronoun and a following noun is perfectly good when the pronoun is in an initial subordinate clause. Consider the contrast between (32) and (33), where the asterisk on (33) indicates that *he* cannot be coreferential with *Lester.*

32. After he drank the vodka, Lester started to feel dizzy.

33. *He started to feel dizzy, after Lester drank the vodka.

Contrasts of this type create problems for the simplest versions of the formalist approach, because they involve identical structural relations. However, they follow immediately from the theory of perspective taking, because a preposed subordinate clause is not a main clause and the process of structure building only requires referentiality for the subject of the main clause. In effect, subordinate conjunctions like *after* in (32) work as cues to place the following material on hold for structure building, until the main clause is encountered. Some additional examples of these effects are given in (34) through (39).

34. *She found a snake near Sue.
35. *Near Sue, she found a snake.
36. *She denied that Martha was a robber.
37. *She liked some of Mary's dates.
38. *He was adored by the students who studied with John.
39. *I think she found a snake near Sue.

In all these examples, clause-initial pronouns that are not protected by placement into an adverbial phrase must be referential so they can serve as the bases for structure building.

The same principle that requires that subjects be referential also applies in a somewhat weakened form to the direct and indirect objects of verbs, as illustrated in (40) through (42).

40. *John told him that Bill was crazy.
41. *I'm willing to give him fifty dollars for Ben's bike.
42. *Him, John's mother likes.

As the object moves into a prepositional phrase, this constraint weakens further:

43. ?People often said to her that Mary was a lunatic.
44. ?John said to him that Bill was crazy.

By the time we reach elements that are no longer in the main clause, as in (45), coreference back to the main clause is not blocked, because elements in a subordinate clause are not crucial perspectives for the structure-building process.

45. The students who studied with him enjoyed John.

This gradient pattern of acceptability for increasingly peripheral clausal participants matches up quite well with the view that the process of perspective taking during structure building requires core participants to be referential.

Further evidence for the gradient nature of the constraint against nonreferential perspectives comes from sentences with special aspect markings, as in (46) and (47).

46. She had just gotten back from vacation, when Mary saw the stack of unopened mail piled up at her front door.
47. *She got back from vacation, when Mary saw the stack of unopened mail piled up at her front door.

Because of the presence of aspectual markers like *had* and *just* in (46), the initial main clause is made relevant for the interpretation of later material. As a result, the possibility is left open that the perspective *she* will be coreferential with later material. Just as relevance markers can increase the openness of a main clause pronoun to coreference, so the openness of a subordinate clause noun for coreference can be decreased by indefinite marking, as in (49).

48. While Ruth argued with the man, he cooked dinner.
49. ?While Ruth argued with a man, he cooked dinner.
50. While Ruth was arguing with a man, he was cooking dinner.

The addition of an aspectual marker of current relevance in (50) overcomes the effect of indefiniteness in (49), again making *man* available as a coreferent for *he*. Gradient patterning of this type provides good evidence that pronominal coreference is under the control of pragmatic factors (Kuno, 1986). Rather than deriving from autonomous formal constraints, we see that the pattern of possible pronominal coreference we have surveyed emerge directly from the forces of perspective and embodiment.

Wh-words introduce a further uncertainty into the process of structure building. In a sentence like (51), the initial *wh*-word *who* indicates the presence of information that needs to be identified.

51. *Who does he hate most?

In this case, it is the pronoun *he*, rather than the initial word *who*, that serves as the starting point for structure building. Because this sentence has no noun to which the pronoun can be bound, it must be bound to some external discourse referent. In any case, the *wh*-word is not a good candidate for the binding of the crucial subject pronoun. However, when there is a pronoun that is not in the crucial subject role, coreference between the *wh*-word and the pronoun is often possible, as in (52) through (56).

52. Who is hated by his brother most?
53. Who thought that Mary loved him?
54. Who hates his mother most?
55. Who said Mary kissed him?
56. Who hates himself most?

In these examples, the *wh*-word can be coreferent with noncentral components, such as objects and elements from embedded clauses. Only coreference with subjects, as in (51), is blocked.

This brief discussion of constraints on coreference has only sampled a few of the most interesting patterns that emerge from a perspective-taking approach to grammar. Kuno (1986) presented a great deal of additional evidence for the importance of pragmatic and functional patterns for additional areas such as reflexive marking and constraints on repeated nominalizations.

Relative Clauses, Conjoined Clauses, and Possessives

Perspective taking also has an important effect on the grammar and processing of various forms of syntactic embedding and conjunction. Let us first look at the impact of perspective on relative clause interpretation. The account presented here was first proposed in MacWhinney (1982) and further elaborated in MacWhinney and Pléh (1988). The predictions of this account can be illustrated by looking at four basic type of relative clauses, given in (57) through (60).

57.	SS:	The dog that chased the cat kicked the horse.	0	switches
58.	OO:	The dog chased the cat the horse kicked.	1	switch
59.	OS:	The dog chased the cat that kicked the horse.	1	switch
60.	SO:	The dog the cat chased kicked the horse.	2	switches

In the SS sentence type, the perspective of the main clause is also the perspective of the relative clause. This means that there are no perspective switches in the SS relative type. In the OO type, the object of the main clause is not the subject of the relative clause. Instead, perspective switches once from the main clause subject (*dog*) to the relative clause subject (*horse*). In the OS type, perspective also switches once. However, in this case, it switches to the main clause object, which then continues as the perspective of the relative clause. In the SO relative clause type, there is a double perspective shift. Perspective begins with the main clause subject (*dog*). When the next noun (*cat*) is encountered, perspective shifts once. However, at the second verb (*kicked*), perspective has to shift back to the initial perspective (*dog*) to complete the construction of the interpretation. Sentences that have further embeddings have even more switches. For example, Sentence (61) has six perspective switches.

61. The dog the cat the boy liked chased snarled. 6 switches

Sentences that have as much perspective switching as (61) without additional lexical or pragmatic support are basically incomprehensible, at least at first hearing.

Studies of the acquisition of relative clauses by children largely support the order of difficulty predicted by the perspective-taking account (MacWhinney, 1982). This predicted order is: SS > OO = OS > SO. This order appears to predict results across a wide variety of experimental paradigms including imitation, comprehension, and sentence memory. In addition, a study of online sentence processing effects in Hungarian (MacWhinney & Pléh, 1988) with adult participants further supported a role for the perspective account. However, there was also evidence in Hungarian for the importance of additional parallel structure effects. In Hungarian, all six orders of the subject, object, and verb are grammatical. In three of these orders (SOV, SVO, and VSO), the subject is the topic; in three other orders (OSV, OVS, and VOS), the object is the topic. When the main clause subject is the topic, the English pattern of difficulty appears (SS > OO = OS > SO). However, when the main clause object is the topic, the order of difficulty is OO > OS = SO > SS. Sentences (62) and (63) illustrate this contrast in Hungarian, using English words:

62. SOV SS: The boy who liked the girl (he) the bike hit.
63. OSV OO: The boy who the girl liked, the bike hit (him).

Sentence (62) illustrates the sentence that is easiest in the SOV word order, when the subject is the topic; whereas (63) illustrates the sentence that is easiest in the OSV word order when the object is the topic. In (62), the initial noun is marked for accusative case in Hungarian. This means that it functions as a patient perspective for both the main and relative clauses.

Perspective maintenance has also been implicated in studies of children's imitations and productions of conjoined sentences (Ardery, 1979; Lust & Mervis, 1980; Slobin & Welsh, 1973). These studies showed that young children find it easier to imitate a sentence like (64), as opposed to one like (65).

64. Mary cooked the meal and ate the bread.
65. Mary cooked and John ate the bread.

In (64), there is no perspective shift, because the perspective of Mary is maintained throughout. In (65), on the other hand, perspective shifts from Mary to John. Moreover, in order to find out what Mary is cooking, we have to maintain both the perspective of Mary and John until the end of the sentence.

We can distinguish structures that require the maintenance of multiple perspectives from those that simply require repeated perspective shifting. Sentence (66) illustrates how the possessive construction can require repeated perspective shifting.

66. My mother's brother's wife's sister's doctor's friend had a heart attack.

In order to determine the identity of this *friend*, we have to trace through a series of social relationships starting with *my mother*. However, once we have traversed one link in this chain, we can drop the initial perspective and shift to the new one. As a result, as long as we can correctly identify the relations involved, this structure is not impossible to process.

Retracing Perspectives

The perspective-taking process also influences ways in which sentences are retraced or reformulated during speech production. MacWhinney and Bates (1978) asked English, Hungarian, and Italian children and adults to describe triplets of pictures involving simple transitive actions. For example, one picture showed (67) and another showed (68).

67. A cat gives flowers to a bunny.
68. A cat gives flowers to a boy.

MacWhinney (1977) found that, for pictures like these, participants sometimes produced retraces like (69) or (70), but never produced retraces like (71) or (72).

69. A bu # a kitty's giving a flower to a bunny.
70. A boy # the cat's giving a boy a flower.
71. A ca # a bunny gets flowers from a cat.
72. A ki # a boy gets flowers from a kitty.

In other words, retracing always moves toward the unmarked perspective of the actor who did the giving, rather than the actor who did the receiving. When we start to describe a picture, we often choose a perspective on the basis of nongrammatical factors such as salience or positioning in the picture (Flores d'Arcais, 1975, 1987; Johnson-Laird, 1968a, 1968b; MacWhinney, 1977; Osgood & Bock, 1977; Pinker & Birdsong, 1979; Sridhar, 1988). However, once we have started to formulate a verb and the rest of the utterance, we may realize that the perspective that we selected was not the best. In such cases, we retrace and begin again with a new, more appropriate perspective.

In this section, we examined various ways in which perspective taking affects grammar and sentence processing on the level of the clause. This discussion passed over many other areas of clausal grammar where perspective taking has a similarly important impact. These additional areas include quantifier scope, word order, and attachment. A fuller account would describe how grammar emerges from perspective in each of these domains. For now, however, we move on to an examination of the fourth and highest level of perspectival organization.

SOCIAL FRAMES

Perspective taking in social and interpersonal frames has its impact not on the grammar of the clause, but rather on the structure of discourse as it is represented through coordination, subordination, propositional chains, and the elaboration of certain lexical and rhetorical structures. Social and interactional frames determine the ways we negotiate points of view, disagreements, and shared understanding between different social agents. The elaboration of cognitive structures to support complex social interactions is certainly not unique to man or to human language. The roots of social perspective taking lie in the basic process of imitation. Young dogs and tigers learn to hunt and kill through imitation. Young beavers learn to build dams through imitation. Young human children learn to walk, talk, and sing through imitation. Imitation involves a particularly direct form of social perspective taking. By taking on the perspective of the parent, the child learns to construct the parent's actions, emotions, and perspectives. Eventually, the child comes to act like the parent. Through observational learning, the young of many species watch adult interactions and acquire age-appropriate role relations. By watching how group members interact, and by assuming alternative perspectives of group members during interactions, a child can learn a great deal about the social world. Finally, perspective is also useful in organizing nonlinguistic plans for group activities, such as hunting, fleeing, or foraging.

It seems unimaginable that the complexity of human society could ever emerge without support from linguistic expression, and herein lies a solution to understanding the great mystery of language evolution. Scholars have long understood the extent to which inner speech supports human cognition. As Plato put it so eloquently in his *Theaetetus,* "The soul in thinking appears to be just talking—asking questions of herself and answering, affirming, and denying. And when she has arrived at a decision, this is called her opinion. I say therefore that to form an opinion is to speak, and opinion is the word spoken—I mean to oneself in silence and not aloud to others." Vygotsky (1962) extended this basic insight by stressing the extent to which inner speech (Sokolov, 1972) derives from the social use of language. In effect, we come to speak with ourselves in ways that we have learned through speaking with others. In concert with Luria (1960, 1975) and others, Vygotsky (1962) elaborated a view of mental functioning that linked inner speech to planning within a social context. The notion of inner speech plays a pivotal role in the account currently being developed. Without access to linguistic expression, animals are able to construct a basic ego-centered social frame. However, inner speech empowers man with ways of operating on the system of social frames in a fuller and more symbolic fashion. Let us examine a few of these systems of linguistic support for social frames.

Social Scenarios

Individual lexical items like *libel, Internet,* or *solidarity* encode social scenarios organized about the perspective of social actors. Let us take the noun *libel* as an example. When we speak of some communication as being *libel* or *libelous,* we mean, roughly, that Speaker A has declared that Speaker B has engaged in some illegal or immoral activity, and that Speaker B has convinced a general Audience C that Speaker A's claims are false and designed to make Audience C think poorly of Speaker A in ways that influence Speaker A's ability to function in public life with Audience C. In fact, the full legal characterization of libel is more complex than this, but the everyday use of the word *libel* has roughly this basic form. This single word conveys a complex set of interacting and shifting social perspectives. To evaluate whether or not a statement is libelous, we have to assume the perspective of Speaker A, Speaker B, and Audience C to evaluate the various claims and possible counterclaims. All of this requires continual integration and shifting of social roles and perspectives.

Implicit Causality

Verbs like *promise, forgive, admire,* and *persuade* encode multiple relations of expectation, benefit, evaluation, and prediction between social actors. To evaluate the uses of these verbs requires flexible perspective taking and coordination. Within this larger group of mental state verbs, one dimension of contrast is known as *explicit causality*. Sentence (73) illustrates the use of the experiencer-stimulus verb *admire*, whereas Sentence (74) illustrates the use of a stimulus-experiencer verb like *apologize*.

73. John admired Mary, because she was calm under stress.
74. John apologized to Mary, because he had cracked under stress.

McDonald and MacWhinney (1995) asked participants to listen to sentences like (73) and (74) while making a cross-modal probe recognition judgment. The probes were placed at various points before and after the pronoun (*he* and *she*). McDonald and MacWhinney found that stimulus-experiencer verbs like *apologize* in (74) tend to preserve the advantage of first mention for the first noun (*John*) as a probe throughout the sentence. However, experiencer-stimulus verbs like *admired* in (73) tend to force a shift in perspective away from the initial perspective (*John*) to the stimulus (*Mary*) right at pronoun. The fact that these perspective shifts are being processed immediately online is good evidence in support of the perspective-taking account of sentence processing.

Expectations and Hypotheticals

Verbs and nouns often characterize complex configurations of social relations within individual clauses. Conjunctions and adverbs are used more to express ways in which clauses interact in terms of presuppositions and perspective. Consider the conjunctions *but* and *although* in sentences like (75) and (76).

75. Mary wanted to win the race, but she felt a need to maintain her allegiance to Helen.
76. Mary wanted to win the race, although she felt a need to maintain her allegiance to Helen.

To understand (75), we have to figure out why Mary's winning of the race would weaken her allegiance to Helen. To understand (76), we additionally have to figure out how Mary thinks she is going to be able to balance her desire to win with her allegiance to Helen.

Language also provides devices for explicit constructions of hypothetical situations. The conjunction *if* is used to establish fictive mental states that very much echo the fictive motion and fictive causality we discussed earlier. Example (77) illustrates this.

77. If I were you, I would share the cookie with me.

To extract the meaning of (77), we need to take the perspective of the speaker and then imagine taking the perspective of the listener. Having done this, we need to understand why the speaker claims that the listener would want to share a cookie.

Mutual Reference

Within larger discourse frames, the establishment of reference for previously mentioned objects and actions relies on devices such as articles and pronouns. The study of these devices has been a major topic in functional linguistics (Haviland & Clark, 1974; Hawkins, 1977a, 1977b; Li & Thompson, 1979; MacWhinney, 1985). These analyses have shown that, in order to make proper use of pronouns and definite articles, we have to assume the perspective of our listener. If we choose to produce a sentence like (78), we need to be sure that our listener knows who *him* is, which car is being mentioned, which key unlocks that car, where the key is located, and where the car is located.

78. Please give him the key to the car.

In order to guarantee successful use of these forms, we have to track our listener's state of knowledge about the objects and positions being mentioned. This requires us to keep track of the conversation from the listener's perspective. As the conversation or narrative progresses, we have to continually update our assumed state of mutual reference to objects and spatial locations, as these form the backbone of a great deal of oral communication.

Theory of Mind

Together, these various devices allow us to talk about a wide range of social perspectives. Within developmental psychology, the study of the ability to take other mental and social perspectives has been discussed in terms of a "theory of mind" (Bartsch & Wellman, 1994). The idea behind theory of mind is that we have to construct a mental model of the knowledge state of other people in order to solve certain problems and communicate successfully. Sentence (79) illustrates the type of embedded representations computed through a theory of mind.

79. Knowing what you expect me to know about what you promised me allows me to surmise that you will not be surprised if I turn down your offer.

Contrasting Perspectives

The various social conventions and forms we mentioned so far have been confined to the lexical level. However, the construction of alternative social perspectives extends far beyond this level to encompass the whole of discourse. To illustrate how these various devices work together to build up larger perspectives, consider Example (80) from Fauconnier and Turner (1996). In Example (80), a contemporary philosopher is imagining a dialog with Kant.

80. I claim that reason is a self-developing capacity. Kant disagrees with me on this point. He says it's innate, but I answer that that's begging the question, to which he counters, in *Critique of Pure Reason,* that only innate ideas have power. But I say to that, what about neuronal group selection? And he gives no answer.

Fauconnier and Turner noted that this brief dialog established three mental spaces—one for the speaker, one for Kant, and one for the projection of the two into a comparison space where the debate occurs.

Example (80) illustrates how persuasion involves negotiation between competing perspectives. On the one hand, speakers must demonstrate an understanding of the listeners' perspectives. At the same time, speakers want to be able to move listeners closer to their perspective. They do this by creating a hypothetical set of intermediary propositions that all can agree to. Then they show that this intermediate perspective could be reconceptualized as being exactly what the speaker believes in the first place. In this way, speakers and listeners move back and forth negotiating perspectives and social frames. Along the way, they rely on lexical, clausal, and discourse structures to cast their viewpoints into the most favorable perspectives.

Multifocal Chains

To build up persuasive and entertaining discourse, we need to control the shifting of perspective between social actors. Sometimes we can organize a narrative chain from a single perspective. For example, Bill could describe his travels through the Florida Everglades totally through the first person. This might work if he were traveling alone through the swamps. However, at his first encounter with another actor, be it an alligator or an egret, there could be a temporary shift in perspective. Although discourses are full of digressions to the perspectives of secondary actors, they typically maintain coherence by relating these excursions back to an ongoing basic chain.

A second type of perspectival organization structures a discourse as a juxtaposition of two or more simultaneous perspectives. This form of organization can involve comparisons and contrasts, or it can simply develop two alternative views of the same set of events. For example, we could describe the events surrounding the Battle of Stalingrad from the perspective of Hitler and the Wehrmacht on the one hand, and Stalin and the Red Army on the other hand. A third form of organization involves the nesting of one full perspective chain within another. For example, within the story of Macbeth, we find nested the play that echoes the planning of the murder of Duncan.

Together, these various methods for maintaining and shifting perspective allow us to construct narratives and conversations that express and develop multifocal perspectives. This multifocality produces memories that are also organized about alternative perspectives. As a result, we can access our knowledge about people and places from alternative viewpoints. Our memories of Rome could be organized around restaurants in which we had eaten, events in Roman history, or ways to get around Rome by bus. The more we know about Rome and the Romans, the more multifocal our memories. Eventually, we can learn to view the city from the viewpoint of people who live in different districts or who have different occupations. This multifocality of representations reflects our expertise in dealing with any subject that we understand well. The more multifocal our representations, the more flexible the thinking and problem solving that depends on them.

MERGING THE FOUR LEVELS

This chapter developed a view of language–thought relations that emphasizes the construction of a human perspective across four major cognitive systems: affordances, spatio-temporal frames, causal action chains, and social frames. Each of these systems establishes a partial cognitive reflection of the entire human being. The affordance system internalizes and adapts to the ways in which humans act on the world using sensation and action. Spatio-temporal frames internalize our mental models of positions, moments, and movements in the world. Causal action chains allow us to encode the activities of the world in terms of our own causative perspective. Social frames allow us to view actions in terms of their personal consequences and implications.

Operating by themselves, these four systems would not give rise to the unitary experience of human consciousness. Without language, our minds would remain prisoners of a certain internal modularity (Fodor, 1983). It is language that provides the real-time, dynamic, symbolic links that merge these four separate perspectives into the integrated human perspective we call consciousness. Language, both in its social form and in the guise of inner speech, links these four separate frames into a functional neural circuit that embodies a complete mental homunculus. It is this complete perspective-taking system that we use to solve scientific problems, form narrations, and develop social relations.

In Examples (1) through (3), at the beginning of this chapter, we examined ways in which language could express interacting and switching perspectives. Let us now consider a more extended example of how language works to blend together information from these four separate systems. This example, given in (83), comes from an Associated Press release of May 20, 1997.

83. A cyclone hammered the Bangladesh coast Monday with the force of "hundreds of demons" leveling entire villages of mud and thatch huts, flooding crops, and killing at least six people.

 Three men and two children were crushed under collapsed buildings or hit by flying pieces of tin roofs in the southern port of Chittagong. One man died in Teknaf, about 110 miles down the coast, when he was blown off his roof, while trying to secure it.

 The storm roared in from the Bay of Bengal with wind gusts of 125 mph, forcing a half-million people to flee their huts and huddle in concrete shelters. Many power and telephone lines were down, so a full account of casualties and damage was not available.

To comprehend this passage fully, we first assume the perspective of the cyclone hammering the coast. We know that storms do not use literal hammers to beat down on the land, but we sense the driving nature of the cyclone pounding the coast. The affordances of hammers, pounding, and rain are fairly clear. We then convert our image of the cyclone to that of hundreds of demons who are now pounding the coast in the guise of a storm. Further concretizing our vision, we now see this demon storm leveling and killing. The perspective now shifts to the people who are being killed. Here the article uses the split perspective of the passive to focus the people against the background of the cyclone and flying roofs. We learn about a man who died in Teknaf. At first his perspective is a passive one (blown off his roof), but then we see him play a more active role (trying to secure it). We also begin to see a shift between spatial perspectives with movements from Chittagong and Teknaf back to the Bay of Bengal. Finally, we shift from the fact that the storm has downed the power lines back to the overall perspective of the writer of the press release who is explaining to us that conditions on the ground made it difficult to write a complete account of this event. Together, these various shifts of perspective give this short press release a rich, dynamic quality that allows us to partially understand key aspects of the catastrophe. This use of dynamic perspective taking and perspective switching substantially enriches our ability to form rich interpretations that support the acquisition of this new information.

NEUROPHYSIOLOGICAL IMPLICATIONS

The claim being made is that the human brain has evolved in a way that allows it to run a high-level simulation of the human body and its positioning in the spatial, social, and causal world. It is this continually running cognitive simulation that constitutes human consciousness. Moreover, language, particularly in the form of inner speech (Sokolov, 1972; Vygotsky, 1962), plays a pivotal role in supporting this continually running perspectival simulation. Language does this by coordinating sensory and motoric systems in posterior brain areas with attentional and planning systems in frontal areas. By continually accessing and refreshing posterior areas, frontal areas allow us to interpret and anticipate experiences in terms of basic affordances. In addition, the frontal cortex is specifically adapted to support dynamic integration of the four perspectival levels we discussed. In particular, frontal cortex has separate mechanisms for refreshing and integrating affordances, spatial referencing, causal action chains, and social frames. In this section, we examine evidence from cognitive neuropsychology that supports this view of cortical processing.

Control of Affordances

A variety of evidence indicates that frontal cortex works together with posterior cortex in a perception–action chain (Neisser, 1976) that allows us to process affordances. In an early study on this topic, Bossom (1965) adapted monkeys to using special eyeglasses that inverted the visual field. After moving about with these eyeglasses for some days, the monkeys became readapted to the upside-down view these glasses provided. When Bossom then lesioned the monkeys at various cortical locations, he found that only lesions to the area of the frontal lobes known as the supplementary eye fields resulted in damage to the readapted visual field. This finding matches up with others that suggest that, even on the levels of affordances and spatial frame processing, perspective switching is controlled by frontal structures that associate perception with action.

In the last few years, imaging studies have provided additional evidence regarding the control of affordance processing. Studies by Parsons et al. (1995), Martin, Wiggs, Ungerleider, and Haxby (1996), and Cohen et al. (1996) showed that when participants are asked to engage in mental imagery, they use modality-specific cortical systems. There is growing evidence for an important role for frontal cortex in supporting strategic aspects of meaning access and generation (Petersen, Fox, Posner, Mintun, & Raichle, 1988; Posner, Petersen, Fox, & Raichle, 1988). Studies using functional magnetic imaging resonance (fMRI) technology have shown that left inferior prefrontal cortex (LIPC) is activated for initial presentations of words, but not for repeated presentations (Demb et al., 1995; Gabrieli et al., 1996). These findings call into question the traditional view of language processing, which locates semantic processing exclusively in posterior errors such as the inferior parietal or the superior temporal gyrus. In addition, lesion studies (Gainotti, Silveri, Daniele, & Giustolisi, 1995), positron emission tomography (PET) studies (Posner et al., 1988), and fMRI analyses (Menard, Kosslyn, Thompson, Alpert, & Rauch, 1996) have shown that right frontal areas are involved in the generation or retrieval of action terms. Together, these studies point to an important role for frontal cortex in generating access cues for the meanings that are eventually expressed by words in general and verbs in particular. Within the current framework, this process is best understood as involving the active generation of a motoric perspective that is compatible with the affordances of particular objects. For example, in the verb generation paradigm, the participant sees a picture of a chair. The task is to activate a verb that is appropriate for this object. To do this, the participant must utilize the affordances of the chair to activate a motoric perspective that is then used to activate a verbal label like *sit.* This interaction between affordances and actions is controlled by areas of the frontal lobes that generate action plans and perspectives.

This view of frontal functioning fits in well with the characterization of processing in the dorsal visual stream as involving an integration between perception and action (Goodale, 1993). Goodale noted that patients with lesions to the dorsal "where" stream have problems not only with locating objects in space, but also with forming hand positions that are appropriate for manipulating these objects. Single-cell recording techniques have shown that there are cells in posterior parietal visual areas that only respond to objects when they are being acted on. These findings support the idea that the dorsal visual stream provides perception–action linkages for processing affordances. These perception–action linkages correspond to what Horowitz and Prytulak (1969) called "reafference," what Teuber (1964) called "corollary discharge," and what Glenberg (1997) called "embodied" perception.

Control of Spatial Perspective

Studies of neurological patients suffering from visual neglect provide striking support for the role of perspective in both affordance and spatial level processing. Behrmann and Tipper (1998) looked at patients with right parietal lesions who showed neglect in the left visual field. When asked to copy a picture with three flowers in flower pots, these participants would typically draw the right flower pot accurately and have problems with the left flower pot. However, when they were then asked to copy a picture of a single flower in a flower pot, they were able to accurately copy one side of the flower but would have trouble with copying the side of the flower on their neglected side. Studies of this type have shown that neglect is based not on absolute properties of the visual field, but on the representation of objects cognitively. This level of field independence is apparently based on primarily parietal mechanisms, or at least connections between parietal and frontal cortex, because the lesions involved are in the parietal lobe. However, there is also evidence for an interaction between frontal and parietal areas in the control of spatial perspective. Using single-cell recording techniques with macaque monkeys, Olson and Gettner (1995) located cells in the supplementary eye field of prefrontal cortex that respond not to positions in the actual visual field, but to positions on objects in visual memory. These results lend further weight to the idea that the prefrontal visual area works together with parietal areas to facilitate object-centered processing of affordances and spatial representations.

Control of Action Chains

It has long been suspected that parts of inferior frontal cortex around Broca's area play an important role in controlling action sequences (Fuster, 1989; Greenfield, 1991). To the degree that language comprehension and production depend on the construction and processing of action sequences, it makes sense that both Broca's area and supplementary motor areas should be involved in supporting language processing. From the viewpoint of perspective theory, it would be easy to suspect that these frontal areas are particularly involved in the construction and support of causal action chains. In fact, recent fMRI work has linked the processing of syntactically complex sentences to Broca's area (Geschwind, 1965; Just, Carpenter, Keller, Eddy, & Thulborn, 1996).

Because language functions simultaneously on so many levels, it is not surprising to find that several frontal areas must all work in concert during language processing. The rich pattern of interconnectivity between frontal areas and from frontal areas to posterior, thalamic, and cingulate areas (Fuster, 1989; Kolb & Whishaw, 1995) underscores the extent to which the frontal system works to integrate a variety of mental facilities, including attention (Cohen & Bookheimer, 1994), memory (Shimamura, Janowsky, & Squire, 1990), inhibition, motor planning, and goal formation, all in the service of perspective taking. Mesulam (1990, p. 610) asked "Why does (prefrontal) area PG project to so many different patches of prefrontal cortex? Why are the various areas of prefrontal cortex interconnected in such intricate patterns?" The perspectival account suggests that the answer to this question lies in the fact that the frontal cortex is not only attempting to integrate perspective across four levels of cognition but also to support the emergent frontal homunculus through access to memory, attention, and systems for inhibiting prepotent responses.

The level of frontal integration we described so far is available in our primate cousins, albeit in a somewhat less elaborated fashion (Wilkins & Wakefield, 1995). What is unique to man is the linkage of this rich frontal system to language. Both cortical and subcortical pathways link frontal premotor cortex to temporal auditory cortex to form a phonological loop (Grasby et al., 1993; Menard et al., 1996; Paulesu, Frith, & Frackowiak, 1993). This loop and the linguistic forms it controls provide an additional bridge between the control architecture of frontal cortex and the affordance and spatial processing of posterior cortex. More important, language links us to our social world and allows us to share in the perspectives of others. These processes of verbal sharing encourage the formation of inner speech that serves to progressively knit together the four levels of perspective taking.

HOW CAN THIS ACCOUNT BE ELABORATED?

This account is just a hypothesis. Although there are hundreds of pieces of linguistic, cognitive, and neurological evidence pointing toward the importance of embodiment and perspective as the central organizing principles of the mind, the current version of the perspective hypothesis needs to be elaborated in much greater detail before it can really be tested. But exactly how should this general claim be cashed out in terms of a specific mechanistic model? Ideally, it would be nice to have a full, simulated model of the human brain. However, evolution has devoted several hundred million years to crafting the basic neural structure and at least another 4 million in building up the specific human adaptations that support language. It may take us a while to catch up with all this handiwork, using our best digital computers. However, we can already begin to see how the notion of embodiment has begun to illuminate work in Artificial Intelligence (Brooks, 1991; Feldman et al., 1996; Harnad, 1990, 1995; Regier, 1996). While this simulation work is progressing, there are several areas in which the empirical claims of the perspective hypothesis can be further elaborated.

From the viewpoint of psycholinguistics, the perspective hypothesis generates many important predictions. Whenever a structure shifts to a marked perspective or forces integration of competing perspectives, it should be difficult to produce, comprehend, imitate, and recall. In fact, this type of prediction has already received extensive support, but it needs to be tested out now against the full range of linguistic structures and psycholinguistic tasks. Not all effects in psycholinguistics can be attributed to perspective, but its influence is pervasive enough to require a complete reexamination of the experimental literature in this new light. Currently, there is no reasonably complete model of sentence processing that properly incorporates perspective-taking effects. However, models developed by Gernsbacher (1990), MacDonald, Pearlmutter, and Seidenberg (1994), and MacWhinney and Bates (1989) could all be adapted in ways that would foreground the impact of perspective on sentence processing.

From the viewpoint of linguistics, the perspective hypothesis unifies a great deal of thinking about functional pressures on language form by Fauconnier, Givon, Kuno, Langacker, Talmy, and others. A theory grounded on perspective and embodiment can provide new motivation for typological theories of language universals as they affect lexical, grammatical, and discourse structure. The individual theories of aspect, pronominal coreference, reflexivization, transitivity, conjunction, and relativization with which linguists are currently working could all be restructured to deal specifically with perspective as a force unifying language and cognition. In this way, linguistics would be drawn more deeply into association with the whole of cognitive science.

From the viewpoint of developmental psychology, the role of perspective in organizing learning reawakens the attention to issues originally debated by Piaget and Vygotsky. Both Piaget (1959) and Vygotsky (1962) recognized the importance of the child's perspective for grounding cognitive development. Piaget viewed this in terms of an egocentric perspective, whereas Vygotsky emphasized social influences on inner speech. The perspective hypothesis views these two approaches as fully compatible. In fact, our understanding of cognitive development would be incomplete without emphasizing both views. Other researchers such as Dewey (1933), Huttenlocher and Presson (1973), Case (1997), and Montessori (1913) emphasized the importance of "learning by doing." These linkages between perception and action are closely compatible with the perspective hypothesis.

From the viewpoint of cognitive psychology, the perspective account matches up well with a number of current research trends. Several years ago, Kolers and Roediger (1984) argued that memories are shaped by the action of encoding. Since then, researchers have increasingly emphasized the impact of embodiment on both memory and categorization. Glenberg's (1997) approach is particularly close to the one developed here. One of Glenberg's important contributions is the notion of "mesh," which emphasizes the extent to which default properties stored in memory interact with new embodied perceptions to give rise to subjective experience and new learning. Glenberg's ideas about mesh match up well with models of schema application in the connectionist framework (McClelland, St. John, & Taraban, 1989; Rumelhart, Smolensky, McClelland, & Hinton, 1986).

By modeling interactions of memory with current embodied perception, cognitive psychologists can make good use of the concept of perspective to generate new experiments and more detailed hypotheses. Within the general area of cognitive psychology, there are further applications of perspective theory to both spatial representation theory and problem-solving theory. In spatial representation theory, there is already a strong tendency to view cognition in terms of conflicting and converging spatial perspectives. The current approach simply rearticulates ideas already common in that field. However, in the field of problem solving, the role of perspective remains largely unexplored. For studies of man–machine interaction, problem representation, and search strategies, the perspective account makes many interesting and testable predictions.

From the viewpoint of social psychology, perspective theory provides an interesting way of rethinking social cognition. Perspective directly expresses basic social concepts such as theory of mind (Flavell & Miller, 1997), social referencing, symbolic interaction (Blumer, 1969), and perspective taking. Rather than viewing social processes in terms of "cold" as opposed to "hot" cognition, perspective theory emphasizes the way in which embodiment unifies hot emotional and instinctual affordances with colder discourse-based structures for social relations. The linkage of social structures to linguistic processes offers a variety of additional ways of conceptualizing the learning and application of roles, rules, and relationship.

Finally, from the viewpoint of cognitive neuropsychology, the implications of the four-level perspectival account of frontal functioning are new and largely unexplored. Through the combined application of imaging techniques such as event-related potentials (ERP) and functional magnetic resonance imaging (fMRI) with data from clinical populations, we can begin the slow process of testing out and elaborating the perspective hypothesis in ways that can possibly reshape our thinking about the human mind. There are also clear implications of this hypothesis for our thinking about the ways in which the human brain developed from the primate brain (Wilkins & Wakefield, 1995). By relating changes in the architecture and connectivity of frontal cortex with posterior and limbic areas to changes across primate species, we can gain a still richer view of the emergence of language from embodied cognition.

REFERENCES

Ardery, G. (1979). The development of coordinations in child language. *Journal of Verbal Learning and Verbal Behavior, 18,* 745–756.

Bartsch, K., & Wellman, H. (1994). *Children talk about the mind.* New York: Oxford University Press.

Behrmann, M., & Tipper, S. P. (1998). Attention accesses multiple reference frames: Evidence from visual neglect. *Journal of Experimental Psychology: Human Perception and Performance.*

Berkowitz, L., & Troccoli, B. T. (1990). Feelings, direction of attention, and expressed evaluations of others. *Cognition and Emotion, 4,* 305–325.

Blumer, H. (1969). *Symbolic interactionism: Perspective and method.* Englewood Cliffs, NJ: Prentice-Hall.

Bossom, J. (1965). The effect of brain lesions on adaptation in monkeys. *Psychonomic Science, 2,* 45–46.

Brooks, R. A. (1991). How to build complete creatures rather than isolated cognitive simulators. In K. VanLehn (Ed.), *Architectures for intelligence* (pp. 225–240). Hillsdale, NJ: Lawrence Erlbaum Associates.

Bryant, D. J., Tversky, B., & Franklin, N. (1992). Internal and external spatial frameworks for representing described scenes. *Journal of Memory and Language, 31,* 74–98.

Carlson-Radvansky, L. A., & Logan, G. D. (1997). The influence of reference frame selection on spatial template construction. *Journal of Memory and Language, 37,* 411–437.

Carreiras, M., Carriedo, N., Alonso, M. A., & Fernández, A. (1997). The role of verb tense and verb aspect in the foregrounding of information during reading. *Memory and Cognition, 25,* 438–446.

Case, R. (1997). The development of conceptual structures. In W. Damon, D. Kuhn, & R. Siegler (Eds.), *The handbook of child development.* New York: Wiley.

Chase, W., & Clark, H. (1972). Mental operations in the comparison of sentences and pictures. In L. W. Gregg (Ed.), *Cognition in learning and memory* (pp. 205–232). New York: Wiley.

Chomsky, N. (1982). *Some concepts and consequences of the theory of government and binding.* Cambridge, MA: MIT Press.

Clark, H., & Clark, E. (1977). *Psychology and language: An introduction to psycholinguistics.* New York: Harcourt, Brace, & Jovanovich.

Clark, H. H. (1973). Space, time, semantics, and the child. In T. E. Moore (Ed.), *Cognitive development and language acquisition* (pp. 28–63). New York: Academic Press.

Cohen, M. S., & Bookheimer, S. Y. (1994). Localization of brain function using magnetic resonance imaging. *Trends in Neurosciences, 17*(7), 268–277.

Cohen, M. S., Kosslyn, S. M., Breiter, H. C., DiGirolamo, G. J., Thompson, W. L., Anderson, A. K., Bookheimer, S. Y., Rosen, B. R., & Belliveau, J. W. (1996). Changes in cortical activity during mental rotation. A mapping study using functional MRI. *Brain, 119,* 89–100.

Cuthbert, B. N., Vrana, S. R., & Bradley, M. M. (1991). Imagery: Function and physiology. *Advances in Psychophysiology* (Vol. 4).

de Leon, L. (1994). Exploration in the acquisition of geocentric location by Tzotzil children. *Linguistics, 32,* 857–884.

De Vega, M. (1994). Characters and their perspectives in narratives describing spatial environments. *Psychological Research, 56,* 116–126.

Delancey, S. (1981). An interpretation of split ergativity and related patterns. *Language, 57,* 626–658.

Demb, J. B., Desmond, J. E., Wagner, A. D., Vaidya, C. J., Glover, G. H., & Gabrieli, J. D. (1995). Semantic encoding and retrieval in the left inferior prefrontal cortex: A functional MRI study of task difficulty and process specificity. *Journal of Neuroscience, 15*(9), 5870–5878.

Dewey, J. (1933). *How we think.* Boston: Heath.

Du Bois, J. (1987). The discourse basis of ergativity. *Language, 63,* 805–856.

Ertel, S., & Bloemer, W. (1975). Affirmation and negation as constructive action. *Psychologische Forschung, 37,* 335–342.

Fauconnier, G., & Turner, M. (1996). Blending as a central process of grammar. In A. Goldberg (Ed.), *Conceptual structure, discourse, and language* (pp. 113–130). Stanford, CA: Center for the Study of Language and Information.

Feldman, J., Lakoff, G., Bailey, D., Narayanan, S., Regier, T., & Stolcke, A. (1996). L_0—The first five years of an automated language acquisition project. *AI Review, 10,* 103–129.

Flavell, J. H., & Miller, P. H. (1997). Social cognition. In W. Damon, D. Kuhn, & R. Siegler (Eds.), *Handbook of child psychology* (pp. 851–898). New York: Wiley.

Flores d'Arcais, G. B. (1975). Some perceptual determinants of sentence construction. In G. B. Flores d'Arcais (Ed.), *Studies in perception* (pp. 343–373). Milan: Martello-Giunti.

Flores d'Arcais, G. B. (1987). Syntactic processing during reading for comprehension. In M. M. Coltheart (Ed.), *Attention and performance VII: The psychology of reading* (Vol. 12, pp. 619–654). Hillsdale, NJ: Lawrence Erlbaum Associates.

Fodor, J. (1983). *The modularity of mind: As essay on faculty psychology.* Cambridge, MA: MIT Press.

Franklin, N., Tversky, B., & Coon, V. (1992). Switching points of view in spatial mental models. *Memory and Cognition, 20,* 507–518.

Fuster, J. M. (1989). *The prefrontal cortex.* New York: Raven.

Gabrieli, J. D. E., Desmond, J. E., Demb, J. B., Wagner, A. D., Stone, M. V., Vaidya, C. J., & Glover, G. H. (1996). Functional magnetic resonance imaging of semantic memory processes in the frontal lobes. *Psychological Science, 7,* 278–283.

Gainotti, G., Silveri, M. C., Daniele, A., & Giustolisi, L. (1995). Neuroanatomical correlates of category-specific semantic disorders: A critical survey. *Memory, 3,* 247–264.

Gernsbacher, M. A. (1990). *Language comprehension as structure building.* Hillsdale, NJ: Lawrence Erlbaum Associates.

Geschwind, N. (1965). Disconnection syndromes in animals and men. *Brain, 88,* 585–644.

Gibson, J. J. (1966). *The senses considered as perceptual systems.* Boston: Houghton Mifflin.

Glenberg, A. (1997). What memory is for. *Behavioral and Brain Sciences, 220,* 1–55.

Glenberg, A. M., Meyer, M., & Linden, K. (1987). Mental models contribute to foregrounding during text comprehension. *Journal of Memory and Language, 26,* 69–83.

Goodale, M. A. (1993). Visual pathways supporting perception and action in the primate cerebral cortex. *Current Opinion in Neurobiology, 3,* 578–585.

Grasby, P. M., Frith, C. D., Friston, K. J., Bench, C., Frackowiak, R. S. J., & Dolan, R. J. (1993). Functional mapping of brain areas implicated in auditory-verbal memory function. *Brain, 116,* 1–20.

Greenfield, P. (1991). Language, tools and brain: The ontogeny and phylogeny of hierarchically organized sequential behavior. *Behavioral and Brain Sciences, 14,* 531–595.

Harnad, S. (1990). The symbol grounding problem. *Physica D, 42,* 335–346.

Harnad, S. (1995). Grounding symbolic capacity in robotic capacity. In L. Steels & R. Brooks (Eds.), *The "artificial life" route to "artificial intelligence": Building situated embodied agents* (pp. 277–286). Mahwah, NJ: Lawrence Erlbaum Associates.

Haviland, J. B. (1993). Anchoring, iconicity, and orientation in Guugu Yimithirr pointing gestures. *Journal of Linguistic Anthropology, 3,* 3–45.

Haviland, S., & Clark, H. (1974). What's new? Acquiring new information as a process in comprehension. *Journal of Verbal Learning and Verbal Behavior, 13,* 512–521.

Hawkins, J. (1977a). The pragmatics of definiteness: Part 1. *Linguistische Berichte, 48,* 1–25.

Hawkins, J. (1977b). The pragmatics of definiteness: Part 2. *Linguistische Berichte, 48,* 27–60.

Hess, D. J., Foss, D. J., & Carroll, P. (1995). Effects of global and local context on lexical processing during language comprehension. *Journal of Experimental Psychology: General, 124,* 62–82.

Horowitz, L., & Prytulak, L. (1969). Redintegrative memory. *Psychological Review, 76,* 519–531.

Huttenlocher, J., & Presson, C. (1973). Mental rotation and the perspective problem. *Cognitive Psychology, 4,* 277–299.

Huttenlocher, J., Smiley, P., & Charney, R. (1983). Emergence of action categories in the child: Evidence from verb meanings. *Psychological Review, 90,* 72–93.

Johnson-Laird, P. (1968a). The choice of the passive voice in a communicative task. *British Journal of Psychology, 59,* 7–15.

Johnson-Laird, P. (1968b). The interpretation of the passive voice. *Quarterly Journal of Experimental Psychology, 20,* 69–73.

Just, M. A., Carpenter, P. A., Keller, T. A., Eddy, W. F., & Thulborn, K. R. (1996). Brain activation modulated by sentence comprehension. *Science, 274,* 114–116.

Karmiloff-Smith, A. (1982). Language as a formal problem space. In W. Deutsch (Ed.), *Child language: Beyond description.* New York: Springer.

Keefe, D., & McDaniel, M. (1993). The time course and durability of predictive inferences. *Journal of Memory and Language, 32,* 446–463.

Keenan, J., MacWhinney, B., & Mayhew, D. (1977). Pragmatics in memory: A study in natural conversation. *Journal of Verbal Learning and Verbal Behavior, 16,* 549–560.

Kintsch, W. (1974). *The representation of meaning in memory.* Hillsdale, NJ: Lawrence Erlbaum Associates.

Klatzky, R. L., Loomis, J. M., Beall, A. C., Chance, S. S., & Golledge, R. G. (1998). Spatial updating of self-position and orientation during real, imagined, and virtual locomotion. *Psychological Science, 9,* 293–298.

Klatzky, R. L., Pellegrino, J. W., McCloskey, B. P., & Doherty, S. (1989). Can you squeeze a tomato? The role of motor representations in semantic sensibility judgments. *Journal of Memory and Language, 28,* 56–77.

Kolb, B., & Whishaw, I. Q. (1995). *Fundamentals of human neuropsychology* (4th ed.). New York: Freeman.

Kolers, P. A., & Roediger, H. L. (1984). Procedures of mind. *Journal of Verbal Learning and Verbal Behavior, 23,* 425–449.

Kuno, S. (1986). *Functional syntax.* Chicago: University of Chicago Press.

Langacker, R. (1989). *Foundations of cognitive grammar. Vol. 2: Applications.* Stanford, CA: Stanford University Press.

Levelt, W. J. M. (1989). *Speaking: From intention to articulation.* Cambridge, MA: MIT Press.

Li, C. N., & Thompson, S. A. (1979). Third-person pronouns and zero-anaphora in Chinese discourse. In T. Givón (Ed.), *Syntax and semantics: Discourse and syntax* (Vol. 12, pp. 311–354). New York: Academic Press.

Lombardi, L., & Potter, M. (1997). The regeneration of syntax in short term memory. *Journal of Memory and Language, 31,* 713–733.

Luria, A. (1960). Verbal regulation of behavior. In M. A. B. Brazier (Ed.), *The central nervous system and behavior.* New York: Macy Foundation.

Luria, A. R. (1975). Basic problems of language in the light of psychology and neurolinguistics. In E. H. Lenneberg & E. Lenneberg (Eds.), *Foundations of language development: A multidisciplinary approach* (Vol. 2, pp. 49–73). New York: Academic Press.

Lust, B., & Mervis, C. A. (1980). Development of coordination in the natural speech of young children. *Journal of Child Language, 7,* 279–304.

MacDonald, M. C., Pearlmutter, N. J., & Seidenberg, M. S. (1994). Lexical nature of syntactic ambiguity resolution. *Psychological Review, 101*(4), 676–703.

MacWhinney, B. (1977). Starting points. *Language, 53,* 152–168.

MacWhinney, B. (1982). Basic syntactic processes. In S. Kuczaj (Ed.), *Language acquisition: Vol. 1. Syntax and semantics* (pp. 73–136). Hillsdale, NJ: Lawrence Erlbaum Associates.

MacWhinney, B. (1985). Grammatical devices for sharing points. In R. Schiefelbusch (Ed.), *Communicative competence: Acquisition and intervention* (pp. 325–374). Baltimore, MD: University Park Press.

MacWhinney, B. (1989). Competition and lexical categorization. In R. Corrigan, F. Eckman, & M. Noonan (Eds.), *Linguistic categorization* (pp. 195–242). New York: Benjamins.

MacWhinney, B., & Bates, E. (1978). Sentential devices for conveying givenness and newness: A cross-cultural developmental study. *Journal of Verbal Learning and Verbal Behavior, 17,* 539–558.

MacWhinney, B., & Bates, E. (Eds.). (1989). *The crosslinguistic study of sentence processing.* New York: Cambridge University Press.

MacWhinney, B., & Pléh, C. (1988). The processing of restrictive relative clauses in Hungarian. *Cognition, 29,* 95–141.

Maki, R. H., & Marek, M. N. (1997). Egocentric spatial framework effects from single and multiple points of view. *Memory and Cognition, 25,* 677–690.

Marslen-Wilson, W. (1975). Sentence perception as an interactive parallel process. *Science, 189,* 226–227.

Marslen-Wilson, W. D., & Tyler, L. K. T. (1980). The temporal structure of spoken language understanding. *Cognition, 8,* 1–71.

Martin, A., Wiggs, C. L., Ungerleider, L. G., & Haxby, J. V. (1996). Neural correlates of category-specific knowledge. *Nature, 379,* 649–652.

McClelland, J. L., St. John, M., & Taraban, R. (1989). Sentence comprehension: A parallel distributed processing approach. *Language and Cognitive Processes, 4,* 287–335.

McDonald, J. L., & MacWhinney, B. J. (1995). The time course of anaphor resolution: Effects of implicit verb causality and gender. *Journal of Memory and Language, 34,* 543–566.

Menard, M. T., Kosslyn, S. M., Thompson, W. L., Alpert, N. M., & Rauch, S. L. (1996). Encoding words and pictures: A positron emission tomography study. *Neuropsychologia, 34,* 185–194.

Mesulam, M.-M. (1990). Large-scale neurocognitive networks and distributed processing for attention, language, and memory. *Annals of Neurology, 28,* 597–613.

Miller, G., & Johnson-Laird, P. (1976). *Language and perception.* Cambridge, MA: Harvard University Press.

Montessori, M. (1913). *Pedagogical anthropology.* New York: Frederick A. Stokes.

Morrow, D. G., Bower, G. H., & Greenspan, S. L. (1989). Updating situation models during narrative comprehension. *Journal of Memory and Language, 28,* 292–312.

Murray, J., Klin, C., & Myers, J. (1993). Forward inferences in narrative text. *Journal of Memory and Language, 32,* 464–473.

Neisser, U. (1976). *Cognition and reality.* San Francisco: Freeman.

O'Brien, E. J., & Albrecht, J. E. (1992). Comprehension strategies in the development of a mental model. *Journal of Experimental Psychology: Learning, Memory, and Cognition, 18,* 777–784.

Olson, C. R., & Gettner, S. N. (1995). Object-centered direction selectivity in the macaque supplementary eye field. *Science, 269,* 985–988.

Osgood, C. E., & Bock, K. J. (1977). Salience and sentencing: Some production principles. In S. Rosenberg (Ed.), *Sentence production: Developments in research and theory* (pp. 89–140). Hillsdale, NJ: Lawrence Erlbaum Associates.

Parsons, L. M., Fox, P. T., Downs, J. H., Glass, T., Hirsch, T. B., Martin, C. C., Jerabek, P. A., & Lancaster, J. L. (1995). Use of implicit motor imagery for visual shape discrimination as revealed by PET. *Nature, 375,* 54–58.

Paulesu, E., Frith, C. D., & Frackowiak, R. S. J. (1993). The neural correlates of the verbal component of working memory. *Nature, 362,* 342–345.

Petersen, S. E., Fox, P. T., Posner, M. I., Mintun, M., & Raichle, M. E. (1988). Positron emission tomographic studies of the cortical anatomy of single-word processing. *Nature, 331,* 585–589.

Piaget, J. (1952). *The origins of intelligence in children.* New York: International Universities Press.

Piaget, J. (1959). *The language and thought of the child.* London: Routledge & Kegan Paul.

Pinker, S., & Birdsong, D. (1979). Speaker's sensitivity to rule of frozen word order. *Journal of Verbal Learning and Verbal Behavior, 18*, 497–508.
Posner, M., Petersen, S., Fox, P., & Raichle, M. (1988). Localization of cognitive operations in the human brain. *Science, 240*, 1627–1631.
Regier, T. (1996). *The human semantic potential.* Cambridge, MA: MIT Press.
Rieser, J. J., Garing, A. E., & Young, M. F. (1994). Imagery, action, and young children's spatial orientation: It's not being there that counts, it's what one has in mind. *Child Development, 65*, 1262–1278.
Rumelhart, D., Smolensky, P., McClelland, J., & Hinton, G. (1986). Schemata and sequential thought processes in PDP models. In J. McClelland & D. Rumelhart (Eds.), *Parallel distributed processing: Vol. 2* (pp. 7–57). Cambridge, MA: MIT Press.
Sachs, J. S. (1967). Recognition memory for syntactic and semantic aspects of connected discourse. *Perception and Psychophysics, 2*, 437–442.
Sanford, A. J., & Moxey, L. M. (1995). Aspects of coherence in written language: A psychological perspective. In M. A. Gernsbacher & T. Givón (Eds.), *Coherence in spontaneous text.* Philadelphia: John Benjamins.
Schank, R., & Abelson, R. (1977). *Scripts, plans, goals, and understanding: An inquiry into human knowledge structures.* Hillsdale, NJ: Lawrence Erlbaum Associates.
Shimamura, A. P., Janowsky, J. S., & Squire, L. R. (1990). Memory for the temporal order of events in patients with frontal lobe lesions and amnesic patients. *Neuropsychologia, 28*(8), 803–813.
Silverstein, M. (1976). Hierarchy of features and ergativity. In R. Dixon (Ed.), *Grammatical categories in Australian languages* (pp. 121–171). Canberra: Australian Institute of Aboriginal Studies.
Slobin, D. I., & Welsh, C. A. (1973). Elicited imitation as a research tool in developmental psycholinguistics. In C. A. Ferguson & D. I. Slobin (Eds.), *Studies of child language development* (pp. 485–497). New York: Holt, Rinehart & Winston.
Sokolov, A. (1972). *Inner speech and thought.* New York: Plenum.
Sowa, J. F. (1984). *Conceptual structures: Information processing in mind and machine.* Reading, MA: Addison-Wesley.
Sridhar, S. N. (1988). *Cognition and sentence production: Cross-linguistic study.* New York: Springer Verlag.
Talmy, L. (1988). Force dynamics in language and cognition. *Cognitive Science, 12*, 59–100.
Tanenhaus, M. K., Spivey-Knowlton, M. J., Eberhard, K. M., & Sedivy, J. C. (1995). Integration of visual and linguistic information in spoken language comprehension. *Science, 268*, 1632–1634.
Teuber, H.-L. (1964). The riddle of frontal lobe function in man. In J. M. Warren & K. Akert (Eds.), *The frontal granular cortex and behavior* (pp. 410–477). New York: McGraw-Hill.
Vendler, Z. (1957). Verbs and times. *Philosophical Review, 56*, 143–160.
Vygotsky, L. (1962). *Thought and language.* Cambridge, MA: MIT Press.
Werner, H., & Kaplan, B. (1963). *Symbol formation: An organismic-developmental approach to language and the expression of thought.* New York: Wiley.
Wilkins, W. K., & Wakefield, J. (1995). Brain evolution and neurolinguistic preconditions. *Behavioral and Brain Sciences, 18*, 161–226.
Zwaan, R. A. (1996). Processing narrative time shifts. *Journal of Experimental Psychology: Learning, Memory, and Cognition, 22*, 1196–1207.

Chapter 9

Social Perspectives on the Emergence of Language

Catherine E. Snow
Harvard Graduate School of Education

The term *social* in the title of this chapter is being used in two senses. In its first sense, *social* refers to the capacities of the infant and young child, which I argue are the source out of which language emerges. In its second sense, *social* refers to the context in which language acquisition occurs. Of course, the social support that adults are inclined to provide to language learners is partially a consequence of the social capacities that infants possess—the degree to which infants are socially appealing creatures. In the chapter, then, I present first an argument about the infant's social capabilities and how they provide a context for the emergence of language, and second about the adult's provision of social support to the learner constructing an emergent language system.

THE INFANT'S SOCIAL CAPACITIES

Discussions of the emergence of language must deal with at least two basic questions: "Emergence from what?" and "Emergence with what help?" Any argument that language emerges as a natural product of development, that is, as a phenomenon without a particular and separate developmental path, must specify what the preconditions are for that emergence, or the domains of accomplishment that make the emergence of this powerful new system possible. Once we have settled what language emerges from, we have a stronger basis for hypothesizing under what conditions of environmental support the emergence is likely to be relatively trouble free.

Semantic Bootstrapping

A recently popular approach to solving the problem of how children learn language has been to invoke some form of bootstrapping—in other words, to identify one domain of precocity that, it is assumed, provides the child with a lever for prying open the mystery of language, or (to mix the metaphor more egregiously) a bit of dry land on which to stand while draining the rest of the swamp. The basic idea behind bootstrapping is clearly quite consistent with a notion of emergence—given that the child has some pre- or nonlinguistic capacity, a new or at least a more complex and elaborated system of language can develop.

Two major hypotheses concerning bootstrapping have been offered: Pinker (1984) coined the term *semantic bootstrapping* for a process first proposed by Macnamara (1972), in which the child is supposed to use cognitive capacities to understand something that is happening while listening to adults talk about that same event; the child's observations of the event and cognitive capacities give the child access to some basis for understanding the structure of the sentences used to describe particular events. So if, while watching a large animal spraying water on a tree, the language learner hears sentences like the following,

(1) a. The elephant is spraying water on the tree
    b. The elephant is spraying water
    c. The elephant is spraying the tree
    d. The elephant is spraying the tree with water

he would presumably be inclined to note that the actor was in first position, the patient mentioned after the verb, two postverbal arguments are possible, that one but not both are obligatory, and so on. Many more such instances, of hearing scenes with actors and patients described in such a way that actors usually came first and patients usually came second, might ultimately lead the child to a generalization, or a rule, that he was dealing with a language that used word order in general, and SVO order in particular, to express major syntactic relations. For this particular scene and these sentences, a rule about SVO order could not be finally settled on, because the possibility of a generalization about animate–inanimate order remains open as well, but soon enough counterinstances to that particular generalization would be encountered (*The elephant sprayed the zookeeper with water*). The semantic bootstrapping hypothesis is, thus, an intellectual cousin of a notion once proposed by Slobin (1991), that canonical descriptions of prototypical scenes might constitute a route into language.

The same child might well, of course, hear this particular scene described in Finnish or in Russian, with varying word orders but reliable morphological marking of the subject–agent and direct object–patient relations. These and other data about the irrelevance of word order and the reliability of suffixes could lead the child to the conclusion that he was meant to be learning a language that marked major syntactic relations morphologically, and that his task as a learner was to figure out the morphological cooccurrences of form and meaning.

Of course, if the child knows most of the open class lexical items in Sentence (1), then the problem of sorting out its grammatical structure by relating it to events observed is greatly simplified; presumably the child thus is able to parse the scene in a way that maps more directly onto the linguistic representation of it. Prior lexical knowledge combines with an understanding of events in the world to provide the semantic analysis from which grammar can be bootstrapped. Within this perspective, it is thus not surprising that grammatical acquisition starts only after some level of lexical sophistication is reached.

The major problem with semantic bootstrapping as a proposed mechanism for language acquisition is, quite simply, that it posits an unlikely domain of precocity. On what grounds should we agree that children are particularly precocious in understanding scenes, events, happenings? How do they become able to distinguish events that need to be described using the local linguistic device for marking subjects and objects from discussions of attributes, expressed using quite different devices (that elephant is very good natured), or intentions (that elephant may well spray us), negations (that elephant would never spray anyone), or any of an enormous list of possibilities? Children have to understand what is going on in the world in order to be able to use semantic bootstrapping, but the claim that they understand the world runs counter to everything we know about very young children. To a large extent, in fact, children learn about the world through learning language, rather than learning language because they already know about the world. In fact, the average 2-year-old is more likely to be learning something about the meaning of *spray* from hearing the sentences in (1) than to be learning about verb argument structure or word order rules. Furthermore, although the language addressed to young children is simplified in all sorts of ways, it certainly is not limited to canonical sentence types nor to descriptions of prototypical scenes (see Bowerman, 1989).

Syntactic Bootstrapping

These and other arguments led Gleitman and colleagues (Gleitman, 1990; Naigles, 1990, 1996) to reject semantic bootstrapping and to propose that children in fact are syntactically precocious, that they use information about the structures in which verbs appear as a source of information about what the verbs might mean, rather than the other way around.

Gleitman and her colleagues carried out an intriguing and varied set of studies demonstrating that there is rather little information in scenes that helps to constrain verb choice, but that there is quite a lot of information in syntactic structures, particularly in cases where one verb is heard in several different structures, about what the verb might be. Thus, a sentence frame like *The elephant is v-ing the tree with water* severely constrains the array of verbs that could fill the empty slot. The verb would have to be a causative one referring to physical motion with change of location—*spray, sprinkle, paint, drench, daub, fill,* and the like. In other words, the sentence constrains the meaning of the verb, rather than the verb meaning illuminating the structure of the sentence.

Gleitman (1990) demonstrated convincingly that adults are quite good at guessing what verbs occurred within particular syntactic frames, although not very good at guessing what verbs cooccurred with particular scenes. Of course, syntactic frames provide information that is helpful to adults in guessing verbs because we already know the cooccurrence constraints and likely argument structures for most verbs in our native languages. The degree to which occurrence in a particular structure is informative to a child who doesn't yet know the language is much less clear. Nor is it entirely clear exactly what is being presumed to be precocious under the syntactic bootstrapping hypothesis—presumably the capacity and the tendency to keep track of cooccurrences between verbs and other expressed structures in the sentences where the verbs occur. Cross-language variability in the specifics of verb–argument structure relations is too high to suggest, for example, that the child is born knowing that *spray* and *sprinkle* fit into the frame in (1), but that *pour, put,* and *move* (also causative verbs involving change of location of the patient) do not, that *run* is intransitive and that *know* takes sentential complements.

Indeed, children are quite good at keeping track of cooccurrences, even meaningless ones. The work of Aslin, Saffran, and Newport (chap. 13, this volume) demonstrates an early capacity to do so, and the ability of children learning languages with gender or noun declensions demonstrates capacities to learn much more complex cooccurrence systems. The brute force cooccurrence tracking that was proposed by Maratsos (1988; Maratsos & Chalkley, 1980) as a mechanism for acquiring word classes and gender may well be working later in development. The specifics of the syntactic bootstrapping proposed by Gleitman, in which the child tracks the argument structure in which verbs occur, also seems quite plausible—as a way to learn about new verbs after a substantial repertoire of verbs and construction types has been amassed. It does not seem plausible as a way to break into grammar.

The more basic problem with both of these versions of bootstrapping is that they are post hoc hypotheses, seizing an aspect of the problem as a source of its solution. In neither case do they fit with what we know of children: that children are neither semantically precocious, nor syntactically precocious, neither in the general sense of semantic and syntactic nor in the much more specific senses required for the proposed bootstrappings to work. Children do not parse, analyze, or understand realities in the world particularly well, and they are notably conservative and limited in their use of novel syntactic structures involving verbs (Goldberg, 1995; Tomasello, 1992). So why would we assume that abilities in either of these domains constitutes the basis of strength on which language is built?

A much more sensible approach is to look at what children are good at and see if their demonstrably precocious abilities can in any sense get stretched to address the problem of language acquisition. I propose in this chapter, then, an account of language development starting from a clearly established fact of infant development—that the one domain of impressive infant precocity is the social—and pursuing the implications of social precocity for a possible account of language development. In particular, I argue for a form of bootstrapping that makes use of young children's pragmatic precocity—precocity in understanding the interpersonal and intentional nature of communication.

SOCIAL PRECOCITY

What do we mean exactly when we say infants are socially precocious? The claim is a multifaceted one, meant to account for facts about infants' early demonstrated capacities to recognize, respond, attend to, and prefer stimuli that are associated with human beings as well as infants' capacities to elicit social responses from adults. I am not, in other words, arguing that infants have well-organized systems of social responsiveness or of social interactive capacity in the first months of life, but rather that a benign conspiracy of infant perceptual and attentional processes and adult responsive tendencies generates social activity that in turn is transformed into social interaction and thus into social, interpersonal understanding well before the onset of language. I am arguing, furthermore, that the social interactive abilities and the social understanding that are the result of those early tendencies and responses provide the platform of precocity from which children enter language.

Recent work by Tomasello and his colleagues highlighted the relation between early social-pragmatic skills and acquisition of language. Tomasello and his colleagues argued the importance of the infant's emerging understanding that other persons are intentional agents (Tomasello, 1995; Tomasello, Kruger, & Ratner, 1993; see also Bruner, 1995) as precursors to lexical development. This understanding distinguishes humans from nonhuman primates (see Tomasello et al., 1993, for a discussion). Understanding that others are intentional agents, infants begin to communicate for two interactive goals. First, they act to ensure mutual attention with persons in their environment, for example, through pointing and showing gestures that emerge before the first word (Bates, Camaioni, & Volterra, 1975). Second, they participate in context-embedded speech games or routines such as peek-a-boo and naming body parts or animal sounds (Bruner, 1983; Ninio & Bruner, 1978; Ninio & Snow, 1996). The fact that children first acquire vocal language for purposes of participating in social interaction rather than as a means for conveying information or even for achieving instrumental ends reflects, we suggest, the social-pragmatic precocity of the young child.

Social-pragmatic precocity is similarly reflected in infants' early social responsiveness (Oller, 1980), preference for human faces (Goren, Sarty, & Wu, 1975), and reactions to speech-like stimuli (Bloom, Russell, & Wassenberg, 1987). Discussions of the evolution of language have not attended sufficiently to the importance of the adult's capacity to socialize the infant into certain ways of communicating, to which a prerequisite is that the infant be an attractive social being. The infant's ability to make eye contact, responses of attention, quieting, and smiling in the presence of talking human faces contributes to his or her attractiveness, as do characteristics of the infant's facial configuration (Jones & Hill, 1993).

In addition to being attractive social stimuli, infants are attracted to social stimuli. A large body of research documents the degree to which infants preferentially attend to sounds that have precisely the characteristics of adult female voices producing baby talk, and the degree to which infants prefer visual stimuli that have the formal characteristics of human faces, ideally human faces engaged in talking and smiling. The social preparedness of the infant to get engaged in language interactions plows fertile ground for learning about communication.

Furthermore, these channels for communication that are privileged by virtue of their stimulus characteristics develop remarkably early in the infant's life. At an age when infants are entirely dependent on others for nutrition, hydration, temperature regulation, mobility, and other basic functions of animacy, they are quite capable of engaging in well-timed vocal turn-taking (Snow, 1977), in imitative behaviors that reveal their understanding of the relations of their own body to adult bodies (Meltzoff, 1993, 1996), in behaviors that reveal they understand the distinction between animate and inanimate stimuli (Trevarthen & Hubley, 1978), in noticing mismatches between visual and auditory channels for talk (Kuhl & Meltzoff, 1982, 1988), and in responding negatively to interactants who show a lack of affect in their faces and a lack of contingency to infant behaviors (Weinberg & Tronick, 1994). The degree to which infants attend to verbal input is revealed by the changes in categorical discrimination of language-specific phoneme boundaries at around 10 months and infants' early preferences for and greater capacities to analyze their own native language (Jusczyk, Cutler, & Redanz, 1993; Jusczyk, Friederici, Wessels, Svenkerud, & Jusczyk, 1993; Mehler et al., 1988; Moon, Cooper, & Fifer, 1993); these input-driven changes could hardly happen if infants were not tuned into the verbal channel as one worth attending to and one in which the details of production were important to note. In fact, infants of 8 months have been shown to prefer to listen to words that occurred in stories read to them only 10 times, as a function of the previous experience (Jusczyk & Hohne, 1997). This incomplete list of capacities in the communicative and protocommunicative domain demonstrates that social-communicative precocity massively outstrips precocity in any other domain of development during the first year of life.

Intersubjectivity is perhaps the most important component of pragmatic precocity. Some, such as Trevarthen and Hubley (1978), would argue that intersubjectivity is present from very early in the 1st year and is in fact innate. Others argue that it emerges only at about 1 year of age, and under the influence of considerable social support, although it is species specific. Whichever view one prefers, it is clear that intersubjectivity is key to the pragmatic basis of language. Intersubjectivity is the construct that makes sense of the claim that communication can occur before conventional language, and that communicative intent can be the source of conventionalized language forms.

IMPLICATIONS OF SOCIAL PRECOCITY FOR THE INCIPIENT LANGUAGE USER

The social interactive experiences the infant has access to during the 1st year of life, or perhaps simple maturation, quite universally (at least as far as can be ascertained) generate a unique, species-specific capacity by the time the child is about 1 year old—the capacity for intersubjectivity, or the understanding that other minds are like one's own. Claims about the onset of intersubjectivity have varied widely in the age assigned and in the accounts given for its sources. Nonetheless, all agree that the achievement of intersubjectivity opens the way to true communication, the production of signals mediated by the expectation that they will be understood as intended. This achievement is grounded in the tendency to interpret others' behaviors as intentional—to imitate adults' actions by aiming at the same end rather than by mimicking their movements (Meltzoff, 1995). The understanding that others' minds are like one's own presumably also opens the way to interest in and acceptance of others' conventionalized means of communications—a potential beginning for real language.

In talking about the emergence of language, though, we as developmentalists have to own up to the dirty little secret of child language—that no one knows how to decide when it begins. Criteria for distinguishing the first word from the other vocal behaviors young children emit have not been established, not because we are lousy methodologists or uninterested in the question, but because, I would argue, there is no principled basis for distinction. In fact, the transition from vocal, semicommunicative behaviors to real, uncontroversial words is a long one that involves many tiny changes. Vihman and Miller (1988) showed, for example, that there is no basis in the vocal characteristics of early words for distinguishing them from babble, and in many children babbling and word use cooccur for many months. Ninio (1993) argued that the communicative intents early words express do not consistently distinguish them from turns in games or other preverbal routinized semicommunicative productions. Given the real lack of distinction, the highly trained specialist in child language can be no more dogmatic or sophisticated in identifying a first word than the average parent who determines that Tuesday's /baba/ is vocal play but Wednesday's /baba/ means "bottle" or even, perhaps, "give me my bottle."

At some point, though, developmental psycholinguists and parents would agree, infants are producing interpretable communicative acts with a frequency that confirms they have developed truly communicative capacities. This ability to communicate does not appear with a pattern suggesting it is a sudden discovery that radically changes behavior; in fact, the frequency of communicative acts produced by very young children is quite low, and the number per unit time of such acts increases steadily during the 2nd year of life—even when the child is given credit for very unsophisticated acts, including clearly nonverbal vocalizations and gestures as communicative acts. In one longitudinal study, we found that the frequency of behaviors produced by normally developing children that could be coded as having some communicative intent increased from 4.4 to 7.9 per 10 minutes between 14 and 20 months, and again to 11.2 at 32 months (Snow, Pan, Imbens-Bailey, & Herman, 1996) despite constant parental rates of communication (Pan, Imbens-Bailey, Winner, & Snow, 1996). Furthermore, a robust characteristic of children with language-handicapping conditions of various sorts, ranging from mental retardation to brain injury, is a lowered frequency of communicative attempts (Feldman, 1992). These data are consistent with the notion that the capacity to communicate, as a source of language, itself emerges gradually.

One might well expect, given that infants are creatures of many wants, that their emerging capacity for communication would immediately be put to use for instrumental purposes—to order adults around, to request objects, to solicit help, to demand attention. Indeed, these directive goals are evident in children's earliest utterances as well as in their preverbal communicative acts (vide the protodeclarative and protoimperative identified by Bates et al., 1975, or the demand vocalizations identified by Carter, 1979). Strikingly, though, a very high proportion of the early words, gestures, and vocalizations of young children is produced in the context of participation in games and game-like formats rather than with directive intent. Intents to convey information do not emerge until even later, well after the first conventional words. Although it may seem counterintuitive to those who think of language as mathetic and of early words as names for things, the most salient need that early conventional communicative means can fulfill for young children is the need to participate in social interaction—waving bye-bye, playing peek-a-boo, exchanging markers of attention while looking at pictures in books, and marking the transfer of objects or the occurrence of an unexpected event. These uses of conventionalized communicative expressions are maximally continuous with the forms of social interaction in which preintersubjective infants engage, in that they are relatively contentless, relatively predictable within their highly constraining social formats, often imitative, and highly situation specific. The earliest words were described by Ninio (1993) as "on the fringes" of the linguistic system, and analyzed by Ninio and Snow (1996) as keywords for social formats, rather than as true, denotative lexical items with symbolic status (see also Ninio, 1994).

These early words, in other words, are not mostly referential—they do not have any semantics per se. Nor are they syntactic, that is, they do not come accompanied by constraints on the syntactic structures into which they can enter, or by word class information. *Uh-oh* is neither verb nor noun nor adverb, it is a marker pure and simple. These early communicative productions express pragmatic intentions, nothing more. It is these intensely social communicative behaviors that children have control over at the time they start to learn about the language system proper, and it is sensible to think that these social, communicative achievements (as flimsy as their linguistic substance is) constitute the bootstraps with which children levitate themselves into language proper.

Not just the earliest words, but also the earliest word combinations, can be explained as the product of the child's attempt to find simple ways to express their communicative intents. Early word combinations typically include one word that expresses a pragmatic force (e.g., *more* for requesting repetition of an activity, *no* for rejection of an object or prohibition of an activity, *mommy* for requesting help) and a second word that specifies the intent further (e.g., *more swing, no milk, mommy tower*). These combinations do not represent semantic or syntactic structures, but rather a direct readout of pragmatic intent (see Ninio & Snow, 1988).

A further source of evidence that social-pragmatic accomplishments might be the bootstrap into language comes from looking at patterns of relation across pragmatic, lexical, and grammatical domains assessed independently. Such a study requires having indices of pragmatic, lexical, and grammatical development that are not confounded, and looking at cross-domain relations both within and across age. Snow et al. (1996) found moderate correlations between indices of pragmatic development at 14 months and size of the lexicon at the same age, and between pragmatic and grammatical measures at 20 months, a finding that is at least consistent with the claim that communicative accomplishments constitute a source of formal language learning. More powerfully, Rollins and Snow (in press) were able to predict children's grammatical status at later ages from frequency of participation in the communicative exchanges of social participation and of regulating attention, for normally developing children and for children with autism. In fact, the only members of the small group of children with autism who made progress in grammar over the period of the study were those who had produced communicative acts intended to regulate attention (see also Rollins, 1994). Directive language use was not related to later grammar. The importance of joint attentional formats as sources of language learning was pointed out by Goldfield (1990) and by Tomasello and his colleagues (Tomasello & Barton, 1994; Tomasello & Farrar, 1986; Tomasello & Kruger, 1992; Tomasello et al., 1993; Tomasello, Strosberg, & Akhtar, 1996); the Rollins and Snow (in press) findings go well beyond Tomasello's work, however, in suggesting that being able to achieve joint attention may also be a prerequisite to making progress in grammar. They suggest, furthermore, that assumptions about modularity—claims that the grammatical system develops independently and is not subject to the influences known to affect other aspects of language—may be exaggerated. Just as grammar is highly correlated with lexicon in normally developing and language-handicapped populations (Bates & Goodman, chap. 2, this volume), so are pragmatic skills correlated with both lexicon and grammar.

I am, thus, arguing that the domain of precocity that a child might use to figure out how the language system works is the pragmatics of communication—the precocious understanding that it is possible to influence another's action by one's own behavior, through a process that involves predicting how the other will interpret what one is doing. This uniquely human level of intersubjectivity leads to the production of speech acts, expressed with increasingly conventional means, thus to the acquisition of forms of expression borrowed from the adult's system, in which they have a structure that goes beyond that of mapping speech act directly onto form. The reliance on pragmatic bootstrapping is, of course, transitional—and it is very likely that reliance on cognitive capacities to analyze what is happening in the world and syntactic capacities to remember and analyze cooccurrence patterns also play a role in later stages of language acquisition, in much the way described in the semantic and syntactic bootstrapping hypotheses. However, these two domains are insufficiently precocious to explain the child's entry into language, which social-pragmatic skills can help us understand.

SOCIAL SUPPORT FROM ADULTS

As stated earlier, *social* in the sense in which I use it in the title of this chapter enters into the argument twice—the first claim is that young children's social capacities and tendencies constitute a domain of precocity that generates the expression of communicative intents. One might well think that pragmatic precocity of sufficient power would lead the child directly into language, providing a basis for bootstrapping as strong as that claimed for semantic and syntactic bootstrapping, respectively. In fact, it seems that there is considerable scope for the quality of the child's social–linguistic environment to affect the speed of language acquisition despite the child's robust pragmatic skill—and this is thus the second place where "social" factors enter into the picture. Furthermore, evidence about the specific features of the linguistic environment that have an effect on language development suggests that they are largely dependent on the child's functioning as an intentional communicative agent. A brief summary is that language development is supported in the early stages by adult attempts to achieve effective communication with the child.

Considerable evidence suggests that adult recognition of and responsiveness to children's communicative intents is demonstrably helpful to children in acquiring language. In fact, all of the factors mentioned in any standard review of what constitutes helpful adult input to children—a child-centered style, a conversation-eliciting style, talking about a joint focus of attention, semantic contingency, provision of expansions and clarification questions, and so forth—presuppose a social, communicative, intentional child attempting to express his or her own intents. In other words, it is the pragmatically effective child with the capacity to express some communicative intents who creates the opening that adults fill with social support.

Traditional descriptions of the role of adult input have focused on the relation of the adult input to the child's meaning (semantic contingency) or to the child's linguistic forms (expansions, clarification questions). I argue that in fact the crucial feature of helpful input is its pragmatics—achieving shared communication—rather than either its propositional or grammatical character, but that a focus on the former makes the latter also more informative. In other words, adult input is helpful because adults share children's presuppositions that language is about accomplishing goals in the world, some of which are intrinsically social and others of which require social mediation, and because adults support children in achieving their goals. The very large body of accumulated data and conclusions about whether and how adult input is modified and whether and how it helps children acquire language needs to be reinterpreted in light of this conception. Accordingly, I review a few selected areas of research in which parental effects on acquisition have been sought, from the perspective of their value in light of the pragmatic bootstrapping capacities of the child.

Negative Feedback

The history of research on negative feedback constitutes all by itself a little case study in historical changes in the dominant models for analyzing child language. Early studies of negative feedback analyzed feedback as information about the language system, whereas studies undertaken after about 1985 analyzed feedback with reference to children's communicative intentions, implicitly accepting the pragmatic underpinnings of language development. Early studies of negative feedback also set up the problem of language learning as a monolithic problem—as if every instance of negative feedback would be a basis for readjusting the entire grammatical system. Later studies presupposed that children learned languages more piecemeal, working on different bits of the system in parallel, tolerating considerable inconsistency across different subsystems, and furthermore, that there were many mechanisms of effect of social interaction and language input. Thus, negative feedback, although helpful, would not need to carry the entire burden of the impact of social interactive effects.

Frequency Effects for Vocabulary

One of the more robust findings concerning the role of language input in language acquisition is that children who hear more words learn more words. This effect is strong enough to penetrate the differences in rate of word learning attributable to conditions under which words are presented, that is, whether during periods of joint attention or not, whether in response to child topic-related utterances or not.

Monolingual, normally developing children entering first grade have been variously estimated to have vocabularies of 3,000 (Dolch, 1936), 6,000 (Chall, 1987), 14,000 (Carey, 1978), and 24,000 (Shibles, 1959) words—a range that confirms the difficulties of giving reliable estimates of the total number of words any individual knows. This range reflects, however, not just difficulty of estimation, but also enormous individual and social class differences in vocabulary size (Hart & Risley, 1995). Smaller vocabularies are typically found among children from lower socioeconomic status families, where parents have less education, less engagement in high-level literacy activities, and fewer economic resources, and homes where there is less talk overall and less child-directed talk in particular (Hart & Risley, 1992; Hoff-Ginsberg & Tardif, 1995).

Differences in the size of children's vocabularies emerge early. Children from lower socioeconomic class families have fewer words than middle-class peers at 18 to 30 months (Arriaga, Fenson, Cronan, & Pethick, 1998) as reflected in the Communicative Development Inventory (CDI; Fenson et al., 1994). Young children have remarkable capacities to acquire new vocabulary rapidly and efficiently; the 15,000-word vocabulary of the middle-class child implies that the child has acquired 12 to 15 new words a day between the age of 3 and school entry. Bilingual children, of course, acquire even more words (although perhaps not quite twice as many) as monolinguals.

The best single predictor of a young child's vocabulary, during the period of early language acquisition when total vocabulary ranges up to 600 words, is density of maternal speech—simply how many words the child hears during a typical hour (Huttenlocher, Haight, Bryk, Selzer, & Lyons, 1991). The amount of talk heard by children in relatively isolated, welfare-dependent, single-parent families is only a small proportion of that heard by children in two-parent, middle-class families (Hart & Risley, 1995; Hoff-Ginsberg & Tardif, 1995), a disparity directly reflected in the children's own vocabulary scores on standardized assessment instruments (Hart & Risley, 1995).

In addition to sheer quantity of talk, there is considerable evidence that early vocabulary acquisition is supported by contingency of adult talk on the child's focus of attention, for children up to about age 3. For example, nouns are most easily learned if mothers name objects that children are looking at or manipulating (Tomasello & Todd, 1983) and verbs are best learned if mothers name the action that is about to happen (Tomasello & Barton, 1994; Tomasello & Kruger, 1992). Such careful tuning of input implies monitoring of child attention and activity and willingness to be responsive to the child's interest.

Beyond Vocabulary Frequency to Vocabulary Richness

An additional set of factors is likely to be implicated in particular in the development of that sector of a child's vocabulary that goes beyond the 3,000 to 5,000 most frequent words in English, words that essentially everyone eventually acquires and that are easily accessible during language production for common use. More rare and sophisticated vocabulary is likely to be found in books rather than in oral language; thus, families that read books with and to their children may well be promoting rare vocabulary acquisition selectively. Furthermore, familial use of sophisticated vocabulary at mealtimes has been shown to relate to children's tested vocabulary scores in subsequent waves of data collection (Beals & Tabors, 1995; Davidson & Snow, 1998; Weizman, 1995).

Sophisticated vocabulary at mealtime tends to occur in the context of extended conversations centered on a single topic, for example, when a narrative or explanation is being produced (Beals, 1997). Thus, the type of talk a family engages in may be critical in generating contexts where more sophisticated vocabulary can be encountered and where enough contextual support is available to help the child learn the meaning of the unfamiliar word. In a study of dinnertable conversations engaged in by low-income families with 5-year-old children, Weizman (1995) found that the density of rare vocabulary items in total talk predicted child vocabulary 2 years later, but that additional considerable variance was explained by the likelihood that the rare vocabulary items were embedded in semantically informative contexts, namely, contexts in which they cooccurred with semantically related words and in which explicit explanations of word meaning were provided.

Frequency Effects on Grammar?

It has been widely argued that, although frequency effects may be apparent for vocabulary, they will be minimal or absent for grammatical development. If grammar is, indeed, a biologically buffered, robust, and independent system, then it is very unlikely to show the same range of variation as a function of quantity or quality of input as vocabulary acquisition.

In fact, the data on social-class differences in language acquisition suggest that working-class children from families where there is less overall talk also show later acquisition of the capacity to produce grammatically complex utterances. The Arriaga et al. (1998) study cited earlier found deficits in the children's reported performance on the sentence complexity scale of the CDI as serious as those on word knowledge. In fact, across a wide variety of studies, encompassing children who vary in social class and children with various sorts of language-handicapping conditions, the correlations between vocabulary and grammar are quite high, suggesting that they are subject to the same set of forces.

Of course, suggesting that children from working-class families show a delay or a deficit in grammatical acquisition involves taking a stand that is unpopular with two quite different groups: (a) those who believe in an innate language acquisition device and thus argue that differences that show up as a function of frequency or of social class are essentially trivial and uninteresting, because they define the core of grammar as precisely that which shows no such differentiation; and (b) those who reject radical innatist positions but nonetheless argue against representing differences in style of talk associated with different social groups as deficits characteristic of the less powerful groups. Because of the vocal political tendencies of this latter group, discussion of social-class differences in language development and language interaction has been largely limited to the domain of vocabulary, where for some reason claims about social class differences are not attended by the same level of controversy as for grammar. Even the very well documented claims that working-class families talk less to their children than middle-class families (e.g., Hoff-Ginsberg & Tardif, 1995) have been treated as somehow controversial. I would argue that it is entirely possible, and tremendously important, to distinguish between socially meaningful variant systems of lexical and grammatical knowledge and amount of lexical and grammatical knowledge. The field of child language assessment has developed a dozen instruments designed to identify language delay, and half a dozen designed to assess vocabulary size. These reflect the existence of a distribution within any given age group of grammatical and lexical capacities, reflecting variation that is correlated with but not entirely explained by social class.

The Home–School Study of Language and Literacy Development is a longitudinal study, now in its 10th year, of a group of low-income, limited-education families, all of whom had a 3-year-old at the start of the study (see Snow, 1991, for an exposition of the theoretical basis of the study). Yearly observations were made of parent–child interaction in the home for the first 3 years of the study, and biannually thereafter. Starting when the children were 5, yearly assessments of language and of literacy skills were carried out (see Snow, Tabors, Nicholson, & Kurland, 1995). The data of interest here are the children's scores on mean length of utterance (MLU) derived from the parent–child interaction data at ages 3 (3;9) and 5 (5;6). MLU measurements were made based on spontaneous speech in interaction with mothers, observed at home during a free-play session that occurred after the observer had been in the home for a while and the parent and child were accustomed to her presence. When the children were 3;9, their mean MLU in this setting was 2.92 (*SD* = 0.67, range 1.17–4.22), an MLU score on the basis of which one would predict an age of 2;20 (with a 1 standard deviation range of 2;3–3;5, according to Table 2 in Miller, 1981). Although MLU norms are not generally an appropriate basis for assessment after about age 4, these same children at 5;6 had an average MLU of 3.46 (*SD* = 0.69, range 1.64–4.96), a mean from which an age of 3;1 would be predicted according to Miller's norms. The IPSyn (Index of Productive Syntax; Scarborough, 1990) was calculated on a random subset of 21 of these children at 3;9, when their mean score was 76.9 (*SD* = 9.70, range 60–94); according to Scarborough's norms, the average

45-month-old should score at about 82 (with a *SD* of between 4 and 6), and a score of 77 is average (using interpolation as a basis for estimation) for a child aged 3;4. Although these data might be interpreted to present the worrying specter of "language deficit" or "deficient code," I would take the much simpler message from them, that low frequency of access to adult talk delays language acquisition for grammar as much as for vocabulary. The children we studied were not deficient in language but were acquiring language more slowly than middle-class peers with large amounts of language input.

These children, although showing enormous variation in oral language abilities as reflected in MLU, had scores that were on average well below those that would be expected from an otherwise comparable group of middle-class children. The lower performance on this measure of grammar is actually even more striking than these children's scores on receptive vocabulary; their mean PPVT (Peabody Picture Vocabulary Test) standard score at age 5 was 93, only slightly depressed from the population norm of 100 (Snow et al., 1995). It does seem, however, that language environments that limit opportunities for vocabulary development also limit opportunities for grammatical development, just as would be expected if grammar and vocabulary were highly correlated rather than being separate modules (see Bates & Goodman, in press).

Beyond Frequency for Grammar

Furthermore, faster and more risk-free acquisition of both grammar and vocabulary occurs when parental input is adjusted in level of complexity and related in topic to the child's talk. Parents who consistently change the topic of talk away from the child's focus, issue directives, or fail to respond to child topics, in general have children who talk later and less complexly than parents who follow up on child utterances with topic-related responses, who extend child topics over several conversational turns, and who avoid initiating new topics when the child is focused on something of interest (see Snow, 1989, for a review).

CONCLUSION

Chapters in this book have shown how the child can use relatively simple mechanisms to solve seemingly quite complex problems. The goal of this chapter has been to show how certain nonlinguistic capacities of the developing child contribute to the emergence of language capacities, including grammar, as well as how the social contexts within which children grow up contribute crucially to the process. The crucial social factors that make language acquisition possible include the child's precocious social capacities and the social-interactive context provided to the developing child by adult caregivers. These precocious social capacities ensure that the child is alert to human faces and human voices, likely to solicit interactions that include adult talk, capable of joint attention, intersubjectivity, and the attribution of intention, and selectively attentive to language input. The specifics of the social-interactive context, although variable across cultures and languages, are universally capable of supporting language acquisition, as in every context, some talk is directed to infants and toddlers, young children's capacities as communicators are acknowledged, and the regularities of the adult language are displayed.

ACKNOWLEDGMENTS

I would like to express my appreciation to Barbara Pan, Kendra Winner, Alison Imbens-Bailey, Jane Herman, Pamela Rollins, and others who worked on Foundations for Language Assessment (which was funded by HD 23388), to Patton Tabors, David Dickinson, Brenda Kurland, and the many others who have contributed to the Home–School Study of Language and Literacy Development (funded by The Ford Foundation, The Spencer Foundation, and The W. T. Grant Foundation).

REFERENCES

Arriaga, R. I., Fenson, L., Cronan, T., & Pethick, S. J. (1998). Scores on the MacArthur communicative development inventory of children from low and middle income families. *Applied Psycholinguistics, 19,* 209–223.

Bates, E., Camaioni, L., & Volterra, V. (1975). The acquisition of performatives prior to speech. *Merrill-Palmer Quarterly, 21,* 205–226.

Bates, E., & Goodman, J. (in press). On the inseparability of grammar and the lexicon: Evidence from acquisition, aphasia, and real-time processing. *Language and Cognitive Processes.*

Beals, D. E. (1997). Sources of support for learning words in conversation: Evidence from mealtimes. *Journal of Child Language, 24,* 673–694.

Beals, D. E., & Tabors, P. O. (1995). Arboretum, bureaucratic, and carbohydrates: Preschoolers' exposure to rare vocabulary at home. *First Language, 15,* 57–76.

Bloom, K., Russell, A., & Wassenberg, K. (1987). Turn taking affects the quality of infant vocalizations. *Journal of Child Language, 14,* 211–227.

Bowerman, M. (1989). Learning a semantic system: What role do cognitive predispositions play? In M. L. Rice & R. L. Schiefelbusch (Eds.), *The teachability of language* (pp. 133–169). Baltimore: Paul H. Brookes.

Bruner, J. (1983). *Child's talk.* New York: Norton.

Bruner, J. (1995). From joint attention to the meeting of minds: An introduction. In C. Moore & P. J. Dunham (Eds.), *Joint attention: Its origins and role in development* (pp. 1–14). Hillsdale, NJ: Lawrence Erlbaum Associates.

Carey, S. (1978). The child as word learner. In M. Halle, J. Bresnan, & G. Miller (Eds.), *Linguistic theory and psychological reality* (pp. 264–293). Cambridge, MA: MIT Press.

Carter, A. L. (1979). Prespeech meaning relations: An outline of one infant's sensorimotor morpheme development. In P. Fletcher & M. Garman (Eds.), *Language acquisition* (pp. 71–92). Cambridge, England: Cambridge University Press.

Chall, J. (1987). Two vocabularies for reading: Recognition and meaning. In M. G. McKeown & M. E. Curtis (Eds.), *The nature of vocabulary acquisition* (pp. 7–17). Hillsdale, NJ: Lawrence Erlbaum Associates.

Davidson, R., & Snow, C. E. (1998). *Social class differences in rare vocabulary.* Unpublished manuscript, Harvard Graduate School of Education.

Dolch, E. (1936). How much word knowledge do children bring to grade 1? *Elementary English Review, 13,* 177–183.

Feldman, H. M. (1992). Early language and communicative abilities of children with periventricular leukomalacia. *American Journal on Mental Retardation, 97,* 222–234.

Fenson, L., Dale, P., Reznick, J. S., Bates, E., Thal, D., & Pethick, S. (1994). Variability in early communicative development. *Monographs of the Society for Research in Child Development, 59*(5, Serial No. 242).

Gleitman, L. (1990). The structural sources of verb meanings. *Language Acquisition, 1,* 3–55.

Goldberg, A. E. (1995). *Constructions: A construction grammar approach to argument structure.* Chicago: The University of Chicago Press.

Goldfield, B. (1990). Pointing, naming, and talk about objects: Referential behaviour in children and mothers. *First Language, 10,* 231–242.

Goren, C. C., Sarty, M., & Wu, P. Y. K. (1975). Visual following and pattern discrimination of face-like stimuli by newborn infants. *Pediatrics, 56,* 544–549.

Hart, B., & Risley, T. R. (1992). American parenting of language learning children: Persisting differences in family-child interactions observed in natural home environments. *Developmental Psychology, 28,* 1096–1105.

Hart, B., & Risley, T. R. (1995). *Meaningful differences in the everyday experience of young American children.* Baltimore: Paul H. Brookes.

Hoff-Ginsberg, E., & Tardif, T. (1995). Socioeconomic status and parenting. In M. Bornstein (Ed.), *Handbook of parenting, Vol. II: Ecology and biology of parenting* (pp. 161–188). Hillsdale, NJ: Lawrence Erlbaum Associates.

Huttenlocher, J., Haight, W., Bryk, A., Selzer, M., & Lyons, T. (1991). Early vocabulary growth: Relation to language input and gender. *Developmental Psychology, 27,* 236–248.

Jones, D., & Hill, K. (1993). Criteria of facial attractiveness in five populations. *Human Nature, 4,* 271–296.

Jusczyk, P. W., Cutler, A., & Redanz, N. J. (1993). Infants' preference for the predominant stress patterns of English words. *Child Development, 64,* 675–687.

Jusczyk, P. W., Friederici, A. D., Wessels, J. M. I., Svenkerud, V. Y., & Jusczyk, A. M. (1993). Infants' sensitivity to the sound patterns of native language words. *Journal of Memory and Language, 32,* 402–420.

Jusczyk, P. W., & Hohne, E. A. (1997). Infants' memory for spoken words. *Science, 277,* 1984–1986.

Kuhl, P. K., & Meltzoff, A. N. (1982). The bimodal perception of speech in infancy. *Science, 218,* 1138–1141.

Kuhl, P. K., & Meltzoff, A. N. (1988). Speech as an intermodal object of perception. In A. Yonas (Ed.), *Perceptual development in infancy* (Minnesota Symposia on Child Psychology, pp. 235–236). Hillsdale, NJ: Lawrence Erlbaum Associates.

Macnamara, J. (1972). Cognitive basis of language learning in infants. *Psychological Review, 79,* 1–13.

Maratsos, M. (1988). The acquisition of formal word classes. In Y. Levy, I. Schlesinger, & M. Braine (Eds.), *Categories and processes in language acquisition* (pp. 31–44). Hillsdale, NJ: Lawrence Erlbaum Associates.

Maratsos, M., & Chalkley, M. (1980). The internal language of children's syntax: The ontogenesis and representation of syntactic categories. In K. Nelson (Ed.), *Children's language: Volume 2* (pp. 31–44). New York: Gardner.

Mehler, J., Jusczyk, P., Lambertz, G., Halsted, N., Bertoncini, J., & Amiel-Tison, C. (1988). A precursor of language acquisition in young infants. *Cognition, 29,* 143–178.

Meltzoff, A. N. (1993). The role of imitation in understanding persons and developing a theory of mind. In S. Baron-Cohen, H. Tager-Flusberg, & D. J. Cohen (Eds.), *Understanding other minds: Perspectives from autism* (pp. 335–366). Oxford, England: Oxford University Press.

Meltzoff, A. N. (1995). Infants' understanding of people and things: From body imitation to folk psychology. In J. L. Bermudez, A. J. Marcel, & N. Eilan (Eds.), *The body and the self* (pp. 43–69). Cambridge, MA: MIT Press.

Meltzoff, A. N. (1996). The human infant as imitative generalist: A 20-year progress report on infant imitation with implications for comparative psychology. In C. M. Heyes & B. G. Galef, Jr. (Eds.), *Social learning in animals: The roots of culture* (pp. 347–370). San Diego, CA: Academic Press.

Miller, J. (1981). *Assessing language production in children: Experimental procedures.* Baltimore: University Park Press.

Moon, C., Cooper, R. P., & Fifer, W. P. (1993). Two-day olds prefer their native language. *Infant Behavior and Development, 16,* 495–500.

Naigles, L. (1990). Children use syntax to learn verb meanings. *Journal of Child Language, 17,* 357–374.

Naigles, L. (1996). The use of multiple frames in verb learning via syntactic bootstrapping. *Cognition, 58,* 221–251.

Ninio, A. (1993). On the fringes of the system: Children's acquisition of syntactically isolated forms at the onset of speech. *First Language, 13,* 291–313.

Ninio, A. (1994). Expressions of communicative intents in single-word period and the vocabulary spurt. In K. Nelson & Z. Reger (Eds.), *Children's language development, Vol. 8* (pp. 103–124). Hillsdale, NJ: Lawrence Erlbaum Associates.

Ninio, A., & Bruner, J. S. (1978). The achievement and antecedents of labeling. *Journal of Child Language, 5,* 1–15.

Ninio, A., & Snow, C. E. (1988). Language acquisition through language use: The functional sources of children's early utterances. In Y. Levi, I. Schlesinger, & M. Braine (Eds.), *Categories and processes in language acquisition* (pp. 11–30). Hillsdale, NJ: Lawrence Erlbaum Associates.

Ninio, A. & Snow, C. E. (1996). *Pragmatic development.* Boulder, CO: Westview.

Oller, D. K. (1980). The emergence of sounds of speech in infancy. In G. H. Yeni-Komshian, J. F. Kavanagh, & C. A. Ferguson (Eds.), *Child phonology* (Vol. 1, pp. 93–112). New York: Academic Press.

Pan, B. A., Imbens-Bailey, A., Winner, K., & Snow, C. E. (1996). Communicative intents of parents interacting with their young children. *Merrill-Palmer Quarterly, 42,* 248–266.

Pinker, S. (1984). *Language learnability and language development.* Cambridge, MA: Harvard University Press.

Rollins, P. R. (1994). *A case study of the development of language and communication skills for six children with autism.* Unpublished doctoral dissertation, Harvard University Graduate School of Education.

Rollins, P. R., & Snow, C. E. (in press). Shared attention and grammatical development in typical children and children with autism. *Journal of Child Language.*

Scarborough, H. (1990). Index of productive syntax. *Applied Psycholinguistics, 11,* 1–22.

Shibles, B. H. (1959). How many words does a first grade child know? *Elementary English, 31,* 42–47.

Slobin, D. I. (1991). Learning to think for speaking: Native language, cognition and rhetorical style. *Pragmatics, 1,* 7–25.

Snow, C. E. (1977). Development of conversation between mothers and babies. *Journal of Child Language, 4,* 1–22.

Snow, C. E. (1989). Understanding social interaction and language acquisition: Sentences are not enough. In M. Bornstein & J. Bruner (Eds.), *Interaction in human development* (pp. 80–103). Hillsdale, NJ: Lawrence Erlbaum Associates.

Snow, C. E. (1991). The theoretical basis for relationships between language and literacy development. *Journal of Research in Childhood Education, 6,* 5–10.

Snow, C. E., Pan, B., Imbens-Bailey, A., & Herman, J. (1996). Learning how to say what one means: A longitudinal study of children's speech act use. *Social Development, 5,* 56–84.

Snow, C. E., Tabors, P. O., Nicholson, P. A., & Kurland, B. F. (1995). SHELL: Oral language and early literacy skills in kindergarten and first-grade children. *Journal of Research in Childhood Education, 10,* 37–48.

Tomasello, M. (1992). *First verbs: A case study of early grammatical development.* Cambridge, England: Cambridge University Press.

Tomasello, M. (1995). Joint attention as social cognition. In C. Moore & P. J. Dunham (Eds.), *Joint attention: Its origins and role in development* (pp. 103–130). Hillsdale, NJ: Lawrence Erlbaum Associates.

Tomasello, M., & Barton, M. E. (1994). Learning words in non-ostensive contexts. *Developmental Psychology, 30,* 639–650.

Tomasello, M., & Farrar, M. J. (1986). Object permanence and relational words: A lexical training study. *Journal of Child Language, 13,* 495–505.

Tomasello, M., & Kruger, A. C. (1992). Joint attention on actions: Acquiring verbs in ostensive and non-ostensive contexts. *Journal of Child Language, 19,* 311–333.

Tomasello, M., Kruger, A. C., & Ratner, H. H. (1993). Cultural learning. *Behavioral and Brain Sciences, 16,* 495–552.

Tomasello, M., Strosberg, R., & Akhtar, N. (1996). 18 month old children learn words in non-ostensive contexts. *Journal of Child Language. 23,* 157–176.

Tomasello, M., & Todd, J. (1983). Joint attention and lexical acquisition style. *First Language, 4,* 197–212.

Trevarthen, C., & Hubley, P. (1978). Secondary intersubjectivity: Confidence, confiding, and acts of meaning in the first year. In A. Lock (Ed.), *Action, gesture and symbol: The emergence of language* (pp. 183–230). London: Academic Press.

Vihman, M., & Miller, R. (1988). Words and babble at the threshold of language acquisition. In M. Smith & J. Locke (Eds.), *The emergent lexicon: The child's development of a linguistic vocabulary* (pp. 154–181). New York: Academic Press.

Weinberg, M., & Tronick, E. (1994). Beyond the face: An empirical study of infant affective configurations of facial, vocal, gestural, and regulatory behaviors. *Child Development, 65,* 1503–1515.

Weizman, Z. O. (1995). *Sophistication in maternal vocabulary input at home: Does it affect low-income children's vocabulary, literacy, and language success in school?* Unpublished doctoral dissertation, Harvard Graduate School of Education, Cambridge, MA.

Chapter 10

Children's Noun Learning: How General Learning Processes Make Specialized Learning Mechanisms

Linda B. Smith
Indiana University, Bloomington

When one looks at all that children come to know so rapidly, so inevitably—knowledge of language, of objects, of number, of space, of other minds—it is easy to conclude that development is driven by mechanisms and principles specific to each domain. There are strong logical arguments for this conclusion. What has to be learned in each domain is unique to that domain. Under the premise that one cannot get something from nothing, the necessary conclusion is that development in different domains must begin with different starting principles. There are also compelling data to support the domain specificity of cognitive development: Children exhibit learning biases specific to the content being learned. Indeed, much contemporary research in cognitive development consists of describing the domain-specific learning biases that guide knowledge acquisition.

This chapter pursues an alternative vision—one that goes beyond description to explanation. The larger idea is that specificity itself *must* be made, constructed out of processes of greater generality. The larger idea is that development creates something more from something much less through the cascading effects of simple processes. This chapter specifically concentrates on the domain-specific knowledge evidenced by early word learners. Children's rapid learning of nouns is clearly driven by knowledge about what kinds of categories and what kinds of word meanings are possible. In brief, young children bring content-specific knowledge to the task of word learning, knowledge that enables them to narrow in on the meaning of a noun from hearing it used to name a single object. This chapter asks: Where does this domain-specific knowledge come from? What processes make it? The answer is general mechanisms of associative and attentional learning.

THE DATA TO BE EXPLAINED: SMART NOUN LEARNING

Consider a commonplace example of young children's remarkable noun learning: A 24-month-old child sees a tractor for the very first time. This particular tractor is big, red, snorting, and pulling machinery. The child is told, "That's a tractor." The referent of *tractor* is clearly underdetermined from this one naming episode. Nonetheless, evidence from experiments and observations indicates that after seeing this one tractor and hearing it named, it is highly likely that the child will in the future correctly recognize and name other tractors, even tractors different from the original in size or color, in not snorting, in not pulling machinery (e.g., Clark, 1973; Mervis, 1987). In brief, from hearing one object named, the child seems to know the whole category.

Laboratory studies using novel objects and novel names have documented this seeming preknowledge of the category named by a noun. In these experimental studies, children are presented with a specially constructed object like the exemplar shown in Fig. 10.1. The children are told its "name," for example, "This is a dax." Then they are shown test objects

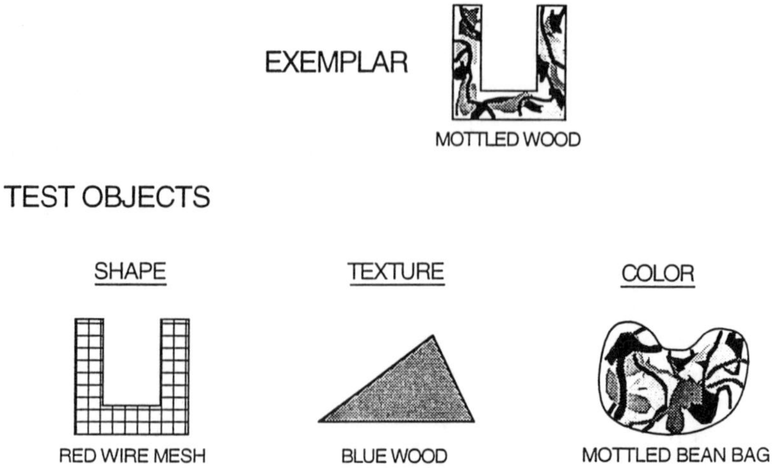

FIG. 10.1. Sample stimuli from a novel word interpretation task. These and virtually all stimuli used in the studies reviewed in this chapter were three-dimensional objects made of wood, wire, or sponge.

such as those also depicted in Fig. 10.1 and asked which of these is also "a dax." The key result is that 2- and 3-year-old children generalize the novel name to objects that are the same shape as the named exemplar. This result has now been replicated many times in many laboratories (see Smith, 1995, for a review).

Critically, children do not attend to shape in nonnaming control tasks. When children are asked to pick out test objects that are "like" or "go with" the exemplar (instead of being asked to generalize a newly learned object name), their choices are not systematically based on shape or on any other single property (e.g., Imai & Gentner, 1977; Landau, Smith, & Jones, 1988; Soja, Carey, & Spelke, 1991). These discrepant behaviors for naming and nonnaming tasks suggest that children know that nouns refer to categories of same-shaped things. Thus, it appears that the shape bias is a domain-specific constraint, one that biases the acquisition of common nouns, words that do in fact typically refer to categories of similarly shaped things (Biederman, 1987; Rosch, 1978).

But what is it exactly that children actually know? What processes implement this biased learning? Before proposing the answer, I briefly summarize the full complexity of children's biased attention to object properties in the task of naming. There is much more to be explained than just a "shape bias."

The Form of the Bias Depends on the Properties of the Named Object

Jones, Smith, and Landau (1991) contrasted children's novel word generalizations when the named objects had eyes and when they did not. When the named object did not have eyes, 3-year-old children generalized the novel name only to objects that were exemplar shaped, but when the objects had eyes, they generalized the name to new instances that matched the exemplar in both shape and texture. Thus, putting eyes on the objects changed the form of the bias in learning object names. Putting eyes on the objects, however, did not at all alter children's categorizations in a nonnaming similarity judgment task. (For related evidence on animacy cues and naming, see also Jones & Smith, 1998.) Soja and her colleagues (1992; Soja et al., 1991) also reported data that show the importance of the kind of object named. In one study, they showed young children stimuli made out of nonsolid material (e.g., hair gel, cold cream). In this stimulus context, 2-year-old children generalized the exemplar's name on the basis of color and texture, ignoring sameness or difference in shape. In sum, when learning names, very young children systematically attend to different properties in different stimulus contexts—forming differently structured categories for different kinds of things.

The Form of the Bias Depends on the Syntactic Context

Children's biased attention to shape in word learning tasks is most robust when the novel word is presented in a count noun frame, "This is a ______," rather than an adjective frame, "This is a ______ thing" (Smith, Jones, & Landau, 1992; Landau, Smith, & Jones, 1992; Waxman, 1994; see also Au & Laframboise, 1990) or a mass noun frame, "This is some ______" (Imai & Gentner, 1997; Soja et al., 1991). Indeed, a mass noun frame recruits attention to material substance rather than shape. Thus, children's smart interpretation of a novel noun incorporates knowledge about specific linguistic forms (see also Waxman, 1994).

Attentional Biases Change With Development

Figure 10.2 summarizes the many developmental experiments that have been conducted on children's biased word learning (Landau et al., 1988, 1992; Smith et al., 1992; Soja, 1992; Soja et al., 1991; Waxman, 1994). Each curve summarizes the developmental pattern given specific stimulus prop-

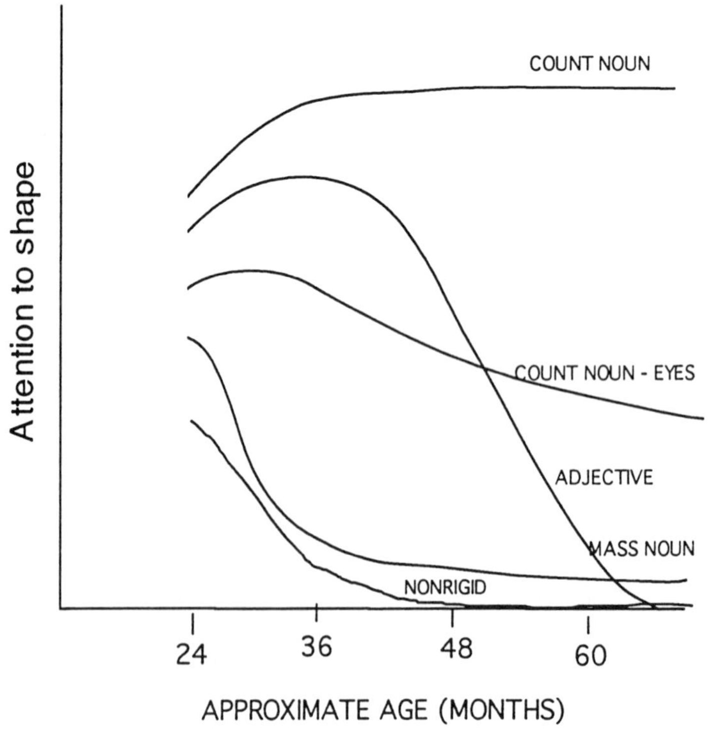

FIG. 10.2. Theoretical developmental trajectories summarizing findings across many experiments.

erties, syntactic context, or both. Briefly, the evidence suggests that by 24 months, there is a weak tendency in naming tasks to attend to shape that gets both stronger with development and more specific to specific contexts. Descriptively, other biases seem to grow out of, differentiate out of, this earlier, less articulated shape bias.

The data summarized in Fig. 10.2 all derive from children learning English. If I were to add the new evidence from children learning other languages—Japanese or Spanish (Imai & Gentner, 1997; Waxman, Senghas, & Benveniste, 1997)—I would have to add other curves. These recent studies suggest that children learning different languages have different attentional biases. They exhibit word learning biases that are smartly specific to the language being learned.

The task for a mechanistic account, then, is to explain how children's attentional biases emerge over the course of word learning and how they come to reflect the properties of the language being learned.

AN ATTENTIONAL LEARNING ACCOUNT

General processes of attentional learning provide an explanation of the origins and mechanisms of word learning biases. One hundred years of experimental psychology have taught us that when one perceptible cue is regularly associated with another, attention to the first automatically recruits attention to the second (e.g., James, 1890/1950; Rescorla & Wagner, 1972). The control of selective attention by associative learning is one of the most widespread and well-documented phenomena in all of psychology. It is a fundamental process, evident in infants, children, adults, and nonhuman animals (e.g., Kruschke, 1992; Lewicki, Hill, & Sasak, 1989; MacIntosh, 1965; Medin & Wattenmaker, 1987; Younger, 1990). It is a process that may also be sufficient to explain young children's smart generalizations of a novel word to new instances.

The viability of this idea is suggested by the strong resemblance between the contextual control of children's attention in novel word learning tasks and the contextual control of selective attention that emerges in well-controlled studies of attentional learning. In such studies, some cue is regularly associated with and predicts the relevance of some other property; after repeated experience, the presence of that first cue automatically recruits attention to the associated property (e.g., Lewicki et al., 1989; MacIntosh, 1965; Rescorla & Wagner, 1972; Younger, 1990). Similarly, in the language learning task, specific linguistic contexts (e.g., "This is a ______" or "This is some ______") in conjunction with specific object properties (e.g., solidity or nonsolidity) predict the relevance of other properties (e.g., shape or color plus texture). These linguistic contexts, then, should be context cues for attention, cues that automatically shift attention in context-relevant ways. Such linguistic context cues would make attention in the context of language learning different from attention in other contexts and would push word learning in the direction of the language being learned.

Note that this associationist explanation affirms the claim of a lexically specific learning bias. It also affirms the claim that children know something about the likely meaning of a noun before they acquire that specific noun. By the present account, however, this domain-specific knowledge emerges from very general learning processes, processes that in and of themselves have no domain-specific content. There are three points in favor of this account that merit recognition:

1. The posited processes require no preknowledge of language and no deliberative thought. This is advantageous because there is much that young children do not know about the language they are learning and about the world and because young children are not skillful problem solvers (see Smith et al., 1992, for more on this point).

2. The posited processes are known to exist. Although some might question whether associative processes are sufficient to account for much in human cognition (e.g., Keil, 1994), their existence is not in question. Associative processes of attentional learning are part of children's biology and thus could be the mechanism behind children's smart interpretations of novel nouns.

3. These processes can be demonstrated to create attentional biases. The hypothesized mechanisms can be shown to work. For example, simulating learned attentional biases specific to specific contexts is easily achieved by connectionist networks of the most generic sort (e.g., Gasser & Smith, 1991; Smith, 1993, 1995).

These three points indicate the plausibility of the idea that children's domain-specific word learning biases originate in domain-general processes. In the next section, I present data from an ongoing series of experiments conducted in collaboration with Susan Jones, Barbara Landau, Larissa Samuelson, and Lisa Gershkoff-Stowe that provide further support for this account.

TESTS OF AN ATTENTIONAL LEARNING ACCOUNT

The proposal is that learned cues that automatically shift attention underlie the entire pattern of results summarized by the changing curves in Fig. 10.2. The idea is that early in word learning, the linguistic context "This is a ______" becomes associated with attention to the shape of rigid things because many of the first nouns that children learn refer to categories of rigid objects similar in shape. However, other more local attentional biases will develop from more local statistical regularities as more words are learned. Attention will become modulated by the presence of eyes, non-rigidity, a mass-noun frame, or an adjectival frame. The long-range goal of our research program is to explain all of this and especially the emerging complexity of word learning biases as children learn more and more words. However, our initial empirical tests concentrated on the origins of children's attention to shape in the context of naming a solid thing. In what follows, I present five hypotheses derived from the Attentional Learning Account and I summarize the preliminary results from the experiments that are testing them.

Hypothesis 1: Early Nouns Refer to Categories of Similarly Shaped Objects

In order for children to learn to attend to shape when forming new nominal categories, it must be the case that many of the first object names learned by young children refer to similarly shaped objects. Experimental analyses of basic-level categories, categories such as *table, cat, bottle,* and *truck,* suggest the plausibility of this assumption (Biederman, 1987; Rosch, 1978). However, by the present account, it is the statistical regularities inherent in the names and categories learned first that create a shape bias and that then make possible the one-trial learning of shape-based nouns. To put it bluntly, in order for the Attentional Learning Account to have any plausibility, most of the count nouns that children learn first—nouns signaled by the syntactic contexts such as "this is a ______" or the plural—*must* name categories of similarly shaped things.

As a first step toward determining whether the count nouns young children know first do name shape-based categories, we asked 20 undergraduates to judge the category structure of all count nouns on the MacArthur Toddler Communicative Developmental Index (MCDI; Fenson et al., 1993, 1994). This is a parent report measure that lists the 625 most common early words and phrases in children's productive vocabulary. The MCDI has been shown to be a reliable and valid indicator of early productive vocabulary (Fenson et al., 1994). The undergraduate raters were specifically asked to judge whether each count noun on the MCDI referred to a category of objects that were "similar in shape," "similar in color," and/or "similar in material substance." The raters were allowed to indicate that none, one, some, or all of these properties were similar across members of the named category. These judgments were used to characterize each count noun on the MCDI. An individual noun was designated as shape based, color based, or material based if 17 of the 20 undergraduates judged

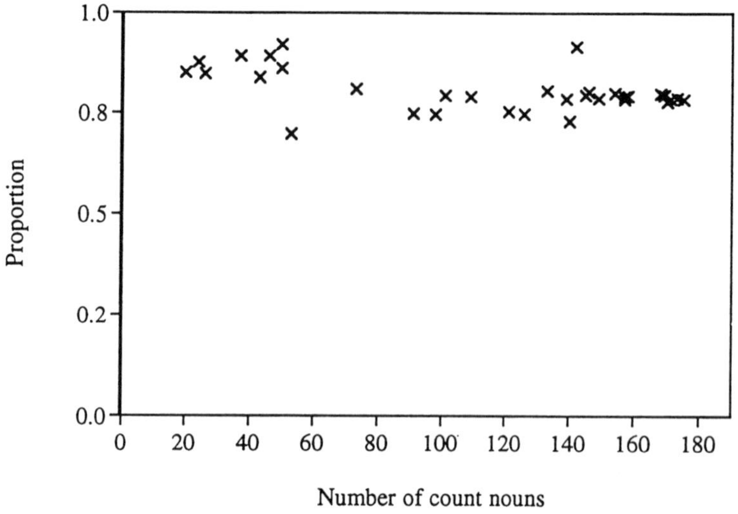

FIG. 10.3. The proportion of count nouns referring to shape-based categories as a function of the number of count nouns known by young children.

the members of the named category to be similar on the designated property.

We then asked the parents of 45 children aged 19 to 30 months to indicate on the MCDI checklist all the words in their children's productive vocabulary. Figure 10.3 shows for each child the proportion of known count nouns that were shape-based categories. As is apparent, whether individual children knew many count nouns or few, most of those count nouns referred to objects of similar shape. Neither material-based nor color-based categories exceeded 40% for any child. This evidence suggests that the count nouns known by young children present the kind of statistical regularities that could create a shape bias.

Hypothesis 2: The Shape Bias Does Not Preexist Word Learning

Apparently, many of the first nouns that children learn, nouns like *table, cat, bottle,* and *truck,* name objects similar in shape. By the Attentional Learning Account, as children learn these words, the regular cooccurrence between the act of naming and attention to shape should cause the act of naming to become a contextual cue that automatically recruits attention to shape. One key prediction that follows from this hypothesis is that a shape bias should not be evident prior to language but should emerge only after the child has learned some number of nouns.

This prediction was tested in a longitudinal study of eight children from 15 to 20 months of age. We tracked the children's vocabulary growth by having parents keep diaries of all new words spoken by their child. We measured the emergence of a shape bias by having the children come into the laboratory every 3 weeks to participate in an artificial word generalization task. At the beginning of the study, the children had very few words in their productive vocabulary (less than 5). At the end of the study, each child had more than 150 words and, for each child, more than half of these were nouns that named concrete objects. Thus, if the shape bias is learned from learning words, children should not show a shape bias at the beginning of the study but should show one at the end—after they have learned some number of object names.

The stimuli used in the laboratory task are those shown in Fig. 10.1. They included an exemplar object made of wood and three test objects that matched the exemplar in either color, shape, or texture. The task began with the experimenter putting the exemplar and three test objects on the table in front of the child. The experimenter picked up the exemplar and said, "This is a dax. Look, this is a dax." Then while still holding the exemplar, the experimenter held out her other hand, palm up and said, "Give me a dax. Give me another dax."

The results are shown in Fig. 10.4. As is apparent, shape choices did not predominate early in the study but reliably did so by the end. More specifically, all eight children began to systematically extend the novel

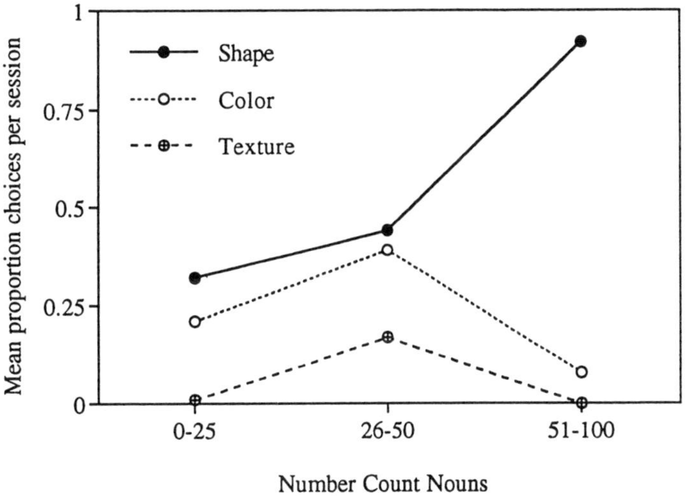

FIG. 10.4. Mean proportion of selected test objects that matched the exemplar in shape, color, or texture as a function of the mean number of object names in the child's productive vocabulary.

word *dax* to the same shape test object after they had 50 count nouns (and about 80 total words) in their productive vocabulary. This point (50 count nouns) in the word learning trajectory is after the spurt in noun acquisitions commonly known as the "naming explosion" as defined by Gopnik and Meltzoff (1987; see also Dromi, 1987; Gershkoff-Stowe & Smith, 1997). The developmental timing of biased attention to shape thus suggests that it may be the consequence of word learning—the consequence of learning some number of names for shape-based categories. Once learned, however, this shape bias should support and sustain rapid word learning.

Hypothesis 3: The Shape Bias Is Lexically Specific When It First Emerges

According to the Associative Learning Account, the shape bias is the product of an associative link between naming and attending to shape. By this account, the shape bias should be lexically specific when it first emerges, evident in naming but not in nonnaming categorization tasks. This hypothesis was tested in a cross-sectional study. This cross-sectional study also serves as a control for the longitudinal study, showing that the repeated laboratory visits in that study did not somehow create the shape bias.

Sixty-four children between the ages of 18 and 24 months participated in the cross-sectional study. They came to the laboratory just once. Productive vocabulary was measured by having parents complete the MCDI. From this measure, children were divided into four groups according to the number of count nouns in their productive vocabulary: 0 to 25, 26 to 50, 51 to 75, and 76 and more count nouns. Half the children at each level of productive vocabulary participated in a novel word generalization task; this naming task was structured similarly to that used in the longitudinal study. Half the children participated in a nonnaming task; all aspects of this task were the same as in the naming task except the exemplar was not named. The experimenter merely held up the exemplar and said, "Look, look at this" and then held out her hand and said, "Give me one."

The key questions of this experiment were whether children systematically select test objects the same shape as the exemplar, whether they do so only in the naming task and not in the nonnaming task, and whether their selective attention to shape emerges only after they have acquired some number of nouns. The data are shown in Fig. 10.5 and as can be seen, the answer to each of these questions is "yes." There is a rise in shape choices as a function of vocabulary growth. Moreover, this rise occurs *after* children have 50 count nouns in their productive vocabulary. Finally, the rise in shape choices is specific to the naming task. Sometime after children have acquired more than 50 count nouns, it is the linguistic context of naming a novel object that recruits attention to shape. These results along

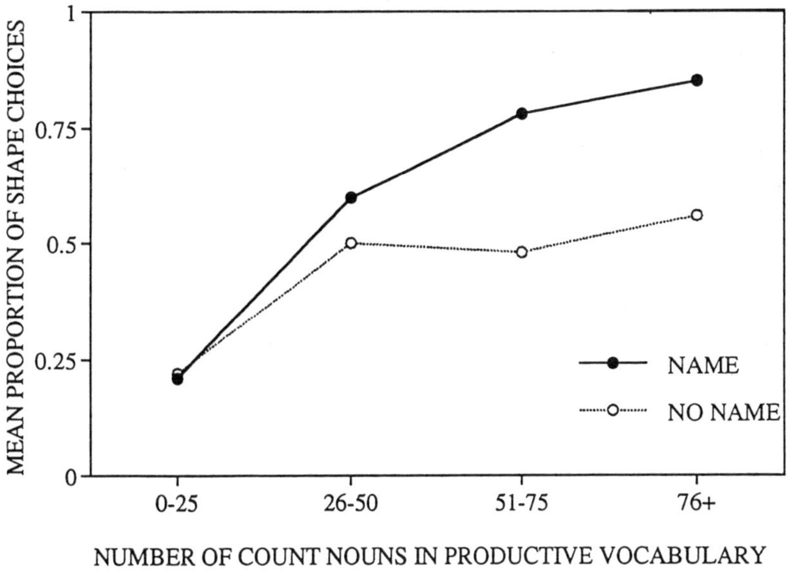

FIG. 10.5. Mean proportion of selected test objects that matched the exemplar in shape in the nonnaming and naming tasks for children grouped according to the number of nouns in their productive vocabulary.

with those of the longitudinal study fit the idea that learning words *creates* a shape bias by creating a contextual cue so regularly associated with attention to shape that the presence of that cue automatically shifts attention to shape.

Hypothesis 4: The Shape Bias Can Be Taught

Correlation, of course, is not causation. Stronger evidence that a lexically specific shape bias is the consequence of learning names for rigid things requires a demonstration that children who have not yet developed a shape bias will acquire one from learning names for shape-based categories. Thus, the goal of this fourth experiment was to create biased attention to shape by teaching lexical categories well-organized by shape to children who did not yet know many words. The participants were eight children aged 17 months who had on average 25 count nouns (range 10–46) in their productive vocabulary by parent report on the MCDI. These children came to the laboratory for 7 weeks and were given extensive training on four different novel categories—all well organized by shape. The top of Fig. 10.6 illustrates the training stimuli for one lexical category.

Each lexical category was trained as follows: The two exemplars for a category were placed on the table and named (e.g., "This is a *zup*. Here is another *zup*."). As illustrated in Fig. 10.6, these two exemplars differed in many ways but were identical in shape. The experimenter and child played with these two objects for 5 minutes, during which time the experimenter repeatedly named the objects (e.g., "Put the zup in the box. Can you put the zup in the wagon?"). Midway in a play session with one pair of exemplars, a nonexemplar for that category (see Fig. 10.6) was briefly placed on the table. The experimenter announced that this just-introduced object was not a member of the category (e.g., "*That's* not a zup!") and then removed it. This nonexemplar matched each exemplar in one nonshape attribute but differed from both exemplars in shape. This nonexemplar thus provides the child with negative evidence as to the kinds of things that are *not* in the lexical category.

For the first 7 weeks of the experiment, the children were trained as described earlier on each of four lexical categories. On Weeks 8 and 9 of the experiment, the children participated in two test sessions that asked them to generalize what had been learned over the first 7 weeks. The first test session, Week 8, measured children's generalizations of the trained lexical categories to new instances. The structure of this task was identical to the novel word generalization task used in the longitudinal and cross-sectional studies described earlier. The stimuli used to test generalization of the *zup* category are illustrated in the middle section of Fig. 10.6. The test began with the experimenter placing one of the trained exemplars on the table along with three novel objects, one that matched the exemplar in material, one in color, and one in shape. The experimenter picked up the exemplar and said, "this is a zup," then requested, "get me a zup." Given the 7 weeks of training, the exemplar is not a novel object for these children nor is the label a novel name. Thus, if the trained children have learned that the specifically trained names refer to objects of a particular shape, they should generalize these already learned names to the novel object that is the same as the exemplar in shape.

On Week 9, the children were tested in a novel word generalization task structured in the same way as the generalization task at Week 8. However, as illustrated by the sample stimulus set at the bottom of Fig. 10.6, all the objects and names were new. This generalization task thus tested the critical prediction that learning specific categories well-organized by shape transforms the act of naming into a contextual cue that automatically shifts attention to shape. If the 7 weeks of intensive training on shape-based categories has caused the linguistic context of naming to automatically cue attention to shape, then these children should form and generalize novel names on the basis of shape.

This experiment also included eight control children. These children were selected at the same time as the children in the trained group; they were 17 months at the start of the 9-week experiment and had on average

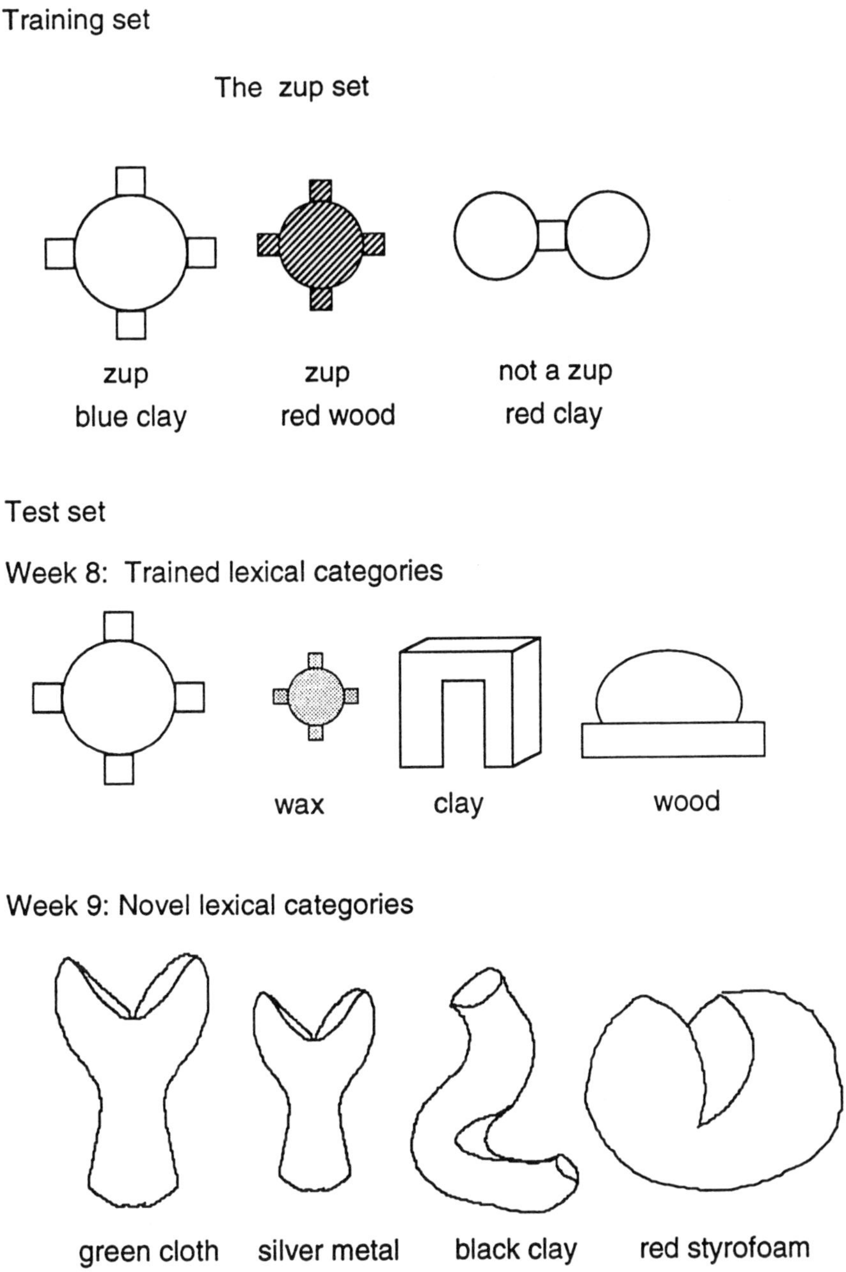

FIG. 10.6. Sample stimuli from the training experiment: top—training stimuli; middle—stimuli for the test of generalization of the trained object name (Week 8); bottom—stimuli for the generalization test for generalization to novel names (Week 9).

22 count nouns in their productive vocabulary (range 8–49). These children, however, did not participate in the 7 weeks of training but returned to the laboratory for the generalization tasks of Weeks 8 and 9, when they and the children in the trained group were 19 months of age. Because the control children had not received intensive training on shape-based lexical categories, the expectation was that these children would not selectively attend to shape in the generalization tasks at either Week 8 or Week 9.

The main results are shown in Fig. 10.7. At Week 8, when the trained children were asked to generalize the trained names to new objects, they did so on the basis of shape. These children had clearly learned that the words we taught them referred to objects of a particular shape. The control children, for whom this was a novel word interpretation task, did not systematically attend to shape.

At Week 9, both the trained and control children heard novel objects named by novel nouns. However, the trained children, but not the

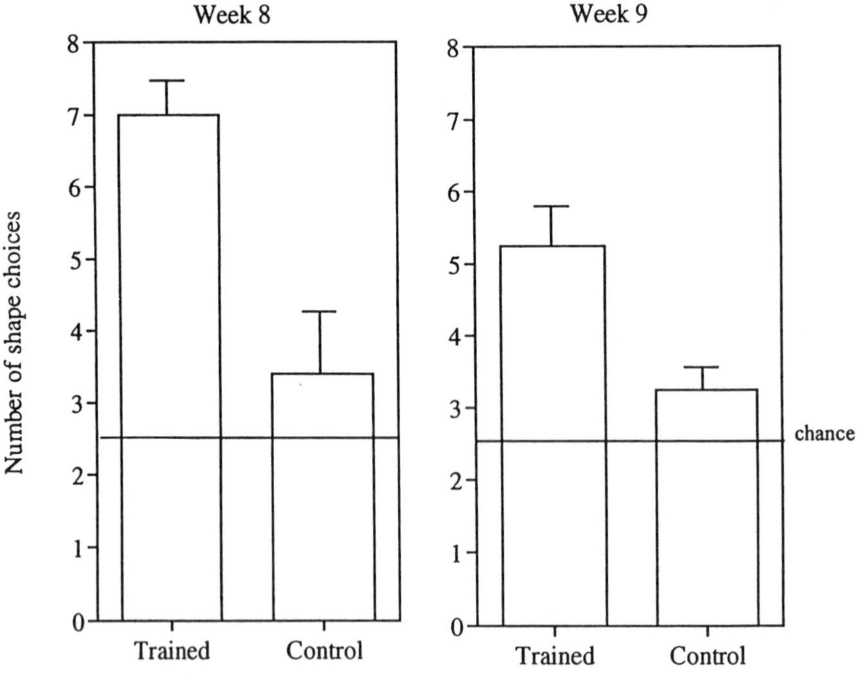

FIG. 10.7. Proportion of choices of test object the same shape as the named exemplar on the two generalization tests: Week 8—trained name and exemplar; Week 9—novel name and novel exemplar.

control children, systematically generalized these newly learned names to other novel objects by shape. In brief, we taught the trained children four categories organized by shape but they learned more than just these categories; they learned to attend to shape when novel rigid objects were named. This generalized attentional shift *is* a learning bias. These children are now biased to induce a shape-based category when a novel object is named.

This precocious bias to link nouns to shape-based categories also appears to have accelerated word learning outside the laboratory for the children in the trained group. The parents of the children in both the trained and control groups were asked to complete the MCDI again at Week 8, indicating all the words now in their children's productive vocabulary. Figure 10.8 shows the change in vocabulary over the 8-week period for the two groups. The children in the training condition showed a 166% increase in number of count nouns known. In contrast, children in the control condition showed only a 73% increase in average number of count nouns. Thus, the children who were taught names for four artificial categories

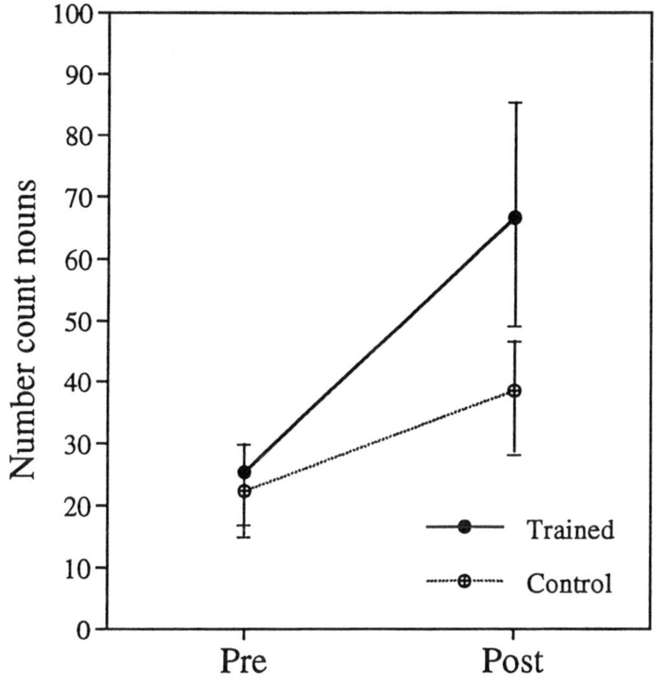

FIG. 10.8. The number of count nouns in children's productive vocabulary at 17 months (pretraining) and at 19 months (posttraining).

well-organized by shape also learned more names for real categories outside the laboratory than did children who did not receive this training. Learning shape-based lexical categories creates a shape bias that in turn promotes the learning of names for more shape-based categories.

Hypothesis 5: Learning About Other Kinds of Words Creates Other Attentional Biases

All the experiments reviewed thus far suggest that children learn to attend to shape in the context of naming by learning count nouns—names that principally refer to categories of similarly shaped things. The learned shape bias then facilitates the learning of other names for shape-based categories. However, children do learn other kinds of words as well, albeit initially with difficulty. Moreover, the evidence suggests that children eventually become facile at learning non-shape-based categories—at least in certain stimulus and linguistic contexts. All these facts are potentially explainable by the Attentional Learning Account. The associative mechanisms proposed here ensure that other smart word learning biases will emerge as long as there are context cues that predict the relevance of specific object properties in the respective contexts.

One test of these ideas examined children's attentional biases in the context of learning novel adjectives. Adjectives present an interesting contrast to the learning of count nouns in that children learn names for things much more rapidly than they learn the dimensional adjectives that label the perceptible properties of those very same things (Gasser & Smith, 1991; Smith, Gasser, & Sandhofer, 1997). Moreover, research in novel word learning tasks suggests that whereas young children (2- to 3-year-olds) often interpret novel adjectives in the same way they do novel count nouns—as referring to shape-based categories—older children (3- to 5-year-olds) systematically shift attention away from shape in the context of a novel adjective used to label an object (Au & Laframboise, 1990; Landau et al., 1992).

The Attentional Learning Account explains the lateness of children's learning of adjectives and the eventual emergence of attentional biases cued by an adjectival syntactic frame by the same mechanisms that explain the emergence of the shape bias. According to the Attentional Learning Account, children start learning about nouns and adjectives in the very same way—with no knowledge about the differences between shape and other properties or the differences between nouns and adjectives. Names for things by this account are not special at the beginning of language learning but become special.

The explanation is straightforward. We have already seen how most of the count nouns that children learn early refer to categories of similarly

TABLE 10.1

The first 10 adjectives in the productive vocabulary of 45 children studied between the ages of 18 and 30 months. The adjectives are listed from earliest acquired by average age in months of the children reported to use the word.

Hot
Bad
Big
Dirty
Mad
Yucky
Awake
Noisy
Good
Little

shaped things. Adjectives, in contrast, do not present the kinds of statistical regularities that would easily create a contextual cue that shifts attention in useful ways. Table 10.1 lists the 10 most commonly known adjectives by 45 children aged 18 to 30 months. Again, word knowledge was assessed by parent report of productive vocabulary on the MCDI. Notice that of the adjectives listed in Table 10.1, many like *awake, bad,* and *yucky* do not refer to simple object properties. The terms that do—*big, hot, noisy*—each refer to unique perceptual properties. Thus, whereas the count-noun syntactic context, "this is a ______," is regularly associated with attention to shape, adjectival syntactic contexts, "this is a ______ thing" or "that's so ______," are not regularly associated with attention to any one property.

Critically, however, the syntactic frames that signal an adjective are regularly associated with *not* attending to shape. Given this statistical regularity, the Attentional Learning Account predicts that once children learn enough adjectives, the syntactic frames that signal an adjective should come to automatically push attention away from shape. This prediction was tested in an experiment with 40 children between the ages of 19 and 35 months. We measured the numbers of count nouns and adjectives in the children's productive vocabulary via the MCDI. All children participated in two tasks, one of which was a novel noun task. The child was shown an exemplar and the experimenter said, for example, "This is a zup. Look at my zup." The child was then shown two test objects, one that matched the exemplar in texture and the other that matched the exemplar in shape, and asked to "Get a zup." The second task was identical in structure except that different objects were used and the exemplar was labeled using a syntactic frame and morphology indicative of an adjective, for example, "This is a riffy one. Look how riffy it is." Then the child was asked which of two test

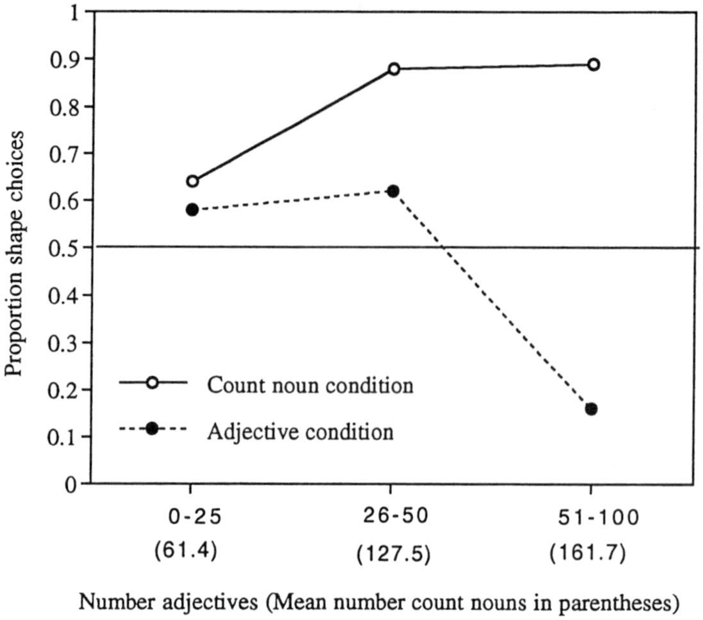

FIG. 10.9. Mean proportion of shape choices in the two conditions as a function of the number of adjectives in productive vocabulary. Mean number of count nouns in the productive vocabulary at the three levels of adjective knowledge is given in parentheses.

objects, one matching the exemplar in texture and the other matching the exemplar in shape, was "a riffy one."

Figure 10.9 shows the results—mean number of choices in the two tasks as a function of the number of adjectives in the children's productive vocabulary. The mean number of count nouns known at the three levels of adjective knowledge is shown in parentheses. Across all three groups of children, there was a rise in the interpretation of a novel count noun as referring to objects of a particular shape. This rise was expected, because children who know more adjectives also know more count nouns. However, even children in the first group—the ones who knew fewest adjectives and fewest count nouns—generalized the novel count noun by shape reliably more than by texture. This again was expected, because these children knew on average more than 60 count nouns—words that typically refer to categories of same-shaped things.

The new results concern the children's performances in the novel adjective generalization task. As is evident, the two groups of children who knew the fewest adjectives showed a tendency to generalize novel adjectives by shape. However, the children who knew the most adjectives, more than 50, systematically and reliably shifted attention away from shape in the novel adjective task and generalized the newly learned adjective to objects with the same texture as the exemplar.

These results strongly fit the idea that nouns and adjectives are initially learned in the very same way. When learning starts, the most pervasive generality in the emerging lexicon is that words refer to same-shaped things, and so early word learners generalize both novel count nouns and novel adjectives by shape. But after first learning many count nouns and then later many adjectives, children come to know that nouns and adjectives are different.

FROM THE MUNDANE TO THE SPECIAL

The proposal put forward in this chapter is that ordinary mechanisms of associative and attentional learning—placed in the context of early language learning—make attentional biases that then promote and speed up the learning of lexical categories consistent with the statistical regularities in that language. The evidence on the emergence and differentiation of the shape bias in early word learning strongly supports this proposal.

To summarize, the main results are the following:

1. Statistical regularities exist among count nouns and the objects they name, and these regularities are of the kind that could create a linguistically cued shape bias: The syntactic frame of a count noun is regularly associated with categories of similarly shaped things.

2. The shape bias does not preexist word learning but emerges over time after children know a substantial number of count nouns. This makes sense; if the shape bias is the product of statistical regularities among count nouns and categories, then children must learn enough count nouns for those statistical regularities to become reliably manifest in their own cognitive processes.

3. The shape bias is lexically specific when it first emerges. This is strongly predicted by the Attentional Learning Account. The act of naming (and the syntactic frames associated with it) is the context cue—the input stimulus—that shifts attention weights.

4. The emergence of the shape bias is accelerated by teaching lexical categories well-organized by shape. The relation between knowing shape-based categories and being biased to learn shape-based categories is not merely correlational, but causally bidirectional. Teaching children new lexical categories that refer to shape-based categories causes these children to increase their attention to shape in the context of hearing of novel objects named, an attentional shift that then promotes the learning of more shape-based categories.

5. Attention away from shape when learning a novel adjective emerges after learning a substantial number of adjectives. Children slowly and laboriously learn adjectives because the statistical regularities inherent in early lexicons organize attention in ways that must make children's initial interpretations of adjectives wrong. However, as each adjective is repeatedly heard and finally learned, the repeated associations between the syntactic frames associated with adjectives and the irrelevance of object shape create a context cue—the adjective frame—that then automatically shifts attention away from shape.

In these ways, in the cascading consequences of mundane and ordinary associative processes, children become smart word learners. All the evidence presented here fits the idea that children start out as quite general learning devices—a bundle of contentless processes—but these processes, through their own activities, change themselves with each word learned until, over time, they are not contentless anymore but instead know how different syntactic categories map onto different meanings. From something much less, general learning processes make something much more.

Words Are Not Initially Special

By the present account, there is nothing originally special about words—or their ability to link to categories or to control attention. It is only because words, the syntactic frames of count nouns, regularly predict the context relevancy of shape that these words come to control attention. The hypothesized processes are truly general and that means that other context cues regularly related to category structure should also come to control attention.

One prediction that follows from this idea is that it should be possible—at least early in word learning—to create nonlinguistic cues that work to organize attention in the same way that linguistic acts do. That is, the regular association of any perceptible cue—hand gestures, whistles, syntactic frames—with the act of referring to categories of objects should come to organize attention. Although this specific prediction has not been tested, Namy and Waxman (1998) reported results that suggest the prediction will be upheld. In this study, very young children (18-month-olds) were presented with objects that were referred to by the experimenter with a nonlinguistic event—a hand gesture—or more conventionally, by an act of naming. These very young word learners were equally likely to associate the nonlinguistic events with the objects as they were the linguistic events and were just as likely to generalize the nonlinguistic as the linguistic event to objects globally similar to the exemplar. This is just as it should be by the Attentional Learning Account: At the start of language learning, words have no special priority over other perceptible events. Older children, however (26-month-olds), did map words to objects more reliably than they mapped gestures to objects. Again, this is as it should be. As children learn more and more words and experience more and more linguistic acts used to refer to objects, language and the act of naming should take strong control over attention to objects—so strong and so automatically, perhaps, that it blocks the learning of other associations or other forces on attention (see Smith et al., 1996, for relevant evidence).

Can General Processes Be All There Is?

Many developmentalists have accepted the idea that the only way the young can develop the concepts of their elders is for the development of those concepts to be strongly constrained by domain-specific mechanisms (see, e.g., Keil, 1994; Markman, 1989). The idea of domain-specific constraints on learning is compatible with the present claim. Indeed, domain-specific word learning biases are the phenomena to be explained. What is new in the present account is the idea that these domain-specific constraints on learning are themselves made out of general, contentless, processes. Some may doubt the validity of this account: not because it cannot explain the data at hand (word learning biases), but because it cannot explain the specialness of human language learning.

DEVELOPMENT PROCESS

How can the specialness of human language learning possibly be explained by generic processes that are not special to language, that are not even special to people? Why don't rats who are good associate learners develop word learning biases? The assumption behind these questions is that the specialness of humans and of language is explainable only by special mechanisms that are not themselves explainable by more general processes. This assumption is contrary to the very idea of development, and indeed, science. It is also contradicted by embryology, which shows repeatedly how universal processes—in their cascading consequences over time—create new and specialized forms. I present three examples.

How Liver Cells and Brain Cells Become Different

One clear example of how general processes make specialized structures is the emergence of body parts and organs in the first weeks after conception (for more details, see Cooke, 1988; Marx, 1984; Wolpert, 1971). The basic facts that we all know are wonderfully more profound than they may initially appear. To review, the initial state is a single cell—the fertilized egg. This cell makes copies of itself; each copy is exactly the same as the next. The cells begin to become different when there are about 10,000 of them amassed in an undifferentiated heap. These differences begin, not inside the individual and identical cells, but outside of them. They begin in gradients over the whole mass. These gradients being of different strengths in different places mark individual cells as different depending on their place in the whole. In this way, the gradients form a prepattern of the body that is to be. The gradients themselves emerge out of the geography of the mass of cells, out of the mechanical and mechanochemical effects of one cell pushing against the next. These chemical gradients thus reflect very general processes. It is these gradients, these general processes, that start specializations by turning on and off the regulating genes in the nuclei of individual cells. The genes that are turned on and then off have their effects by making proteins; in so doing, they change again the local chemical geography of identical cells. These changes create the context for more changes and for more triggering events. All of embryology is like this: A causal chain of individually contentless events, beginning with quite mundane biochemical effects, creates with near certainty the specialness of arms and legs and livers and brains.

The reason liver cells are not like brain cells is not because the processes that make liver cells are unique to liver cells—at least not in the beginning. Development is the process of getting something new from the cascading effects over time of more general processes. In this example, the general processes are biochemical and mechanical. In the case that comprises the centerpiece of this chapter, the general processes that make word learning biases are psychological ones: associative learning and attention. But in both cases, the history and collective effects of generic processes make specialized structures.

Why Leopards Do Not Have Tiger Stripes

The mathematician J. D. Murray (1988, 1993) provides a second example: an elegant model of how between-species differences can be created by quantitative differences in the same developmental process. Murray's model concerns the ontogeny of mammalian coat markings—the developmental processes that make the complex spots and stripes of leopards, tigers, and giraffes; the more simple stripes of skunks and raccoons; and the soft shadings of ungulates. Murray showed how a single mechanism can account for all the variation. The mathematical structure of the mechanism is modeled by a nonlinear equation of the reaction-diffusion type. Put simply, the interactions between the chemical reaction and its rate of diffusion are highly nonlinear, meaning that sometimes the reaction proceeds in a stable manner and at other values, the reaction is unstable and no pigment is formed. The key variables are the geometry and size of the surface over which the reaction occurs. The nonlinearity as a function of these variables leads to either a smooth or patchlike pattern of reaction productions on the surface.

The power of Murray's simple model is illustrated in Fig. 10.10. These are the results of the simulations of the equation with set parameters varying only the body size over which the chemical dynamics work. As a body is scaled up more than 50,000 times (e.g., from mouse size to elephant size), a regular series of patterns emerges—from the solid color of small animals through simple patterns to spots, and back to a nearly uniform coat. In real animals, more than body size matters—the reaction rates and

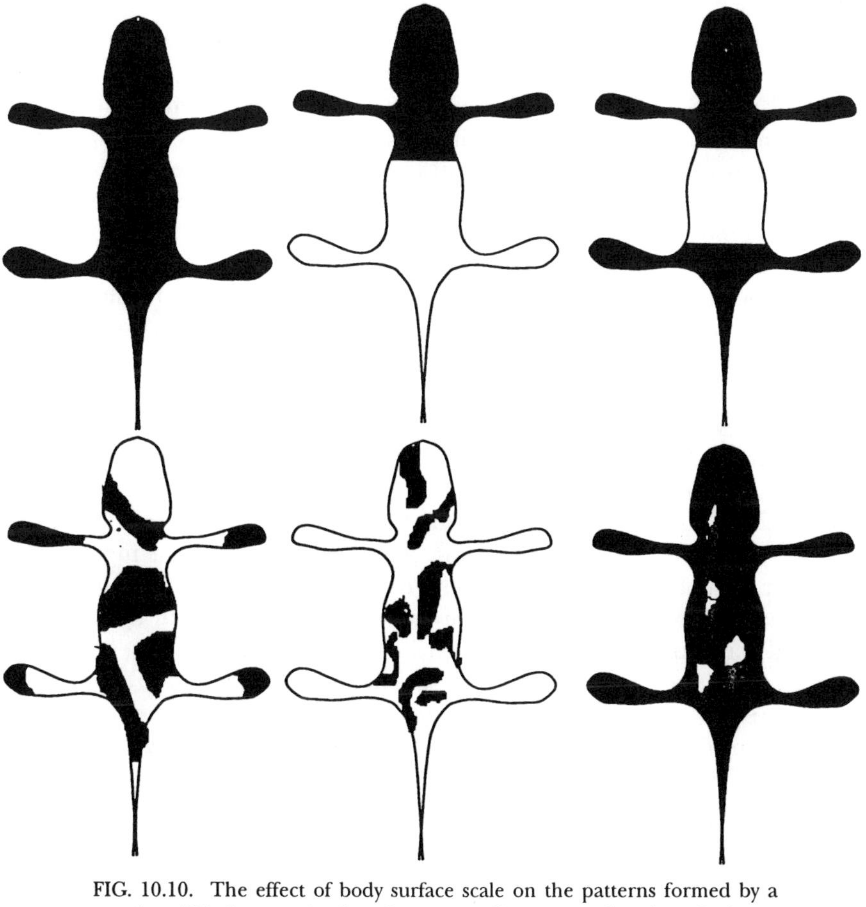

FIG. 10.10. The effect of body surface scale on the patterns formed by a reaction–diffusion mechanism for mammalian coat coloration. Redrawn from Murray (1993).

timing of the process are absolutely critical as well. Variations on these parameters lead to even more diverse coat patterns than those shown in Fig. 10.10.

The key point is this: Small differences in the same general processes can lead to dramatically different outcomes. Thus, a theory that postulates the same general processes across species is neither making the claim that there are no differences between species nor that one can turn one kind of animal into another. Indeed, a theory of how seemingly small differences in the timing, scale, and history of complexly interacting but universal processes would seem to be the ultimate goal of a complete theory of development.

Why Rats Do Not Have People Eyes

The third example is the elegant work on the development of the mammalian eye by Barbara Finlay and colleagues (Kelling, Sengelaub, Wickler, & Finlay, 1989; Wickler & Finlay, 1989). There are dramatic structural differences in the eyes of different mammals—differences that make the visual lives of different mammals distinct. Moreover, these distinct visual capabilities appear to be adaptations that fit the ecological niche of each species. One answer to the question of why different mammals have different kinds of eyes is the functional one: The eyes of different mammals differ because they have evolved to see in different contexts. But there is also the mechanistic answer, one that specifies the developmental processes that make eyes in each individual animal. Evolution could have created species-unique developmental mechanisms, different mechanisms for each different eye. But it did not.

Through an elegant series of cross-species developmental experiments, Finlay and colleagues found that there is one general set of processes that make all mammalian eyes. The dramatic differences in the structural properties of the eye cross-species result from small tweakings in the developmental timing of inputs, cell growth, and cell death. Evolution has its effect through developmental processes. Small changes in the developmental trajectory—because of their cascading and constraining effects on what can happen next—create big functional differences and specialized structures.

In sum, can the specialness of human language learning possibly be explained by generic processes that are not specific to language, not even to humans? If human cognition is a biological process, if it has a material cause, then it is made of processes—of bits and pieces of matter and connections—that are themselves much less than what they yield. Understanding how this is so is to understand development.

CONCLUSION

By the Attentional Learning Account, word learning biases that constrain and propel learning in certain directions are themselves made out of general associative and attentional processes. Each new word learned by a child changes what that child knows about learning words—adding to, strengthening, weakening associations among linguistic contexts and attention to object properties. In the end, word learning looks special and predestined. But specialness and destiny are themselves made out of more ordinary stuff.

ACKNOWLEDGMENT

The research discussed in this chapter was supported by NIH Grant HD28675.

REFERENCES

Au, T. K., & Laframboise, D. E. (1990). Acquiring color names via linguistic contrast: The influence of contrasting terms. *Child Development, 61,* 1808–1823.

Biederman, I. (1987). Recognition by components: A theory of human image understanding. *Psychological Review, 94,* 115–147.

Clark, E. V. (1973). What's in a word: On the child's acquisition of semantics in his first language. In T. E. Moore (Ed.), *Cognitive development and the acquisition of language* (pp. 42–86). New York: Academic Press.

Cooke, J. (1988). The early embryo and the formation of body pattern. *American Scientist, 76,* 35–41.

Dromi, E. (1987). *Early lexical development.* New York: Cambridge University Press.

Fenson, L., Dale, P., Reznick, J. S., Bates, E., Hartung, J., Pethick, S., & Reilly, J. (1993). *MacArthur Communicative Development Inventories.* San Diego, CA: Singular.

Fenson, L., Dale, P., Reznick, J. S., Bates, E., Tahl, D., & Pethick, S. (1994). Variability in early communicative development. *Monographs of the Society for Research in Child Development, 59*(5, Serial No. 242).

Gasser, M., & Smith, L. B. (1991). The development of a notion of sameness: A connectionist model. In *Proceedings of the 13th Annual Conference of the Cognitive Science Society* (pp. 719–723). Hillsdale, NJ: Lawrence Erlbaum Associates.

Gershkoff-Stowe, L., & Smith, L. B. (1997). Naming errors and emerging retrieval processes: A study of early changes in lexical processing. *Cognitive Psychology, 34,* 37–71.

Gopnik, A., & Meltzoff, A. N. (1987). The development of categorization in the second year and its relation to other cognitive and linguistic developments. *Child Development, 58,* 1523–1531.

Imai, M., & Gentner, D. (1997). A cross-linguistic study of early word meaning: Universal ontology and linguistic influence. *Cognition, 62,* 169–200.

James, W. (1950). *The principles of psychology, Vol. 1.* New York: Dover. (Original work published 1890)

Jones, S. S., & Smith, L. B. (in press). How children name objects with shoes. *Cognitive Development.*

Jones, S., Smith, L., & Landau, B. (1991). Object properties and knowledge in early lexical learning. *Child Development, 62,* 499–516.

Keil, F. C. (1990). Constraints on constraints: Surveying the epigenetic landscape. *Cognitive Science, 14,* 135–168.

Keil, F. C. (1994). Explanation, association, and the acquisition of word meaning. In L. R. Gleitman & B. Landau (Eds.), *Lexical acquisition* (pp. 169–198). Cambridge, MA: MIT Press.

Kelling, S., Sengelaub, D., Wickler, K., & Finlay, B. (1989). Differential elasticity of the immature retina: A contribution to the development of the area centralis? *Visual Neuroscience, 2,* 117–120.

Kruschke, J. K. (1992). ALCOVE: An exemplar-based connectionist model of category learning. *Psychological Review, 99,* 22–44.

Landau, B., Smith, L., & Jones, S. (1988). The importance of shape in early lexical learning. *Cognitive Development, 3,* 299–321.

Landau, B., Smith, L., & Jones, S. (1992). Syntactic context and the shape bias in children's and adults' lexical learning. *Journal of Memory and Language, 31,* 807–825.

Lewicki, P., Hill, T., & Sasak, I. (1989). Self-perpetuating development of encoding biases. *Journal of Experimental Psychology: General, 118,* 323–338.

MacIntosh, N. J. (1965). Selective attention in animal discrimination learning. *Psychological Bulletin, 64,* 125–150.

Markman, E. M. (1989). *Categorization and naming in children: Problems of induction.* Cambridge, MA: MIT Press.

Marx, J. L. (1984). The riddle of development. *Science, 226,* 1406–1408.

Medin, D. L., & Wathenmaker, W. D. (1987). Category cohesiveness, theories, and cognitive archeology. In U. Neisser (Ed.), *Concepts and conceptual development* (pp. 25–62). Cambridge, England: Cambridge University Press.

Mervis, C. B. (1987). Child-basic object categories and early lexical development. In U. Neisser (Ed.), *Concepts and conceptual development: Ecological and intellectual factors in categorization* (pp. 201–233). New York: Cambridge University Press.

Murray, J. D. (1988). How the leopard gets its spots. *Scientific American, 258,* 80–87.

Murray, J. D. (1993). *Mathematical biology* (2nd ed.). Berlin, Germany: Springer-Verlag.

Namy, L. L., & Waxman, S. R. (1998). Words and gestures: Infants' interpretations of different forms of symbolic reference. *Child Development, 69,* 295–308.

Rescorla, R. A., & Wagner, A. R. (1972). A theory of Pavlovian conditioning: Variations in the effectiveness of reinforcement and nonreinforcement. In A. H. Black & W. F. Prokasy (Eds.), *Classical conditioning II* (pp. 35–51). New York: Appleton-Century-Crofts.

Rosch, E. (1978). Principles of categorization. In E. Rosch & B. Lloyd (Eds.), *Cognition and categorization* (pp. 28–46). Hillsdale, NJ: Lawrence Erlbaum Associates.

Smith, L. B. (1993). The concept of same. *Advances in Child Development and Behavior, 24,* 216–253.

Smith, L. B. (1995). Self-organizing processes in learning to learn words: Development is not induction. *The Minnesota Symposia on Child Psychology, Volume 28. Basic and applied perspectives on learning, cognition, and development* (pp. 1–32). Mahwah, NJ: Lawrence Erlbaum Associates.

Smith, L. B., Gasser, M., & Sandhofer, C. (1997). Learning to talk about the properties of objects: A network model of the development of dimensions. *Psychology of Learning and Motivation, 36,* 220–256.

Smith, L. B., Jones, S. S., & Landau, B. (1992). Count nouns, adjectives, and perceptual properties in children's novel word interpretations. *Developmental Psychology, 28*, 273–289.

Smith, L. B., Jones, S., & Landau, B. (1996). Naming in young children: A dumb attentional mechanism? *Cognition, 60*, 143–171.

Soja, N. (1992). Inferences about the meanings of nouns: The relationship between perception and syntax. *Cognitive Development, 7*, 29–46.

Soja, N., Carey, S., & Spelke, E. (1991). Ontological categories guide young children's inductions of word meaning: Object terms and substance terms. *Cognition, 38*, 179–211.

Waxman, S. R. (1994). The development of an appreciation of specific lineages between linguistic and conceptual organization. In L. Gleitman & B. Landau (Eds.), *The acquisition of the lexicon* (pp. 229–250). Cambridge, MA: MIT Press.

Waxman, S. R., Senghas, A., & Benveniste, S. (1997). A cross-linguistic examination of the noun-category bias: Evidence from French- and Spanish-speaking preschool-aged children. *Cognitive Psychology, 32*, 183–218.

Wickler, K. C., & Finlay, B. L. (1989). Developmental heterochrony and the evolution of species differences in retinal specializations. In B. L. Finlay & D. R. Sengelaub (Eds.), *Development of the vertebrate retina* (pp. 227–246). New York: Plenum.

Wolpert, L. (1971). Positional information and pattern formation. *Current Topics in Developmental Biology, 6*, 183–223.

Younger, B. (1990). Infants' detection of correlations among feature categories. *Child Development, 61*, 614–621.

Chapter 11

Emerging Cues for Early Word Learning

Roberta Michnick Golinkoff
University of Delaware

Kathy Hirsh-Pasek
George Hollich
Temple University

How do infants break the word learning barrier and learn their first words? How (if at all) do their word learning strategies change with development? The answer to these questions begins with the study of the youngest word learners in the last trimester of the 1st year of life. It has, however, proven very difficult to devise methods that can reliably assess early word learning in a controlled setting with such young children. This chapter addresses these questions and attempts to make progress along these fronts. First, we introduce a set of six principles that Golinkoff, Mervis, and Hirsh-Pasek (1994) posited to account for word learning in the *developmental lexical principles framework*. Second, we offer a thumbnail comparison of alternative theoretical approaches. Third, and finally, we present a new method, the *Interactive Intermodal Preferential Looking Paradigm* (Hirsh-Pasek, Golinkoff, Rehill, Wiley, & Brand, 1997; Hollich, Hirsh-Pasek, & Golinkoff, in press) that permits us to study early word learning in a new way. To illustrate our theoretical approach and the new paradigm, results from experiments on the origins of the principle of reference (Golinkoff et al., 1994) are described. Before beginning, however, we ask the reader to suspend belief and to identify with the following example.

Imagine that your friend Anne is invited to someone's house for a brunch. She is standing in the kitchen, chatting with her host and hostess, as things are being brought out to the table. Her hostess says, "Could you get the caponata?" Anne is clueless. What is caponata? Her hostess is involved in several different conversations so Anne doesn't want to interrupt and ask. What does she do? First, Anne probably looks at her hostess to see where she's looking and perhaps gesturing. Because her hostess was gesturing vaguely in the direction of the refrigerator (although she was looking into the sink), Anne has her first clue. She opens the refrigerator door and peers in. What is she looking for? Anne is not even sure. Without realizing it, Anne is looking for something that is unfamiliar, something for which she doesn't already have a name. Anne sees a bowl of brownish stuff that she can't identify. Ah ha! This must be the caponata.

We've all experienced such episodes—be they in someone else's kitchen or in the hardware store when we're told we need a "ristobop" to fix the toilet and we are clueless as to what it is or where to find it. We, as adults, have very sophisticated strategies for learning new names, strategies that we become vaguely aware of only when something goes wrong.[1]

Some of the cues Anne relied on seem more basic than others. For example, Anne assumed, at a very fundamental level, that the word *caponata* was being used to refer to some object in the world. That is, she knew that words are used to refer—this is the principle of *reference.* It is hard to imagine language learning without the central principle of reference. Reference allows a word to symbolize, or stand for, an object, action, or event. Furthermore, words have a status different from other sounds that are associated with objects such as the beep of the microwave or the ring of the telephone. These sounds occur at the same time that the object is present and embody a "goes with" relation. Words function differently than sounds in that they have a "stands for" relation to what they label. Words do not need to occur contemporaneously with the objects, actions, and events they represent. Rather, words stand for their referents even when the referents appear in a totally different context than the original usage and even when the referents are not present. Second, Anne used the principle of *extendibility.* If Anne's hostess had said "There's more caponata" as an indirect request to bring it out too, Anne would have assumed that similar looking greenish stuff on a shelf of the refrigerator was probably also in the same category. That is, Anne knows that most words do not refer to a single exemplar but to categories of objects. Thus, when we call a dog *dog,* we are really using *dog* generically to refer to a class of similar animals. It could be otherwise: Each word could label only the original exemplar, as is the case when we call our own dog *Fido.* Memory would soon be exceeded if each object, event, and action in the world had its own unique label. Probably by the end of the 1st year of life, children have reached at least a primitive realization that words

[1]An analogy can be made here with the Gricean maxims of communication (Grice, 1975). We become aware of the maxims only when they are violated. For example, when someone elaborates in far more detail than is necessary, we notice that a maxim is being breached: Tell the listener no more than he needs to know. It is as if the fabric of word learning—or communication—only becomes clear when there is a rent in it.

label more than just the original exemplar. However, they may at first be unsure about the basis for object label extension.

Third, Anne probably assumed at first that the word *caponata* referred to an object, using the principle we call *object scope.* Object scope has two parts: Words refer to objects over actions or events, and words refer to whole objects as opposed to referring to a part of an object or an object's attributes. (Markman & Wachtel, 1988, posited a similar principle called *whole object.*) This is one place where Anne parts company from the 1-year-old novice word learner. Anne's linguistic experiences allow her to look for either an object or a substance when she hears a novel noun. Young children, in contrast, are predisposed to interpret novel words as object labels.

These first three principles—reference, extendibility, and object scope—are sufficient to get the infant's word learning off the ground. None of these require much linguistic sophistication. Yet they are foundational to the word learning process. Nonetheless, they only allow the young child to learn words in a laborious, one-at-a-time fashion, nowhere near approaching the rapid word learning that occurs after the vocabulary spurt. Because the character of word learning changes around the time of the vocabulary spurt, it is obvious that these three principles alone cannot account for the word learning process. Therefore, reference, extendibility, and object scope occupy what Golinkoff et al. (1994) referred to as the first tier of their word learning model. These evolve into more sophisticated word learning principles that define the second tier. The first tier principle of reference evolves into the principle of conventionality (Clark, 1983). Whereas reference states that consistent phonological forms (words) map to entities in the environment (via the children's representations of those entities), the principle of conventionality makes it clear that for communication to proceed successfully, those consistent phonological forms better match the ones used by others in the environment. For example, if young children are to be understood outside the family circle, they must abandon their invented words in favor of the more widely used terms. Similarly, the first tier principle of extendibility allows the young child to apply newly learned words to nonidentical exemplars that share either perceptual similarity or thematic relations with the original referent. Extendibility evolves into the second tier principle called *categorical scope,* which refines extendibility by removing doubts about the basis for extension. The principle of categorical scope states that words label taxonomic categories first, at the basic level, and only later at the superordinate level (Golinkoff, Shuff-Bailey, Olguin, & Ruan, 1995). (Markman & Hutchinson, 1984, suggested a similar principle called the *taxonomic assumption.*) Thus, on hearing caponata requested yet again, Anne knew to look for something that resembled the caponata and was probably the same kind of substance, rather than assuming that caponata meant the special implement it was served with (a thematic relation). Finally, whereas the first tier principle of object scope allowed the child to map new terms to objects (as opposed to actions), and to whole objects at that, the second tier principle of novel name–nameless category (N3C) causes the child to search out a nameless object referent as soon as a novel word is heard. Thus, for example, Anne assumed that when she heard the novel name *caponata* it should map to an unnamed object category. Markman's (1989) principle of mutual exclusivity (see also Merriman & Bowman, 1989) is similar to N3C, although N3C does not presuppose that children avoid having two names for things. The six principles just discussed are graphically depicted in Fig. 11.1.

In sum, the character of word learning changes from the end of the 1st year when it is slow and piecemeal to the end of the 2nd year when children can produce as many as nine new words a day. After reviewing the literature on word learning, we chose these six principles because they appeared to be necessary and sufficient for word learning to take place. Taking a broad view of word learning in the first 2 years of life, it becomes apparent that young children have important insights about word learning that were not being captured by existing principles in the literature.

The two-tiered model of lexical principles is a way of explaining how word learning begins and how it might change over development. The first tier of lexical principles helps get word learning off the ground during the last trimester of the 1st year of life. The second tier of principles builds on the first tier. The second tier is constructed by children as they increasingly utilize features of the linguistic and nonlinguistic input that they were not sensitive to earlier. Thus, each lexical principle is itself a product of learning that can then be used to enable more efficient word learning.

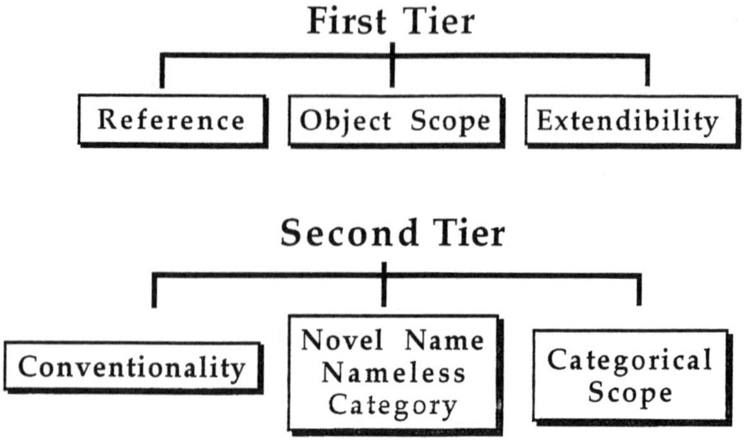

FIG. 11.1. Six lexical principles in the developmental lexical principles framework (Golinkoff et al., 1994).

A THUMBNAIL COMPARISON OF ALTERNATIVE THEORETICAL APPROACHES

It is at this point—the presentation of a constraint or two for word learning—that other theoretical approaches that draw on constraints or principles end their story. The implicit assumption is that there is enough information available in the *linguistic stream* and in the word learning principles that are either present from the start (Markman, 1989) or learned (Smith, Jones, & Landau, 1996), to help children learn new object words. However, the information in our homespun example of Anne's caponata experience is more than just linguistic information. The example was rich in social cues (e.g., eye gaze and nonverbal gestures) that learners could also exploit for word learning. Our approach, the developmental lexical principles approach, is not to stop here but rather to acknowledge both a constraints position and a social-environmental position. Theories of word learning can only succeed if they are hybrid theories, combining lexical principles with theories about domain-general attentional processes and social-pragmatic cues.

This point becomes obvious when considering the indeterminacy of reference. There are a surprising number of difficulties in figuring out what someone is talking about when they point and refer to an object. These difficulties were amply demonstrated by the philosopher Quine (1960). Although we utter the word *rabbit* as the rabbit scurries by, the word *rabbit* could potentially refer to any number of things, from the whole rabbit, to the rabbit parts, to the ground the rabbit was traversing. With an indeterminate number of word-to-world mappings, how do children, by the age of 20 months, learn up to nine new words a day?

Current solutions to the Quinean conundrum come from word learning theories that fall into three camps. Constraint theorists, using the rabbit example, argue that word learners face a massive induction problem. Rather than sifting through the myriad of possible mappings between a word and a referent, children are cognitively and pragmatically constrained to entertain certain hypotheses for word meanings over others. Led by scientists like Markman (1989), Clark (1983), Merriman and Bowman (1989), and others, these researchers hold that children have a set of domain-specific constraints, biases, or principles that guide the attachment of new labels to referents. Thus, children escape the Quinean problem because they are more likely to focus on the whole rabbit, for example, than on the infinite number of possible alternative meanings for the word.

The domain-general approach to word learning (Smith, chap. 10, this volume; Smith et al., 1996) is in some ways compatible with our own—especially with its emphasis on the development of lexical principles. Principles are not present full-blown from the start but emerge during the course of the child's experience in word learning. If there is nothing there from the start, however, these theorists must explain what gets word learning off the ground to begin with. How does the child ever start to make inferences about a word's meaning? Because word learning biases are rooted in forming associations and not in any species-specific attentional biases, the domain-general view suffers from another potential problem. It offers no constraints on the number or kind of principles that a child could have.

Finally, in stark contrast to the constraint theories are the social-pragmatic theories, led by Baldwin (1991, 1993), Tomasello and his colleagues (e.g., Tomasello & Barton, 1994; Tomasello & Farrar, 1986), and Harris (1992), among others, who argued that Quine's example is not an appropriate analysis for early word learning. Children face no induction problem, the argument goes, because they are guided toward the correct word-to-world mappings by skilled conversational partners (their parents) who use social cues like joint attention and eye gaze to direct their young apprentices. With appropriate social supports and a socially sophisticated child who can read pragmatic cues, children can easily discern that *rabbit* applies to the entire rabbit and not to the other, nonrelevant characteristics of the scene. The social-pragmatic theorists contend that they do not need the constraint theorists. In fact, the constraint view and the social-pragmatic perspective are considered to be diametrically opposed to one another. Either the child has an induction problem and is blessed with word learning constraints *or* the child is reliant on the social environment for guidance in word-to-world mappings. Yet, we argue that the social-pragmatic researchers need the constraints theorists. Otherwise, how can they account for why the child assumes that it is the whole object that is being labeled or that words apply to categories? Children could make any number of other assumptions about how words work but they don't. Likewise, the constraint theorists need the social-pragmatic theorists. Without social-pragmatic input, children would have no idea which of the many unnamed whole objects around them the speaker intends to be the referent of the new label. Social cues help the child determine which object is being labeled.

Thus, we adopt a position that embraces findings from both the constraints and social-pragmatic literatures. Lexical constraints, we argue, are the products of developmental processes rather than the engines of that development. These constraints or principles emerge in full form as children, over developmental time, differentially weigh all of the available inputs—be they social, perceptual, temporal, or linguistic. Our position is designed to examine multiple influences on word learning (as in the caponata example), rather than focusing on a single influence in an either–or approach. In our work in progress, we take the charge of moving away from an either–or view of word learning quite seriously and present a fourth, hybrid emergentist alternative.

The key point of our model is that all of the principles are not available from the start of word learning and that all cues are not created equal. For example, children do not start word learning with the principle of N3C. Mervis and Bertrand (1994) showed that the N3C principle is not in place until after the vocabulary spurt. The authors tested 19-month-old children, some of whom had and some of whom had not experienced a vocabulary spurt. They presented the children with two objects, one whose name they knew and a novel object whose name they did not know. Prior to the vocabulary spurt, when children were asked to retrieve an object requested with a novel name, they did not assume that it mapped to the unnamed object. However, if they had had a vocabulary spurt, they readily selected the unnamed object to be the referent of the novel name.

The same is true for the principle of conventionality—it is also not present from the start of word learning. There is ample evidence in the literature that children create their own words for things and gradually drop these in favor of more conventional terms (Clark, 1983). For example, one of Mervis's sons (see Golinkoff et al., 1994) called pacifiers *pops.* At some point, however, he dropped *pops* and switched to the conventional term *pacifier.* In other words, the principle of conventionality is only adopted after the child has compiled a sizable vocabulary.

Finally, Clark (1983) showed that early in lexical acquisition, the child often uses a word to label a fuzzy set of exemplars, bound together most often by common shape (Smith, 1995), but sometimes by common usage and association (thematically). For example, Guillaume's (1927) son said the French word for "breast" at 11 months. He used this word not only to ask for the breast but to ask for a biscuit, to refer to a red button, to the point of an elbow, to an eye in a picture, and to his mother's face in a photograph (cited in Bloom & Lahey, 1978). Diffuse extension under the principle of extendibility gives way to extension based on taxonomic category membership, first at the basic level and later at the superordinate level (Golinkoff et al., 1995).

The hybrid emergentist view captures the development of the lexical principles, describing the shifts from first tier to second tier principles that are reflected in the examples cited earlier. Under the hybrid view, the child differentially taps into a coalition of cues available in the input to construct ever more complex principles for word learning. These cues might be temporal cues (what appeared first), perceptual cues (which object is moving), or social cues (mom is looking at that object). Furthermore, the types of cues that children come to rely on change over time. This view too, has precedence in the literature in the work of Baldwin (1991, 1993). Baldwin found that although social cues to referential intent are always present when children are offered new words, it is not until around 18 months of age that they are able to use these cues in the service of word learning.

In the hybrid view, lexical principles are built up from coalitions of cues and change as the child comes to mine different coalitions of these cues. The caponata example indicates how far adults have come compared to children learning their first words. However, for infants learning their first words, having only first tier lexical principles, many cues that make up the coalition have to be present and in alignment in order for word learning to occur. For example, whereas adults can often make sense of contradictory information (e.g., in the caponata example, the hostess gestured vaguely to the refrigerator while looking into the sink), children would probably be confused in this situation because the cues do not agree. Children's discovery and exploitation of the coalition of cues for word learning are exactly what we are beginning to study.

PRINCIPLES DEVELOP NOT JUST ACROSS TIERS BUT WITHIN A TIER

We have come to realize that there is not only a developmental progression from Tier 1 to Tier 2 principles, but also that each of the principles has its own course of development. It is imperative that we look for the origins of the Tier 1 principles and that we come to think of the model not as a set of static principles, but as a set of principles that develop along a continuum as can be seen in Fig. 11.2.

Using the principle of reference as an example, we argue that children assume from the start that a word maps to an object, action, or event and

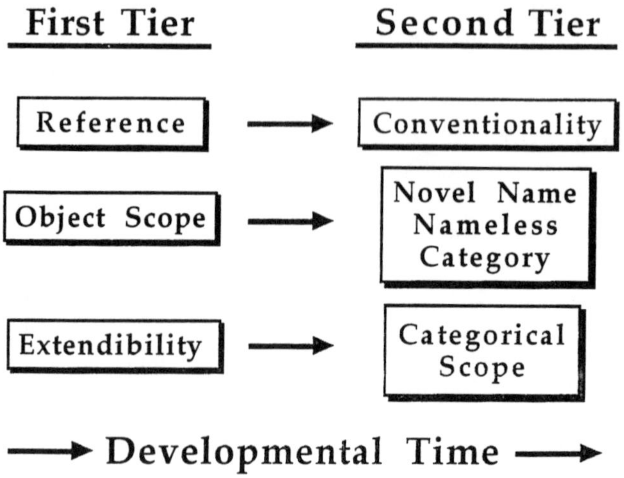

FIG. 11.2. Lexical principles develop within a tier and build on each other across tiers.

that a word can be extended (the principle of extendibility).[2] Without these very basic principles, the child could not get word learning started. However, what exactly it *means* to refer remains to be worked out by the child in the course of development. Children begin with an immature principle of reference, assuming that a word "goes with" an object. Children do not assume that the word "stands for" the object yet as adults do. A mature principle of reference, by contrast, requires that a word stand for an object and that it be mapped to the referent that the speaker (as opposed to the hearer) has in mind. Thus, the basis for attaching a label to a referent changes in the course of development. Another way to say this is that the very same act of reference may result in the identification of different referents, depending on the level of development of the principle of reference.

Our current work attempts to track these changes and the way in which the social-pragmatic and cognitive cues influence children's word learning heuristics. We hypothesize that infants who are first learning words can attend to a number of relevant inputs in their environment, including social cues, perceptual salience, and temporal cues. However, the very young child, with an immature principle of reference, cannot necessarily use all of these cues to establish reference. Instead, we hypothesized that the infant at the beginning of word learning is drawn by perceptual salience when attaching a word to a referent. That is, a novel word "goes with" the most interesting object in the context. Older, more sophisticated, word learners, in contrast, may be able to use even subtle social cues like eye gaze to "read" the speaker's intent when affixing a label to a referent—even when the object being labeled is the more boring alternative in the context. Before describing a study that pitted the cue of perceptual salience against the cue of eye gaze for determining reference, we describe a new method we developed to enable the study of the very earliest stages of word learning.

THE INTERACTIVE INTERMODAL PREFERENTIAL LOOKING PARADIGM

Our new method for investigating early word learning is based on the Intermodal Preferential Looking Paradigm developed by Golinkoff and Hirsh-Pasek (Golinkoff, Hirsh-Pasek, Cauley, & Gordon, 1987; Hirsh-Pasek & Golinkoff, 1996) to study lexical and syntactic comprehension. That

[2]This does not imply that extendibility is innate. Indeed, Dromi's (1987) diary study of her daughter's early language development suggests that word learning may begin in the absence of extendibility. A number of Keren's early words were underextended to just the original exemplar.

paradigm shows two video events simultaneously on two side-by-side televisions and plays a single linguistic message that matches only one of the events. The dependent variable is visual fixation: Does the child look longer at the event that matches the linguistic message than at the event that does not match what they are hearing? Although this method has proven quite successful in probing the origins of grammar and lexical comprehension (Golinkoff & Hirsh-Pasek, 1995; Hirsh-Pasek & Golinkoff, 1996), we needed a new method that was both tightly controlled and easy to alter. We needed a method that would allow us to systematically introduce different kinds of cues for word learning in different combinations. For example, the original paradigm does not readily lend itself to the study of social cues like object handling or eye gaze; also, without making new movies, we could not introduce additional cues. Finally, for infants around 1 year of age, we thought that word learning might work best if it was more immediate and not mediated by the medium of videotape.

Borrowing from Baldwin's (1991, 1993) successful "bucket task," our intermodal preferential looking paradigm (Golinkoff et al., 1987), and Fagan's (1971; Fagan, Singer, Montic, & Shepard, 1986) infant intelligence test, we arrived at the paradigm shown in Fig. 11.3. Infants are seated on their blindfolded mother's lap facing the experimenter and our testing apparatus. After some preexposure to the toys—both familiar toys on some trials and novel toys on others—the toys are fixed with Velcro onto one

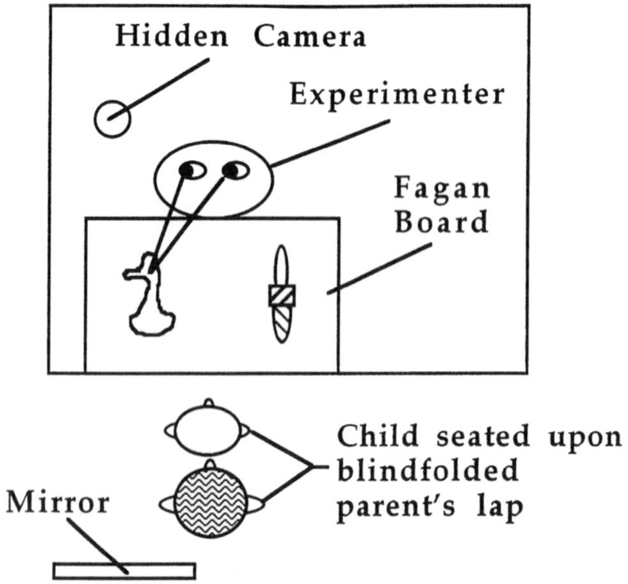

FIG. 11.3. A graphic depiction of the Interactive Intermodal Preferential Looking Paradigm.

side of a two-sided blackboard (40 cm × 50 cm) approximately 5 inches apart. The board can be rotated almost 180° so that the toys can go in and out of view for a specified period of time. Importantly, the board is out of the child's reach and is high enough so that the experimenter can hide behind the board while children are inspecting the toys during test trials. Therefore, the experimenter cannot inadvertently influence the child about which is the "correct" toy. A video camera on a tripod above and behind the experimenter records the child's visual fixation of the stimuli and a mirror reflection of the objects on the board. Coding is done offline after the child leaves.

Using this apparatus, it is possible to examine word knowledge and word learning in a controlled setting using both familiar and novel test objects. For example, familiar object trials allow us to indirectly ask whether the child can "play our game." If children cannot look at the correct familiar object when it is asked for by name, it is very unlikely that they could succeed with novel objects in a word learning task. Another purpose the familiar trials serve is that they acclimate children to the task. Whereas testing with familiar objects is important to make sure that children can function in the paradigm, it is the use of novel objects that allows us to ask central questions about the word learning process. Unfamiliar novel objects given novel names and presented under various conditions permit us to probe which cues children use and in what combinations to assist their word learning.

Both familiar and novel trials begin with a period of object exploration in which the child has an opportunity to play with the test objects. This is followed (in the case of the trials in which novel objects are introduced) by a check on object salience, a training phase in which the experimenter attempts to teach a name, and a testing phase to see if the name offered has been mapped to the object.

Table 11.1 reviews the sequence that occurs on the trials in which novel objects are used. In the exploration phase, children are presented with two novel objects, one at a time, for exploration. The objects are not named at that time. In the present study, infants were offered a "boring" toy and an "interesting" toy to play with, each for 26 sec. Then the two objects appeared side-by-side on the board to test for stimulus salience. In the following training trials, the experimenter first captured children's attention by locking eye gaze with them. Then, with both toys displayed but out of the child's reach, the experimenter gazed fixedly at the target toy and labeled it five times. Using infant-directed speech, the experimenter would say, for example, "Eve, this is a danu. See the danu?" Children's visual fixation responses during the training trials indicated whether they could even follow the eye gaze of the experimenter as the toy was being labeled. Finally, in the test trials, the experimenter asked for the object

TABLE 11.1
Sequence of Events in Presentation of Trials With Novel Objects

Exploration (26 sec):		**(Interesting Toy)**
Exploration (26 sec):		**(Boring Toy)**
Salience (6 sec): **"Eve, look at the board!"** **"What do you see?"**	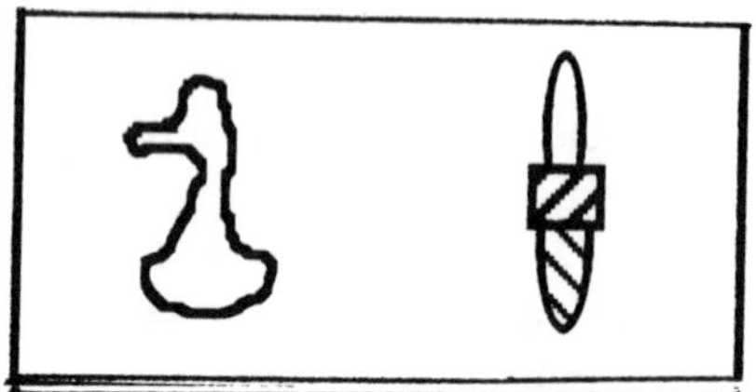	
Salience (6 sec): **"Eve, look at the board!"** **"What do you see?"**		
Training (≈ 16 sec): **"Eve, look at the modi."** **"It's a modi, a modi."** **"Eve, see the modi!"**	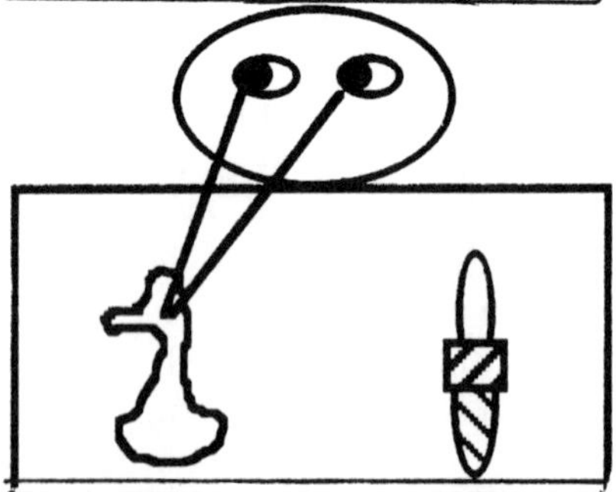	
Testing (6 sec): **"Eve, where's the modi?"** **"Do you see the modi?"**	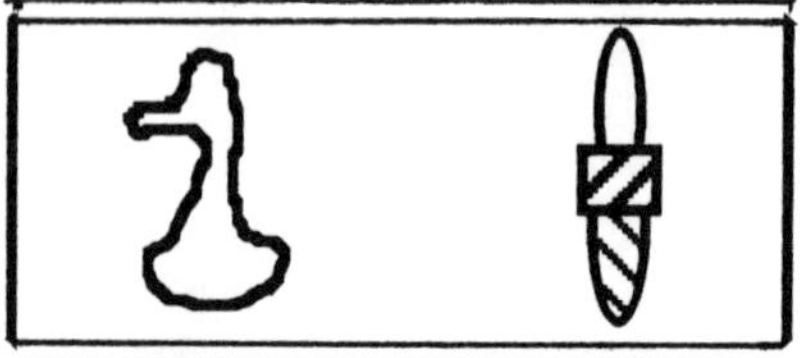	
Testing (6 sec): **"Eve, where's the modi?"** **"Do you see the modi?"**	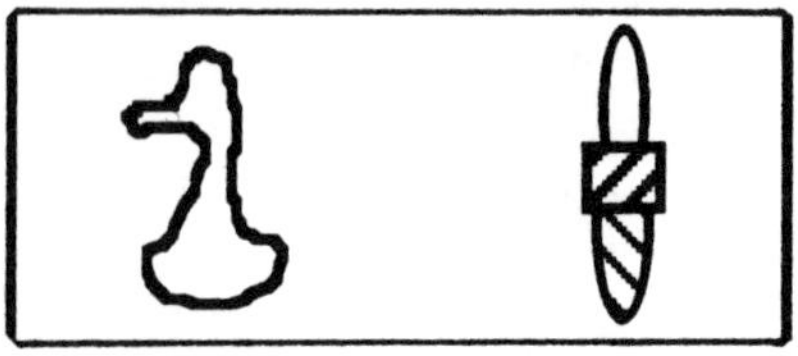	

that was labeled during training, once again getting the child's attention first. For example, the experimenter might say, "Eve, where's the danu? Can you find the danu?" If children actually used eye gaze to decide which toy was being labeled, they should look more to the object that was being requested by name than to the object that was not being requested.

A number of variables were counterbalanced, such as whether the boring and interesting toys were on the left or right side of the board and which toy was offered first. The independent variables were gender, age, type of toy (interesting or boring), and condition (coincident vs. conflict). In the coincident condition, the toy that coincided with children's preferences—the interesting toy—was labeled. In the conflict condition, the toy that did not coincide with the children's preferences—the boring toy—was labeled. The dependent variable was looking time to each toy in three phases of the design: the saliency phase, the training phase, and the testing phase. Finally, the logic of the design, as with our other intermodal preferential looking paradigm (Golinkoff et al., 1987; Hirsh-Pasek & Golinkoff, 1996), was that children will choose to look at objects that match the linguistic stimulus more than they look at objects that do not match the linguistic stimulus. Of course, this assumes that toddlers have paired up the label with the appropriate toy. If they fail to link the label to the appropriate referent, visual fixation time should be distributed equally to both toys or disproportionately to the toy that children consider to be more attractive.

Children at three ages were tested: 12 to 13 months, 19 to 20 months, and 24 to 25 months. As in all our joint research, half of the children were tested at the University of Delaware and half were tested at Temple University.

DOES THE METHOD WORK?

To determine whether the method was a viable one, children's responses to the two familiar test trials were examined. At each age, children looked significantly more at the target item (i.e., the item requested) than they did at the nontarget item (see Fig. 11.4). Thus, even the 12-month-old children were "playing the game."

Two other points about the new method are of interest. First, even the youngest children distribute their looking times to examine both stimuli. That is, even when one object is clearly more attractive than the other, children inspect both objects. Second, not only is this method successful for 12-month-olds, but there is very little participant loss (less than 10%). Because participant loss in studies with infants can run as high as 50%, this is good news!

It appears, then, that the 3-D intermodal preferential looking paradigm is a robust method that will enable the field to probe very early word

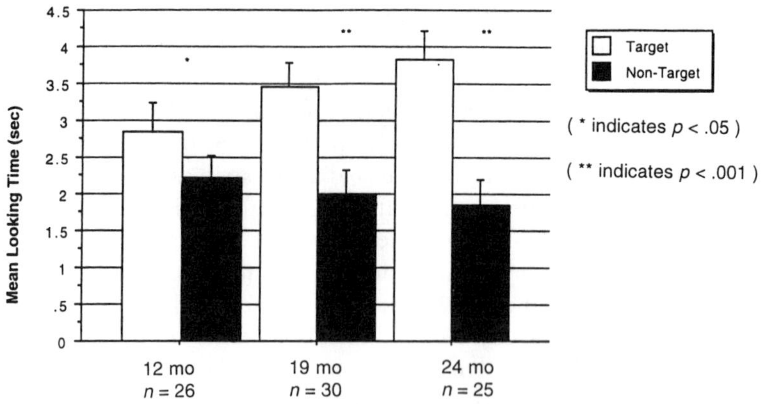

FIG. 11.4. Mean visual fixation time (in sec) by age to the target and nontarget toy in the familiar sets.

learning and to explore the changing dynamics of word learning over time.

TESTING THE HYPOTHESES

Recall that our interest in conducting the study was to see whether the principle of reference moves from an immature to a mature state. We hypothesized that very young children, with an immature principle of reference, would be drawn by perceptual cues when attaching a word to a referent—that the word might "go with" the most interesting perceptual object in the immediate context. We further hypothesized that older children with a more mature principle of reference might use subtle social cues like eye gaze and would thus read the speaker's intent when affixing a label to a referent—even when the object to be labeled was the more boring alternative. Thus, we put the cue of perceptual salience in conflict with the cue of eye gaze in a labeling situation.

Two questions were addressed in this experiment. First, when can children follow the subtle social cue of eye gaze? That is, when do they even appreciate that one can follow another's gaze to a focal point in the context? Second, when can children use this cue to figure out which of two toys is being labeled? Perhaps one of the reasons word learning occurs so slowly at first is that they cannot use another's eye gaze to discern what is being labeled.

To examine these questions, it was necessary to first establish that our intuitions about which was the boring and which was the interesting toy were correct. As Fig. 11.5 shows, results indicated that across all three age

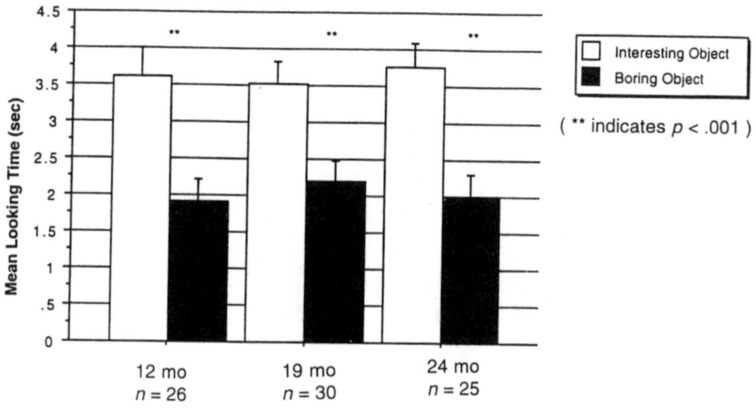

FIG. 11.5. Mean visual fixation time by age to the interesting and boring objects during the saliency trials.

groups, children did indeed look more at the interesting toy than the boring toy.

Given this confirmation in the saliency trials, we next asked whether young children could even follow the social cue of eye gaze to help them in determining the speaker's intended referent. A simple associationistic theory of word learning predicts that children should attach a new word to the first object they see. Baldwin (1991, 1993) found that babies resist doing this when the experimenter acts as though she intends to label an object different than the first one revealed. Thus, Baldwin's work suggests that by 19 months of age, children can follow social eye gaze, overriding cues such as temporal contiguity for word learning.

Data from the training trials reveal whether children could follow the experimenter's eye gaze. As Fig. 11.6 shows, only at the two oldest ages do children appear to be following the experimenter's gaze. In contrast, the 12-month-olds seem oblivious, remaining fixated on the interesting object whether the experimenter looked there or not.

It could be argued, however, that for the older two groups, the true test of gaze following is what occurs in the conflict condition where the child is asked to follow the experimenter's gaze to the boring object. Again, as seen in Fig. 11.7, the 12-month-olds do not seem to follow the experimenter's gaze despite the fact that the experimenter makes eye contact first with the children and then tries to drive their looking response to the boring toy. By 19 and 24 months, however, significant looking toward the boring toy occurs in the training trials.

Having established that 19- and 24-month-olds can follow social eye gaze, the next question is whether they can use social eye gaze to determine

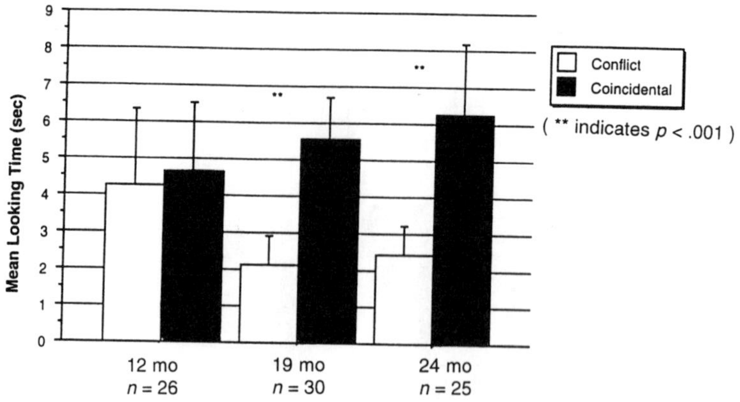

FIG. 11.6. Mean visual fixation time by age and condition during the training trials to the interesting object.

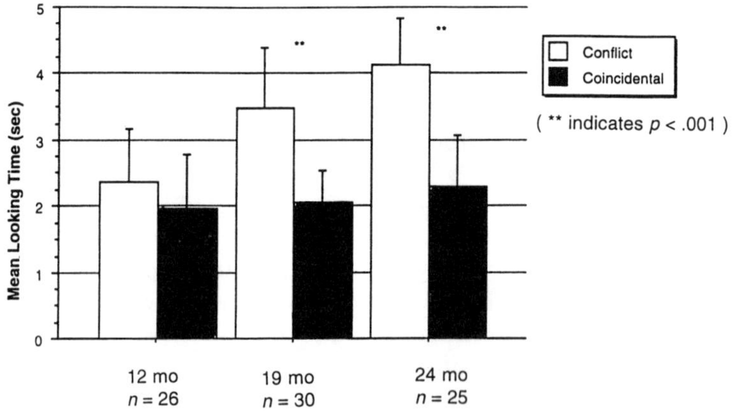

FIG. 11.7. Mean visual fixation time by age and condition during the training trials to the boring object.

which object is being labeled. The first way to address the question is to ask whether, across age, children looked at the interesting toy more than at the boring object in the coincident condition. As can be seen in Table 11.2, it appears that all participants—including the 12-month-olds—are looking to the interesting object when it is requested by name. Perhaps even the youngest age group has succeeded in mapping the novel name to the interesting object.

Once again, however, the true story is revealed in the conflict condition, the condition in which the boring object received the label. Here, 12-month-olds look at the interesting object significantly more than they look at the target, the boring object. Does this mean that the 12-month-olds

TABLE 11.2
Mean Visual Fixation Time to Target and Nontarget by Age and Condition During the Test Trials

Condition	*Age (in months)*		
	12	*19*	*24*
Coincident			
Target (interesting	3.01*	3.70*	3,61*
Nontarget (boring)	1.22	1.27	1.60
Conflict			
Target (boring)	1.43*	2.06	2.85*
Nontarget (interesting)	2.84	2.56	2.46

*$p < .05$.

attached the label to the interesting toy as we had predicted, using the cue of perceptual salience? Although this is possible, we think it unlikely because the 12-month-olds did not follow the experimenter's eye gaze to the interesting object during the training trials when the object was labeled. A simpler explanation is that the youngest group just preferred to look at the interesting toy. On the other hand, it is possible that these children attached the label to the interesting toy because they looked at it significantly more during test trials in both conflict and coincident conditions. One way to test this possibility would be to allow these children to become familiar with an additional novel toy with roughly equal salience to the original interesting toy. Then when asked to look at the interesting object when it was requested by name, and when given a choice between the new salient toy and the original interesting toy, children should look at the original interesting toy more if they had mapped a name to it. Studies like this are currently being conducted in our laboratories.

What do the 19-month-olds do in the conflict condition when the boring toy is the target that receives the name? They look at the interesting toy somewhat more but the difference is not significant (M = 2.56 to the interesting vs. M = 2.05 to the boring). The sophisticated 24-month-olds reverse this trend. They look at the target (i.e., the boring toy) significantly more (M= 2.87) than they look toward the interesting toy (the nontarget; M = 2.46).

Another approach to the same data can be gained by examining how children responded to the same toy when it appeared in the conflict and in the coincident conditions. Recall that children saw exactly the same objects in both conditions; the only difference between conditions was in the direction of the experimenter's gaze as she labeled the object. Thus, in the coincident condition, the experimenter labeled the interesting toy (a clacker) while the more boring object (the bottle opener) was present; in the conflict condition, however, the experimenter labeled the bottle opener in the presence of the interesting clacker. Any difference in how long the children look at the interesting or boring toy in either condition must be a function of which toy was labeled. Did children look longer at the interesting clacker in the coincident condition when it was asked for by name than they looked at that same object when it appeared in the conflict condition in which it was not requested by name?

The answer depends on the child's age. The 12-month-olds do not spend significantly more time looking at the interesting toy in the coincident than in the conflict condition. By 19 and 24 months, however, children are showing a clear effect of the cue of eye gaze on word learning. They look at the interesting object significantly more when it is requested in the coincident condition than in the conflict condition when it is not being requested. This finding already suggests that the social cue of eye gaze wins out over the cue of perceptual salience by the time children are 19 and 24 months of age. Is this pattern upheld in the arguably more difficult conflict condition?

The answer is yes. This analysis indicates that the 19- and the 24-month-olds are affected by the labeling. That is, they look longer at the boring toy in the condition in which it is requested than in the condition in which it is not requested. The 12-month-olds, in contrast, seem relatively unaffected by the labeling. Although their looking time at the boring toy increases in the conflict condition by .30, this value does not reach significance.

What these findings appear to indicate is that children are becoming more sensitive to social cues over time and can use them in a labeling task. They are still lured by the cue of perceptual salience, but they are weighing social information more heavily in figuring out which object is being labeled. It should be noted that these results appear to be robust because they have been replicated in a control experiment. In that experiment, the side on which the target object appeared during the test trial was switched. That is, if the target appeared on the left of the board during salience and training, its position was then switched to the right of the board during the test trials. Results were upheld despite the unexpected switch of sides at test.

WHAT IS THE SIGNIFICANCE OF THIS WORK?

To conclude, three main issues will be discussed. First, we review the developmental story these data seem to tell and the utility of the new method. Then we describe the theoretical implications of these findings. Finally, we ask how data like these may help us to understand the development of lexical principles and word learning in a richer, more complex way.

The study presented is among the first in a series of experiments designed to look at the emerging lexical principles of Tier 1 as they develop over time. We examined two cues thought to play an important role in the development of reference (eye gaze and perceptual salience). We hypothesized that children might begin to attach words to objects by simply noting what is perceptually salient in the environment and by attaching the word to the most obvious, salient object. With time, children would come to more heavily weight social inputs as critical cues to word learning, coming to use adults' social cues to locate the objects being labeled. Were our original hypotheses confirmed? That is, did the cue of perceptual salience take precedence over the cue of social eye gaze at the youngest age? Conversely, was social eye gaze weighted more heavily than perceptual salience at the older ages?

The 12-Month-Olds

The first important point for making sense of the 12-month-olds' behavior is that they were clearly "playing our game." They looked more to the familiar object requested by name than to the familiar object that was not requested. This means that we cannot blame the method on their possible failure to learn the novel words. Second, we had predicted that the label would be attached to the interesting object regardless of whether it was labeled or not. Although this may have occurred, we are not convinced because the children did not follow the experimenter's gaze during even the coincident condition training trials. However, it is possible that the use of social eye gaze in these particular circumstances confused the 12-month-olds. Prior research (e.g., Butterworth & Grover, 1990; Scaife & Bruner, 1975) suggested that by 12 months of age, infants could follow their mothers' eye gaze to one of several targets. It is unclear what in this task kept children from following the experimenter's gaze to the target object—especially in the coincident condition where she looked at the object they liked best. A possible indication of their confusion is that the only phase of the experiment in which the 12-month-olds did not significantly prefer the interesting object was the training trials. To disambiguate the 12-month-old results, we need to run the condition mentioned earlier as well as another condition in which the experimenter provides a label while looking at the child with both objects present. Will the child assume that the experimenter, looking to neither toy, is labeling the interesting object?

Yet another reason the 12-month-olds may not be learning the novel names is that they may need to have more cues in the coalition present and more of these cues in alignment. The cues available in this experiment were minimal and two cues (perceptual salience and eye gaze) were purposely put into conflict. Would the 12-month-olds show learning if an additional cue, such as object handling, was added?

A final possibility is that we may still find that perceptual salience is weighted more heavily than social cues for attaching a label when the principle of reference is immature. Perceptual salience is but a relative concept. The objects selected in this study were roughly the same size and made of the same material—plastic. Perhaps using an interesting object that was even more compelling, relative to the boring object, such as a highly textured, much larger object, would have produced clearer results from the 12-month-olds.

The 19-Month-Olds

After 7 more months of word learning experience, the 19-month-olds are no longer seduced by perceptual salience and can clearly follow eye gaze. They also show that they can use eye gaze to discern which object is being labeled. However, in the first analysis, which compared visual fixation time to the target and nontarget in the conflict condition, their visual fixation differences did not reach significance in favor of the boring object. Nonetheless, overall, these results confirm those offered by Baldwin (1991, 1993) in that it appears that children can capitalize on the cue of social eye gaze for word learning by 19 months of age.

The 24-Month-Olds

These children appear to be in possession of a mature principle of reference. They follow the experimenter's eye gaze during training and they look at the target object more than the nontarget in both analyses. With the exception of studies by Woodward, Markman, and Fitzsimmons (1994) and Waxman and Markow (1996), most researchers have investigated word learning in children who are 24 months of age and older. The vast majority of our literature has thus missed out on earlier, critical developments in word learning that occur when lexical principles are being constructed. By 24 months of age, according to the developmental lexical principles approach (Golinkoff et al., 1994), children are already in possession of the six lexical principles necessary for word learning.

Theoretical Implications of the Present Work

One message from this program of research is that it is now possible for us to look at the emergence of word learning skills. The interactive intermodal paradigm makes it possible to examine the coalition of cues surrounding the early word learner. As we shift our focus downward, it be-

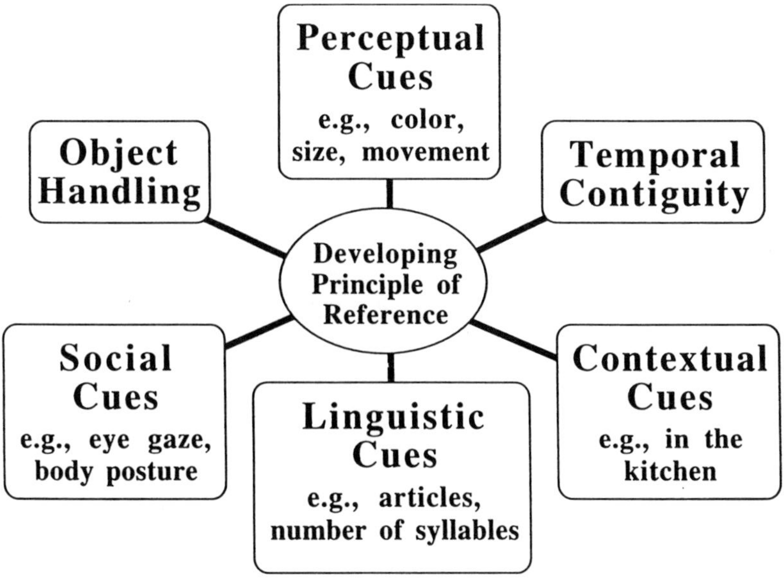

FIG. 11.8. The coalition model for word learning illustrated for the principle of reference. The child is surrounded by a coalition of cues, the weightings changing with development.

comes clear that seemingly incompatible approaches might all be necessary to explain word learning.

Why haven't we seen the advantage of this polygamous union before between social-pragmatic theorists and constraint theorists? Partly because researchers prefer to work from a particular theoretical vantage point and partly because the methods that exist were insufficient to study very early word learning.[3] The interactive intermodal preferential looking paradigm appears to be one way to assess children's earliest word learning. It permits us to offer different cues from the coalition of cues in isolation, in competition, or in alignment with each other.

Our position is that the inputs available in a referential act form a coalition of cues (as seen in Fig. 11.8) to which children assign differential weights as they move from being only immature word learners with rudimentary lexical principles toward skilled word learners with more mature lexical principles. As a graphic analogy to how the development of the principle of reference works, imagine that different cues in Fig. 11.8 light up with differential intensity (analogous to weightings) as the child con-

[3]See Waxman and Markow (1996) for another method used with 12-month-olds in a task involving linguistic stimuli. That method also used a measure of attention (time spent exploring objects haptically and visually) as the dependent variable.

structs the principle of reference. Early on, when the child has only an immature principle of reference, the perceptual cues and perhaps temporal contiguity are lit up. Certainly linguistic cues such as the reflexes associated with the different form classes are less important for the 1-year-old than they will be even by the middle of the 2nd year of life. For example, Waxman and Markow (1996) reported that 12- and 13-month-olds appear to treat nouns and adjectives interchangeably. Nor is it likely that 1-year-old children are relying heavily on social cues such as eye gaze, or on contextual cues, as in where the act of naming takes place. By the time the child has a mature principle of reference, however, the figurative lights on some of these cues have become dimmer. For example, the work of Baldwin (1991, 1993) and Tomasello and Farrar (1986) indicated that temporal contiguity is no longer weighted as a cue to word learning. Neither do the perceptual cues light up, as shown in the present research. Instead, social, contextual, and linguistic cues light up to guide the child in early word mapping. With the interactive intermodal preferential looking paradigm, we are now in a position to study how weightings are assigned.

One criticism that may be raised against our emphasis on children's use of correlated cues in the input is that we are making the young organism too complex. Is there any evidence that children, using what we have elsewhere called *guided distributional learning* (Hirsh-Pasek & Golinkoff, 1996), can look for and mine correlations among multiple sources of information in the input? Recent work by Saffran, Aslin, and Newport (1996) and Morgan, Shi, and Allopenna (1996) in the area of speech perception along with work by Younger and Cohen (1983, 1986) in visual categorization are sufficient to make this case. Infants are capable of sensitivity to subtle cues in both the auditory and visual domains and to cues that function in correlation with other cues.

The position we have taken on the development of lexical principles is really quite similar to our position on the development of language comprehension (Golinkoff & Hirsh-Pasek, 1995; Hirsh-Pasek & Golinkoff, 1996). In the latter case, multiple sources of input such as prosody, semantics, and syntax are weighted differentially over the course of the emergence of language comprehension. Once again, different areas light up with differential intensity, although it is important to note that as in word learning, each type of information is available to the child from the outset. Just as in word learning, however, availability is not the same as accessibility. The child cannot use all these sources of information from the beginning and allocates more attention to some sources over others at first.

There is much information available in the coalition of cues when an act of reference takes place—as in the caponata example. Children need to figure out *which* cues they are being offered, and *how* to weight them, in order to decide *which* object in the environment is being labeled. The weightings of these cues change over the course of development as the children hone their strategies for word learning. The principles that guide word learning then fall out or emerge as the child gains more experience in word learning.

In sum, we propose that it is time to rethink word learning, to look at the origins of word learning, and to see how multiple cues interact to create the climate for the emergent principles that will help children navigate through the problem space that Quine (1960) so aptly described. We offered a new method to accomplish this ambitious goal—the interactive intermodal preferential looking paradigm—a method that makes few response demands on infants because it utilizes a response already in their repertoire, namely, visual fixation. We also offered a new theoretical framework based on the developmental lexical principles approach (Golinkoff et al., 1994), a framework that has now been modified to recognize that each of the word learning principles itself undergoes development, becoming refined as a result of word learning experience. If we have accomplished anything, we hope to have convinced the reader that we cannot make progress in understanding word learning without embracing its complexity.

ACKNOWLEDGMENTS

We thank Rebecca Brand, Cindy Hankey, and Camille Rocroi for their invaluable assistance on this project. Special thanks to Allison Golinkoff and He Len Chung for their help with editing. The work reported herein is supported by Grant SBR9601306 to the first two authors from NSF and by NICHHD Grant HD25455-07 to Hirsh-Pasek.

REFERENCES

Baldwin, D. A. (1991). Infants' contributions to the achievement of joint reference. *Child Development, 62,* 875–890.

Baldwin, D. A. (1993). Infants' ability to consult the speaker for clues to word reference. *Journal of Child Language, 20,* 395–418.

Bloom, L., & Lahey, M. (1978). *Language development and language disorders.* New York: Wiley.

Butterworth, G., & Grover, L. (1990). Joint visual attention, manual pointing, and preverbal communication in human infancy. In M. Jeannerod (Ed.), *Attention and performance XIII* (pp. 605–624). Hillsdale, NJ: Lawrence Erlbaum Associates.

Clark, E. V. (1983). Meanings and concepts. In J. H. Flavell & E. M. Markman (Eds.), *Handbook of child psychology: Vol. III. Cognitive development* (pp. 787–840). New York: Wiley.

Dromi, E. (1987). *Early lexical development.* Cambridge, England: Cambridge University Press.

Fagan, J. (1971). Infant recognition memory for a series of visual stimuli. *Journal of Experimental Child Psychology, 11,* 244–250.

Fagan, J., Singer, L., Montic, J., & Shepard, P. (1986). Selective screening device for the early detection of normal or delayed cognitive development in infants at risk for later mental retardation. *Pediatrics, 78,* 1021–1026.

Golinkoff, R. M., & Hirsh-Pasek, K. (1995). Reinterpreting children's sentence comprehension: Toward a new framework. In P. Fletcher & B. MacWhinney (Eds.), *The handbook of child language* (pp. 430–461). London: Blackwell.

Golinkoff, R. M., Hirsh-Pasek, K., Cauley, K., & Gordon, L. (1987). The eyes have it: Lexical and syntactic comprehension in a new paradigm. *Journal of Child Language, 14,* 23–45.

Golinkoff, R. M., Mervis, C. V., & Hirsh-Pasek, K. (1994). Early object labels: The case for a developmental lexical principles framework. *Journal of Child Language, 21,* 125–155.

Golinkoff, R. M., Shuff-Bailey, M., Olguin, K., & Ruan, W. (1995). Young children extend novel words at the basic level: Evidence for the principle of categorical scope. *Developmental Psychology, 31,* 494–507.

Grice, H. P. (1957). Meaning. *The Philosophical Review, 66,* 377–388.

Guillaume, P. (1927). Les débuts de la phrase dans le langage de l'enfant [The beginnings of the sentence in children's language]. *Journal de Psychologie, 24,* 1–15.

Harris, M. (1992). *Language experience and early language development.* Hillsdale, NJ: Lawrence Erlbaum Associates.

Hirsh-Pasek, K., & Golinkoff, R. M. (1996). *The origins of grammar: Evidence from early comprehension.* Cambridge, MA: MIT Press.

Hirsh-Pasek, K., Golinkoff, R. M., Rehill, J. L., Wiley, J. G., & Brand, R. (1997, April). *Mapping words to referents: Multiple cues for word learning.* Paper presented at the meeting of the Society for Research in Child Development, Washington, DC.

Hollich, G., Hirsh-Pasek, K., Golinkoff, R. M. (1996, December). Introducing the 3-D intermodal preferential looking paradigm: A new method to answer an age-old question. Paper presented at the Australian Conference on Methods in Language Acquisition.

Markman, E. M. (1989). *Categorization and naming in children.* Cambridge, MA: MIT Press.

Markman, E. M., & Hutchinson, J. E. (1984). Children's sensitivity to constraints on word meaning: Taxonomic vs. thematic relations. *Cognitive Psychology, 16,* 1–27.

Markman, E. M., & Wachtel, G. F. (1988). Children's use of mutual exclusivity to constrain the meaning of words. *Cognitive Psychology, 20,* 121–157.

Merriman, W. E., & Bowman, L. (1989). The mutual exclusivity bias in children's word learning. *Monographs of the Society for Research in Child Development, 54*(Serial No. 220).

Mervis, C. B., & Bertrand, J. (1994). Acquisition of the novel name-nameless category (N3C) principle. *Child Development, 65,* 1646–1663.

Morgan, J. L., Shi, R., & Allopenna, P. (1996). Perceptual bases of rudimentary grammatic categories: Toward a broader conceptualization of bootstrapping. In J. L. Morgan & K. Demuth (Eds.), *Signal to syntax* (pp. 263–283). Hillsdale, NJ: Lawrence Erlbaum Associates.

Quine, W. V. O. (1960). *Word and object.* Cambridge, England: Cambridge University Press.

Saffran, J. R., Aslin, R. N., & Newport, E. L. (1996). Statistical learning by 8-month-old infants. *Science, 274,* 1926–1928.

Scaife, M., & Bruner, J. S. (1975). The capacity for joint visual attention in the infant. *Nature, 253,* 265–266.

Smith, L. B. (1995). Self-organizing processes in learning to learn words: Development is not induction. In C. A. Nelson (Ed.), *Minnesota Symposium for Child Development* (pp. 1–32). Mahwah, NJ: Lawrence Erlbaum Associates.

Smith, L. B., Jones, S. S., & Landau, B. (1996). Naming in young children: A dumb attentional mechanism? *Cognition, 60,* 143–171.

Tomasello, M., & Barton, M. (1994). Learning words in non-ostensive contexts. *Developmental Psychology, 30,* 639–650.

Tomasello, M., & Farrar, M. J. (1986). Joint attention and early language. *Child Development, 57,* 1454–1463.

Waxman, S. R., & Markow, D. B. (1996). Words as invitations to form categories: Evidence from 12- to 13-month-old infants. *Cognitive Psychology, 61*, 257–302.

Woodward, A., Markman, E., & Fitzsimmons, C. (1994). Rapid word learning in 13- and 18-month olds. *Developmental Psychology, 30*, 553–556.

Younger, B. A., & Cohen L. B. (1983). Infant perception of correlations among attributes. *Child Development, 54*, 858–867.

Younger, B. A., & Cohen, L. B. (1986). Developmental changes in infants' perception of correlations among attributes. *Child Development, 57*, 803–815.

Chapter 12

Competition, Attention, and Young Children's Lexical Processing

William E. Merriman
Kent State University

The model of toddlers' and preschool-age children's lexical processing that I am developing goes by the acronym CALLED, which stands for Competition, Attention, and Learned LExical Descriptions. Although the utility of acronyms can be debated, at least this one provides a transparent mnemonic for what the model is primarily intended to explain, namely, how children learn what things are called.

The heart of the model is a device that forms associations between representations of features of the world and representations of spoken words, and can retrieve words when presented with objects, scenes, or events. The device is very similar to that of the Competition Model of MacWhinney and colleagues (Bates & MacWhinney, 1987; MacWhinney, 1987, 1989; McDonald & MacWhinney, 1991) but has been altered to accommodate the acquisition and use of multiple names for things (see Merriman, 1998, and Merriman & Stevenson, 1997, for earlier versions of the model). The unique feature is that it allows the competition between words to be affected by learned attentional responses to words, as well as by other forces that direct attention. Thus, the first two letters of CALLED concern processes that are central to the device, namely, competition and attention.

My plan is to describe the way in which this device learns, comprehends, and produces words. Because attention is central to these processes, the many factors that determine how attention will be distributed over the dimensions of a stimulus are reviewed first. I also show how the workings of the device can account for several phenomena that have been attributed to two lexical operating principles, namely, Shape or Categorical Scope (Golinkoff, Mervis, & Hirsh-Pasek, 1994; Landau, Smith, & Jones, 1988; Mervis, 1987), and Mutual Exclusivity (Markman, 1989; Merriman & Bowman, 1989). Both of these principles will be reinterpreted as emergent properties of the way in which the device operates on linguistic input.

I do not say much about the Learned LExical Descriptions part of CALLED. This component takes into account the child's occasional experience of hearing and retaining statements of semantic fact (e.g., "A whale is not a fish"). When an element from such a statement is subsequently presented or retrieved, the statement may itself be retrieved. So when asked of a particular whale, "Is this a fish?", a youngster may retrieve the stored fact that a whale is not a fish, and answer, "No." Although such fact retrieval may have some influence, it is not the primary basis for very young children's word comprehension or production decisions. The output of the associative device is the main engine.

Word Learning as Adjusting Feature and Dimension Connections: The Basic Ideas

According to CALLED, every time a child hears a word used for something or uses it for something himself or herself, mental connections are strengthened between an auditory representation of the word and representations of features of the referent (including those it is made of as well as those that characterize its surrounding context). A particular connection is strengthened only if the feature in question is attended to near the time that the word is encoded.

The presentation or production of a word for something also causes increases in the strength of mental connections between the word's representation and representations of the dimensions of the attended-to features. For example, the child who hears the novel name *cardinal*, used for a cardinal, and happens to attend to the bird's color, experiences a strengthening of two connections, one between *cardinal* and the dimension of color, and the other between *cardinal* and the value from that dimension, red. The assumption that responses become associated with both the features and dimensions of stimuli is found not only in attention theories of animal discrimination learning (Sutherland & Mackintosh, 1971) but also in several current accounts of category learning in full-grown members of our own species (Anderson, 1990; Kruschke, 1992; Nosofsky, 1984).

Whenever a word is encountered in input, attention is hypothesized to shift in the direction of the dimensions to which the word is most strongly connected. Dimension connections thus affect word comprehension. They also affect production. A word will be produced only if attention happens to focus on the dimensions to which the word is most strongly connected.

Factors That Influence Attention to the Features of a New Word's Referent

The following determinants of attention seem particularly important:

- The stimulus dimensions that occupied the learner's attention right before the referent was presented (dimensional inertia)
- The dominant dimensions of stimuli found in similar situations in the past and of stimulus representations that are most similar to the referent
- The relative distinctiveness of the features of the referent
- Pragmatic and linguistic cues
- Acts by the speaker that highlight a particular feature of the referent

I elaborate on the first three factors, which are hypothesized to operate even when a referent is encountered outside of a linguistic or communicative context. (For discussions of pragmatic and linguistic cues, see Bloom & Keleman, 1995; Tomasello, 1995; and Woodward & Markman, 1997. Regarding feature highlighting, see Banigan & Mervis, 1988; Merriman, 1986; and Merriman & Kutlesic, 1993.) In a later section, I propose an additional determinant of attention that is motivated by the child's desire that words characterize their exemplars well (the Shared Distinctive Feature Hypothesis).

(1) Dimensional Inertia. The tendency to continue to attend to a dimension after a stimulus change is generally greater than the tendency to attend to that dimension for the first time after the change. A child should be more likely to attend to the brightness of a ball, for example, if he or she had just encoded the brightness of a cube rather than encoded some other dimension of the cube, such as its compactness.

Support for the construct of dimensional inertia comes from research demonstrating that both the immature and mature members of many species, including Homo sapiens, show more positive transfer from one set of discrimination problems to another when the positive cue for each set (the cue associated with the correct answer) comes from the same rather than a different dimension (Dickerson, Novik, & Gould, 1972; House & Zeaman, 1962; Sutherland & Mackintosh, 1971). That is, an intradimensional shift tends to be mastered more quickly than an extradimensional one.[1] For example, if length is the relevant dimension for the first set of problems, the second set will be learned faster if the positive cue for these is also a particular length (e.g., the correct choice is always the 7-inch object) rather than, say, a particular color (e.g., the correct choice is always the blue one).

The organism is assumed to learn to attend to the relevant dimension in solving the first set of problems, then to maintain this attentional response when the second set is presented. The intradimensional shift is learned more quickly because this dimension maintains its relevance, whereas some other dimension becomes relevant in the case of an extradimensional shift.

Two factors are hypothesized to affect dimensional inertia. First, the longer a dimension has been the focus of attention prior to the change in the stimulus, the greater its inertia. Indirect support for this proposal comes from work by Daniel Anderson and colleagues on children's TV viewing (see Burns & Anderson, 1993, for a review). A central finding, which has been dubbed the *inertia of attentional engagement*, is that the child's likelihood of maintaining any particular look at the screen increases the longer the look has been sustained. My suggestion is that such inertia is a property of attention to any dimension of a changing stimulus or succession of stimuli.

Second, the tendency to maintain attention to a dimension over a stimulus change should be directly proportional to the psychological size, or salience, of the change in the attended-to dimension relative to the sum of the sizes of the changes in every dimension of the stimulus. Big changes attract attention more readily than little ones. If a child is attending to the color of a red ball, for example, he or she should be more likely to maintain attention to color if the next object is (a) a green cube rather than a green car, (b) a blue cube of the same size as the ball rather than a blue cube of a different size, and (c) a green ball rather than another red ball.

(2) Dimensional Dominance. Despite its inertial tendencies, attention shifts quite frequently. The pull or dominance of a particular dimension in a situation depends on what the child attended to in similar situations

[1]An intradimensional shift should not be confused with a reversal shift. The latter involves maintaining a set of problems but interchanging the positive and negative cue (e.g., the correct alternative becomes the object that is 5 inches tall rather than the one that is 3 inches tall). Reversal shifts present special problems, such as having to unlearn feature-response associations, which make them more difficult than other types of shifts in some situations, especially for younger children (see Coldren & Colombo, 1994).

in the past and the status of the dimension in the cohort of stimulus representations evoked by the situation. The more frequently, recently, and reliably that attention to a particular dimension has cooccurred with perception of a valued stimulus in similar contexts, the greater the likelihood that the dimension will attract attention in the current situation. Every time a hungry animal observes that a stimulus feature precedes the delivery of food, for example, the strength of the animal's tendency to attend to the dimension to which the feature belongs increases. Consistent with these claims, the greater the training on the first set of problems in a discrimination learning shift paradigm, the more rapid the learning of both intradimensional and reversal shift problems (the ones in which the relevant dimensions are not changed over the shift; Eimas, 1966a, 1966b; Sutherland & Mackintosh, 1971).

Regarding stimulus cohort, initial nonselective encoding of a stimulus and its surrounding context should cause the activation of a set of potential representations of the stimulus. Even in fairly young children, the vast majority of these evoked representations will be strongly associated with different names. The most heavily weighted dimensions of the most strongly activated representations in the cohort will tend to become dominant in the final encoding of the referent. For example, the very first time that a toddler encounters a male cardinal, it should evoke representations of familiar kinds of things that are most similar to it, namely, other birds.[2] The strongest dimensions of these kinds should be given the most weight in his or her encoding of the cardinal. For example, shape dimensions should be dominant over size because words for near neighbors such as *bird, robin,* and *duck* have stronger connections to shape dimensions than to size.

(3) Feature Distinctiveness. A child's attention will also be drawn to those features of a stimulus that are markedly different from the features of the stimuli in the evoked cohort. The child is assumed to have stored some representation of the frequency distribution of the features from those dimensions that characterize the most activated stimulus representations in the cohort. The scale characteristics of each dimension (e.g., nominal, ordinal, interval) are maintained in the frequency distribution such that, if the features bear similarity relations to one another, the more similar features are located nearer one another in the representation than are less similar features. For any particular dimension, the frequency distribution may just reflect the cumulative strengths of the word–feature connections for every feature of the dimension (summed over the most activated words). The distinctiveness of a feature increases as its distance from the features in the frequency distribution increases.

---

[2]Activation of representations does not necessarily cause them to enter consciousness.

Consider again the toddler who sees a male cardinal for the first time. Although the brightness and hue dimensions of color may not be as dominant in his or her representations of other birds, the distinctiveness of the cardinal's values on these dimensions will draw the child's attention. Thus, although the child will attend to the cardinal's shape because this dimension is dominant in stored representations of familiar birds, he or she will also attend to color dimensions because no familiar bird possesses such a striking shade of red.

As my cardinal examples show, the encoding of a stimulus will be affected by both dimensional dominance and feature distinctiveness. The contributions of these two factors are independent. If two features are equally distinctive, then more attention will be devoted to whichever dimension is more dominant. If two dimensions are equally dominant, then more attention will be devoted to whichever feature is more distinctive. For example, if two balls evoke similar cohorts, but ball A has a more distinctive color than ball B, then color will be weighted more heavily in the child's representation of A than B. Also, if a ball's shape is as distinctive as its color (i.e., vis-à-vis the distribution of the features from these two dimensions in the evoked cohort), then its shape will be weighted more heavily than its color because shape is more heavily weighted than color in the cohort.

Word Learning as Adjusting Feature and Dimension Connections: Specific Proposals

Adjusting Feature Connections. In keeping with a widely shared assumption in connectionist models of learning, the degree of strengthening of a particular word–feature connection that comes about from a single experience of their cooccurrence will be assumed to be inversely proportional to the strength of the existing connection. The nearer the strength to the upper limit that a connection can possibly attain (i.e., the smaller the distance from asymptotic strength), the less the increment. This assumption is consistent with the intuition that a surprising word–feature cooccurrence will have a greater impact on a connection than an expected cooccurrence will have.

Attentional responses may be partly responsible for the distance-from-asymptote rule. When a particular word–feature connection is already at asymptote, the cooccurrence of the word and feature will be unremarkable to the child. Because he or she devotes scarcely any attention to the feature, the connection will change very little. However, when the connection is far from asymptote, the cooccurrence is noteworthy, and the attention that the feature attracts will boost its connection to the word. The degree to which a connection strength is incremented depends in part on the amount of attention devoted to the feature when the word is uttered.

The distance-from-asymptote rule cannot depend entirely on attention, however. If it did, then there would be no limit to how strong a connection could become if a person complied with a request to concentrate on a feature from a dominant dimension as it was presented repeatedly. Because connections are supposed to correspond to functional properties of the brain, there must be a physical limit on how large they can become. (Metcalfe, 1993, made a similar argument about the need to constrain the values that features take on in her composite associative memory model.) The distance-from-asymptote rule enforces this limit.

Adjusting Dimension Connections. Change in the strength of word–dimension connections also follows the distance-from-asymptote rule and depends on the amount of attention devoted to a feature. Consider the child who has developed a strong tendency to attend to color in response to *cardinal.* If this child hears this word said of yet another male cardinal, barely any increase should occur in the strength of the *cardinal*–color connection, which is already near asymptote. The small change that occurs in such cases corresponds to the child's tendency to quickly shift attention away from a dominant dimension after having confirmed the presence of its expected feature. The child redirects attention to weaker dimensions where the features are less predictable. The longer he or she spends attending to a dimension in response to a word, the greater the increment in that dimension's connection to the word. Note that strength of a word–dimension connection will only predict whether a word directs attention to that dimension rather than another dimension, not how much time is spent encoding a feature from a dimension.

The tendency to shift attention away from the predictable features of dominant dimensions toward the features of other dimensions can be understood as a special case of feature distinctiveness influencing attention. By my definition of feature distinctiveness (a feature's distance from the features in the frequency distribution for the evoked stimulus cohort), predictable features are not distinctive.

Because more attention will be devoted to the less predictable features, a weak dimension can potentially gain strength relative to a strong one. The two could eventually become equals, possessing the same likelihood of being the first dimension that a child attended to in response to hearing the word. If the predictable feature from each dimension were present in a stimulus, both would be encoded in quick succession, however. Herein lies the means by which redundant cues for identifying a word's exemplars can be acquired.

The strength of any particular word–dimension connection depends on how frequently and recently the child has attended to that dimension when he or she has either used the word or heard it used in the past. It ought to be nearly perfectly positively correlated with the collective strength of the connections of the word to all features from the dimension, because attending to a feature causes strengthening of both feature and dimension connections.

Attentional Response to a Poor Fit Between Familiar Word and Attested Exemplar

What happens to word–dimension connections when a familiar word is heard for something that seems incompatible with the word's meaning? Assuming that such surprising input is accepted by the child, which must happen at least occasionally, the attentional response should depend on the size of the perceived incompatibility. If it is small, the youngster should try to shift attention so as to repair the word's representation. If it is large, he or she should establish a second meaning for the word.

(1) Minor Incompatibilities Trigger Search for Shared Distinctive Features. Suppose a little boy hears the familiar word *cardinal* used, for the first time in his experience, for the brownish female of the species. Suppose also that no one tells him that the bird is the female, and he does not induce this fact on his own. The child should attend to the surprising feature, the brownish color, causing the strength of *cardinal*'s connection to the dominant dimension, COLOR, to increase, but not by much because the connection is already near asymptote. Dissatisfied by the mismatch with the expected feature, he should then check other dimensions. If his attention settles on a feature from one of these, the strength of the word's connection to this feature's dimension should increase by more than the increase in the strength of its connection to the dominant dimension.

What determines the dimension to which attention will shift and whether it will then settle or shift again? First, the relative dominance of the other dimensions will be important. For example, in the case of *cardinal*, the dimension +/− HAS A CREST may have some strength (although presumably less than COLOR) and so attention would shift to it. Second, the child will favor a feature that is nondistinctive vis-à-vis the word's representation (i.e., matching a feature of previous exemplars) but distinctive vis-à-vis other words' representations. For example, the feature [+ has a crest] is likely to be nondistinctive regarding previously seen cardinals but distinctive regarding representations of other kinds of birds. I refer to this last proposal as the Shared Distinctive Feature hypothesis.

(2) Major Incompatibilities Result in Homophone Induction. The child needs to distinguish an exemplar of a second sense of a word from an unexpected exemplar of the first sense of a word. That is, he or she needs to react differently to hearing a flying rodent called a *bat* (when this term has only been used for a piece of sports equipment in the past), for example, than to hearing a brownish bird called a *cardinal*. In the CALLED model, a differential reaction comes about because the attentional response to a word is not solely determined by the strength of word–dimension connections. The five factors discussed in the previous section on influences on attention (dimensional dominance, feature distinctiveness, etc.) also play a role.

Consider the child who knows *bat* only as a name for a piece of sports equipment. When this child sees the flying rodent type of bat in a particular context, a cohort of similar stimulus representations (e.g., owl, rat, butterfly) will be activated. Assuming that no dimension has established much momentum in the situation, dimension dominance and feature distinctiveness will primarily determine which dimensions get the most attention.

The child is then told that the animal is a bat. The word should divert some activation toward the strongest dimensions associated with the piece of sports equipment, but because the flying rodent either lacks these dimensions or possesses features on them that greatly mismatch those typical of baseball bats, the activation of these should quickly dissipate. The dimensions determined by comparison to the evoked cohort (i.e., owl, rat, etc.), as well as the features on these dimensions, should become associated with *bat*.

Children might have difficulty acquiring a homophone if the word were introduced before the exemplar of its new sense (e.g., if they were told, "I'm going to show you a bat," then shown the flying rodent). Depending on the time interval between word and referent presentation, substantial activation could accrue to the dimensions and features associated with the word's familiar sense (the piece of sports equipment) before the referent was encountered. If so, the children might be troubled by the mismatch between the referent and what they expected to see. By contrast, when the referent is presented before the word, the activation of a representation for the referent prevents the word from diverting much activation to its more familiar sense (see Miikkulainen & Mayberry, chap. 5, this volume, for a related proposal).

Acquisition of a second sense for a word should not generally undermine the word's power to evoke its first sense. If the word is presented in isolation, the child may think of the second sense, rather than the first sense or both senses. However, if the word is presented in a context that is relevant only to the first sense (e.g., "He's been known to throw his bat" regarding a baseball player), the context should evoke a cohort of representations that includes exemplars of the first sense, but not the second. In such situations, the word will cause attention to shift to the dimensions and features associated with its first sense just as rapidly as if the second sense had never been acquired.

One implication of my arguments is that a child need not be told that a familiar word has another meaning for him or her to construct one for it. Consistent with this position are documented cases of false homonyms, that is, of inappropriate additional meanings having been constructed for terms (see Vosniadou & Brewer, 1992, for a discussion of the inappropriate second meaning that some grade schoolers give to the term *earth*).

Word Comprehension in CALLED

Let us consider what a child does when asked whether some word applies to something. Suppose, for example, the child is asked, "Is this a bird?" in reference to a picture of a sparrow. The test word, the referent and its context, and dimensional inertia will jointly determine the dimensions of the sparrow to which the child pays greatest attention. The word directs attention according to the relative strengths of its connections to various dimensions. Initial nonselective encoding of the referent and its context evokes a cohort of near neighbor words, which may include the test word, and this cohort directs attention via dimension dominance and feature distinctiveness. Because of dimensional inertia, there will also be some tendency for whatever dimensions were activated immediately before the word and referent were presented to remain activated.

As in MacWhinney's (1987) Competition model, the comprehension decision is based on a variant of the choice rule developed by Luce (1959). The probability of accepting the word for the referent is directly proportional to $A_{\text{test word}}/(A_{\text{all words}} + \text{noise})$, where $A_{\text{test word}}$ = activation of the test word that results from encoding the referent and its context, and $A_{\text{all words}}$ = total activation of all words in the vocabulary (including the test word) that results from this act of encoding. Whether a child accepts the word depends on whether this activation fraction exceeds some threshold value that varies according to the child's cautiousness.

My previous descriptions of CALLED did not include a noise component in the denominator. I am grateful to Terry Regier for pointing out that my original model implied that a child who knew only one word would extend it to everything, because for this child, $A_{\text{known word}} = A_{\text{all words}}$. The noise component prevents this from happening.

The extent to which a particular feature of the stimulus activates a particular word depends on three things: (a) degree of match of the feature to a feature representation that is connected with the word; (b) strength of the relevant feature–word connection; and (c) amount of attention directed to the dimension to which the feature belongs. This last factor is a point of departure from MacWhinney's (1987) model. Attention has a multiplier effect on feature strengths, serving to either minimize or magnify their impact.

By allowing attention to modulate the impact of feature strengths, the system has the potential to accept multiple names more readily. When asked, "Is this a sparrow?" and "Is this a bird?" of the same sparrow, for example, MacWhinney's (1987) model will say "Yes" to both questions only if a low, or incautious, criterion for $A_{\text{test word}}/(A_{\text{all words}} + \text{noise})$ is adopted. Many of the sparrow's features are strongly associated with *bird* and many are strongly associated with *sparrow*. The denominator reflects both of these sets of strong associations, making it large, and the fraction small. In contrast, because dimension strengths of the test word influence attention, the impact of matches with the strongest features of the test word on its strongest dimensions are amplified and the impact of matches with the strongest features of the other words on other dimensions are attenuated.

As an illustration, assume that the strongest dimensions of *sparrow* are COLOR OF FEATHERS and SIZE, and the strongest features from these dimensions are [dull brown] and [small], respectively. Let the strongest dimensions of *bird* be various shape dimensions, +/– HAS FEATHERS, +/– FLIES, and the strongest features on these dimensions be those most typical of birds. When asked of a sparrow, "Is this a bird?," activation travels along *bird*-dimension connections to cause attention to focus on the strongest dimensions of *bird*. The activation of *bird* that results from the match between the sparrow's features on these dimensions with the features most strongly connected with *bird* is thus magnified. *Sparrow* receives little activation because little attention is directed to the features of the sparrow that are most strongly associated with this word. Because $A_{\text{all words}}$ is not much greater than $A_{\text{test words}}$, *bird* is accepted.

When asked of the same bird, "Is this a sparrow?," the *sparrow*-dimension connections cause attention to focus on the strongest dimensions of *sparrow*. Activation of *sparrow* is magnified and activation of *bird* is minimized, causing $A_{\text{test word}}/(A_{\text{all words}} + \text{noise})$ to be high, which results in acceptance of *sparrow*. The value of the main component of the denominator, $A_{\text{all words}}$, varies with the test word in CALLED, but not in MacWhinney's (1987) model.

Although CALLED has greater potential to allow acceptance of multiple names for things, my claim that dimensional inertia also influences attention complicates predictions because dimensional inertia can work against such acceptance. When *bird* and *sparrow* are tested for the same referent in quick succession, for example, there will be some tendency for the dimensions most activated by the first word tested to remain active during the second word's test. The effect is to increase the competition from the first word in this test (increasing the size of the denominator). Acceptance of the second word will depend in part on whether the second word's connections to its most distinctive dimensions (i.e., the ones not shared with the first word) are strong enough to have a greater impact on attention than whatever dimensional inertia remains from the test of the first word.

CALLED is intended to capture the intuition that when one considers whether something has a particular name, one tends to examine those features most diagnostic of that name. With the exception of exact synonyms, words with overlapping extensions should tend to have different diagnostic dimensions, making these extensions learnable by the associative device in the model. (Exact synonyms may only be learnable by the LLED component. The child may have to hear language in which one term is applied to the other, for example, "A sofa is the same thing as a couch," and be able to retrieve such descriptions.) Generally, flexibility of attention will be critical to learning and to retrieving more than one name for something. Accepting a name for something will depend on how well that name characterizes that thing relative to how well other names characterize it when attention is restricted to just certain aspects of the thing.

ADJUSTING DIMENSION CONNECTIONS REVISITED: ENCODING EXEMPLARS OF SECOND LABELS

My account of how a child might learn the extensions for words such as *bird* and *sparrow* presupposes that the strongest dimensions of each word will be different. But are there any constraints or mechanisms that ensure that this will happen? Given my claims about the role of dimension dominance in attention, why doesn't the child who knows *bird* and hears *sparrow* for the first time, for example, encode the referent of this new word according to the dominant dimensions of *bird*, and thereby fail to learn the word? In answering this question, I extend the Shared Distinctive Features hypothesis to the case of second label learning.

First, a child's encoding of the referent of the new word *sparrow* should not only be influenced by the dominant dimensions of *bird*, but also by the four other factors I identified as influencing attention: dimensional inertia, feature distinctiveness, and so forth. To the extent that these direct attention away from the dominant dimensions of *bird, sparrow* will be learnable. Of course, on those occasions where these factors conspire to direct attention toward the dominant dimensions (a possibility for all of them except feature distinctiveness), children will be less likely to learn *sparrow*. One- and 2-year-olds have been observed to learn labels for objects that they can already name less readily than labels for unfamiliar kinds of objects in certain circumstances (Liittschwager & Markman, 1994; Merriman, Marazita, & Jarvis, 1993; Mervis, 1987).

Second, because each time a child uses a word, the dimensions that he or she happens to attend to become more strongly connected to the word, *sparrow* should become more strongly connected to the nondominant dimensions of *bird* over time. To see how this works, suppose a dominant and a nondominant dimension of *bird* (e.g., +/– HAS FEATHERS and COLOR OF FEATHERS, respectively) have equal weight in a child's encoding of *sparrow,* and that the child has 50 occasions to name a sparrow over several months' time. On some of these occasions, factors such as dimensional inertia, pragmatic cues, and so forth, will tilt the balance of attention toward the dominant dimension of *bird,* causing the child to call the sparrow "bird." According to the CALLED model, these events will alter the feature and dimension connections for *bird,* but leave the ones for *sparrow* unchanged. On other occasions, the balance will tilt toward the nondominant dimension of bird, in many instances causing the child to call the sparrow "sparrow." Whenever the child does this, the connection of *sparrow* to the nondominant dimension will become stronger. Thus, the connection to the nondominant dimension builds muscle over time, whereas the connection to the dominant dimension does not.

Extending the Shared Distinctive Feature Hypothesis to Second Labels

Finally, there is evidence that even before their second birthdays, children are dissatisfied when the features of a new word's referent are ones that are already strongly associated with a familiar word. For example, in an extensive diary of her 1-year-old son's language, Mervis (1987) noted numerous instances in which Ari resisted the introduction of new names for objects to which he had overextended other names. In most cases, he did not learn the new name until he discovered or was shown an attribute of the object that distinguished it from appropriate exemplars of the name that he had overextended. For example, he objected to his mother's use of the word *pump* for a depicted hand pump, insisting it was a mixer, until she had him imagine the handle being pushed down and water pouring out of it. See Banigan and Mervis (1988), Mervis (1987), and Mervis and Mervis (1988) for further evidence of the power of such distinctive feature highlighting to overpower children's resistance to second labels.

Children develop a gut-level reaction to the value of the activation fraction that a label evokes in a particular situation (i.e., to $A_{word}/[A_{all\ words} + noise]$). High values elicit positive reactions and low values elicit negative ones. I already proposed that children consider the value of $A_{familiar\ word}/(A_{all\ words} + noise)$ when judging the acceptability of a familiar label for a referent. The evaluative function of this fraction is also implied by the Shared Distinctive Features hypothesis. Hearing a familiar label for something that has a deviant feature on a dominant dimension is hypothesized to dissatisfy the child and compel him or her to search for shared distinctive features that will raise the value of the activation fraction.

The extension of the Shared Distinctive Features hypothesis to second label acquisition is straightforward. The child reacts to a such a label by searching its referent for distinctive features, specifically ones not weighted heavily in the representation of the first label's extension. If such features are discovered, they will receive considerable attention, causing them to be weighted heavily in the representation of the second label's extension. Consequently, future exemplars of this label will only be recognized as such if they manifest these features (i.e., share them with the original exemplar).

When a new label is presented and attention focuses on features of its referent that are not already strongly associated with another word, the value of the activation fraction for the new label will not be that high (because there is no preexisting connection between the distinctive features of the referent and the label) but it will be above baseline. (Baseline is slightly above zero because there is noise in the system.) When attention focuses on features of a referent that are strongly connected to another word, however, the value of the fraction for the new label will fall below baseline. The connections between the referent's features and the familiar label for the referent cause the denominator of the fraction for the new label to swell, making the fraction very small.

The attentional response entailed by the Shared Distinctive Features hypothesis is adaptive (Anderson, 1990). Comprehension of a label for its attested exemplar will depend on the activation fraction that the label and exemplar jointly evoke. Thus, it is rational to direct encoding of the exemplar in a way that maximizes the chances of changing dimension and feature weights to values that will yield a higher activation fraction when the exemplar is reencountered. This encoding tendency serves two primary goals of the child, namely, learning to accept and learning to retrieve the label for the exemplar.

The evaluative response to the value of $A_{word}/(A_{all\ words} + \text{noise})$ is learned via covariation detection. Children's experience is such that when persons accept familiar words for things, the activation fractions that the word and referent jointly evoke tend to be high, and when they do not, the evoked activation fractions tend to be low.

Once the activation fraction acquires this visceral, evaluative significance, then any attentional response that tends to raise the value of this fraction should be intrinsically reinforcing. The tendency to search for distinctive features in the referent of a novel label, and to search for shared distinctive features in the referent of a familiar label, should be acquired primarily through intrinsic negative reinforcement. When such searches succeed, the value of the associated activation fraction is raised, terminating the dissatisfying state that had resulted from perception of the low value.

A second, related mechanism may also contribute to the acquisition of the tendency to search for distinctive features in the exemplar of a second label. When such a label is presented for something, children often respond by producing the name they already know for it (Macnamara, 1982). The acceptability of their own label (the value of its activation fraction) is likely to register as being greater than that of the novel label, causing the youngsters to wonder why the familiar one was not used. By shifting attention to distinctive features of the referent, the acceptability value for the new label should increase relative to that for the familiar label, reducing the children's puzzlement.

The Shared Distinctive Features hypothesis is generally compatible with Clark's (1987) Principle of Contrast, which characterizes children as assuming that every word has a unique meaning. CALLED makes no commitment for or against this principle, however. If some situation were discovered in which children had little difficulty accepting exact synonyms, then this would be a problem for the Contrast principle, but not for CALLED. Exact synonyms are potentially learnable by the LLED component when input consists of statements in which one term describes the other. The closest thing to the principle of Contrast in CALLED is the tendency for the CA component (the associative device) to establish distinctive word–dimension connections because of the acquired habit of searching for and dwelling on shared distinctive features in the referents of words.

Word Production in CALLED

According to CALLED, production is similar to comprehension, except that the child's attention is not influenced by the test word. When the child is asked, "What is this?" in reference to something, the test word is what the child is being asked to provide.

Therefore, only the referent, its context, and dimensional inertia determine the dimensions of the referent that receive the most attention. The child's likelihood of producing any particular word should be directly proportional to the activation fraction, $A_{\text{that word}}/(A_{\text{all words}} + \text{noise})$, with this fraction varying according to changes in the distribution of the child's attention over the dimensions of the referent. Articulatory obstacles (e.g., sounds that are difficult for the child to produce), phonological priming, and the density of word representations along phonological dimensions in long-term memory (Luce, Pisoni, & Goldinger, 1990) will also affect a word's production likelihood.

Because naming depends on the distribution of attention, it should be possible to get a child to produce more than one name for something by directing his or her attention. Horton (1983) developed a procedure for eliciting multiple names that not only exploits this dependence of production on attention, but also takes advantage of dimensional inertia. The procedure involves modeling incorrect names for a picture, each from a different hierarchical level, so that each elicits a different correction. For example, a preschooler might be shown a dandelion and told, "This is not a rose, it's a what?" "Dandelion," would be a common reply. The child might then be told of the same picture, "This is not a tree, it's a what?" The child would have some tendency to say, "Flower." Variants of this procedure have also been employed by Waxman and Hatch (1992) and Deak and Maratsos (1996) to successfully evoke multiple names from 3- and 4-year-olds.

According to CALLED, when the incorrect name is modeled, the dimension connections for this name direct the child's attention toward the dimensions most diagnostic of this name. Because of dimensional inertia, these dimensions remain fairly strongly activated as the child attempts to retrieve the correct name for the referent. Thus, the child shows a tendency to retrieve a name from the same hierarchical level as the modeled name because words from the same level tend to have their most diagnostic dimensions in common.

THE SHAPE PRINCIPLE AS A CONSEQUENCE OF THE DOMINANCE OF BASIC LEVEL DIMENSIONS

Having outlined how the CA component of CALLED learns, comprehends, and produces words, I want to show how two operating principles that children have been hypothesized to follow in their word learning can be construed as emergent properties of the operation of this component. That is, these operating principles (Shape and Mutual Exclusivity) need not be the products of insight nor be represented in a direct form (i.e., as retrievable rules) in the child's knowledge base.

Several investigators have proposed that youngsters are disposed to interpret novel count nouns as labels for shape-based object categories. This operating principle has been given a variety of names—Shape (Landau, Smith, & Jones, 1988); Child Basic Category (Mervis, 1987); and Categorical Scope (Golinkoff et al., 1994). According to CALLED, the principle derives from the primacy of familiar basic-level names and their dominant dimensions in children's long-term memories. Because individual objects are referred to by basic-level names more often than by other types of names (Anglin, 1977; Rosch, Mervis, Gray, Johnson, & Boyes-Braem, 1976), familiar basic-level names develop stronger associations with their dominant dimensions (parts, shape or the way in which the parts are configured, and functions) and with features from these dimensions than other familiar terms develop with their corresponding dominant dimensions and features. This difference in association strength accounts for the superiority of basic-level over other types of names in children's production and comprehension (Rosch et al., 1976).

When children encounter a novel object, it tends to evoke a cohort of representations of objects and their associated names (e.g., a unicycle might activate representations of bicycles, tricycles, and wheels). This evocative tendency is especially pronounced when a novel count noun is introduced because children have learned that count noun syntax signals that the word is a name for an object rather than for something else. Given the greater association strengths for basic-level names, the most strongly activated name representations in the cohort will be those for basic-level names. Because of dimension dominance, children's attention will be drawn to the most heavily weighted dimensions in the evoked basic-level representations, namely, overall shape, parts, and functions. These dimensions and the features from them will thus receive the most weight in the representation established for the novel noun. (Research on the Shape principle has mostly used test sets in which shape has been confounded with parts and functions. For evidence that each of these types of information has some influence on young children's interpretation of count nouns, see Corrigan & Schommer, 1984; Gathercole, Cramer, Somerville, & Jansen op de Haar, 1995; Gentner, 1978; Merriman, Scott, & Marazita, 1993; Ward, Becker, Hass, & Vela, 1991.) Thus, novel count nouns tend to be interpreted as names for shape-based categories, or at least categories whose most diagnostic dimensions tend to be correlated with shape.

Landau, Smith, and Jones (1988, 1992; Smith, chap. 10, this volume) put forward a similar attentional learning hypothesis to explain why toddlers begin their vocabulary development by emphasizing shape slightly more strongly than other properties in the interpretation of any kind of new word, then as linguistic experience accumulates, sharpen this bias for count nouns and eliminate it for adjectives. Experience makes the covariation between words' syntactic forms and their typical semantics clear to them. Because most of their first-learned count nouns designate shape-based object categories, toddlers develop a habit of attending to the shape of an object whenever a new count noun is used for it. (Smith and colleagues do not propose that the object activates a cohort of basic-level name representations in this situation, however.) In contrast, the first adjectives to be learned designate properties from a variety of dimensions, and so new instances of this form class do not evoke a strong bias to attend to one dimension over another.

Ward et al. (1991) found that overall shape was less important in 4-year-olds' generalization of a name for an unfamiliar kind of animal when the creature lacked both bilateral symmetry and a face than when it possessed these features. This result can be explained in terms of differences in the cohorts evoked by the two types of creatures. Children know the names of many bilaterally symmetric animals that have faces, but know none or few for ones that lack both of these features. Thus, the shape and the other dominant dimensions of familiar basic-level animal names have little impact on the children's name generalization in the case of the bizarre-looking animal.

Differences in evoked cohort can also explain why rigid shape is more important in children's interpretation of a name for an unfamiliar kind of inanimate thing than in their interpretation of a name for an unfamiliar kind of animal (Jones, Smith, & Landau, 1991). Basic-level animal kinds have a greater potential for deformation than basic-level inanimate kinds. A typical animal has more parts that can bend, move, sag, squinch, and so forth, relative to its other parts than does a typical inanimate object. Compare a dog to a vacuum cleaner. Thus, rigid shape will be a more dominant dimension in the encoding of a novel object name when its referent is inanimate rather than animate.

The CALLED model also provides an explanation for Taylor and Gelman's (1989) finding that 2-year-olds' extension of a novel count noun relied more exclusively on shape when the noun had been introduced for an unfamiliar rather than a familiar kind of object. When the noun was a first label, it was generalized to all like-shaped objects, but when it was a second label, it was only extended to objects that matched the training object in both shape and other properties (e.g., color).

This result is actually overdetermined in the CALLED model. It follows from both the general power of distinctive features to attract attention and children's tendency to deliberately search for features that will distinguish a second label's exemplars from those of a first label. The second of these influences was already described. Regarding the first, the shape of an unfamiliar kind will necessarily be more distinctive (i.e., deviant with respect to the shapes in the object's evoked cohort) than the shape of a familiar kind. The most strongly activated members of the familiar object's cohort will have the same basic shape as it does. Therefore, because the shape of the unfamiliar kind is both distinctive and from the dominant dimension, nearly all of the child's attention will be drawn to it. In contrast, attention to the familiar kind will be split between the more distinctive nonshape features and the dimension-dominant shape feature.

This analysis leads to a prediction that contradicts Taylor and Gelman's (1988) general conclusion that second labels tend to be generalized by 2-year-olds less broadly than first labels. The prediction is that if test sets were constructed in a certain way, toddlers would select more objects as exemplars of a second than a first object label. Because shape should be weighted less heavily in the representation of a second label, somewhat more change in shape should be tolerated when generalizing a second label. Evaluation of this prediction would require a test set that contained several objects that were only moderately similar to the training referent in shape but identical to it on some other salient dimension(s), and few or no objects where the opposite was true. Taylor and Gelman's test sets, which were not constructed to evaluate this prediction, consisted of objects whose shapes were either identical to or quite different from that of the training example. Thus, the prediction has yet to be put to the test.

If it were confirmed, the result would also support the contention of CALLED that 2-year-olds do not necessarily have an implicit understanding of semantic hierarchies. Contrary to Taylor and Gelman's (1989) conclusion, they may not represent the object category denoted by a second label as a subset of the basic-level category denoted by the label they already know.

THE MUTUAL EXCLUSIVITY PRINCIPLE AS A CONSEQUENCE OF COMPETITIVE RETRIEVAL

According to many theorists (Au & Glusman, 1990; Markman & Wachtel, 1988; Merriman & Bowman, 1989), children and adults tend to assume, in the absence of contradictory evidence, that two words will not refer to the same thing. This claim rests on three empirical effects: children's greater difficulty learning second as opposed to first labels for things, their tendency to map novel labels onto unfamiliar rather than familiar kinds, and their tendency to restrict their generalization of familiar labels in response to learning new labels. All three effects can be construed as emerging from the operation of the CA component of CALLED.

Rejecting or Failing to Learn Second Labels

I already touched on this phenomenon in my discussion of the forces that bias word–dimension connections toward distinctiveness. The CA component can only retain a second label from a single training episode if attention is devoted to features that are not already strongly associated with the first label. Very short retention intervals are the exception. Immediately after training, associations between the second label and the features of the referent will be stronger than the associations between the first label and these features. However, the second label's associations will lose strength very rapidly. Unless additional training trials are presented, these associations will become so much weaker than those of the first label that the child will be unable to retrieve the second label for the referent.

Because the label that the child already knows is prominent in the cohort of representations that the object evokes, the child will give some weight to the dominant dimensions of this label in his or her representation of the training exemplar of the second label. Unless the child can shift attention to dimensions that are not dominant in the representation of first label, the value of the activation fraction for the second label will be very low. The lower this value, the less likely the child is to accept the second label for its training exemplar, either when it is first introduced or when it is subsequently tested. Research showing the positive effect of distinctive feature highlighting in second label training (Banigan & Mervis, 1988; Mervis, 1987; Mervis & Mervis, 1988) is consistent with this claim.

Regier (personal communication, 1997) pointed out that several forces should cause the value of the $A_{\text{all words}}$ term in the activation fraction for a second label to increase with age. The number of other words that have been heard used for the referent, as well as the frequency with which those other words have been heard, should increase with exposure to language. These increases should thus cause the denominator to swell. Also, because there is noise in the system, every word that a child knows should receive at least a tiny amount of activation by the referent, which means that the more words the child knows, the greater the size of the denominator. Because the size of the activation fraction is inversely proportional to the size of the denominator, the implication is that the tendency to reject or fail to learn second labels should increase with age. Studies of young children's second label learning indicate that the reverse is true, however (Liittschwager & Markman, 1994; Merriman & Bowman, 1989; Mervis, 1987).

The contradiction is resolved rather easily. Improvements in control of attention that occur with age, together with both a continued strengthening of the learned bias to search for distinctive features for second labels and an increasing tendency to encode episodic context, are hypothesized to more than offset the negative impact of the child's growing knowledge base. Older children should be better able to combat the competition from familiar words because they are more likely to seek out, discover, and dwell on features that are uniquely associated with the second label, including features that are unique to the training referent's episodic context. To the extent that unique features, and their dimensions, are weighted heavily in the representation of the second label's referent, the size of the denominator in the activation fraction should be low. Perner and Ruffman (1995) provided evidence that the general tendency to encode episodic context increases during the preschool years.

Liittschwager and Markman (1994) found that 24-month-olds who were taught a second label for an object learned it as well as those who were taught a first label. However, those who were taught two second labels (one for each of two different kinds of objects) did not learn these as well as those who were taught two first labels. The investigators speculated that when presented with a single second label, the children interpreted input as clearly overriding the Mutual Exclusivity default assumption but that when presented with two labels of this sort, "the evidence against Mutual Exclusivity . . . may have been forgotten or confused as children tried to keep track of the information and objects presented to them" (p. 967).

An alternative explanation is suggested by the CALLED model. Suppose the children have some tendency to encode the episodic context of the training event (i.e., the who, where, and when of the event). When only a single second label is trained, these episodic cues become associated with the label and its referent. To the extent that attention is devoted to these cues at training and test, the activation fraction, $A_{\text{second label}}/(A_{\text{all labels}} + \text{noise})$, will be high because these cues have not been associated with any other word or referent that the child knows. However, when two second labels are trained, the episodic cues are now associated with both labels and their respective training referents, because both were presented by the same person in the same situation at the same time of day. When one of the labels is subsequently tested, the newly formed connections between episodic cues and training referents, as well as between episodic cues and labels, will cause each word to seem as appropriate for one referent as for the other. The denominator of the activation fraction for each label should be about twice as large as the numerator because one label should be activated nearly as much as the other by each training referent.

Mapping Novel Labels Onto Novel Kinds

When asked to find the exemplar of an unfamiliar name, youngsters are more likely to select something they cannot already label rather than something they can. (The earliest demonstrations were reported by Hutchinson, 1986; Markman & Wachtel, 1988; and Vincent-Smith, Bricker, & Bricker, 1974; the youngest group to show it has been 18- to 20-month-olds; Mervis & Bertrand, 1994.) For example, they pick a garlic press over a cup when asked, "Which one is a zav?"

According to CALLED, the child's likelihood of choosing the unfamiliar kind should be proportional to how much it activates the novel name relative to how much the familiar object activates this name. Essentially, the Luce rule is applied to two activation fractions, which are themselves instances of the Luce rule (Luce, 1959). The value of $A_{\text{novel name}}/(A_{\text{all words}} + \text{noise})$ for the unfamiliar kind is compared to the value of this fraction for the familiar kind. Even though the name is novel, it receives some activation from each object because there is noise in the system and because the syntactic frame that surrounds the name in the test question, "Which one is a ___?", supports assigning the name to an object rather than to an attribute or action. Although $A_{\text{novel name}}$ is tiny for both objects, the denominator term, $A_{\text{all words}}$, is much larger for the familiar kind than for the unfamiliar kind. Because the activation fraction for the familiar kind is much less than that for the unfamiliar kind, children select the unfamiliar kind as the referent of the novel noun.

The current account is quite different from the one offered by Golinkoff et al. (1994) and Mervis and Bertrand (1994), who proposed that children do not consistently favor the unfamiliar kind until the Novel Names for Nameless Categories principle becomes operative at 18 to 20 months of age. This principle, which differs from Mutual Exclusivity in that it only concerns the interpretation of novel names when as yet unnamable objects are present, becomes operative once children have the insight that every object has a basic-level name.

The CALLED model makes no appeal to insight. The model does imply, however, that the effect ought to become stronger as the learned connections between familiar kinds and their familiar names grow stronger with age. The stronger these connections, the greater the difference between the value of $A_{novel\ name}/(A_{all\ words} + noise)$ for the familiar kind and the value of this fraction for the unfamiliar kind. There should also be a marked boost in the effect once children become capable of reliably producing familiar names for familiar kinds at 18 to 20 months of age (Dapretto, 1995). According to CALLED, the connections between a word and the attended-to features of its referent are strengthened whenever the child produces the word for the referent. So when a child is shown a cup and a garlic press, and is asked, "Which one is a zav?", the degree to which the cup activates *zav* (i.e., the value of the activation fraction, $A_{zav}/[A_{all\ words} + noise]$) will be much lower if the child spontaneously calls the cup "cup" than if he or she does not.

Restricting Familiar Names in Response to Learning New Ones

Children sometimes respond to hearing a second label for something by deciding that they cannot, in fact, already name the referent. That is, they reinterpret the first label so that it no longer applies (Gelman, Wilcox, & Clark, 1989; Merriman, 1986; Merriman & Bowman, 1989; Merriman & Stevenson, 1997). (See Merriman, 1998, for practical reasons for ignoring the distinction drawn by Merriman & Bowman, 1989, between familiar name correction, which involves rescinding a previous decision that a familiar name applies to something, and familiar name restriction, which only involves avoiding generalizing the name to the stimulus in the first place.) This restriction effect is predicted by the Mutual Exclusivity principle, but not by the Novel Names for Nameless Categories principle.

After a new name is presented for a stimulus, the likelihood of accepting the familiar name for that stimulus should decline. Because the new name's activation, $A_{new\ name}$, gets added to $A_{all\ words}$ (the main term in the denominator of the activation fraction), the value of the activation fraction declines. The new word becomes one more competitor with the familiar name, potentially weakening the power of the stimulus to retrieve the familiar name.

The size of the decline in acceptance of the familiar name (i.e., the size of the restriction effect) will depend on the extent to which the strongest dimensions in the test of the familiar name overlap with the strongest dimensions established for the novel name. The effect should be smaller if distinctive features of the stimulus are primarily encoding during the acquisition of the novel name than if they are not. In the studies by Mervis and colleagues (Banigan & Mervis, 1988; Mervis, 1987; Mervis & Mervis, 1988) in which distinctive features were highlighted during second label training, the 2-year-olds showed no restriction effect. In contrast, Merriman and Stevenson (1997), who did not highlight features during training, observed a restriction effect in this age group. (See their article for an analysis of previous failures to demonstrate this effect in toddlers.)

The size of the effect should also depend on the value of the activation fraction for the familiar name before the novel name is learned. If this value is far above the child's threshold of acceptability, then the increase in the denominator that comes about from learning the new name may not be sufficient to cause the value to fall below threshold (i.e., to cause the familiar name to be deemed unacceptable). In Merriman and Bowman's (1989) studies, the introduction of a second label for an object caused children and adults to restrict the familiar name from the object only if the object was an atypical exemplar of the familiar name. They were too certain that typical exemplars had their familiar names (e.g., that an 18-wheeler was a truck) to be dissuaded by hearing them referred to by new names.

Assuming that the new and the familiar name are tested in close succession, dimensional inertia should influence the restriction effect. The dimensions that receive the most activation in the test of one name should have some residual activation during the test of the other name, and so should the feature connections to the first-tested name. Thus, the restriction effect should be larger if the familiar name is tested immediately after the novel name is trained or tested than if a delay is introduced. (Similarly, failure to pass a test of retention of novel name training should be greater if the name is tested immediately after the familiar name is tested than if a delay is introduced.) These implications regarding test order and test interval are consistent with the small empirical literature in which such variables have been manipulated (e.g., Savage & Au, 1996; see Merriman, 1998, for a review).

SUMMARY

The associative device at the heart of CALLED is very similar to that of the Competition Model, which was developed by MacWhinney and colleagues. The primary difference is that lexical competition is not only affected by learned word–feature connections, but also by learned word–dimension connections and by the way in which attention is distributed over the dimensions of a referent at any given moment.

Because attention is hypothesized to play such an important role in lexical decisions, a large section of this chapter was devoted to factors that direct children's attention in situations where they might hear or use words. Five factors were identified and three were elaborated on (dimensional inertia, dimensional dominance, and feature distinctiveness). The Shared Distinctive Features hypothesis, which concerned an attentional response to certain kinds of lexical input, was also proposed. According to this hypothesis, children shift attention to new dimensions in search of distinctive features whenever they hear a familiar word for something that has an unexpected feature on a dominant dimension or hear a novel word for something that they can already name well.

A noteworthy feature of CALLED is its capacity to acquire many-to-one mappings, both homophones (more than one kind of referent for the same word) and overlapping terms (more than one word for the same referent). Despite this capacity, the model's default assumptions are that a familiar word will be used with its familiar sense (i.e., that it will not be a homophone) and that something that can already be labeled will not be called by another name (i.e., that labels will be mutually exclusive).

Regarding Mutual Exclusivity, CALLED's associative device generates its three observable effects: greater difficulty learning second labels than learning first labels, the tendency to map novel labels onto unfamiliar rather than familiar kinds, and the disposition to restrict generalization of familiar labels in response to learning new labels. According to CALLED, the Mutual Exclusivity principle is neither the product of insight nor linguistically specific innate knowledge nor a stored rule. Rather, it is an emergent property of a retrieval system that is intrinsically competitive.

Several claims regarding CALLED's handling of multiple names for the same referent have some support, but deserve direct empirical tests. First, input that highlights a distinctive feature of a referent should have an impact on each of the three Mutual Exclusivity effects. Second, these effects should also be influenced by the increase that occurs during the preschool years in the tendency to encode episodic context. Finally, from an early age, children should develop an evaluative response to the value of the activation fraction that is evoked by the use of a label in a situation, motivating their acquisition of the habit of searching for distinctive features in the referents of such labels. That is, children's conformity with the Shared Distinctive Features hypothesis ought to increase with age.

Like Mutual Exclusivity, the Shape principle also emerges from the operation of the associative device, but for different reasons. Shape is a dominant dimension in most of the first object names that children learn.

When a novel object is referred to by a novel count noun, a cohort of representations of the most similar types of familiar objects is evoked. Because attention is influenced by the dominant dimensions in the most strongly activated representations of the cohort, shape is usually emphasized in the construal of the novel noun's referent. Factors that have been found to attenuate the power of shape are accommodated by noting the presence of representations in the cohort in which shape is not dominant and by appealing to the impact of feature distinctiveness on attention.

Although the CALLED model is promising, much work needs to be done. Little is known about how the many factors that direct attention combine with one another. I have yet to specify how the LLED component operates or changes with development, or how its output is integrated with that of the associative device. Some account also needs to be given of how the child reconciles the joint product of LLED and the associative device with his or her naive theoretical beliefs and other kinds of knowledge in making decisions about what things are called.

ACKNOWLEDGMENTS

Discussions with Steve Fountain and Maria Zaragoza, and in particular, Terry Regier and Brian MacWhinney, helped me to develop many of the ideas in this chapter. Terry and Brian also provided some very useful comments on a draft. Much valuable intellectual stimulation has also come from the students with whom I have had the pleasure of working: Roger Bolger, Julie Evey, Lorna Jarvis, Cathy Lowe, John Marazita, Nausheen Momen, Colleen Stevenson. And as usual, "In all ways acknowledge Him . . ." (Prov. 3:6).

REFERENCES

Anderson, J. R. (1990). *The adaptive character of thought.* Hillsdale, NJ: Lawrence Erlbaum Associates.

Anglin, J. (1977). *Word, object, and conceptual development.* New York: Norton.

Au, T. K., & Glusman, M. (1990). The principle of mutual exclusivity in word learning: To honor or not to honor? *Child Development, 61,* 1474–1490.

Banigan, R. L., & Mervis, C. B. (1988). Role of adult input in young children's category evolution: 2. An experimental study. *Journal of Child Language, 15,* 493–504.

Bates, E., & MacWhinney, B. (1987). Competition, variation, and language learning. In B. MacWhinney (Ed.), *Mechanisms of language acquisition* (pp. 157–194). Hillsdale, NJ: Lawrence Erlbaum Associates.

Bloom, P., & Keleman, D. (1995). Syntactic cues in the acquisition of collective nouns. *Cognition, 56,* 1–30.

Burns, J. J., & Anderson, D. R. (1993). Attentional inertia and recognition memory in adult television viewing. *Communication Research, 20,* 777–799.

Clark, E. V. (1987). The principle of contrast: A constraint on language acquisition. In B. MacWhinney (Ed.), *Mechanisms of language acquisition* (pp. 1–34). Hillsdale, NJ: Lawrence Erlbaum Associates.

Corrigan, R., & Schommer, M. (1984). Form versus function revisited: The role of social input and memory factors. *Child Development, 55,* 1721–1726.

Dapretto, M. (1995, April). *A new perspective on the naming explosion.* Paper presented at the biennial meeting of the Society for Research in Child Development, Indianapolis, IN.

Deak, G., & Maratsos, M. (1996, April). *Preschoolers produce multiple words for unfamiliar objects.* Paper presented at the annual Stanford University Child Language Research Forum, Palo Alto, CA.

Dickerson, D. J., Novik, N., & Gould, S. A. (1972). Acquisition and extinction rates as determinants of age changes in discrimination shift behavior. *Journal of Experimental Psychology, 95,* 116–122.

Eimas, P. D. (1966a). Effects of overtraining and age on intradimensional and extradimensional shifts in children. *Journal of Experimental Child Psychology, 3,* 348–355.

Eimas, P. D. (1966b). Effects of overtraining, irrelevant stimuli, and training task on reversal discrimination learning in children. *Journal of Experimental Child Psychology, 3,* 315–323.

Gathercole, V. C. M., Cramer, L. J., Somerville, S. C., & Jansen op de Haar, M. (1995). Ontological categories and function: Acquisition of new names. *Cognitive Development, 10,* 225–251.

Gelman, S. A., Wilcox, S. A., & Clark, E. V. (1989). Conceptual and lexical hierarchies in young children. *Cognitive Development, 4,* 309–326.

Gentner, D. (1978). What looks like a jiggy but acts like a zimbo? A study of early word meaning using artificial objects. *Papers and Reports on Child Language Development, 15,* 1–6.

Golinkoff, R. M., Mervis, C., & Hirsh-Pasek, K. (1994). Early object labels: The case for lexical principles. *Journal of Child Language, 21,* 125–155.

Horton, M. S. (1983, April). *The development of hierarchical and contrastive organization in natural category domains.* Paper presented at the biennial meeting of the Society for Research in Child Development, Detroit, MI.

House, B. J., & Zeaman, D. (1962). Reversal and nonreversal shifts in discrimination learning in retardates. *Journal of Experimental Psychology, 63,* 444–451.

Hutchinson, J. E. (1986). Children's sensitivity to the contrastive use of object category terms. *Papers and Reports on Child Language Development, 25,* 49–55.

Jones, S. S., Smith, L. B., & Landau, B. (1991). Object properties and knowledge in early lexical learning. *Child Development, 62,* 499–516.

Kruschke, J. K. (1992). ALCOVE: An exemplar-based connectionist model of category learning. *Psychological Review, 99,* 22–44.

Landau, B., Smith, L. B., & Jones, S. S. (1988). The importance of shape in early lexical learning. *Cognitive Development, 3,* 299–321.

Landau, B., Smith, L. B., & Jones, S. S. (1992). Syntactic context and the shape bias in children's and adults' lexical learning. *Journal of Memory and Language, 31,* 807–825.

Liittschwager, J. C., & Markman, E. M. (1994). Sixteen- and 24-month-olds' use of mutual exclusivity as a default assumption in second-label learning. *Developmental Psychology, 30,* 955–968.

Luce, R. D. (1959). *Individual choice behavior.* New York: Wiley.

Luce, P. A., Pisoni, D. B., & Goldinger, S. D. (1990). Similarity neighborhoods of spoken words. In G. T. M. Altmann (Ed.), *Cognitive models of speech processing: Psycholinguistic and computational perspectives* (pp. 122–147). Cambridge, MA: MIT Press.

Macnamara, J. (1982). *Names for things: A study of human learning.* Cambridge, MA: MIT Press.

MacWhinney, B. (1987). The competition model. In B. MacWhinney (Ed.), *Mechanisms of language acquisition* (pp. 249–308). Hillsdale, NJ: Lawrence Erlbaum Associates.

MacWhinney, B. (1989). Competition and lexical categorization. In R. Corrigan, F. Eckman, & M. Noonan (Eds.), *Linguistic categorization*. New York: Benjamins.

Markman, E. M. (1989). *Categorization and naming in children: Problems of induction.* Cambridge, MA: MIT Press.

Markman, E. M., & Wachtel, G. F. (1988). Children's use of mutual exclusivity to constrain the meanings of words. *Cognitive Psychology, 20,* 121–157.

McDonald, J., & MacWhinney, B. (1991). Levels of learning: Concept formation and language acquisition. *Journal of Memory and Language, 30,* 407–430.

Merriman, W. E. (1986). Some reasons for the occurrence and eventual correction of children's naming errors. *Child Development, 57,* 942–952.

Merriman, W. E. (1998). CALLED: A model of early word learning. In R. Vasta (Ed.), *Annals of child development* (Vol. 13; pp. 67–112). London: Jessica Kingsley.

Merriman, W. E., & Bowman, L. L. (1989). The mutual exclusivity bias in children's word learning. *Monographs of the Society for Research in Child Development, 54*(3–4, Serial No. 220).

Merriman, W. E., & Kutlesic, V. (1993). Bilingual and monolingual children's use of two lexical acquisition heuristics. *Applied Psycholinguistics, 14,* 229–249.

Merriman, W. E., Marazita, J., & Jarvis, L. H. (1993, April). *On learning two names for the same thing: The impact of mutual exclusivity violation on two-year-olds' attention and learning.* Paper presented at the biennial meeting of the Society for Research in Child Development, New Orleans, LA.

Merriman, W. E., Scott, P., & Marazita, J. (1993). An appearance-function shift in young children's object naming. *Journal of Child Language, 20,* 101–118.

Merriman, W. E., & Stevenson, C. M. (1997). Restricting a familiar name in response to learning a new one: Evidence for the mutual exclusivity bias in young two-year-olds. *Child Development, 68,* 349–366.

Mervis, C. B. (1987). Child-basic object categories and early lexical development. In U. Neisser (Ed.), *Concepts and conceptual development: Ecological and intellectual factors in categorization* (pp. 201–233). Cambridge, England: Cambridge University Press.

Mervis, C. B., & Bertrand, J. (1994). Acquisition of the novel name–nameless category (N3C) principle. *Child Development, 65,* 1646–1662.

Mervis, C. B., & Mervis, C. A. (1988). Role of adult input in young children's category evolution. I. An observational study. *Journal of Child Language, 15,* 257–272.

Metcalfe, J. (1993). Novelty monitoring, metacognition, and control in a composite holographic associative recall model: Implications for Korsakoff amnesia. *Psychological Review, 100,* 3–22.

Nosofsky, R. (1984). Choice, similarity, and the context theory of classification. *Journal of Experimental Psychology: Learning, Memory, and Cognition, 10,* 104–114.

Perner, J., & Ruffman, T. (1995). Episodic memory and autonoetic consciousness: Developmental evidence and a theory of childhood amnesia. *Journal of Experimental Child Psychology, 59,* 516–548.

Rosch, E. H., Mervis, C. B., Gray, W., Johnson, D., & Boyes-Braem, P. (1976). Basic objects in natural categories. *Cognitive Psychology, 3,* 382–439.

Savage, S. L., & Au, T. K. (1996). What word learners do when input contradicts the mutual exclusivity assumption. *Child Development, 67,* 3120–3134.

Sutherland, N. S., & Mackintosh, N. J. (1971). *Mechanisms of animal discrimination learning.* New York: Academic Press.

Taylor, M., & Gelman, S. A. (1988). Adjectives and nouns: Children's strategies for learning new words. *Child Development, 59,* 411–419.

Taylor, M., & Gelman, S. A. (1989). Incorporating new words into the lexicon: Preliminary evidence for language hierarchies in two-year-old children. *Child Development, 60,* 625–636.

Tomasello, M. (1995). Pragmatic contexts for early verb learning. In M. Tomasello & W. E. Merriman (Eds.), *Beyond names for things: Young children's acquisition of verbs* (pp. 115–146). Hillsdale, NJ: Lawrence Erlbaum Associates.

Vincent-Smith, L., Bricker, D., & Bricker, W. (1974). Acquisition of receptive vocabulary in the toddler-age child. *Child Development, 45*, 189–193.

Vosniadou, S., & Brewer, W. F. (1992). Mental models of the earth: A study of conceptual change in childhood. *Cognitive Psychology, 24*, 535–585.

Ward, T. B, Becker, A. H., Hass, S. D., & Vela, E. (1991). Attribute availability and the shape bias in children's category generalization. *Cognitive Development, 6*, 143–167.

Waxman, S. R., & Hatch, T. (1992). Beyond the basics: Preschool children label objects flexibly at multiple hierarchical levels. *Journal of Child Language, 19*, 153–166.

Woodward, A., & Markman, E. M. (1997). Early word learning. In W. Damon, D. Kuhn, & R. Siegler (Eds.), *Handbook of child psychology, Vol. 2: Cognition, perception and language* (pp. 371–420). New York: Wiley.

Chapter 13

Statistical Learning in Linguistic and Nonlinguistic Domains

Richard N. Aslin
Jenny R. Saffran[1]
Elissa L. Newport
University of Rochester

By common definition, emergence means "to come forth from concealment or obscurity" (Webster's Dictionary). In the context of this book, emergence also implies "without prescription or stipulation." That is, in contrast to a developmental process that unfolds according to a prescribed plan or blueprint contained within the organism, an emergentist view holds that a variety of biases, some quite subtle, and some residing as much in the environment as in the organism, might coalesce to produce a phenotype so constrained that it is often characterized as innate. Such an emergentist view has considerable appeal, provided that one can conduct appropriate empirical investigations to reveal just what the constraints are, when they operate, and how they interact.

But it is also important to remain open to more prescriptive possibilities, even if they fly in the face of emergentist wisdom. Among the cases of development that are reasonably well understood, some do appear to emerge by complex nature–nurture interactions, but some do not. There *are* examples of human behaviors that by the classic definition of innate are both present at birth and independent of postnatal experience, and whose character is determined by relatively direct prescription. Consider the well-known case of color vision, in which color-normal adults have three classes of cones, each with different but overlapping sensitivities to wavelength. Less well known is the fact that the average spectral charac-

[1]Now at the University of Wisconsin–Madison.

teristics of reflected light from the environment can be described by three principal components, which account for 99% of the variance in that reflected light (Judd, MacAdam, & Wyszecki, 1964). These three principal components, when appropriately weighted and combined, closely match the spectral sensitivities of the three cone photopigments (Baylor, 1987). In the absence of developmental data, one might conclude that photopigments emerge postnatally to match the statistics of the environment. Alternatively, one might conclude that evolutionary pressures have selected photopigments that are matched to the average visual environment, thereby eliminating the need for further environmental tuning. Without denying the role played by experience in the interpretation of chromatic stimuli, we believe it is safe to conclude that in the domain of photopigments, the second *nativist* conclusion is by far the better explanation.[2]

One might argue that such examples of direct, nonemergentist innate mechanisms are too low level; but consider a case in the domain of object perception. The fact that we have two eyes separated horizontally in our head means that certain patterns of retinal stimulation will always be present. One such pattern is the interocular difference in occlusion of far surfaces by near objects. Each eye is prevented by a near object from seeing a slightly different part of the background; these regions are therefore seen only by one eye. Under normal viewing conditions, adults are entirely unaware of the differently occluded regions of space and do not report seeing them at all. However, when presented with stereograms in which these two portions of the retinal image are reversed for the two eyes (i.e., when each eye is presented with the region normally seen by the opposite eye), the viewer reports that the scene no longer makes sense (Shimojo & Nakayama, 1990). In other words, adults are sensitive to this constraint and expect it to be present and instantiated in a particular way. Infant data are not available, so we do not know whether this constraint is learned or innate. But we (and we suspect many others working in the area) would not be surprised if infants could display this ability without learning, or other forms of postnatal experiential influence. Our point is simply that we should not reject out of hand the possibility that evolutionary pressures may create mechanisms that are present at birth and independent of experience, and that result from relatively direct stipulation. We also should not reject out of hand the possibility that very rapid learning mechanisms, some highly specialized, may have evolved to solve particular tasks. In contrast to what some have concluded, we believe the nature–nurture

---

[2]The photopigments are undoubtedly synthesized by a complex interactive biological process. Nonetheless, from the perspective of behavior and systems-level structure, the photopigments are directly stipulated, and do not develop from an interplay between visual experience and a complex set of visual constraints.

debate is perfectly legitimate and poses questions that get to the heart of any developmental mechanism. The debate should be approached not by dismissing certain possibilities, but rather by conducting carefully designed empirical investigations that can help to illuminate and distinguish the underlying mechanisms (Spelke & Newport, 1998).

The nature–nurture debate plays itself out with perhaps no greater fury than in the area of language acquisition. Our own view is as follows: There are clearly parts of language acquisition influenced heavily by linguistic experience, as well as parts of language acquisition influenced heavily by native tendencies of the child. Depending on what is meant by "heavily" and by "native tendencies," no one in the field would disagree with this statement. There are, however, strong differences focused on two related issues: how important (and interesting or revealing) linguistic experience and learning may be in the acquisition of certain parts of languages, and what type of innate tendencies combine with them. Emergentist views of language acquisition argue for the importance of learning from a rich linguistic environment and for the indirect and general nature of the innate contributions to this process. Traditional nativist views of language acquisition argue for innate knowledge of the dimensions along which languages vary, emphasizing both the substantive and linguistically specific nature of the innateness and also the directive role of this knowledge in the learning process. We find ourselves in the somewhat odd position of being convinced that both learning and innate tendencies are crucial, but seeing surprisingly little definitive evidence concerning how either the learning or the innateness might be implemented in the human child. Most important, whereas we are certain that there are substantial aspects of language acquisition that are at least partly dependent on innate factors, we are willing to entertain the possibility of either direct or indirect nativism, hoping that we and others can in the future provide evidence that will distinguish the alternatives from one another. Indeed, we find it surprising that so many are unwilling to entertain both possibilities. So why are these two possibilities so unaccommodating?

On the traditional nativist side of language acquisition, it seems that learning has received relatively little attention for several reasons (see also Seidenberg, 1997, for discussion of these issues). First, in the face of a predominantly empiricist bias in the field, in both the 1950s and the 1990s, it has seemed important to many to emphasize those findings that implicate innate factors. Explanations for how learning might work have not been the focus of this field since the 1950s. Second, available theories of learning have historically been extremely simple and largely inadequate to explain the acquisition of complex behavioral systems. Indeed, there are still no well-articulated learning theories capable of accounting for the development of complex cognitive processes. Third, as an empirical matter, we have largely underestimated both the information that might be computed from linguistic input (see Mintz, Newport, & Bever, 1995; Saffran, Newport, & Aslin, 1996) and also the remarkable learning and computational capacities of infants (see chaps. by Johnson; Bertenthal & Clifton; Kellman & Banks; Aslin, Jusczyk, & Pisoni; and Haith & Benson in Kuhn & Siegler, 1998). On the one hand, these new empirical findings may change the balance of our attention to various types of mechanisms. On the other hand, however, they make only more serious the problem of learning as initially articulated by nativists, namely, that the number of potential analyses is infinite, whereas the performance of human infants seems remarkably focused and computationally acute.

On the traditional empiricist side of language acquisition, it seems that innate mechanisms have likewise received relatively little attention, for several reasons. First, as a matter of taste, there is a widespread and understandable excitement about explanations that produce outcomes indirectly and without stipulation, and a disappointment with accounts that explain X by saying X is innate. Second, there is among psychologists a skeptism that "knowledge" could be innate and a related preference by training and background for probabilistic and quantitative tendencies, or stimulus preferences and biases, rather than absolute rules and principles. Third, as an empirical matter, in underestimating the remarkable capacities of human infants, we may also underestimate the extent to which their ability to learn is itself an innate propensity, one that does not characterize every species at every age.

Where does our own research program fit into this debate? By prior background we come from subfields interested in innate and initial abilities: infant speech perception, infant vision, critical periods, and creolization. But we also have always found ourselves interested in mechanisms of plasticity, mechanisms that integrate perceptual (or linguistic) experience with initial states. Our larger goal in the present research is to shed some needed light on those parts of language acquisition that clearly involve learning, and perhaps as well to suggest how this learning might ultimately be integrated with innate tendencies. To begin this line of work, we purposely chose a domain within language acquisition—word segmentation—where listening experience *must* play a dominant role. No one believes that words are innate; they must be learned from linguistic input. Second, there are several quite different ways in which words could be learned, some rather simple and others more complex, as we summarize later. Several recent computational models of word segmentation attempted to explore the efficacy of these different sources of information (Aslin, Woodward, LaMendola, & Bever, 1996; Brent & Cartwright, 1996; Christiansen, Allen, & Seidenberg, 1998). If we could demonstrate that learning is both complex and rapid, then we would raise the possibility that new types of learning and computational mechanisms might be playing an important role in language acquisition.

We noted that our research has sometimes been absorbed into one of the prevailing camps in ways at odds with our own intentions. It is therefore important for us to be very clear about several key points. We are *not* claiming that a sophisticated learning mechanism demonstrated in one domain of language acquisition must of necessity be involved in all aspects of language acquisition. We are also *not* claiming that precisely the same learning mechanism must be employed at all levels of language. What we are suggesting is that there may be a range of learning mechanisms, exemplified by the one we are studying in word segmentation, that may be interestingly different than those previously considered in language acquisition, and that may make the learning half of the language acquisition equation worthy of more attention. At the same time, we are also claiming that *all* forms of learning must be innately constrained. Our sensory and perceptual systems, even early in development, are so sophisticated that the potential set of discriminable aspects of the environment that could be associated with one another is computationally explosive. Even the simple task of correlating two stimulus events must involve the selection of those two events and the computation of their correlation over the thousands of other competing events and their respective correlations. Our agenda is to discover and account for some of the constraints.

Interestingly, our studies of word segmentation were inspired, in part, by a chapter from the 1969 Carnegie Mellon Symposium on Cognition by Hayes and Clark (1970). Linguists have long defined words, as well as other units of languages, by distributional means: Words are sequences of sounds that stably occur together (Harris, 1955). Hayes and Clark (1970) sought to test whether this notion could be implemented by listeners. In their study, a small number of noises (warbles and glides) were organized into sequences. By analogy to speech, 12 of the noises were "consonants" and 7 were "vowels"; noises from these two categories were alternated to form "consonant–vowel syllables"; and four "words" were created from sequences of "syllables" (three 4-syllable words and one 3-syllable word). The words were then randomly ordered and concatenated into a continuous stream, with no pauses or other cues to word boundaries. After 45 minutes of listening to this uninterrupted stream of noises, adults could reliably discriminate 4-word sequences with pauses added at the word boundaries from 4-word sequences where pauses were added at nonword boundaries. Hayes and Clark (1970) concluded that,

> humans do, in fact, have a clustering mechanism able to segment artificial speech. It is a mechanism which (a) can segment completely unutterable sounds, (b) works on "speech" that has no semantic and no significant syntactic structure, and (c) requires relatively little time—about three-quar-

> ters of an hour in our experiments—to come to at least some parsing of speech. It seems to us that these are important properties of a mechanism that would be useful to a child first trying to sort out the sounds he hears around him. (p. 230)

Hayes and Clark (1970) were careful to point out that a "clustering mechanism is almost certainly not the only device used by children" (p. 230) for word segmentation. Other commonly suggested sources of information for word segmentation include the fact that some words are presented in isolation, thereby eliminating the segmentation problem entirely (Bloomfield, 1933). However, more recent research has shown that words are rarely if ever presented in isolation, even in infant-directed speech (Woodward & Aslin, 1990). Thus, isolated words could only serve as an entry point for learners to bootstrap the remainder of the word-segmentation process. Another proposed mechanism for word segmentation is the pairing of sounds with meaning, particularly via reference to concrete objects (Osgood & Sebeok, 1965). Although such a mechanism undoubtedly is used in language acquisition, meanings can only be paired with sounds if those sound units have been appropriately extracted from fluent speech. Thus, the initial process of word segmentation cannot rely heavily on sound–meaning pairs. A third proposed mechanism for word segmentation is prosodic regularity, most notably the Metrical Segmentation Strategy (Cutler & Norris, 1988). While it is certainly the case that in individual languages there are prosodic cues to word boundaries (e.g., in English the trochaic or strong–weak stress pattern is present in more than 80% of multisyllabic nouns), and infants are sensitive to such cues (Morgan, 1994, 1996; Morgan & Saffran, 1995; Echols, Crowhurst, & Childers, 1997), prosodic information is both language specific and highly variable. As pointed out by Cole and Jakimik (1980), word segmentation is an interesting problem because no single cue reliably denotes a word boundary, even within a given language. Thus, without denying the importance of these other sources of information for word segmentation, we sought to explore further the distributional information alluded to by Hayes and Clark (1970) because it appeared to be a robust and universal cue to word boundaries and therefore might serve as an initial mechanism for extracting candidate sound sequences from fluent speech.

Hayes and Clark (1970) provided only a brief account of the clustering process by which sounds are grouped into words: "These abstract mechanisms are able to measure crude correlations and to differentiate between the strong interphoneme correlations found within words and the weaker correlations across word boundaries" (p. 223). This statement is based on a suggestion made much earlier, by Harris (1955), for how linguists might discover the words in an unfamiliar language. Harris suggested that, at the ends of words, a very large number of sounds might be possible successors.

In contrast, within words, the number of successor sounds would be more limited. In our own work, we converted this notion into a more precise statistic: *transitional probability* (see also Chomsky, 1955/1975; Goodsitt, Morgan, & Kuhl, 1993; and Johnson, 1965, who used Transitional Error Probability to define phrasal constituents in sentences). This statistic involves calculating the probabilities that certain sounds follow other sounds and using this information to infer word boundaries. Sound pairs with high transitional probabilities should be more likely to occur word internally than to span a word boundary, and low transitional probabilities reflect the fact that sounds beginning a word are relatively unconstrained. For example, in the two-word sequence *pretty baby,* there are three transitional probabilities across the four syllables. Over a corpus of English, the probability that *ba* will follow *ty* is lower than either of the two word-internal transitional probabilities (*ty* given *pre* or *by* given *ba*). These differences in transitional probabilities follow from the fact that words have coherence. One can move a word to a different position within an utterance, but one cannot interrupt it or move part of it without also changing its meaning. For example, Sentences (1), (2), and (3) are acceptable in English, but Sentence (4) is not:

(1) Look at mommy's *pretty baby.*

(2) Isn't my *baby pretty?*

(3) That's a *pretty* ugly *baby*!

(4) *How *pre baby ty* you look today.

It is important to point out that the sounds making up a word may also occur in other contexts, as illustrated in Sentences (5) and (6). As a result, transitional probabilities will rarely be 1.0 within a word and will never be zero at word boundaries. However, the usefulness of transitional probabilities for word segmentation resides in the ability of learners to detect differences that will occur within versus between words. If these differences are reliable over a corpus, then they could serve as a cue to word segmentation. That is, in the examples shown in Sentences (1) through (6), does *pre* predict *ty* more strongly than *ty* predicts *bay?*

(5) Let's *pre*tend to look out the *bay* window.

(6) His diet consists of hear*ty ba*sic foods.

Our initial attempt to examine the usefulness of transitional probabilities for word segmentation involved a study of adults presented with an artificial language (Saffran, Newport & Aslin, 1996). Much like Hayes and Clark (1970), our language consisted of multisyllabic "words" concatenated in random order for a total of 21 minutes of exposure. However, rather than using nonspeech noises, our words were composed of speech sounds generated by a text-to-speech synthesizer (MacInTalk). Four consonants (*b, p, d, t*) and three vowels (*a, I, u*) were combined to create 11 consonant–vowel syllables that, in turn, were combined to create six 3-syllable words: *babupu, dutaba, pidabu, tutibu, patubi,* and *bupada.* The only restriction on our randomization sequence across the 21-minute corpus was that no word was repeated in immediate succession. A sample of the transitional probabilities between adjacent syllables from the corpus is shown in Fig. 13.1. Notice that although there is variability both within and between words, the transitional probability spanning word boundaries is characterized by a dip or local minimum. At issue, then, is the ability of adult listeners to utilize the pattern of transitional probabilities to segment the continuous stream of speech into the six words of this artificial language.

Hayes and Clark's (1970) postfamiliarization testing procedure only allowed them to say that subjects were somewhat above chance in clustering sounds into words. Our own testing procedure differed in a number of ways from Hayes and Clark in order to reveal more precisely whether subjects acquired the statistical structure of the corpus for word segmentation. We presented subjects with pairs of three-syllable strings (a word

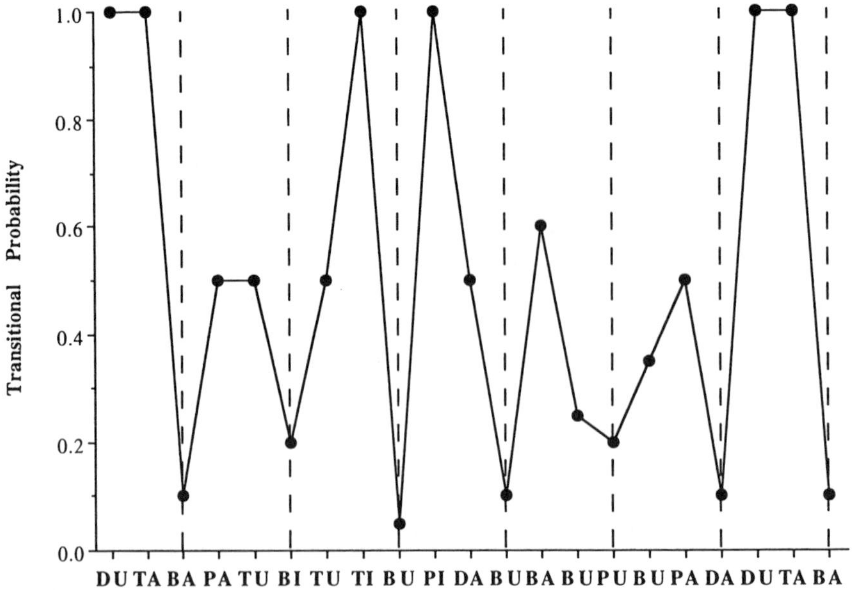

FIG. 13.1. Transitional probabilities for successive syllable pairs across a sample of the language corpus from Saffran, Newport, and Aslin (1996). The vertical dashed lines indicate the syllable pair that spans a boundary between two 3-syllable words.

vs. a similar string that was not a word). For one group of subjects, each word from the corpus was paired with a nonword; that is, a three-syllable string composed of syllables from the language, but which had never occurred in that order in the 21-minute corpus (e.g., *tudata* or *batipa*). For the other group of subjects, each word from the corpus was paired with a part-word, defined as a three-syllable string consisting of two of the syllables from a word in their correct positions, plus a third syllable that did not occur in that position. Thus, in this more difficult part-word condition, subjects had to discriminate between a three-syllable string whose order matched precisely with a word in the corpus (e.g., *dutaba*) and a three-syllable string where two of the three syllables matched a word in the corpus (e.g., *bitaba*).

The results from this initial study of adults were quite straightforward. Subjects in both the nonword condition (76% correct) and the part-word condition (65% correct) performed significantly better than chance in selecting the word as more familiar. Thus, in support of the tentative conclusions reached by Hayes and Clark (1970), we found that adults could segment a continuous stream of syllables into groups based on the distributional characteristics of the corpus, and after only 21 minutes of exposure (half that used by Hayes and Clark). The putative mechanism by which adults succeeded on this task is the computation of transitional probabilities across successive syllables.[3]

Despite these encouraging results from adults, it is not clear whether children acquiring language have similar capacities and actually use them when listening to fluent speech. Our second study (Saffran, Newport, Aslin, Tunick, & Barrueco, 1997) therefore was aimed at a more relevant target population: namely, young children. On the one hand, one might expect young children to perform more poorly than adults on this word-segmentation task because they typically have immature attentional and information-processing skills. On the other hand, evidence of a sensitive period in language acquisition (e.g., Johnson & Newport, 1989) suggests that young children are superior to adults in learning a second language, including portions of that language's phonological structure. We chose to study 7- to 8-year-olds because they are still within the sensitive period but have sufficient verbal and attentional skills to perform the task.

One aspect of our procedure did require modification, however. It became apparent that 7- to 8-year-olds would not sit still for 21 minutes of exposure if they were asked to attend to the artificial language. Moreover, children do not acquire natural languages by sustained attention and explicit learning. Therefore, we presented the artificial language corpus to

[3]There are other statistics (e.g., conditional entropy) that are functionally equivalent to the computation of transitional probabilities.

children (and to adult controls) while they were engaged in the task of creating a color drawing on a computer screen using the program KidPix. The same language we had used with adults in our previous study was presented to 7- to 8-year-olds and to adults while they were coloring. Indeed, subjects thought their task was to create pictures. They were told that there would be sounds playing in the background, but they were not told to learn them or even to listen to the sounds. After 21 minutes of coloring, they were tested on the same word versus nonword task that had been used with one group of adults in our previous study. Both the adults (59% correct) and the children (59% correct) performed significantly above chance, choosing the familiar words over the nonwords. These results are both impressive, because the subjects performed the learning implicitly, and somewhat disappointing, because their performance was poorer than in our previous study of adults. It is also noteworthy that the children performed as well as the adults in this implicit learning task.

Despite the success of this study of children, we felt it was important to replicate and extend it by testing both children and adults after more extensive exposure to the artificial language. Therefore, we kept the task exactly the same but increased the exposure to 42 minutes by presenting the 21-minute corpus (and coloring) on two successive days. Performance on the test trials after 42 minutes was significantly better than chance for both the adults (73% correct) and the children (68% correct). Importantly, the performance of the adults in this extended implicit learning paradigm was now quite similar to their performance after 21 minutes of exposure in the explicit learning paradigm. In addition, the performance of the adults and the children remained equivalent, indicating that the additional exposure had the same effect at both ages. Thus, not only did this second study verify that children can segment words from fluent speech based solely on statistical information from a continuous corpus, but it also showed that this statistical learning can proceed implicitly. Finally, although we found no evidence for an age effect in these studies of implicit learning, it is important to note that the equivalent performance of children and adults is impressive because it rules out the possibility that children are inferior to adults on artificial language-learning tasks. Further research will reveal whether the performance of children under these testing conditions is actually an underestimate of their capacity for statistical learning.

Given strong evidence that adults and children can use statistical information alone to extract multisyllabic words from a continuous speech stream, we directed our attention to the age range in which initial attempts at word segmentation are most critical. As summarized by Hayes and Clark (1970) nearly 30 years ago, "To complete the case, experiments like the present ones must be repeated, under the appropriate conditions, on children of about a year old. The technicalities of these experiments, of course, would be very difficult" (p. 232). Since 1970, considerable progress has been made to resolve these difficulties, and several lines of research with infants have demonstrated that they are sensitive to the distributional properties of their native language input.

A comprehensive survey of the findings on infants' sensitivity to their native languages was provided within the past year (Aslin, Jusczyk, & Pisoni, 1998; Jusczyk, 1997). Of most relevance to the present context are preferential listening studies showing that infants are attuned to the phonetic (Kuhl, Williams, Lacerda, Stevens, & Lindblom, 1992; Werker & Tees, 1984), prosodic (Hirsh-Pasek et al., 1987; Jusczyk, Cutler, & Redanz, 1993), phonotactic (Friederici & Wessels, 1993; Jusczyk, Friederici, Wessels, Svenkerud, & Jusczyk, 1993), and biphone frequency (Jusczyk, Luce, & Charles-Luce, 1994) properties of their native language. These studies suggest that infants in the first 9 months of life are extracting some aspects of the distributional properties of the sound structure of their native language. Indeed, the process by which they are acquiring these properties may be analogous to the statistical learning that we demonstrated in our studies of 7- to 8-year-olds and adults. The crucial piece of evidence for this claim would involve showing that infants, like our child and adult subjects, can acquire distributional, or statistical, properties of linguistic input when other aspects of that input are removed or controlled.

The methodological advance that enabled us to investigate word segmentation in infants was provided by Jusczyk and Aslin (1995), who modified the preferential listening technique to assess rapid auditory learning. The preferential listening technique (Kemler Nelson et al., 1995) presents an infant, seated on her mother's lap, with a series of auditory stimuli that have been divided into two categories. Exemplars from one of these two categories are presented on each trial from one of two loudspeakers, which is selected randomly from trial to trial. A trial begins with the infant fixating a central blinking light that is extinguished as a blinking light near one of the two loudspeakers is illuminated. When the infant shifts gaze from the central light to the blinking side light, an experimenter (unaware of the trial type and testing condition) signals the computer to present the repeating sounds from the loudspeaker. Sounds continue to repeat until the infant looks away or until a predefined maximum trial duration is met. Trials continue for each of the two sound categories until the infant has provided sufficient data to determine if there is a preference for one sound category over the other (typically 8–12 trials).

Jusczyk and Aslin (1995) added to this technique a familiarization phase immediately preceding the test phase. This addition permits the use of the technique to assess preferences induced by the familiarization exposure. They reported that as little as 45 seconds of listening to a series of sentences, within which a target word was embedded, was sufficient to induce a listening preference for that familiar word. This finding was important not only methodologically, but also because it demonstrated that 8-month-old infants could recognize an auditory stimulus (the word *cat, dog, bike,* or *feet*) presented in isolation based on a brief exposure to a similar auditory stimulus embedded in fluent speech. The basis for this word segmentation, however, was unclear because the natural speech tokens contained multiple sources of information for word boundaries.

The goal of our first study of infants (Saffran, Aslin, & Newport, 1996) was to limit the information available for word segmentation to the statistics of the sequences of syllables, as we had done in our previous studies of adults and young children. Based on the methodology developed by Jusczyk and Aslin (1995), we familiarized each infant with 2 minutes of an artificial language corpus. Because this exposure was considerably shorter than the 21- and 42-minute exposures used with adults and children, we simplified the artificial language in two ways. First, we used four rather than six 3-syllable words. Second, each of the 12 syllables making up the four words was unique; that is, each syllable was used in only one position within one word. Thus, the transitional probabilities of the two syllable pairs within each word were 1.0. Because the order of the words in the corpus was random (with the constraint of no successive repetition), the transitional probabilities for syllable pairs spanning a word boundary were 0.33. Another important feature of the experimental design was the counterbalancing of familiarization and test items (see Table 13.1). In this first study, each infant was tested with two of the four words from the language corpus and two nonwords made up of familiarization syllables in a novel order. Thus, within nonwords, the transitional probabilities for the two syllable-pairs were 0.0. To ensure that any postfamiliarization listening preferences for words versus nonwords were not the result of intrinsic preferences for the specific test items, a second group of infants was familiarized with a different set of four words (see Table 13.1). This second language was constructed so that its words were identical to the nonwords in the first language. Similarly, the words in language one were identical to the nonwords in language two. This design resulted in identical test items for both groups of infants; the only difference was which test items were familiar and which were novel. Thus, any listening preferences for words versus nonwords that were present across both languages must have been based on the learning that occurred during familiarization.

There were no differences between the two language groups in this first infant study, and so the results were pooled across the two groups of 12 eight-month-olds. Importantly, listening times did differ significantly between the word and nonword test items. As shown in Table 13.2, infants

TABLE 13.1
Design of the Two Infant Studies in Saffran, Aslin, and Newport (1996)

	Group A	*Group B*
Experiment 1		
Words	dapiku tilado buropi pagotu	tupiro golabu bidaku padoti
Test words	dapiku tilado	tupiro golabu
Test nonwords	tupiro golabu	dapiku tilado
Experiment 2		
Words	pabiku tibudo golatu daropi	tudaro pigola bikuti budopa
Test words	pabiku tibudo	tudaro pigola
Test part-words	tudaro pigola	pabiku tibudo

listened longer to the novel nonwords than to the familiar words. Although this novelty effect is common in studies of infant visual (Bornstein, 1985) and auditory (Jusczyk, 1985) discrimination, they differ in direction from the Jusczyk and Aslin (1995) results, where infants listened longer to the familiar words than to the unfamiliar words. Similar novelty preferences were obtained in other studies using a familiarization phase followed by a preferential listening phase (e.g., Echols et al., 1997). The important point, however, is that infants listened differentially to the words and nonwords, thereby indicating that they can discriminate between them. This

TABLE 13.2
Mean Listening Times in Seconds *(SE)* to the Test Items by 8-Month-Old Infants in the Saffran, Aslin, and Newport (SAN; 1996), the Aslin, Saffran, and Newport (ASN; 1998), and the Johnson, Saffran, Aslin, and Newport (JSAN; 1998) Studies

Study	*Words*	*Nonwords/Part-words*
SAN (1996) Experiment 1	7.97 (0.41)	8.85 (0.45)
San (1996) Experiment 2	6.77 (0.44)	7.60 (0.42)
ASN (1998)	6.78 (0.36)	7.36 (0.42)
JSAN (1998)	5.88 (0.45)	6.92 (0.48)

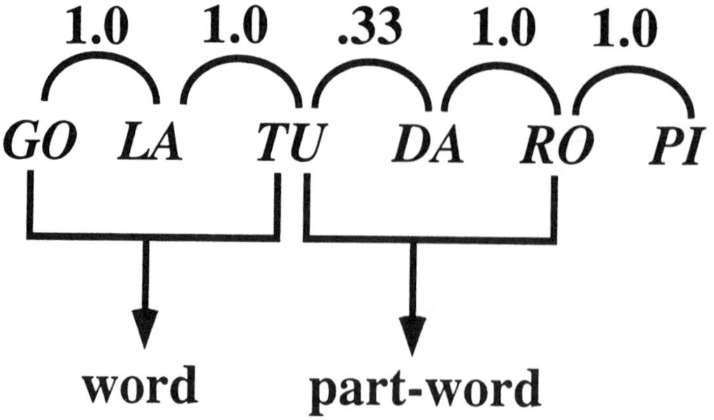

FIG. 13.2. Sample trisyllabic words and transitional probabilities for the second infant study in Saffran, Aslin, and Newport (1996).

discrimination can only be attributed to the extraction of information about the statistics of the artificial language corpus, especially given the counterbalanced design. Thus, these results provide compelling evidence that 8-month-olds can group sequences of syllables based solely on their distributional properties.

Because all of the syllables in the word and nonword test items had been presented with equal frequency in the familiarization corpus, the results of this first infant study cannot be attributed to the first-order statistic of individual syllable frequency. However, because nonwords were composed of syllables in a sequence that never occurred in the familiarization corpus, the results could be due merely to discriminating this sequential difference. A second study of 8-month-olds was, therefore, conducted to explore more closely the basis for infants' statistical learning of syllable grouping and especially to determine whether infants are capable of computing the more complex statistics of the corpus. The design of the familiarization corpora was identical to the first study, with 2 four-word languages and counterbalancing of the test items (see Table 13.1). The sole difference from Study 1 was the manner in which the three-syllable test items were constructed. As shown in Fig. 13.2, the words were identical to the words in the familiarization corpus, with transitional probabilities of 1.0 for the two within-word syllable pairs. The other test items were, however, much more similar to words than in our previous study. These test items were part-words, consisting of the final syllable of one word and the first two syllables of another word. Thus, in contrast to the nonwords from Study 1 that had never occurred in the familiarization corpus, these part-words had in fact occurred in the familiarization corpus, when the two words from which they were formed happened to occur in the proper order. The transitional probabilities for the part-words were thus well above 0.0. This study, therefore, asks whether infants can make a much more difficult discrimination, between syllable sequences with very high transitional probabilities and sequences with one high and one lower transitional probability. Figure 13.2 illustrates the contrast between words and part-words.

As in Study 1, there were no differences between the two groups of 12 infants, and their results were pooled. Table 13.2 shows that infants in this second study did listen significantly longer to the novel part-words than to the familiar words. Thus, not only did we replicate the novelty effect from Study 1, but, more important, we also demonstrated that 8-month-olds can perform a more sophisticated analysis of the statistics of the artificial language corpus than simply noting whether a syllable sequence occurred or did not occur.

However, this study does not entirely resolve whether infants are computing a transitional probability statistic or its equivalent.[4] Although the words and part-words of this study do differ in transitional probability (as illustrated in Fig. 13.2), they also differ in another way: There were 45 tokens of each word in the familiarization corpus. However, because the part-words are each formed by the juncture of two particular words in sequence, there were only 15 tokens of each part-word in the corpus. Infants' listening preferences, therefore, could have been based on these differences in syllable cooccurrence frequency rather than on the differences in syllable transitional probabilities.

Actually, either of these computations is quite complex, and therefore either is important as a demonstration of infants' rapid statistical learning. Nonetheless, it is of some interest to determine more precisely the particular computation infants are performing. Moreover, transitional probabilities are in a class of especially complex and theoretically significant statistics, which normalize cooccurrence frequency by the overall frequency of the individual syllable. Because such conditional probabilities are both complex and particularly revealing of structure, we conducted a third infant study to determine whether infants were capable of such a computation.

In this study of 8-month-olds (Aslin, Saffran & Newport, 1998), two of the four words presented during the familiarization corpus were more frequent than the other two. The test items consisted of the two less-frequent words (presented 45 times each) and the two part-words that spanned the word boundary between the two more-frequent words (presented 90 times each). Thus, in this 3 minute familiarization corpus, the two test words and the two part-words were presented 45 times each and therefore could not be discriminated by syllable cooccurrence frequency.

[4]There are other statistics (e.g., conditional entropy) that are functionally equivalent to the computation of transitional probabilities.

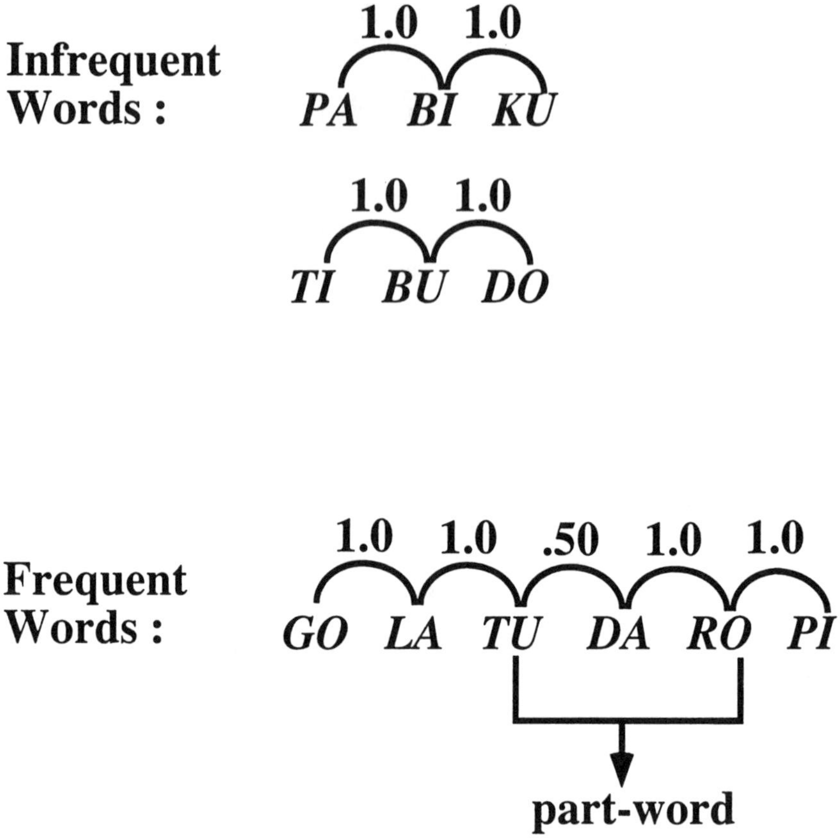

FIG. 13.3. Sample word pairs and transitional probabilities for the frequency-equated study of infants in Aslin, Saffran, and Newport (1998).

However, as shown in Fig. 13.3, the transitional probabilities for the syllable pairs within words were 1.0 and 1.0, whereas the transitional probabilities for the syllable pairs within part-words were 0.50 and 1.0. Therefore, information for syllable grouping in this study consisted solely of transitional probabilities and not differences in the frequency of syllable cooccurrences.

As in the previous two infant studies, there was no difference between the two counterbalanced groups, and results were pooled across the sample of 30 eight-month-olds. Table 13.2 shows that listening times for the novel part-words were significantly greater than for the familiar words. These results demonstrate that infants can rely solely on transitional probabilities to segment multisyllabic words from fluent speech, when the frequency of cooccurrence of syllables is equated. Computation of this transitional probability statistic, based on a mere 3 minutes of exposure to syllables presented without interruption at a rate of 3 per second, is a remarkable feat.

Although these results build on the previous decade of research in infant speech perception, which documented that distributional aspects of the native language are extracted over the course of the first 6 to 12 months of life, the speed and complexity of the infants' computations revealed by the present findings were quite unexpected. In our publication of the results from the first two infant studies (Saffran, Aslin, & Newport, 1996), we were enthusiastic about our findings, "Our results raise the intriguing possibility that infants possess experience-dependent mechanisms that may be powerful enough to support not only word segmentation but also the acquisition of other aspects of language" (p. 1928). However, we did not mean to suggest that the same *kinds* of statistical analyses employed to solve the word segmentation problem could solve other problems of language learning, such as the acquisition of syntax. Rather, our results raise the possibility that infants may be capable of performing other kinds of complex statistical analyses that might be pertinent to linguistic analysis. Our ongoing research examines this question. Moreover, we did not mean to suggest that experience-dependent mechanisms alone could be sufficient, neither for word segmentation nor for other aspects of language. As we noted, "Linguistic structure cannot be learned through undirected analyses of input sentences, no matter how complex or numerous these analyses may be. Such analyses must in some fashion be focused or oriented by innate predispositions of the learner; otherwise, there is no way to explain why human infants are the only learners who can acquire human languages or why languages recurrently develop certain types of structures" (Saffran, Aslin, & Newport, 1997, p. 1181).

At the time we completed these studies, it was unclear "whether the statistical learning we observed is indicative of a mechanism specific to language acquisition or of a general learning mechanism applicable to a broad range of distributional analyses of environment input" (Saffran, Aslin, & Newport, 1996, p. 1928). One way to approach this question of stimulus specificity is to examine statistical learning in a different domain or modality. Recent evidence from our laboratory bears on that question (Johnson, 1997). We constructed a "language" made of pure-tone sequences, analogous to the artificial speech language used in our previous studies. The structure of the language was identical to that in Saffran, Newport, and Aslin (1996) and Saffran, Newport, et al. (1997), except that pure tones substituted for the syllables in the six words of the language (see Table 13.3). The resulting tone stream sounded like *Close Encounters of the Third Kind,* and bore no resemblance to speech. Adults exposed to this tone language for 21 minutes nonetheless performed identically to the adults exposed to the speech language. That is, they judged as familiar the tone words over the tone nonwords with the same accuracy as adults had judged words over nonwords in Saffran, Newport, and Aslin (1996).

TABLE 13.3
Correspondence Between the Syllables and the Tones (in Musical Notation within a Single Octave) Used to Create "Words" in the Adult and Infant Studies (Only One of the Counterbalanced Conditions Is Shown for Each Study)

Study	*Speech Words*	*Tone Words*
Adults	babupu	A D B
	dutaba	G G# A
	pidabu	D# E D
	tutibu	C C# D
	patubi	F C F#
	bupada	D F E
Infants	pabiku	A F B
	tibudo	F# A# D
	golatu	E G D#
	daropi	C G# C#

Thus, the ability to rapidly extract auditory sequences and form units, or groups, from a continuous stream of sounds is not unique to linguistic materials.[5]

Of course, one could argue that any evidence from adults' learning of artificial languages bears only indirectly on language acquisition because adults have sophisticated learning mechanisms that may not be indicative of how language learning occurs in the natural environment. A superior test of whether statistical learning of the type reported here is unique to language or shared with other domains would involve infants. To that end, we recently completed a study (Johnson, Saffran, Aslin, & Newport, 1998) identical to the second experiment in Saffran, Aslin, and Newport (1996) but using tones rather than speech. Two groups of infants were exposed to 3 minutes of a tone language identical in structure to the two speech languages used in Saffran, Aslin, and Newport (1996). Twelve unique pure tones were substituted for the 12 unique syllables to form the four words of each tone language (see Table 13.3). After familiarization, each infant was presented with tone words and tone part-words. We chose the more difficult part-word test for our first infant tone study because we wanted to determine if infants could extract the more complex statistics than those needed to solve the word versus nonword task. As in our study of adults' learning of a tone language, the infants in this study did extract the tone

[5]Peter Gordon suggested during the discussion following our presentation at the Carnegie Mellon Symposium on Cognition that some languages employ tonal characteristics, and therefore our study demonstrating tonal grouping may not, in fact, represent a nonlinguistic test of statistical learning. While we recognize that some phonemic contrasts are tonal, we would argue that the similarity between our tonal stimuli and linguistic materials is so minimal as to render any auditory materials insufficient to serve as nonlinguistic controls.

words, as indicated by significantly longer listening times to tone part-words over tone words (see Table 13.2). Thus, the statistical learning mechanism used by adults and infants appears to be capable of computations on both linguistic and nonlinguistic materials. These findings, in turn, suggest that, for at least the level of language involved in word segmentation, the acquisition process has capitalized on a more general statistical learning mechanism that can operate on a range of auditory materials. Whether this mechanism is limited to the auditory modality, or can operate on any patterned sensory input, is currently being investigated in our laboratory. Also under investigation is whether the types of computations performed across modalities are constant or varying as a function of the materials and the processing abilities of learners in these modalities.

In summary, we have shown in a series of studies of adults, children, and infants that sequential auditory patterns, composed of both speech and tonal elements presented in rapid succession, can be grouped solely on the basis of their distributional properties. The statistic that characterizes this grouping is the transitional probability between adjacent elements in the auditory stream. Such a statistic, or one essentially equivalent, is logically sufficient for at least certain parts of word segmentation (cf. Harris, 1955) and has now been empirically verified as available even to 8-month-old infants. However, the segmentation of words from the speech stream is a rather rudimentary aspect of language structure. One challenge for the future is to explore other, more complex and less immediately sequential statistics that may characterize higher levels of linguistic structure (see also Maratsos & Chalkley, 1980; Mintz et al., 1995). We also conducted studies of both adults and children to examine distributional, or statistical, learning at the level of phrase structure (Morgan, Meier, & Newport, 1987; Morgan & Newport, 1981; Saffran, 1997). Although it remains unclear how much of language acquisition can be accounted for by such sophisticated learning mechanisms, we believe that our work has drawn attention to the plausibility of considering statistical learning mechanisms as part of the battery of analytic abilities that infants bring to the problems of early development.

In conclusion, we wish once more to reiterate our cautions about the fallacy of considering statistical learning mechanisms as though there could be unconstrained and open-ended learning of whatever regularities a rich linguistic environment happens to offer. Successful accounts of language acquisition, whether emergentist or traditionally nativist in flavor, must, in our opinion, attend to the central point of Chomskian linguistics. As we stated, "Chomsky's point was not that there is no such thing as learning; rather, it was that unconstrained learning mechanisms will not, by themselves, correctly learn just those things that every human baby learns" (Saffran, Aslin, & Newport, 1997, p. 1276). Much of our ongoing work investigates constraints on learning within a statistical framework, asking, for example, which types of computations human learners readily perform and which they do not (see, e.g., Newport, in press; Saffran, 1997). Insofar as this enterprise is successful, it may suggest that "some aspects of early development may turn out to be best characterized as resulting from innately biased statistical learning mechanisms rather than innate knowledge" (Saffran, Aslin, & Newport, 1996, p. 1928). But whatever one's particular theory, the problem of language acquisition, as Chomsky has noted, is one that demands an account of the constraints that permit learning to succeed.

ACKNOWLEDGMENTS

This chapter is based on a presentation at the 28th Carnegie Mellon Symposium on Cognition (May 29–31, 1997) entitled "Emergentist approaches to language." Preparation of this chapter and support of the research described herein was provided by the National Science Foundation (SBR-9421064 and a Graduate Research Fellowship) and the National Institutes of Health (DC00167).

REFERENCES

Aslin, R. N., Jusczyk, P. W., & Pisoni, D. B. (1998). Speech and auditory processing during infancy: Constraints on and precursors to language. In D. Kuhn & R. S. Siegler (Eds.), *Handbook of child psychology, Volume 2: Cognition, perception, and language* (5th ed., pp. 147–198). New York: Wiley.

Aslin, R. N., Saffran, J. R., & Newport, E. L. (1998). Computation of conditional probability statistics by 8-month-old infants. *Psychological Science, 9,* 321–324.

Aslin, R. N., Woodward, J. Z., LaMendola, N. P., & Bever, T. G. (1996). Models of word segmentation in fluent maternal speech to infants. In J. L. Morgan & K. Demuth (Eds.), *Signal to syntax: Bootstrapping from speech to grammar in early acquisition* (pp. 117–134). Mahwah, NJ: Lawrence Erlbaum Associates.

Baylor, D. A. (1987). Photoreceptor signals and vision. *Investigative Ophthalmology and Visual Science, 28,* 34–49.

Bloomfield, L. (1933). *Language.* New York: Holt, Rinehart & Winston.

Bornstein, M. H. (1985). Habituation of attention as a measure of visual information processing in human infants: Summary, systematization, and synthesis. In G. Gottlieb & N. Krasnegor (Eds.), *Measurement of audition and vision in the first year of postnatal life: A methodological overview* (pp. 253–300). Norwood, NJ: Ablex.

Brent, M. R., & Cartwright, T. A. (1996). Distributional regularity and phonotactic constraints are useful for segmentation. *Cognition, 61,* 93–120.

Christiansen, M. H., Allen, J., & Seidenberg, M. S. (1998). Learning to segment speech using multiple cues: A connectionist model. *Language and Cognitive Processes, 13,* 221–268.

Chomsky, N. (1975). *The logical structure of linguistic theory.* New York: Plenum. (Original work published 1955)

Cole, R. A., & Jakimik, J. (1980). A model of speech perception. In R. A. Cole (Ed.), *Perception and production of fluent speech* (pp. 133–163). Hillsdale, NJ: Lawrence Erlbaum Associates.

Cutler, A., & Norris, D. G. (1988). The role of strong syllables in segmentation for lexical access. *Journal of Experimental Psychology: Human Perception and Performance, 14,* 113–121.

Echols, C. H., Crowhurst, M. J., & Childers, J. B. (1997). The perception of rhythmic units in speech by infants and adults. *Journal of Memory and Language, 36,* 202–225.

Friederici, A. D., & Wessels, J. M. I. (1993). Phonotactic knowledge and its use in infant speech perception. *Perception and Psychophysics, 54,* 287–295.

Goodsitt, J. V., Morgan, J. L., & Kuhl, P. K. (1993). Perceptual strategies in prelingual speech segmentation. *Journal of Child Language, 20,* 229–252.

Harris, Z. S. (1955). From phoneme to morpheme. *Language, 31,* 190–222.

Hayes, J. R., & Clark, H. H. (1970). Experiments in the segmentation of an artificial speech analog. In J. R. Hayes (Ed.), *Cognition and the development of language* (pp. 221–234). New York: Wiley.

Hirsh-Pasek, K., Kemler Nelson, D. G., Jusczyk, P. W., Wright Cassidy, K., Druss, B., & Kennedy, L. (1987). Clauses are perceptual units for young infants. *Cognition, 26,* 269–286.

Johnson, E. K. (1997). *Statistical learning of non-linguistic stimuli: Implications for language acquisition.* Unpublished senior honors thesis, Department of Brain and Cognitive Sciences, University of Rochester.

Johnson, E. K., Saffran, J. R., Aslin, R. N., & Newport, E. L. (1998, April). *Statistical learning of non-linguistic stimuli by 8-month-olds.* International Conference on Infancy Studies, Atlanta.

Johnson, J. S., & Newport, E. L. (1989). Critical period effects in second language learning: The influence of maturational state on the acquisition of English as a second language. *Cognitive Psychology, 21,* 60–99.

Johnson, N. F. (1965). The psychological reality of phrase structure rules. *Journal of Verbal Leaning and Verbal Behavior, 4,* 469–475.

Judd, D. B., MacAdam, D. L., & Wyszecki, G. W. (1964). Spectral distribution of typical daylight as a function of correlated color temperature. *Journal of the Optical Society of America, 54,* 1031–1040.

Jusczyk, P. W. (1985). The high-amplitude sucking technique as a methodological tool in speech perception research. In G. Gottlieb & N. Krasnegor (Eds.), *Measurement of audition and vision in the first year of postnatal life: A methodological overview* (pp. 195–222). Norwood, NJ: Ablex.

Jusczyk, P. W. (1997). *The discovery of spoken language.* Cambridge, MA: MIT Press.

Jusczyk, P. W., & Aslin, R. N. (1995). Infants' detection of the sound patterns of words in fluent speech. *Cognitive Psychology, 29,* 1–23.

Jusczyk, P. W., Cutler, A., & Redanz, N. (1993). Preference for the predominant stress patterns of English words. *Child Development, 64,* 675–687.

Jusczyk, P. W., Friederici, A. D., Wessels, J., Svenkerud, V. Y., & Jusczyk, A. M. (1993). Infants' sensitivity to the sound patterns of native language words. *Journal of Memory and Language, 32,* 402–420.

Jusczyk, P. W., Luce, P. A., & Charles-Luce, J. (1994). Infants' sensitivity to phonotactic patterns in the native language. *Journal of Memory and Language, 33,* 630–645.

Kemler Nelson, D. G., Jusczyk, P. W., Mandel, D. R., Myers, J., Turk, A., & Gerken, L. A. (1995). The headturn preference procedure for testing auditory perception. *Infant Behavior and Development, 18,* 111–116.

Kuhl, P. K., Williams, K. A., Lacerda, F., Stevens, K. N., & Lindblom, B. (1992). Linguistic experiences alter phonetic perception in infants by 6 months of age. *Science, 255,* 606–608.

Kuhn, D., & Siegler, R. S. (Eds.). (1998). *Handbook of child psychology, Volume 2: Cognition, perception, and language.* New York: Wiley.

Maratsos, M., & Chalkley, M. A. (1980). The internal language of children's syntax: The ontogenesis and representation of syntactic categories. In K. Nelson (Ed.), *Children's language* (Vol. 2, pp. 127–213). New York: Gardner.

Mintz, T. H., Newport, E. L., & Bever, T. G. (1995). Distributional regularities of form class in speech to young children. In J. N. Beckman (Ed.), *Proceedings of NELS 25* (Vol. 2, pp. 43–54). Amherst, MA: Graduate Linguistic Student Association.

Morgan, J. L. (1994). Converging measures of speech segmentation in preverbal infants. *Infant Behavior and Development, 17,* 389–403.

Morgan, J. L. (1996). A rhythmic bias in preverbal speech segmentation. *Journal of Memory and Language, 35,* 666–688.

Morgan, J. L., Meier, R. P., & Newport, E. L. (1987). Structural packaging in the input to language learning: Contributions of prosodic and morphological marking of phrases to the acquisition of language. *Cognitive Psychology, 19,* 498–550.

Morgan, J. L., & Newport, E. L. (1981). The role of constituent structure in the induction of an artificial language. *Journal of Verbal Learning and Verbal Behavior, 20,* 67–85.

Morgan, J. L., & Saffran, J. R. (1995). Emerging integration of sequential and suprasegmental information in preverbal speech segmentation. *Child Development, 66,* 911–936.

Newport, E. L. (in press). Reduced input in the acquisition of signed languages: Contributions to the study of creolization. In M. DeGraff (Ed.), *Language creation and change: Creolization, diachrony, and development.* Cambridge, MA: MIT Press.

Osgood, C. E., & Sebeok, T. A. (1965). *Psycholinguistics: A survey of theory and research.* Bloomington: Indiana University Press.

Saffran, J. R. (1997). *Statistical learning of syntactic structure: Mechanisms and constraints.* Unpublished doctoral dissertation, University of Rochester.

Saffran, J. R., Aslin, R. N., & Newport, E. L. (1996). Statistical learning by 8-month-olds. *Science, 274,* 1926–1928.

Saffran, J. R., Aslin, R. N., & Newport, E. L. (1997). Reply to five letters to the editor on the topic of "acquiring language." *Science, 276,* 1177–1181, 1276.

Saffran, J. R., Newport, E. L., & Aslin, R. N. (1996). Word segmentation: The role of distributional cues. *Journal of Memory and Language, 35,* 606–621.

Saffran, J. R., Newport, E. L., Aslin, R. N., Tunick, R. A., & Barrueco, S. (1997). Incidental language learning: Listening (and learning) out of the corner of your ear. *Psychological Science, 8,* 101–105.

Seidenberg, M. S. (1997). Language acquisition and use: Learning and applying probabilistic constraints. *Science, 275,* 1599–1603.

Shimojo, S., & Nakayama, K. (1990). Real world occlusion constraints and binocular rivalry. *Vision Research, 30,* 69–80.

Spelke, E. S., & Newport, E. L. (1998). Nativism, empiricism, and the development of knowledge. In R. M. Lerner (Ed.), *Handbook of child psychology, Volume 1: Theoretical models of human development* (5th ed., pp. 275–340). New York: Wiley.

Werker, J. F., & Tees, R. C. (1984). Cross-language speech perception: Evidence for perceptual reorganization during the first year of life. *Infant Behavior and Development, 7,* 49–63.

Woodward, J. Z., & Aslin, R. N. (1990, April). *Segmentation cues in maternal speech to infants.* Paper presented at the biennial meeting of the International Conference on Infancy Studies, Montreal.

Chapter **14**

The Emergence of Phonology From the Interplay of Speech Comprehension and Production: A Distributed Connectionist Approach

David C. Plaut
Christopher T. Kello
Carnegie Mellon University

How do infants learn to understand and produce spoken language? Despite decades of intensive investigation, the answer to this question remains largely a mystery. This is, in part, because although the use of language seems straightforward to adult native speakers, speech recognition and production present the infant with numerous difficult computational problems (see Lively, Pisoni, & Goldinger, 1994). First of all, processing speech is difficult both because it is extended in time and because it is subject to considerable variability across speakers and contexts. Moreover, even with an accurate representation of the underlying phonetic content of a heard utterance, mapping this representation onto its meaning is difficult because the relation of spoken words to their meanings is essentially arbitrary. On the output side, the infant must learn to produce comprehensible speech in the absence of any direct feedback from caretakers or the environment as to what articulatory movements are required to produce particular sound patterns. Finally, the processes of learning to understand speech and learning to produce it must be closely related (although certainly not synchronized; Benedict, 1979) to ensure that they eventually settle on mutually consistent solutions.

In this chapter, we formulate a general framework for understanding how the infant surmounts these challenges, and we present a computational simulation of the framework that learns to understand and produce spoken words in the absence of explicit articulatory feedback. Our initial focus is on addressing the relevant computational issues; we postpone consideration of how the approach accounts for specific empirical phenomena until the General Discussion section.

The framework, depicted in abstract form in Fig. 14.1, is based on connectionist–parallel distributed processing (PDP) principles, in which different types of information are represented as patterns of activity over separate groups of simple, neuron-like processing units. Within the framework, phonological representations play a central role in mediating among acoustic, articulatory, and semantic representations. Critically, phonological representations are not predefined but are learned by the system under the pressure of understanding and producing speech. In this way, the approach sidesteps the perennial question of what the specific "units" of phonological representation are (see, e.g., Ferguson & Farwell, 1975; Menn, 1978; Moskowitz, 1973; Treiman & Zukowski, 1996). Representations of segments (phonemes) and other structures (onset, rime, syllable) are not built in; rather, the relevant similarity among phonological

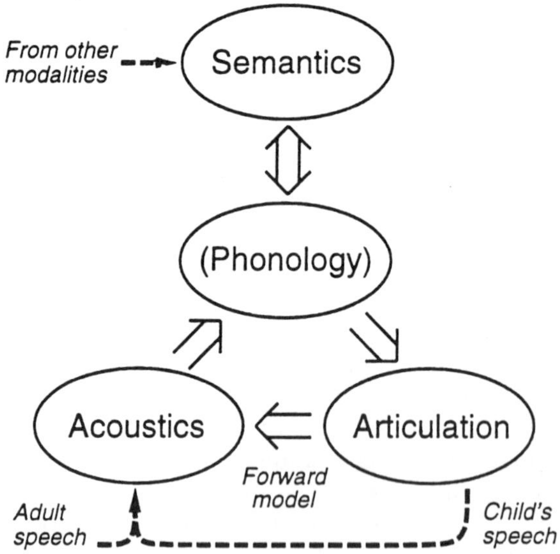

FIG. 14.1. An abstract connectionist framework for phonological development. Ovals represent groups of processing units, and arrows represent mappings among these groups. The intermediate or "hidden" representations that mediate these mappings, and the specific sets of connections among unit groups, are omitted for clarity (see Fig. 14.2 for details). Although "Phonology" is also a learned, hidden representation and therefore listed in parentheses, it it singled out because it plays a unique role in performing the full range of relevant tasks. The dashed arrows indicate sources of input—either acoustic input from speech generated by an adult model or by the system itself, or semantic input, assumed to be derived from other modalities, such as vision.

representations at multiple levels emerges gradually over the course of development (also see Lindblom, 1992; Lindblom, MacNeilage, & Studdert-Kennedy, 1984; Nittrouer, Studdert-Kennedy, & McGowan, 1989). Also note that the system lacks any explicit structures corresponding to words, such as logogens (Morton, 1969) or "localist" word units (Dell, 1986; McClelland & Rumelhart, 1981). Instead, the lexical status of certain acoustic and articulatory sequences is reflected only in the nature of the functional interactions between these inputs and other representations in the system, including semantics (see Plaut, 1997; Van Orden & Goldinger, 1994; Van Orden, Pennington, & Stone, 1990, for discussion). Although the current work focuses on the comprehension and production of single words, the general approach is inherently sequential and, thus, intended to be extensible to higher levels of language processing.

Using distributed representations for words has important—and seemingly problematic—implications for both comprehension and production. In the current formulation, comprehension involves mapping time-varying acoustic input onto a more stable semantic representation (via phonology), whereas production involves generating time-varying articulatory output from a stable phonological "plan" (possibly derived from semantics). The problem is as follows. Distributed connectionist models are strongly biased by similarity; because unit activations are determined by a weighted sum of other activations, similar input patterns tend to cause similar output patterns. This property is a boon in most domains, which are largely systematic, because it enables effective generalization to novel inputs (see, e.g., Plaut, McClelland, Seidenberg, & Patterson, 1996). It poses a particular challenge in the current context, however, because of the lack of systematicity between the surface forms of words and their meanings; acoustic–articulatory similarity is unrelated to semantic similarity. This challenge is not insurmountable—distributed connectionist models can learn arbitrary mappings, even for reasonable-sized vocabularies (e.g., a few thousand words; see Plaut, 1997), although they require a large number of training presentations to do so. Learning an unsystematic mapping is even more difficult, however, when the relevant surface information is extended in time. For example, as the initial portion of the acoustic input for a word comes in (e.g., the /m/ in MAN), its implications for the semantics of the word depend strongly on the acoustics for the final portion of the word (e.g., the final /n/; cf. MAT, MAP, MAD, etc.). However, by the time this final portion is encountered, the initial acoustics are long gone.

The obvious (if vague) answer to this problem is memory. The system must somehow retain earlier portions of the input so that they can be integrated with later portions in order to map a representation of the entire word onto semantics. The critical questions, though, are exactly how this is done and how it is learned. In our view, the answers to these questions are of fundamental importance for understanding the nature of phonological representations.

To solve this problem, we adopt (and adapt) the approach taken by St. John and McClelland (1990, see also McClelland, St. John, & Taraban, 1989) in confronting a similar challenge relating to lexical and syntactic ambiguities in sentence comprehension: The information that resolves a point of ambiguity often comes much later in a sentence. St. John and McClelland (1990) trained a simple recurrent network to take sequences of words forming sentences as input and to derive an internal representation of the event described by the sentence, termed the *Sentence Gestalt.* Critically, the Sentence Gestalt representation was not predefined but was learned based on feedback on its ability to generate appropriate thematic role assignments for the event (via a "query" network). For our purposes, there are two critical aspects of their approach. The first and most straightforward is the use of a recurrent network architecture in which the processing of any given input can be influenced by learned, internal representations of past inputs. The second is more subtle but no less important. From the very beginning of a sentence and for every word within it, the current (incomplete) Sentence Gestalt representation was pressured to derive the correct thematic role assignments of the entire sentence. It was, of course, impossible for the network to be fully accurate at early stages within a sentence, for exactly the reasons we have been discussing: the correct interpretation of the beginning of a sentence depends on later portions that have yet to occur. Even so, the network could be partially accurate—it could at least improve its generation of those aspects of the role assignments that did not depend on the rest of the sentence. In doing so, it was pressured to represent information about the beginning of the sentence within the Sentence Gestalt, thereby indirectly making it available to bias the interpretation of the rest of the sentence as necessary. In this way, the "memory" of the system was not any sort of buffer or unstructured storage system but was driven entirely by the functional demands of the task and the interdependence of different types of information.

The same approach can be applied at the level of comprehending single words from time-varying acoustic input. As acoustic information about the very beginning of the word becomes available, and throughout the duration of the word, the system can be trained to activate the full semantic representation of the entire word (which, we assume, is made available from other modalities of input, such as vision). As with sentence-level comprehension, this cannot be done completely accurately, but the network can be pressured to derive whatever semantic implications are possible from the available input to that point (e.g., ruling out some semantic features and partially activating others). Moreover, the network will activate the full representation as soon as the word can be reliable distinguished from all other words (i.e., its uniqueness point; cf. Marslen-Wilson's, 1987, Cohort model). This type of processing fits naturally with evidence supporting the immediacy of online comprehension processes (e.g., Eberhard, Spivey-Knowlton, & Tanenhaus, 1995; Marslen-Wilson & Tyler, 1980; Sedivy, Tanenhaus, & Spivey-Knowlton, 1995).

Within our framework, phonology (like the Sentence Gestalt) is a learned, internal representation that plays a critical role in mediating between time-varying acoustic input and stable semantic representations (see Fig. 14.1). In particular, we assume that a phonological representation of an entire word builds up gradually over time under the influence of a sequence of acoustic inputs, but that, at every stage, the current approximation is mapped to semantics in parallel. Note that, although the phonological representation encodes the pronunciation of an entire word simultaneously, it must nonetheless retain whatever order and content information in the original acoustic signal is necessary for deriving the correct semantic representation. In this way, learned phonological representations compensate for the detrimental effects of sequential input in learning an unsystematic mapping by integrating and recoding time-varying information into a more stable format. Put simply, phonological representations instantiate the "memory" necessary to map acoustics to semantics.

Analogous issues arise in the production of articulatory sequences from a stable phonological plan (Jordan, 1986). In this case, the system must keep track of where it is in the course of executing an articulation so as to apply the appropriate contextual constraints. As an extreme example, consider the word Mississippi /mɪsɪsɪpi/. Without clear information about having completed both the second and third syllables, the system might very well continue on with /mɪsɪsɪsɪsɪ . . . /. Thus, both comprehension and production require a recurrent network architecture that is capable of integrating information over time in mapping time-varying surface forms to and from more stable internal (phonological) representations.

There is, however, a more fundamental problem to solve regarding production. This problem stems from the fact that the environment provides no direct feedback concerning the appropriate output patterns for production (i.e., the articulations necessary to produce certain sounds). In a sense, the system must discover what sequences of articulatory commands produce comprehensible speech. A critical assumption in the current approach is that the process of learning to generate accurate articulatory output in production is driven by feedback from the comprehension system—that is, from the acoustic, phonological, and semantic consequences of the system's own articulations (see also Markey, 1994; Menn & Stoel-Gammon, 1995; Perkell, Matthies, Svirsky, & Jordan, 1995; Studdert-Kennedy, 1993). Deriving this feedback is made difficult, however, by the fact that, whereas the mapping from articulation to acoustics is well defined, the reverse mapping is many-to-one (Atal, Chang, Mathews, & Tukey, 1978). That is to say, essentially the same acoustics can be produced by many different articulatory configurations. For example, if no exhalation is allowed, then any static position of the tongue and jaw will result in silence. Silence maps to many possible articulatory states, but each of those articulatory states maps only to silence. From the perspective of control theory, the mapping from proximal domain (articulation) to the distal domain (acoustics) is termed the *forward* mapping, whereas the reverse is termed the *inverse* mapping (see Jordan, 1992, 1996). When the inverse mapping is many-to-one, as in this case, it constitutes a "motor equivalence" problem. This problem must be solved if the link between articulation and acoustics is to support the acquisition of speech production.

Our solution to the motor equivalence problem is based on a computational method developed by Jordan and Rumelhart (1992; see Markey, 1994, for an alternative approach based on reinforcement learning). The method capitalizes on the fact that, although one cannot deterministically translate distal to proximal *states,* one can translate distal to proximal *errors.*[1] This is accomplished by first learning an internal model of the physical processes that relate specific articulations to the acoustics they produce (recall that the articulation-to-acoustics mapping, although complicated, is well defined). This *forward model* must be invertible in the sense that acoustic error for a given articulation can be translated back into articulatory error—a natural instantiation of this would be back-propagation within a connectionist network (Rumelhart, Hinton, & Williams, 1986). Such a model can be learned by executing a variety of articulations, predicting how they each will sound, and then adapting the model based on the discrepancies between these predictions and the actual resulting acoustics. In the infant, we assume that an articulatory–acoustic forward model develops primarily as a result of canonical and variegated babbling in the second half of the first year (Fry, 1966; Oller, 1980; see Vihman, 1996, for review, and Houde, 1997; Wolpert, Ghahramani, & Jordan, 1995, for empirical evidence supporting the existence of forward models in human motor learning). Note that the strong reliance on learning within the current approach contrasts sharply with accounts in which the perceptuomotor associations involved in speech production are assumed to be specified innately (e.g., Liberman & Mattingly, 1985).

The learned forward model plays a critical role within our framework by providing the necessary feedback for learning speech production (also see Perkell et al., 1995). Specifically, the forward model is used to convert acoustic and phonological feedback (i.e, whether an utterance sounded

---

[1]Although we will describe Jordan and Rumelhart's (1992) method in terms of error-correcting learning, it is applicable to any supervised learning framework.

right) into articulatory feedback, which is then used to improve the mapping from phonology to articulation. We assume that learning to produce speech takes place in the context of attempts to imitate adult speech and attempts to produce intentional utterances driven by semantic representations. In imitation, the system first derives acoustic and phonological representations for an adult utterance during comprehension (see Fig. 14.1). It then uses the resulting phonological representation as input to generate a sequence of articulatory gestures. These gestures, when executed, result in acoustics that are then mapped back onto phonology via the comprehension system. The resulting discrepancies between the original acoustic and phonological representations generated by the adult and those now generated by the system itself constitute the error signals that ultimately drive articulatory learning. In order for this to work, however, these distal errors must be converted to proximal errors (i.e., discrepancies in articulation). This is done by propagating phonological error back to acoustics and then back across the forward model (which mimics the actual physical processes that produced the acoustics from articulation) to derive error signals over articulatory states. These signals are then used to adapt the production system (i.e., the mapping from stable phonological representations onto articulatory sequences) to better approximate the acoustics and phonology generated by the adult. Intentional naming involves similar processing except that the initial input and the resulting comparison are at the level of semantics rather than at acoustics and phonology.

In summary, in the current work we develop a framework, based on connectionist–PDP principles, for understanding the interplay of comprehension and production in phonological development. Comprehension is instantiated as a mapping from time-varying acoustic input onto a more stable internal phonological representation of the entire word that is mapped simultaneously onto its semantic representation. In production, the same phonological representation serves as the input or plan for generating time-varying articulatory output. Articulatory feedback is not provided directly but is derived by the system itself from the consequences of self-generated speech using a learned forward model of the physical processes relating articulation to acoustics.

These processes can be instantiated in terms of four types of training experiences: (a) *babbling*, in which the system produces a range of articulations and learns to model their acoustic consequences; (b) *comprehension*, in which acoustic input from an adult is mapped via phonology onto a semantic representation; (c) *imitation*, in which the system generates articulations in an attempt to reproduce the acoustic and phonological representations it previously derived from an adult utterance; and (d) *intentional naming*, in which the system uses a semantic representation (perhaps derived from vision) to generate articulations via phonology and then compares this semantic representation to the one produced by comprehension of the system's own utterance.

In the remainder of this chapter, we develop a computational simulation of the framework that, although simplified, serves to establish the viability of the approach. We discuss the implications of the framework for a variety of empirical findings on phonological development in the subsequent General Discussion section.

SIMULATION

Given the considerable scope of the framework depicted in Fig. 14.1, a number of simplifications were necessary to keep the computational demands of the simulation within the limits imposed by available computational resources. The most fundamental of these was that instead of using continuous time and a fully recurrent network (Pearlmutter, 1989), the simulation used discrete time and a simple recurrent network (hereafter SRN; Elman, 1990).[2] This change results in a drastic reduction in the computational demands of the simulation, because once the states of context units are set, processing in an SRN is entirely feedforward. The drawback of this simplification is, of course, that we cannot capture the true temporal complexities of articulatory and acoustic representations, nor their interactions with phonological and semantic representations. In addition, variability due to speaker pitch and rate was not included—these are issues to be addressed by future work.

In order to reformulate the general framework in Fig. 14.1 as an SRN, certain architectural changes are necessary. Specifically, in the framework, the mappings between phonology and semantics are assumed to be bidirectional and interactive. Given that processing in an SRN must be feedforward, the input mapping (from phonology to semantics) and the output mapping (from semantics to phonology) must be separated and implemented with separate units and connections. The resulting architecture (ignoring hidden and context units) maps output semantics → output phonology → articulation ⇒ acoustics → input phonology → input semantics (where "⇒" corresponds to the forward model). It is important to keep in mind, however, that the division of input and output representations for phonology and semantics is not intended to imply that these representations are actually separate in child and adult speakers—to the

[2]An SRN differs from a fully recurrent network primarily in that performance error is attributed to activations only for the current and immediately previous time step but not further back in time (see Williams & Peng, 1990). Also, in an SRN, computing the output for a given input involves a single pass through the network, whereas in a fully recurrent network, it typically involves multiple iterations as the network settles to a stable state.

contrary, we claim that the same representations underly both comprehension and production. Accordingly, the functional correspondence of the SRN architecture to the more general framework is maintained by running only subsections of the network and by copying unit states and targets as appropriate. This ensures that, for both semantics and phonology, the representations on the input and output sides of the network are identical.

Finally, the implementation includes neither a physical articulatory apparatus that produces real sound nor an auditory transducer that generates acoustic inputs from sound. Rather, these physical processes were approximated by coupled equations that map any combination of values over a set of articulatory variables onto a particular set of values over a set of acoustic variables (see following section). These values are what the network's articulatory and acoustic representations encode. Considerable effort was spent to make these equations as realistic as possible while staying within the constraints of computational efficiency.

Despite these simplifications, the implemented simulation nevertheless embodies a solution to the fundamental computational challenges of speech comprehension and production discussed previously. To the extent that it succeeds in learning to understand and produce words, it provides support for the more general framework and approach to phonological development.

Network Architecture

Figure 14.2 shows the fully recurrent version of the general framework and the specific architecture of the implemented simple recurrent network version. The recurrent version (Fig. 14.2a) is equivalent to Fig. 14.1 with the addition of the groups of hidden units and connections that carry out the mappings among acoustics, semantics, and articulation. The implemented version (Fig. 14.2b) has a general feedforward structure, starting from the upper right of the network and continuing clockwise to the upper left. In addition, as an SRN, the states of particular groups of units on the previous time step are copied to additional *context* units and thus are available to influence processing on the current time step. It is by virtue of connections from these context units that the network can learn to be sensitive to nonlocal temporal dependencies in the task (see Elman, 1990, for discussion). Note that the actual context units are not shown in the figure; rather, the connections from context units are depicted as recurrent or feedback projections (shown as thin dashed arrows) from the source of the copied activations. Also note that there is one exception to this: In addition to a standard projection (solid arrow) from Articulation to the hidden units within the forward model, there is also a feedforward context projection

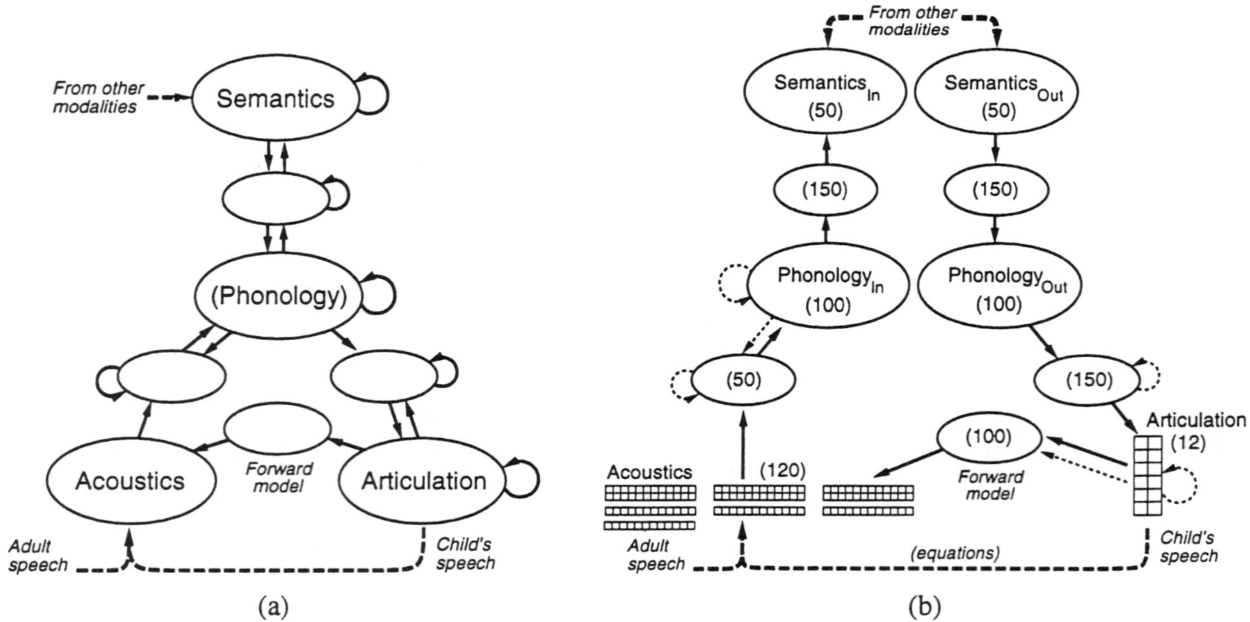

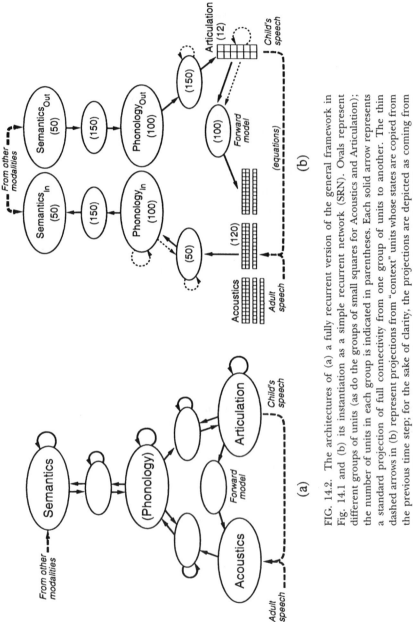

FIG. 14.2. The architectures of (a) a fully recurrent version of the general framework in Fig. 14.1 and (b) its instantiation as a simple recurrent network (SRN). Ovals represent different groups of units (as do the groups of small squares for Acoustics and Articulation); the number of units in each group is indicated in parentheses. Each solid arrow represents a standard projection of full connectivity from one group of units to another. The thin dashed arrows in (b) represent projections from "context" units whose states are copied from the previous time step; for the sake of clarity, the projections are depicted as coming from the source of the copied states rather than from separate context units (which are not shown). The thick dashed arrows represent external input: semantic patterns from other modalities (targets for comprehension; inputs for intentional naming), acoustic input sequences from an adult, and the acoustics generated by the system's own articulations.

(dashed arrow). These two arrows are intended to indicate that the patterns of activity over Articulation from both the current and previous time steps are provided as input to the forward model. Functionally equivalent groups that were split for the purposes of implementation as an SRN, but would be a single group within a fully recurrent implementation, are named with the subscripts *in* and *out* for clarity (e.g., $\text{Phonology}_{in,}$ $\text{Semantics}_{out)}$.

During comprehension and production, only Acoustics and Semantics_{out} receive external input, and only Semantics_{in} has externally specified targets. All of the remaining groups in the network, with the exception of Articulation, are "hidden" in the sense that their representations are not determined directly by the training environment but develop under the pressure of performing the relevant tasks accurately. Articulation has an unusual status in this regard. It has a predefined representation in the sense that unit activations have fixed and externally specified consequences for the resulting acoustics, and it is driven externally during babbling (see subsequent section). On the other hand, the network itself is given no information about the implications of this representation; it must learn to generate the appropriate activations based solely on observing the consequences of these activations (much like actions on a musical instrument have predefined acoustic consequences, but a musician must learn which combination of actions produce a particular piece of music).

Corpus

The network was trained on the 400 highest (verbal) frequency monosyllabic nouns and verbs in the Brown corpus (Kučera & Francis, 1967) with at most four phonemes ($M = 3.42$). Words were selected for presentation during training in proportion to a logarithmic function of their frequency of occurrence. As the main goal of the current simulation was to establish the viability of the general approach, little effort was made to structure the vocabulary of the model to correspond to the actual language experience of infants and young children. The restriction to monosyllables was for reasons of simplicity and because monosyllables dominate the production of children acquiring English (Boysson-Bardies et al., 1992; Vihman, 1993); note, however, there there is nothing in the current implementation that precludes applying it to multisyllabic or even multiword utterances.

Representations

The following descriptions provide a general characterization of the representations used in the simulation. Many details have been omitted for clarity, particularly with respect to the articulatory and acoustic representations and the mapping between them—see Plaut and Kello (1998) for full details and equations.

Articulatory Representations. The articulatory domain was carved into discrete events, roughly at points of significant change in articulation.[3] Each event was represented with six articulatory degrees of freedom based on configurations of oral–facial muscles that are more or less directly relevant to speech. Each dimension was a real value in the range [−1,1], corresponding to a static state in time. Three constraints entered into our choice of dimensions: (a) they needed to capture the physical similarities and differences in producing different phonemes in English, as well as the variations in producing the same phoneme in different contexts; (b) they had to lend themselves to engineering the equations that map articulation to acoustics; and (c) they had to be mostly independent of each other, in terms of muscular control, to avoid complications of building dependencies into the network architecture.

The six articulatory degrees of freedom are as follows (the labels are used in the example representations shown in Fig. 14.3):

1. *Oral Constriction (ORC).* This corresponds to the maximal amount of air flow for a given articulatory state. It represents the combined effects of constricting articulators such as the jaw and parts of the tongue. In general, vowels have low oral constriction, approximants have moderate constriction, fricatives have high constriction, and stops have complete constriction.

2. *Nasal Constriction (NAC).* Because nasal constriction is primarily controlled by raising and lowering the soft palate (Ladefoged, 1993), this dimension directly corresponds to the height of the soft palate.

3. *Place of Constriction (POC).* This corresponds to the location of the maximal point of constriction for a given articulatory state. Location is coded from front to back, with the most front value equal to a labial POC, and the most back value equal to a glottal POC. With moderate to high amounts of oral constriction, POC codes place of articulation for consonant-like articulations. With little oral constriction, articulation becomes vowel-like and POC has no effect on acoustics.

4. *Tongue Height (HEI).* This roughly codes the maximal closeness of the tongue to the roof of the mouth, but only when there is little oral constriction. Tongue height is directly related to the openness of a vowel.

---

[3]As pointed out earlier, discretization of time was a simplification introduced to permit the the use of an SRN architecture. We believe that continuous dynamics would more accurately capture a number of relevant phenomena.

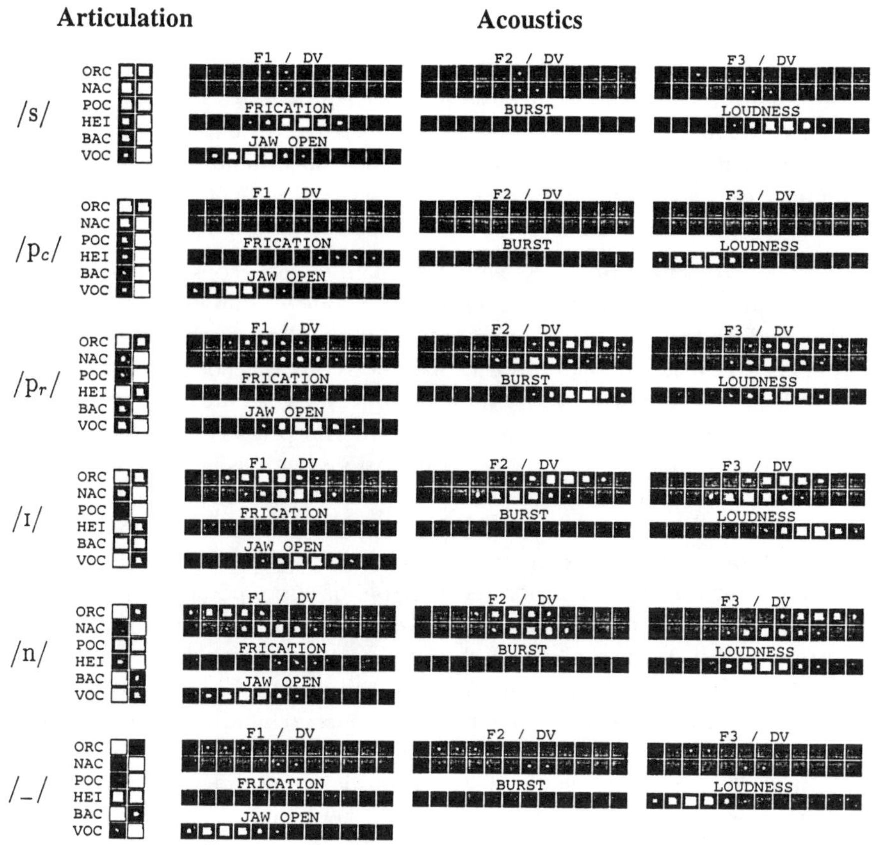

FIG. 14.3. The sequence of articulatory (left) and acoustic (right) events corresponding to an adult utterance of the word SPIN. In the simulation, articulatory degrees of freedom are subject to intrinsic variability within permissible ranges; for illustration purposes, this variability was not applied to the depicted events. These events were, however, still subject to both perseverative and anticipatory coarticulation. Each acoustic event is determined by both the current and previous articulatory event (which, for the first, is a copy of the current event). See the text for definitions of each unit group.

5. *Tongue Backness (BAK).* This is directly related to vowel backness. As with tongue height, it only takes effect when there is little oral constriction.

6. *Voicing (VOC).* This corresponds to a combination of glottal opening and vocal chord constriction, given that our model assumes constant pulmonary pressure for the sake of simplicity.

Each articulatory degree of freedom in the network was coded by two units whose activities fell in the range [0,1]. The value for each degree of freedom was coded by the signed difference between these values, having a possible range of [−1,1]. Note that the same value can be coded by different combinations of unit activities; the network can learn to use any of these. Finally, the network represented both the past and current articulatory event in order to capture articulatory change information that has consequences for acoustics.

Acoustic Representations. As with articulation, the acoustic domain was divided into discrete events. We chose 10 "acoustic" dimensions based on aspects of the speech environment that are generally thought to be relevant to speech perception. The choice of dimensions was constrained by the same factors as the articulatory dimensions. The word *acoustic* is placed in quotes because, although sound is certainly the primary perceptual–proprioceptive domain of speech, oral dimensions such as jaw openness also play a role. For example, newborns pay special attention to certain mouth posturings (Meltzoff & Moore, 1977), and 3- to 4-month-old infants are aware of the relation between certain facial and vocal activities (see Locke, 1995, for review). We incorporated the role of visual perception–proprioception by including a visual dimension of jaw openness in our acoustic representation. In fact, our model provides an additional reason for why infants might pay such close attention to the mouth: Visual speech helps to reduce the motor equivalence problem, thus facilitating the acquisition of both the comprehension and production of speech.

Another important aspect of our acoustic representation is that the dimensions were normalized for overall speaker variations such as rate and pitch (but random variation and coarticulation were incorporated). Researchers have shown that infants as young as 2 months can normalize for speaker variation (Jusczyk, Pisoni, & Mullennix, 1992; Kuhl, 1983). Although this simplification seems reasonable, we believe that the mechanism for speaker variability is an important part of understanding phonological development, and we intend to incorporate this into future versions of the model.

Unlike the articulatory degrees of freedom, each acoustic dimension had an accompanying *amplitude* value corresponding to the degree to which information on that dimension was present in a given acoustic event. For example, first formant frequency was an acoustic dimension, yet not all acoustic signals have formant structure (e.g., a voiceless fricative such as /s/). In this case, the degrees of freedom corresponding to formants would be assigned very low amplitudes in our encoding.

The 10 acoustic dimensions are as follows (note that we have included here some aspects of the articulation-to-acoustics mapping; further detail is provided later):

1–3. *First through third formant frequencies.* Because these are normalized, they essentially code frequency position relative to a particular formant and a particular speaker. In general, the amount of periodicity in the putative acoustic wave form determines the amplitudes of these dimensions.

4–6. *First through third formant transitions or derivatives.* These code the normalized amount of rise or fall in each formant from the previous to the current acoustic state. Their amplitudes are identical to those for the corresponding formant frequency.

7. *Frication.* This is a composite of the frequency, spread, and intensity of very high frequency, nonperiodic energy. Previous research suggests that all of these measures play a role in distinguishing different fricative sounds, although the exact relations are unclear (see Lieberman & Blumstein, 1988, for review). We simplified matters by collapsing these variables into one acoustic dimension. Frication is present when oral or nasal constriction, or both, is slightly less than fully constricted.

8. *Burst.* This dimension is a simplification analogous to frication: a composite of acoustic measures that are involved in distinguishing plosive releases of different places of articulation. Bursting is present when a sufficiently large positive change occurs in oral or nasal constriction.

9. *Loudness.* This codes the overall amount of acoustic energy in a given event (normalized for speaker and stress). For example, silence has very little or no energy, fricatives have little energy, nasals have significantly more, and vowels have the most. The amplitude value for loudness is redundant and therefore permanently set to one.

10. *Jaw openness.* This dimension reflects the size of the mouth opening for a given articulatory state and was computed based on the amount and place of oral constriction. We chose jaw openness because it is relatively visible (and presumably salient), but because speakers cannot normally see their own jaw, this dimension also represents the analogous proprioceptive signal. Because the jaw is always somewhere along the continuum of openness, the amplitude value was unnecessary and therefore set to one.

Each of the 10 acoustic dimensions was represented in the network with a separate bank of 12 units, laid out in one dimension corresponding to the [−1,1] range of possible dimension values. A specific acoustic value was encoded by Gaussian unit activity with mean equal to the value and fixed variance. Unit activities were determined by sampling this Gaussian at the 12 equal-spaced intervals indicated by the unit positions within the bank. The total activity (i.e., the area under the Gaussian) was set to equal the amplitude of that acoustic dimension. Whereas articulation was represented by both a past and current articulatory vector in order to capture change information, an acoustic event contains dimensions that directly code change in time. Therefore, the network represented a single acoustic event that changed over time.

Articulation-to-Acoustics Mapping. The translation from two articulatory events (past and current) to an acoustic event consisted of 10 equations, 1 for each acoustic dimensions. Each equation was written solely in terms of one or more of the articulatory degrees of freedom. The functions ranged from primarily linear and consisting of one or two variables, to highly nonlinear and consisting of four or five variables. We do not present the details of the equations here (see Plaut & Kello, 1998) but we outline the major relations they embodied.

1. Formant frequency is determined primarily by either tongue height and backness, or by POC. In addition, nasal constriction tends to lower the first formant frequency (Lieberman & Blumstein, 1988).
2. Formant transitions are based on change in oral or nasal constriction, or both, in combination with change in the dimensions relevant to formant frequencies. The relation between place of articulation in a plosive release and the following vowel played a major role in determining these equations (see Liberman, 1996).
3. The amplitudes of the six formant dimensions are based on a combination of voicing and both oral and nasal constriction.
4. The frication and burst values are determined by place of articulation. The amplitudes of these dimensions are based on current (and, for bursting, also previous) oral and nasal constriction values.
5. Loudness is determined by a combination of all six articulatory degrees of freedom.

To illustrate the articulatory and acoustic representations and the mapping between them, Fig. 14.3 shows the sequence of events corresponding to an "adult" utterance of the word SPIN /spIn/ (see the "Adult Utterances" subsection for a description of how such sequences are generated).

Babbling. In our theoretical framework, babbling serves to train a forward model to learn the relation between articulation and acoustics. The system uses this model to convert acoustic error to articulatory error to incrementally improve its own productions during imitation and intentional naming. A given babbling episode consisted of a string of articulations generated stochastically from a model of babbling behavior that combined canonical and variegated babbling. This model was intended to approximate the articulatory effects of a bias towards mandibular (jaw) oscillation in the oral behavior of young infants. This oscillatory bias has been proposed as a fundamental constraint on early speech development (Davis & MacNeilage, 1995; Kent, Mitchell, & Sancier, 1991; MacNeilage, in press; MacNeilage & Davis, 1990) and is consistent with the central role of rhythmic behavior in motor development more generally (Thelen, 1981; Thelen & Smith, 1994). The generated articulatory sequences reflected both reduplicated babbling (to the extent that POC remained constant across the articulatory string) and variegated babbling (to the extent that POC changed).

Specifically, each instance of babbling was composed of five articulatory events. Four of the six degrees of freedom in the first event of a sequence were given random values; the remaining two—oral and nasal constriction—were random but their probabilities were weighted toward the endpoints (i.e., −1 and 1, which correspond to completely closed and opened, respectively). Each subsequent event in a sequence was generated by sampling from a Gaussian probability distribution centered around the previous values for five of the six degrees of freedom (producing a bias toward gradual change); oral constriction was stochastic but weighted toward the opposing sign of the previous value, thus exhibiting a bias toward oscillation. The resulting articulatory sequence constituted a babbling utterance used to train the articulatory-acoustic forward model, as described later.

Adult Utterances. Adult word utterances were derived from canonical strings of phonemes, each ending with a null or silent phoneme. Note that, although the canonical forms were represented as phonemes, the resulting acoustic events did not have a one-to-one correspondence with phonemes. Moreover, each articulatory event underlying an acoustic pattern was subject to considerable intrinsic variability and was shaped by multiple phonemes due to coarticulatory influences.

The procedure for generating an instance of an adult utterance of a word was as follows. The word's phoneme string was first converted into a sequence of articulatory events. Most phonemes corresponded to a single articulatory event, although plosives and diphthongs were coded as two events (except that the second, "release" event of the first of two adjacent plosives was deleted). The articulatory event(s) corresponding to a phoneme were defined in terms a range of permissible values over the articulatory degrees of freedom. The center and size of each range was estimated from the role and importance that a given degree of freedom plays in producing a given phoneme (based on phonetic research drawn largely from Ladefoged, 1993). A specific utterance was generated by randomly sampling from a Gaussian distribution centered on the ranges for each phoneme and clipped at the endpoints. The randomly determined initial values for each articulatory event were then adjusted based on both perseverative and anticipatory coarticulation. For a given event, each degree of freedom was first pulled toward the specific values of previous events, with the strength of this pull scaled by the number of intervening events and the value range of the perseverative influence. Then, each degree of freedom was pulled toward the canonical values of the subsequent events (i.e., the range midpoints, before their values were randomly generated), scaled by the same factors. Finally, the coarticulated values were forced to be within their respective ranges. The resulting string of articulatory events was input to the articulation-to-acoustics equations to generate a string of acoustic events. In generating the first acoustic event, the first articulatory event was interpreted as both the current and previous articulatory state, analogous to allowing for articulatory preparation before beginning an utterance. Note that, although the articulation-to-acoustics equations are deterministic, adult utterances of a given word exhibited considerable variability due to the random sampling of articulatory degrees of freedom within the permissible range for each articulatory event. Moreover, individual tokens of the same phoneme varied both from this random sampling and from the coarticulatory influences of surrounding phonemes.

Semantic Representations. No attempt was made to design semantic representations that captured the actual meanings of the 400 words in the training corpus. Rather, artificial semantic representations were developed that, although constituting only a very coarse approximation to the richness and variability of actual word meaning, nonetheless embodied the core assumptions behind the challenges of comprehension and production: namely, that semantic similarity is unrelated to acoustic–articulatory similarity.

Specifically, the semantic representations of words were generated to cluster into artificial semantic "categories" (Chauvin, 1988; Plaut, 1995, 1997). Twenty different random binary patterns were generated over 50 semantic features, in which each feature had a probability $p_a = .2$ of being active in each prototype. Twenty exemplars were then generated from each prototype pattern by randomly altering some of its features; specifically, each feature had a probability of .2 of being resampled with $p_a = .2$. The effect of this manipulation is to make all exemplars within a category cluster around the prototype, and for all semantic patterns to have an average of 10 active features (range 6–16) out of a total of 50. The resulting 400 semantic patterns were then assigned to words randomly to ensure that the mappings from acoustics to semantics and from semantics to articulation were unsystematic.

Training Procedure

As mentioned earlier, the system undergoes four types of training experiences: babbling, comprehension, imitation, and intentional naming. Although each of these is described separately, it is important to keep in mind that they are fully interleaved during training.

Babbling. The role of babbling in our framework is to train an articulatory–acoustic forward model; the only parts of the network involved in this process are Articulation, Acoustics, and the hidden units between them (see Fig. 14.2). First, a particular sequence of articulations corresponding to an instance of babbling was generated (as described under "Representations"). This sequence was then passed through the articulation-to-acoustics equations to produce a sequence of "actual" acoustic patterns. The articulations also served as input to the forward model (see Fig. 14.2), which generated a sequence of predicted acoustic patterns. The discrepancy or error between the actual and predicted acoustics at each step, measured by the *cross-entropy*[4] between the two patterns (Hinton, 1989), was then back-propagated through the forward model and used to adjust its connection weights to improve its ability to predict the acoustic outcome of the given articulations. In this way, the forward model gradually learned to mimic the physical mapping from articulatory sequences to acoustic sequences (as instantiated by the articulation-to-acoustics equations).

Comprehension. Comprehension involves deriving the semantic representation of a word from a sequence of acoustic patterns corresponding to an adult utterance of the word (generated as described under "Representations"). Given such an utterance, the network was trained to derive the semantics of the word in the following way. Prior to the first acoustic event, the context units for Phonology_{in} and for the hidden units between Acoustics and Phonology_{in} (see Fig. 14.2) were initialized to states of 0.2. (Note that there are no context units between Phonology_{in} and Semantics_{in}—this means that, although the pattern of activity over phonology changes as acoustic input comes in, this activity must map to semantics in parallel.) Then, each acoustic event was presented successively over Acoustics, and the activations of all units between Acoustics and Semantics_{in} were computed. For each event, the resulting semantic pattern was compared with the correct semantics for the word and the resulting error was propagated back through the network to Acoustics to accumulate weight derivatives for connections in this portion of the network (including the connections from context units). After processing each event, the activities of the Phonology_{in} units and the Acoustics-to-Phonology_{in} hidden units were copied to their corresponding context units, to influence processing of the next acoustic event. After the last acoustic event was presented (corresponding to silence), the accumulated weight derivatives were used to adjust the weights to improve comprehension performance on subsequent

[4]The cross-entropy between a pattern of activation over a set of units and their target activations is given by $-\sum_i t_i \log_2(a_i) + (1 - t_i)\log_2(1 - a_i)$, where a_i is the activity of unit i and t_i is its target.

presentations of the word. Because error was based on the discrepancy of the generated and correct semantics from the very beginning of the acoustic input sequence, the network was pressured to derive information about the semantics of the incoming word as quickly as possible.

Imitation. Imitation involves using a phonological representation derived from an adult utterance as input to drive articulation, and comparing the resulting acoustic and phonological representations with those of the adult utterance. Imitation could, in general, be based on any adult utterance, including those without any clear semantic referent. However, for practical reasons (i.e., to avoid having a much larger training corpus for imitation than for comprehension), training episodes of imitation were yoked to episodes of comprehension in the simulation.

Specifically, after having processed an adult utterance of a word for comprehension, the final phonological pattern over Phonology_{in} was copied to Phonology_{out} (see Fig. 14.2; recall that these correspond to the same group in the general framework). The phonological pattern then served as the static input plan for generating an articulatory sequence. All of the context units between Phonology_{out} and Phonology_{in} were initialized to states of 0.2. The network then computed unit activations up to and including Articulation. This articulatory pattern and the one for the previous step (which, for the first step, was identical to the current pattern) were mapped through the forward model to generate predicted acoustics. At the same time, the articulatory patterns were used to generate an actual acoustic event via the articulation-to-acoustics equations. The discrepancies between the network's actual acoustics and those predicted by the forward model were used to adapt the forward model, as during babbling. In addition, the actual acoustics were mapped by the comprehension side of the network to generate a pattern of activity over Phonology_{in}. The error between the activations generated by the network and those generated by the adult were then calculated both at Phonology_{in} and at Acoustics.[5] The phonological error was back-propagated to acoustics (without incrementing weight derivatives) and added to the acoustic error. The combined error was then back-propagated through the forward model (again without incrementing derivatives) to calculate error for the current articulatory pattern. This error was then back-propagated to Phonology_{out} and weight derivatives were accumulated for the production side of the network. At this point, the relevant unit activations were copied onto context units,

[5]Note that the use of a direct comparison between the acoustics generated by the adult and those generated by the network assumes a considerable amount of pre-acoustic normalization. It should be noted, however, that training imitation using comparisons only at the phonological level results in only marginally worse performance (see Plaut & Kello, 1998).

and the pattern over Phonology_{out} was used to generate the next articulatory event. This process repeated until the network produced as many articulatory events as there were acoustic events in the imitated adult utterance (note that a more general strategy would be to continue articulating until a number of silent acoustic events are produced).

Intentional Naming. The final type of training experience included in our general approach to phonological development is the intentional generation of an utterance on the basis of semantic input (perhaps derived from another modality). In the current simulation, however, the ability was trained only indirectly.

Again, for reasons of efficiency, intentional naming was yoked to comprehension. After the network was trained to comprehend a given word, the correct semantic pattern for the word was then presented as an input pattern over Semantics_{out} (this pattern had been assumed to be available as targets over Semantics_{in}). This input pattern was then mapped by the network to generate an output pattern over Phonology_{out}. The error between this pattern and the one over Phonology_{in} coding the entire adult utterance (again, these should be thought of as the same group) was then back-propagated to Semantics_{out}, and the corresponding weights were adapted to improve the network's ability to approximate its own phonological representation of the adult's utterance given the corresponding semantics as input. Note that the targets for the task change as the network's own phonological representations evolve during the development of comprehension; the output side of the system must nonetheless track this change. Eventually, both the comprehension and production systems converge on being able to map the same phonological representation both to and from semantics. In fact, this training procedure was intended to approximate the effects of bidirectional interactions between phonology and semantics in a fully recurrent version of the system.

Once the system has the capability of mapping a semantic representation onto a phonological representation, training during imitation enables this phonological pattern to be mapped to an analogous one on the input side, which can then be mapped to the corresponding semantics due to training during comprehension. In this way, the network can be tested for its ability to map a semantic pattern via phonology to an articulatory sequence which, according to its own comprehension system, sounds the same and means the same as the intended utterance. The entire mapping (from Semantics_{out} to Semantics_{in}) was not, however, explicitly trained because the resulting back-propagated error derivatives would be very small (due to the large number of intervening layers of units) and because children seem relatively insensitive to the semantic plausibility of their own utterances (e.g., the *fis* phenomenon; Berko & Brown, 1960; Dodd, 1975; Smith, 1973).

Testing Procedure

The network was trained on 3.5 million word presentations and babbling episodes. Although this may seem like an excessive amount of training, children speak up to 14,000 words per day (Wagner, 1985), or over 5 million words per year. For each word presentation, the network was trained to comprehend the word and then to imitate the resulting acoustics and phonology. The network also produced and learned from an unrelated babbling sequence. Although, in actuality, the onset of babbling precedes clear attempts at imitation and falls off as production skill increases, the model engages in both babbling and imitation throughout training. Babbling and early word production do, in fact, overlap in time to a large degree (see Vihman, 1996), and the phonetic inventory that children use when beginning to produce words is drawn largely from the inventory of sounds produced during babbling (Vihman & Miller, 1988). Moreover, some babble-like utterances may result from undeveloped speech skills during attempts to imitate or intentionally produce words. Such attempts nontheless constitute opportunities for learning the relation between articulation and acoustics; as mentioned previously, our network adapts its forward model during both babbling and imitation. As it turns out, the performance of the forward model achieves a reasonable level of accuracy fairly quickly, so continuing to include babbling episodes throughout training has little impact on performance.

After every 500,000 word presentations during training, the network was evaluated for its ability to comprehend and imitate adult speech and to produce comprehensible intentional utterances. Because there was intrinsic variability among adult utterances, the network was tested on 20 instances of each of the 400 words in the training corpus. Performance on each task was based on whether each stimulus could be accurately discriminated from all other known words, using a *best-match* criterion over semantics and, for imitation, also over phonology. Specifically, when applied to semantics, the network was considered to comprehend a word correctly if its generated semantics matched the correct semantics for that word better (in terms of normalized dot product) than the semantics for any other word in the training corpus. The best-match procedure over phonology was a bit more complicated, as there are no predefined phonological representations for words against which to compare the network's utterance. Moreover, due to intrinsic variability, different adult instances of a word generated somewhat different phonological representations during comprehension. Accordingly, the best-match criterion was applied to phonology by comparing the phonological pattern generated by the network's utterance of a word with the phonological representations generated by all 8,000 adult utterances (20 instances of 400 words) and considering the network's utterance correct if the best-matching adult utterance was one of the 20 instances of the word.

Much of the most important evidence on the nature of phonological development comes from an analysis of children's speech errors (Ingram, 1976; Menn, 1983; Smith, 1973; see Bernhardt & Stemberger, 1997, for review). Although a comprehensive account of the systematicity and variability of child speech errors remains a long-term goal of the current approach, an initial attempt can be made by examining the nature of the network's errors in comprehension, imitation, and intentional naming. Specifically, if the best match to the network's utterance was the representation of a word other than the stimulus, the network was considered to have made an error, which was then evaluated for phonological or semantic similarity, or both, with the stimulus.[6] For these purposes, an error was considered phonologically related if it differed from the stimulus by an addition, deletion, or substitution of a single phoneme, and it was considered semantically related if its assigned semantic pattern came from the same artificial category (see the earlier "Representations" section).

Results

Due to space limitations, we present only a subset of the results derived from the network (see Plaut & Kello, 1998, for a more comprehensive presentation). In particular, we omit a full characterization the performance of the forward model. This model is acquired fairly rapidly, achieving reasonable performance within the first 1 million (M) word presentations and babbling episodes. Moreover, its ability to predict the acoustic consequences of articulatory events is ultimately very accurate, producing an an average cross-entropy per event of less than 0.39 summed over the 120 Acoustic units (cf. 33.7 at the beginning of training). When inaccurate, it tends to produce Gaussian activity over the acoustic banks with greater variance than in the actual acoustic signal, which is a natural indication of reduced confidence in the underlying dimension value.

Correct Performance. Figure 14.4 shows the correct performance of the network over the course of training on comprehension, imitation, and intentional naming using the best-match criterion. First note that comprehension performance improved relatively rapidly, reaching 84.3% correct

[6]This way of defining speech errors allows for only word responses, which is clearly inadequate. Determining nonword error responses is problematic, however, because the acoustic sequences generated by the network cannot be interpreted directly. Plaut and Kello (1998) addressed this problem by training a separate network to map sequences of acoustic events onto sequences of phonemes, analogous to a trained linguist listening to and transcribing speech.

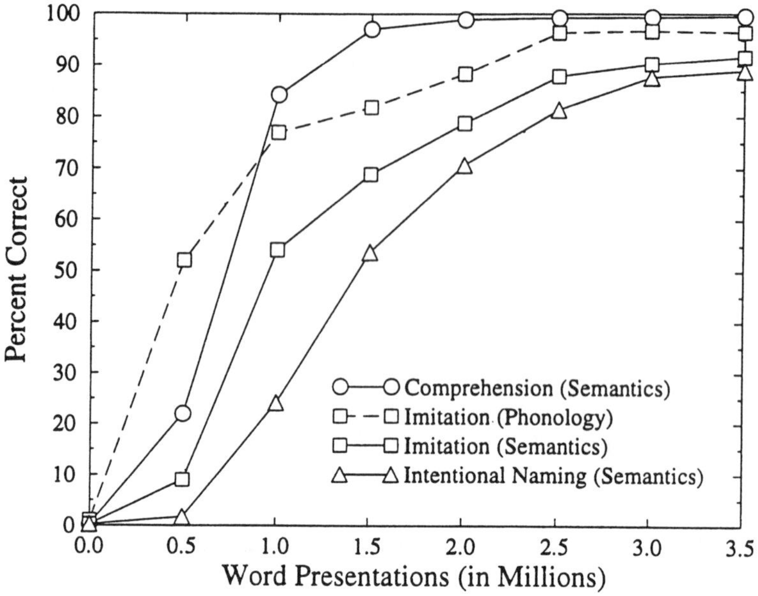

FIG. 14.4. Correct performance of the network in terms of a best-match criterion on comprehension (at semantics), imitation (at both phonology and semantics), and intentional naming (at semantics) over the course of training.

by 1M word presentations and 99.6% by 3.5M presentations. This level of performance is impressive given the lack of systematicity in the mapping between acoustics and semantics and the considerable intrinsic variability of adult utterances. Relative to comprehension, competence in production developed more slowly: When evaluated at semantics, the network was only 54.2% correct at imitation by 1M presentations, although it did achieve 91.7% correct by 3.5M presentations. Intentional naming was slightly poorer than imitation throughout training, eventually reaching 89.0% correct. This is not surprising, as the task involves mapping through the entire network and was not trained explicitly.

When evaluated at phonology, imitation performance was more accurate, achieving 96.5% correct by 3.5M word presentations. The rapid rise in best-match imitation performance at phonology at 0.5M presentations is due to the fact that phonological representations are relatively undifferentiated at this point.

Overall, the network achieved quite good performance at both comprehension and production. The fact that comprehension precedes production in the model stems directly from the fact that learning within the production system is driven by comparisons over representations within the comprehension system. The excellent performance on imitation, particularly at phonology, demonstrates that feedback from the comprehension system via a learned forward model can provide effective guidance for articulatory development. The findings provide encouraging support for the viability of our general framework for phonological development.

Error Analysis. To further characterize the network's performance, we analyzed the errors made by the network under the best-match criterion after 3.5M word presentations. As described earlier, an error response was considered semantically related to the correct (target) word if it belonged to the same category, and phonologically related if it differed from the target word by the addition, deletion, or substitution of a single phoneme. Based on these definitions, errors were classified as *semantic* (but not phonological), *phonological* (but not semantic), *mixed* semantic and phonological, or *miscellaneous* (neither semantic nor phonological, although many such errors exhibited phonological similarity that failed to satisfy our strict definition).

Table 14.1 presents the percentage of error occurrences for each of the types and for each task, as well as the chance rates of occurrences of each error type. Calculating the chance probability of a semantic error was straightforward, as there were five equiprobable categories. The chance probability for a phonological error was determined empirically by computing the rate of phonological relatedness among all pairs of trained words. The chance rate of a mixed error was simply the product of these two probabilities (i.e., we assumed independence, given that semantic patterns were assigned to words as phoneme strings randomly).

In general, the network showed a strong bias toward phonological similarity in its errors compared with the chance rate, for both comprehension

TABLE 14.1
Error Rates and Percentage of Error Types for Various Tasks, and Chance Rates

		Error Type			
Task	*Error Rate*	*Semantic*	*Phonological*	*Mixed*	*Miscellaneous*
Comprehension	0.45	14.1 (0.71)	85.3 (32.8)	0.0 (0.00)	0.0 (0.00)
Imitation	3.52	10.1 (0.51)	74.3 (28.6)	1.9 (4.75)	13.7 (0.18)
Intentional naming	11.0	40.9 (2.05)	11.4 (4.4)	0.0 (0.00)	47.7 (0.62)
Chance		20.0	2.6	0.4	77.0

Note. Each value in parentheses is the ratio of the observed error rate to the chance rate listed at the bottom of the column. Performance was measured after training on 3.5 million word presentations. Error rate is based on 20 instances of adult utterances of each of 400 words (8,000 total observations) for comprehension and imitation, and one instance of intentional naming (because the network's own articulations are not subject to variability). Comprehension and intentional naming were evaluated at semantics, whereas imitation was evaluated at phonology.

and imitation (although this is based on relatively few errors in the former case). Comprehension and imitation also produced semantic errors below chance, whereas the rates for intentional naming were well above chance. Interestingly, the rate of mixed errors in imitation, although low, was almost five times the chance rate, consistent with a general preference in production for errors sharing both semantic and phonological similarity with the target (see, e.g., Levelt, 1989).

Although comprehension errors were rare, when they occurred they typically involved the additional of a final plosive (most commonly /t/ or /d/) to yield a higher frequency word (e.g., PASS /pæs/ → PAST /pæst/), presumably because utterance-final silence was misinterpreted as the closure event of the plosive, and the system is insufficiently sensitive to the acoustics of the release. This type of error was also common in imitation, presumably because its feedback during training was derived from comprehension. Imitation also produced a number of multichange errors that appear to be phonetically conditioned (e.g., GAVE /geɪv/ → CAME /keɪm/), and some evidence of cluster reduction (e.g., FLAT /flæt/ → MATCH /mætʃ/), although the corpus provided very few opportunities to observe the latter.

At the phoneme level, there were far more errors on consonants than on vowels and, among consonants, a relatively higher error rate on fricatives, affricates (e.g., /tʃ/), and /ŋ/ (as in RING). These errors involved both additions and deletions; when they were deleted, they were often replaced by a plosive. In fact, plosives accounted for more than half of the total number of insertions. By contrast, the liquids /r/ and /l/ were deleted occasionally but never inserted. These characteristics are in broad agreement with the properties of early child speech errors (e.g., Ingram, 1976).

Although these error analyses are preliminary and are significantly limited by allowing only word responses, they suggest that the current approach can be applied fruitfully to understanding the nature of children's speech errors.

GENERAL DISCUSSION

Infants face a difficult challenge in learning to comprehend and produce speech. The speech stream is extended in time, highly variable, and (for monomorphemic words) bears little systematic relation to its underlying meaning. Articulatory skill must develop without any direct instruction or feedback, and comprehension and production processes must ultimately be tightly coordinated.

This chapter outlines a general framework, based on connectionist–parallel distributed processing principles, for understanding how the infant copes with these difficulties, and presents an implemented simulation that, although simplified relative to the framework, nonetheless instantiates its fundamental hypotheses. In particular, two key properties of the framework and implementation reflect a close interplay between comprehension and production in phonological development. The first is that both comprehension and production are subserved by the same underlying phonological representations. These representations are not predefined but emerge under the combined pressures of mediating among acoustic, semantic, and articulatory information. The second key property is that the necessary articulatory feedback for the production system is derived from the comprehension system. Specifically, proximal (articulatory) error is derived from the distal (acoustic and phonological) consequences of articulation via a learned articulatory–acoustic forward model (also see Jordan, 1996; Perkell et al., 1995). The simulation demonstrates that a model instantiating these properties can, in fact, learn to cope with time-varying, variable speech in comprehension and use the resulting knowledge to guide production effectively in imitation and intentional naming. Moreover, its pattern of errors, although not matching child speech errors in detail, does show the appropriate general trends, suggesting that the approach may provide a computationally explicit basis for understanding the origin of such errors.

The bulk of this chapter focused on the nature of the computational problems posed by phonological development and on the formulation of a particular approach for solving these problems. At this stage in the work, relatively little attention has been directed at relating the simulation, and the more general framework, to specific empirical phenomena concerning phonological development in infants and young children. In the remainder of this chapter, we consider three categories of empirical phenomena—the relation between comprehension and production, the time course of speech acquisition, and the phonetic content of speech errors—and briefly address how our approach might account for some of the more central findings in each. Whereas many of these points are addressed directly by the existing framework and implementation, some of them constitute important directions for future research.

Relation Between Comprehension and Production

One of the most basic findings in phonological development is that skilled word comprehension precedes skilled word production (Benedict, 1979; Reznick & Goldfield, 1992; Snyder, Bates, & Bretherton, 1981). This finding has prompted speculation that a certain skill level of comprehension is necessary for production skills to advance. Our model embodies this notion in terms of the maturity of phonological representations that map acoustic input onto semantics. The internal representations must begin to stabilize in comprehension before their input to the production system becomes useful for learning articulation. Our approach differs from Vihman's (1996) idea of an "articulatory filter," in which the articulatory system mediates which words the child can perceive, remember, and therefore produce. Our framework holds that the perception and comprehension of speech can develop somewhat independently of the articulatory system, although the mature system must eventually mediate both tasks with the same underlying phonological representations.

Another finding that points towards a link between development in comprehension and production is that the phonetic distribution of late babbling (i.e., by 10 months) is influenced by the ambient language (Boysson-Bardies et al., 1992). When beginning to imitate and speak from intention, a child's utterances, as well as those of our network, will tend to sound like babble (i.e., highly variable exploration of articulation) because the link between phonology and articulation has not yet developed. If the adult characterizes these early attempts at speech as babble, then indeed babbling will tend to have phonetic characteristics of the ambient language. Similarly, the phonetic characteristics of early word production overlap to a large degree with the characteristics of a given infant's babbling (Stoel-Gammon & Cooper, 1984; Vihman, Maken, Miller, Simmons, & Miller, 1985). Given that the instantiation of babbling in the current model is not influenced by the developing phonological representations, the model does not account for this finding, but we plan to address it in future extensions.

Time Course of Speech Acquisition

A second major area of investigation in phonological development relates to the order of acquisition of various speech production skills. We consider two findings to be of particular importance. The first is that infants often have a small repertoire of *protowords* late in the babbling phase but prior to true word production (Menyuk & Menn, 1979; Stoel-Gammon & Cooper, 1984; Werner & Kaplan, 1984). Protowords are characterized by relatively stable patterns of vocalization that serve to communicate broad distinctions between situations (e.g., request an object vs. request social interaction). As discussed earlier, distributed networks have an inherent tendency to map similar input patterns onto similar output patterns; this bias is overcome only gradually in learning an unsystematic mapping. In the current context, this means that broadly similar semantic patterns will map initially onto similar phonological patterns. If the phonological patterns are similar enough, they will be heard as the same utterance (i.e., a protoword).

The second finding is an example of the ubiquitous phenomenon of U-shaped learning: As the child learns to produce more words, production of originally well-learned words often regresses (Vihman & Velleman, 1989). More generally, articulation increases in variability and decreases in phonetic accuracy as development progresses, although this trend reverses as articulatory skills approach mature levels. This pattern is generally interpreted as indicating a shift from a whole-word system to a more systematic, segmentally based one (see Jusczyk, 1997; Vihman, 1996). A number of researchers (e.g., Jusczyk, 1986; Lindblom, 1992; Studdert-Kennedy, 1987; Walley, 1993) have pointed to the growth of receptive vocabulary as exerting a powerful influence on the degree to which phonological representations become segmental. Early on, relatively undifferentiated, "wholistic" phonological representations may suffice for discriminating among the few words known to the child. However, as the number and similarity of words that must be represented increase, there is greater pressure to develop a more systematic encoding of the relevant distinctions. Insofar as the same phonological representations subserve both comprehension and production (as in the current framework), the emergence of more segmental representations through pressures on comprehension should also be manifest in production.

Another class of time-course phenomena concerns the order in which skilled performance is achieved for various phonological units (e.g., vowels, consonants, and consonant clusters). A coarse-grained example is the finding that the proportion of consonants in intentional–imitative utterances is low early on and increases as the number of words produced increases (Bauer, 1988; Roug, Landberg, & Lundberg, 1989; Vihman et al., 1985). Our framework does not account for this directly, but there are two factors that bias vowel-like articulations during early imitation and intentional naming in our model. First, our articulatory representations have a built-in bias toward the center value of each degree of freedom, mimicking a physical bias of least articulatory effort. This bias causes oral constriction to be somewhat open (i.e., vowel-like) by default. Second, when the model begins to compare its own acoustics with those of the adult, it learns quickly that it must vocalize in order to produce most types of sounds. This coarse learning precedes learning the more complicated articulatory relation involved in producing consonants. The combination of these two factors creates an early bias toward vowel-like sounds during imitation and intentional speech, which is overridden as the system gains greater control of the articulatory degrees of freedom.

Another, finer grained example is that labials are produced more often in the first word productions than in babbling (Boysson-Bardies & Vihman, 1991). In learning to produce labial consonants (compared with more orally internal articulations), infants can use the visual feedback of labial articulations in addition to feedback derived from acoustics (see Vihman, 1996). The acoustic level of representation in our model includes a visual dimension that corresponds to jaw openness, which is most active for labial articulations. The additional visual information for labials should cause words with primarily labial articulations to be produced accurately sooner than other words because the error signal from labial productions is richer than from less visible articulations.

A similar finding is that children master the production of stops before fricatives and affricates (Menn & Stoel-Gammon, 1995). In the physical mapping from articulation to acoustics in our model, the range of oral constriction values that produces frication is much smaller that the range that produces the component events of a plosive sound (i.e., closure followed by release). Second, mandibular oscillation during babbling produces a bias favoring closure-release sequences that approximate plosives. This, in turn, causes the forward model to learn the articulatory–acoustic relation for plosives before fricatives. The forward model will thus provide more accurate articulatory feedback for plosives than for fricatives as the system learns to produce words.

Phonetic Content of Speech Errors

Detailed analyses of speech errors have provided some of the most important constraints on theories of phonological development. Perhaps the most basic and widespread types of errors that children make during the early stages of word production are ones of simplification or reduction. Menn and Stoel-Gammon (1995) listed three such error types that we address in this section: (a) stops are substituted for fricatives, (b) consonant clusters are reduced to single consonants, and (c) voiceless initial stop consonants are deaspirated (e.g., TOE is heard as DOE).

That plosives are mastered before fricatives is relevant to the first point. If the production system cannot activate the articulatory representations precisely enough to produce fricatives, then plosives are the likely alternative. With respect to consonant reduction, both acoustic and articulatory factors may be involved. The acoustic similarity of BOND and BLOND, for example, is very high, which means that learning distinct phonological representations for them will be difficult. The similar representations that such contrasts will drive may be sufficiently distinct for driving different semantics but not different articulations. On the articulatory side, vowels and consonants constrain somewhat complementary sets of articulatory degrees of freedom. Consequently, consonant clusters permit relatively less coarticulation—and hence entail greater difficulty—compared with transitions between consonants and vowels (see also Kent, 1992). Also, the bias to produce simple over complex onsets may, in part, be due to their generally higher frequency of occurrence in speech. Finally, the deaspiration of initial unvoiced stops may be explained by articulatory difficulty (i.e., a least-effort bias).

Conclusion

In conclusion, we propose a distributed connectionist framework for phonological development in which phonology is a learned internal representation mediating both comprehension and production, and in which comprehension provides production with error feedback via a learned articulatory–acoustic forward model. An implementation of the framework, in the form of a discrete-time simple recurrent network, learned to comprehend, imitate, and intentionally name a corpus of 400 monosyllabic words. Moreover, the speech errors produced by the network showed similar tendencies as those of young children. Although only a first step, the results suggest that the approach may ultimately form the basis for a comprehensive account of phonological development.

ACKNOWLEDGMENTS

This research was supported by the National Institute of Mental Health (Grant MH47566 and the CMU Psychology Department Training Grant on "Individual Differences in Cognition") and the National Science Foundation (Grant 9720348). We thank Marlene Behrmann, Brian MacWhinney, Jay McClelland, and the CMU PDP Research Group for helpful comments and discussions. Correspondence may be directed either to David Plaut (plaut@cmu.edu) or to Chris Kello (kello@cnbc.cmu.edu), Mellon Institute 115—CNBC, Carnegie Mellon University, 4400 Fifth Avenue, Pittsburgh, PA 15213–2683.

REFERENCES

Atal, B. S., Chang, J. J., Mathews, M. V., & Tukey, J. W. (1978). Inversion of articulatory-to-acoustic transformation in the vocal tract by a computer sorting technique. *Journal of the Acoustical Society of America, 63,* 1535–1555.

Bauer, H. (1988). The ethological model of phonetic development: I. *Clinical Lingistics and Phonetics, 2,* 347–380.

Benedict, H. (1979). Early lexical development: Comprehension and production. *Journal of Child Language, 6,* 183–201.

Berko, J., & Brown, R. (1960). Psycholinguistic research methods. In P. H. Mussen (Ed.), *Handbook of research methods in child development* (pp. 517–557). New York: Wiley.

Bernhardt, B. H., & Stemberger, J. P. (1997). *Handbook of phonological development.* New York: Academic Press.

Boysson-Bardies, B. de., & Vihman, M. M. (1991). Adapatation to language: Evidence from babbling of infants according to target language. *Journal of Child Language, 67,* 297–319.

Boysson-Bardies, B. de., Vihman, M. M., Roug-Hellichius, L., Durand, D., Landberg, I., & Arao, F. (1992). Material evidence of infant selection from target language: A cross-linguistic phonetic study. In C. A. Ferguson, L. Menn, & C. Stoel-Gammon (Eds.), *Phonological development: Models, research, implications* (pp. 369–391). Timonium, MD: York Press.

Chauvin, Y. (1988). *Symbol acquisition in humans and neural (PDP) networks.* Unpublished doctoral dissertation, University of California, San Diego.

Davis, B. L., & MacNeilage, P. F. (1995). The articulatory basis of babbling. *Journal of Speech and Hearing Research, 38,* 1199–1211.

Dell, G. S. (1986). A spreading-activation theory of retrieval in sentence production. *Psychological Review, 93,* 283–321.

Dodd, B. (1975). Children's understanding of their own phonological forms. *Quarterly Journal of Experimental Psychology, 27,* 165–173.

Eberhard, K. M., Spivey-Knowlton, M. J., & Tanenhaus, M. K. (1995). Eye movements as a window into real-time spoken language comprehension in natural contexts. *Journal of Psycholinguistic Research, 24,* 409.

Elman, J. L. (1990). Finding structure in time. *Cognitive Science, 14,* 179–211.

Ferguson, C. A., & Farwell, C. B. (1975). Words and sounds in early language acquisition. *Language, 51,* 419–439.

Fry, D. B. (1966). The development of the phonological system in the normal and deaf child. In F. Smith & G. A. Miller (Eds.), *The genesis of language.* Cambridge, MA: MIT Press.

Hinton, G. E. (1989). Connectionist learning procedures. *Artificial Intelligence, 40,* 185–234.

Houde, J. F. (1997). *Sensorimotor adaptation in speech production.* Unpublished doctoral dissertation, Massachusetts Institute of Technology, Department of Brain and Cognitive Sciences, Cambridge.

Ingram, D. (1976). *Phonological disability in children.* London: Edward Arnold.

Jordan, M. I. (1986). Attractor dynamics and parallelism in a connectionist sequential machine. *Proceedings of the 8th Annual Conference of the Cognitive Science Society* (pp. 531–546). Hillsdale, NJ: Lawrence Erlbaum Associates.

Jordan, M. I. (1992). Constrained supervised learning. *Journal of Mathematical Psychology, 36,* 396–425.

Jordan, M. I. (1996). Computational aspects of motor control and motor learning. In H. Heuer & S. Keele (Eds.), *Handbook of perception and action: Motor skills.* New York: Academic Press.

Jordan, M. I., & Rumelhart, D. E. (1992). Forward models: Supervised learning with a distal teacher. *Cognitive Science, 16,* 307–354.

Jusczyk, P. W. (1986). Toward a model of the development of speech perception. In J. S. Perkell & D. H. Klatt (Eds.), *Invariance and variability in speech processes.* Hillsdale, NJ: Lawrence Erlbaum Associates.

Jusczyk, P. W. (1997). *The discovery of spoken language.* Cambridge, MA: MIT Press.

Jusczyk, P. W., Pisoni, D. B., & Mullennix, J. (1992). Some consequences of stimulus variability on speech processing by 2-month old infants. *Cognition, 43,* 253–291.

Kent, R. D. (1992). The biology of phonological development. In C. A. Ferguson, L. Menn, & C. Stoel-Gammon (Eds.), *Phonological development: Models, research, implications* (pp. 65–90). Timonium, MD: York Press.

Kent, R. D., Mitchell, P. R., & Sancier, M. (1991). Evidence and role of rhythmic organization in early vocal development in human infants. In J. Fagard & P. H. Wolff (Eds.), *The development of timing control and temporal organization in coordinated action* (pp. 135–149). Oxford, England: Elsevier Science.

Kučera, H., & Francis, W. N. (1967). *Computational analysis of present-day American English.* Providence, RI: Brown University Press.

Kuhl, P. K. (1983). Perception of auditory equivalence classes for speech in early infancy. *Infant Behavior and Development, 70,* 340–349.

Ladefoged, P. (1993). *A course in phonetics.* Orlando, FL: Harcourt Brace.

Levelt, W. J. M. (1989). *Speaking: From intention to articulation.* Cambridge, MA: MIT Press.

Liberman, A. M. (1996). *Speech: A special code.* Cambridge, MA: MIT Press.

Liberman, A. M., & Mattingly, I. (1985). The motor theory of speech perception revised. *Cognition, 21,* 1–36.

Lieberman, P., & Blumstein, S. E. (1988). *Speech physiology, speech perception, and acoustic phonetics.* Cambridge, England: Cambridge University Press.

Lindblom, B. (1992). Phonological units as adaptive emergents of lexical development. In C. A. Ferguson, L. Menn, & C. Stoel-Gammon (Eds.), *Phonological development: Models, research, implications* (pp. 131–163). Timonium, MD: York Press.

Lindblom, B., MacNeilage, P. F., & Studdert-Kennedy, M. (1984). Self-organizing processes and the explanation of phonological universals. In B. Butterworth, B. Comrie, & Ö. Dahl (Eds.), *Explanations for language universals.* Berlin, Germany: Mouton.

Lively, S. E., Pisoni, D. B., & Goldinger, S. D. (1994). Spoken word recognition: Research and theory. In M. A. Gernsbacher (Ed.), *Handbook of psycholinguistics* (pp. 265–301). New York: Academic Press.

Locke, J. L. (1995). Development of the capacity for spoken language. In P. Fletcher & B. MacWhinney (Eds.), *The handbook of child language* (pp. 278–302). Oxford, England: Blackwell.

MacNeilage, P. F. (in press). The frame/content theory of evolution of speech production. *Behavioral and Brain Sciences.*

MacNeilage, P. F., & Davis, B. L. (1990). Acquisition of speech production: The achievement of segmental independence. In W. J. Hardcastle, & A. Marchal (Eds.), *Speech production and speech modelling.* Dordrecht, Netherlands: Kluwer Academic.

Markey, K. L. (1994). *The sensorimotor foundations of phonology: A computational model of early childhood articulatory and phonetic development* (Tech. Rep. CU-CS-752-94). Boulder: University of Colorado, Department of Computer Science.

Marslen-Wilson, W. (1987). Functional parallelism in spoken word-recognition. *Cognition, 25,* 71–102.

Marslen-Wilson, W., & Tyler, L. D. (1980). The temporal structure of spoken language understanding. *Cognition, 8,* 1–71.

McClelland, J. L., & Rumelhart, D. E. (1981). An interactive activation model of context effects in letter perception: Part 1. An account of basic findings. *Psychological Review, 88,* 375–407.

McClelland, J. L., St. John, M., & Taraban, R. (1989). Sentence comprehension: A parallel distributed processing approach. *Language and Cognitive Processes, 4,* 287–335.

Meltzoff, A. N., & Moore, M. K. (1977). Imitation of facial and manual gestures by human neonates. *Science, 198,* 75–78.

Menn, L. (1978). Phonological units in beginning speech. In A. Bell & J. B. Hooper (Eds.), *Syllables and segments.* Amsterdam: North-Holland.

Menn, L. (1983). Development of articulatory, phonetic, and phonological capabilities. In B. Butterworth (Ed.), *Language production* (Vol. 2, pp. 3–50). New York: Academic Press.

Menn, L., & Stoel-Gammon, C. (1995). Phonological development. In P. Fletcher & B. MacWhinney (Eds.), *The handbook of child language* (pp. 335–359). Oxford, England: Blackwell.

Menyuk, P., & Menn, L. (1979). Early strategies for the perception and production of words and sounds. In P. Fletcher & M. Garman (Eds.), *Language acquisition: Studies in first language development.* Cambridge, England: Cambridge University Press.

Morton, J. (1969). The interaction of information in word recognition. *Psychological Review, 76,* 165–178.

Moskowitz, B. A. I. (1973). The acquisition of phonology and syntax: A preliminary study. In K. J. J. Hintikka, J. M. E. Moravcsik, & P. Suppes (Eds.), *Approaches to natural language.* Dordrecht, Netherlands: Reidel.

Nittrouer, S., Studdert-Kennedy, M., & McGowan, R. S. (1989). The emergence of phonetic segments: Evidence from the spectral structure of fricative-vowel syllables spoken by children and adults. *Journal of Speech and Hearing Research, 32,* 120–132.

Oller, D. K. (1980). The emergence of the sounds of speech in infancy. In G. Yenicomshian, J. F. Kavanagh, & C. A. Ferguson (Eds.), *Child phonology 1: Production.* New York: Academic Press.

Pearlmutter, B. A. (1989). Learning state space trajectories in recurrent neural networks. *Neural Computation, 1,* 263–269.

Perkell, J. S., Matthies, M. L., Svirsky, M. A., & Jordan, M. I. (1995). Goal-based speech motor control: A theoretical framework and some preliminary data. *Journal of Phonetics, 23,* 23–35.

Plaut, D. C. (1995). Semantic and associative priming in a distributed attractor network. *Proceedings of the 17th Annual Conference of the Cognitive Science Society* (pp. 37–42). Hillsdale, NJ: Lawrence Erlbaum Associates.

Plaut, D. C. (1997). Structure and function in the lexical system: Insights from distributed models of naming and lexical decision. *Language and Cognitive Processes, 12,* 767–808.

Plaut, D. C., & Kello, C. T. (1998). *A distributed connectionist approach to phonological development.* Manuscript in preparation.

Plaut, D. C., McClelland, J. L., Seidenberg, M. S., & Patterson, K. (1996). Understanding normal and impaired word reading: Computational principles in quasi-regular domains. *Psychological Review, 103,* 56–115.

Reznick, J. S., & Goldfield, B. A. (1992). Rapid change in lexical development in comprehension and production. *Developmental Psychology, 28,* 406–413.

Roug, L., Landberg, I., & Lundberg, L. J. (1989). Phonetic development in early infancy: A study of four Swedish children during the first eighteen months of life. *Journal of Child Language, 16,* 19–40.

Rumelhart, D. E., Hinton, G. E., & Williams, R. J. (1986). Learning internal representations by error propagation. In D. E. Rumelhart, J. L. McClelland, & the PDP Research Group (Eds.), *Parallel distributed processing: Explorations in the microstructure of cognition. Volume 1: Foundations* (pp. 318–362). Cambridge, MA: MIT Press.

Sedivy, J. C., Tanenhaus, M. K., & Spivey-Knowlton, M. J. (1995). Integration of visual and linguistic information in spoken language comprehension. *Science, 268,* 1632.

Smith, B. L. (1973). *The acquisition of phonology: A case study.* Cambridge, England: Cambridge University Press.

Snyder, L. S., Bates, E., & Bretherton, I. (1981). Content and context in early lexical development. *Journal of Child Language, 6,* 565–582.

St. John, M. F., & McClelland, J. L. (1990). Learning and applying contextual constraints in sentence comprehension. *Artificial Intelligence, 46,* 217–257.

Stoel-Gammon, C., & Cooper, J. A. (1984). Patterns of early lexical and phonological development. *Journal of Child Language, 11,* 247–271.

Studdert-Kennedy, M. (1987). The phoneme as a perceptomotor structure. In A. Allport, D. MacKay, W. Prinz, & E. Scheere (Eds.), *Language perception and production.* New York: Academic Press.

Studdert-Kennedy, M. (1993). Discovering phonetic function. *Journal of Phonetics, 21,* 147–155.

Thelen, E. (1981). Rhythmical behavior in infancy: An ethological perspective. *Developmental Psychology, 17,* 237–257.

Thelen, E., & Smith, L. B. (1994). *A dynamic systems approach to the development of cognition and action.* Cambridge, MA: MIT Press.

Treiman, R., & Zukowski, A. (1996). Children's sensitivity to syllables, onsets, rimes, and phonemes. *Journal of Experimental Child Psychology, 61,* 193–215.

Van Orden, G. C., & Goldinger, S. D. (1994). Interdependence of form and function in cognitive systems explains perception of printed words. *Journal of Experimental Psychology: Human Perception and Performance, 20,* 1269.

Van Orden, G. C., Pennington, B. F., & Stone, G. O. (1990). Word identification in reading and the promise of subsymbolic psycholinguistics. *Psychological Review, 97,* 488–522.

Vihman, M. M. (1993). Variable paths to early word production. *Journal of Phonetics, 21,* 61–82.

Vihman, M. M. (1996). *Phonological development: The origins of language in the child.* Oxford, England: Blackwell.

Vihman, M. M., Maken, M. A., Miller, R., Simmons, H., & Miller, J. (1985). From babbling to speech: A re-assessment of the continuity issue. *Language, 61,* 397–445.

Vihman, M. M., & Miller, R. (1988). Words and babble at the threshold of lexical acquisition. In M. D. Smith & J. L. Locke (Eds.), *The emergent lexicon: The child's development of a linguistic vocabulary.* New York: Academic Press.

Vihman, M. M., & Velleman, S. L. (1989). Phonological reorganization: A case study. *Language and Speech, 32,* 149–170.

Wagner, K. R. (1985). How much do children say in a day? *Journal of Child Language, 12,* 475–487.

Walley, A. C. (1993). The role of vocabulary development in children's spoken word recognition and segmentation ability. *Developmental Review, 13,* 286–350.

Werner, H., & Kaplan, D. (1984). *Symbol formation: An organismic-developmental approach to language and the expression of thought.* Hillsdale, NJ: Lawrence Erlbaum Associates.

Williams, R. J., & Peng, J. (1990). An efficient gradient-based algorithm for on-line training of recurrent network trajectories. *Neural Computation, 2,* 490–501.

Wolpert, D. M., Ghahramani, Z., & Jordan, M. I. (1995). Forward dynamic models in human motor control: Psychophysical evidence. In G. Tesauro, D. S. Tourtezky, & T. K. Leen (Eds.), *Advances in neural information processing systems* 7 (pp. 43–50). Cambridge, MA: MIT Press.

Chapter 15

The Emergence of Faithfulness

Joseph Paul Stemberger
University of Minnesota

Barbara Handford Bernhardt
University of British Columbia

Any theory of language development, whether emergentist or nativist, must address the child's phonological development. A child's pronunciation of words is often quite different from an adult's, in a way that does not obviously reflect the phonological system of the target adult language, but which makes sense from a cross-linguistic perspective on the phonological systems of adult languages in general. In this chapter, we provide an overview of the phenomena of phonological development and sketch how they can be accounted for within the Optimality Theory variant of Bernhardt and Stemberger (1998). We argue that the main mechanisms within this approach (constraints) are almost certainly emergentist in nature.

This chapter focuses on speech production during the acquisition of meaningful speech rather than on speech perception or the babbling period. We assume that, at least for children with normal hearing, the child's perception of the adult pronunciation is by and large accurate by the time the child begins to produce words. Furthermore, we believe that, in the babbling period, the child learns the basics about that mapping from acoustics to articulation, and we therefore do not discuss issues regarding that developmental process (but we note that those issues are not yet worked out in any coherent fashion).

WHAT NEEDS TO BE ACCOUNTED FOR IN PHONOLOGICAL DEVELOPMENT

Pronunciations of words in early child language development (especially before 30 months, but as late as 5 or 6 years of age for particular aspects of the pronunciation) are frequently very different from the pronunciations of adult speakers of the target language. We would like to stress the great range of variation across individuals. There are few generalizations about phonological development that hold true for all young children learning English, especially generalizations about particular sounds or sequences of sounds. The following examples illustrate just a few possible pronunciations of a few words, based on the patterns reported in the literature for individual children; some of the pronunciations for the final word are hypothetical.

WORD	ADULT PRONUNCIATION	CHILD PRONUNCIATIONS		
pocket	[ˈpʰɑ:kət]	[baː]	[ˈbatə]	[ˈbahə]
		[batʰ]	[ˈbaba]	[ˈgakə]
giraffe	[ʤəˈɹæːf]	[daː]	[datʰ]	[βaː]
		[dəˈwæt]	[ˈʤɪɹEf]	
mailed	[meɪɫd]	[maɪ]	[maʊ]	[mat]
		[meɪjoʊd]	[meɪmoʊd]	[mɛmbəd]

Depending on the complexity of the sounds and sequences of sounds that a word has, the word's pronunciation may be quite similar to the adult pronunciation for almost all children from the beginning, or may at first be unrecognizable (from an adult perspective) for most children. Looking across children, however, there are a number of generalizations that can be drawn.

The most obvious observation is that the child's pronunciation overall is not very faithful to the adult pronunciation, in a way that suggests simplification:

- Classes of speech sounds (e.g., fricatives) may be absent.
- Words may contain fewer phones than the adult pronunciations.
- There may not be any codas.
- There may not be any consonant clusters.
- Possible sequences of phones may be fewer than in adult speech.
- There are often fewer contrasts than in adult speech.

The examples given earlier demonstrate various aspects of the lack of faithfulness. In the word *pocket*, this lowered degree of faithfulness can be reflected in the lack of particular segments, such as word-initial voiceless (aspirated) stops ([b] for /p/) or velars ([t] for /k/ in [batə]), or in reduced syllable *number* ([baː] and [bat^h]), or type (coda-less syllables). Constraints on phone sequences (e.g., if /p/ cannot be followed by /k/ later in the word) can lead to replacement of the /k/ by some other phone ([ˈbahə]) or to the assimilation of one of the phonemes to the other ([ˈbaba] or [ˈgakə]). In the word *giraffe*, which has a weak–strong stress pattern that is divergent from the more typical English strong–weak pattern, the initial unstressed syllable may be deleted ([dat^h]), or the stress may be produced more "regularly" on the first syllable ([ˈdʒɪɹəf]). The word *mailed* shows how sequence constraints can influence output. If the sequence /eɪl/ cannot be produced within a single syllable, the word may be produced as two syllables. If, additionally, the child has a very restricted range of allowable syllable types, the second syllable may be required to have an onset. An onset consonant may be derived by lengthening the glide portion of the diphthong /eɪ/ into the second syllable ([meɪjoʊd]) or by duplicating the word-initial consonant ([meɪmoʊd]).

When a child's phonological system has a limited range of contrasts, there may be an overreliance on *defaults* (patterns that are very frequent). In terms of place of articulation, velar (and even labial) consonants may be replaced by alveolars ([t] for /k/), the most frequent place of articulation in adult languages (e.g., Paradis & Prunet, 1991; Stemberger, 1992). These defaults may be different in different parts of the word (Bernhardt & Stemberger, 1998; Dinnsen, 1996). In terms of stress, words may default to the most frequent pattern of the language: in English, a strong–weak pattern. There is one exception to such reliance on defaults: When one consonant assimilates to another, the typical default is often eliminated and the nondefault appears for both phones in the child's pronunciation (as in *duck* /dʌk/ [gʌk] and *top* /tɑp/ [bap]).

Although child phonology usually shows simplification patterns, occasionally children's productions are more complex than the adult targets. For example, a syllable may be added in order to pronounce a consonant that would otherwise be in a coda or consonant cluster: *book* /bʊk/ [bʊkə] or *play* /pleɪ/ [pəleɪ]. A single consonant may be expanded into a cluster, for example, /d/ showing up as [nt] ([bɛnt] for *bed* /bɛd/, as in Clark & Bowerman, 1986), or /m/ as [mb] in the hypothetical *mailed* [mɛmbəd].

It should also be noted that the child's pronunciation can sometimes be more faithful to the word than the typical pronunciations of adults. Bernhardt and Stemberger (1998) pointed out phonological processes observed in word combinations in adult speech (e.g., *want you* [wɑntʃuː]) that may be absent in a child's speech; the child faithfully produces the consonants (as in [wɑntjuː]). However, greater faithfulness than in adult speech is the exception, not the rule.

Finally, although children's productions often differ from the adult targets, the phenomena that are observed are strikingly similar to the phenomena of adult phonology. Restrictions on children's speech (e.g., the lack of codas) are often common in adult languages. Further, the child's "repairs" (that change the pronunciation so that it obeys the observed restrictions) are often found in (nontarget) adult languages, in combinations of morphemes or words. These repairs also often resemble the sorts of changes in pronunciation that occur historically. By and large, there is very little about the child's pronunciation that is found only in child language. (See Stemberger, 1996, for discussion of the few characteristics that are restricted to child language.)

Over time, the child's pronunciation changes to become more and more faithful to the adult pronunciations. Most of these developmental changes are pure improvements; the pronunciations of all words become closer to the adult targets or remain unchanged. In a minority of cases (perhaps no more than 5 or 10 instances across a child's entire phonological development), the pronunciations of at least some words become less faithful to (some aspect of) the adult pronunciations than had earlier been the case. This is commonly called *u-shaped learning*, but in the child phonology literature is more often referred to as *regression*. Most regressions involve some form of trade-off: one aspect of the pronunciation improves, while another aspect deteriorates. For our purposes here, we distinguish between two common types of regression: correlated changes versus independent changes. In correlated changes, a regression occurs that is related to a change elsewhere in the child's phonological system, as in the following example:

balloon	[buːn]	>	[bəluːn]
black	[bæk]	>	[bəlæk]

At both time points, the child lacks consonant clusters such as /bl/. At the earlier point, the child simplifies the cluster to a single consonant [b]; the resulting pronunciation is unfaithful to the number of consonants in the word, but is faithful to the number of vowels. At this point, the child never produces word-initial unstressed syllables. At the later point, the child now produces initial unstressed syllables. This allows a new pronunciation of /bl/ as [bəl]; this is more faithful to the consonants of the adult target, but less faithful to the syllable structure of the word (a trade-off). However, regressions can also be independent of any other change in the child's system, as in the following:

balloon	[bəluːn]	>	[bəluːn]		
black	[bæk]	>	[bæk]	>	[bəlæk]

Here, initial unstressed syllables appear long before the child begins to produce /bl/ with an epenthetic unstressed vowel. This is the same trade-off regression as in the correlated change, but it does not reflect any other changes in the child's system. We distinguish between the two types of regression because some approaches to learning (Tesar & Smolensky, 1995) can account only for correlated regressions, as we discuss later.

Much research in the developmental literature has paid minimal attention to facts of phonological development, even when they are particularly relevant. In the examples given previously, we included the [mɛmbəd] pronunciation of *mailed* because this has been the subject of discussion in the literature. The connectionist past-tense learning model of Rumelhart and McClelland (1986) produced *mailed* as [mɛmbəld]. Pinker and Prince (1988) characterized that pronunciation (and the pronunciations of three other words) as "grossly bizarre" (p. 124) and "quite removed from the confusions we might expect people to make" (p. 125). In fact, people (at least when they are children) may produce such forms. The fact that the Rumelhart and McClelland (1986) model produced such forms suggests that it is not too far removed from reality (rather than the reverse), although of course it is a problem for the model if the system cannot progress from those forms toward the adult target. In order to evaluate models of development, we must take phonological development seriously, and any adequate model must be able to handle the types of phenomena sketched earlier. An adequate model must especially be able to account for the extreme variability across children. It must also explain where the following come from: elements, constraints, and defaults. Such theories are still under construction, and in the next section we outline the theory and approach we take to account for the data and phenomena of child phonology.

OPTIMALITY THEORY (OT)

The approach that we take here is a variant of Optimality Theory, originally developed by Prince and Smolensky (1993). We follow the version of the theory presented in Bernhardt and Stemberger (1998). Unlike most versions of OT, our version uses transparent terms, has fewer constraints, and takes into account what is known about human cognition. We believe that the concepts employed by a theory must be justified; to this end, we try to provide a motivation for all constraints. OT is in many ways a fusion between earlier linguistic theories and (local) connectionist models. Our version falls closer to the connectionist end of the continuum, because we deal with activation levels and their consequences for the system.

In our view, OT is a high-level description of the language system, which also could be described at a more detailed level using a connectionist model. We feel that it is of value to work at the higher level at this time for a number of reasons. First, the theory allows us to pinpoint particular types of information that seem to be relevant for a given phenomenon. This can guide the construction of lower-level models, in that modelers need to be careful to include the appropriate information in some form. Second, the theory allows humans to examine, systematize, and explain data without doing simulations. This is of practical value. Clinical applications of any theory that requires computer simulation are still minimal. In our view, OT offers a useful tool for exploring language in general and language acquisition in particular, thus setting up possibilities for clinical application. No theory is of lasting value, but while examining data within the framework of the theory, new insights into the data emerge.

The basis of OT is the use of *constraints* rather than rules. Rules within language are procedures that construct representations and alter them in particular ways. Constraints, in contrast, are limitations on what is possible in a system. Constraints can also lead to the alteration of a representation such that information is lost or added. From a cognitive–psychological perspective, however, the mechanisms are quite different. We return to the relation between rules and constraints shortly.

Within an OT approach to speech production, the pronunciation of a word is determined solely by constraints, interacting with the "input representation" (the "underlying form" that is stored in long-term memory). Constraints fall into two basic subtypes:

(1) Most constraints are purely constraints on output. They can be paraphrased in prose as generalizations such as the following:

"There are no codas."

"Nothing may be [C-Dorsal]." (No "dorsal" consonants; i.e., no [k], [g], [ŋ], [x], [ɣ])

If the speaker obeys an output constraint, then a particular element or structure either cannot be present in the output (the actual pronunciation) or must be present in the output.

(2) Some constraints do not address just the output, but rather the relation between the input and the output. These are known as faithfulness constraints. There are basically three aspects to faithfulness:

"Don't delete anything."

"Don't insert anything."

"Don't change the order of anything."

There is a delicate balance between faithfulness constraints and output constraints. Faithfulness constraints tend to maintain distinctions between different lexical items, whereas output constraints reduce the number of possible contrasts between words. Indeed, no speaker can obey both faithfulness constraints and output constraints (unless all input representations already obey all relevant output constraints; but no adult language quite reaches that state, and all children are far away from that state).

This leads us to another important characteristic of OT: Constraints can be violated. Speakers do not necessarily abide by a given constraint at all times. Another constraint may force a speaker to violate the first constraint. For example, the constraint against coda consonants is violated in the word *cat* /kæt/; faithfulness to the /t/ forces the coda to be produced. However, the constraint against codas may show up in a more subtle form: in some particular set of circumstances (such as unstressed syllables), codas may be disallowed. All speakers of all languages have the same set of constraints, but not all constraints are important enough to affect the output. The importance of a constraint is reflected in its *ranking*: high-ranked constraints are highly constraining; low-ranked constraints are less constraining and are overridden by high-ranked constraints.

Some versions of OT (e.g., McCarthy & Prince, 1995; Prince & Smolensky, 1993) presuppose a single ranking of all constraints, with a strict dominance between all constraints. Constraint A is always ranked higher than Constraint B, in all circumstances. Further, one violation of Constraint A is always more important than violations of Constraint B, whether Constraint B is violated once or 10 times. In our view, both of these characteristics are unimportant parts of the theory that significantly contribute to the complexity and awkwardness of the theory. They can be abandoned without any great consequences. However, we note that the analyses that we present can easily be translated over into a theory that has these characteristics, as long as one is willing to multiply the number of constraints in the system greatly and to make use of constraints with no obvious functionality. Because our interests lie with human cognition, we assume that the ranking of constraints is more flexible (and is correlated with activation levels; see subsequent sections).

One difference between rules and constraints (at least, as usually practiced within OT) is that constraints are less complex. OT unpacks rules and distributes them across a set of simple constraints (much as connectionist models take the concepts of symbolic models, such as words, and distribute them across a set of simple units). As in connectionist models, complex behavior is not encoded directly into the units (the constraints), but rather arises though the interaction of many simple units. Consider the phenomenon of Final Devoicing, wherein obstruent consonants are always voiceless at the end of a syllable (as in Slovenian *voz* 'wagon (nom. sg.)' [vos] vs. *voza*' wagon (gen. sg.)' [voza]). A typical statement of a rule would be the following:

$$[-\text{sonorant}] \rightarrow [-\text{voiced}] / \_\_\_ {}_{\sigma}]$$

This is a procedure that identifies all obstruents in codas, and alters them so that they are voiceless. In OT, this would translate into the following:

(1) There is no [+voiced] in codas.
(2) Underlying [+voiced] survives.
(3) PRIORITY: Obey (1), violate (2).

A rule can be viewed as a set of (at least partially conflicting) constraints, along with a statement about which constraints are obeyed and which are violated. By unpacking the rule, however, the overall dynamics of the system is changed, and we end up with a system that has significantly less power. In a rule-based system, each rule has an independent token of a constraint, which can behave in a way that is entirely unrelated to the way that other tokens of the constraint behave. This means that Constraint A can be ranked higher than Constraint B in one rule, but that Constraint B can be ranked higher than Constraint A in another rule. In OT, in contrast, there is only one token of each constraint, and only one ranking that is allowed for the whole phonological system. As a result, there are sets of rules that in principle could not easily be translated into OT.

By unpacking rules, we also allow fairly easily for all constraints to be satisfied simultaneously. Although rules do not require lengthy serial derivations, in practice linguistic theories made extensive use of such seriality. With a mathematical model that makes no pretensions toward cognitive–psychological reality, massive seriality is fine. However, within actual human beings, massive seriality is a problem. Touretzky (1986) pointed out that there is a "100-step problem" in neural netware: Given typical times needed to perform actions or to perceive events, there can be no more than about 100 serial steps in processing. Linguistic theories such as that of Chomsky and Halle (1968) and Kiparsky (1982) in principle can never be implemented within a human brain, without changing the most basic characteristics of the theory. With simultaneous constraint satisfaction, as in OT, seriality is much reduced. OT thus allows for a symbolic theory that resolves the 100-step problem. This makes it a much more desirable theory than most alternative linguistic theories.

There are things that are lost in OT, however. These are, interestingly, generally the same things that are lost in connectionist models. (a) Clarity and simplicity of description is lost. It can be difficult to follow all the interactions of constraints needed to describe a complex pattern, even though a rule would be simple to understand. (b) Convenience is lost. In rule-based systems, every rule is in theory independent of every other rule, and it is possible to work on just a small portion of the phonological system. In OT, however, every constraint in theory interacts with every other constraint. In order to work on one phenomenon, it is often necessary to develop a picture of a much larger portion of the phonological system. Whereas the researcher may have more confidence that the final analysis is a more accurate description of a given phonological system, it certainly places a greater burden on the researcher. (c) OT as we have described it is simply not powerful enough. If rules are unpacked into a simple set of constraints (with one token of each constraint in one fixed ranking), then it becomes impossible to describe some patterns that in fact occur. For example, consider again Final Devoicing. There are three relevant constraints that we address here (but additional possibilities also exist): (a) Underlying [+voiced] features must be present in the output: Survived(+voiced); (b) No vowels may be inserted: Not(V-Root). (Actually, this constraint rules out all vowels, unless they are supported by other constraints, such as the faithfulness constraint Survived(V-Root).); (c) The feature [+voiced] is not allowed in outputs: Not(+voiced). There are three functionally different rankings of these constraints; the optimal output is determined by which constraint is ranked lowest. We show the different rankings in a visual display that we call a *constraint table* (but which is called a *tableau* elsewhere in the literature). The input form is given in the upper left cell of the table. Possible output candidates (pronunciations) are given in the top row. Relevant constraints are listed in the left-most cell of lower rows. If a given output candidate violates a given constraint, an asterisk is placed in the appropriate cell. If that violation is "fatal" (because it involves a high-ranked constraint that cannot be violated), an exclamation point is placed after the asterisk, and a special border is placed around the cell. Cells in lower rows are then lightly shaded (10%), to denote that violations within those cells are not important. The optimal output candidate (that violates only low-ranked constraints) is also given a special border to draw attention to it. The following constraint table derives the (correct) pronunciation [bɛd] from *bed* /bɛd/:

/bɛd/	bɛd	bɛt	bɛdə
Survived(+voiced)		*!	
Not(V-Root)			*!
Not(+voiced)	*		

Not(+voiced) is low-ranked relative to faithfulness constraints that cause [+voiced] to survive and prevent the insertion of a vowel (Not(V-Root)). This is the constraint ranking that allows the faithful production of the word, without alteration. If the lowest-ranked constraint is Survived(+voiced), however, then it is more optimal to delete the feature [+voiced], and the /d/ is produced as voiceless [t].

/bɛd/	bɛd	☞ bɛt	bɛdə
Not(V-Root)			*!
Not(+voiced)	*!		
Survived(+voiced)		*	

This is common within many adult languages and is also frequently observed in the speech of young children learning English.

Alternatively, if the constraint against inserting a vowel is lowest ranked, then a final vowel can be inserted. The [+voiced] does not appear in a coda, and thus does not violate Not(+voiced).

/bɛd/	bɛd	bɛt	☞ bɛdə
Survived(+voiced)		*!	
Not(+voiced)	*!		
Not(V-Root)			*

This analysis, however, leads to a ranking paradox. As discussed earlier, there is supposed to be a single ranking of each constraint, but this is clearly not the case here. In onsets (as with the /b/ in *bed*), [+voiced] survives, implying the ranking:

Survived(+voiced) » Not(+voiced)

When there is Final Devoicing in a coda, however, [+voiced] is deleted, implying the ranking:

Not(+voiced) » Survived(+voiced)

The rankings are different in different positions of the syllable. It is not possible to make a single generalization about the survival of the feature [+voiced] using a single set of simple constraints in a single ranking. OT must be made more complex in some way. There are two ways in which this can be accomplished: allow for more complex constraints, or allow for multiple rankings of the same constraints.

Different types of complex constraints might be posited. For example, there could be multiple tokens of each constraint, with one token holding on onsets, one token holding on codas, and so forth:

$\text{Survived}_{\text{Onset}}$(+voiced)
$\text{Survived}_{\text{Coda}}$(+voiced)

If $\text{Survived}_{\text{Onset}}$ is ranked higher than Not, then voicing survives in the onset consonant. If $\text{Survived}_{\text{Coda}}$ is ranked lower than Not, then [+voiced] is not allowed in a coda, and the feature can delete. By having two slightly different tokens of the same constraint, we allow for two different rankings, and thus can handle the complexity of the observed pattern. Alternatively, a special constraint can be created that conjoins two simple constraints (Smolensky, 1997):

Not(Coda)&Not(+voiced)

This conjoined constraint is violated only if both component constraints are violated at a single location in the output form. In the word *bed*, the /b/ does not violate Not(Coda) and thus does not violate the conjoined constraint; [+voiced] /b/ is thus allowed in the output. The /d/, however, does violate Not(Coda), and consequently the [+voiced] feature is disallowed and deleted. There is a drawback to both of these alternatives, however. One of the crucial goals of the theory is to unpack rules into simple constraints. These alternatives constitute a retreat back toward rules, by packaging independent tokens of two constraints together as a complex constraint. OT is maintained, but at the cost of abandoning a central part of the theory. We feel that that part of the theory is a good one and should not be abandoned casually.

The second resolution of this problem posits multiple constraint rankings. There may be different constraint rankings in different parts of the syllable or word. In the worst case, we could simply stipulate the rankings in different positions in the word, but we do not feel that that would be explanatory or interesting. It is far better if the different rankings can be derived from an independent characteristic of onsets and codas. Bernhardt and Stemberger (1998) argued that the rankings reflect different levels of activation in different parts of the syllable or word, as established by research within psycholinguistics. We return to this later following a discussion of the origin of constraints, a central concern for this chapter.

UNIVERSALITY AND THE ORIGIN OF CONSTRAINTS AND CONSTRAINT RANKINGS

Linguistic theories most often emphasize characteristics of language that are universal for all (adult) human languages. It is most often assumed that the elements of phonology (features) and structures (segments, syllables, feet, etc.) are universal: that there is a single set of features, defined identically for all languages. In OT, it is assumed that all basic constraints are universal and are present in all languages (whether an effect can be observed or not). Linguists often talk as if universality entails a nativist approach to language. However, the assumption of nativism most often ends with an assertion of nativism. There are no sophisticated arguments for phonology arguing that a nativist approach is necessary. One often hears the complaint that there is as yet no completely explicit full account of phonological universals from an emergentist perspective, but that is also true of the nativist perspective. We argue here (see also Bernhardt & Stemberger, 1998; Stemberger, 1996) that a nativist account of phonological constraints is extremely unlikely, from the perspective of evolutionary biology. Anyone wishing to take a nativist approach must present an explicit account of how an innate set of phonological constraints could have become universal among human beings. We are skeptical that a satisfactory nativist account is currently possible.

There is some indication that features at least are not strictly universal. This is reflected in debates within linguistic theory about the best set of features to use. The feature [+continuant] is one of the more notable points of debate. There are easily three possible competing versions of this feature (where most phonologists would presuppose that only a single version should ever be used):

[+continuant]: There is continuous airflow
- (a) Through the oral cavity
- (b) Through the oral cavity, over the center of the tongue
- (c) Through the vocal tract

The question of which version is the real one should affect the way particular classes of sounds behave.

Consider first version (a) versus version (b). With version (a), the lateral /l/ is [+continuant], because there is continuous airflow through the oral cavity. However, unlike most sounds with oral airflow, laterals direct air around the sides of the tongue, not over the midline. With version (b), that difference in airflow is recognized, and /l/ is [−continuant]. There are languages in which /l/ patterns with stops and nasals, suggesting that they are [−continuant]. In other languages, however, /l/ patterns with trills and glides, which are [+continuant]. Bernhardt and Stemberger (1998) concluded that /l/ most commonly acts like fricatives and glides in language acquisition, rather than like stops and nasals. If either version (a) or version (b) is assumed to be universal, there will be patterns in some languages (and some children) that will be puzzling and hard to explain. Perhaps some languages (and some children) use version (a), but other languages (and children) use version (b).

Now consider version (c) versus versions (a) and (b). With versions (a) and (b), fricatives (/s/, /f/, etc.) are [+continuant] but nasals (/n/, /m/, etc.) are [−continuant]; fricatives and nasals have no manner of articulation features in common. This means that fricatives and nasals are quite dissimilar and should rarely pattern together or interact, in adult languages or in phonological development. Bernhardt and Stemberger (1998) noted that this is often the case. When fricatives or nasals are impossible in a child's system, they are most often replaced by stops and rarely replace one another. Assimilations of manner between fricatives and nasals are uncommon across children. It works well to assume version (a) or (b) for most children. However, there are (rare) reports of children who substitute [n] for /z/, for example, or produce nasals with frication at the nares (a "nasal snort"; Bernhardt & Stemberger, 1998) as substitutions for fricatives. This is difficult to explain if nasals and fricatives have no manner features in common but makes sense with version (c), where any continuous airflow through the vocal tract (whether through the oral cavity or through the nasal cavity) defines a phone as [+continuant].

Arguments about features of other speech sounds have also arisen in the literature. Are glides like /w/ and /j/ [−consonantal] or [+consonantal]? Are /h/ and /ʔ/ [−sonorant] or [+sonorant]? Are alveolar trills [+anterior] or [−anterior]? All of this uncertainty suggests that there may be variability in feature definitions. Different languages (and different children) appear to have slightly different definitions for features. In that case, there is no strict universality of features.

Are constraints universal? This is certainly a possibility. However, universality cannot be proven. If a language shows no overt evidence that a particular constraint exists, that nonevidence is compatible with the presence of a constraint (ranked too low to have any observable effects) or with the absence of that constraint. But let us accept the claim that all constraints are universal. Universality does not have to derive from innateness. It may instead derive from the universality of other characteristics of human beings: vocal tract design, perceptual systems, cognitive systems, and aerodynamics. We address this later. To our knowledge, no one has presented an explicit account of how a universal set of constraints could be innate, and we argue here that a nativist account is unlikely and unnecessary. A nativist perspective also has some unpleasant consequences that go against the main thrust of linguistic theory throughout the 20th century.

At the turn of the last century, linguists were forced to address the issue of whether some languages were inferior to others. It was popularly held that Indo-European languages like English and French were inherently superior to indigenous languages of other continents. Boaz (1911) addressed this issue and argued that all languages were inherently equal.

(He also argued against the version of nativism that was current at the time, which held that differences between languages were innate. This is different from the currently popular version of nativism, which holds that the similarities between languages are innate.) Linguists have taken the inherent equality of languages as an important part of their worldview for most of this century. Unfortunately, a nativist view of constraints seems to lead us back to the notions of the 19th century: Some languages are inferior (from the standpoint of communication and of biology) to other languages. It is unclear how the set of constraints that we must deal with in phonology could be universal without an assumption of the basic inferiority of some languages. Our argument has several parts.

First, most constraints appear to make sense from a functional point of view. Faithfulness constraints, if strictly enforced, would lead to a single pronunciation for a given morpheme in all combinations of morphemes and words, and would never allow two morphemes with different representations in long-term memory to be pronounced identically in the output. This would clearly facilitate and simplify lexical access, reducing ambiguity and giving a stable acoustic form for a given morpheme that could be used directly to access that item from memory. Archangeli and Pulleyblank (1994), Hayes (1996), and Bernhardt and Stemberger (1998) argued that all output constraints may make sense from a functional perspective. Archangeli and Pulleyblank (1994) devoted an entire book to the feature [ATR] (Advanced Tongue Root), arguing that because it is phonetically difficult to advance the tongue root when producing low back vowels, [+ATR] low back vowels are ruled out by high-ranked constraints in most languages. They also argued that it is difficult to produce high vowels without advancing the tongue root (for mechanical reasons), with the result that [–ATR] high vowels are ruled out by high-ranked constraints in most languages. Although arbitrary and difficult-to-explain constraints are sometimes posited (e.g., Generalized Alignment; McCarthy & Prince, 1993), most constraints make sense from a functional perspective. If all or most constraints are functional this must be taken into account in arguments about nativism.

Most arguments that language is innate are based on the claim that the phenomena being discussed are arbitrary (see Pinker & Bloom, 1990). If a characteristic makes no sense from a functional perspective, then there seems to be little reason why it would be present in all human languages, unless it were innate. This sort of argument for nativism cannot hold if the constraints are all or mostly functional. If they are functional, the argument for nativism becomes more complex, as it must be shown that the functionality is not sufficient to lead to the characteristic being universal in all human languages without innateness.

If all or most constraints make sense from a functionalist perspective, there are only two possible ways to account for that universality. The first explanation is to assume that the functionality of the constraints is accidental. Purely by accident, as these constraints arose through random mutations, almost all of the constraints turned out to be functional; but that functionality was an accident and did not affect the origin or spread of those constraints throughout the species. Such an accident seems extremely unlikely and is not worth pursuing.

The only alternative is to assume that the functionality derives from natural selection. All organisms have large numbers of functionally useful characteristics, and the literature on evolutionary biology is filled with arguments of how that functionality could result in the spreading of a characteristic throughout a population. Basically, an individual with the functional characteristic is at an advantage in terms of reproductive fitness and is more likely to have offspring (or is likely to have more offspring); individuals with the functional characteristic out-reproduce individuals without that characteristic. In relation to characteristics of language, then, individuals with a particular constraint would have greater reproductive fitness than individuals who have no relevant constraint or who have the opposite constraint.

With that background in mind, consider the following constraint:

NotCo-occurring(+sonorant,–voiced): Sonorants must be voiced.

Sonorants (vowels, glides, liquids, and nasals) are voiced in most languages. Even in languages in which they can be voiceless, most sonorants are in fact voiced. Why would this constraint be universal, from a nativist perspective? Presumably, voiceless sonorants would have to interfere with communication. One could perhaps stretch one's imagination to the point of considering that individuals using voiceless vowels might not be heard when shouting about danger and therefore might be less likely to survive. With fewer of them to produce offspring, the language might die out. Such languages would be inferior for the purposes of communication, with biological consequences.

However, there are languages that have voiceless sonorants in addition to voiced ones:

[sɯ̥ʃi]	'sushi'	(Japanese)
[m̥ɪ̥t^{h}ɪg]	'tree'	(Ojibwe)

If having voiceless sonorants impairs the communicative efficiency of a language, then that must hold true for languages such as Japanese and Ojibwe, which are consequently inferior languages. It is hard to imagine that this is the case. The "distance" between specific language phenomena and reproductive fitness is very far, and thus the implementation of a nativist account is very difficult in real terms. Anyone who wants to maintain that constraints are innate needs to work out a plausible evolutionary account of how functional constraints became universal.

There is a subargument that is also seen in the arguments about the innateness of language. We refer to this as "the problem of being high ability." The argument runs that if a speaker is capable of doing everything, the language system would be impossible for some reason. Chomsky (see Piatelli-Palmarini, 1980) used this argument for syntax. He maintained that a learner never gets enough evidence for the particular patterns that hold true of a language. In a language designed for high-ability speakers, in which the patterns that are possible are arbitrarily unrelated to the patterns used by other languages, a learner cannot acquire those patterns uniquely; the limited data that a learner is exposed to are too ambiguous and could reflect many different underlying rules. There is nothing wrong with such systems from a perceptual or production point of view but only from the perspective of learning.

Superficially similar arguments involving phonology are actually of a very different nature, due to the differences between phonology and syntax. In syntax, sentences are often produced that have never been produced before, and it is often assumed that few sentences are memorized as units. In phonology, most words have been produced before, and the sounds of a given morpheme are simply memorized by the speaker. If one word has a voiced sonorant but another has a voiceless sonorant, there is no learning problem; the learner simply memorizes which words have which sound, as an arbitrary characteristic of the word. Thus, any problem that arises from allowing everything is not due to learning, but to some inherent problem with being able to produce both voiced and voiceless obstruents.

One must ask, however, why being high ability should be a problem. What advantage is there to being unable to do everything to which you are exposed? Why should the ability to produce both marked and unmarked segments lead to impaired communication and fewer offspring? This seems unlikely. We return to the problem of being high ability subsequently.

Functionality of Constraints

In the previous section, we discussed the functionality of constraints in relation to universality. We expand the discussion of functionality in this section as a prelude to further discussion on learning. As indicated previously, in our view, all constraints are functionally motivated and would have to exist in any communicative system. The relative rankings, however, are only sometimes functionally motivated; some rankings are random or arbitrary, differing across languages and across children during acquisition.

The primary functions of constraints are communicative (governing the transfer of information from the speaker to the listener) and cognitive (governing the processing of information during speech production), although a few constraints may have a phonetic (articulatory or acoustic) motivation. The rankings of constraints either have communicative functions, or are grounded in phonetics, or are random or arbitrary.

An important part of any communicative system is to allow for the transfer of information from the speaker to the listener. There must be constraints on speech production that reflect the need to communicate information. First, and most important, all information about the lexical item's pronunciation should be expressed phonetically. Given that lexical items have distinct representations in long-term memory, the expression of all lexically idiosyncratic information keeps lexical items distinct, thereby reducing the amount of ambiguity and leading to fewer failures of communication. The more that the system ignores faithfulness and imposes a standard shape on all words, the more ambiguity there will be. There is presumably some limit on ambiguity that can be tolerated. As a result, faithfulness constraints (preventing deletion, insertion, and reordering) must be present and ranked fairly high (for adult speech). It is difficult to imagine any system involving any form of imitation without constraints enforcing faithfulness, and language is no different.

Another constraint on communication is one that reduces redundancy. A given piece of information should (ideally) be expressed only once. We see the effects of this constraint (SinglyExpressed) at many levels in the language system. Bock (1982) argued for it on a semantic–lexical level: A given piece of semantic information is expressed in only one lexical item in the sentence. It is operative in morphology; an affix is generally added only once, so that the plural of the word *dog* is *dog-s*, rather than **dog-s-es*. Phonologically, a given segment is generally produced only once. There is only one /p/ in *apple* (/æpl/), not two (*[pʰapu]), nor is the final /p/ of the word *up* articulated twice ([ˀʌpʰ], not *[ˀʌpʰpʰ].

Bernhardt and Stemberger (1998) and others have pointed out that faithfulness constraints are often initially ranked fairly low. Children learn to reproduce adult speech faithfully only with practice (learning). Bernhardt and Stemberger also noted that children occasionally duplicate information incorrectly, both affixes and phonemes. When such is the casc (uncommonly), they must learn to express elements only once, as in the target. Nativist approaches make no predictions of any sort about faithfulness. All faithfulness constraints could be high ranked, which would be strong evidence for a nativist account. But all faithfulness constraints could alternatively be low ranked (which also never happens) or ranked randomly, so that some faithfulness constraints are ranked high and some are ranked low (the actual state of affairs). Emergentism, on the other hand, makes correct predictions about faithfulness (in which faithfulness constraints are both high ranked and low ranked). Emergentism could be falsified with respect to faithfulness but is not. Nativism makes no predictions and therefore is compatible with the facts; but it cannot be falsified, in principle.

Many linguists have presupposed that constraints should be phonetically motivated (Archangeli & Pulleyblank, 1994; Hayes, 1996). They suggest that ease of articulation is an important consideration: There should be constraints against anything that is articulatorily difficult to produce (and perhaps against things that are perceptually difficult to perceive). For example, voicing is harder to produce in codas, for aerodynamic reasons, and therefore a constraint against voicing within codas is reasonable. However, there is a problem with how this could be learned by a child, in an emergent fashion. If a child has never produced a coda, how does he or she know that voicing is difficult in codas, making repairs (from the outset) that cannot just be low-level failures to voice. As noted earlier, a vowel can be added after the voiced consonants so that it is not final and voicing is easier (*bed* [bɛdə]), or the voiced stop as a whole can be deleted (*bed* [baː]). In order for constraints to emerge from ease of articulation, the child must attempt to produce a very wide range of sounds, and we know that they do not (Locke, 1983; Vihman, 1996). In our opinion, few constraints, if any, exist for articulatory reasons.

It is also possible that constraints exist in order to make perception easier. For example, voicing might be harder to perceive in codas, and thus a constraint would prevent voicing in codas. Again, we do not think that constraints of this sort could emerge during the learning process. A child with normal hearing *can* hear voicing in codas, as can the adults around the child. It does not make sense to argue that a child would eliminate some feature from his or her production of words that he or she can hear, when its elimination causes communication problems with adults.

In our view, the second major motivation for constraints is cognitive, by which we mean "deriving from constraints on information processing." In speech production, there are costs to accessing any information, and the costs vary with the item being accessed. (For example, more resources are needed to access low-frequency words than to access high-frequency words.) For speech production, resources are needed to do the following, and thus there are constraints against them:

- Produce a gesture (Not; Stemberger, 1991, reported frequency effects of phonemes in speech errors)
- Combine two gestures at the same time (NotCo-occurring)
- Combine two gestures in a sequence (NoSequence)
- Immediately repeat a gesture (NotTwice)

- Prolong a gesture (SinglyLinked)
- Interrupt a gesture and return to it later (Uninterrupted)

If the constraint is high ranked, many resources are needed. If the constraint is low ranked, few resources are needed. The optimal pronunciation optimizes the amount of resources needed. In addition, there are effects of primacy and recency, leading a speaker (including young children) to give priority to information early in the word or utterance (Priority(Left)) or late in the word or utterance (Priority(Right)).

Frequency and Activation

If constraints reflect the use of cognitive resources, then the ranking of constraints should be correlated with resource use. If an element requires few resources, constraints against that element should be low ranked. This implies that high-frequency elements and sequences (which require fewer resources) should in general be mastered earlier by children than low-frequency elements and sequences. It also implies that the highest frequency elements should function as defaults once a sufficient degree of learning takes place. In adult English (as in many languages), the following are all of high frequency (beginning even in babbling):

obstruents	(not sonorants)
coronals	(not labials or velars)
voiceless obstruents	
stops	
SW stress	(not WS)

For a great majority of young children, these values act as defaults (Bernhardt & Stemberger, 1998). Sonorant consonants may be replaced by obstruents, but the reverse is less common. Velar and even labial consonants may be replaced by alveolar consonants, but the reverse is uncommon. Obstruents generally devoice, with voicing being less common. Fricatives and nasals may become stops, and the reverse is uncommon across children. Most English-learning children favor initial stress, although an occasional child favors initial unstressed syllables. The majority of children show defaults (which are learned early as targets and then substitute for other elements) that are of high frequency in the target language. This follows easily from an emergentist perspective but is an accident within a nativist perspective.

Other aspects of resource use can be seen in the ranking of constraints. Positions in the word or syllable that are high in activation tend to show higher faithfulness (in both adult and child phonology) than locations that are low in activation. Through decades of work in psycholinguistics (see e.g., Levelt, 1989), we have independent information about word and syllable positions that are high or low in activation:

HIGH:	onset	stressed	word-initial	
LOW:	coda	unstressed	word-final	second position

There is evidence from adult phonology (Alderete et al., 1996) and child phonology (Bernhardt & Stemberger, 1998) that faithfulness is ranked high in those domains that have high activation, but low in those domains that have low activation. For example, children are often unable to produce as wide a range of consonants in word-initial unstressed syllables (as in *balloon* and *giraffe*) as in word-initial stressed syllables; a child may be able to produce the affricate /ʤ/ in stressed syllables (*jet*), but not in unstressed syllables (*giraffe*).

One interesting application of this can be found in consonants in second position in word-initial consonant clusters. Stemberger and Treiman (1986) showed that consonants in second position have higher error rates than consonants in first position, even controlling for the identity of the consonant. They argued that consonants have lower activation levels in second position. In adult English, there are few constraints on sequences of consonants in CVC syllables. However, in CCVC words, there are many constraints restricting the similarity of the second consonant and the final consonant:

CVC:	/pɑp/	/mæn/	/ɹɛɹ/
C<u>C</u>VC:	*/spɑp/	*/smæn/	*/kɹɛɹ/

There are constraints on the repetition of features in consonants, holding across consonants separated by a vowel: NotTwice(Labial), NotTwice(+nasal), and so forth. Faithfulness is ranked high in the first consonant of the word and overrides these constraints, which consequently are violated frequently in adult English. Faithfulness is ranked lower in the second consonant of the word, and hence many features are impossible in that position; faithfulness is overruled by sequence constraints. The correlation between activation levels (which reflect how easy it is to access a given piece of information, in performance models) and the ranking of faithfulness constraints (which reflect how easy it is to output a given piece of lexical information) is predicted in an emergentist approach. It is not predicted in a nativist approach, but can of course be stipulated as an arbitrary characteristic of human language. Again, emergentism makes a correct prediction, whereas nativism makes no prediction at all.

The correlation between activation level and faithfulness (especially with Survived) may also account for more subtle aspects of acquisition. Bernhardt and Stemberger (1998) reported three different types of interactions between different features in the same segment. First, a marginal feature may be possible in some segments, but not in others. If two marginal (especially low-frequency or late-learned) features are present in the same segmental target, both may be deleted from the segment. For example, /f/ may be pronounced as [t] (losing the features [+continuant], as is reasonable if fricatives are impossible in the system, and [Labial]); the loss of the feature [Labial] may be surprising, if [p] is a possible output in the system. In one child that Bernhardt and Stemberger (1998) discussed, [Labial] was only weakly established in codas, and was lost when combined with the impossible feature [+continuant]. Dell (1985) argued that the different features in a segment reinforce each other. It follows that the loss of one feature decreases the activation level of all remaining features, by removing that reinforcing activation. The loss of reinforcing activation to a marginal feature can drop it below a threshold, and the feature may fail to survive. Second, a marginal feature may in general not be possible at all, but reinforcing activation from a strongly established (high-activation) feature may be enough to allow the marginal feature to survive. Consequently, the feature [+nasal] may be possible in combination with the strongly established feature [Labial] (in /m/ as [m]), but not in combination with a weakly established feature [Dorsal] (as in /ŋ/ as [k]). Third, competing output features inhibit each other and thus decrease each other's activation levels. Sometimes the competitors damage each other sufficiently that neither one is produced. This has been observed (but only rarely) in the acquisition of consonant clusters. The child may produce single consonants (with /CV/ as [CV]) but delete both members of a cluster (with /CCV/ as [V]). Such interactions that suggest the effects of activation levels (with reinforcement and competition) are not that common in development but are challenging for a version of OT that does not explicitly link faithfulness and activation levels.

Negative Versus Positive Constraints

One aspect of constraints as described in current versions of OT seems difficult for an emergentist approach. The output constraints that we have been dealing with are generally phrased in a negative fashion: Not(+voiced), Not(C-Dorsal), NotCo-occurring(+voiced,C-Dorsal), and so forth. There are a very large number of constraints, each of which addresses a very specific phonological element. How and why would constraints of that nature (specifically addressing the difficulties inherent with each individual item) simply emerge during development? It seems to us that this is simply not expected.

The problem vanishes, however, if constraints are recast as statements on what is possible (rather than negative constraints on what is impossible):

Possible(+voiced), Possible(+voiced,C-Dorsal), and so forth. (Some constraints such as Survived are already positive constraints, but they function necessarily in competition with negative constraints prohibiting faithfulness.) In an emergentist system, nothing is possible until a learner learns how to produce it. As a result, there will be very few possible outputs at first. In general, faithfulness will be low. This is not just a characteristic of language learning; it holds for the acquisition of any type of skill or knowledge (including dancing, cycling, and chess). Nothing is ruled out because there is something undesirable about being able to produce it. Rather, faithfulness is low until practice builds up the ability to do many things. There is no problem with being high ability, and no advantage to being low ability, but everyone starts out being low ability.

Faithfulness is related to resources in the following way. If many resources are needed, then Survived is ranked low and Not is ranked high. The element is deleted from the word and is never inserted in the word. If an intermediate amount of resources are needed, Survived is ranked high and Not is ranked fairly high. An element is not deleted (and is faithfully produced when it is a part of the word's underlying representation), but too many resources are needed for the element to be inserted where it does not belong. If few resources are needed, Survived is high ranked and Not is low ranked. An element is so easy to produce that it is never deleted when it belongs there and can be inserted even when it does not belong there, if other constraints require the presence of some element in that position.

The Initial State: Variability Across Children

It is still necessary to account for the extreme variability across children. We assume that there is a partially random component to the initial set-up of the system. Different children can have different initial random states. Thus, what is difficult or easy to produce will vary across children. (This is also true in other domains, such as music or chess.) Once learning commences, other factors come into play. High-frequency elements (which have more learning trials or "practice") tend to be learned earlier. For example, Ingram (1989) reviewed the evidence concerning the acquisition of the same speech sound by children learning different languages; specific speech sounds are learned earlier in languages in which they are of high frequency but later in languages in which they are of low frequency. In addition, children learn at different rates, which introduces further individual variation. Children may also have different levels of tolerance for degree of difference from the adult target in their own speech. Some children appear to avoid producing speech sounds until they can be produced accurately (Schwartz & Leonard, 1982), whereas others produce the sounds as best they can. Factors such as these can influence the child's system and lead to considerable variation across children in phonological development.

An interesting issue is why faithfulness is initially so low in a child's early speech. Smolensky (1996) recently addressed this issue. He argued that faithfulness should initially be low ranked, in order for adults to have as few abilities as possible. He further argued that being high ability is quite detrimental for performance. If all outputs were possible, then the *neighborhood densities* (the number of words that are phonologically similar to each other) for words would in general be quite low (with the same number of words as in any actually known language system, but with thousands of times as many neighborhoods, and words distributed across all of those additional neighborhoods). This would lead to less efficient lexical retrieval (because high-density neighborhoods have been shown to facilitate lexical retrieval), which would be harmful for communication.

For this argument to work, the initial low ranking for faithfulness must be innate. (Presumably, earlier humans who started out life with high-ranked faithfulness did less well in life and had fewer children, so that low-ability human beings have prevailed.) We do not believe that it could work within an emergentist perspective. Neighborhood density is always initially low for a child, when only a few words are known. Whether faithfulness is ranked high or low would not affect lexical access, if neighborhoods are sparse anyway. This problem can only matter for the adult system, but must be implemented in the child system. There is no (obvious) emergent way to design the child system to solve problems that do not arise until much later in development. In an emergent system, current problems are resolved, not future ones. As a result, this explanation requires a nativist approach.

Smolensky's (1996) approach has some problems, however. Not all faithfulness constraints are in fact low ranked; some begin high ranked. Exactly how is this restriction implemented? Further, some faithfulness constraints are ranked higher than in adult speech. Whereas adult speakers of North American English convert /t/ into taps between vowels, children often do not:

eated: adult [ˀiːɾEd] child [ˀiːtəd] (cf. *eat* [ˀiːt])

Does Smolensky's hypothesis allow for the fact that faithfulness can be ranked higher for children than for adults? Finally, actual adult systems do not make equal use of all possible neighborhoods; some neighborhoods are filled with large numbers of words, whereas others are sparse or even empty. Even if a high-ability adult could produce any conceivable speech sound or sequence of sounds that is observed in any human language, that does not mean that all such sounds and sequences would occur or be common if they did occur. In adult English, there are high-frequency phonemes ([t], [aɪ], [ɪ]) and low-frequency phonemes ([tʃ], [ɔɪ], [ʊ]). Certain phonemes are rare in word-final position; this is especially true for the coda of an unstressed syllable, where some phonemes ([t] and [n], as in *bucket* and *button*) are common, but others are quite rare ([p] and [d], as in *ketchup*, *naked*, and very few other words). In adult English, faithfulness for /p/ and /d/ is high ranked, but there are nonetheless few words with such phonemes in codas in unstressed syllables. There is no problem with such phonemes when they do occur, but they are rare. It seems unlikely that the low neighborhood densities of words like *ketchup* and *naked* cause communication problems (and lower the reproductive fitness of speakers of English). The low initial ranking of many faithfulness constraints is probably not related to neighborhood densities in adult speech.

Thus, although the high-ability problem may induce a nativist explanation, the high-ability problem in actuality does not appear to be real. There is a simpler and less controversial emergentist account of why faithfulness is initially low ranked. As with all other learned skills, faithfulness starts out low. With practice, people improve at such skills. Language is no different from any other skill in this respect.

Learning Constraint Rankings of the Target Language

Any model of acquisition must be able to account for the fact that children ultimately attain a system that approximates that of the adults from which they learned the language. In OT, the same constraints are involved at all ages. However, children begin with constraint rankings that, as a whole system, are different from those of adults. Some of the constraints may be ranked just as in the target adult language, but other constraints are ranked differently. The improperly ranked constraints must be reranked, in order to achieve the adult system. There are a number of possible approaches to this.

Tesar and Smolensky (1995) argued that constraints can only be reranked lower ("demotion"), never higher ("promotion"). The system can identify which constraints are ranked too high. Some constraints are violated in the target adult pronunciation; if those constraints are ranked too high in the child's system, the pronunciation with those violations is nonoptimal and thus cannot occur. When violations are incorrectly fatal, the constraint is ranked too high and must be reranked lower. Tesar and Smolensky argued that only demotion can provably succeed. It is always possible to recognize that a constraint is ranked too high, because violations are fatal that should not be fatal. However, it is not always possible to identify a constraint that is ranked too low. It is generally the case that an output is compatible with several constraints being ranked too low, but only one of those constraints may be the one that is ranked incorrectly. Faced with this indeterminacy, the system must "guess" which constraint is ranked too low and may choose the wrong one. It can be shown that systems may sometimes fail to settle on the target ranking.

Although this mathematical approach is admirably explicit, it unfortunately rules out certain types of regressions that occur. Earlier, we divided regressions into *correlated regressions* (which cooccur with another change in the system) and *independent regressions* (which do not cooccur with another relevant change).

Correlated regressions can be handled easily through constraint demotion. Consider the example mentioned previously, in which the cluster /bl/ undergoes a trade-off regression, from [b] at Point 1 to [bəl] at Point 2, at the same time that word-initial unstressed syllables appeared in the child's system:

balloon	[buːn]	>	[bəluːn]
black	[bæk]	>	[bəlæk]

Although both consonants are correctly present at Point 2, there is now a vowel error that was not present at Point 1. This correlated regression can derive from the following constraint ranking, with the changes indicated:

Prominent(Foot,Left) Survived(V-Root) NotComplex(Onset)	← Demote to *bottom*
Survived(C-Root)	
Not(V-Root)	
Not(C-Root)	

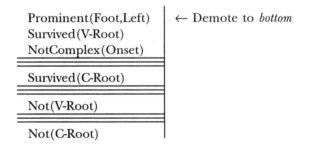

The highest ranked constraint rules out initial unstressed syllables. By reranking it low, initial unstressed syllables become possible. Complex onsets are still impossible, ruling out clusters. However, the relative ranking between Survived(C-Root) and Not(V-Root), which previously made no difference at all, now determines that a vowel will be inserted between the consonants, in preference to the deletion of a consonant. Insertion had been impossible earlier, because initial unstressed syllables were impossible. This is fully an improvement in words with an initial unstressed syllable but is a trade-off regression in words with a consonant cluster. In later learning, NotComplex(Onset) must be reranked lower in order for consonant clusters to appear. Correlated regressions are quite possible even if constraint reranking is limited to demotion.

Independent regressions, however, cannot be handled via constraint demotion alone. Consider the following independent regression:

balloon	[buːn]	>	[bəluːn]		
black	[bæk]	>	[bæk]	>	[bəlæk]

This involves the same changes as noted earlier, except that word-initial unstressed syllables are possible long before the child begins to epenthesize a vowel in consonant clusters. When vowel epenthesis begins, it is not a response to any other general change in the system but relates to the drive for faithfulness to the segments in the target. This happens through the following ranking and reranking:

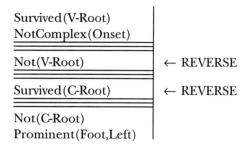

Survived(V-Root) NotComplex(Onset)	
Not(V-Root)	← REVERSE
Survived(C-Root)	← REVERSE
Not(C-Root) Prominent(Foot,Left)	

The problem in this case is that NotComplex(Onset) is ranked too high. Not(V-Root) is also ranked high, because vowels are not inserted randomly. Critically, Survived(C-Root) is ranked too low. If NotComplex(Onset) were to be demoted below Survived(C-Root), the child would accurately produce words with clusters. But this has not yet happened in this case. Instead, vowel epenthesis occurs, allowing production of both the [b] and the [l] of /bl/. Not(V-Root) ends up lower ranked than Survived(C-Root), but there is no obvious and inherent motivation for a demotion that allows epenthesis rather than deletion in response to the complexity constraint. On the other hand, there is motivation for promotion of the faithfulness (Survived) constraint. This promotion is motivated by the need to produce the /l/ of /bl/. Independent regressions of this type can only occur if constraints can be re-ranked higher.

We are unsure as to how constraints are generally reranked. They may always be reranked higher. Although it is not provable that such a learning strategy will converge with the target adult system, it seems that constraint promotion is needed to account for the actual learning of children. We suggest that the typical way that children learn the ranking of constraints is to rerank faithfulness constraints so that faithfulness increases. This can work well in an emergent system using positive constraints. Possible(X) (or Survived(X)) is simply reranked higher and higher until X is possible enough that it appears in the child's pronunciation. The drive toward increasing faithfulness is arguably the main change in a learner's system. Whether it will prove to be the only type of change remains to be seen.

INTERFACING PHONOLOGY AND ARTICULATION

In our approach, we have side-stepped what is undoubtedly one of the most difficult aspects of phonological development. How exactly is the cognitive system affected by how much effort something takes in production? How does articulatory difficulty affect higher level planning of the word? The system is clearly affected at a high level. A difficult-to-produce segment (such as a word-final voiced stop) can be deleted as a unit (as in *bed* [baː]). Such high-level deletion would not be expected at a low level; one would rather expect that the target voiced stop would be produced as a stop (preserving most aspects of the pronunciation) but with poor laryngeal control. Just how is the cognitive system affected by peripheral motor effects?

We do not know the full answer to these questions, but we believe that *coupling* within an interactive system may play some role. It is reasonable to assume that feedback from the periphery is needed to construct and maintain motor programming. Such feedback may extend to higher cognitive levels of planning. In order to plan an output, some feedback from the periphery may be required. If there is too much resistance from the periphery, it may be impossible to achieve the associated cognitive state, so that the system instead settles into a different output state where there is less resistance. There are analogous coupling effects in physical systems. If you attempt to whistle into a large tube in which the volume of air significantly outmasses the lips and the air within the oral cavity, the natural resonances of the tube can interact with the sound source in the oral cavity and prevent the production of those frequencies at which the tube will not resonate. We suggest that something similar may occur in the interaction of the cognitive system and speech production. More research is clearly indicated to determine whether this is feasible. If it is, it undoubtedly plays a role in an emergentist account of phonological development (and of speech production in general).

SUMMARY OF MAIN POINTS

This chapter provided a general overview of phenomena in phonological development within the OT (constraint-based) approach of Bernhardt and Stemberger (1998). We asserted that constraints are functional and that nativist accounts of constraints are very unlikely to be plausible from an evolutionary point of view. The constraints themselves emerge from communicative function and information processing, not from phonetics. The constraint rankings, however, can be random or additionally influenced by phonetic difficulty (primarily in articulation, but also possibly in perception). Faithfulness to the adult target generally begins low ranked, because children possess no innate phonological skills and must learn to do everything. Faithfulness does not start out low ranked because there is something inherently problematic about speakers being high ability and able to produce a wide range of speech sounds and sequences. Faithfulness can be ranked higher in child systems than in the target adult system because of the initial random state of the system. The ranking of faithfulness constraints is correlated with the amount of activation that is present (in general, and in the particular part of the word that is relevant). Change largely involves reranking faithfulness higher (promotion). There are developmental patterns (especially independent regressions) that cannot be accounted for if constraint demotion is the only mechanism for change.

There is as yet no complete account of phonological development that can handle all known effects of the acquisition of phonology. In particular, how the child manages to relate acoustic information with articulatory information is unclear. It is also unclear how peripheral effects on the difficulty of producing a segment can affect high-level cognitive levels that plan output, although coupling between the different systems may be involved. This chapter by Bernhardt and Stemberger (1998) represents a beginning attempt to lay out the phenomena that need to be accounted for within a constraint-based framework, suggesting that an emergentist account of those phenomena is more plausible than a nativist account.

REFERENCES

Alderete, J., Beckman, J., Benue, L., Gnanadesikan, A., McCarthy, J., & Urbanczyk, S. (1996). *Reduplication and segmental umarkedness.* Unpublished manuscript, University of Massachusetts.

Archangeli, D., & Pulleyblank, D. (1994). *Grounded phonology.* Cambridge, MA: MIT Press.

Bernhardt, B. H., & Stemberger, J. P. (1998). *Handbook of phonological development: From the perspective of constraint-based nonlinear phonology.* San Diego, CA: Academic Press.

Boas, F. (1911). *Handbook of American Indian languages* (Bureau of American Ethnology Bulletin 40). Washington, DC: Smithsonian Institute.

Bock, J. K (1982). Towards a cognitive psychology of syntax: Information processing contributions to sentence formulation. *Psychological Review, 89,* 1–47.

Chomsky, N., & Halle, M. (1968). *The sound pattern of English.* Cambridge, MA: MIT Press.

Clark, E. V., & Bowerman, M. (1986). On the acquisition of final voiced stops. In J. A. Fishman, A. Tabouret-Keller, M. Clyne, B. Krishnamurti, & M. Abdulaziz (Eds.), *The Fergusonian impact, Vol. 1: From phonology to society* (pp. 51–68). Amsterdam: Mouton/de-Gruyter.

Dell, G. S. (1985). Positive feedback in hierarchical connectionist models: Applications to language production. *Cognitive Science, 9,* 3–23.

Dinnsen, D. A. (1996). Context effects in the acquisition of fricatives. In B. Bernhardt, J. Gilbert, & D. Ingram (Eds.), *Proceedings of the UBC international conference on phonological acquisition* (pp. 136–148). Somerville, MA: Cascadilla Press.

Hayes, B. (1996, April). *Can optimality theory serve as the medium for a functionally-guided phonology?* Paper presented at the Milwaukee Conference on Linguistics, Milwaukee, WI.

Ingram, D. (1989). *First language acquisition: Method, description, and explanation.* Cambridge, England: Cambridge University Press.

Kiparsky, P. (1982). From cyclic phonology to lexical phonology. In H. van der Hulst & N. Smith (Eds.), *The structure of phonological representations* (Part 1, pp. 130–175). Dordrecht, Netherlands: Foris.

Levelt, W. J. M. (1989). *Speaking: From intention to articulation.* Cambridge, MA: MIT Press.

Locke, J. (1983). *Phonological acquisition and change.* New York: Academic Press.

McCarthy, J., & Prince, A. (1993). Generalized alignment. In G. Booij & J. van Marle (Eds.), *Yearbook of morphology* (pp. 79–153). Dordrecht, Netherlands: Kluwer.

McCarthy, J. J., & Prince, A. S. (1995). Faithfulness and reduplicative identity. In J. Beckman, L. Dickey, & S. Urbanczyk (Eds.), *University of Massachusetts Occasional Papers in Linguistics 18: Papers in Optimality Theory* (pp. 249–384). Amherst, MA: Department of Linguistics.

Paradis, C., & Prunet, J.-F. (1991). Asymmetry and visibility in consonant articulations. In C. Paradis & J.-F. Prunet (Eds.), *The special status of coronals* (pp. 1–28). San Diego, CA: Academic Press.

Piatelli-Palmarini, M. (1980). *Language and learning: The debate between Jean Piaget and Noam Chomsky.* Cambridge, MA: Harvard University Press.

Pinker, S., & Bloom, P. (1990). Natural language and natural selection. *Behavioral & Brain Sciences, 13,* 707–784.

Pinker, S., & Prince, A. (1988). On language and connectionism: Analysis of a parallel distributed processing model of language acquisition. *Cognition, 28,* 73–194.

Prince, A. S., & Smolensky, P. (1993). Optimality theory: Constraint interaction in generative grammar (Rutgers University Cognitive Sciences Center Tech. Rep. 2). Piscataway, NJ: Rutgers University.

Rumelhart, D., & McClelland, J. (1986). On learning the past tenses of English verbs. In D. Rumelhart & J. McClelland (Eds.), *Parallel distributed processing: Explorations in the microstructure of cognition* (Vol. 1, pp. 216–271). Cambridge, MA: Bradford Books.

Schwartz, R. G., & Leonard, L. B. (1982). Do children pick and choose? An examination of phonological selection and avoidance in early lexical acquisition. *Journal of Child Language, 9,* 319–336.

Smolensky, P. (1996). *The initial state and 'richness of the base' in optimality theory* (Tech. Rep. JHU-CogSci-96-4). Baltimore: Johns Hopkins University, Department of Cognitive Science.

Smolensky, P. (1997, May). *Constraint interaction in generative grammar II: Local conjunction.* Paper presented at the Johns Hopkins Optimality Theory Workshop, Baltimore.

Stemberger, J. P. (1991). Apparent anti-frequency effects in language production: The addition bias and phonological underspecification. *Journal of Memory and Language, 30,* 161–185.

Stemberger, J. P. (1992). Vocalic underspecification in English language production. *Language, 68,* 492–524.

Stemberger, J. P. (1996). The scope of the theory: Where does beyond lie? In L. McNair, K. Singer, L. M. Dobrin, & M. M. Aucoin (Eds.), *Papers from the parasession on theory and data in linguistics, CLS 23* (pp. 139–164). Chicago: Chicago Linguistic Society.

Stemberger, J. P., & Treiman, R. (1986). The internal structure of word-initial consonant clusters. *Journal of Memory and Language, 25,* 163–180.

Tesar, B., & Smolensky, P. (1995). The learnability of optimality theory. In R. Aranovich, W. Byrne, S. Preuss, & M. Senturia (Eds.), *Proceedings of the 13th West Coast Conference on Formal Linguistics* (pp. 122–137). Stanford, CA: Center for the Study of Language and Information.

Touretzky, D. S. (1986). BoltzCONS: Reconciling connectionism with the recursive nature of stacks and trees. *Proceedings of the 8th Annual Conference of the Cognitive Science Society.* Hillsdale, NJ: Lawrence Erlbaum Associates.

Vihman, M. M. (1996). *Phonological development: The origins of language in the child.* Cambridge, MA: Basil Blackwell.

Chapter 16

The Emergence of Language From Serial Order and Procedural Memory

Prahlad Gupta
Gary S. Dell
Beckman Institute for Advanced Science & Technology
University of Illinois at Urbana–Champaign

In every spoken language, the words have two fundamental properties.[1] First, they are temporal sequences; in the articulatory domain, a word is a sequence of gestures, and in the auditory domain, a sequence of sounds. Second, the relation between this serially ordered sequence and the word's meaning is arbitrary. Words with similar meaning do not typically have similar forms.

It is a truism that the nature of language has shaped the way that it is learned and processed. It is also generally agreed that the reverse is true; learning and processing constraints have profoundly influenced language. In this chapter, we start with the fact that words are serially ordered temporal sequences arbitrarily related to meaning, and ask how these properties reflect and are reflected in the processing system. Specifically, in the first section, we suggest that some aspects of vocabulary structure can be linked to the fact that words are sequences. Along with this, we will consider the production of words and introduce a simple recurrent network model that relates some speech error phenomena to the sequential nature of words. This account of sequence and speech errors embodies a view in which many aspects of language learning can be understood as proceeding via the gradual, experience-driven adjustment of connection weights between levels of representation. In the second section, we examine parallels between this

[1]We are using the term *word* informally and intuitively. We are not referring to a specific constituent such as the phonological word.

general view of language learning and implicit or procedural memory. In particular, we suggest that the systematic aspects of language learning are continuous with the mechanisms of procedural memory and show that the simple recurrent network model that accounts for speech errors can also account for important phenomena in the domain of procedural memory. In the third section, we situate our speech error model in the cognitive system and situate our discussion of procedural memory more concretely in the context of language. We discuss how word forms can be acquired and associated with arbitrary meanings. We suggest that the seemingly unitary process of learning a new word can be fractionated into two components that rely on two quite different memory systems and learning mechanisms. The discussion centers on the relation between the sequential and arbitrary aspects of words and on the correspondence of these aspects of word learning with the procedural and declarative memory systems. Overall, we propose in this chapter that important aspects of language can be viewed as emerging from serial order and from procedural memory.

WORDS AS TEMPORAL SEQUENCES

Recently, *Scientific American* published a debate between. Stephen Hawking and Roger Penrose on the fate of the universe (Hawking & Penrose, 1996). The article started with an assumption that both debaters accepted: The "big bang," the rapid expansion at the beginning of the universe, and the "big crunch," when everything collapses together again at the end, will likely look very different. The big crunch will not be the big bang in reverse. However, if this is true, there is a puzzle. The laws of physics, as we know them, are symmetric in time. Consequently, there is no explanation for the assumed asymmetry on a cosmological scale. So, why will the end of the universe be different from the beginning? The article did not offer a definitive answer. Nonetheless, it was agreed that something must provide the universe with temporal asymmetry.

The debate in *Scientific American* leads into the first question that we ask: Why are the beginnings of words different from their ends? If we break words down into sequences of phonemes or features, we find several temporal asymmetries in the vocabulary. For example, languages have positional phonotactic constraints. Certain sounds (e.g., /ŋ/ or /ʒ/ in English) cannot begin words, whereas others (e.g., /h/ and many short vowels in English) cannot end them. Furthermore, the constraints on sound combinations differ at the beginning and ends of words (and syllables). The onset–rime organization of syllables is an example. Within a syllable there are many more constraints between the vowel and following (coda) consonants than between the vowel and preceding (onset) consonants. In

English CVC words, for example, the consonant /r/ can precede any vowel, but it cannot follow most vowels (Kessler & Treiman, 1997).

The differences between words' beginnings and ends require us to postulate some temporal asymmetry. Fortunately, in cognitive science, we are not burdened with a theory whose laws are indifferent to time's arrow. Instead, the production or recognition of a sequence is inherently asymmetric because of memory. We remember the past much better than we can predict the future. As we process a sequence we have a better representation of prior context, specifically of elements in the sequence that have already been processed, than we do of subsequent context. On the assumption that representations of context guide our processing, there is reason to expect differences between the beginnings and ends of words.

The sequential asymmetries in the lexicon are reflected in speech production errors. First, consider positional phonotactic constraints. Speech errors are exquisitely sensitive to these constraints. Slips in which a phoneme occurs in a phonotactically illegal position, such as *neck* spoken as *ngeck,* are rare in comparison to cases such as *meck* for *neck,* in which the wrong sound occupies a legal position. Stemberger (1983), for example, found that less than 1% of phonological errors were phonotactically deviant.

Another example of a speech error effect tied to sequence concerns the onset–rime asymmetry. The onset and rime constituents of syllables appear to act as units in errors. Consider the phrase *smell bad,* whose constituent structure is illustrated in Fig. 16.1. One is more likely to see the exchange of the rime constituents /ɛl/ and /æd/ (*smad bell*), or the onsets /sm/ and /b/ (*bell smad*), than exchanges of other contiguous groups of sounds such as /smɛ/ and /bæ/ (*bal smed*).

A final speech error phenomenon linked to sequence is the onset bias. Most phonological speech errors involve the movement or substitution of word-initial consonants. In English, for instance, around 80% of consonant exchanges involve word-initial sounds (Shattuck-Hufnagel, 1987). Although some languages (e.g., Spanish) do not exhibit a word-onset bias, their errors nonetheless have a strong syllable-onset bias (Berg, 1991)

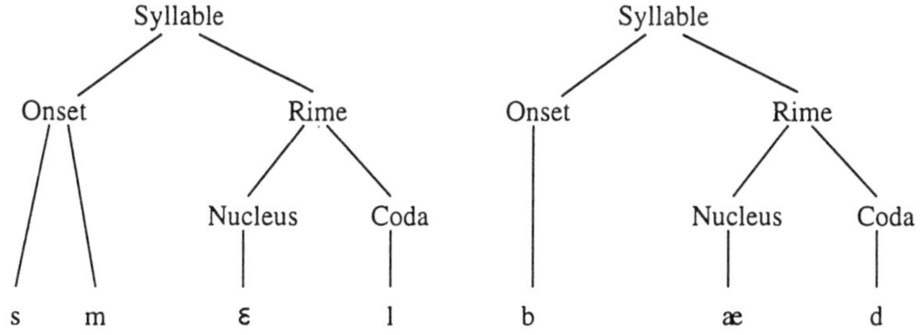

FIG. 16.1. Phonological constituent structure of the example phrase *smell bad.*

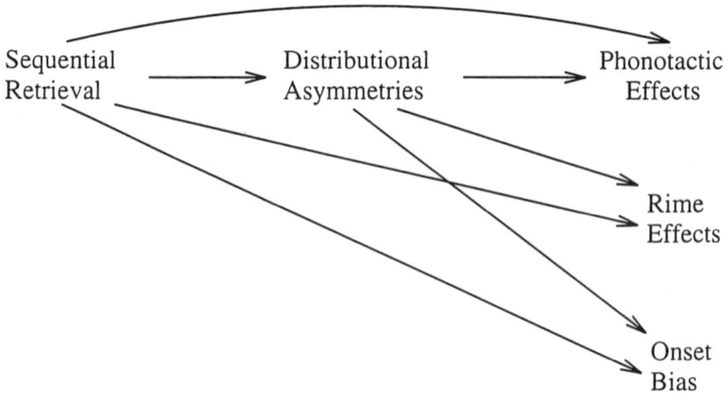

FIG. 16.2. Causal links hypothesized between the sequential nature of words, distributional asymmetries in the lexicon, and speech errors.

Figure 16.2 illustrates the causal links that we hypothesize between these speech error effects and the serially ordered nature of words. The causal structure has two parts. First, we hypothesize that the fact of temporal sequence leads to distributional asymmetries in the vocabulary. Specifically, we claim that the need to retrieve the sounds of words in sequence favors a vocabulary with asymmetries such as an onset–rime organization. Second, we argue that the speech error effects derive jointly from the asymmetries in the vocabulary and directly from the sequential nature of retrieval during production. In the next two subsections, we flesh out these claims, beginning with the link between serial order and the vocabulary.

Vocabulary Structure, Sequential Cueing, and Interference

The fact that words are temporal sequences has consequences for how they are perceived and produced. One consequence is the sequential cueing assumption: Sounds that have already been processed serve as cues that guide subsequent processing. So, after hearing or retrieving the first sounds of a word, the processing system is biased toward later sounds that are consistent with this prior context. Because it emphasizes the constraint imposed by prior context, the sequential cueing assumption is temporally asymmetric. Prior context is hypothesized to be a more powerful cue than subsequent context. We can most definitely see this asymmetry in word recognition, where decades of research have shown that the initial sounds of an acoustic string have a disproportionate impact on the candidate words that are actively considered (Marslen-Wilson & Zwitserlood, 1989).

Sequential cueing also may apply to sound retrieval during production. Sevald and Dell (1994) asked speakers to say word pairs as many times as they could during a 4-sec interval. The word pairs either shared two initial sounds (CAT CAB), one initial sound (CAT CUB), one final sound (CAT BUT), or two final sounds (CAT BAT). The pairs that were similar at the beginning were much harder to recite than those that were similar at the end. The effects were stronger when two sounds were shared rather than one. Figure 16.3 shows the difference in the production time per syllable for the pairs sharing two initial sounds and the pairs sharing two final

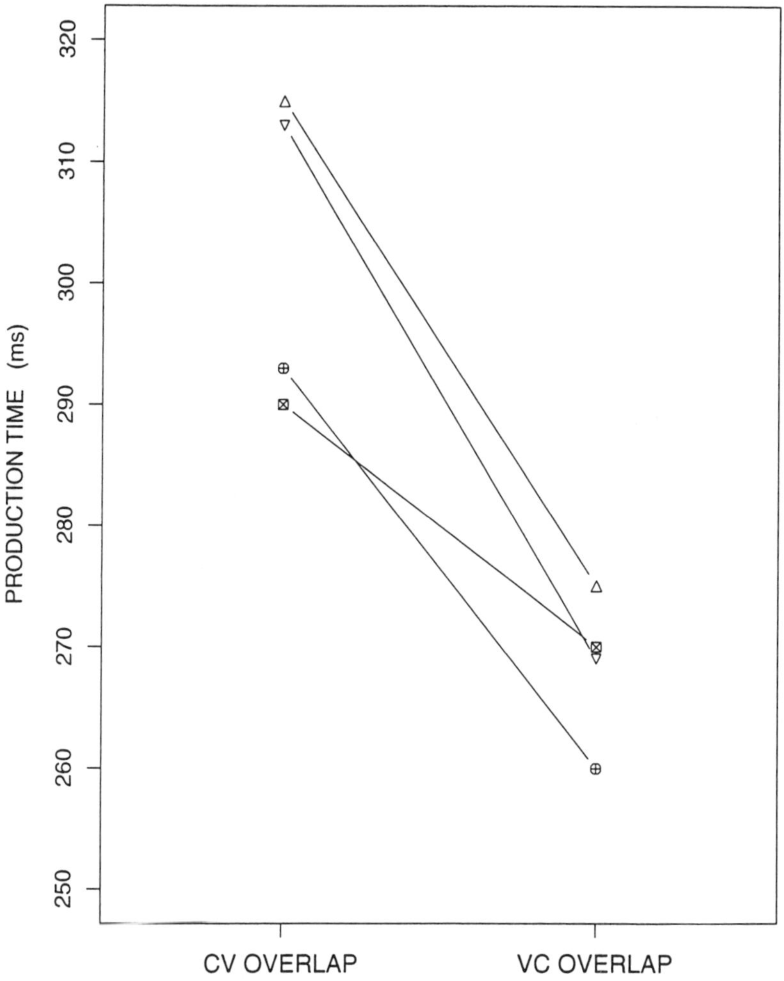

FIG. 16.3. Production time per syllable in repetition of pairs of CVC words that are the same either at the beginning (CV overlap) or at the end (VC overlap). The four lines plot the difference for four different groups of word pairs. Within each group, the word pairs were constructed from a particular set of consonants and vowels. Redrawn from Sevald and Dell (1994).

sounds. The 40-msec difference is quite large considering that the average production time for a syllable is less than 300 msec.

The difficulty that speakers have in reciting word sequences with common initial sounds can be called the *sequential interference effect.* It reflects, according to Sevald and Dell (1994), the greater cueing power of prior over subsequent context. When a speaker is seeking the final sound of the word CAT, for example, the already retrieved /kæ/ acts as a retrieval cue. However, when saying CAT CAB CAT CAB etc., this cue is equally associated with /t/ and /b/ and hence is a source of interference, rather than being a benefit. Interference is much less in evidence, however, when the word pair is similar at the end, as in CAT BAT. Here, the distinguishing sounds, /k/ and /b/, are followed rather than preceded by identical contexts. There is less interference because subsequent within-word context is not represented as strongly as prior context.

The repeated recitation of a word pair can be conceptualized as rapid retrieval from a minilexicon consisting of two words. The results of Sevald and Dell (1994) then suggest that it is easier to produce words from a minilexicon of CAT and BAT than one with CAT and CAB. A related point can be made about word recognition. A CAT-BAT lexicon would be associated with faster recognition than a CAT-CAB one. Generally speaking, on the assumption that words do share sounds, it is best that the common sounds be at the end. Applying these observations to language-sized lexicons suggests that some vocabularies are better than others. A good vocabulary would contain word sets such as CAT, BAT, SAT, RAT, MAT, and so on, whereas a bad one would have sets like CAT, CAN, CAB, CAD, and CAP. To put it another way, a good lexicon's words are not randomly distributed in phonological space. Instead, words should have neighbors sharing sounds at the end rather than neighbors sharing sounds at the beginning.

Real lexicons appear to be organized in exactly this way. Kessler and Treiman (1997) analyzed the sound distribution in the English CVC lexicon, focusing on differences between the ends of words—the VCs—and the beginnings—the CVs. The set of VCs is quite restricted. Several possible VCs, such as /Un/ or /iŋ/, do not occur at all, whereas others such as /æt/ or /ab/ are much more likely than would be expected from the frequency of their constituent sounds. The CVs, in contrast, are largely unrestricted; just about any initial consonant can be followed by any vowel. Moreover, the frequency of a particular CV is predictable from the frequency of the consonant and vowel. A consequence of these facts is that, on average, CVC words have more VC neighbors than CV neighbors.

We suggest that the structure of the vocabulary has been shaped by the sequential nature of words, in particular by the interference that results when competing words share initial sounds. In traditional phonological theory, the distributional asymmetries noted by Kessler and Treiman have been explained by the assumption that syllables have an onset–rime hierarchical organization. Because the VC of a CVC word is a single constituent, there are more restrictions between the vowel and the coda than between the vowel and the onset. These restrictions are expressed by cooccurrence rules that allow or prohibit particular sound combinations in the rime. Our view is different. The onset–rime organization in the vocabulary emerges from sequential factors. So, we would explain the distributional facts by appealing to the processing consequences of sequentiality, rather than by assuming an onset–rime structure. Specifically, we suggest that forces on vocabulary evolution such as the need for rapid retrieval favor redundancy toward the ends of words, leading to neighborhood structures in which a selected set of endings (rimes) recur.[2]

An important aspect of Kessler and Treiman's (1997) analysis favors an account of distributional asymmetries in terms of sequential factors instead of an assumption that syllables possess an onset–rime organization. Kessler and Treiman found that the restrictions on VCs were graded rather than absolute. In addition to nonoccurring VCs such as /Un/, there are several VCs whose frequency in the vocabulary is much less than would be expected. For instance, /ʌl/ occurs in significantly fewer words than would be expected. (See also Frisch, 1996, for other evidence for graded phonotactic constraints and for the influence of sequential factors on these constraints). One might explain the graded nature of the constraints by proposing that the cooccurrence rules only indirectly reflect a universal a priori onset–rime organization. However, it is more parsimonious, in our view, to dispense with the a priori and treat onset–rime structure as emergent from sequential processing. The mechanism is simply that more difficult words, for example, those whose neighbors have common beginnings as opposed to common endings, are less likely to be used and, hence, will tend to drop out across generations. This would presumably be a gradual probabilistic process and so one would expect to see the graded cooccurrence restrictions that Kessler and Treiman found.

Our linkage of distributional asymmetries in the lexicon to factors such as sequential interference is speculative. We have no direct evidence for the hypothesized evolutionary mechanism. However, what is not speculative is the fact that the statistical structure of the word-form lexicon influences perception and production. Sound combinations that are common in the

---

[2]To make this account really work, we would need a mechanism for the sound distributions in single-syllable words to transfer to the syllables of multisyllabic words, because onset–rime organization is about syllables rather than words. PDP models of the production and recognition of phonological sequences (e.g., Plaut & Kello, chap. 14, this volume; Dell et al., 1993) may have such a mechanism based on shared weights, but this remains to be seen because the models have not yet been applied to multisyllabic words.

lexicon are easy to perceive and produce (Levelt & Wheeldon, 1994). In the following section, we turn to the second half of the causal chain presented in Fig. 16.2 and show how the distributional asymmetries can explain the speech error effects.

The Speech-Error Model

The model that we review here (Dell, Juliano, & Govindjee, 1993) is a simple recurrent network model of word-form retrieval. For our purposes, it has three key properties: it retrieves words as sequences of phonological features; it uses prior context to guide the retrieval of the sequence (and hence embodies the sequential cueing assumption); and it is sensitive to the statistical structure of the word-form lexicon through its learning mechanism.

Figure 16.4 shows the architecture. There are four layers of units: input, hidden, output, and context. The input layer represents the word to be spoken as a distributed pattern of activation (1s and 0s). The output consists of a bank of units, one for each of 18 phonological features. Sequences of features are produced by means of recurrent one-to-one connections from the output and hidden layers to the context layer. There were two sets of context units, internal context units, whose activations were copies of the hidden layer's activation on the previous pass through the network, and external context units, whose activations derive analogously from the output units. The context units thus serve as a dynamic memory for prior

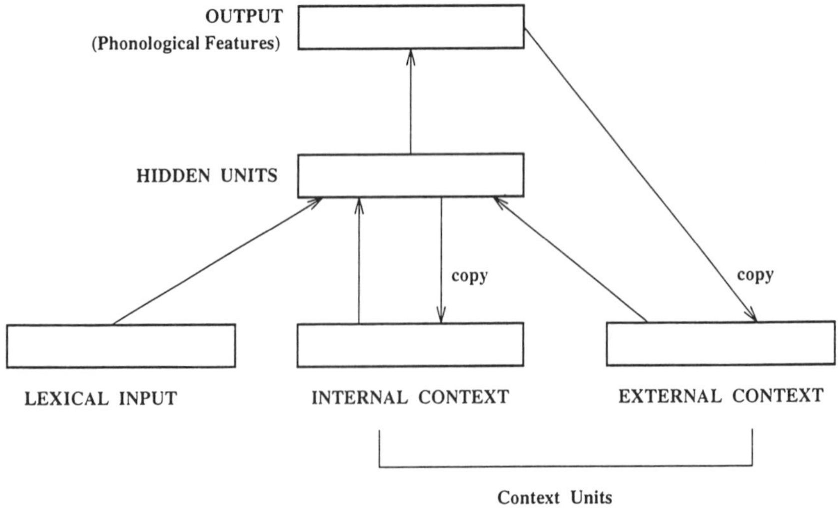

FIG. 16.4. Simple recurrent network model of word-form retrieval and speech errors (redrawn from Dell et al., 1993).

context and act as input along with the static input layer to cue for the appropriate features throughout the production of the word.

Specifically, the production of a word involves the following steps, illustrated here using CAT. The input pattern for CAT is entered on the input units, the internal context units are initialized to zero, and the external context units are set to .5, a pattern that symbolizes a word boundary. Activation then spreads to the output features via the hidden units. The target output is the feature set for the first phoneme, here /k/. To the extent that the output deviates from the target, weights are adjusted by backpropagation (Rumelhart, Hinton, & Williams, 1986). Then the output and hidden layer activations are copied to the external and internal context units, respectively. Hence, after the output of /k/, the context units represent the state of /k/ just having been retrieved, instead of their original state that marked the beginning of the word. This change in the context then allows for the production of /æ/ in the next forward pass through the network. The process continues until the end of the word, the final target being the word boundary pattern. The model was trained by repeatedly presenting short English words (1–3 phonemes), and adjusting the weights until performance was mostly correct.

The modeling goals were to explain certain speech error facts. These included the phonotactic regularity of errors, the tendency for multiphoneme errors to coincide with syllabic constituents such as the rime, and the tendency for errors to occur at the beginnings of words. Earlier, we suggested that these three error effects are related to the sequential nature of words and distributional asymmetries in the lexicon resulting from sequence.

If noise is introduced to the connection weights, the model produces realistic phonological errors, and these errors exhibit the three effects in question. First, the erroneous sequences obey the phonotactic constraints of English. Versions of the model that were trained on representative samples of English words made errors that were phonotactically legal between 90% and 100% of the time. For example, the model might produce *gat* or *cot* instead of *cat* but rarely *ngat* or *ctt*. Second, the model exhibits sensitivity to the rime constituent. Its multiple-phoneme substitution errors are about two or three times more likely to involve rime (VC) constituents (e.g. *bed* slips to *big*) than CV combinations (e.g., bed slips to *mad*). Finally, the model's errors showed the onset effect. Errors involving single consonants involved word onsets more often than other consonants (between 59% and 78% were onsets) even though there were slightly more nononset than onset consonants in the training vocabularies.

Why does the model produce these speech error effects? In general, the model's errors are sensitive to the structure of English words because it is trained on English words. The superimposed weight changes associated with the training set create sequential schemata, pathways in activation space that reflect common sequences of features. When the model makes an error it tends to stick close to those pathways, or move to other well-worn paths in the vicinity. That is why the errors obey phonotactic constraints. The reason that the model's errors sometimes involve rime units is also due to the structure of the training set. When that set mirrors English in having a restricted set of rimes each of which is part of several words, the occurring rimes then become part of the well-worn paths in the model. When output jumps from its target path to another, that path is likely to be one that is frequently taken, that is, one corresponding to a common rime.

The tendency for errors to obey phonotactic constraints and to coincide with rimes arises in the model simply because the model responds directly to the statistics of its training set. Any distributional asymmetries in the training set are reflected in the model's behavior. Hence, these two error phenomena relate to the sequential nature of words only indirectly, through properties of the vocabulary. The third error effect, the onset effect, comes directly from the model's sequential properties. Because the model uses prior context as input, the first sound is more difficult to retrieve than the others. Consequently, there are more errors involving onset consonants. At the beginning of a word, the context units' activation is completely uninformative about the features to be retrieved. The lexical input must be relied on entirely to signal the features of the first phoneme. However, as more and more of the word is retrieved, the context units become more helpful. There is simply greater constraint later on in the word than at the beginning.

In summary, the speech-error model allows us to see how error effects that are associated with the sequential structure of words arise. We claim that any model in this domain must, first, be sensitive to the statistics of the sound patterns in the vocabulary, including patterns that are temporally asymmetric, and second, the model must itself produce output in sequence with an emphasis on the cues provided by prior context. Simple recurrent networks, in general, have both of these properties.

To conclude our discussion of speech errors and sequence, we turn to a new experimental finding that highlights people's abilities to learn sound distributions and how those distributions affect errors.

Learning Sequences of Sounds

As noted previously, the reason why speech errors adhere to phonotactic constraints is, in our view, that these errors reflect experience with the statistical patterns in the vocabulary. However, patterns occur at many levels of generality. For example, one can speak of patterns that are true for the entire language. The facts that /h/ is an onset or /ŋ/ is a coda are true for all of English (and many other languages, for that matter.) There are also patterns that apply only to a subset of words, such as the location of stressed syllables in English verbs. Ultimately, one can speak of "patterns" that are so specific that they apply to single words. For example, CAT is a CVC word with two voiceless stop consonants: /k/ as onset, /t/ as coda, and /æ/ as the vowel.

One can view some speech error effects in terms of very local patterns. The most common phonological speech errors involve the movement of sounds from one syllable or word to another, such as *leading list* for *reading list* or *black bloxes* for *black boxes* (Fromkin, 1971). Typically, these movement errors exhibit what is called the syllable-position effect: When a sound moves from one place to another, it retains its position in the syllable.[3] So, in *leading list* the erroneous /l/ in *leading* is an onset just like its source in *list*.

We suggest that the syllable position effect and the fact that errors obey positional phonotactic constraints are related phenomena. They just refer to constraints at different levels of generality. Consider the fact that /h/ is always a syllable onset when one is speaking English. This is a language-wide constraint, and errors adhere to it, as seen in the absence of any errors with /h/ as a coda. Next, consider the fact that /k/ is always an onset when one is saying the word CAT. This is a local constraint, one that is true only for CAT. An error in the vicinity of CAT, involving the production of /k/, will nonetheless preserve the onset status of /k/. For example, *the cat chases* might be spoken as *the cat cases*. The migrating /k/ preserves the position it is constrained to occupy in its originating word. In this way, the syllable position effect can be thought of as adherence to a local constraint in the vicinity of that word. Adherence to language-wide positional phonotactic constraints is simply a more general application of this principle: Substituting phonemes obey the constraints on positions in which they can occur in the language.

The syllable position and phonotactic effects can be thought of as two ends of a continuum of breadth of constraint. The syllable position effect is at the narrow end and adherence to phonotactics is at the wide end. The often discussed distinction between rules and exceptions is analogous. A rule applies widely, and exceptions locally. So, the past tense for English is *ed*, but the past tense of the word *come* is *came*. Moreover, the regularities in English past tense morphology fall on a continuum between rules and exceptions and include a variety of subregularities such as the *ring–rang, sing–sang, drink–drank* cluster.

If breadth of constraint is truly a continuum, we ought to be able to find a speech error effect that is in the "middle" between the syllable-

---

[3]Sometimes the constraint is formulated in terms of word position; see Meyer (1992).

position effect and error adherence to language-wide phonotactics. An experiment by Dell, Adams, Reed, and Meyer (1998) provided exactly this. They showed that speech errors in an experimental paradigm exhibit the syllable-position effect, language-wide phonotactic effects, and a new effect, sensitivity to learned experiment-wide constraints on the position of sounds within the syllable.

The experimental participants were given a simple task: They had to recite four-syllable lists three times in a row in time with a metronome. They did this for four 1-hour sessions, each of which was associated with the recitation of 96 different lists. Each syllable in the lists was a CVC and included the vowel /ɛ/. The eight consonants in each list always included exactly one of each of the following: /h/, /ŋ/, /f/, /s/, /n/, /m/, /k/, and /g/. For example, one string was *hes feg meng ken.*

There were three sets of constraints on the location of the eight consonants in each list, language-wide, experiment-wide, and list-wide constraints. The language-wide constraints concerned /h/ and /ŋ/. Because /h/ is an onset and /ŋ/ is a coda in English, these constraints were present in the experimental lists as well. The experiment-wide constraints concerned /f/ and /s/. For each experimental participant, the syllable position of these two sounds was held constant across the experiment. Half of the participants only experienced /f/ as an onset and /s/ as a coda, and half only experienced the reverse. These experiment-wide constraints thus represented a level of constraint that is less general than the language-wide constraints. The relevant context is "syllables in this experiment" as opposed to "syllables in English." The list-wide constraints applied to the other four sounds, /n/, /m/, /k/, and /g/. Because each sound occurs exactly once in a list, each of these four sounds is experienced as either an onset or a coda for this list. However, the next list may change the sound's syllable position. The list-wide constraints are therefore the least general, the relevant context being "syllables in this list."

The effect of the three constraints was assessed simply by determining whether the speakers' errors during the recitation of the lists obeyed or violated the constraint. As expected, the language-wide constraints were upheld without exception. There were 498 cases in which the erroneously spoken sound was /h/ or /ŋ/ (e.g., *meng ken* → *meng keng*) and in every case, the sound appeared in a phonotactically legal position. Thus, this provides an experimental demonstration of the phonotactic legality of errors.

Next, consider the list-wide constraints. Here, the errors involved the production of /n/, /m/, /k/, or /g/ instead of a target sound. These errors could obey or violate list-wide constraints. For example, *meng ken* spoken as *meng men* upholds the constraint that /m/ is an onset for this list. If these syllables are spoken instead as *meng kem,* the error violates the constraint that /m/ is an onset. The results showed an imperfect adherence to the constraint: 873 illegal to 323 illegal errors, 73% adherence. Thus, list-wide constraints are not upheld to the extent that language-wide constraints are, which is what one would expect from a system that responds directly to the strength of constraint. Notice that this result constitutes an experimental demonstration of the syllable-position effect: A moving sound tends to retain its syllable position. However, we are conceptualizing this effect in terms of a constraint of narrow breadth.

The key result of the experiment concerns experiment-wide constraints. That is, do the errors in which /f/ and /s/ replace target sounds obey the experiment-wide constraints on the position of these sounds? If there is zero sensitivity to the experiment-wide constraint, then we would expect the errors involving /f/ and /s/ to be legal at about the same rate as those testing for the sequence-wide constraint (73%). This is because the experiment-wide constraint implies sequence-wide constraint. On the other hand, if language-wide constraints reflect nothing more than recent experience with the distribution of the sounds /h/ and /ŋ/ in the experiment, then one would expect the experiment-wide results to be as exceptionless as the language-wide ones.

It turned out that the language-wide constraints were very strongly upheld, but were not exceptionless. There were 276 relevant legal errors (e.g., *meng* spoken as *feng* for participants for whom /f/ was an onset) and only 3 illegal ones (e.g., *kem* spoken as *kef*). This level of adherence—nearly 99%—suggests a highly adaptive production system, one that is constantly updating its knowledge of the position of sounds within syllables. Moreover, the fact that the experiment-wide comparison fell between the language-wide and sequence-wide ones tells us that breadth of constraint is, in fact, graded. The constraints with wider applicability are more likely to be upheld in errors.

Another aspect of the results with the experiment-wide constraint is that they illustrate implicit learning. When one erroneously produces an /f/, one is clearly not deliberately accessing the knowledge about whether /f/ is an onset or a coda. There is no time for such deliberation and, moreover, what was produced was an error rather than the intended sound. Further evidence for the implicit nature of the learning was provided by two other findings. First, the experimental participants reported no awareness of the distribution of the key sounds /f/ and /s/ at the end of the experiment. Second, half of the participants were told the rule about the distribution of /f/ and /s/ at the beginning of the experiment; their error data did not differ from the participants who were not informed.

In summary, the experiment tells us that the production system responds to experience. Error adherence to sound patterns, and perhaps other manifestations of knowledge about sound patterns, are products of implicit learning from experience with the sequential patterns in the vocabulary and may, in fact, be largely due to recent experience. It is worth noting that these conclusions are quite in line with the simple recurrent network model that we have reviewed here. If learning is always assumed to be "on," and there is a component of the input that reflects the situation (e.g., being in a particular experiment), the model's weights will come to be sensitive to the sound patterns in that situation.

So far in the chapter, we have discussed how onset–rime distributional asymmetries in the lexicon may arise from the needs of sequential processing. We also showed that some speech-error effects derive jointly from the asymmetries and other distributional statistics in the vocabulary and directly from the sequential nature of retrieval during production. We described experimental results showing that many phonological constraints in language are the result of learning contingencies at multiple levels of temporal structure. In the rest of this chapter, we argue that these kinds of phenomena are really manifestations of domain-general procedural learning mechanisms, deployed within the specific domain of language. We show that similar effects arise in nonlinguistic sequential domains and can be accounted for by essentially the same incremental learning mechanisms as described earlier. We focus particularly on how sensitivity to multiple levels of structure directly reflects experience with the distributional statistics of the vocabulary in nonlinguistic domains, just as in linguistic domains.

LANGUAGE LEARNING AND PROCEDURAL MEMORY

The foregoing discussion of speech errors and sound-sequence learning incorporates a view of language learning that has been increasingly adopted in recent years. According to this view, many aspects of language learning can be understood as proceeding via the gradual, experience-driven adjustment of connection weights between levels of distributed representation. This view has been applied to aspects of language as varied as sentence comprehension (McClelland, St. John, & Taraban, 1989), inflectional morphology (Gupta & MacWhinney, 1992; Hoeffner, 1992; MacWhinney & Leinbach, 1991; Rumelhart & McClelland, 1987), phonology (Dell et al., 1993; Gupta & Touretzky, 1994), and reading (Plaut, McClelland, Seidenberg, & Patterson, 1996; Seidenberg & McClelland, 1989), and it is also incorporated in many of the models described in this volume. This is, of course, the view of learning and cognitive processing embodied in the Parallel Distributed Processing (PDP) framework (McClelland & Rumelhart, 1986; Rumelhart & McClelland, 1986).

These same kinds of learning mechanisms have also, however, been proposed for another domain of cognition, namely, implicit or procedural memory. One of the most significant developments in the study of human memory over the last 2 decades has been the discovery of a dissociation between two different kinds of memory systems, referred to as explicit versus implicit memory (Schacter, 1987) or declarative versus procedural memory (Cohen, 1984; Cohen & Squire, 1980). Dissociations between procedural and declarative memory were originally discovered in amnesics (Cohen & Squire, 1980) and have since also been documented in normal populations (e.g., Graf & Schacter, 1985). Declarative memory refers to memory for arbitrarily related collections of representations, such as episodes, or factual knowledge. Implicit or procedural memory includes the acquisition of skills that are acquired gradually over several sessions of practice and facilitation or priming in processing of a stimulus following prior exposure to that stimulus (e.g., Squire, 1992). Much of the interest in procedural or implicit memory arises from the fact that a great deal of everyday human learning appears to have just this character, occurring gradually as a result of practice over many exposures. This is, of course, precisely the view of language learning described previously. In fact, it has been hypothesized (e.g., Cohen, 1984; Cohen & Eichenbaum, 1993) that procedural memory is based on the continual, experience-driven tuning of processing elements, similar to the experience-driven adjustment of connection weights in PDP networks. Thus, within the domain of memory research, one major human memory system, procedural memory, has been characterized as operating via the same principles that are incorporated in many recent models of language. A similar view of procedural memory is inherent in the work of some of the architects of the PDP framework (e.g., McClelland, McNaughton, & O'Reilly, 1995; McClelland & Rumelhart, 1985).

Bringing these ideas together, we hypothesize that those aspects of language learning that can be characterized as gradual, experience-driven tuning are in fact forms of procedural memory, a suggestion that has also been made by a number of other researchers (e.g., Cleeremans, 1993; Reber, 1993). This suggestion extends the domain of procedural memory to encompass many of the systematic aspects of language learning and implies that these aspects of language learning can be viewed as *emerging* from the mechanisms of procedural memory.

If this view is correct, it should be possible to use the same kinds of computational models that have been proposed for language, to account for phenomena in the domain of procedural memory. In what follows, we discuss how a model very similar to the model of speech errors described earlier (Dell et al., 1993) can yield insight into aspects of procedural memory. In our earlier discussion of this model, the focus was on the temporal aspects of processing, manifested in such phenomena as speech errors. We now focus instead on how such a system might develop. Let us suppose that the model is exposed to a number of word forms in each period of time. In each period of time (such as a day), some of these word forms are ones that have previously been encountered, whereas some of the word forms are novel, as depicted in Fig. 16.5a. Let us further suppose that the model's task is simply to spell out each input word form representation, as a sequence of output phonemes or phonological features (see Fig. 16.4). How might the system's basic ability to perform this task develop? Figure 16.5b shows the pattern of results that we might expect. The ability to spell out familiar forms would improve greatly, as a result of multiple exposures to these forms; this is depicted by the lower curve in Fig. 16.5b. Additionally, we would expect cumulative practice to result in generalized performance improvement, as a result of continual adjustment of connection weights in the system. That is, we would expect the model to become more effective at the process of spelling out word forms in general, irrespective of whether they were familiar or not. This is shown in the upper curve in Fig. 16.5b.

This examination of the effects of repetition on novel and familiar stimuli is precisely what is studied under the general heading of "skill learning" and "repetition priming" in the implicit memory literature. Figure 16.5c schematizes an experimental paradigm that is commonly used in studies of repetition priming (e.g., Kirsner & Speelman, 1996; Logan, 1990; Schwartz & Hashtroudi, 1991). In this paradigm, participants are required to respond in some way to each stimulus with which they are presented. Each block of stimuli is comprised of a number of "unique" stimuli that appear exactly once throughout the experiment and a number of "repeating" stimuli that appear in every block. Figure 16.5d illustrates the phenomena of interest in such studies: improvement in performance on unique stimuli (termed *skill learning*) and the greater facilitation of performance on repeating stimuli over performance on unique stimuli (this difference being *repetition priming*).

There appears to be a clear analogy between the developmental effects we would expect in our PDP model of speech errors and the study of skill learning and repetition priming as aspects of procedural memory. In the remainder of this section we examine this analogy further, by discussing skill learning and repetition priming in a specific procedural memory task, with a view to making two points. First, we show that learning occurs at multiple levels of structure in this procedural memory task, just as in the sound-sequence learning experiment of Dell et al. (1998) described earlier. In the sound-sequence task, we observed sensitivity to distributional statistics at the level of experiment-wide constraints, list-wide constraints, and language-wide constraints. We describe a procedural memory task in which, similarly, sensitivity to sequential constraints arises at multiple levels. Second, we show that a simple recurrent network essentially identical to the Dell et al. (1993) model can account for these and other results from the procedural memory task. These two demonstrations emphasize the conti-

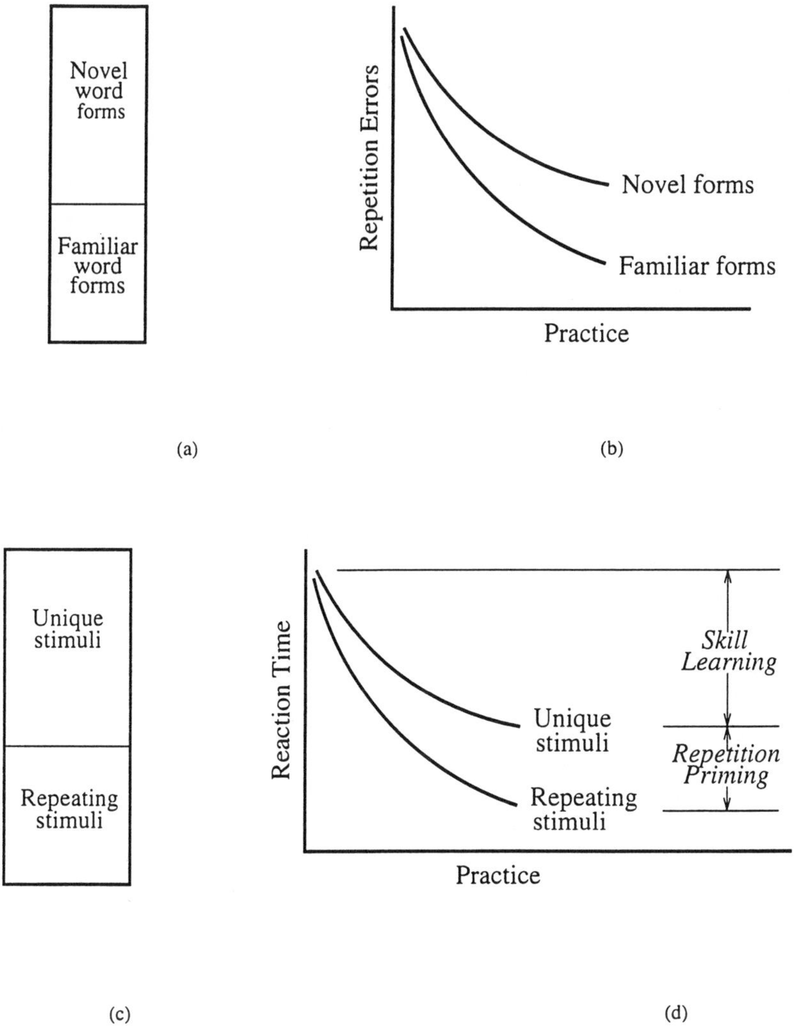

FIG. 16.5. Comparison of expected development of the ability to repeat word forms, in a sequential PDP model, with issues in the study of two procedural memory phenomena, skill learning and repetition priming: (a) hypothetical regimen of environmental exposure for the PDP system; (b) expected schedule of development; (c) regimen of experimental practice in a typical procedural memory task; (d) measures of interest in such procedural memory paradigms.

nuity of the phenomena and mechanisms of procedural memory with those of language learning.

Skill Learning and Repetition Priming

We focus on the digit entering task (Fendrich, Healy, & Bourne, 1991), in which both skill learning and repetition priming have been studied. We describe a version in which 5-digit numbers (e.g., *49385*) were presented individually to participants, who entered these numbers on a computer numeric keypad (Poldrack, 1995, Experiment 1a). No feedback was provided for the response. After entering the number, the participant pressed the enter key, which triggered the next trial after a 1-sec interval. Participants were instructed not to correct errors. Some numbers appeared multiple times during the experiment (repeating items) whereas other items appeared only once (unique items).

Training stimuli were chosen from the set of all possible 5-digit numbers by placing three constraints on them. First, only the digits 1 through 9, were allowed (i.e., the digit 0 was not used). Second, digits could not repeat immediately (e.g., *44* never appeared as part of a number). Third, 5-digit numbers were constrained to obey certain first-order transitions between digits, as follows. For each of the digits 1 through 9, there are 8 possible (different) digits that can follow it. For each digit, 4 of these 8 possible transitions were chosen at random. The set of 36 chosen transitions (4 transitions for each of the 9 digits) comprised one full transition rule set. There was also a complementary transition rule set comprised of the other 36 transitions (4 complementary transitions for each of the 9 digits). Figure 16.6 illustrates such transition rule sets for the digit 1. Five-digit numbers were constrained to obey one or other of these transition rule sets. Half of the participants in each experiment were trained on 5-digit numbers that followed one transition rule set, and the other half were trained on items following the complementary rule set.

The experiment (Poldrack, 1995, Experiment 1a) consisted of three sessions, each consisting of 12 blocks. The structure of the experiment is summarized in Table 16.1. Forty-eight 5-digit strings were presented in each block. However, the composition of the 48 stimuli in a block varied across sessions. In Session 1, each block consisted of 12 repeating stimuli, that is, stimuli that appeared once in every block throughout Session 1 and also throughout the experiment ("S1 Repeats"). The remaining 36 stimuli in each block of Session 1 were unique stimuli, that is, stimuli that appeared once, in only that one block and that did not appear in any other block in the experiment ("S1 Uniques"). In Session 2, each block consisted of the 12 repeating stimuli from Session 1; 12 new repeating stimuli that appeared in each block in Session 2 and through the rest of

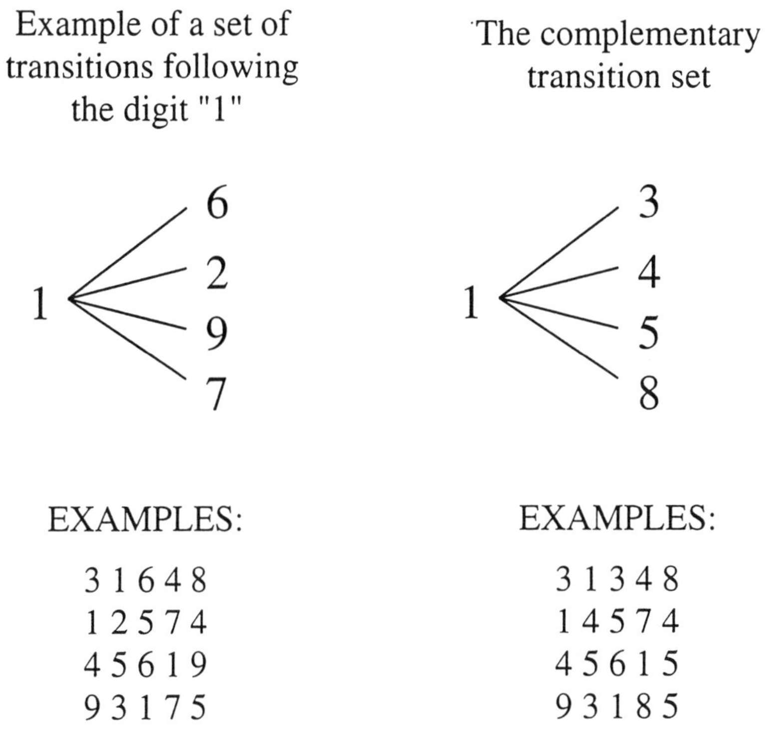

FIG. 16.6. Example of transition rules used in the digit entering task of Poldrack (1995, Experiment 1a).

TABLE 16.1
Structure of the Digit Entering Task of Poldrack (1995, Experiment 1a)

	Trial Type	*Number of Stimuli per Block*
Session 1	S1 Repeats	12
	S1 Uniques	36
Session 2	S1 Repeats	12
	S2 Repeats	12
	S2 Uniques	24
Session 3	S1 Repeats	12
	S2 Repeats	12
	S3 Uniques	12
	New Rule Uniques	12

the experiment ("S2 Repeats"), and 24 unique stimuli ("S2 Uniques"). In Session 3, each block consisted of the 12 Session 1 repeating stimuli, the 12 Session 2 repeating stimuli, and 12 unique stimuli ("S3 Uniques"). In addition, each block in Session 3 contained a further 12 unique stimuli that did not conform to the transition rule structure of all the other stimuli ("New Rule Uniques"). That is, all the stimuli in all three sessions of the experiment conformed to a particular set of transition rules, except for the Session 3 New Rule Uniques, which conformed to the complementary rule set.

Response times were separated into two components, latency for the first keystroke, and interkeystroke interval. Our concern is with interkeystroke interval (IKI), the average interval between each keystroke subsequent to the first. Figure 16.7 illustrates pertinent results from Poldrack (1995, Experiment 1a). The horizontal axis shows blocks of practice whereas the vertical axis shows participants' performance as measured by mean IKI per block. The four curves in the upper part of the figure show (from the top downward) performance on S3 New Rule Unique stimuli, performance on Old Rule Unique stimuli, performance on S2 Repeat stimuli, and performance on S1 Repeat stimuli. Skill learning was measured as the improvement in performance on Old Rule Uniques over the course of the experiment. That is, skill learning at block *n* is the difference between performance on Old Rule Uniques at Block 1 and performance on Old Rule Uniques at Block *n*. This measure is plotted as the upper of the two curves in the lower part of the figure. Repetition priming at Block *n* was measured as the difference between performance on Old Rule Unique stimuli and performance on S1 Repeat stimuli, both measured at Block *n*. This measure is plotted as the lower of the two curves in the lower part of the figure.

The following effects are noteworthy. First, there is marked improvement in performance on both Repeating stimuli and Old Rule Unique stimuli across blocks in Fig. 16.7. Second, there is a clear increase in skill learning across blocks, seen in the decrease in IKI for Old Rule Unique items across blocks and also seen in the plot of skill learning in the lower part of the figure. There clearly is also repetition priming, as shown by the difference between performance on Old Rule Unique stimuli and performance on S1 Repeat stimuli at each block and as also shown by the plot of repetition priming in the lower part of the figure. Third, repetition priming can be observed at different levels of skill learning: In addition to repetition priming for the S1 Repeats introduced at the beginning of the experiment, there is also repetition priming for S2 Repeats, which were introduced only in Session 2. The latter effect can be seen in the divergence in performance between S2 Repeat stimuli and Old Rule Unique stimuli, following introduction of the S2 Repeat stimuli in Block 13. Fourth, there is negative transfer to the New Rule Unique stimuli introduced in Session

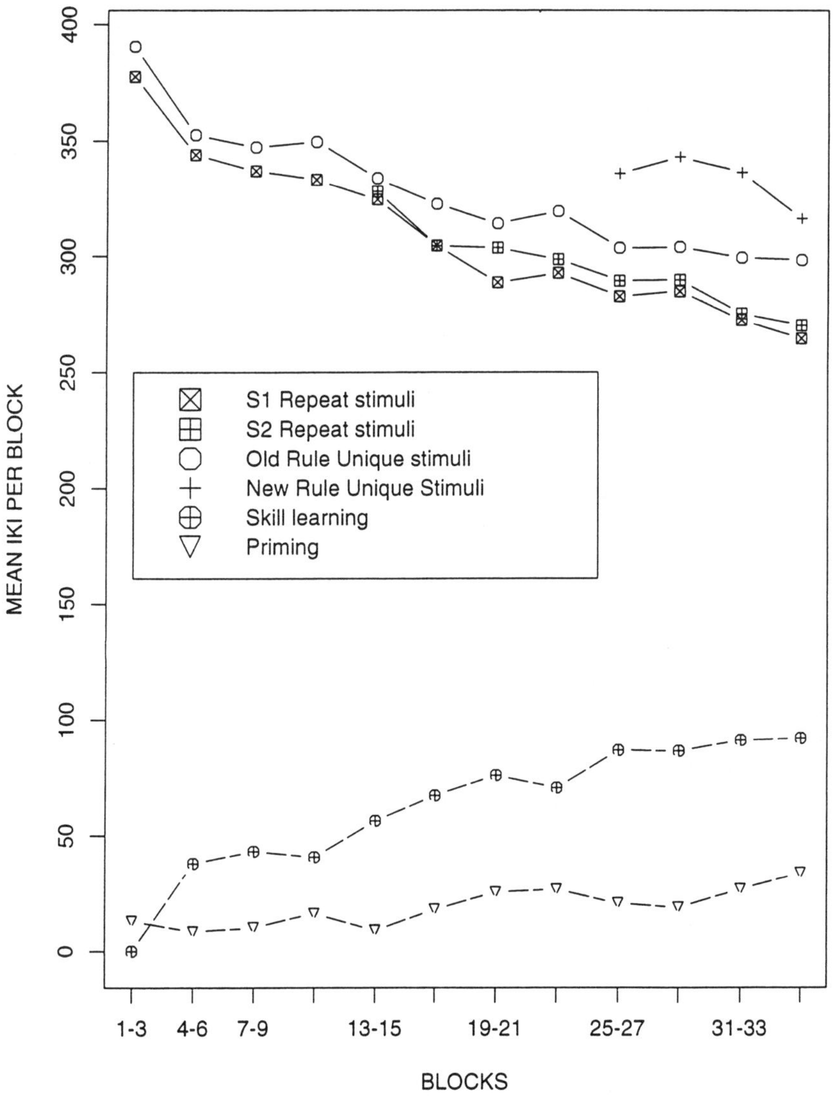

FIG. 16.7. Key results redrawn from the digit entering task of Poldrack (1995, Experiment 1a).

3. The only difference between the Old Rule Unique stimuli and New Rule Unique stimuli is in the familiarity of the specific 2-digit transitions they incorporate. The negative transfer effect therefore indicates that participants learned something about the 2-digit transition structure of the Old Rule Unique stimuli. That is, part of what they learned were subitem regularities within the stimuli.

For present purposes, one of the most significant aspects of these results is that participants appear to learn structure at multiple levels, just as in the sound-sequence learning experiment of Dell et al. (1998) described earlier in this chapter. In that experiment, the pattern of speech errors revealed participants' sensitivity to within-experiment regularities as well as to within-list regularities. These multiple levels of sensitivity necessarily must have developed during the course of the experiment. In Poldrack's (1995) results, participants learned regularities at both the 5-digit level and the 2-digit level during the course of the experiment. Sensitivity to the former is shown by superior performance on Repeating over Unique stimuli. Sensitivity to the latter is shown by superior performance on Old Rule Unique stimuli over New Rule Unique stimuli, in Session 3.

Figure 16.8 illustrates the architecture of the model that Gupta and Cohen (1997) used to simulate the digit entering task. The model is a simple recurrent network (Cleeremans, Servan-Schreiber, & McClelland, 1989; Elman, 1990; Jordan, 1986) and is essentially the same as the model of Dell et al. (1993). The task for the present model was formulated to have the same structure as the digit entering task. In each trial in the digit entering task, participants were presented with a 5-digit number, which they were required to convert into a sequence of keyboard strokes representing the sequence of digits comprising the 5-digit number. Similarly, the input to the model was a representation of a 5-digit number, and the model's task was to produce a sequence of outputs representing the sequence of digits in the input.

The input was represented as a pattern of activation over five banks of units that constituted the input layer, as shown in Fig. 16.8. Each of these

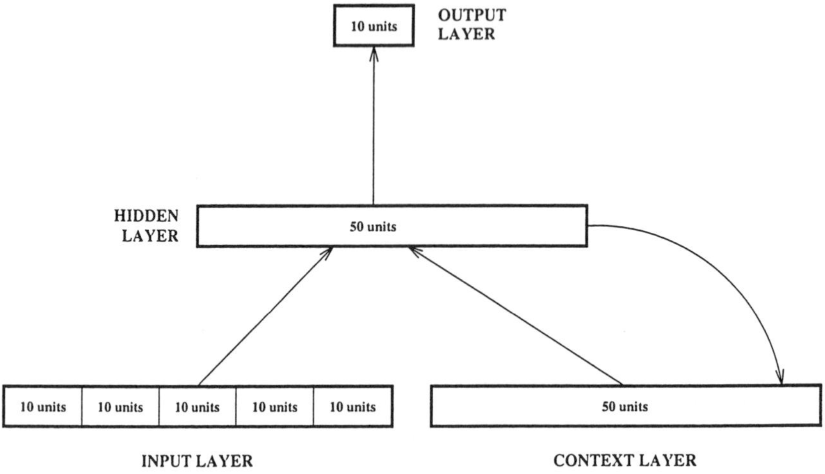

FIG. 16.8. Architecture of the model of the digit entering task (Gupta & Cohen, 1997).

banks comprised 10 units representing the digits 0 through 9, with each unit representing a specific digit. Thus, the 5-digit string *49683* was represented as a pattern of activation in which the 5th unit in the first bank of units was active (representing the occurrence of *4* as the 1st digit in the string); the 10th unit in the second bank of units was active, representing the occurrence of *9* as the 2nd digit in the string; the 7th unit in the third bank was active, representing the occurrence of *6* in third position; the 9th unit in the fourth bank was active, representing the occurrence of *9* as the 4th digit; and the 4th unit in the fifth bank was active, representing the occurrence of *3* as the 5th digit. All other units in the 50-unit input layer were inactive. The output layer consisted of a single bank of 10 units, representing the digits 0 through 9, with each output unit representing a specific digit. When presented with an input pattern of the kind described previously, the network's task was to spell out the input as a sequence of activations at the output layer. For example, for the input *49683,* the network's task was to activate, in sequence, the output layer units representing the digits *4, 9, 6, 8,* and *3.*

At the first step in processing this input, activations from the input layer and from the context layer were propagated forward to the hidden layer, and activations from the hidden layer in turn were propagated forward to the output layer. This resulted in some pattern of activation at the output layer. An error signal was generated, representing the distance of this actual activation pattern from the target pattern, in which the output unit representing *4* should be maximally activated and all other output units inactive. Back propagation of error (Rumelhart et al., 1986) was then used to adjust the strength of connection weights throughout the system.

At the next step in processing the input, the activation of hidden layer units was copied to the context layer (Elman, 1990), and the network was now expected to produce as output the 2nd digit in the input string. Note that the input pattern representing the digit string *49683* was still present. As on the first step of processing, the actual output produced by the network was compared with the target output for the 2nd digit, and connection weight strengths adjusted so as to reduce the magnitude of error. Processing continued in this way for three further time steps, at which the network's task was to output the 3rd, 4th, and 5th digits, respectively, of the input. At the end of the fifth time step, the context layer was cleared, and the next 5-digit input string was presented for the network to spell out.

The model was used to simulate results from the digit entering task of Poldrack (1995, Experiment 1a) summarized earlier. Sixteen participants took part in that experiment. One complete simulated "replication," accordingly, comprised 16 runs of the model. Each run of the model consisted of three parts. First, weights in the system were initialized to random values, corresponding to variation between participants. Second, the model was trained on 1,000 5-digit strings, which were randomly chosen from the set of all possible 5-digit strings but excluded strings that would appear in the actual experimental simulations. This training consisted of four *epochs*, i.e., four cycles of presentation of the 1,000-stimulus set. The model's task at each 5-digit stimulus presentation was to spell out the sequence of digits comprising the string. This second step of pretraining was intended to provide the model with a preexperimental level of skill approximately equivalent to that of participants entering the experiment. At the end of preexperimental training, the model was correctly able to spell out 85.3% of novel 5-digit inputs, which corresponded quite well with the 86.98% accuracy of human participants on unique stimuli in the first block of the digit entering task.

The third step consisted of the actual experimental phase of the simulation run. The structure of this third phase precisely mirrored the structure of the digit entering task (Poldrack, 1995, Experiment 1a), which was summarized in Table 16.1. Thus, in the first epoch of a simulation, the model was presented with 48 stimuli (5-digit strings) that obeyed a particular transition rule structure. Twelve of these stimuli were to repeat throughout the simulation (S1 Repeats), whereas the other 36 stimuli would not be presented again during the simulation (S1 Uniques). As explained previously, the model's task at each 5-digit stimulus presentation was to spell out the sequence of digits comprising the string, just as in the experiment with human participants. Thus, Epoch 1 in the simulation corresponded to Block 1 in the Experiment. In the second epoch of a simulation, the 12 S1 Repeat stimuli were presented again, and 36 novel stimuli were also presented. Thus, Epoch 2 corresponded to Block 2. In analogous fashion, each epoch in the simulation mirrored the corresponding block of the experiment. It may be worth noting that the model's task in response to presentation of a 5-digit string was the same during Step 2 (pretraining) and Step 3 (experimental simulation). The only difference was that the presentation of stimuli during Step 3 had a carefully controlled structure, identical to that in the digit entering task (Poldrack, 1995, Experiment 1a).

In the digit entering task, the specific stimuli in each category (S1 Repeats, S1 Uniques, etc.) were carefully counterbalanced across the 16 participants (Poldrack, 1995, Experiment 1a). In simulations, the model was run once with each of these actual sets of stimuli. Thus, one simulation run consisted of: (a) random weight initialization, (b) pretraining for 4 epochs, and (c) simulation of the 36 Blocks of Experiment 1a, using one of the 16 stimulus sets actually presented to participants. A set of 16 such runs constituted one simulated replication of Experiment 1a. Twenty such replications were run and the results averaged. Simulation results were measured by mean squared error per digit, which was the mean squared difference between the target output pattern and the actual output pattern for every digit. For example, performance on unique stimuli in Epoch 1 of the simulations was measured by the squared error per digit, averaged over all digits presented in Epoch 1, averaged over all 16 simulated participants, averaged over all 20 replications. This measure was found to be linearly related to the IKI measure used in the behavioral experiments.

Figure 16.9a redisplays the results from Poldrack (1995, Experiment 1a). Figure 16.9b shows the corresponding simulation results (Gupta & Cohen, 1997). As can be seen, the simulations provide a good fit to the data and exhibit all of the phenomena characteristic of the empirical results. First, there is improvement in performance on both unique and repeating stimuli across blocks. Second, we see clear indication of both skill learning and repetition priming. Third, the effects of repetition can be observed even after significant skill learning has occurred, as shown by performance on the new repeating items (S2 Repeats) introduced in Session 2. Fourth, there is negative transfer to stimuli that follow the complementary transition rule structure, in Session 3. These results confirm that the kinds of incremental learning mechanisms widely employed as accounts of language learning can also account for procedural memory phenomena.

LEXICAL LEARNING AND PROCEDURAL AND DECLARATIVE MEMORY

How can we concretize the notion that aspects of language learning are forms of procedural memory? In this section, we present a simplified view of the lexical system in language. We use this framework to situate our model of speech errors within a broader context and to situate our discussion of procedural memory more firmly within a linguistic setting.

Our view of the lexical system is depicted in Fig. 16.10. According to this view, when the sequence of speech segments ("input phonemes") constituting a word is presented as input to the lexical system, this sequence of inputs leads to activation of an internal representation of the word form. We assume that this internal representation is phonologically structured and that it is distributed over many processing units. The mapping from sequences of input sound segments to internal representations is the "input phonology" mapping. The internal word form representation, once activated, can lead to the playing out of a sequence of "output phonemes," corresponding to the process of saying (producing) the word. The mapping from internal word form representations to sequences of output phonemes is the "output phonology" mapping. In addition to participating in the input and output phonology mappings, internal word form representations also have associative links to and from the level of semantic representations. Thus, when a word form representation is activated, it evokes activation of any semantic representation that may be associated with the word form.

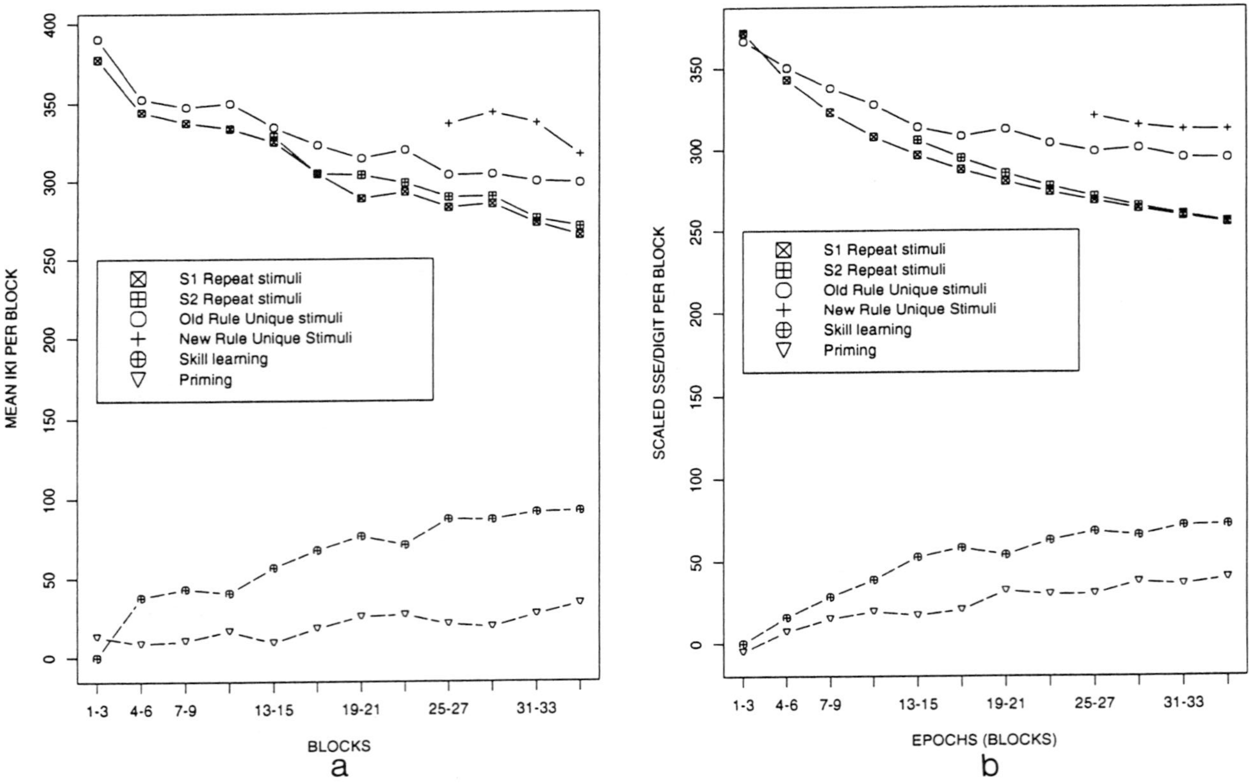

FIG. 16.9. Comparison of experimental and simulation results: (a) results from the digit entering task (Poldrack, 1995, Experiment 1a); (b) simulation results (Gupta & Cohen, 1997).

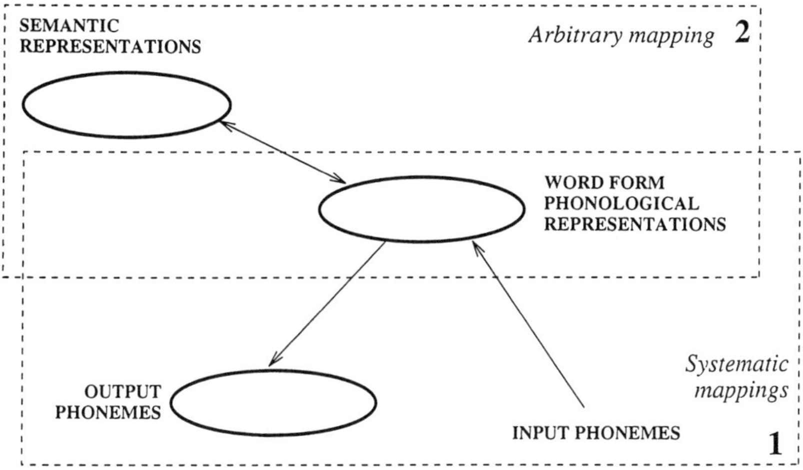

FIG. 16.10. One view of the lexical system in language and the nature of the mappings involved.

Conversely, when a semantic representation is activated, it leads to activation of any associated word form level representation.

The output phonology mapping is implemented in the cognitive system by a transducer that learns to approximate the mapping through experience-driven, incremental tuning. The kind of transducer we envisage is the system of weighted connections that mediates between two levels of representation in a PDP network. The incremental tuning is the kind of adjustment of connection weights that occurs in PDP networks. Similarly, the input phonology mapping and the two mappings between internal word form representations and semantics are also implemented by transducers that are incrementally tuned by experience.

The system we outlined is comprised of systematic as well as arbitrary mappings, as shown in Fig. 16.10. The input and output phonology mappings are both systematic, in that similar sequences of input phonemes map onto similar internal word form representations, and similar word form representations map onto similar sequences of output phonemes. However, as we noted at the beginning of this chapter, it is a fundamental property of all spoken languages that the mapping between word forms and meanings is arbitrary, in that similar word form representations are not guaranteed to map onto similar meanings, and vice versa. For example, the similar-sounding word forms *carlin, car,* and *marlin* do not map onto similar meanings. Conversely, the similar semantics of the objects "cup" and "glass" do not map onto similar-sounding word forms. Of course, in most languages, there are partial regularities in the mapping. For example, inflectional morphology leads to certain aspects of meaning (e.g., plural number) being expressed consistently in a particular fashion (by adding *-s*, for example, in English). Nevertheless, the mapping is for the most part arbitrary.

How does the simple recurrent network model of speech errors described earlier fit in with the view of the lexical system we have just presented? Figure 16.11 illustrates the correspondence. In Fig. 16.11, a simplified version of the Dell et al. (1993) model is shown inverted, with its input layer at the top and its output layer at the bottom. Its input layer corresponds to the word form level of representation in the present lexical system whereas its output layer corresponds to the present output phoneme layer. The model additionally has a recurrent hidden layer not depicted in Fig. 16.10. Comparison of Fig. 16.11 with Fig. 16.10 should make it clear that the Dell et al. (1993) model is in effect an implementation of the present output phonology mapping. It instantiates one of the systematic mappings in the lexical system and is precisely the kind of transducer we envisaged.

The import of our observations about systematic versus arbitrary mappings becomes clearer when we consider the fact that learning a new word can in general be a fast process. Research on "fast mapping" indicates that children as young as 4 years of age can learn the association between a novel word form and its referent, given only one or two exposures to the pairing (Carey, 1978; Dollaghan, 1985), and certainly, adults have the ability to learn new words with very little repetition. Learning a new word requires establishment of a new entry in each of the transducers in the lexical system. Therefore, if the word is to be learned within one or two exposures, then this requires that new entries be established in each of the transducers with only one or two exposures.

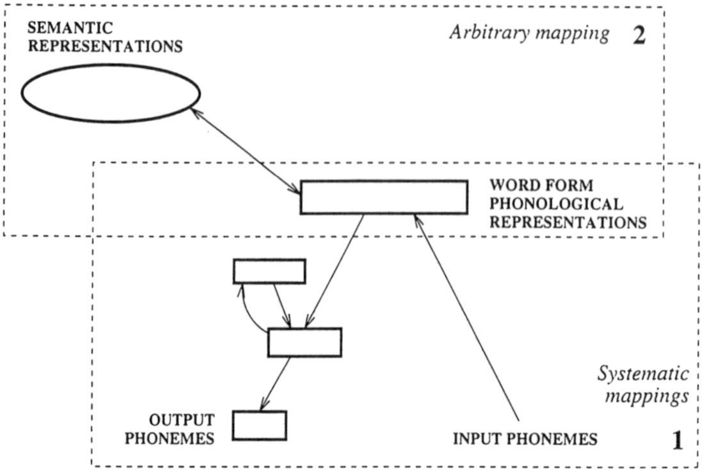

FIG. 16.11. Situating the Dell et al. (1993) model of speech errors within the lexical system.

Let us first consider the transducer that implements the output phonology mapping. Given that word form level representations are distributed, and given that the output phonology mapping is systematic, it follows that this transducer can generalize. It automatically has the ability to transduce a novel word form representation into the correct sequence of output phonemes. Thus, in the output phonology mapping, fast learning comes for free, as a process of similarity-based generalization. The same is true of the input phonology mapping. To see this, consider the human ability to repeat nonwords. Nonword repetition requires mapping from the novel input phoneme sequence to a novel word form level representation via the input phonology transducer, and then spelling out the novel word form representation as a novel sequence of output phonemes, via the output phonology transducer. The fact that humans can easily repeat nonwords shows that there must be generalization in both the input and output phonology mappings. This is not true, however, of the mapping from word forms to meaning, or from meaning to word forms, because these are arbitrary mappings. Similarity-based generalizations cannot determine the correct word form level representation for a novel semantic representation, or vice versa (although it can support productive inflectional processes, as previously noted). Furthermore, the connection weight changes needed to establish a new entry in these two transducers can be large. Gradual, incremental tuning processes will not suffice to make such large weight changes within one or two exposures. However, if we try to make the large necessary weight changes nongradually, previous entries in the transducers will be overwritten, given that the representations are distributed. Some other learning mechanism is needed for the mappings between word forms and semantics, to reconcile the conflicting requirements of fast learning and distributed representations.

To reiterate, the incremental, experience-driven tuning of connection weights provides a sufficient basis for fast learning in the systematic input and output phonology mappings. However, some additional mechanism is needed for fast learning in the arbitrary mappings between word forms and semantics. This distinction is reminiscent of the previously mentioned dissociation between explicit versus implicit or declarative versus procedural memory. Recall that declarative memory refers to memory for arbitrarily related collections of representations. For example, the set of representations comprising the memory of a past event or "episode" are forms of declarative memory (e.g., Squire, 1992), as is the factual knowledge that the capital of Madagascar is Antananarivo. Procedural memory includes the acquisition of skills that are acquired gradually over several sessions of practice, and facilitation or priming in processing of a stimulus, following prior exposure to that stimulus (e.g., Squire, 1992). There is considerable agreement about the neural basis of the dissociation between declarative and procedural memory. The declarative memory system is believed to be subserved by the hippocampus and related medial temporal lobe structures. These structures provide for the initial encoding of memories involving arbitrary conjunctions and also for their eventual consolidation and storage in neocortex (e.g., Cohen & Squire, 1980; Mishkin, Malamut, & Bachevalier, 1984; Squire, Knowlton, & Musen, 1993). The procedural memory system, which provides for the learning and processing of motor, perceptual, and cognitive skills, is believed to be subserved by learning that occurs in neocortex and in the basal ganglia (e.g., Cohen & Squire, 1980; Mishkin et al., 1984; Squire et al., 1993).

It has further been suggested that there is a functional reason for the existence of two memory systems (McClelland et al., 1995). According to this view, the neocortex processes distributed representations. Such representations have the desirable property of providing a basis for similarity-based generalization. However, in a computational system employing distributed representations, learning of arbitrary associations must be slow and interleaved, if the system is not to suffer from "catastrophic interference," the overwriting of previously existing knowledge (McClelland et al., 1995; McCloskey & Cohen, 1989). Episodes and new facts (i.e., the kinds of arbitrary associations that constitute declarative memory) therefore cannot be encoded swiftly via slow cortical learning. It has been proposed that the role of the hippocampus is to convert distributed representations into localist nonoverlapping ones and to establish fast mappings between such converted representations. That is, the hippocampus performs fast learning, based on orthogonalized representations, and thus provides a basis for the swift encoding of arbitrary associations of the kind that comprise episodic and factual information (McClelland et al., 1995). Neocortex and hippocampus thus perform complementary learning functions and provide the basis for procedural and declarative memory, respectively.

It thus appears that the two different kinds of mechanisms required in lexical learning map quite well onto the functional roles assigned to procedural and declarative memory. This suggests that the input and output phonology mappings in our lexical system may be subserved by procedural learning, but that the mappings between word forms and meaning must invoke the mechanisms of declarative memory. To elaborate, the locus of the various phonological and semantic representations can be viewed as being cortical tissue (Blumstein, 1995; Gupta & MacWhinney, 1997; Kandel & Schwartz, 1985). Incremental tuning of the weighted connections between these cortical representations occurs automatically, following exposure to each conjunction of representations. This tuning occurs in all the transducers shown in Fig. 16.11—the input phonology transducer, the output phonology transducer, and the transducers between word forms and semantics. Although such tuning provides a sufficient basis for generalization and fast learning in the input and output phonology transducers, it cannot support fast learning in the transducers between word forms and semantics. It needs to be augmented by hippocampally mediated learning processes that are not represented in Fig. 16.11 but that are added in Fig. 16.12. The cortical representations are relayed to the hippocampus where they are bound together rapidly in the form of orthogonalized representations. In the long term, however, the binding of semantic and word form representations to each other must occur in the connections between the cortical representations, and this process of consolidation proceeds slowly because cortical learning is slow (Cohen & Eichenbaum, 1993; McClelland et al., 1995). Once established cortically, a particular binding can be thought of as having become proceduralized.

Two predictions follow from the view we outlined. First, under conditions of impairment in declarative memory, it should be difficult to learn new word meanings quickly. Second, even if declarative memory is impaired, it should nevertheless be possible for procedural learning to occur in the input and output phonology transductions; we might expect such tuning to be manifested in the form of repetition priming. These are in fact precisely the kinds of impairments observed in hippocampal amnesics. Such patients are virtually unable to learn new word meanings (e.g., Gabrieli, Cohen, & Corkin, 1988; Grossman, 1987), which is an indication of their impairment in declarative memory. However, these same patients exhibit intact repetition priming for both known and novel words (e.g., Haist, Musen, & Squire, 1991), which is an indication of their relatively spared procedural memory. These results support the hypothesis that phonological learning proceeds via cortical procedural learning mecha-

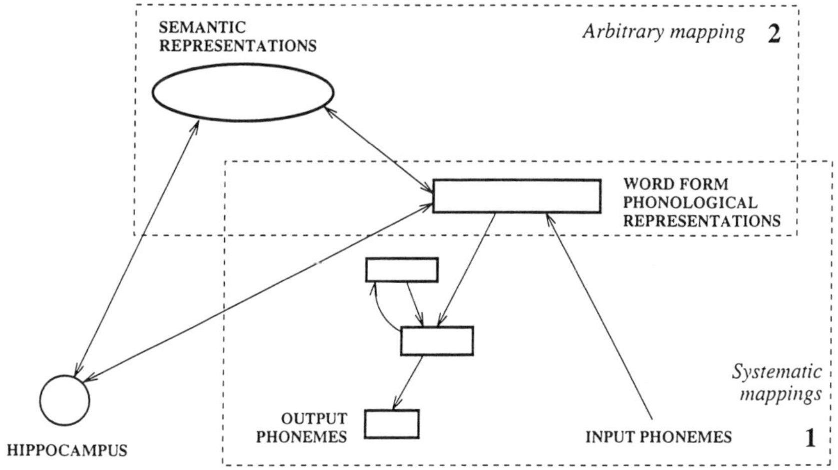

FIG. 16.12. Hypothesized role of the hippocampus in lexical learning.

nisms, whereas learning the mapping between word forms and meaning relies additionally on hippocampal declarative memory.

CONCLUSIONS

We began this chapter with the observation that in all spoken languages words are temporal sequences arbitrarily related to meaning, and we asked how these properties reflect and are reflected in the processing system. We suggested that the processing mechanisms necessary to deal with the serially ordered nature of words play a role in the emergence of distributional asymmetries in the lexicon. Specifically, we claimed that the need to retrieve the sounds of words in sequence favors a vocabulary with asymmetries such as an onset-rime organization. We then argued that some speech error effects derive jointly from the asymmetries and other distributional statistics in the vocabulary and directly from the sequential nature of retrieval during production. We reviewed a simple recurrent network model that implements such an account of speech error phenomena. We also presented new experimental results supporting the view that many phonological constraints in language are the result of learning contingencies at multiple levels of temporal structure.

We then suggested that those aspects of language learning that can be characterized in terms of the slow, incremental tuning of connection weights may in fact be forms of procedural memory. We focused particularly on how sensitivity to sequential constraints can arise at multiple levels in procedural memory tasks, similar to the sensitivity to multiple levels of constraint observed in our sound-sequence learning task. We described the application of a simple recurrent network (similar to the speech-error model) to data from a procedural memory paradigm, and showed that the model provides an excellent account of the empirical results. The similarity in effects and the applicability of the kinds of incremental learning mechanisms proposed for language processing to the domain of procedural memory emphasizes the continuity of the phenomena and mechanisms of procedural memory with those of language learning.

Finally, we situated our speech error model in the lexical system and provided a specific example of the role of procedural memory in language learning. We argued that the existence of different kinds of mappings in the lexical system leads to a pressure for two different mechanisms to support fast learning. We suggested that these mechanisms can be identified with those of procedural and declarative memory and showed that the available neuropsychological data are consistent with this hypothesis. The seemingly unitary process of learning a new word thus appears to draw on two rather different systems of learning and memory.

Overall, our discussion in this chapter suggests that important aspects of language can be viewed as emerging from serial order and from procedural memory, and that lexical learning draws on the mechanisms of procedural as well as declarative memory.

ACKNOWLEDGMENTS

This work was supported by a Beckman Institute Fellowship to the first author, and by NSF Grant SBR 93-19368 and NIH Grants DC-00191 and HD-21011. We are grateful for the advice of David Adams, Kathryn Bock, Barbara Church, Neal Cohen, Victor Ferreira, Zenzi Griffin, Brian MacWhinney, Antje Meyer, Kevin Miller, Gregory Murphy, and Kristopher Reed. Correspondence and requests for reprints may be addressed to either author, at the Beckman Institute, University of Illinois at Urbana–Champaign, Urbana, Illinois 61801.

REFERENCES

Berg, T. (1991). Phonological processing in a syllable-timed language with pre-final stress: Evidence from Spanish speech error data. *Language and Cognitive Processes, 6,* 265–301.

Blumstein, S. E. (1995). The neurobiology of the sound structure of language. In M. S. Gazzaniga (Ed.), *The cognitive neurosciences* (pp. 915–929). Cambridge, MA: MIT Press.

Carey, S. (1978). The child as word learner. In M. Halle, J. Bresnan, & G. Miller (Eds.), *Linguistic theory and psychological reality* (pp. 264–293). Cambridge, MA: MIT Press.

Cleeremans, A. (1993). *Mechanisms of implicit learning: Connectionist models of sequence processing.* Cambridge, MA: MIT Press.

Cleeremans, A., Servan-Schreiber, D., & McClelland, J. (1989). Finite state automata and simple recurrent networks. *Neural Computation, 1,* 372–381.

Cohen, N. J. (1984). Preserved learning capacity in amnesia: Evidence for multiple memory systems. In L. R. Squire & N. Butters (Eds.), *Neuropsychology of memory* (pp. 83–103). New York: Guilford.

Cohen, N. J., & Eichenbaum, H. (1993). *Memory, amnesia, and the hippocampal system.* Cambridge, MA: MIT Press.

Cohen, N. J., & Squire, L. R. (1980). Preserved learning and retention of pattern analyzing skill in amnesia: Dissociation of knowing how and knowing that. *Science, 210,* 207–209.

Dell, G. S., Juliano, C., & Govindjee, A. (1993). Structure and content in language production: A theory of frame constraints in phonological speech errors. *Cognitive Science, 17,* 149–195.

Dell, G. S., Reed, K. D., Adams, D. A., & Meyer, A. S. (1998). *Speech errors, phonotactic constraints, and recent experience.* Unpublished manuscript.

Dollaghan, C. (1985). Child meets word: "Fast mapping" in preschool children. *Journal of Speech and Hearing Research, 28,* 449–454.

Elman, J. L. (1990). Finding structure in time. *Cognitive Science, 14,* 179–211.

Fendrich, D. W., Healy, A. F, & Bourne, L. E. (1991). Long-term repetition effects for motoric and perceptual procedures. *Journal of Experimental Psychology: Learning, Memory, and Cognition, 17,* 137–151.

Frisch, S. (1996). *Similarity and frequency in phonology.* Doctoral dissertation, Northwestern University, Linguistics Department, Evanston, IL.
Fromkin, V. (1971). The nonanomalous nature of anomalous utterances. *Language, 47,* 27–52.
Gabrieli, J. D. E., Cohen, N. J., & Corkin, S. (1988). The impaired learning of semantic knowledge following bilateral medial temporal-lobe resection. *Brain, 7,* 157–177.
Graf, P., & Schacter, D. (1985). Implicit and explicit memory for new associations in normal and amnesic subjects. *Journal of Experimental Psychology: Learning, Memory, and Cognition, 11,* 501–518.
Grossman, M. (1987). Lexical acquisition in alcoholic Korsakoff psychosis. *Cortex, 23,* 631–644.
Gupta, P., & Cohen, N. J. (1997). *Skill learning, repetition priming, and procedural memory: Theoretical and computational analysis.* Manuscript submitted for publication.
Gupta, P., & MacWhinney, B. (1992). Integrating category acquisition with inflectional marking: A model of the German nominal system. In *Proceedings of the Fourteenth Annual Conference of the Cognitive Science Society* (pp. 253–258). Hillsdale, NJ: Lawrence Erlbaum Associates.
Gupta, P., & MacWhinney, B. (1997). Vocabulary acquisition and verbal short-term memory: Computational and neural bases. *Brain and Language, 59,* 267–333.
Gupta, P., & Touretzky, D. S. (1994). Connectionist models and linguistic theory: Investigations of stress systems in language. *Cognitive Science, 18,* 1–50.
Haist, F., Musen, G., & Squire, L. R. (1991). Intact priming of words and nonwords in amnesia. *Psychobiology, 19,* 275–285.
Hawking, S. W., & Penrose, R. (1996). The nature of space and time. *Scientific American, 275*(1), 60–65.
Hoeffner, J. (1992). Are rules a thing of the past? Learning the past tense in an attractor network. In *Proceedings of the Fourteenth Annual Conference of the Cognitive Science Society* (pp. 861–866). Hillsdale, NJ: Lawrence Erlbaum Associates.
Jordan, M. I. (1986). *Serial order: A parallel distributed processing approach* (Report 8604). La Jolla: Institute for Cognitive Science, University of California, San Diego.
Kandel, E. R., & Schwartz, J. H. (Eds.). (1985). *Principles of neural science* (2nd ed.). New York: Elsevier.
Kessler, B., & Treiman, R. (1997). Syllable structure and the distribution of phonemes in English syllables. *Journal of Memory and Language, 37,* 295–311.
Kirsner, K., & Speelman, C. (1996). Skill acquisition and repetition priming: One principle, many processes? *Journal of Experimental Psychology: Learning, Memory, and Cognition, 22,* 563–575.
Levelt, W. J. M., & Wheeldon, L. (1994). Do speakers have access to a mental syllabary? *Cognition, 50,* 239–269.
Logan, G. D. (1990). Repetition priming and automaticity: Common underlying mechanisms? *Cognitive Psychology, 22,* 1–35.
MacWhinney, B., & Leinbach, J. (1991). Implementations are not conceptualizations: Revising the verb learning model. *Cognition, 40,* 121–157.
Marslen-Wilson, W. D., & Zwitserlood, P. (1989). Accessing spoken words: The importance of word onsets. *Journal of Experimental Psychology: Human Perception and Performance, 15,* 576–585.
McClelland, J. L., McNaughton, B. L., & O'Reilly, R. C. (1995). Why there are complementary learning systems in the hippocampus and neocortex: Insights from the successes and failures of connectionist models of learning and memory. *Psychological Review, 102,* 419–457.
McClelland, J. L., & Rumelhart, D. E. (1985). Distributed memory and the representation of general and specific information. *Journal of Experimental Psychology: General, 114,* 159–188.
McClelland, J. L., & Rumelhart, D. E. (Eds.). (1986). *Parallel distributed processing, Vol. 2: Psychological and biological models.* Cambridge, MA: MIT Press.
McClelland, J. L., St. John, M., & Taraban, R. (1989). Sentence comprehension: A parallel distributed processing approach. *Language and Cognitive Processes, 4,* 287–335.

McCloskey, M., & Cohen, N. J. (1989). Catastrophic interference in connectionist networks: The sequential learning problem. In G. H. Bower (Ed.), *The psychology of learning and motivation* (Vol. 24, pp. 109–165). New York: Academic Press.

Meyer, A. S. (1992). Investigation of phonological encoding through speech-error analyses: Achievements, limitations, and alternatives. *Cognition, 42,* 181–211.

Mishkin, M., Malamut, B., & Bachevalier, J. (1984). Memories and habits: Two neural systems. In G. Lynch, J. McGaugh, & N. Weinberger (Eds.), *Neurobiology, of learning and memory* (pp. 65–77). New York: Guilford.

Plaut, D. C., McClelland, J. L., Seidenberg, M. S., & Patterson, K. (1996). Understanding normal and impaired word reading: Computational principles in quasi-regular domains. *Psychological Review, 103,* 56–115.

Poldrack, R. A. (1995). *The relationship between skill learning and repetition priming.* Unpublished doctoral dissertation, Department of Psychology, University of Illinois, Urbana-Champaign.

Reber, A. S. (1993). *Implicit learning and tacit knowledge: An essay on the cognitive unconscious.* New York: Oxford University Press.

Rumelhart, D., Hinton, G., & Williams, R. (1986). Learning internal representations by error propagation. In D. Rumelhart & J. McClelland (Eds.), *Parallel distributed processing, Vol. 1: Foundations* (pp. 318–362). Cambridge, MA: MIT Press.

Rumelhart, D. E., & McClelland, J. L. (1986). *Parallel distributed processing, Vol. 1: Foundations.* Cambridge, MA: MIT Press.

Rumelhart, D. E., & McClelland, J. L. (1987). Learning the past tenses of English verbs: Implicit rules or parallel distributed processes? In B. MacWhinney (Ed.), *Mechanisms of language acquisition* (pp. 195–248). Hillsdale, NJ: Lawrence Erlbaum Associates.

Schacter, D. (1987). Implicit memory: History and current status. *Journal of Experimental Psychology: Learning, Memory, and Cognition, 13,* 501–518.

Schwartz, B. L., & Hashtroudi, S. (1991). Priming is independent of skill learning. *Journal of Experimental Psychology: Learning, Memory, and Cognition, 17,* 1177–1187.

Seidenberg, M. S., & McClelland, J. L. (1989). A distributed, developmental model of word recognition and naming. *Psychological Review, 96,* 523–568.

Sevald, C. A., & Dell, G. S. (1994). The sequential cueing effect in speech production. *Cognition, 53,* 91–127.

Shattuck-Hufnagel, S. (1987). The role of word-onset consonants in speech production planning: New evidence from speech errors. In E. Keller & M. Gopnik (Eds.), *Motor and sensory processes of language* (pp. 17–51). Hillsdale, NJ: Lawrence Erlbaum Associates.

Squire, L. R. (1992). Declarative and nondeclarative memory: Multiple brain systems supporting memory and learning. *Journal of Cognitive Neuroscience, 4,* 232–243.

Squire, L. R., Knowlton, B., & Musen, G. (1993). The structure and organization of memory. *Annual Review of Psychology, 44,* 453–495.

Stemberger, J. P. (1983). *Speech errors and theoretical phonology: A review.* Bloomington: Indiana University Linguistics Club.

Author Index

C

D

H

I

J

M

N

Subject Index

STEAM TURBINES

MERCHANT BOOKS